ASTROANALYSIS

Scorpio

October 23–November 22

The American AstroAnalysts Institute

BERKLEY BOOKS, NEW YORK

The publishers regret that they cannot answer
individual letters requesting personal horoscope information.

AstroAnalysis
SCORPIO

PRINTING HISTORY
Berkley trade paperback edition / September 2000

Cover design by Segal Savad
Text design by Tiffany Kukec

The Penguin Putnam Inc. World Wide Web site address is
http://www.penguinputnam.com

ISBN: 0-425-17565-0

BERKLEY®
Berkley Books are published by The Berkley Publishing Group,
a division of Penguin Putnam Inc., 375 Hudson Street,
New York, New York 10014.
BERKLEY and the "B" design are trademarks
belonging to Penguin Putnam Inc.

PRINTED IN THE UNITED STATES OF AMERICA

10 9 8 7 6 5 4 3 2 1

CONTENTS

CHAPTER ONE

The Art of AstroAnalysis

It is not enough to describe you simply as an Aries, Taurus, Gemini or any other Sun Sign. You are an individual, a unique personality. Quite obviously you can't be lumped in with millions of others born all over the world in the same month and told: "That's you!" Astrology is not that superficial.

In addition to the Sun, other major planetary influences were acting at the time of your birth. It is these that make all the difference(s) and, together with the Sun Sign, add up to that unique individual, you.

Astrologers have always recognized this. So, of course, have many of the vast numbers of people who enjoy reading about their character descriptions. These descriptions, though basically true and often uncannily accurate, are too wide of the mark to be wholly satisfactory for the serious horoscope reader.

Yet to obtain greater accuracy—that is, a really personal character analysis—you would either have to go to a professional astrologer or wade through a mind-bending mass of figures and technical jargon. Until now!

AstroAnalysis has been devised to provide every single reader with his or her own personal astrological particulars and their detailed interpretations.

The key to AstroAnalysis is the three sets of planet tables prepared for you.

First are the Cusp Charts, which are simplified Sun Tables. These Cusp Charts enable you to determine your true Sun Sign.

Second are the Ascendant Tables provided on blue-colored pages. The Ascendant Tables enable you to determine your Ascendant, your Rising Sign.

Third are the Planet Tables provided on pink-colored pages. The Planet Tables enable you to find the Signs where the other nine planets were located on your birth date.

The three sets of tables are easy to follow. All you need to know is your birth date and time of birth, or the birth date and time of anyone you wish to AstroAnalyze.

How This Book Is Organized

This book contains much more than the tables, of course. Here in the opening chapter you will become familiar with the art of AstroAnalysis. You will learn some basic astrology vocabulary too—the Zodiac, the Houses of the Zodiac, the horoscope.

Subsequent chapters are arranged in a natural sequence. Chapter 2 gives the meaning and influence of the cusp. Chapter 3 provides Cusp Charts from 1910 through 2015 so you can find your true Sun Sign. Then, for those of you born on the cusp, Chapter 4 describes its significance for your character.

Chapter 5 is an in-depth study of your Sun Sign personality. Chapter 6 on love and romance and marriage and friendship is one of the most comprehensive guides ever published. It describes how you can expect to get along with a man or woman born under any of the Signs, including your own.

Rounding out your Sun Sign personality are Chapters 7 and 8 describing your work and health prospects. Chapter 9 displays an astro check list of your positive and negative qualities.

Chapters 10 and 11 on parents and children follow. Here is an analysis of each Sign as parents, then a general description of the traits and needs of children born under the various zodiacal signs.

Chapters 12 and 13 cover the Ascendant, which is the Rising Sign. Chapter 13 is one of the most penetrating and complete studies ever written on the ascendant personality for each of the 12 zodiacal signs.

Chapter 14 on planetary influences highlights all ten planets, including the Sun, and provides key words to summarize each planet's influence. Then Chapters 15 through 23 cover the nine remaining planets, from Moon through Pluto. Each chapter discusses the meaning and significance of the planet in the various zodiacal signs.

Chapters 24 and 25 enable you to create your own astro profile and construct your own horozope chart. Or you can create a profile and chart for anyone else born under the same Sun Sign as you. Here are helpful hints and graphics, a world map showing all the time zones, conversion features, the Ascendant Tables (blue) and the Planet Tables (pink).

Elements of AstroAnalysis

Every AstroAnalysis begins with the Sun Sign. In some astrological guides only the Sun Sign is given. But in order to personalize and individualize your horoscope, AstroAnalysis uses not one but three standard astrological references. They are:

1. Sun Sign. The Sun Sign represents your basic character. (Use Cusp Charts to know your true Sun Sign.)
2. Ascendant, the Rising Sign. The Rising Sign represents self-image and shows how other people see you. (Use Blue Ascendant Tables.)
3. Planets in the Signs. Besides the Sun, nine other planets influence your patterns of thought and behavior, modifying the Sun Sign influence. (Use Pink Planet Tables.)

The art of AstroAnalysis lies in being able to synthesize these results. Put another way, it's obvious that if you know your basic character traits and potential (Sun Sign), if you have the advantage of seeing yourself as you appear to others (Ascendant), if you understand your likely patterns with the risks and rewards that may flow therefrom (Planets)—you will be in a much better position to assert your talents, correct your shortcomings, exploit your natural possibilities, bring greater harmony into your relationships with others. You will be able to live a richer and more meaningful life.

You then don't have to look for salvation in strange beliefs and doctrines, or to escape in drugs and self-delusion. With this knowledge, you will be yourself. And to the degree that this self-realization becomes permanent and profound, you will be the master of your fate, a stable personality and an individual well worth having around.

Sun Sign

No two people born under the same Sign are identical. Each type is subject to numerous modifications wrought by the environment, both physical and social, and by heredity. The royal daughter and the under-privileged child born at the same moment in palace and slum will have the same basic thinking and urges, but their vastly different circumstances and conditioning will modify the essential purity of the type.

So, as important as the basic Sun Sign character is, it is only part of the story. The all-important influence of the Ascendant, which is the Rising Sign, is another vital consideration.

Ascendant Sign

The Ascendant is the Sign that was rising (ascending) on the eastern horizon at the time of your birth. The Ascendant is often called the Rising Sign, and it is the second major influence in the formation of your personality.

The Rising Sign, or Ascendant, represents your response to the environment, and often denotes a particular body type or facade. The Ascendant also shows how you appear to other people.

In the Blue Ascendant Tables you will see the Rising Sign given for each hour of every day during your birth month. If you don't know the time of your birth, try to reach someone, perhaps a relative, who does know. If that fails, there's a good chance you can determine your Rising Sign by reading the descriptions in Chapter 13 (Ascendant Personalities: Rising Sign Types).

Planets in the Signs

Remember, the Sun is only *one* influence, though it is by far the most important. Our material existence depends on it absolutely, which is why its position in the Zodiac determines the basic type. But there are nine other planets whose positions in the horoscope modify the basic Sun Sign character. When you read about these, you'll find a short introduction to each planet that shows some surprising correlations between ancient myths and verifiable facts.

You will also read the significance for you of each planet—Moon, Mercury, Venus, Mars, Jupiter, Saturn, Uranus, Neptune, Pluto—in the Sign you have found by using the Pink Planet Tables. The tables show you where all nine planets were on your birth date. Each planet will reside in a particular Sign of the Zodiac for the day of your birth. Sometimes two or more planets will be in the same Sign on your birth date. And it is not unusual for someone to have four or five planets in the same Sign!

It might help the skeptical to know that modern Astrology does not suggest that the planets themselves rule our destinies. The planets are merely dynamic parts of the electromagnetic field in which we exist—a scientific fact. Their constantly altering angular position to the Earth and to each other correlates with distinct changes in human and cosmic affairs.

Unique Features and Benefits of AstroAnalysis

When you use the colored Planet Tables and references, you will be drawing on the skills of a group of highly experienced international astrologers. It took over two years to reduce the complex calculations of all of the planet movements during a 106-year period to a simplified table format that uses only words (except for the birth date and Moon time.)

When you read the various chapters of AstroAnalysis that relate to your astro profile, your personal horoscope, you will discover many things. You will discover the kind of career you are best suited for: you may have a flair for selling or perhaps you have a scientific bent. You may be a born leader or prefer a background role. You will learn why you are a whiz at math and music, but find it hard to compose prose or poetry.

You will understand why you feel sympathy for some people but not for others. You will have clues to why some people attract you, either sexually or intellectually, and why others turn you off, leave you cold or even repel you.

With the other books in the *AstroAnalysis* series, you can AstroAnalyze your friends (and others who may not be so friendly). All you need to know is the day and year of their birth. It can be fun. It certainly will be revealing.

You will discover who your real friends are, and who would be a natural ally. You will get insights about the types of people who can be depended on in business as well as the people who might be unreliable or tricky in business. And, of course, the conspicuous advantage of knowing a rival's innate strengths and weaknesses does not need to be stressed.

Frequently, when making an AstroAnalysis, you will notice that an individual's character clashes with his or her personality. This will help you to understand aggressive and contradictory behavior patterns that otherwise would be baffling. With your new insight, you will be able to ameliorate relationships between husband and wife, partners, co-workers, friends—generally eliminate friction between people who live or work together. Children can be encouraged along positive lines and guided toward a future that provides full scope for their natural abilities and aptitudes.

Every one of us has negative qualities. No type is all good. The planets' effects sometimes result in pretty rotten behavior. But always we retain our individuality and the capability of exercising our free will. It is for you alone to judge which parts of your character revealed in this work need accentuating, changing or correcting. The aim of AstroAnalysis is merely to draw attention to the possibilities and some of the alternatives.

In evaluating what you read and how you apply it, you will be demonstrating your aptitude for AstroAnalysis. The challenge is for you to reach a fairly correct conclusion about a person using your judgment, understanding and intuition based on what you have discovered in these books. Remember, there is a constant pushing and pulling in our natures, which makes each of us react differently to similar events. The potential and the conflicts you will read about and assess are what make us complex, intriguing, interesting personalities—in other words, individuals.

The Zodiac

Astrology is based on the Zodiac. The word is from the Greek *zodiakos*, which is from zoion (animal) and *kirkos* (circle)—a circle of animals. This alludes to the ancients naming of the heavenly constellations after various animals.

Astrology is indebted to the ancients, who saw in the symbolism of the stars the existence of the spatial Zodiac. But there is no connection—except symbolically—between the two.

The Zodiac is a group of stars (constellations) in space centered against the Sun's *apparent* path around the Earth. These constellations are divided into 12 equal segments, called Signs of the Zodiac. What we are actually dividing up is the Earth's path around the Sun. But from our frame of reference on Earth, it seems as if the Sun is circling the Earth. So we say it is the Sun's apparent path.

The Signs

Astrology regards these 12 Signs inherent in space as patterns of human characteristics. Among them they represent the 12 psychological types of people or the 12 ways in which human individuality expresses itself. The Signs are:

Aries the Ram	*Libra the Scales*
Taurus the Bull	*Scorpio the Scorpion*
Gemini the Twins	*Sagittarius the Archer*
Cancer the Crab	*Capricorn the Goat*
Leo the Lion	*Aquarius the Water Bearer*
Virgo the Virgin	*Pisces the Fishes*

So the first quality of zodiacal space is that it contains 12 distinct divisions of character.

The Houses

The second quality of space—still represented by the Zodiac—is that it contains 12 basic spheres of human activity. These are called Houses and are numbered from 1 to 12.

The Houses and an abbreviated description of their meanings are:

1st Persona, facade, body type, self-centered interests, outlook on life.

2nd Possessions, money, gain or loss, earning power, basic security.

3rd Communication with the environment, close relatives, neighbors, letters, speech, short trips, intellect.

4th Home, childhood, the unconscious, traditions, the psychological self.

5th Self-projection, pleasure, love affairs, children, sensual enjoyment, creativity, ideas, talent.

6th Employment, health, harvest, duty, service, pets, diet, daily tasks, hygiene, basic necessities, self-fulfillment.

7th The husband or wife, partners, contracts, war, marriage, divorce, legal matters, social awareness.

8th Death, legacies, shared feelings, the sex urge, psychoanalysis, the partner's resources, taxes, the afterlife.

9th Religion, long journeys, philosophical speculation, dreams, foreign countries, publicity, organized sport.

10th Public standing, fame, attainment, career or profession, status, corporations, government.

11th Impersonal relationships, group activities, friends, idealism, humanitarian objectives, unexpected happenings.

12th Sacrificial service, exile, karma, hidden agenda, unfinished psychic business, secret wisdom, secret motives, hidden enemies, sorrow, trouble.

Each House has an affinity with a Sign, beginning with Aries.

The two qualities of space together form the Zodiac—like circles slowly rotating one inside the other. When an energy source (a planet) is in one of the divisions or Signs, it throws that particular character inward into a life situation (House), and the combined image appears on the Earth at the center as the individual within the environment.

The Planets

Then there are the ten planets (the Sun and Moon are called planets) always radiating in particular Signs and Houses. The result is fascinating diversity—or human existence as we know it. And it takes the art of AstroAnalysis to sort it out into patterns.

It is obvious that the type of energy a planet radiates—and its angular position in relation to the Signs, Houses and other planets—will also have a substantial bearing on the resultant Earth image. Accordingly, the characteristic energies of each of the planets have to be borne in mind. These are:

Sun Power, self-expression, generosity, individuality.

Moon Response, fluctuation, mood, sensitivity, sympathy.

Mercury Communication, mind, intelligence, discernment.

Venus Attraction, unity, harmony, beauty, evaluation, assets, materiality.

Mars Activity, energetic expression, self-assertion, heat, enterprise.

Jupiter Expansion, optimism, foresight, luck, opportunity.

Saturn Limitation, restriction, reason, order, sensitivity, discipline.

Uranus Drastic change, independence, originality, inventiveness.

Neptune Transcendence through dissolution, immateriality.

Pluto Resurrection, elimination, renewal, resolution, transformation.

The planets energize the Signs and Houses and the kaleidoscope of life results.

The Horoscope

The horoscope is a reference map. It shows exactly where the planets were in the Zodiac at the time of the person's birth. As with an ordinary map, if the salient features are identified, a fair assessment can be made of the terrain in advance and obvious obstacles can be avoided.

The horoscope is a map, not only of the character, urges and inclinations working in a person but also of the forces acting to create him or her as a human being. What is in the map will always be the fundamental physical and psychological self.

If the time of an event can be fixed, the space characteristic or nature of it may also be determined. The horoscope is Astrology's way of writing science's space-time theory in relation to people and events.

With 10 planets distributed around the 12 Signs of the Zodiac and charted in horoscope form, a starting point has to be found from which to begin to read.

Starting Point: The Ascendant

The starting point in constructing a horoscope is the Ascendant, the Rising Sign. The Ascendant is actually the planet Earth. Generally speaking, the Earth is not considered among the planets because it is the focal point of the horoscope. But it also affects our lives through the Zodiac, and the way it does this is by energizing the Ascendant, the Rising Sign.

The Ascendant is the point at which the Earth meets space at the individual's place of birth—the horizon. Because of the Earth's rotation, a different Sign of the Zodiac rises on the horizon about every two hours. As mentioned earlier, you need to have a fairly accurate idea of your birth time in order to determine your Rising Sign.

The Ascendant, your Rising Sign, dictates how you appear to other people. It is your fate, which can't be avoided, your environment (family, home and hereditary circumstances). In many cases, the Rising Sign will be different from the Sun Sign. This explains why we often feel totally different from how we act, why we are misunderstood and misunderstand others, and why we have a conscience.

The Rising Sign part of your character, which you present to the world, is in many ways as important as your Sun Sign character. You don't always have to reveal your Sun Sign character, although it remains intrinsically you and it is what you may always feel inside you as yourself. The Sun Sign is what you must become—eventually. The Rising Sign is what you are now, and what you must use in your struggle to transcend.

The importance of the Ascendant, the Rising Sign, is recognized in AstroAnalysis to full extent. Chapter 13, so comprehensive it could be a book in itself, is an in-depth study of each of the 12 Rising Sign types.

Locating Planets Moon through Pluto

The next most important planet in the horoscope is the Moon. This is our emotional self, our deep-rooted past that extends back through childhood, through the maternal influence, beyond memory into the unconscious wisps of other time-space con-

tortions. We respond from the Moon in us with instinct and sensibility.

The positions in the horoscope of all the other planets must be located to get a complete picture. In natural solar system order come Mercury, Venus, Mars, Jupiter, Saturn, Uranus, Neptune, Pluto. Once each planet is located—where the planet was when you were born—that position can be studied in Chapters 15 through 23.

Relation Between Planets and Signs

For the professional astrologer, there are many other considerations in the horoscope that must be taken into account. For instance, each planet "rules" a Sign, sometimes two Signs. Some planets have part ownership, or co-rulership, of a Sign. A planet in its own Sign is said to be in "dignity" and at "home" there. A planet at home in its own Sign is stronger than in other Signs.

Planets are said to be "exalted" in certain Signs, which means the planet is extra powerful there than in other Signs. Planets can be in "detriment" in certain Signs, which means they are out of harmony there. And planets can be in "fall" in certain Signs, which means the planet's influence is weakened there.

Such relationships among the planets will be important in your horoscope. Astrologers call these relationships *aspects*, and denote the aspects as "good," "adverse" and "neutral." Good aspects are the stable planetary relationships, the clear-flowing, easy-to-combine energies. Adverse aspects are the stress aspects, the struggle to grow and integrate conflicting forces and seemingly opposing facets of character.

Good aspects and adverse aspects together are the creative raw material of human personality and spiritual growth. Chapters 15 through 23 on the planets describe the aspects, helping you to evaluate the forces influencing your personality and potential growth.

The Signs themselves have various properties and qualities. Each has an elemental nature, which is either fire, earth, air or water. The fire Signs—Aries, Leo, Sagittarius—are ardent and volatile. Earth Signs—Taurus, Virgo, Capricorn—are practical and cautious. Air Signs—Gemini, Libra, Aquarius—are intellectual and communicative. Water Signs—Cancer, Scorpio, Pisces—are intuitive and sensitive.

Each Sign is either positive (Aries, Gemini, Leo, Libra, Sagittarius, Aquarius) or negative (Taurus, Cancer, Virgo, Scorpio, Capricorn, Pisces). The Signs are also divided according to qualities called cardinal, fixed and mutable. The cardinal Signs—

Aries, Cancer, Libra, Capricorn—are outgoing. The fixed Signs—Taurus, Leo, Scorpio, Aquarius—are resistant to change. Mutable Signs—Gemini, Virgo, Sagittarius, Pisces—are adaptable and versatile.

Free Will and Astrology

Does Astrology preclude free will? This is a question that concerns many people when they begin to understand cosmic significance.

One of the problems is that many of us mistake choice for free will. Astrology shows that there is more than considerable difference between the two.

We all know that at any moment of choice we are free. Otherwise we could not perform as responsible beings. We may have reasons for feeling one thing and choosing to be another—fear, consideration for someone, love—but we are free to choose when the opportunity is presented. Only this is a very limited freedom. A person's choice usually amounts to: will I or won't I stop or go? speak or be silent? say yes or no? Two alternatives obviously do not constitute much of a choice. This limited choosing certainly could not be equated with freedom.

This limited choosing, where we feel the burden of our worldly obligations and frequently choose the way of duty rather than what we feel is right for us, is presented by the Ascendant Sign. You will remember that this is the second most important factor in the horoscope: the character or personality we show to the world and our environment—rich or poor, orphaned or cherished, healthy or unhealthy—is determined by the Earth's relation to the Zodiac at the moment of birth. Limited choice is limited freedom, the condition of our worldly existence.

Will is quite a different quality. It is represented by the Sun Sign, the character we are becoming by means of our personality and worldly situation. The position of the Sun is the most important point of the horoscope.

Our will, like the Sun, sits behind our choosing personality like an old-fashioned king watching the antics of his prime minister making limited decisions. As was said earlier, the Sun character is what we always feel inside as ourselves. We can fool everyone else, perhaps, but we can't fool it. We get away with our limited choosing, but it won't make us happy or contented for long. We have to choose again, and go on choosing, to enjoy this limited freedom of the Ascendant.

But if through our Ascendant situation we have found a purpose to our lives, we will have the will to do or to be something. Choosing, then, will never really foul us up because we will choose according to our purpose, which is related to our Sun character. An extraordinary thing about purpose is that it has no object. Choice, which is of the Earth-bound Ascendant Sign, always has an object, a goal, an end in mind.

If our purpose is to be kind, we will never have to choose what to do—we'll be kind. Unlike those who choose an object or a goal, we will never face the question of what to do when enough has been acquired or the goal has been reached. How can we ever be kind enough when every moment of our life is a new opportunity for kindness?

Purpose is timeless and an individual seldom has anything in particular to show for it. Purpose is both willing and free—in other words, free will—and it shines like the Sun above the Earth.

Every one of us is a mixture of his or her Sun character and Ascendant Sign. That is why there are so many nice people around.

CHAPTER TWO

Sun Sign and the Cusp

Many readers are sure they know what their Sun Sign is. But some people born at the *cusp,* or edge, of a Sign have difficulty determining their true Sun Sign.

The cusp represents the borderline, the boundary between one Sign and another Sign. As any planet, in this case the Sun, moves from one Sign to the next Sign, there is a time during a day when the planet is at or on the cusp.

Remember, in Astrology the Sun is considered to be a planet moving in space through each Sign of the Zodiac. Throughout a year the Sun spends approximately one month in each Sign. But the day on which the Sun leaves one Sign and enters the next Sign varies from year to year.

That is why AstroAnalysis provides Cusp Charts for all readers. The Cusp Charts are simplified Sun Tables. They show the cusp dates—the days on which the Sun Sign changes—for every year from 1910 through 2015.

You can use the Cusp Charts in the next chapter to determine your true Sun Sign, or that of a friend or relative. The Cusp Charts tell you the precise days on which the Sun enters and leaves each of the 12 Signs of the Zodiac every year.

The Cusp Influence

The influence of the cusp is evident not only on the exact day of the cusp but also for several days. The cusp influence starts two to three days before the end of one Sign, then lasts for two to three days after the beginning of the next Sign.

Some astrologers say that if you were born when one Sign was giving way to the next Sign, then you were influenced by both Signs. The cusp influence persists for about six or seven days.

The Cusp Period

Listed below is the cusp period for all 12 Signs of the Zodiac. See if you belong to one of these cusp periods. If you do, read about your cusp-born personality in Chapter 4. You may find an aspect of your personality—and a key to your character—you never before suspected!

Aries and Taurus • *April 17–23*	**Libra and Scorpio** • *October 20–26*
Taurus and Gemini • *May 17–23*	**Scorpio and Sagittarius** • *November 19–25*
Gemini and Cancer • *June 18–24*	**Sagittarius and Capricorn** • *December 18–24*
Cancer and Leo • *July 19–25*	**Capricorn and Aquarius** • *January 17–23*
Leo and Virgo • *August 19–25*	**Aquarius and Pisces** • *February 16–22*
Virgo and Libra • *September 20–26*	**Pisces and Aries** • *March 17–23*

Cusp Charts

YEAR	ARIES MAR.- APR.	TAURUS APR.- MAY	GEMINI MAY- JUNE	CANCER JUNE- JULY	LEO JULY- AUG.	VIRGO AUG.- SEPT.	LIBRA SEPT.- OCT.	SCORPIO OCT.- NOV.	SAGITTARIUS NOV.- DEC.	CAPRICORN DEC.- JAN.	AQUARIUS JAN.- FEB.	PISCES FEB.- MAR.
1910	22-20	21-21	22-21	22-23	24-23	24-23	24-23	24-22	23-22	23-20	21-19	20-21
1911	22-20	21-21	22-22	23-23	24-23	24-23	24-24	25-22	23-22	23-20	21-19	20-21
1912	21-19	20-20	21-21	22-22	23-23	24-22	23-23	24-22	23-21	22-20	21-19	20-20
1913	21-20	21-21	22-21	22-23	24-23	24-23	24-23	24-22	23-21	22-20	21-18	19-20
1914	21-20	21-21	22-21	22-23	24-23	24-23	24-23	24-22	23-22	23-20	21-18	19-20
1915	22-20	21-21	22-22	23-23	24-23	24-23	24-24	25-22	23-22	23-20	21-19	20-21
1916	21-19	20-20	21-21	22-22	23-23	24-22	23-23	24-22	23-21	22-20	21-19	20-20
1917	21-20	21-21	22-21	22-22	23-23	24-23	24-23	24-22	23-21	22-20	21-18	19-20
1918	21-20	21-21	22-21	22-23	24-23	24-23	24-23	24-22	23-22	23-20	21-18	19-20
1919	22-20	21-21	22-21	22-23	24-23	24-23	24-23	24-22	23-22	23-20	21-19	20-21
1920	21-19	20-20	21-21	22-22	23-22	23-22	23-23	24-22	23-21	22-20	21-19	20-20
1921	21-20	21-21	22-21	22-22	23-23	24-23	24-23	24-22	23-21	22-20	21-18	19-20
1922	21-20	21-21	22-21	22-23	24-23	24-23	24-23	24-22	23-22	23-20	21-18	19-20
1923	22-20	21-21	22-21	22-23	24-23	24-23	24-23	24-22	23-22	23-20	21-19	20-21
1924	21-19	20-20	21-21	22-22	23-22	23-22	23-23	24-22	23-21	22-20	21-19	20-20
1925	21-20	21-21	22-21	22-22	23-23	24-23	24-23	24-22	23-21	22-20	21-18	19-20
1926	21-20	21-21	22-21	22-23	24-23	24-23	24-23	24-22	23-22	23-20	21-18	19-20
1927	22-20	21-21	22-21	22-23	24-23	24-23	24-23	24-22	23-22	23-20	21-19	20-21
1928	21-19	20-20	21-21	22-22	23-22	23-22	23-23	24-22	23-21	22-20	21-19	20-20
1929	21-20	21-21	22-21	22-22	23-23	24-23	24-23	24-22	23-21	22-20	21-18	19-20
1930	21-20	21-21	22-21	22-23	24-23	24-23	24-23	24-22	23-22	23-20	21-18	19-20
1931	22-20	21-21	22-21	22-23	24-23	24-23	24-23	24-22	23-22	23-20	21-19	20-21
1932	21-19	20-20	21-21	22-22	23-22	23-22	23-23	24-22	23-21	22-20	21-19	20-20

YEAR	ARIES MAR.-APR.	TAURUS APR.-MAY	GEMINI MAY-JUNE	CANCER JUNE-JULY	LEO JULY-AUG.	VIRGO AUG.-SEPT.	LIBRA SEPT.-OCT.	SCORPIO OCT.-NOV.	SAGITTARIUS NOV.-DEC.	CAPRICORN DEC.-JAN.	AQUARIUS JAN.-FEB.	PISCES FEB.-MAR.
1933	21-20	21-21	22-21	22-22	23-23	24-23	24-23	24-22	23-21	22-19	20-18	19-20
1934	21-20	21-21	22-21	22-23	24-23	24-23	24-23	24-22	23-22	23-20	21-18	19-20
1935	22-20	21-21	22-21	22-23	24-23	24-23	24-23	24-22	23-22	23-20	21-19	20-21
1936	21-19	20-20	21-21	22-22	23-22	23-22	23-23	24-21	22-21	22-20	21-19	20-20
1937	21-20	21-20	21-21	22-22	23-23	24-22	23-23	24-22	23-21	22-19	20-18	19-20
1938	21-20	21-21	22-21	22-23	24-23	24-23	24-23	24-22	23-22	23-20	21-18	19-20
1939	22-20	21-21	22-21	22-23	24-23	24-23	24-23	24-22	23-22	23-20	21-19	20-21
1940	21-19	20-20	21-21	22-22	23-22	23-22	23-23	24-21	22-21	22-20	21-19	20-20
1941	21-19	20-20	21-21	22-22	23-23	24-22	23-23	24-22	23-21	22-19	20-18	19-20
1942	21-20	21-21	22-21	22-23	24-23	24-23	24-23	24-22	23-21	22-20	21-18	19-20
1943	22-20	21-21	22-21	22-23	24-23	24-23	24-23	24-22	23-22	23-20	21-19	20-21
1944	21-19	20-20	21-21	22-22	23-22	23-22	23-23	24-21	22-21	22-20	21-19	20-20
1945	21-19	20-20	21-21	22-22	23-23	24-22	23-23	24-22	23-21	22-19	20-18	19-20
1946	21-20	21-21	22-21	22-22	23-23	24-23	24-23	24-22	23-21	22-20	21-18	19-20
1947	21-20	21-21	22-21	22-23	24-23	24-23	24-23	24-22	23-22	23-20	21-18	19-20
1948	21-19	20-20	21-21	22-22	23-22	23-22	23-23	24-21	22-21	22-20	21-19	20-20
1949	21-19	20-20	21-21	22-22	23-22	23-22	23-23	24-22	23-21	22-19	20-18	19-20
1950	21-20	21-21	22-21	22-22	23-23	24-23	24-23	24-22	23-21	22-20	21-18	19-20
1951	22-20	21-21	22-22	23-23	24-23	24-23	24-24	25-23	24-22	23-20	21-19	20-21
1952	21-20	21-21	22-21	22-22	23-23	24-23	24-23	24-22	23-21	22-21	22-19	20-20
1953	21-20	21-21	22-21	22-23	24-23	24-23	24-23	24-22	23-22	23-20	21-18	19-20
1954	22-20	21-21	22-21	22-23	24-23	24-23	24-23	24-22	23-22	23-20	21-19	20-21
1955	22-20	21-21	22-22	23-23	24-23	24-23	24-24	25-23	24-22	23-20	21-19	20-21
1956	21-20	21-21	22-21	22-22	23-23	24-23	24-23	24-22	23-21	22-21	22-19	20-20
1957	21-20	21-21	22-21	22-23	24-23	24-23	24-23	24-22	23-22	23-20	21-18	19-20
1958	22-20	21-21	22-21	22-23	24-23	24-23	24-23	24-22	23-22	23-20	21-19	20-21
1959	22-20	21-21	22-22	23-23	24-23	24-23	24-24	25-23	24-22	23-20	21-19	20-21

The first date shows when the Sun enters a Sign, the second date when the Sun leaves the Sign. Example: in 1933 the Sun entered Aries on March 21 and left Aries on April 20.

YEAR	ARIES MAR.-APR.	TAURUS APR.-MAY	GEMINI MAY-JUNE	CANCER JUNE-JULY	LEO JULY-AUG.	VIRGO AUG.-SEPT.	LIBRA SEPT.-OCT.	SCORPIO OCT.-NOV.	SAGITTARIUS NOV.-DEC.	CAPRICORN DEC.-JAN.	AQUARIUS JAN.-FEB.	PISCES FEB.-MAR.
1960	21-20	21-21	22-21	22-22	23-23	24-23	24-23	24-22	23-21	22-21	22-19	20-20
1961	21-20	21-21	22-21	22-23	24-23	24-23	24-23	24-22	23-22	23-20	21-18	19-20
1962	22-20	21-21	22-21	22-23	24-23	24-23	24-23	24-22	23-22	23-20	21-19	20-21
1963	22-20	21-21	22-22	23-23	24-23	24-23	24-24	25-23	24-22	23-20	21-19	20-21
1964	21-20	21-21	22-21	22-22	23-23	24-23	24-23	24-22	23-21	22-21	22-19	20-20
1965	21-20	21-21	22-21	22-23	24-23	24-23	24-23	24-22	23-22	23-20	21-18	19-20
1966	22-20	21-21	22-21	22-23	24-23	24-23	24-23	24-22	23-22	23-20	21-19	20-21
1967	22-20	21-21	22-22	23-23	24-23	24-23	24-24	25-22	23-22	23-20	21-19	20-21
1968	21-20	21-20	21-21	22-22	23-23	24-22	23-23	24-22	23-21	22-20	21-19	20-20
1969	21-20	21-21	22-21	22-23	24-23	24-23	24-23	24-22	23-22	23-20	21-18	19-20
1970	22-20	21-21	22-21	22-23	24-23	24-23	24-23	24-22	23-22	23-20	21-19	20-21
1971	22-20	21-21	22-22	23-23	24-23	24-23	24-24	25-22	23-22	23-20	21-19	20-21
1972	21-19	20-20	21-21	22-22	23-23	24-22	23-23	24-22	23-21	22-20	21-19	20-20
1973	21-20	21-21	22-21	22-22	23-23	24-23	24-23	24-22	23-22	23-20	21-18	19-20
1974	22-20	21-21	22-21	22-23	24-23	24-23	24-23	24-22	23-22	23-20	21-19	20-21
1975	22-20	21-21	22-22	23-23	24-23	24-23	24-24	25-22	23-22	23-20	21-19	20-21
1976	21-19	20-20	21-21	22-22	23-23	24-22	23-23	24-22	23-21	22-20	21-19	20-20
1977	21-20	21-21	22-21	22-22	23-23	24-23	24-23	24-22	23-21	22-20	21-18	19-20
1978	21-20	21-21	22-21	22-23	24-23	24-23	24-23	24-22	23-22	23-20	21-19	20-20
1979	22-20	21-21	22-21	22-23	24-23	24-23	24-24	25-22	23-22	23-20	21-19	20-21
1980	21-19	20-20	21-21	22-22	23-22	23-22	23-23	24-22	23-21	22-20	21-19	20-20
1981	21-20	21-21	22-21	22-22	23-23	24-23	24-23	24-22	23-21	22-20	21-18	19-20
1982	21-20	21-21	22-21	22-23	24-23	24-23	24-23	24-22	23-22	23-20	21-18	19-20
1983	22-20	21-21	22-21	22-23	24-23	24-23	24-23	24-22	23-22	23-20	21-19	20-21
1984	21-19	20-20	21-21	22-22	23-22	23-22	23-23	24-22	23-21	22-20	21-19	20-20
1985	21-20	21-21	22-21	22-22	23-23	24-23	24-23	24-22	23-21	22-20	21-18	19-20
1986	21-20	21-21	22-21	22-23	24-23	24-23	24-23	24-22	23-22	23-20	21-18	19-20
1987	22-20	21-21	22-21	22-23	24-23	24-23	24-23	24-22	23-22	23-20	21-19	20-21

YEAR	ARIES MAR.-APR.	TAURUS APR.-MAY	GEMINI MAY-JUNE	CANCER JUNE-JULY	LEO JULY-AUG.	VIRGO AUG.-SEPT.	LIBRA SEPT.-OCT.	SCORPIO OCT.-NOV.	SAGITTARIUS NOV.-DEC.	CAPRICORN DEC.-JAN.	AQUARIUS JAN.-FEB.	PISCES FEB.-MAR.
1988	21-19	20-20	21-21	22-22	23-22	23-22	23-23	24-22	23-21	22-20	21-19	20-20
1989	21-20	21-21	22-21	22-22	23-23	24-23	24-23	24-22	23-21	22-20	21-18	19-20
1990	21-20	21-21	22-21	22-23	24-23	24-23	24-23	24-22	23-22	23-20	21-18	19-20
1991	20-20	20-21	21-21	21-23	23-23	23-23	23-23	23-22	22-22	22-20	20-18	18-20
1992	20-19	19-20	20-20	20-22	22-22	22-22	22-22	22-21	21-21	21-20	20-19	19-20
1993	20-19	19-20	20-21	21-22	22-22	22-22	22-23	23-21	21-21	21-19	19-18	18-20
1994	20-20	20-21	21-21	21-22	22-23	23-23	23-23	23-22	22-21	21-20	20-18	18-20
1995	20-20	20-21	21-21	21-23	23-23	23-23	23-23	23-22	22-22	22-20	20-18	18-20
1996	20-19	19-20	20-20	20-22	22-22	22-22	22-22	22-21	21-21	21-20	20-19	19-20
1997	20-19	19-20	20-21	21-22	22-22	22-22	22-23	23-22	22-21	21-19	19-18	18-20
1998	20-20	20-21	21-21	21-22	22-23	23-23	23-23	23-22	22-21	21-20	20-18	18-20
1999	20-20	20-21	21-21	21-23	23-23	23-23	23-23	23-22	22-22	22-20	20-18	18-20
2000	20-19	19-20	20-20	20-22	22-22	22-22	22-22	22-21	21-21	21-20	20-19	19-20
2001	20-19	19-20	20-21	21-22	22-22	22-22	22-23	23-22	22-21	21-19	19-18	18-20
2002	20-20	20-21	21-21	21-22	22-23	23-22	23-23	23-22	22-21	21-20	20-18	18-20
2003	20-20	20-21	21-21	21-23	23-23	23-23	23-23	23-22	22-22	22-20	20-18	18-20
2004	20-19	19-20	20-20	20-22	22-22	22-22	22-22	22-21	21-21	21-20	20-19	19-20
2005	20-19	19-20	20-21	21-22	22-22	22-22	22-23	23-22	22-21	21-19	19-18	18-20
2006	20-20	20-21	21-21	21-22	22-23	23-23	23-23	23-22	22-21	21-20	20-18	18-20
2007	20-20	20-21	21-21	21-23	23-23	23-23	23-23	23-22	22-22	22-20	20-18	18-20
2008	20-19	19-20	20-20	20-22	22-22	22-22	22-22	22-21	21-21	21-20	20-19	19-20
2009	20-19	19-20	20-21	21-22	22-22	22-22	22-23	23-22	22-21	21-19	19-18	18-20
2010	20-20	20-21	21-21	21-22	22-23	23-23	23-23	23-22	22-21	21-20	20-18	18-20
2011	20-20	20-21	21-21	21-22	23-23	23-23	23-23	23-22	22-21	22-20	20-18	18-20
2012	20-19	19-20	20-20	20-22	22-22	22-22	22-22	23-21	21-21	21-20	20-19	19-20
2013	20-19	19-20	20-21	21-22	22-22	22-22	22-23	23-22	22-21	21-19	19-18	18-20
2014	20-20	20-21	21-21	21-22	22-23	23-23	23-23	23-22	22-21	21-20	20-18	18-20
2015	20-20	20-21	21-21	21-23	23-23	23-23	23-23	23-22	22-22	22-20	20-18	18-20

CHAPTER FOUR

Scorpio on the Cusp

You are about to read all about your Scorpio personality. Are you truly a Scorpio? Did you check the cusp charts in Chapter 3 to be sure? The charts tell you the precise days on which the Sun entered and left your Sign of Scorpio for the year you were born.

Even so, if you were born near the end of one Sign or near the beginning of the next Sign, there is a cusp influence operating as described in Chapter 2. Glance back there to see the Scorpio cusp periods.

If your birthday falls sometime during the fourth week of October, at the beginning of Scorpio, will you still retain the traits of Libra, the Sign of the Zodiac before Scorpio? What if you were born during the third week or early fourth week of November, at the end of Scorpio? Are you more like Sagittarius, the Sign of the Zodiac that comes next after Scorpio?

If you were born at the beginning of Scorpio, you may want to read the *AstroAnalysis* book for Libra as well as Scorpio, for Libra holds the keys to much of the complexity of your spirit and reflects many of your hidden weaknesses, secret sides, and unspoken wishes.

You have a keen way of making someone feel needed and desired, whether you care deeply or not. Sex is a strong directive in your life. You might turn your charm and seductiveness toward gaining a merely superficial relationship. You could use your sexual magnetism and love magic to win people over for the sheer purpose of being seen as partnered in a respectable couple.

You can love with an almost fatal obsession, a bigger-than-both-of-you type thing. You may blind your eyes to basic incompatibilities just to keep the peace in a relationship—then suddenly declare war.

No one in the whole Zodiac is as turned on to the passions of life as you are. You can survive any crisis, for deep in your spirit lie the seeds of immortality and you know it. Above all you are the symbol that life goes on—the personification of awakening passion.

If you were born at the end of Scorpio, you may want to read the *AstroAnalysis* book for Sagittarius as well as for Scorpio. You are the symbol of the human mind awakening to its higher capabilities. What you are leaving behind is greed, blind desire, and shallow lust, as you awaken to your own ability to learn, to create, and to understand.

You want to travel, see new places, see how people live, figure yourself out, acquire knowledge—yet you are often not quite ready to take the plunge. When you shift your behavior patterns significantly and permanently, new worlds open up and you turn on to immortality and the infinite possibilities of your own mind.

Whether you were born at the beginning or at the end of Scorpio, yours is a lifetime reflecting a process of subtle transformation. Your life on Earth will symbolize a significant change in consciousness, for you are either about to enter a whole new way of living or are leaving one behind.

CHAPTER FIVE

Scorpio Personality

There's no point in beating around the bush: Scorpio is the Sign of sex in its pure, elemental form. Not sexual appetite; it is far more potent and meaningful than that. Scorpio men and women are human volcanoes of intense primal energy. The burning question for them throughout their lives is which way to release it—creatively or destructively?

The temptation to go to extremes is enormous here. No other Sign gives the individual such an awesome capability for good or evil. Perhaps that's why Scorpio is the only one of the twelve Signs with three astrological symbols—the Eagle, the Serpent and the Scorpion. Like the Eagle, Scorpios can soar to exalted heights of service to mankind. They can be as wise as the Serpent and extremely successful in worldly affairs. Or they can be as devilish in their methods and motives as the poisoned-tailed Scorpion.

It is usually the scorpionic and sexual side of this mysterious and fascinating Sign that achieves notoriety. This is naturally irritating to the very intelligent and reflective individuals born in October to November who, perhaps like yourself, represent the typical Scorpio character.

To ascertain just how pure a type you are, it is essential to take into account all the planetary positions given for your birthday in this book. These are clearly set out in the Pink Tables. Because the natural Scorpio urge is to go to one extreme or the other more so than any other Sign, these modifications are terribly important in making a correct AstroAnalysis.

The key to the Scorpio character is an insatiable desire to get at the truth. This urge can become distorted and badly corrupted, but it is present in every true Scorpio. In the underdeveloped type, the impulse becomes a search for self-satisfaction. Then there are no limits to the depths that may be plumbed. At any level of development, Scorpio is single-minded in whatever he or she undertakes. If it's sensual gratification, there will be no letup in the pursuit.

In the typical Scorpio person, the desire for the truth is recognizable in the way he or she is always endeavoring to get to the bottom of things. You Scorpios are the instinctive detectives of this world. You don't talk much unless it is about a pet subject. You listen, at least until you have summed up the situation or the people you are with.

You can ask the most direct and embarrassing questions without blinking an eye. Your skill at handling and dealing with difficult and downright offensive people is incredible. You know just what to do, just what to say. You despise hypocrisy and affectation. Anyone with something to hide should avoid a confrontation with a Scorpio. Your intuition and understanding of human nature is phenomenal. You have a way of asking the right question at the worst possible time.

Although you Scorpios are experts at unraveling the secrets in other people's lives, you manage to keep your own affairs very much to yourself. You relish secrecy. You revel in the cat-and-mouse game. You enjoy deliberately sparking the curiosity of others and then blocking their attempts to find out more. If anyone dares to try to pry into your affairs or take any liberties with your psyche, you get very haughty.

You are proud of your subtlety and skill at conducting intrigue. Nothing pleases you more than to prove your intellectual superiority in a contest of wits. You are not dependent on the acclaim of an audience, either. If your performance satisfies you, that is enough. In an extroverted world where ego satisfaction often depends on applause and admiration, you are a very difficult character to understand.

You are proud but not egotistical, dramatic but not ostentatious. You are a little bit too self-sufficient and durable for mere mortals to empathize with. No one ever really gets to know you.

You rarely volunteer information of any kind. But when asked a question, you will give a straightforward answer. When you do share a confidence with another individual, it will be a minor matter as far as you are concerned. And it will be because you want to encourage that person to talk.

To you, life is a pretty serious business. You are always working toward some aim or patiently waiting for the next move. You may appear relaxed and amiable in company, but you are always the center of your own existence. This attitude has given Scorpio the reputation of being selfish, self-centered and more than usually calculating.

That this is an accurate characterization no one knows better than you, but you are not necessarily immoral, as your critics try to make out. Rather, you are supremely self-aware. You are never little-boy or little-girl lost. You know exactly where you are. Other people may like to lose themselves, to forget the real world for a while and be comforted in silly and sentimental ways. Not you. You are no romantic when it comes to essentials. You can't bear to kid yourself. You want the truth, no matter how it hurts.

At first meeting, it is obvious that a typical Scorpio man or woman has something instinctively serious on his or her mind. It shows first in the eyes. The gaze is penetrating and compelling, uncommitted but very, very personal. There is a calmness to the face, a quiet intensity. In an instant, Scorpio seems to see all that matters in a person; something indefinable is communicated. The recipient of a Scorpio gaze usually feels immediate attraction or repulsion. Scorpios are such powerful personalities that their presence can often be felt in a room. They are certainly not the type that can ever be ignored.

If you are a typical Scorpio, you are intensely critical and skeptical. You can't help seeing faults and failings in others. Unfortunately, you are not so talented at perceiving your own. You have a stinging tongue when you want to use it. No other Sign is a match for your biting sarcasm.

You are very fixed in your ideas and absolutely convinced they are correct. It's true, you are often right. Your golden rule is not to accept anything unless you've proved it to your own satisfaction. You listen to what others have to say but you don't readily believe them. In you, there's always a degree of reserve and doubt, which sometimes comes across as suspicion or distrust. Frequently you are just plain disdainful and contemptuous when others try to convince or impress you.

In your search for what counts, you have learned to accept facts only. You are wary of opinions and impressions. Experience has taught you that others are easily conned, that they are far too willing to accept without question. You know better. You

check everything out. You're pretty sure of yourself. And it shows in your bluntness, which can be quite brutal on occasions. You can't stand fools.

One drawback to your pragmatic self-certainty is that you may fail to move with the times. You are inclined to stick to your views permanently. You won't listen to the advice of others, no matter how overwhelming their experience. Over the years, you become inflexible and with power or authority, a law to yourself. Too often you make the same mistakes over and over again. You don't mind a bit of pain and suffering to gain your ends, but what you're likely to overlook is that things don't have to be done the same way all the time!

As long as you are not opposed and don't have an ax to grind, you are a very likable person. You are helpful and courteous. You have good taste, a civilized outlook and an innate appreciation of the artistic and cultural side of life. People can overlook your rather caustic remarks because what you say usually contains the truth. The fact that people don't always like to hear the truth about themselves doesn't prevent them from admiring your straight-from-the-shoulder style.

Of course, you make enemies, more than most. You are too independent and outspoken. When you've got the bit in your teeth, you don't care what others think. You won't compromise or pull your punches. You stand by what you say because if it weren't true, you wouldn't have said it. You'll never back down on a matter of principle.

No authority can hope to compel you against your will more than temporarily. Eventually you will win out because you will continue to scheme and undermine long after everyone else has tired of the fight and wants to call it a day. In some ways, you are as invincible as you are implacable. Victory sometimes comes to you by default. No one else cares enough. Times change. You don't.

There was a Scorpio woman with an adult son and two younger daughters. She was an excellent mother and a widow. It was common knowledge that if anything ever happened to her, the bulk of her sizable estate would go to her son. She took ill. Her son made the mistake of mentioning in passing that he'd lost two thousand dollars in business over the weeks through visiting his mother. She died a couple of years later. In the will, she left the son two thousand dollars only, with no explanation. She'd changed her will in favor of her daughters the day after he made his remark.

You are the sort of person whose unconquerable nature can inspire others. Weaker characters gain strength from your example. Some who unwisely try to match your physical endurance collapse with exhaustion. When your mind is made up, you seem to be able to go on forever. Nothing daunts you, no added burden is too great. You personify indomitability.

Yet, paradoxically, you can be quite lazy; you can sit back and seem to take it easy for very long periods. You won't exert yourself for anything or anyone that doesn't interest you. You'll only go through the necessary motions and spend your time in introspection. Too much self-study can have odd effects on a Scorpio. One is you may lose all interest in life and will your own death. The volcano must express itself or explode.

Sometimes you will take someone who has a problem under your wing. You are generous and patient when your sympathy is aroused, a steadfast and staunch friend. You never go back on your word. You seldom make promises of your own volition, but when you do, you keep them. You help bring out the best in others.

Your most outstanding quality is your persistence and determination to reach your goals. It is characteristic of you Scorpio people to fix your objectives years ahead and to tenaciously work toward them irrespective of the difficulties. You have a one-track mind. You don't go around obstacles or try to remove them; you confront them and destroy them. Anything in your path gets flattened, no matter how long it takes.

This is not such an easy Sign for a woman to be born under. It is too dominant, masterful and unyielding for the female element to cope with comfortably. The Scorpio woman has to learn to pull her punches in her close relationships. She can seldom be herself with a man and get away with it for very long, even in these liberated days. She is very good for any male she links up with, though. Even if the association doesn't last, he will be a far wiser man when it's over. She will teach him much about himself.

If you look at a diagram of the Zodiac, you'll notice that Scorpio, the eighth Sign, is exactly opposite Taurus, the second Sign. This has a particular significance for you. You and Taurus have one thing in common. You are both intensely possessive. But there is this difference. Taurus loves to possess objects and money. This is because the first six Signs are concerned mainly with personal activities and in building up the individual ego. You love to possess people. Scorpio is among the last six Signs, which are more concerned with activities entered into with others.

You direct your feelings toward people. You are jealous and react violently to the feelings they cause in you and which you share. Although you enjoy creature comforts, you are not a materialistic person. What you gather are feelings, and you hold to them with even more emotional zeal than Taurus clings to money and belongings.

Scorpio is a water Sign, which means it is unfathomable and charged with high-pitched unstable emotionality. Taurus is a solid, phlegmatic earth Sign. Your energy is like an arresting shriek, Taurus energy is a bear hug. It's the same primal urge expressed by opposite temperaments.

You are bold, self-willed and love adventure. Your courage in the face of danger is magnificent. You are an excellent leader, a born strategist, an astute tactician. In an emergency, you are cool, calm, decisive. You think and act simultaneously. Your powers of observation are acute. You are practical and shrewd. Your mind works more constructively under moment-to-moment pressure than when you are making decisions based on your strong likes and dislikes. Here your capacity to hate and detest can take over and become a cold fury of absurd prejudice. In this mood, Scorpio may sink the ship and go down with it just to destroy the engineer.

Your self-control is tremendous. If ever you go off the rails in any way, it's because you wish to, not because you've lost your restraint. The exception is when your emotions are suddenly inflamed and you lash out or act on impulse. In these brief moments, you can do a terrible lot of damage to your own life and to other people's. Once you lose your cool, your judgment is either hopelessly impaired or completely subjugated by your passion. Fortunately, this happens rarely. Most of the time you maintain a facade of well-regulated control. Inside you are usually in turmoil, not because of any doubts or uncertainty, but because of the sheer intensity of your feelings. Still, no one would guess.

In weaker Scorpio types, this self-repression, instead of galvanizing the individual into productive effort, creates a smoldering resentment. Normal healthy expression becomes impossible. Vehement passions are generated, helped by a brooding imagination. An emotional venom reminiscent of the Scorpion's paralyzing poison builds up. No Sign is as relentlessly vindictive, cruel or sadistic as Scorpio raw and unregenerate. These characters never forget an injury, even an imagined one. Whereas others may be content to forget a wrong once the person who committed it is out of their life, unregenerate Scorpios will wait years for the moment of retaliation. These individuals are quite capable of engineering complex conspiracies to bring about another's downfall. Their power to harm is concealed in subtlety. They can be friendly and helpful while plotting mercilessly. Here emotion contorts the Scorpio search for truth into the craving for retribution. The vendetta is a truly Scorpio iniquity if ever there was one.

There is much nobility in your character if only it can be released. No other Sign can love with the grandeur of the Scorpio individual who has managed to open the floodgates of his or her heart. You have the capacity for total devotion to a cause or a person. Scorpio men and women make the most inspired mystics. Their spiritual fervor and insights into higher truths can raise the consciousness and faith of others. If they can overcome the peculiar possessiveness of their affections, learn to forgive and release those who have hurt them, they can fervently love all of humanity. If not, their repressive nature makes them unconsciously despise mankind.

At heart, you are altruistic. You wish to heal your fellow man, to remove his doubts and uncertainties, to give him wings to fly like the eagle above the earth's limitations. For this reason, your type is often among the world's finest psychiatrists and surgeons. You are naturally adapted to probe or cut to remove the mental hangups and physical causes that prevent men and women from being what they are or ought to be. But before Scorpio can overcome the ills of the world, it must first conquer itself. This is indeed the Sign of the phoenix that rises transformed from its own ashes.

You have a fineness of taste that is evident in your home. You are rather traditional. As a rule, you prefer older and more elegant furniture to modern contemporary styles. You like your home to be a place apart from the world and its problems. You enjoy entertaining, but very selectively. You do not appreciate people who casually drop in uninvited. You rather enjoy formality. You are a sophisticated host or hostess, but enjoy letting your hair down in the right company as the evening progresses. You are likely to drink or smoke too much.

The Scorpio man is not likely to be numbered among the ten best-dressed males. In fact, he's rather lax in his sartorial habits. Unless he's got a mate or date who cares, he's apt to forget to have his trousers pressed. He's the type who gives his shoes a quick rub on the back of his socks. He's convinced that people are more concerned with what's inside the package than with the wrapping.

Lady Scorpio is inclined to be a bit old-fashioned in her choice of clothes. That is, she'll wear the latest gear in her youth, but when that's over, she'll tend to stick to the same styles. What she wears may suit her perfectly, but how can a woman look really smart in picture hats and corsages? A modern Scorpio woman is likely to wear the most masculine jeans and other old gear and still manage to look sexier than any female at the party. She knows instinctively that she doesn't have to try to look good to attract men. She knows about the bees and the honeypot. Some Scorpio women buy their clothes piecemeal instead of coordinating a look. In a moment of impulse, they may invest in a smashing outfit, and then wear last season's shoes with it. They are very good with colors but a bit square on image.

For pastimes, you Scorpio people like activities where you can use your body or put your intuition to practical use. Your tremendous energy and stamina, plus your natural ability to think and act at the same time, make you extremely proficient at active, competitive sports. Given a choice, you usually prefer water sports. Both men and women like to keep in good shape. Remarkably enough, you often look older than your years in youth and younger in middle age.

The powerful libidinal energies of the Scorpio person are often very successfully released in artistic pursuits. You are very progressive in these fields. It is likely that you are quite ingenious in adapting existing art forms to your own ideas. You are inclined to pull down the established order and replace it with a different version of itself. You introduce depth and greater meaning. Whether it's in art, poetry or literature, your work suggests a new dimension. When you get involved in art, it is not just a pleasing aesthetic experience. It's a labor of love into which you pour your energies with passionate intensity. To many of you, it is a therapeutic necessity. There is no such thing as a halfhearted Scorpio in any of the arts.

If you are a typical Scorpio person, you have a deep-seated interest in the occult. You may try to deny it, especially in your brasher younger years, but eventually it will intrigue you because all that is mysterious and unsolved fascinates you. You dream of discovering the secrets of life beyond the rational. You look for the keys to life contained in the esoteric disciplines and pseudo-sciences.

You may not be a psychic investigator or clairvoyant, but you sense the reality of the spiritual and psi worlds. You are intrigued by discussions on magic, witchcraft and primitive cults. Astrology means more to you than you would probably ever admit. You know and feel things that make you realize your perception reaches beyond the senses. It won't surprise you to learn that Scorpio is the Sign associated with flying saucers, a mystery yet to be solved.

Sometimes Scorpio men and women are considered a bit morbid. Others can't understand your interest in questions concerning life and death, which often amounts to preoccupation. This is not surprising. Scorpio, as well as being the Sign of sex, is the Sign of death and regeneration. You Scorpios are not the least afraid of death as a physical ending. You are concerned with it as a psychological mystery that constantly taunts you to find the solution within yourself. The reason you don't fear death is that instinctively you know it is only a concept. You seek to demolish it, to release its hold on your psyche, with the same intensity with which you attack everything else.

Similarly, your strong sexual feelings are nothing more than the primal urge to penetrate to the roots, to be at one with something, to identify with your source, whatever that may be, in a final ecstatic forgetfulness. If this sounds a bit flaky to you, you are not a true Scorpio. Only a true Scorpio can understand the weird profundity of his or her feelings.

As lovers, Scorpio men and women are superb. Your responses to the various Signs are discussed in detail in the next chapter. Briefly, Scorpio people are built to probe the mystery of sex. At this stage of human evolution, this irrepressible energy is expressed mainly in physical ways. As a result, Scorpio individuals are highly sensual. You are sexually magnetic, you give deep satisfaction, but your chances of forming a happy permanent relationship are not too good. Sexual fulfillment with your partner may be wonderful, but the psychological side of a relationship may prove difficult.

Scorpios are demanding, domineering and fiercely jealous mates You often find it hard to resist a secret love affair. Despite your better judgment, you often yield to the impulse of passion and mystery, even if you are happily married. You may not, but it's always a lusty possibility, more so than with any other Sign.

Few Scorpios seem to escape tragedy or disaster in their love life. Those who can sublimate their intense erotic desires in artistic or productive ways and free their imagination of constant erotic images have a chance at making a reasonably happy marriage. It depends substantially on compatibility, so it would be advisable for you to check out your mate in the appropriate book of this series.

An interesting astrological tradition exists concerning the Sign of Scorpio, which some authorities maintain is the most important of the twelve. Way back in the forgotten past, before the Age of Atlantis, there were only ten Signs in the Zodiac. Virgo and Scorpio were one; Libra didn't exist.

At this time, apparently, there was only the human spirit—a kind of unisex entity—comprising both the masculine and the feminine principles. The immortals in their wisdom split the then sixth Sign (Virgo-Scorpio) in two by inserting Libra (the balancing Sign) in between. Virgo, of course, is the Sign of the Virgin and represents Eve. Scorpio, of course, is Adam and represents the pure sex drive. It's clearly no accident that Libra, which now stands between them, is the Sign of partnership and marriage.

According to the ancient esoteric teaching, we human spirits for a few billion years have been living out our incarnations not as whole beings but as our male and female halves. We must learn how to be reunited in spirit. By seeking union only through the physical body, we're apparently getting nowhere fast and binding ourselves to the earth. Love alone, through the true partnership principle epitomized by Libra, is the link and the way.

Scorpios have a highly developed intellect and a sharp, resourceful mind. Subjects you are interested in you learn very quickly. Your unquenchable desire to dominate often induces you to take on a job or duty that others would avoid. You want power, sometimes at any price. Your memory is excellent. You make a point of being well informed on the topics you discuss and the projects you undertake. You absorb facts easily and pay close attention to the details of a proposition.

You are a thorough and systematic thinker though sometimes narrow in your approach. Your preconceived ideas are both your strength and your weakness. You never go off half-cocked, but are sometimes inclined to delay matters. Your gift for visualization reveals defects in plans and possible problems long before they are evident to others. Your imagination sometimes gets out of control, and you daydream about your love life. But as a rule, you keep your thinking straight and very down to earth.

One overriding fault is that you separate your life into various compartments, meaning you don't think in an integrated way. You can have two opposing feelings about one subject because you concentrate on aspects and not the total picture. This is one reason why you are so dogmatic. You don't admit grays to your vision, just blacks and whites, likes and dislikes. You can't weigh one fact against another. Instead you sift and isolate facts and consider them individually, in succession.

You are very quick, though, to discern what is relevant. What you want, you pursue; what you don't want, you shun; what opposes you, you demolish. Consideration is a compartment called the self: you are self-made and self-existing. This is a simple code for living at either the highest or the lowest level of human aspiration.

Sometimes you appear to be a very stubborn person, like your opposite Sign Taurus, which is renowned for obstinacy. But your obstinacy has a different root: you are just very hard to influence. Anyone who thinks he can win you over to an idea by the hard sell, or even the soft sell, will be sorely disappointed. You fortify yourself against outside influence by learning everything about a subject you are interested in. In your opinion, there's only one way to do something you're involved in, and that's your way!

Despite your calm and composed manner, you have difficulty keeping still for long. Your nervous energy often makes you an inveterate doodler, leg swinger or finger tapper.

You are one of these admirable people who don't think that life owes them a living. In fact, you don't expect much from other people, especially in the way of favors and handouts. You don't resent life's adversities because you're determined to make the best of things even in the worst of circumstances. This trait is particularly evident in the Scorpio woman. When hard times hit, she is quite prepared to share economic and other responsibilities with her mate. And she won't complain if she's got to go without things in order to bring up her children properly.

Is there such a creature as a lonely Scorpio person? Indeed there is. Loneliness usually arises from early rejection by a mother or father or both, or later parental figures. The rejection grows into resentment of all others. A love-hate complex can develop regarding the opposite sex. Even amid intense physical intimacy, Scorpio can be joyless, loveless and lonely. However, true Scorpio courage can enable such people to face up to their deeper resentments and fears. Then they can rid themselves of their constricting and repelling emotionalism and discover the joy and fulfillment of loving from the heart.

CHAPTER SIX

Scorpio in Love and Friendship

What will Scorpio expect from love? What will Scorpio give to a partnership? What will a partner give in return? Where does friendship fit? This chapter provides a profile of romantic Scorpio, a compatibility guide for Scorpio, and an account of Scorpio as a friend.

The Scorpio Woman

Deep. Dominant. Dynamite. Dangerous. Direct.

If Scorpio wants to have an affair with you, she'll let you know. She'll sum you up as a male the instant she meets you; she'll know your weaknesses and your strengths.

This woman is deeper, sexier and more realistic than any other woman you'll ever meet. And she has a voracious sexual and emotional appetite. Boys had better not apply to be her lover.

The Scorpio female is a very puzzling combination of contradictions and extremes. She is highly intelligent and intensely physical. She loves to be complimented and appreciated, but resents flattery. She doesn't like to be criticized, but can dish it out bluntly to others.

She has the cultured type of mind that appreciates the civilized and educated side of things. She's not arty, yet she understands art and probably collects it. She loves mysteries, especially the occult.

Scorpio will attract you as soon as she enters the room. She has a reserved, aloof poise. Her look of interest is a deep penetrating gaze that reaches down into the depths of your being. You'll sense she's seeing things that even you don't know are there. She is. One of her unique armaments is her ability to divine a man's soul.

No male will ever put one over on her unless she is bemused by her emotions. Then she's a hopeless case of surrender to her own self-indulgent desires. Otherwise she keeps control of any romantic situation. She is quite capable of having affair after affair without her feelings being the least bit involved. Her body and its desires are one thing. Her emotional self is another. She keeps them in two separate compartments. If they ever get mixed up, it's dynamite.

A Scorpio woman is very direct. If she's married and needs an affair because her husband can't satisfy her passions, she'll tell you it's only your body she wants. Take it or leave it. She won't want you falling in love with her and making trouble. It's quite an experience to meet such an extraordinary woman.

If you marry her and are true, your Scorpio lady will also be loyal. But you will have to be intensely virile to satisfy her sexual needs.

She will go to no end of trouble to make the home comfortable and attractive; she is very talented at selecting furnishings. She will adore her children, but she won't put them before you. She's rather old-fashioned in her homemaking ideas and will endeavor to do everything correctly and in the best of taste.

She's jealous. And she's dangerous. Don't try to kid her along. If you cross her, she'll be on your doorstep at midnight letting all the neighbors know just what a so-and-so you are. Or she'll call the office and tell your boss a couple of secrets you've confided to her. Or she might just flatten you with a saucepan. Anything to hurt, anything to get even. This is a volcano of a woman you're thinking about.

She doesn't give a hoot what other people think when she's made up her mind to do something. She's courageous. Her ideas are fixed. She either loves, hates, or is indifferent to something, and that's that.

She's not the type to have many girlfriends. She spends a lot of her time just assessing people and not becoming intimate, let alone close.

She won't put you on a pedestal. She'll see you exactly as you are. She won't kid herself, and she certainly won't allow you the luxury of self-delusion. In three words, this woman can deflate any pretentious male or female. She's not a gossip. She doesn't confide in others. She's a bit distrustful of everyone. She's learned that most people are fools because all fools are people. She doesn't give anyone the benefit of the doubt.

Scorpio needs friction in her love relationships to keep them sufficiently alive and satisfying. This gives meaning she can feel. She adores an argument with her man, the stimulus of bared, ferocious passion.

For her lover, the making up afterward—because she is so sexually proficient and desirable in her uncharacteristic surrender—is not infrequently ecstatic. Great. But can you stand the emotional workup to it? That's a question you're going to have to answer.

The Scorpio Man

Deep. Dominant. Magnetic. Passionate. Demanding.

Scorpio is not usually an easy man to get along with in a permanent relationship, unless he feels contented. He'll never be mastered or changed, so if you're a persistently dominating type of woman, or if you have hopes of reforming him after marriage, forget it. Your life together could be hell.

This guy has a subtle yet distinctive magnetism. When you meet him for the first time, he'll either turn you on or make you want to run a mile. The trouble is, even when you're running from him, you may want to look back. He's interesting. Arresting. When he makes an approach, you're either for him or against him. You can't ignore him. The vibes this man sends out are heavily sexual. You have to respond.

You'd better understand right from the start that there are two Scorpio men. In no other Sign are the differences between the evolved and the immature type so important to the woman who is thinking of marriage or a long-term affair.

The undeveloped type can be a bully and a brute. He will use his suave Scorpio manner and sharp intellect to impress a woman, but his ulterior motives are sex or domination. This guy wants power over people. Men are quick to shun him, but his powerful physical appeal and disarming surface charm gull many women. He's not an easy man to get away from. He can be unscrupulous, violent, jealous, vindictive, cruel and revengeful. At the first sign that he's a baddie, you had better start running.

The good Scorpio guy, although a powerful personality, manages to direct his energies into productive channels. Sex is extremely important to him, but it doesn't occupy his entire life. Given the right woman, he will settle down. In fact, this man can make a good husband. He loves his home and will do everything in his power to give the right woman all she desires.

Yet he will always remain a law unto himself— that is, he will cooperate, but only so far. He insists on making all the major decisions. Once he sets his mind on an objective, he will never give up; no one will dissuade him. But he is sincere and honest. He can't stand duplicity. You must be open with him.

If you marry a Scorpio man, you may be lonely at times. He doesn't make many friends, and those he has have to be intelligent and able to discourse on the subjects that interest him.

He's a wonderful businessman. You should have some opportunities to play hostess when he invites clients home to help him swing a deal. But unless there's a good practical reason, he likes to keep his business and private life as separate as possible.

His home is his haven. He expects his woman to be there always. He doesn't like surprise parties and similar lighthearted intrusions.

He's very possessive, suspicious and jealous. He won't tolerate infidelity. He will never forgive the woman who betrays him. Once she puts her foot out the door to meet another man, she'd better keep going.

If you love this man, he'll give you the feeling you need never fear anything again. So self-sufficient is he that he seems capable of standing alone against any odds. His determination makes him almost invincible. Almost!

His emotions are his weakness. He is impulsive where they are concerned. He has a fearful temper. When aroused, he is likely to do anything. When in love, he will throw caution to the wind and consider nothing more important than reaching his love mate.

He often makes the same mistakes in romance over and over again. His passionate nature seems to drive him on regardless of the consequences. When he finds himself in romantic competition, he can endure tremendous aggravation for long periods while working patiently at undermining the opposition.

Scorpio is not a flirt. He has two things on his mind: sex and finding the right mate. He won't confuse you. If you are all he's looking for in a woman, there's no reason why life together with this strange and often brilliant man should not work out—if he is the evolved type. Just be sure you AstroAnalyze the other influences working in his horoscope because you can't afford to make a mistake here.

Scorpio Compatibility Guide

Each description of a partner, or potential partner, is based on their Sun Sign. For a closer look see the relevant *AstroAnalysis* book. Then you can AstroAnalyze your partner and discover new clues to his or her personality.

Scorpio Woman—Aries Man

If you are the type of Scorpio woman who needs friction to keep your close relationships alive, then link up with an Aries man. He likes to dominate, so do you. You cannot stand to be told what to do. Traits like yours conflicting with those of Aries are pretty good for openers.

You both know how to dish it out. On first meeting, the sparks are likely to fly. When it comes to verbal battles, you're both as hot and fiery as a volcanic explosion.

There are many things that will attract you to Aries, although you may not like to admit it even to yourself. He has an air of stability. You'll get the impression he would know what to do in a crisis. He seems very sure of himself without being aggressive.

People find you hard to fathom. You seem mysterious even to your close friends. The Ram will find your aura magnetic. You are the type of woman who instantly appeals to him, even though he will instinctively know you are going to be quite a handful.

It is difficult to work out just how long you would last together. There would always be an underlying tension in the union.

Even though you may be deeply in love, you will want to test each other all the time. You will bring out the fighter in him and vice versa.

If an Aries man has set his sights on you, he will certainly battle to win your love. This is a quality you admire in a man because, deep down, you're a bit of a romantic. The idea of a dream prince willing to try to overcome all the obstacles between you is very appealing.

You have ambition, although it can be misdirected at times. It is possible for Scorpio people to channel their talents and energies into pointless and nonproductive projects. This is where the Ram could help you. If you would take good advice for once in your life, this man could put you on the right track.

You are both spontaneous and abandoned lovers. Physically you will have no problems. However hurtful your verbal battles may be on occasions, you should always be able to make it up in the bedroom. And how sweet it will be.

You could not call an Aries man subtle. You will realize after two or three dates with him that your basic attitudes toward life are very different. If you can learn to respect each other's opinions, you will have overcome the major stumbling block to permanent happiness.

A single-minded Scorpio woman may become worried by the Aries haste to change things. You will think him crazy when he gives up a steady job to earn less money elsewhere. The fact is he feels he has to rise to new challenges to keep alive. He can't stand being trapped in a routine for very long.

He doesn't go for the out-of-date or antique. He loves the latest in everything. He's very gadget-conscious and is fascinated by any mechanical devices he can tinker with and improve.

Aries men love children. They make fine fathers. Kids take to the Aries dad like ducks to water.

You may find a man born under the first Sign of the Zodiac too demanding. He will always be questioning you, and you can't stand constant cross-examinations. On his part, he will be confused by your occasional sullenness and changes of mood. He always tries to do the right thing, though, and this will endear him to you.

Even if he doesn't always manage it, he will try to understand you. Remember this, and you will find it much easier to forgive this likable boyish character for some of his tactlessness.

Scorpio Woman—Taurus Man

Look at any picture of the Zodiac, and you'll notice that your Sun Sign is opposite Taurus. You know all about the attraction of opposites, and this could well be what draws you two together. He is a real man. He's the sort of guy you can turn to when you've got a problem. You will always feel secure in his company.

One of the difficulties for a water baby like you in this Taurus-Scorpio linkup is that you can't stand to admit you need anyone's help. No matter what sort of situation you get yourself into, you like to sort it out unaided.

This fighting attitude is all well and good, but it's not what love is all about. Occasionally you must put trust in people. You have to be willing to take a chance of getting hurt if you are going to become deeply in involved in a relationship.

You should not be too doubtful about the Bull. If he gives his word, he will usually stick to it. He is not the game playing type of man you are likely to meet elsewhere in the Zodiac.

You will infuriate each other, of course. His stubbornness will drive you mad. Your black moods will seem to him like adolescent tantrums.

You will always know where you stand with a Taurus man. He doesn't use a line in order to attract or impress a woman.

If he meets you at a party, or even approaches you while you're walking down the street (he's aggressive enough to do that), he will come straight out with what is on his mind: sex. He might ask you around to his place for dinner or suggest you have a crazy weekend in Vegas. You might feel like slapping his face. But you will have to admire his honesty.

He will know how to wine and dine you. Although a very astute businessman, he is never tight with money where the opposite sex is concerned. He will take you to the best restaurants and make sure you have a wonderful time.

Friends will warn you about a Taurus man. They'll say he's a womanizer and will break your heart if you give your love to him. Find out for yourself. It's true he has an eye for pretty girls, but basically that's because he's searching for someone to give him the roots and security that every Taurus man deeply needs.

It is amazing how quickly this man settles down when he finds what he wants. You will love the home he provides. He will not interfere with the way you manage financial matters because he trusts your Scorpio shrewdness. He will be proud to bring people home to dinner.

Taurus is noted for his jealousy—a quality you also possess in abundance. If either of you were to fool around after settling down together, it's likely you'd split up pretty quickly.

Being an honest Scorpio woman, you might find it difficult to give this man the flattery that makes him hum. Perhaps if you love him enough, you'll find it in you to praise him, realizing that by boosting his confidence you will make it possible for him to achieve greater things.

You both love kids. As parents, you will find you basically agree on how children should be brought up. As a pair, you must beware of being too strict with your children.

Scorpio Woman—Gemini Man

As friends, you would be a great pair. As business associates, you would be a fantastic combination. As lovers, you will have problems.

It's possible that when you first meet Gemini you'll decide he's a guy you couldn't trust as far as you could throw him. But then you'll discover you are drawn to him against your better judgment.

If he falls for you, you'll have great difficulty shaking him off your trail. Once Gemini really wants something, he usually gets it.

He can be very childlike. He's like the little boy tugging at Mommy's arm to get the bicycle he sees in the shop window. Even though Daddy can't afford it, he usually gets his way.

If you do eventually fall under his spell, beware! Gemini is a great user of people. He takes everything he can from them. He sucks them dry and then moves on to pastures new. Don't misunderstand. He doesn't do this purposely. He just doesn't understand what motivates him and needs constant changes of scene—variety.

It is very difficult for this man to form a permanent relationship. When he goes cold on something, you won't see him for dust. He doesn't like to face up to responsibilities. He hates feeling trapped.

If he does something to hurt you, your suffering will be great. You might try every ploy in the book to get him to settle down. You might even end up feeling rather sorry for him because you will realize he is getting nowhere fast.

A Gemini man tends to live for the moment. He doesn't relish the idea of making definitive decisions—decisions that would bind him to a positive course of action.

If he is in a group at a party, you can bet he will be the one doing all the talking. He will forget all about you, sitting in the corner waiting for some attention and affection.

He is a constant flirt. He will promise you undying love and mean it. This is what is so difficult about the Twins. You can't call him a liar, because you'll be able to see by the look in his eyes that he means the words he is saying at the moment he is saying them.

In sheer frustration, the smart Scorpio woman may decide to give him up. That is not because you don't love him anymore, but because you'll realize he's not ever going to do you any good.

Is there any chance of your getting it together in marriage? Well, perhaps, if you meet this man when he has had a great deal of experience of life and realized he can't go on chasing rainbows forever. Then there is a possibility you'll find true happiness. There will still be differences, of course, because basically you are very different types.

He's generous. On a date, he will insist on paying for everything even if he can't afford it. His generosity can become downright foolish. You are much better at money management than he, and you're a shrewd saver.

Gemini loves going deeply into subjects, and so do you. Romance is necessary for him. For all his blunders and irresponsibility, you will have to treat him with gentleness and affection.

He won't take your Scorpio moodiness all that seriously, which is probably a good thing. His sense of humor will help you to laugh at yourself.

He gets on terribly well with people younger, than himself probably because he has such a youthful attitude toward life.

It is Gemini's youthfulness that makes him a wonderful father, being both a playmate and a parent to the children.

Scorpio Woman—Cancer Man

You will have much in common with this man. Both of you were born under water Signs. So you should have the same sort of rhythms and composure. You will understand his moods and will certainly have a good deal of sympathy for him when he gets down in the dumps, which is often for Cancer.

One of your problems might be that you will have a negative effect on each other. Unless you surround yourself with positive constructive people, you tend to sink terribly low. It is exactly the same for your Cancer man.

You both tend to be dreamers. You could spend many evenings talking about what might have been if only. Such reminiscences are all very interesting, but is it going to get you anywhere?

He tries to be steady. He desires security. Cancer always appears to end up making the most dreadful mistakes, though. The way he tells the story of his life you will get the impression that the whole world has ganged up against him to plan his downfall.

He needs affection and he needs looking after. He also needs a strong woman to give him a kick occasionally and tell him to get out and on with it.

You do need a powerful man. It is not an easy task to beguile a Scorpio woman. It would appear to be beyond the capabilities of most Cancer men to keep you interested.

He's a fussy Crab, especially when it comes to romance. He has to desire a woman strongly before he makes a play for her. He is unlikely to get involved in many casual affairs.

It is in the home that you will both function best. You will love having quiet evenings together. Cancer is highly domestic. He will enjoy doing the cooking, especially for gala occasions. You will be amazed at how capable he is in the kitchen.

Cancer won't mind your continuing with a career after marriage if that is what you desire. He will be quite capable of looking after the kids if he is left to cope alone.

You both enjoy entertaining, though you prefer to have a few well-chosen friends over than to host large gatherings.

This man often has a great deal of artistic talent within him. Many people born under this Sign have turned out to be famous writers or musicians who earn fortunes in their lifetime.

You must try not to take each other too seriously. Always look on the bright side of things.

Be sure he invests his money wisely. He is careful with loot, perhaps too careful. He's likely to put his cash in extra-safe government bonds that pay good interest but do not show capital appreciation.

If you love him and are prepared to give as much as you take, this could be a happy and lasting relationship. He will rarely step out of line because he would hate to jeopardize his marriage for a passing fancy.

Cancer will see to it that you are always provided for. He will pay the bills on time even if he has to work all hours to do so.

He makes a wonderful and loving father. Perhaps he is better with girls than boys. But very often the Scorpio mother is better with boys than girls, so you should balance each other out as loving parents.

At times, you'll think he is overindulging the children—and he probably is. But he does have a fine way of nurturing youngsters through kindness and understanding so that they grow up with an appreciation of basic values. For instance, he's a great believer in courtesy and moral rectitude. He thinks these are the qualities that hold the family and society together.

Scorpio Woman—Leo Man

Much will depend on the picture you have built up of your dream man. With Leo it is important that you are searching for a leader—a man who will look after you, protect you, enlighten you and occasionally dominate you.

As an honest Scorpio, you must ask yourself a number of serious questions before you get deeply involved. If you are too wrapped up in yourself and your own opinions to change—even when you know deep down it is for the best—it would be wise to forget any further involvement.

Leo is a no-nonsense type. He will not meekly submit to your moods or tantrums. One thing you can be sure of is that whatever admonishment and guidance he metes out will be with your best interests at heart. He will not be trying to satisfy his own ego.

He can be a bit of an actor. He loves to make a dramatic effect. Basically, he needs lots of loving and fussing. The Lion likes to have his mane ruffled and to be tickled under the chin. You will soon see through his posing and strutting and realize that he is basically a wonderfully soft and sensitive man.

He can be aggressive. His temper is just as frightening as your Scorpio rage when it is aroused. He's tenacious, too. If he decides you are his woman, he'll stalk you until you submit. When the Lion is in love, it is impossible to ignore him or pretend he isn't there.

Let us hope your ideal man is not the sort who will meekly submit to your strong Scorpio will. This is doubtful since you don't admire weakness, even if you do put up a struggle before you commit to an equal.

Leo is a hard worker. He does not like to remain idle for long. He's always coming up with new ideas. Let us hope your Leo man gets to the top in his career. People born under this Sign hate to take orders. They always feel their ideas are best. Very often they are proved right.

He can be a bit of a showoff. He is inclined to become egotistical when things are going his way. This is where you will come in. One or two stinging remarks from you will remind him that he is only human after all.

He's great to go out on the town with. When you are courting, he'll really give you the treatment. Leos have the knack of appearing to have money when they are actually low on funds. It's wonderful the way they can put on a show when they haven't got two cents to rub together.

Leo is very possessive. He will not like to let you out of his sight. He won't be happy about your having an independent career once you are married if it's going to interfere with your focus on him and the home life he wants.

It's terribly important to him to be the number-one interest in your life. He will want you to be waiting to throw your loving arms around him when he comes home from the office. He will enjoy telling you what a successful day he had.

The physical side of your relationship should be quite something. He's a passionate lover. As a passionate Scorpio woman, you will know just how to excite and satisfy him.

Don't get too annoyed at his flirtations because they are unlikely to be serious. It's part of Leo's character to play up to the prettiest woman in the room.

He's very good with kids. He doesn't usually desire a large family, only the number he feels he can handle properly and teach. He's a great one for giving kids instruction in practical matters. He's both strict and indulgent, depending on how he feels at the time.

Scorpio Woman—Virgo Man

You won't find it easy to get it together with a Virgo man, though he will have many qualities you can't help but admire. He is serious, dedicated, a man of his word. He would never welsh on a promise. He is certainly honorable.

It would appear, however, that he's a little too tame for a dynamite Scorpio woman like you. You like some drama and excitement in your life.

He's terribly fussy and pedantic. He's also a stickler for hygiene. He can't stand dust on the windowsill or dirty dishes in the kitchen sink.

Having rather a mischievous streak, you will find it difficult not to tease your earth-bound Virgo lover. Don't ever underestimate him, though. Remember he is ruled by Mercury, and therefore has a very quick mind.

He is a logical man. He believes that you acquire talent by hard work rather than being born with it. He admires people who strive to get to the top in their careers. He tends to write off people like pop stars as useless members of society.

He is devoted to the old-fashioned ways, the tried-and-true traditions. If you are looking for a level-headed man, a fellow with his feet planted firmly on the ground, then look no further.

Virgo doesn't do anything on the spur of the moment. If you decide to get married, he won't go for your idea of rushing into it. Everything will have to be planned down to the last detail. The invitations must be printed, the wedding cake designed. Everything must be just right.

He's a bit hesitant where love is concerned. When you start to date him, you may feel that first goodnight kiss is never coming. He doesn't believe in rushing anything. He feels that love should grow slowly. He will want to get to know you really well before he commits himself.

But once there, his love is unselfish. He will want to do everything possible for you. He tends to put his woman on a pedestal.

As a Scorpio you are the no-nonsense type, so you may find his overly sedate ways rather irritating. He is quite mannered because he often finds it necessary to put on an act to conceal his basic fear and insecurity. He will not allow many people to get close to him.

Virgo will always face up to his responsibilities, even if he occasionally finds them distasteful. He is neither a shirker nor a quitter.

He is a good son to his parents. He is likely to have great respect for his father in particular and his elders in general.

His lovemaking may be a bit too tepid for a sensual Scorpio like you. You are much more physical than he is. You will have to have great patience with him in bed and teach him to let himself go. He can be a bit of a prude where sex is concerned.

If you are able to overcome your various problems together, you'll find you have a devoted and loving husband. Although you may feel many men are more exciting, you will find him more dependable than most. This is sort of relationship that will gain in strength over the years.

He loves his home comforts. He will be happy to do his fair share of the domestic chores. He will want you to pursue your own interests and have your own friends. He's neat in appearance and quite capable of looking after himself. Virgos are never sloppy dressers.

Virgo will make a fine father, though he might not want kids until you've had a few years of married life together.

Scorpio Woman—Libra Man

You will enjoy being the company of a smooth Libra man. He certainly knows how to treat a woman. He is a good talker.

But whether he is a strong enough type of man for you is a question you will have to ask yourself. It is true you like your man to put you before anything else. Libra has many interests. He is also a bit of a dreamer.

As an alluring Scorpio you will be a mystery to him. He may not be able to cope with your moods. He can't stand arguments.

This man is interested in people, people from all walks of life. He blows hot and cold. One moment, he will be all over you; the next, he'll seem strangely distant and aloof. He becomes bored terribly quickly. If

you want to keep this man, you'll have to keep him guessing, which is no problem for secretive Scorpio.

You are a fairly possessive woman. If you throw scenes because he has arrived home late, he won't be able to take it.

He is a true romantic. It is possible for you to have a sexual relationship without becoming emotionally involved. Not so a Libra. If he is not in love, or at least convinced himself he's in love, he simply can't work up any interest.

You will find his mind fascinating. He knows how to tell a story. He is fickle. Being a Scorpio who likes to know where you stand with a man, you could easily get your heart broken if you go overboard here.

He hides his depressions, doesn't like others to see him when he is down in the dumps. The reason he tries to put on a brave front is that he feels the world situation is bad enough without adding his personal gloom.

You could be driven to physical violence by his flirting ways. He simply can't help playing up to a pretty woman. You will have to learn to turn a blind eye when you are out on a date together.

Libra can be vague. He will hardly notice all the effort you put into keeping the home running. He takes such things for granted. But when you wear a new dress, he'll always notice.

It's amazing how cold and ruthless a Libra can be when he has to face adversity.

It doesn't take this man long to get over an affair that goes wrong. He bounces back pretty quickly after having suffered a rough time.

Your physical relationship should be good. He will love your uninhibited Scorpio way of making love. He likes a woman who comes on strong, so he won't mind your taking the lead in the bedroom.

There is a lot you can learn from a Libra. He is a good talker, and you'll discover he can interest you in subjects that previously had no appeal. He's ambitious without being pushy. He is capable of fighting his way to the top. Once he has made up his mind on a positive course of action, he sticks to it.

Life with your Libra man will not be roses all the way. There is bound to be a certain amount of conflict. Periods of strife could help to keep your union alive. You will need to be interested in his work because his job is likely to be very important to him.

He will not try to pry into your secrets. He will understand that there are certain things about your past you want to remain buried.

It could be that you will have to make most of the important decisions in this liaison. You will have to be prepared to take on quite a lot of the responsibility for the children, the finances and the running of the household.

Financially, there will be a few ups and downs. A Libra is not good at budgeting.

He will be very fair with the children. He will make sure they are very well provided for.

Scorpio Woman—Scorpio Man

It seems natural that people born under the same Sign be instantly attracted to each other. After all, they share numerous personality traits. But very often this is not the case. Either we recognize and abhor in the other person our own weaknesses, or the union has no mystery.

In the case of Scorpio-Scorpio, you need have no such worries. You are likely to be instantly attracted to each other.

Chances are you'll fall for each other on first meeting. It is quite likely this will begin mainly as a physical attraction. As you get to know each other better, you'll find you both have much more to offer. Your love will be passionate on both a mental and a physical plane.

You will recognize each other's weaknesses, all right. But in understanding your partner, you will also come to terms with your own hangups.

Like you, he is jealous and possessive. He is a real fighter for what he believes in. You like a man who lays his cards on the table.

His lovemaking can be bawdy and aggressive or gentle and caressing.

You must both watch your raging Scorpio tempers. You will have to treat your man with the same respect you expect from him.

He is, of course, a very direct person. He will fight to the end for what he believes in. He is perfectly capable of quitting a good job if he feels he is not being treated fairly.

You should understand him well enough to be able to channel his fire and determination into worthwhile endeavors. In Scorpio unions if you are not working for each other's good, you will destroy each other and probably yourselves into the bargain.

He is not a great romantic, but then, you're usually not enamored of the soft-talking sweet-music kind of lover. Your sex scene is unlikely to become dull. It will be a matter of pride to both of you to bring satisfaction to your partner.

Love without jealousy doesn't exist for either of you. You both like to feel your partner is desired by others. But in order to keep this relationship alive, it is essential that neither of you become seriously involved with another.

Home is an important place for you both. There will be many nights when you will be content to stay in, plan your next mutual strategic move, then imagine sweet victory ahead.

As a woman, you can be very hard on yourself. Your understanding Scorpio man will help you to overcome this self-criticism. You find it hard to allow any man to make the important decisions, but you'll feel you can trust your Scorpio mate more than most.

He will adore your passion. He likes his woman to be all woman, not little-girl-lost.

People rarely get the better of him in business. He is very shrewd at psyching out others.

He will be terribly ambitious for his children and will do all he can to make sure his kids get to the top in whatever career they enter. Scorpio men are sometimes heavy-handed with the discipline. If he has a son, he may try to turn him into a carbon copy of himself.

If you can stick together through the difficult times, you will help each other to become better and wiser human beings.

Scorpio Woman—Sagittarius Man

When you first meet him, he'll seem to have many of the qualities you demand in a man. He has a powerful personality, a certain magnetism and a good sense of humor—which will never be directed against his woman. But if you contemplate settling into any kind of personal relationship, certain major obstacles must first be overcome.

He is rather frightened of losing his freedom. He is hard to catch and harder to live with. He has to be constantly on the go. You do like to have your quiet moments. Sagittarius finds it very difficult to stay in even on a cold winter's evening. You may begin to doubt the depth of his love when he constantly suggests that you ask friends over.

This is a man who can't bear to be trapped. He refuses to make plans for the future. He is a wonderer, a gypsy at heart, and he can never get his fill of adventure.

He needs a strong woman behind him, and as a Scorpio you are certainly that. But you will have to ask yourself the serious question of whether you are prepared to play mother as well as wife to the guy you choose as a partner.

He needs lots of looking after. You will have to

be prepared to go to bed alone some nights because he will want to have his evenings out with the boys. You are not a shy Scorpio woman who likes to stay home every night of the week. But the sort of outside stimuli he appears to want might not appeal to you.

You are possessive and you are jealous. It might be difficult for you to accept the fact that he needs so many other people.

You needn't worry too much about his having an affair, though. Once you are living together, this is unlikely because he is surprisingly a one-woman man. Also, he will probably come to depend on you far too much to put your relationship in jeopardy. He will flirt with women, but this will be to boost his ego more than anything else.

He is lots of fun. You will never have a dull moment when out at parties with him. He is a great storyteller and his company is very much in demand. A crowd will often gather around him. He seems so bright and full of energy.

Sagittarius is, as a rule, a good earner. There is a serious side to him. As long as his energy is channeled in purposeful ways, he can live a fairly settled life.

You don't like to play a background role. You are very much an individual. As a Scorpio sometimes you are a loner. You will have to decide whether you can make any man the main reason for your existence. You are likely to get bored following him around. He isn't the sort of man who takes to being dominated.

As you get to know him well, you will discover much of his antics are just a front. He is actually desperately shy. He puts on an act for others so they won't discover the real him.

There are bound to be quite a few arguments. But life will most certainly not be dull.

It might be a good idea for you to keep your own career going if you do get married to the Archer. He won't mind your having outside interests. It will probably do him good to have to get his own meals on occasions and not always take you for granted.

With this man, you'll find your marriage becomes better as you get older.

With kids, Sagittarius is pretty hopeless and can rarely manage to give them the time they need. He tries hard, but he's never quite able to get close to them. You won't think his fun-loving party-guy image is a very good example for them.

Scorpio Woman—Capricorn Man

Capricorn is an extremely complex individual. He has great difficulty coming to terms with himself, let alone others. He wants love desperately, but he's afraid of it. To a certain extent, he is insecure. He finds it hard to trust anyone with his heart.

He is an emotional and passionate creature. And if you take the trouble to get to know him well, you will discover he is as sincere and straightforward as they come. He can't help covering up what he truly feels. He finds it necessary to put on a front when meeting people for the first time.

He does tend to be rather conservative in his outlook on life. In many ways, he could seem too prim and proper for a forward-looking Scorpio woman like you. You are the kind of woman who will fascinate him, though. Your very sexuality will make him want to get to know you really well.

He will also be rather envious of your habit of speaking your mind without worrying what others may think of you. One of Capricorn's basic personality problems is that he so desperately wants to be liked.

A Capricorn man often marries rather late in life. He can be very fussy and terribly set in his ways. He needs to be loved and admired. Basically, he is a logical person rather than an intuitive one. The longer you are in his company, the more complex you will discover he is.

He is an extremely hardworking person. His career is usually important to him. Whatever he takes on, he wants to do well.

He is probably the most loyal type of all the Signs of the Zodiac. If he tells you he loves you, you can bet your last dollar he's serious. He is a romantic who fervently believes in true love. At times, he has difficulty facing up to the world as it really is. He feels let down if friends don't live up to his expectations.

In his youth, he can be a bit wild; it's as though he's having his last fling first. In maturity, he doesn't get on too well with people who don't take life seriously. He loves a deep discussion, which you as a profound Scorpio woman can initiate. You will find his mind is quick. He is usually a good conversationalist when he has something to say.

Your Capricorn man will be proud of you as a homemaker. He will adore the way you make the house attractive and comfortable to live in. He is careful with money. As a pair, you should have no trouble providing for the future.

He will not expect you to tie yourself to the kitchen sink. If you wish to continue working after marriage, that will be okay with him. He couldn't expect you to make a sacrifice he's not prepared to make himself.

There is a passionate side to his nature, but it needs bringing out. You will have to help him lose his inhibitions in bed. If you desire him enough, this should be no problem. Keep telling him he is the greatest lover in the world, and it will not be long before that is exactly what he is.

He will want to defend you against the outside world. Surprisingly enough, you will like the protective attitude coming from this man. So many people feel you are capable of looking after yourself and fighting your own battles.

Capricorn will make a fine father for your children. He will try to bring up his kids with the right values. He believes in discipline and good manners. Living with this man will not always be easy, but you will never doubt the depth of his feelings.

Scorpio Woman—Aquarius Man

Aquarius is a very outward-looking person. He is interested in the world around him to such an extent that his family life and personal life often suffer a great deal.

He loves discussion. He is usually highly intelligent and capable of putting his point of view across most forcefully. But when it actually comes to making any really important changes, it is often another story.

He is more interested in tomorrow than today. He knows how the world should be. He looks for the best in people. He thinks it is possible to change human nature.

You may find him a fascinating guy. His views will certainly interest you. When it comes to a permanent relationship, though, it is difficult to tell how long you would last together.

You like someone with a positive views on things, but you also hold to definite opinions. This is the sort of man who would confuse you.

Aquarius is very broad-minded. He always tries to see things from everybody's point of view. He is neither jealous nor possessive.

You may sometimes wonder if he is at all concerned where you have been when you come in late. The simple fact is he will feel you are perfectly capable of looking after yourself. He'll think you're old enough to decide how you should run your own life. That's a very adult way of looking at it, and a mature Scorpio woman like you will agree.

It is true, of course, that love changes a man. If he feels you really do need protection, he might make it his life's work to provide you with all your needs and shelter you from the big bad outside world. He's a bit of an extremist, sometimes even a downright fanatic.

Can your basic differences in attitude be overcome? Just because he doesn't agree with your philosophy doesn't mean to say he will stop loving you. But it doesn't make it any easier to stay together when two people hold opposing views on everything except the love they share.

Aquarius needs a cause. He finds it difficult to reveal his true feelings at the personal level. He often hides behind a placard or a slogan. Often it is hard to find the real man. As a Scorpio you are much more straightforward. You tend to tell people what you think about things. If they don't like your candor, that's tough.

Aquarius is the sort of man who has loads of acquaintances but very few close friends. You may get rather fed up with the constant comings and goings in the household. He may not even notice when you are ready for bed if he is in the middle of a heated debate.

He won't be very good at coping with your moods, either. When you get down in the dumps, he's likely to tell you to snap out of it and think about all the people in the world who are worse off than you are. He's not a bully or a brute, though. He is, in fact, a very gentle man.

He won't be able to understand your deep interest in the home. He is unlikely to notice the care you have taken with decorations and furnishings. He needs a stable influence in his life. Yet if you provide it, he might take you for granted.

Still, Aquarius can be a good family man once the children arrive. He will understand them as much as he will love them.

If you care deeply enough for your Aquarius mate, you might be able to work up some enthusiasm for his various projects. However, think very carefully before you marry him.

Be sure that you have a lot more going than a purely physical attraction. Have a wild affair with him, enjoy his zany company and particularly his crazy friends. But give yourself time to find out whether it's an impossible dream.

Scorpio Woman—Pisces Man

Your friends who take an interest in zodiacal relationships between men and women may pooh-pooh the idea that a Scorpio woman could ever get deeply involved with a Pisces man.

Actually, you have much more in common than appears at first sight. To begin with, you are both water Signs, which creates an emotional understanding if not an affinity. Also, you both have a profound interest in the occult and life and death. Moreover, you are both moved by your impulses rather than by any logical thought processes. Finally, you both have a vivid imagination and you both love change.

This man is likely to have a special sort of appeal. He is artistic and can get carried away by beautiful poetry and music. One reason you would tend to be such a good combination is that as a Scorpio you are so much more realistic than Pisces. He needs someone to bring him down to earth with a bump on occasions.

He is romantic, but not in a mushy way. He is sincere, and that is terribly important to you.

He will do his best to look after you. But you had better face up to the fact early on that you are likely to go through a few rough stretches with your Pisces man.

He is not petty. He will always consider your feelings before he makes any decision that would affect you.

At times, he will be amazed at your Scorpio energy. He is a bit of a dreamer and may find it difficult to understand why you rush around so much.

Whatever work he does, he is likely to bring to it a distinctly individualistic approach. Very often you will find that a man born under the Sign of the Fishes has a creative kind of job. He isn't very good at knuckling down to routine. He needs more than mere financial reward to spur him on.

Don't question his motives too much. He doesn't like to be cross-examined. If you love him, he will expect you to accept him as he is.

People born under the Sign of Pisces are the idea type. He will always be on the lookout for something new. He will take a chance on a project or an invention even if it may be rejected.

In your courting days, he will make you feel like a million dollars. He knows how to wine and dine a woman. This man also has the happy knack of being able to choose the sort of surroundings that will appeal to the woman he is taking out. He will not try to foist his tastes or opinions on you.

Pisces will understand your dark Scorpio moods and do his best to cope with them. He will always have the time and patience to allow you to talk yourself out of your depressions.

He can be changeable, and you may find this side of his nature rather difficult to live with. He may seem determined to get to the top one day, and the next suddenly become lethargic and lose all interest in his career.

You also are subject to sudden ups and downs. Let's hope you manage to have these in turn rather than simultaneously. You'll find, though, that when your Pisces man knows he's the anchor in a relationship and things start going wrong, he'll rise to the occasion magnificently. He's got a lot more strength and staying power than his manner suggests.

He needs security as much as you. He won't object if you wish to keep up with your career as long as it doesn't interfere with your being a good and loving mate.

Pisces will need your firm grip on the family when the children start growing up. As a father he is too permissive with kids and will spoil them.

Most of all, he will need you as a woman, and that is the most important thing in the world to a passionate Scorpio.

Scorpio Man—Aries Woman

Quite a few differences will have to be overcome if a union with an Aries woman is going to last for very long. To be honest, after you've been with her a while, she could drive you absolutely crazy. She's not as feminine as you like your women to be. She, like you, prefers the role of the dominant partner. Still, love can find a way.

She is terribly ambitious. You like to be the breadwinner. You will have to ask yourself seriously if you would be happy with a woman who follows her own interests as much as your Aries is going to want to do.

Although motherhood appeals to her, she will probably want to continue with her work for quite a long time after marriage and postpone having a family. When she does have children, Aries become wonderfully involved in their activities.

You like to take the aggressive role with a woman. An Aries female may be too forward for your liking. If she's attracted to you, she may well suggest the first date. This sort of tactic tends to scare off the Scorpio man.

This woman goes into things feet first. She's no diplomat. She comes out with exactly what is on her mind. You do like to be pampered and made a fuss of. Underneath your tough exterior, you Scorpio males are a bit soft, especially where women are concerned.

She finds it hard to stay put. The nervous energy she burns up in a day is quite amazing.

The lady Ram hates to be given guidance. She can't take criticism, even if it is well meant. You like to protect your woman and advise her when she goes wrong. This attitude toward the female sex would not be acceptable here.

Don't get the wrong idea, though. For all her ambition and drive, she is extremely nervous and sensitive. She does her best to hide her emotions and her vulnerability.

Your sex scene is apt to be pretty hot. You will definitely click in bed. She is almost as passionate as you are. As a swinging affair, you could have a ball together. Whether your love would go any deeper is open to question.

The Aries woman is quite complex. She's terribly jealous, but then, so are you. She's quite capable of resorting to violence if pushed far enough. An argument between you two could turn into a flaming battle.

Basically, she would have no trouble playing the role of homemaker. The real trouble is that there are so few men she feels it is worth sacrificing her independence for.

Aries can be promiscuous. It's not easy for a woman born under the first Sign of the Zodiac to settle for one guy. She may, in fact, live with two or three men before she makes her choice. This might play on your jealous Scorpio mind.

Her lovemaking is warm and spontaneous. She will want to be on your arm all the time if you are her man. She will desire to share in your success. She'll want to share your problems, too, and is capable of going through the hard times as well as the good. She's a survivor.

Aries loves a party. She is great at entertaining. She is also extremely generous. She would do anything for a friend in need of help. Her spontaneous way of giving will impress you.

Your house would be well furnished. She's got imagination when it comes to decorating. And she's a good cook.

If you have the patience to accept her moods and tantrums, you could be happy together.

Scorpio Man—Taurus Woman

It is possible you would hit it off with Venus-ruled Taurus. She loves the domestic scene and she is a great homemaker. Like you, she is not too keen on change. She will be prepared to settle down to being a housewife and mother without many qualms.

She possesses a very strong personality. You may find her a little hard to handle. She digs her heels in when anyone tries to tell her what to do. Still, she's as straight as a die. A very down-to-earth female, she always lays her cards on the table.

You may get the wrong idea about Taurus on first meeting. Chances are she will appear to be totally absorbed in her career. You will be amazed at how quickly she is prepared to give all that up when she meets the man who can give her a secure and stable home.

She may try to interfere in your business activities, which is not likely to go over too well with the secretive Scorpio. You like to keep home and work in distinctly separate compartments. When she asks if you've had a good day at the office, she'll want you to inform her of the minutes of your important meetings.

If you do score with a Taurus woman, you won't be disappointed with her lovemaking. She's all woman. She'll make you feel all man.

Possessions are quite important to her. She also likes a comfortable home life. You're fond of your creature comforts, too, and shouldn't have any trouble providing her with all she needs.

This woman takes people for what they are without being at all demanding or judgmental. You tend to be rather critical of others and to make snap judgments.

She is likely to have a great affinity with nature. As a rule, Taurus is extremely fond of animals, especially dogs, and is bound to want to have one or two pets. If you haven't got a garden, she'll want a window box or some indoor plants.

You'd better watch that roving eye, Scorpio. The lady Bull won't tolerate your getting involved with another woman even if it's only on a casual basis. This is one area where she will not be quick to forgive. And she is not an easy woman to fool. She'll sense it if you are trying to put a fast one over on her.

If she loves you, she'll stand by you come what may. She's not the type to run for the lifeboat at the first sign of a storm.

She likes her food. As a rule, you will find a Taurus cutting out the frills when she's in the kitchen. All the rich and savory ingredients, the heartier the better appeal, and she heaps it on.

Your Taurus woman likes her surroundings to be soft and feminine. You may have to get used to a pink bedroom. You'll also have to be prepared to live with the teddy bear she's had since she was two years old. She's a great hoarder and extremely sentimental.

Taurus is a bit of a plodder. She refuses to be rushed into making important decisions. Her restraining influence could be good for you. If you have an impulsive streak, she may make you think twice about important matters.

She will adore doing things for you. As long as she feels she is the only woman in your life, she'll remain faithful.

She can take care of herself if she has to. She's fantastic at facing up to reality. She likes straightforwardness even if it hurts.

She'll fight to get the best for her kids. You'll make a first-rate parent combination. With Scorpio and Taurus in charge, your children are likely to be well balanced.

Scorpio Man—Gemini Woman

It's hard to see how you would last very long together because you do appear to be completely opposite types. Fortunately, there are other influences working in both horoscopes that may help.

Don't forget that Gemini is the Sign of the Twins. Two of her! You may find this dual personality just too much to cope with.

This woman finds it difficult to stick at things. She is always on the move. You will find it tough going keeping up with her moods. She's full of new ideas. It's difficult to get a word in edgewise because she's such a chatterbox.

She also blows hot and cold. One moment, she'll be the most passionate woman you've ever met. The next, she might be engrossed in a magazine or talking on the phone.

You like to know where you stand with women. You're in for some surprises this time. Her sudden fluctuations will drive you right up the wall.

Gemini is even more of a flirt than you are. Whereas you make your intentions clear from the start when you desire someone, she can be a bit of a tease. She'll play footsie under the table, flutter her flirtatious eyes and let you drive her all the way home. Then she'll open the door, let herself in and shut you out before you can make another move.

She likes to be constantly active. She tends to live in the future. She loves people and enjoys meeting folks from all walks of life. She adores being surrounded by admirers. The center of attraction is what Gemini is always aiming to be.

Most Scorpio men can't help but be attracted to this shooting star. But give yourself plenty of time to think about it before you ask her to be your wife.

Gemini would not be prepared to sit at home all day while you are at work. Do you think you could live with a woman who'll want to keep up her outside interests and old friends?

Gemini is likely to be artistic. If she could stick to one subject for any reasonable length of time, she'd most likely have a very successful career. But routine terrifies her. She doesn't want to be tied down. Being a creative woman, she runs from the thought of a nine-to-five office job.

Other people find her fascinating. She usually has lots of chums. You must not get jealous at the number of telephone calls she gets from male friends. She will tell you these relationships are purely platonic. More often than not, she'll be telling the truth.

Don't try to work out what makes her tick. If you are really gone on this Mercury-ruled woman, you'll have to accept her for what she is and leave it at that.

Don't get angry with her. And don't try to change her. Watch that dark Scorpio temper of yours. She needs kindness and understanding, not the heavy-handed approach. You will not win this one's heart by being aggressive.

Don't keep asking her if she loves you, either. She prefers her man to play a bit hard to get. If you're all over her, it will be too easy for her. She treats love as a game. It's not that she can't fall like a ton of bricks, it's just that she seldom finds the right man.

Gemini is a romantic at heart. She loves to be in love with the idea of love.

Basically, she is yearning for peace of mind and security. Have patience with her and in time she will settle down.

With children, she will mature. The responsibilities of motherhood will make her realize that she can't be a party girl all her life.

Scorpio Man—Cancer Woman

Of all the twelve Signs of the Zodiac, the Cancer woman is perhaps the most likely to be the dream girl of a Scorpio male. She will have almost everything you desire. She needs protection, she loves her home, her mission in life is to look after the man she loves, and she makes a fantastic mother.

You like to dominate, and she likes a masterful guy. There are few men who can control her, but you appear to fit the bill.

You will need to have quite a lot of patience with her. She's a woman of many moods.

She can be terribly extravagant, too. Although she's quite astute at managing a budget, she can go off the rails from time to time with a massive spending spree. Clothes are her great weakness, especially if she's a city woman. She'd buy a new outfit every day of the week if she could. Her closet is likely to be packed with many different fashions.

When it comes to clothes, the Scorpio man is a bit sloppy. You tend to be absentminded about putting on a clean shirt and polishing your shoes. A Cancer woman will make sure you are always looking your best. And she'll do it unobtrusively. She'll do everything she can to turn you into a well-dressed man. If you really love her, you'll go along with it and probably enjoy your new image.

She needs security. Cancer can get very down in the dumps. She does not like to live alone. She will turn to you for protection and understanding when things get too much for her. You will have that special talent for calming her down and, more important, for cheering her up.

You will share the same sort of interests. As a Scorpio you need your home to be a place to escape to after a hard day's work. She will like nothing better than preparing your favorite dishes and spending the evening alone with you.

Don't ever let your Cancer lady down. She is likely to believe everything you say, not because she follows blindly, but because she wants to have faith in you. She will put you on a pedestal. She will stand up for you at all times. No one will dare to say a word against you in her presence.

Don't ever nag her or be overly critical. She can't stand to be bullied. She gets upset very easily. The pain she feels when her emotions are aroused is very deep. Don't ridicule her. Take her seriously when you know she's being sincere.

She would be terribly upset if you were to get involved with another woman after you had pledged yourself to her. If she has built her world around you, she will be absolutely shattered. Then things will never be quite the same again no matter how much you change your ways.

She loves to be spoiled with presents. Buy her occasional chocolates or roses to show how much you appreciate all the things she does for you. She will never take you for granted.

Don't play little-boy-lost. She's got no time for a man who is searching for his mother. More than likely, she's looking for her daddy.

People born under Cancer usually have great respect for their parents and like to visit them often. Even if you don't get on well with her side of the family, it would be in your best interests to keep your mouth shut and make the best of it.

It's quite likely you'll have a large family. The Cancer woman is a devoted mother. In caring for and bringing up children, there is none better.

Scorpio Man—Leo Woman

If you can take a woman who has an independent streak as wide as a freeway, you should hit it off with a Leo.

She is a positive, no-nonsense type. She is quick to sum up people. You will have to be straight with her, or you won't keep her. There will be no room here for your usual Scorpio jealousy and possessiveness. She simply won't put up with that sort of behavior. If you persist, she'll consider you extremely adolescent and not her type.

Your Leo lady won't be dominated. If you try it, she'll show you the door. She is logical and matter-of-fact in her approach to life. Certainly there is a sentimental side to her nature, but it's always tempered with the practical.

Other woman are often extremely jealous of the Lioness. They wish they had the nerve and strength of character to conduct their lives the way she does. She is not bothered by catty remarks. After all, she is the Queen of the Jungle. What comes first with her is to be true to herself. You'll admire this quality because as a Scorpio you too believe in sticking to one's principles.

Leo is likely to be a leader among her friends. She's often full of bright suggestions about how to spend an evening. She's glamorous and feline. She likes bright lights, spotlights, lots of yellow and gold. She shines like a diamond when she's the center of attraction.

In bed, you'll find her a fireball. She is a physical creature. To her, lovemaking must never become routine. She needs an imaginative lover.

As a Scorpio male, you are probably on the lookout for a homemaker. Check your priorities, and you'll find this is high on the list. But don't expect an old-fashioned homemaker if you link up with a Leo. She mightn't stray, but she certainly likes to roam around. She has a very inquiring mind and will want to go on developing it and acquiring more knowledge all her life.

Although this woman may appear soft and cuddly on the surface, don't be taken in. When she is aroused, she can be quite stormy.

The Lioness won't be prepared to stand by and watch you playing up to other women. Don't try to get away with anything. She has an uncanny knack of being able to read her lover's mind. This could be a bit discomforting for a guy like you, who has such a vividly erotic imagination.

Her tastes are expensive, though not extravagant. She's artistic. It's quite likely she will be able to save you money running the household. She's very good at making things herself. She will certainly make domestic life very comfortable. Where she could cause you to dig deep into your pocket is in entertainment. She loves dining at good restaurants and will expect to be taken to the movies or the theater at least twice a week.

Leo can be a whiz at sports, and she's quite a fighter. You might have some problem getting the upper hand in any games you play.

If you have an important business deal to clinch, be sure to take your Leo woman along. She's capable of charming any man when she puts her mind to it. Share the decision making, don't be quite so demanding and overpowering, and this woman could do a lot for you.

She may not be too eager to have children early in the marriage. It is highly unlikely that you'll ever have a large family.

If you are well-heeled, you will probably be able to overcome your differences. But if you're never going to make a pile of money, it might be best to cross all the Leo women you know out of your little black book.

Scorpio Man—Virgo Woman

You are likely to be confused by a Virgo woman. In many ways, you are a secretive type. But this woman has even more hidden depths. Virgo takes a lot of getting to know. She can be terribly shy and reserved.

She is particular about her man. Romance is not something she enters into lightly. She's unlikely to have a lot of boyfriends in her life. She finds some difficulty in showing her feelings.

Of course, if you are really crazy about her and have the patience to bring her along slowly, this could be a successful liaison. People are often unfair to this damsel. So many in this day and age expect to make it to the bedroom before they even know a person's name. But Virgo doesn't play that game.

You will discover you have come across one woman here who believes in courtship and good manners. She has standards and she lives by them.

Don't rush the romance. Get to know her first. Be her friend. You will have to take your time wooing this lady. Basically, she is a perfectionist. She has to be sure of her man before she will give herself to him. The question is, can you stand the long preamble?

You'd better smarten yourself up a bit, too. Nothing offends a Virgo woman more than slovenly dress. She won't go out with you if you turn up looking like someone on his way to the poorhouse. She'll feel you don't care very much about her if you don't make a special effort to look presentable.

Don't ask her back to see your etchings. She won't find those corny old ploys amusing. You'll just

have to keep your passionate Scorpio nature under control for a little longer than usual. Try not to criticize her or dominate her. If you can't accept the way she is, it would be best to forget all about it. She's not one to change her ways to suit a man.

Virgo does not like to show her feelings in public. She's likely to blush bright red if you hold her hand at the bus stop or get romantic when her friends are around. She is interested in true love. To her way of thinking, second best just isn't worth bothering about.

You are not the tidiest of men around the house and that could cause problems. Virgo can't stand things to be in disarray. You tend to be a bit messy. You like to spread. Her efficiency could drive you up the wall.

If you are a true Scorpio type, lovemaking is one of the major forces in your life. A Virgo woman could be too cool for you. You will have to be sophisticated and smooth to get her in the mood on occasions.

She'll be very shy about going out with you. When you first date her, it might be a good idea to make it a foursome.

She puts great emphasis on good manners, considerateness and loyalty. She honors much of the past and sticks to her childhood friends.

You'd better keep to the straight and narrow if she does become your woman. Virgo can't tolerate hypocrisy and double standards.

Love can conquer all, of course. If you are wild about Virgo, you can both overcome your differences. You could be just the man to bring her out.

She will do her best to be a good wife. You will always be able to bring friends back in the sure knowledge that your home will sparkle. She's fond of preparing food and is most certainly not an extravagant woman.

Like you, she believes in bringing up children strictly. Just be careful that between the two of you they get enough cuddling and affection.

Scorpio Man—Libra Woman

Your patience will be sorely tried with a Libra because she is forever changing her mind. Her main problem is she always sees two sides to every argument. On the other hand, you could be absolutely marvelous for each other. If you are prepared to give a little and not be so sure of your opinions, she will certainly make you wiser.

She is charming and she is extremely feminine. It is possible she'll be one of the few women who could actually have you eating out of her hand. You will find her sexy and irresistible.

Good luck if you are a Scorpio man with nerves of steel. She will confuse you. Just when you think you have won her, she's quite likely to tell you she doesn't want to get too serious with any man. There is still so much she wants to do in life!

It's quite possible you will discover your Libra sweetheart is a career woman. She can be a wife and mother, but she won't be prepared to make her whole life revolve around you.

Being possessive, you may not take too well to the idea of her having outside interests and friends. Libra is vitally interested in life and people. She's very quick to sum up other folks' strengths and weaknesses.

You two might find you are better equipped to handle a passionate affair than to spend the rest of your natural life together.

She's a woman through and through. Lots of guys fall for her, and she often has the field to choose from. As a Scorpio you enjoy a bit of competition. It flatters your ego to think other men would like to be in your shoes. You are a determined guy, and what you want you usually get.

This woman does not put on airs. Libra is a seeker of truth and likes to be honest with herself. This causes problems, though. What she believes today she might not tomorrow. When she's emotional, she can kid herself. She gets carried away with enthusiasm and imagines things are better than they are.

You may find it frustrating that your Libra partner is always surrounded by crowds of people. You could have some difficulty in getting time on your own with her.

There's quite an astute head on those seductive shoulders. This Sign is often extremely good at business. If you can stand her going out to work, it's possible she'll bring a fair amount of cash into the family coffers.

She might keep you waiting for hours when you're going out together. She takes ages to make up her mind about what to wear. If you've got an important appointment, it might be an idea to set the clocks back an hour when she's not looking.

You like your home comforts and will have no complaints about your artistic Libra lady.

She won't try to boss you around, and she will expect to be given the same sort of personal freedom by you. She is fond of beautiful clothes and furnishings. Her surroundings are important to her and must be in harmony with her moods.

You will have to earn her love. The way to do that is by trusting her. She will not be able to give herself to you completely if she feels you are a possessive person. You will have to want her happiness first and foremost.

She is a particularly generous person and will shower you with expensive gifts when you are courting her. Even when you are married, she will save money to buy you quality presents for your birthday and special occasions. She genuinely delights in giving to her mate.

She loves kids and will be more than eager to have a family. As a mother Libra has few peers.

When you get to know your Libra lady really well, you'll consider yourself extremely lucky to be her man.

Scorpio Man—Scorpio Woman

Can you put up with someone who is as powerful, aggressive, possessive and jealous as you are? The thought of a Scorpio-Scorpio linkup is quite a mind blower.

Since sex is the force that drives you both, from the physical point of view you are likely to get on fantastically.

When this woman's temper gets the better of her, you'd better run, though. She can't stand to be criticized or told what to do. To be honest, there could be violence if you both lose your cool at the same time.

Scorpio is deep and intuitive. She usually has an interest in the occult and things mysterious. Some people find her fascination with matters connected with life and death rather morbid.

She is very honest with other people. When she thinks you have done something worthwhile, she will praise you to the skies. She wants her man to be successful. But she won't be prepared to kid herself or you if you don't make it. She won't pay false compliments, either.

You may find her brand of honesty rather brutal. Scorpio males like to be flattered sometimes, but the Scorpio woman will not be coy with you.

This woman has a tremendous amount of tenacity. When she makes up her mind to do something, she does it. No one gets in her way.

You know all about the Scorpio jealousy, so don't two-time her. One must feel sorry for the man who is foolish enough to get involved with another woman when he is going steady with a Scorpio. She'll get even with him no matter how long she has to wait.

Of course, life with this woman will be pretty bumpy. If you can make that first passion last, marriage might work. She is a very independent woman, though, and hates to have to rely on other people—especially a man—for anything.

Don't embarrass her in public. She can't stand to have ugly scenes in front of her friends. If you have any criticism to make of her, then wait until you both get home and give it to her straight. If there is a grain of truth in what you say, there's a very good chance she will admit it.

You will have to come to some arrangement as to who wears the trousers. She can be quite dominant if she senses weakness in a man.

A Scorpio woman is capable of excesses, and this is where you could be bad for each other. When one partner does not know when to stop, it is a good thing if his or her opposite number can be a restraining influence. You both have a great curiosity about life. If you were to get involved in heavy drinking bouts or drug taking together, the results could be disastrous.

You are unlikely to tire of her in the bedroom. She knows how to win a man and how to keep him. She has a vivid imagination and enjoys playing sex games.

Never cross her because she has as much capacity for revenge in her nature as you have. You know how you seethe when another person plays a dirty trick on you. She feels exactly the same.

It could be you will find life with someone born under the same Sign as you a little too draining. You prefer your domestic scene to be peaceful. Probably you require a woman who is a little more obviously feminine. You should have a closer look at the other influences in her horoscope before you commit.

When children come along, you could find yourself relegated to second place. The Scorpio woman makes a good mother, but she can be overprotective of her offspring.

Scorpio Man—Sagittarius Woman

Here is a woman who is hard to track down, but it seems likely that Sagittarius will be attracted to a man like you. She needs someone who is self-assured and confident. She wants a man she can believe in. She is very cheery and always tries to look on the positive side of life.

You will have to watch that explosive Scorpio temper of yours. When a fiery Sagittarius woman is provoked, she can be quite a volcano herself.

She is straightforward. It would be extremely good for you to marry someone like her. She will make sure you face up to yourself.

She likes to keep on the move. She is also a bit of

a mystery. It is not easy to get to know her.

She's very outspoken and capable of standing up for her rights. You will find the way she deals with difficult people most refreshing. You're expert at handling disagreeable types, so you can't help but admire the Sagittarius style.

Although you are a pretty astute businessman, you're not too good at dealing with everyday problems. This is where your fire lady will come in. She's excellent at shopping and budgeting. No tradesperson will be able to cheat her.

It is in her dealings with friends that she may turn to you for help. She does have an unfortunate way of saying the wrong thing at the wrong time to people she loves. You might be able to advise her on how to be a little more diplomatic.

A Sagittarius individual has a habit of making a remark that can bring an interesting discussion to an abrupt end. You could be sitting around for hours debating a fascinating subject with your cronies, when suddenly your Sagittarius woman will toss in a couple of her special observations, and the room will come to a painful silence. Don't get the wrong idea. There is nothing malicious about her. It's just that when tact is required, she prefers honesty.

She can be impatient. Even when she hasn't got anywhere in particular to go, she has a tendency to rush.

With a weak man, she can get a bit bossy. It's unlikely she will try this with a strong Scorpio man like you.

If you have to go away on business, you can feel confident she'll be able to run the house and look after herself and the kids.

Sagittarius is the faithful type, definitely a one-man woman.

Don't try to get your way by shouting. She's very reasonable and will try to go along with your ideas as much as she can.

People born under this Sign are often somewhat marriage-shy. They think twice before they give up their independence.

It would be wise for you to allow her to keep on with her career after marriage. She will become rather insular if she is home all day with little to occupy her mind.

Your love life should not give you any reason to complain. She needs a man who can take the lead. The sexy Scorpio is sure to stir her.

With children, she is terrific. A Sagittarius mother will make sure that any talents a child has are developed.

Even if you don't wind up marrying this woman,

you and Sagittarius will probably go on being friends long after the affair is over.

Scorpio Man—Capricorn Woman

Many people have called Capricorn inhibited or frigid. This is simply not true. Perhaps the reason so few men fail to arouse her is that they don't know how to treat her.

It is true that she can be cold if she meets a guy who does not know how to excite her. But she can be an absolute whirlwind of passion. Even a sexy Scorpio like you may be taken aback by her insatiable appetite for sex.

She will like the fact that you are ambitious and a hard worker. Success is quite important to Capricorn. She is attracted to talent, not because she wants reflected glory, but because she she can't abide people who have little to offer.

If you win her, she will be faithful. She will do everything she can to ensure the marriage is a success. If, however, you let her down, there is no telling what she'll do. She might go straight out and have an affair herself—partly to get back at you and partly to experience what you have experienced.

She's hung up on security, just like you. As a pair, you won't have too many problems putting the shekels in the bank.

A Capricorn woman is clever enough to play little-girl-lost if she sees it makes you happy.

Don't try handing her a line. She is interested in true love, not a casual affair. Don't neglect her. She will pout and make big scenes if you have too many late nights out with the boys.

Basically, she is responsible about money. But if you happen to be broke, she'll give you her last cent and pawn her jewelry for you. For this woman, love is a total commitment, and she expects it to be the same for her man.

The Capricorn woman is a wonderful hostess. She is just the sort of woman you will want around if you have to do a lot of business entertaining. She knows how to make people laugh and can bring a twinkle to the eye of most men. She likes to be well thought of.

The Capricorn woman is efficient yet glamorous. Whatever her background, her innate elegance will shine through.

She loves parties, and you might get a bit bored with the number of people she wants to invite over. When she knows you are tired and want to be alone with her, she'll make sure you are not disturbed.

She doesn't like to waste time. She will make sure she keeps busy all day. She is generally very thorough in what she does.

Let's hope you get along well with her family because she is likely to be very close to them and have lots of favorite uncles and aunts, too. Relatives are important to her, and she will be particularly proud of them if they have achieved any sort of fame or recognition.

Marriage always improves a Capricorn person. For one thing, it stops any introverted tendencies from getting out of control.

Sometimes Capricorn women marry relatively late because they get stuck on some guy who is not free and out of loyalty won't leave him. They often have some sad or unhappy love experiences behind them.

Kids will love their Capricorn mother, but she won't stand for any nonsense from them.

Scorpio Man—Aquarius Woman

Chances are you'll find an Aquarius woman almost impossible to understand. Unless there are other favorable influences working in your individual horoscopes, this woman's progressive ideas and attitude toward life would be difficult for you to live with for very long. You would be well advised to check the AstroAnalysis book for Aquarius to be sure.

It may take you some time to discover what she's really like. She'll probably always remain something of a mystery to you.

Her mood changes are difficult to keep up with. You do like to know where you stand with a woman. And, perhaps more important, you want someone who will provide you with a secure and stable home life.

Aquarius is independent by nature. She likes to stand up for herself and can't bear to admit that even she at times might need a dependable man to fall back on.

An Aquarius woman is a bit of a revolutionary and quite a feminist in her way. The Water Bearer is out to put the world to rights. She's a brave one and will battle hard for what she believes in.

Certainly there will never be a dull moment in your life if you do get involved romantically with this woman.

There is something magical about her. She believes in freedom. But if you ask her to define that word, she might have some difficulty.

When you come home after putting in a full day's work, it could be that your supper will be waiting for you on the table but your dear lady will be nowhere to be seen. You will be left on your own.

When she does turn up, you'll probably discover she's been out helping someone less fortunate than herself or enlisting aid for one of her causes. One doesn't wish to paint a gloomy picture, but your married life could be like this.

She is unconventional. Home to her is where she unrolls her sleeping bag. She is not that interested in comfort. She certainly would not be content to sit at home all day attending to the routine affairs that make up the average housewife's life.

She is likely to get many proposals of marriage. An Aquarius woman has a great personality and people are magnetically drawn to her. Perhaps if you meet her when she is past her banner-waving days, she will be ready to settle down.

Don't introduce her to your boss if you work for a large corporation because she will probably cross-examine him on how he makes his profits and what he pays his workers. There goes your bonus for another year!

She isn't as crazy as she seems. Often many of her ideas are accepted by the more conservative members of society in years to come. She is ahead of her time.

Marriage is a big step for this woman. You'd better sort out your differences before you contemplate slipping the ring on her finger.

As a mother Aquarius will be a great teacher as well as a great friend to the children.

Unlike you, she's not a jealous person. Your Scorpio possessiveness will be difficult for her to understand. She won't question you if you don't get home on time. She doesn't have a suspicious mind.

She's capable of going for long spells without making love. She can channel her energy into other things.

Scorpio Man—Pisces Woman

Never tell this woman she won't be able to succeed in what she's attempting. She needs to have her confidence built up, not shattered.

When a Pisces woman enters your life, you may wonder why you have spent so long searching for the right woman. In so many ways, you will be good for each other. There is much you have in common. Remember, you are both water Signs, which gives you emotional similarity.

If you land the Fish, you'll think you're a lucky guy.

Pisces has a fantastic imagination and is full of ideas. Her intuition is astonishing at times. She would never dream of trying to boss or dominate you. But if you ever ask her advice, even if it's about matters that are not of special interest to her, it is likely she'll come up with some interesting thoughts.

It is when she is trying to come to terms with herself that she experiences problems. So often in life she feels she has reached a crossroads. She can always see the possibilities offered in taking the other path. She is a seeker after truth, ever striving for honesty.

Pisces is very much a woman. You will fancy her like mad. She will boost your ego and give you all the confidence you need to go out and wrestle with your work problems.

You will have to get her to accept more responsibility for herself. This will be for her own good. As a Scorpio you are a protective mate. But you must insist that she make certain decisions on her own.

Pisces can't help going out of her way to give a hand to others when they are down on their luck. She has a deep feeling for the sufferings of mankind. Not that she is gullible about it. She will quickly realize if someone is not doing enough to get himself or herself out of a hole.

Her clothes sense is wonderful. She knows what suits her. You must boost her in this area, too, and get her to buy clothes she admires.

In love, Pisces is devoted. Once she has decided that you are her man, that will be it. A career is not all that important to her. She will find interests outside the home to occupy herself while you are at work. But she will always be around when you need her. You will definitely come before all else.

You will never be bored in her company. Although she changes moods very quickly, you are not likely to find this inconstancy more than you can bear.

Pisces believes deeply in goodness. Just being with her will make you a better person. She will be a driving force. Any success you achieve in your career will be done for her just as much as for yourself.

She's not the sort to blame others when things go wrong. She'll stand by you through the bad times as well as the good.

Mind you, it will not always be a bed of roses. Pisces can act up like a spoiled brat on occasions. You will sometimes have to reprimand her for behaving like a kid. She can be extremely selfish, too, especially when she doesn't get her own way.

Never let her get the feeling she is trapped or confined; she can become too introverted then. It is important to take her out at least once a week and insure she meets interesting people.

As your wife, she'll look up to you as head of the family. As a mother she would never dream of disagreeing with your decisions about the children, although she may tell you when you are alone together that you were perhaps a little harsh.

Scorpio as a Friend

Scorpio people can be the most demanding friends of all. They are basically loners, they won't share their feelings, and they want everything their way. They expect their friends to be as intense about their interests as they are. If not, they're out. A Scorpio doesn't have a friend around unless he or she has something to give.

As harsh as this sounds, it's the key to the extraordinary personality of the pure Scorpio type. Fortunately, the pure type is always modified by other factors in the horoscope, although the essential framework remains.

Scorpio seldom gives an opinion unless it's asked for, and doesn't accept the views of others without investigation. Scorpios themselves have fixed opinions and stick stubbornly to them.

This makes Scorpios exceedingly obstinate. Their amazing willpower makes them unbending psychological beings. They keep their attitudes intact in separate watertight compartments so there is no overlapping. Scorpio people know exactly what is in each department of their mind, but have little idea of what they add up to as a whole. If they did, they would be more tolerant, more forgiving, more failing, more human.

It is not easy for Scorpio to attract true friends because he and she do not have a great need for them. And what is not needed, normally becomes expendable under stress.

But Scorpio generally does have a compulsive desire to satisfy the sex drive, which is intensely strong in him or her. This drive in this remarkable Sign may go to the opposite extreme and propel Scorpio, still alone, to the self-denying heights of mystical experience. But usually the Scorpio man or woman directs libidinal energies in one way or another into love. So he or she really needs a lover, and will serve or treat that person according to that need.

So what is it that Scorpio needs in a friend? An echo of his or her own idea, a sounding board, a captive audience? The problem is, Scorpio's friends usually need Scorpio, and this places them in a most unenviable position.

The Scorpio personality is intensely magnetic to some people; to others, it is exceptionally repulsive. Those who are attracted frequently have great feelings of love and devotion, which the Scorpio person probably does not require. To remain in Scorpio's company, friends must indulge this generally selfish, tyrannical, vindictive, suspicious, scheming, stubborn, quite often cruel and violent personality.

But, of course, there are always exceptions, produced by positive and favorable influences elsewhere in the chart. These more developed Scorpio types—when not emotionally aroused—are staunch and sympathetic friends. They will work and fight courageously on behalf of a friend. Weaker companions often draw inspiration and strength from their dauntless determination and patience.

However, when Scorpio individuals encourage a friendship, it usually means they have an ulterior motive. For instance, the friend is likely to be a personal friend of Scorpio's boss. Scorpios have an astonishing gift for weighing situations and seeing who will come out on top—and therefore who is the best person to cultivate—in a future power struggle. Their ability for intrigue is unmatched by any other zodiacal type, for there is no limit to their strategic cunning and wily patience when self-interest is involved.

The Scorpio person can passionately and devotedly serve a cause or a person he or she loves—and be just as violent in his or her hatred or loathing of either.

Scorpios can be cruel and vengeful enemies. And yet, by the strange quirks of opposites that distinguish this Sign, they are capable of devoting themselves with the same tireless yet repressed passion to a friend or even a colleague. You take a lottery ticket when you select Scorpio. The odds are against you, but someone wins somewhere every draw.

If friendship is understood to be based on trust and sharing, Scorpio friendships do not have a lot going for them. Ask Scorpio, for he or she has that chilling and detached honesty that would probably agree.

CHAPTER SEVEN

Scorpio in Work, Money, and Business

As a Scorpio you have just about all that it takes to succeed in any profession or job you set your mind to. But it's amazing how often people born under your Sign mess up their careers through tactlessness. You can't help putting your foot in it, blurting out a truth nobody wants to hear, upsetting just about everyone who counts. Unless there are strong mitigating factors elsewhere in your horoscope, you'd be better off choosing a career where your advancement depends on the fewest number of people.

Job and Career

In your own business or as a professional consultant, you should certainly be successful. Your straightforward and often blunt manner is less likely to offend those who are paying for your opinion than a superior. Still, you've got to start somewhere before you set up on your own.

The sooner you can find a boss or powerful figure who likes or admires you, one whose good books you can concentrate on staying in, the better. The more people you've got to please, the riskier are your chances.

You do possess immense personal magnetism, apart from your other considerable talents. As a rule, you should have no trouble getting a job; the problem of holding it will rest purely on personal relations. Those who take to you will tend to overlook your tactlessness provided you don't go too far. They can't help but admire your conscientiousness, drive and tireless energy, or the speed with which you are able to learn and assimilate.

You are extremely well suited for scientific research, medicine, journalism, investigation, industrial or political espionage, psychiatry and archeology.

These fields will allow you to employ your natural talent for unearthing hidden information and finding out what others are doing behind the scenes. There are many other careers in this category that will offer you a fine opportunity for success.

Being natural investigators interested in benefiting all mankind, you Scorpios are often found in the forefront of laboratory programs intended to solve major problems such as a new source of energy, the global food shortage and biological scourges like cancer and heart disease.

Because of your avid interest in the occult and the mysteries of life and death, you are often leaders in parapsychology and similar investigative fields. You write and publish books about your findings. Usually you are specialists.

Scorpios will work indefatigably to find a cure or an answer. When dedicated, you are oblivious to failure, time or money. You will persevere long after others have given up or despaired. Frequently you are publicly honored for your discoveries.

You have a distinct flair for investment. You should be able to make a career as a broker, financial consultant or accountant. The foreign exchange or investment department of a bank or brokerage may offer you the scope you need. Scorpios are also proficient auctioneers. You can spot a bargain anywhere.

You are the natural builder of the Zodiac. But your vision in this respect is vast. You are not interested in building a house or two. You want to transform the environment, turn deserts into farmland, build whole towns, community centers, shopping and office complexes. If you enter the construction industry, you are apt to rise to a position of considerable power and influence. If you don't see the opportunity for this, you'll probably quit and try something else. As a builder, you always favor the boldest, the biggest and the most dramatic improvements.

Your imagination is excited by travel to other countries and strange places. You also have a strong affinity for water and the sea. Many Scorpio individuals earn their living working with boats and on ships. A naval career is not an uncommon choice.

Other factors in your horoscope may make you adaptable for work connected with the mining, engineering or chemical industries. You are skillful with machines and instruments. Any inventive flair in this direction should be cultivated.

Your cool nerve, manual dexterity and innate desire to heal often make you a top-flight surgeon. Many people born under your Sign are also found in the butchering trade.

You don't like doing heavy manual work for a living. You prefer to use machines. You'll dig a trench in the back garden just for the wonderful stimulus of getting your muscles working. But you're too intellectual to be content with a purely physical role.

The same talents that make you such an admirable and clever worker make the Scorpio character most successful at villainy. People born in October and November are among the most notorious crooks in the country. To the criminally minded, the thrill of outsmarting the other guy, especially matching wits with the defenders of the law and all their resources, is an irresistible challenge. Scorpio hoods often rise to gang leadership where power is measured in life and death and bloody vengeance. Others operate in the vague area between the legal and the illegal, the thrill being to remain respectable and accepted by the solid citizenry.

As a boss, you are a smoothie and something of a tyrant. You know exactly how to handle everyone on your staff. You can be tough, real tough. You can tear a man or woman to shreds with the edge of your tongue. You can make them wish you were dead. And yet no one you reprimand will crack because you are a great judge of character and know precisely how much each individual can take and still learn. You possess an extraordinary ability for making people you like stronger while you are tearing at their weaknesses.

Of course, it's a different matter when you're dealing with an antagonist. But with your chosen subordinates, you take a deep-seated interest. You are not just concerned with them as working units but as people. They often love you even though they mightn't like you. They admire your quiet, cool efficiency. They respect your candor and hatred of duplicity. They are intensely loyal. You make sure they realize they are your team. They also know you would make a terrible enemy. They are happy to be on your side when a fight looms.

The secret, of course, is that you never hire anyone unless he or she is a certain type. You have to like the person, and discern that their psychic chemistry fits with your own. All this is revealed to you in your first look. One deep gaze into their eyes, and you know everything.

If you take over a department, it's not long before you've weeded out the unacceptables. You may kick them upstairs or out the door. But however you get rid of them, they'll be banished to the outer regions and never enter your orbit again. You are instantaneous and implacable in your likes and dislikes.

As an employee, you don't necessarily want to be the boss. At least not right away. You're a realist. Apart from being the most consistently energetic and resourceful person around the place, you never want to make a move until you're absolutely ready. And that means knowing the business, whatever it is.

You will take orders. You will do a job over and over to satisfy a fastidious boss without feeling any impatience or ill will. You may think the boss got hold of the wrong end of the stick, but this opinion will make no difference to your work. The boss is the boss, and you accept his or her right to have things done their way. That is, as long as you can see clearly that under this boss you are going places. You are a person who fixes goals well in advance. You are more concerned with the inevitability of the end than with the irritations in between.

You don't expect any special favors as an employee, only what is due you. You have a good opinion of yourself, but it is based on an honest assessment of your worth and capabilities. You're not a boaster, a showoff or a clown. Compliments don't impress you much. You see instantly through flattery.

Your whole attitude is purposeful and workmanlike. You are forever learning and moving ahead on the strength of that knowledge. You are extremely loyal to your employer. You are a company man or woman, not a maverick.

However, when the time comes, as it must for

you to make your push for power, you will discard all previous alliances. You will change sides without compunction and work just as earnestly and conscientiously for the opposition. You are committed only to your own goals. While these happen to coincide with those of an employer, you can be counted on never to let him or her down.

If you were born between October 22 and October 31, you are inclined to be dictatorial and domineering. No obstacle will delay your career for long. You should try to be more patient, understanding and tolerant of others. Your impulsive and headstrong methods are likely to create more opposition than is necessary. You have great self-control once you learn to use it.

You should be able to accumulate a fair amount of property during your working life. Involvement with large construction projects should provide a suitable outlet for your abundance of energy. You need to think big and operate on a grand scale. You should try to associate with people who are bright and sharp.

Business partnerships can be profitable provided you curb your urge to take over completely. You usually think in terms of large groups of people and have a way of handling them. Sales work, where you have a large area or network to supervise, is likely to be rewarding.

If you were born between November 1 and November 11, you should make a competent and forceful teacher in any field that interests you. You are likely to prefer employment with a very large organization and to gradually make your way to the top.

You are tenacious. And once you've chosen a course, your life should become much more settled. The early years may be notable for their lack of direction. You may have to try numerous jobs before finding what you want. You possess a dynamic personality and should cultivate the friendship and support of people in authority who like you.

Your executive skills and judgment are excellent. You will probably gravitate to a financial or organizational career. You have a marked ability for laying down guidelines that others can follow. Your associates should be people who are interesting, dramatic and able to discuss most subjects. You have a powerful desire to keep learning and broadening your knowledge.

If you were born between November 12 and November 23, you have a good mind for legal technicalities. You can judge people and affairs with great

accuracy. You intuition in business matters is quite remarkable.

You are inclined to be highly emotional with strong romantic leanings. Sometimes you are aggressively ambitious, other times philosophically placid. There is much that is contradictory in your nature, particularly when your emotions are involved. You have to avoid impulsive moves.

You may be successful in an artistic or dramatic field, and you should be able to write with great power and imagination.

You are likely to be attracted to work that allows you to influence the public. Your personality is magnetic and sympathetic. You may be able to carve a career in publishing or politics. Given the chance, you are likely to rise to a position of considerable popularity or authority.

Money

Money seems to come to you fairly easily, mostly because your hardworking nature ensures an above-average income. Scorpio people often receive inheritances, but the sums are sometimes smaller than anticipated.

You are a shrewd financial manipulator. You understand budgeting, fiscal policies and complex appropriations better than most. Running a household is child's play to you.

You spend freely on your home and personal comfort, but you are not especially generous. However, many of the world's most famous philanthropists who set up anonymous foundations for the public benefit turn out to be Scorpios.

By a strange quirk, the more Scorpios spend on themselves and their families, the more money comes their way.

As a Business Partner

As a business partner Scorpio has tremendous qualities such as unlimited patience, superhuman endurance and a passionate drive to get at the truth. But the scalding nature of their temperament makes them very difficult candidates for partnership. Fortunately, the Scorpio character is rarely met in its pure state. The pure type is usually modified by the positions of the other planets in the horoscope.

The first thing that amazes about Scorpio men and women is their penetrative intelligence. They go straight to the heart of the matter with an economy of words and astonishing accuracy. You won't even get around to a discussion with a prospective Scorpio partner if he or she doesn't think you're very bright. But if Scorpio has an ulterior motive, he or she will mentally note all your weak spots with terrifying insight, butter you up and prepare to dispose of you to best advantage.

But if the partnership is desirable, Scorpios will want to get down to business immediately and be told exactly what preparations have been made, the objectives and the market potential. Here is where you'll need to have done your homework. Scorpio has an uncanny gift of assessing the chances of success and failure for an enterprise.

They can look years ahead and see future developments, anticipate trends. And they will analyze your scheme on the spot with computerlike precision. If the plan is any good, Scorpio will probably appreciate the possibilities better than you, at least the long-term ones. This makes Scorpio an exceptionally handy business partner.

You will be impressed by Scorpio's thoroughness. This guy or gal never goes off half-cocked. Everything is worked out, analyzed, schemed beforehand—particularly the strengths and weaknesses of the personalities involved. The shrewdness of the Scorpio mind is almost inconceivable.

Scorpio is both strategic and tactical, often using unscrupulous means to achieve a desired end. This tendency might be carried to diabolical lengths. But your partner is probably a modified type. To outwit your rivals, you couldn't have the assistance of a more fertile, cunning and relentless mind.

Your Scorpio partner's incredible power of persistence may weary even you. He or she never, ever gives up. Whereas the Taurus partner will persevere with great plodding determination, your Scorpio partner will keep up such high-pitched pressure that the opposition will usually give up, give in, compromise or surrender in some way just to escape the perpetual nerve-pinching pain.

Scorpios seem quite unaffected by the exertion and tension involved in maintaining such pressure. They can keep it up for years. They have such massive and enduring constitutional strength that to win they will literally press on to the point of their own destruction, which is normally far beyond any other individual's.

Out of all this emerges Scorpio's reputation for dependability. They do not accept challenges lightly; they dismiss fools; they manipulate and struggle to the death. Such a temperament, if nothing else, has to be dependable.

Scorpios respond from fixed opinions. One opinion may oppose another. But since the mind can have only one conscious thought at a time, no serious conflict arises. Scorpios will defend their conflicting views with implacable severity, which is aimed at destroying an antagonist rather than considering the logic of the argument.

If you, as Scorpio's partner, dare to point out their inconsistency, they might erupt into a vituperative rage. Perhaps they will create another secret, seething department in their mind with you as a possible target for some future vengeful action that only a Scorpio could sweetly contemplate.

Scorpios will expect you to work as hard as they do. If you, or members of your staff, try to keep pace, you probably will endanger your health!

Scorpio is no diplomat. They believe in going directly to the point. They will tell you, or perhaps even your top client, a raw-boned home truth without the slightest regard for personal feelings. They are contemptuous of displays of emotion and expect everyone to be as dispassionate as they are on the surface. Inside Scorpio twists and creaks with personal dissatisfaction and repressed desire. They want desperately to rise above burning feelings but are not sure how to do this except by suppressing one or more fiery emotions.

Scorpio finds it difficult to adapt to new conditions. Once you've fixed your mutual aims, Scorpio wants to go on, come what may. You may wish to take advantage of a profitable year and enjoy an extra vacation—but not Scorpio. There must be no letup until the objective is achieved. If they feel their position may be weakened by an absence, they won't take a vacation for years if necessary.

Your partner loves power. It is this desire that drives Scorpio. Their thirst for it seems unquenchable. Scorpio is a budding tyrant whose own opinion is what is right.

Sometimes the Sign produces the ennobled human being. Here power works for the good and serves wonderful purpose. But in the lesser Scorpio mortal, it is their own selfish purposes that count. Financially, this may lead to fiddling and recklessness on a ruinous scale.

Although your Scorpio partner possesses great personal magnetism, he or she is unlikely to be a favorite among your clientele. Here is a type who attracts people or turns them off. There is no in between, only extremes. You should consider if this credential qualifies or disqualifies Scorpio from being your business partner.

CHAPTER EIGHT

Scorpio Health

If you are a typical Scorpio your attitude to life is the chief factor determining the state of your health. So strong is your willpower that you can actually will yourself to recovery. So pernicious is your power to resent and hate that you can poison yourself with your own emotions.

Generally your constitution is robust, rugged and healthy. No other Sign in the Zodiac has at its disposal as great a reserve of sheer tenacious energy. Your health is largely a question of what you do with it.

There is always a danger that people born under your Sign will push themselves beyond physical endurance once they've resolved to accomplish something. Scorpios are such demons for devoted effort that they can ignore the normal limitations and end up with a breakdown of some sort. You should always remain conscious of the fact that your will is far stronger than your body.

You are also a person who is prone to illnesses brought about by self-indulgence. Few Scorpios are ever able to satisfy their lust for total experience by sticking to norms. Moderation and normal living leave them with energy to burn. They work hard, they play hard, and still they can usually physically outdistance associates.

Excessive drinking is often a problem. Sometimes you make a habit of eating too much. You know you shouldn't, but it is your nature to dismiss the protests of your body and to make it serve you as you please.

There is a strong self-destructive urge in the Scorpio character. You don't deliberately set out to damage yourself. You just refuse to acknowledge any limits. You want to experience all there is in life. Often this search for sensation and knowledge leads to dangerous experimentation with drugs. Occult phenomena, with their self-charging emotional energies and weird rites of invocation, are likely to interest you. The changes in perception that emotional stimulus and narcotics induce can be fascinating for Scorpio. Sexual excess you also find difficult to resist.

If you are a typical Scorpio, you don't have any patience at all where illness is concerned. You are more inclined to ignore a complaint than go to the doctor. This can be dangerous because you tend to dismiss the serious symptoms as well as the trivial. Since you are a realist, if incapacitated by illness, you will take quick remedial action. The trouble is, you may wait too long.

Your most vulnerable part is the stomach. Various disturbances are likely in the digestive system as a result of excesses. It is difficult for you to overcome internal toxic effects. Once a poison is in your body, it is hard to eradicate it. A buildup of any kind, even constipation, is to be avoided.

The reproductive organs are also governed by your Sign. So is the bladder, urethra and rectum. You are also susceptible to minor ailments affecting the head and throat. Nasal congestion, adenoids and sinus trouble are not uncommon. Children born under this Sign frequently suffer from recurring bouts of throat trouble until well into their teens.

It is advisable not to expose yourself to cold or dampness without taking sensible precautions. You are accident-prone, so be extra careful around fire and sharp objects. Being a fixed Sign, you tend to suffer from rheumatism with age. Colds and influenza can drag on and make life miserable and you irritable. Find healthful outlets against brooding and worry in order to avoid depression.

Scorpio individuals are the stuff that heros and heroines are made of. They are disdainful of personal danger when principles are involved. They will suffer without complaint for what they believe in.

CHAPTER NINE

Scorpio Astro Check List

Following you will find a list of words usually linked to Scorpio. On the left-hand side of the page are those qualities generally considered negative. On the right side you'll find the positive traits of the Scorpio nature. Being as honest as you can, put a check mark beside each trait that best describes you.

Then add up the number of check marks on the left and on the right. If the number on the left exceeds the number on the right by ten, then you are truly way out of whack, and must hasten to restore balance to your life. If on the other hand, you have checked ten more traits on the right-hand side than on the left, you are an excellent example of a well-balanced Scorpio. Congratulations to you!

If every year you can erase one check mark on the left-hand column and add one to the right, you are proceeding well along the road to happiness and fulfillment.

NEGATIVE	POSITIVE
❑ Sarcastic	❑ Creative
❑ Vengeful	❑ Magnetic
❑ Obsessive	❑ Intense
❑ Jealous	❑ Loyal
❑ Envious	❑ Honorable
❑ Possessive	❑ Passionate
❑ Obstinate	❑ Determined
❑ Destructive	❑ Competitive
❑ Treacherous	❑ Prolific
❑ Fanatical	❑ Fertile
❑ Ruthless	❑ Steel-willed
❑ Controlling	❑ Dedicated to healing
❑ Brooding	❑ Enduring
❑ Repressed	❑ Regenerating
❑ Unfulfilled	❑ Spiritually healthy
❑ Sexually unexpressed	❑ Sexually fulfilled
❑ Selfish	❑ Generous
❑ Materialistic	❑ Inventive
❑ Death-oriented	❑ Respectful of life
❑ Uncaring	❑ Protective
❑ Dangerous	❑ Brave
❑ Violent	❑ Penetrating
❑ Extremist	❑ Thorough
❑ Scheming	❑ Magical
❑ Suspicious	❑ Seductive
____ TOTAL	____ TOTAL

CHAPTER TEN

Parents

The following descriptions of the various Signs as parents are based on the position of the Sun, the most powerful influence in the horoscope. Most people conform to the solar influence. However, variations do occur because of the placement of the other planets at the time of birth. And, of course, the birth Sign of the child will also be an important consideration.

For a closer examination of these factors, it is advisable to study the individual parent's and child's horoscopes, which are available for every Sign in *AstroAnalysis*. All you need to know is the person's date of birth.

Since some Signs are naturally more and less compatible with others, you can obtain a fairly accurate idea of how parents and children will hit it off by reading the pertinent descriptions for each.

The Aries Parent

The Aries parent is kind, generous and fairly strict. The Aries woman often makes a better parent than the Aries man. Neither is particularly sympathetic or understanding; Aries people have difficulty seeing things through a child's eyes, possibly because they want too much to be proud of their offspring.

But the Aries woman takes parenting very much to heart. She's determined to bring up her children the way she thinks is right, even if it kills her—or drives her neighbors crazy, which is more likely.

Aries mothers have some very advanced ideas about child rearing. Their methods are often unconventional. They believe in teaching their youngsters initiative from the outset. And that may include permitting the three-year-old pride of the household to toddle over and pour himself a cup of coffee from Aunt Nellie's best bone-china set. Or to get busy with a pair of scissors or a crayon, perhaps on the wallpaper, while mother's attention is elsewhere. Not that an Aries is irresponsible. Far from it. But

one freedom is likely to lead to another in the child's eyes, and she is impelled to go along with it. Still, it's the child that counts with her, and you've got to admire the way she tries to prepare him to cope with the practical side of life without putting a stranglehold on his self-expression.

The Aries dad is somewhat different. He's also progressive, extremely proud of his offspring and wants the very best for them. But he won't allow kids to take over his whole life the way some fathers do. They occupy a very special place in his affections and he'll see they never want for any material things. But he's a busy man, and although he'll do his best to satisfy their emotional needs, he's not particularly good at it—consciously anyway. But children usually love him and they do delight in the way he'll do things they enjoy on the spur of the moment.

The Aries father tends to become impatient and irritable under the constant demands of his children. Both parents believe that experience is a great teacher. If the child has to burn himself to learn not to touch the hot stove, then the attitude is, okay, let's let him get on with it. Mother is the softer and more efficient parent of the two. But they're both wonderful examples to the growing child of initiative and independence.

The birth Sign of the child, of course, will have a large bearing on the success of the individual Aries parent.

The Taurus Parent

Taurus men and women adore their children and make them the center of family life. But these loving and affectionate people are far too wise in normal circumstances to put the children before their mate. In fact, this question just doesn't arise with them. They manage in a wonderfully sensible way to make the family a unit. And the youngsters usually grow up with a keen respect for the virtues of family life based on their Taurus parent's example. These children often go on to make happy marriages themselves.

It's not surprising, therefore, that Taurus is frequently considered to be the ideal mom or dad. These people are kindhearted and sympathetic personalities with a deep, intuitive understanding of those they love. As homemakers, they are generally considered to be without peer as a rule.

Because of their sensitive nature, they are conscious at all times of the emotional impact that unpleasant scenes and quarreling have on children. They have their marital disagreements, of course, but would rather lose an argument—or eat humble pie for a while—than disturb the tranquillity of the home.

Their views on child rearing are rather conventional. They believe generally in the old-fashioned way—teaching children good manners, good behavior and good morals right from the start. Freedom and independence, they feel, are qualities of character natural to children who feel loved and secure. If they are given correct values—and who, asks the Taurus parent, would argue against goodness and kindness as the golden rule?—then youngsters will have a firm foundation on which to build for themselves.

One of the secrets of the Taurus success as a parent is that he or she loves home life; the domestic routine is never a bore, as it is to several other zodiacal types. Home, to these people, is not just a place to sleep and eat—it's a place to live in with as much comfort, elegance and harmony as is humanly possible.

Taurus parents are acutely aware of surroundings and the importance of environment on a child's development. They prefer to make their home in a suburb well away from the city, or ideally in the country.

Most Taurus have a strong protective instinct. They are among the last people to seek a divorce because they fear it would unsettle the children. They will endure considerable personal hardship for the sake of a growing family.

The birth Sign of the child, of course, will have a large bearing on the success of the individual Taurus parent.

The Gemini Parent

Parenthood is not an easy role for a typical Gemini man or woman. Their temperament and outlook are generally too youthful and adaptable to impart the solid direction and psychological security so necessary for a developing personality. Children who compare Gemini's example of restless activity and nervous excitement with conventional ideas of steady citizenship may become confused and uncertain of themselves.

The Gemini mother is likely to make a better fist of it than the Gemini dad. These versatile women are inclined to carry on with an outside activity after marriage, but when the children come along, they will probably realize they can't manage both. Or can they? There's no telling with ingenious, energetic Gemini. These women, although appearing domestically slack at times, loathe untidiness and are very fussy about how their home is run. What they would prefer is to have someone else do the housekeeping while they get out and on with their other interests.

Both parents love their children, but they're not prepared to make them their whole life. To do so, they feel, would be to give the youngsters a wrong impression of what living is all about. They are deeply interested in their children's intellectual development. They don't believe they should have second-hand ideas and values stuffed into them. They believe in free speech, free thought and independence—and this is what they try to teach their offspring. After all, that's what democracy is about, isn't it?

Geminis put a lot more thought than emotion into their relationships with children. Critics may say they show a deficiency of heart. They tend to reason with them rather than try to "feel" with them. Emotionally, the Twins and their children may be miles apart.

The Gemini father is very quickly bored by the routine of family life. He's inclined to go out as often as possible, and may even seek an occupation that requires him to spend odd days away from home. However, he has a great deal of affection for his children as well as his home base. He is apt to rush in after a short absence in a flurry of expectation and excitement, stimulating everyone (especially the youngsters) to fever pitch.

The Gemini father may at times be unduly strict. He is likely to put on a display of irate authority to cover up his own feelings of uncertainty and insecurity.

Both Gemini parents find, as a rule, that they are able to guide their children more effectively by creating a restful atmosphere in the home.

The birth Sign of the child, of course, will have a large bearing on the success of the individual Gemini parent.

The Cancer Parent

A person born under Cancer often feels he or she is the best mom or dad in the world. Cancers do have some remarkably fine parental qualities (some even say that Cancer is the personification of motherhood), yet they are at the opposite extreme to Gemini: Cancer is all heart or feeling and not enough reason.

Both Cancer parents love their children in a most possessive, effusive and sentimental way. They are determined to nourish and protect them—and often succeed in almost suffocating them with affection in the process.

The Cancer parent is completely devoted to home and family. Every other activity is incidental to this one great absorbing idea. While the children are growing up, they receive every consideration. Nothing is too much trouble; no desired object is denied them while there is any money available.

The Cancer mom and dad are of much the same temperament. But since this is a mothering Sign, the characteristics generally fit the woman better than the man. He's moody, changeable, sentimental and too often oblivious to the exacting demands he makes on his family in exchange for his devotion to them. If you call him selfish, he will be flabbergasted, then highly indignant—and reel off incontrovertible evidence of all the sacrifices he's made for his family over the years. Yet his family might feel that despite his loving kindness, he has cheated them emotionally—that the price he has extorted in sympathy, approval and recognition of his virtues down the years was just not worth it. His fussiness around the home, insistence on accepted forms of behavior and corrective criticism may make the children nervous and self-conscious paragons. He can't seem to see beyond his own feelings of devotion and worthiness.

The Cancer mother will indulge and coddle her children with doting kindness, and then punish them with undue severity when they are naughty. Her moods change abruptly with irritation. Then this woman, who normally serves her children day in and day out and regards it as a privilege, will flare into a near-hysterical outburst. The children are often left bewildered and puzzled by this adult inconsistency.

Cancer parents need to exercise more reasoning and control over their fluctuating emotions if they are to balance their love with wisdom.

The birth Sign of the child, of course, will have a large bearing on the success of the individual Cancer parent.

The Leo Parent

Leo is the Sign of children. So it is to be expected that both the Leo man and the Leo woman make fairly good parents.

They are exceedingly ambitious for their off-spring. They want them to succeed in everything they attempt and are prepared to ensure that they enjoy every possible advantage. They won't take the initiative from their youngsters, but they will let them know they expect big things from them.

The success of these tactics depends to a great degree on the character of the child. If some of the zodiacal types are driven too hard or too much is expected of them, their development will probably be impaired or they will become resentful of the parent in later years.

Fortunately, Leo is also the Sign of deep love. The parent's ambitions for the children are usually tempered with profound affection and understanding. A typical Leo won't push a child beyond safe limits. Leo's style is more showmanship than shovemanship.

Children, whatever their Sign, can't help but be aware of the strength and loving concern of these parents. They will frequently indulge their offspring with extravagance, yet usually manage to attach some sort of condition that encourages a responsible attitude toward life. Despite their strong desire to be able to show off their youngsters to others, when it comes down to fundamentals, they want what is best for each child.

Leo parents (particularly dad) are likely to run the home as though it were their own private kingdom. Unless they receive homage and attention from their family, they are apt to become silent and sulky or stride off in a huff. This is more a device for drawing attention to the ingratitude of loved one (who really should know better!) than moodiness or brooding. Once the acknowledgments are forthcoming, the whole household smiles again.

When Leo parents feel a visitor or friend is receiving more attention and admiration than they are from their offspring, they'll sometimes do ridiculous things to go one better. Junior may enjoy this, but the effects of such egocentric contests on his outlook are hard to gauge.

Leo parents have a habit of going from one extreme to another with their children; they either lavish too much attention on them or demand too much.

The birth Sign of the child, of course, will have a large bearing on the success of the individual Leo parent.

The Virgo Parent

Virgo men and women make first-rate parents, although their mates may have to see to the emotional development of the children because this side of child rearing is not one of Virgo's strong points.

These parents are practical, neat and orderly. They

teach their children admirably how to cope with the problems of everyday life. They are especially mindful of diet and careful to instill in youngsters the necessity for cleanliness and good hygiene.

The Virgo mother instructs her youngsters from an early age in the virtues of good manners, tidy appearance and moral behavior. She doesn't believe in waste and makes sure that the children, both boys and girls, do their share of the chores around the house and learn to be methodical.

Sometimes she's a bit tight with the purse-strings where small personal luxuries are concerned. Occasionally, though, she is unexpectedly indulgent, particularly when she feels the child has earned a treat. Her youngsters never want for necessities, and they always have good, nutritious food to eat.

Virgo mothers and fathers encourage their children right from the start to save for a rainy day. They are not social climbers nor particularly ambitious for themselves, but they do with all their heart want to see their children get a good start in life. They are very much aware of the benefits of a good education and will themselves help with lessons at home. They can grasp a subject very quickly from a textbook and have a knack for explaining things in clear, concise, and logical concepts.

Both Virgo parents want their children to stand on their own two feet, and will do everything possible to encourage this. However, they are apt to overlook a child's emotional needs because they feel the practical side is more important in the youngster's development. It is not easy for them to demonstrate love and affection. Although highly sensitive within themselves, they find it very difficult to show their real feelings. Although they love and care deeply for their offspring, a child may miss the warmth of cuddling and close physical contact.

The Virgo mom and dad both have a strong tendency to nag children. They may also be very possessive and fail to extend the freedom of choice in play that other children normally enjoy.

The birth Sign of the child, of course, will have a large bearing on the success of the individual Virgo parent.

The Libra Parent

Libras make excellent parents, probably the best of all the zodiacal types. They have an affinity with children that shines through their relationships in many delightful ways. They love to play with them. As the youngsters grow up, they genuinely enjoy having them and their young friends around. They help with the entertainment and can join in games and conversation without appearing to be intruding.

Basically, Libra men and women treat children with the same consideration and regard for dignity that they extend to their own many friends. They are gentle and patient; persuasive rather than pushy. They know instinctively what is right for a child, but would rather guide him to choose for himself than put an object into his hands with a ready-made explanation.

Because Libras are very fair, they won't allow themselves to inflict their own hangups and prejudices on a developing mind; nor do they permit others to intrude in this way. They can be surprisingly adamant and forceful if an adult—whatever his position—attempts to bully or tyrannize a child. Although they are the last people to go looking for a fight, they are the first to resist injustice in any form.

The Libra parent loves beauty and harmony and will do all in his or her power to awaken similar feelings in the children. Libras endeavor to interest their children early in one of the arts—say music or painting—believing that this will aid their higher development and enable them to mix with creative and socially refined people. They are not snobs by any means, but they do appreciate sophistication and culture, so they can't help but endeavor to educate their children along many of these same lines.

Libras have a way of making instruction interesting for children. And children do their best to please them. These individuals make loving and affectionate parents, but not stupid ones. They don't spoil their young ones by overindulging them in material possessions or waiting on them hand and foot. They believe in moderation in all things. Gushing sentiment and insincere platitudes cut no ice with them.

Having an independent and spontaneous nature themselves, Libras endeavor to see that these qualities are not inhibited in the young personality. They will never attempt to hold back or delay progress out of jealousy.

The birth Sign of the child, of course, will have a large bearing on the success of the individual Libra parent.

The Scorpio Parent

The Scorpio parent usually runs a tight family ship. Oh, these moms and dads are generous enough, keenly solicitous of the physical and moral welfare of their children and intent on providing a good home for them with every modern convenience. No one could say they aren't deeply devoted, but they are rarely capable of appreciating the child's point of view. Everything must be as they divine it. The result is often a rigid and unyielding discipline that cramps the child's style.

Scorpio is one of the clearest-thinking, no-nonsense Signs of the Zodiac. It seems a pity these men and women can't always humanize their gift for dealing with realities when it comes to child rearing.

Their function as parents is to help form an integrated personality through which the reality of the youngster's character can unfold. But too often the Scorpio parent's stern methods of discipline disintegrate the child's personality. The child's main concern, then, is to obey—it is, after all, his or her best means of defense. The personality such a child presents to the family may have no relationship at all to his or her inner state. Some children of Scorpio parents wait only for the day when they can quit the rigorous regimen of their home. Others may be so intimidated that they grow up repressed and cowardly.

The Scorpio dad is often the worse offender of the two parents. He frequently runs his home like an old feudal baron, insisting that his wife as well as his children follow his instructions to the letter. The overbearing and tyrannical methods that he often employs to become a successful businessman are imposed on his household.

The Scorpio mother is a great homemaker and she idolizes her children. As long as she is in love with her husband, all is relatively well. But if the marriage breaks up or if she falls in love with another man, she will usually follow the dictates of her passionate nature. Although the children's material needs will be looked after in every respect, their psychological development may be seriously impaired.

Both parents are likely to suffer from inordinate and irrational jealousy, which may intensify their urge to restrict their child's personal freedom.

The birth Sign of the child, of course, will have a great bearing on the success of the individual Scorpio parent.

The Sagittarius Parent

The Sagittarius man is usually too in love with his own freedom to make a really good father. He's a great sport, a fine companion and a real man's man. But when it comes to supervising children, he's usually a dead loss. He gets impatient with his own family. He wants to be out and about, roaming and sharing his ideas and comradeship with the rest of humanity.

The Sagittarius mother is a much more stable and settled character as far as the home and parenthood are concerned. She has a deep inner wisdom and a lot of common sense, which allow her to bring up her children in a balanced way. She also believes in freedom, but is more inclined to regard it as a state of mind than as the absence of any physical restriction; she teaches her children accordingly.

Both parents are intellectual types, have a broad outlook and are usually well informed on world affairs. They are also likely to approach religion from a philosophic rather than dogmatic angle, and to encourage their children to be tolerant of the opinions of others but to make decisions for themselves.

Both mother and father are splendid influences from a moral point of view. Although sometimes bluntly outspoken, their frankness and honesty are among their finest attributes. They are also good-hearted, kind and generous, but not foolishly so (except dad sometimes when he's out with the boys).

The children of Sagittarius parents will probably be more at ease confiding their personal problems to their mother. Dad, although just as capable of giving sound and helpful advice, may become a little uneasy when intimate matters are discussed. He prefers to stay clear—if possible—of emotional problems concerning his family. He feels more comfortable if his wife deals with them and lets him know the happy result when it's all over! Both parents will see that their youngsters take an early interest in sports and get plenty of exercise and fresh air. With a Sagittarius parent, a child is almost sure to develop great affection for animals of all kinds.

The birth Sign of the youngster, of course, will have a great bearing on the success of the individual Sagittarius parent.

The Capricorn Parent

The personality of the Capricorn parent ranges between two extremes. On the one hand, these people may be too indulgent with their children. On the other, they may be unduly stern, demanding and forbidding.

The Capricorn woman, especially, finds motherhood an outlet for her often cruelly repressed emotions. Capricorn is nowhere near as self-sufficient as the individuals born under this Sign usually manage to convey.

Generally speaking, Capricorn parents do have a deep love for their children and regard them as necessary to complete a marriage. The parents' own childhood is often memorable for its unstable conditions, particularly in the relationship between their mother and father. They tend to retain vivid emotional impressions of any unhappiness suffered in those days and endeavor to protect their own children from such similar and painful experiences.

However, the less mature Capricorn parent, especially dad, may have been so bitterly affected by his past that he is unsympathetic and intolerant of his own children. He is likely to impose rules that restrict normal pleasures and emphasize responsibility and duty. He may justify his harshness by saying it is for the children's own good. This parent may feel he enjoys the respect of his children, when in fact they fear him and in later years may detest him.

The Capricorn mother is frequently very ambitious for her offspring. She will see that they are always well dressed when going out, but may not worry so much when they're around the house. She will tend to nag continually, trying to improve their speech, their manners and their behavior. Her object is to make them more socially acceptable and popular. She will take a close interest in their education and insist on homework (as well as chores about the house) being done.

Both parents may be possessive or jealous. Those who spoil and indulge their own youngsters may find that they are irritated by other people's children.

Capricorn mothers and fathers will instruct their children to be careful with money, although they themselves may be quite unwise in their spending habits.

The birth Sign of the child, of course, will have a large bearing on the success of the individual Capricorn parent.

The Aquarius Parent

Aquarius men and women make wise and mature parents. They are intent on allowing the child to develop as himself or herself and not as a carbon copy of either mom or dad.

Aquarius is the Sign that rules brotherhood and understanding, and Aquarius parents base their relationships with their children on these qualities. Although intensely devoted to them, they keep their emotional distance. The child is never stifled or confused by displays of jealousy or the inconsistencies of sickly sentimentality.

The Aquarius mother and father both encourage their youngsters to be intellectually fearless, to question rather than blindly accept the opinions of others. The children are taught to be keen and considerate rather than purely competitive. These people desire their children to succeed as much as any parent, but they put less emphasis on materialistic values and egocentric pride. The Aquarius parent likes first to think of his or her child as a successful human being.

Aquarius are gentle and reasonable with children. They endeavor at all times to awaken the youngster's interest so that he feels he is making his own way under their sympathetic and helpful supervision.

Both are exceedingly independent, with strong ideals and humanitarian feelings. Their views on child rearing are often well ahead of the times, and may be criticized by conventional members of the family. But they are firm in their beliefs and will not allow in-laws or other relatives to interfere.

When it comes to discipline, both parents are likely to have an enlightened and original approach. They are usually most reluctant to resort to corporal punishment. They find it difficult to rebuke children who are too young to heed an appeal to reason. They are sometimes accused of being permissive by stalwarts of the old school.

The Aquarius mother will usually manage to dress her children in a distinctive way. She will encourage them to be honest and not to compromise with their conscience. The child with an Aquarius parent will be brought up with a high regard for loyalty to family and friends.

The birth Sign of the youngster, of course, will have a large bearing on the success of the individual Aquarius parent.

The Pisces Parent

Pisces mothers and fathers are both gentle and loving. But it's debatable whether they are really up to coping with the practical demands of their parenthood.

No one derives more pleasure from their children than these parents. They wait on their charges hand and foot, listen sympathetically to their small talk and problems, welcome their friends and spoil them in every way.

The problem is they are reluctant to face up to the often unpleasant and disagreeable side of parenthood—training and discipline. The child is frequently so indulged that unless the other parent is strong and determined, the child will grow up thoroughly spoiled and unreasonably demanding in his or her personal relationships.

However, there is a saving grace. These people do all in their power to encourage their children to be socially acceptable. It is extremely important to Pisces own happiness and contentment that their offspring be liked by others.

So although they may adroitly sidestep the nasty and serious business of disciplining youngsters, they will use their splendid gifts of persuasion to inculcate the social graces—correcting speech, manners, deportment and so forth at every opportunity.

Both the Pisces mother and father are inclined to crack emotionally under pressure in the home or in disharmonious surroundings. Trying to cope with intractable young children or willful teenagers is apt to send them screaming for the door—or the bar.

Pisces parents usually imagine they are good parents, and they are more than half right. But for the sake of their mate, as well as for their children, it will pay them to learn to be a little less softhearted and permissive.

There is no doubt that the children of Pisces have a rare opportunity to be associated with spiritually uplifting influences. Also, their parents' fondness for all that is artistic and aesthetically pleasing can have a most beneficial effect on children's developing personalities.

If tangible direction is lacking, there is certainly no absence of love, affection and a subtle appreciation of beauty and graciousness in the home of a Pisces parent.

The birth Sign of the child, of course, will have a great bearing on the success of the individual Pisces parent.

CHAPTER ELEVEN

Children

The following descriptions of children born under the various Signs are based on the position of the Sun, the most powerful influence in the horoscope. Most individuals conform to the solar influence. However, variations do occur because of the placement of the other planets at the time of birth. And, of course, the birth Signs of the parents will also be reflected in the child's conditioning.

For a closer examination of these factors, it is advisable to study the individual child's and the parents' horoscopes, which are available for every Sign in *AstroAnalysis*. All you need to know is the person's date of birth.

Since some Signs are naturally more and less compatible with others, you can obtain a fairly accurate idea of how parents and children will hit it off by reading the pertinent descriptions for each.

The Aries Child

The Aries child is extremely bright (sometimes brilliant) and usually very advanced for his or her age.

Too much applause and reference to the child's precocity by admiring adults is likely to make him strive to outdo himself and overexcite his nervous system. This could result in sleeplessness, supersensitivity and an overcritical approach to his playmates and later all his associates.

The Aries child is high-strung and needs to be intelligently quieted. His mind is so alert to the possibilities for action in his environment that he finds it difficult to concentrate on one thing for very long. He begins new interests with great enthusiasm, but usually veers off well before they are finished. Sometimes it is because he has discovered the challenge is within his capabilities and so loses interest in it. But if a toy or game is beyond him, he will petulantly turn his back on it—or perhaps break it or throw it away. He should be taught to apply himself to finish what he starts. The chances of success will be greater

in an atmosphere where he feels there is due recognition of the importance of what he is doing.

From the start, these youngsters should be taught the advantages of slowing down without inhibiting their spontaneity. Their excited, sudden movements are apt to lead to more than their share of accidents. They will usually be recovering from a bruise, scald or cut somewhere on their body. It is terribly important for Aries boys and girls to be physically active; it helps to work off the excess nervous energy that subtracts from their powers of concentration. But they need to learn the value of deliberate, measured movement as against unrestrained hustle and bustle; their parents should inculcate in them a sense of grace and rhythm, which their impulsive actions seldom allow.

Sports are good for the Aries child and he or she is usually proficient at them. It is wise to have children coached from an early age so that they express themselves with style and expertise. Abounding energy and desire to succeed will prevent them from becoming performing cogs in a wheel. Either they'll get to the top of the team or they'll quit and try another activity until they make their mark.

In none of his activities should the Aries child be encouraged to show off. If restraint or discipline is required, it should be exercised tactfully so it won't injure the youngster's pride. Aries is a fiercely proud Sign, and this is the key to the nobility that can readily be developed in this character.

It is important that this type of child be allowed to discover things for himself and not constantly be told what to do. He likes to experiment. Too much supervision and interference make him resentful. He learns from making mistakes. He might make the same mistake more than once (which can be rather exasperating for a parent), but this is his style. He packs a lot of experience into his life. He is attracted by the challenge rather than by the end result.

The Aries child often reveals creative talents quite early. These should be nurtured and developed as soon as they appear, without stressing the competitive angle.

One of the main problems is an overactive imagination. Young Aries should be taught not to exaggerate and to learn to describe objects and events as they really are, not as he or she fancies them to be.

The Taurus Child

Taurus is usually a lovely child, both to look at and in disposition. But he has some very definite characteristics that are not immediately discernible. These need to be understood, especially by his teachers, for him to develop in a normal, balanced way.

Above everything else, young Taurus need love and affection. They are deeply sensitive and unsure of themselves inside. They often give the appearance of being wonderfully self-assured, but this is to compensate for their uncertainty, which can amount almost to an inferiority complex at times.

Taurus are not intellectual beings, essentially. They live on their feelings, which need to be constantly stimulated by the demonstration and knowledge that they are loved and appreciated. You can't just tell a Taurus child that you love him or her. You have to show it in physical terms by cuddling and petting—or with caring actions. If you don't do this, the child will become more and more indifferent, and as he gets older, will turn to sensual self-indulgence as a substitute for the loving stimulation he missed as a child. Failing this, Taurus may become increasingly stolid, and, in maturity, a rather dull and uninteresting person.

Young Taurus has exceptional willpower, which may, at times, reveal itself as a fearful obstinacy. If he digs in his toes, no argument or threat will shake him. He can be absolutely unreasonable. Again, only an appeal to his emotional self is apt to make him relent. Should he ever lose his temper, it could be a devastatingly memorable occasion.

He is an extremely modest child and tends to underrate his own abilities. He should not be criticized to make him "do better" because criticism will only make him feel more inferior and then, perhaps, defiantly overconfident and prone to making silly mistakes. He responds much better to praise and encouragement.

Taurus children are not studious types. Normal education methods don't work so well with them. To learn, it is vital that they have their feelings aroused so they can take a genuine interest in the subject. These boys and girls need to relate to topics through their senses; if they're to learn about nature,

they must examine the specimen, touch it, smell it. With arithmetic and other abstract subjects, the teacher must find a way of exciting them into participation with demonstrations, models. The failure to realize this often leads to branding the Taurus child a slow learner, when he is, in fact, nothing of the sort.

Friendship and playmates are very important to Taurus youngsters. If they can't mix with children they like, they will slow down physically and mentally, and may easily become lazy and indifferent. Having a great love of pleasure (because it helps them learn to be intellectual creatures), they might choose companions who teach them bad habits.

Properly handled and encouraged, the Taurus child quickly puts aside his timidity and becomes a friendly and congenial little person. He is likely to be artistic with his hands and any sign of this should be cultivated.

The Gemini Child

Gemini children are usually filled with restless, nervous energy. It comes from their minds, which are like delicately tuned electronic instruments. They simply can't keep still, mentally or physically. They must be constantly engaged in something that interests them. Parents and teachers may find this an exhausting business, mainly because these lovable little imps lose interest more quickly than most children. And when that happens, and no one's around, their capacity for mischief is almost unbelievable!

Young Gemini is an exceedingly bright child. He or she learns instantaneously and has an alert, inquiring mind that demands to know the reason behind everything that catches his or her attention.

As often as practical, Gemini children should be answered factually and not put off because the question happens to be irrelevant. This is the way they absorb, and every fact goes into their formidable memory, where it will be recalled as soon as it's required. In a very short time, you can teach a Gemini child practically anything.

He may not be physically strong in his early years because his whole system is under the continual tension of febrile nervous activity. As his body adapts to this, he will get stronger, until finally, in maturity, his health will be dictated largely by his state of mind. Just as Gemini can stage remarkable recoveries when new and novel interests appear, so he can become listless when assailed by boredom and depression.

The pure Gemini child needs plenty of exercise, but usually not in the form of rough and strenuous sports. His lithe, agile body and quick actions enable him to excel in games requiring thought and technique rather than brute strength and endurance.

It is especially necessary for these boys and girls to get as much sleep and rest as possible. But this is usually easier said than arranged. At bedtime, the aim should be to avoid excitement that stimulates the imagination. Stories and television shows should be carefully selected. Horror movies and the like are almost certain to cause nightmares and extreme anxiety. The child may be afraid of the dark well into his or her teens.

Gemini youngsters frequently exaggerate and tell outrageous lies—with remarkable plausibility. Their imagination is so active and vivid that they live out adventures and dramas in their heads and can't (or would rather not) separate fiction from reality.

They make excellent actors, able to mimic sounds and reproduce the characteristics of people they observe. Sometimes these children suffer from a slight speech impediment—the brain is too fast for the vocal equipment. But with patience and understanding, this can be overcome. Otherwise, the Gemini child is usually well advanced in his speech and comprehension. He may be a terrible chatterbox, though.

A child of this Sign is more intellectual than sentimental and may sometimes be slow at showing love and affection.

The Cancer Child

The Cancer child looks for love and a placid existence. These boys and girls are extremely sensitive and timid. Even though they crave to make friends, their retiring nature renders it difficult to make the first move. They do not enjoy being alone; they need to feel they belong. A Cancer child will cling tenaciously to anyone who loves him. The most difficult parental task is to push this sensitive little creature gently forward into the world.

Although the Cancer child is not necessarily the smartest or brightest of children, he possesses innate talents that a sensible upbringing will help make manifest. The tendency for late development makes the formative years extremely important for them.

Young Cancer responds remarkably to adults who show they have faith in him. For those who love him, he will do almost anything. A responsive and understanding parent or teacher will try to arouse his interest in games and activities that he can confidently share with other children. He should not be left to feel lonely. The object is to coax the child out, to make him more independent and outspoken. It is best to encourage him to do as much as possible for himself and let him feel he is actually achieving results. These should be praised and appreciated.

Cancer children are splendidly conscientious when they have been entrusted with a task. Psychologically, the reason for this is they are in constant need of approbation and learn quickly that one way of guaranteeing this is to do a job assiduously.

These children are not studious and intellectual, although they may become so in adulthood. They learn through their feelings. Unless they are very clearly associated with sensation, concepts and ideas confuse them. They need to smell a flower, to sing a song, to taste a piece of fruit if they are going to be taught about these things. You can't assume that a Cancer child has got the idea of a subject from a verbal description—which would suffice for most other children.

Cancer is the Sign of the senses and intuition, so the child's intellectual development depends on emotional understanding. Once a parent or teacher manages to arouse an absorbing interest in him, the Cancer child may apply himself to this subject for the rest of his life. Great artistic and creative careers may be begun with the right treatment of these finely balanced little people.

Otherwise, the younger person of this Sign is tempted to become introverted and live off his own emotions—moody, changeable and lethargic.

Being exceedingly sensitive, the Cancer child is easily discouraged and takes criticism much to heart. Worry may upset his stomach. He is also apt to suffer from colds and chills. His health in his earlier years may be indifferent. He may pick at his food and cry more than most youngsters.

Cancer children are usually competent at making handicrafts. In later years, they often show an extraordinary flair for business coupled with an intensely ambitious spirit.

The Leo Child

The Leo child has a vast amount of vital and mental energy at his or her disposal. It is important for parents and teachers to see that this is directed along positive lines. This youngster, because of his forceful determination, is apt to find that success comes fairly readily. He may get so carried away with applause and admiration that he overlooks the value of accomplishment itself.

Young Leo has a natural gift for leadership and will assert this as his or her right in the presence of other youngsters. The problem is a tendency to become domineering, to throw his weight around unnecessarily, show off and generally bore everyone within earshot with his boasting. In some cases, little Leo becomes "little Caesar" and exhibits a distinct love of power, which may be harmless in a child but is an objectionable quality in an adult.

The Leo child is an active and lovable little person. Quite apart from the early ego flexing, there is a dignity and nobility to his nature. His unquestionable courage becomes obvious early. Although as disobedient as any child, he will seldom resort to mean and spiteful actions. He or she will probably only have to be told once that it is dishonest to tell tales. This child's sense of loyalty is ingrained and at times may be carried to absurd lengths.

Leos are deeply affectionate children and, despite their love of display and applause, are keenly sensitive. Their intuition is often remarkable. They have a great sense of pride and yet are quick to forget and forgive. Once they make up their minds to do something, they are unswervingly determined.

A Leo child often acts impulsively, especially where pleasure is concerned, finding it very difficult to turn down an opportunity to enjoy himself. When playing, he is likely to lose all sense of time and arrive home at nine o'clock at night for his evening meal. He has a love of the great outdoors and is likely to acquit himself well at all kinds of sports.

Young Leo, although enjoying his periods of seclusion, will usually be found among groups and clubs where he can demonstrate his organizing ability and powers of leadership.

Parents of the Leo teenager should endeavor to have him trained in any profession or line of work he shows an interest in. He has a great capacity for learning, not by gathering and memorizing information but by inquiring and understanding its significance. He is never really satisfied unless he comprehends the reason for an action or instruction. A natural commander of men and women in the making, Leo will never be a shallow echo of another person's caprices.

The Leo youngster has a deep-seated ambition to get to the top even though he or she may not understand this inner drive. This child's considerable energies and diverse talents work better harnessed in a definite direction, whether in the arts, literature, politics, journalism, science or executive management.

Young Leo also benefits from a good example. Conversely, he or she should not be allowed to fall into bad company.

The Virgo Child

Virgo children are worriers. They take the smallest disappointments very seriously. They want to be liked, and yet have an unfortunate way of upsetting others by being unduly critical and faultfinding. A Virgo child is often exasperated and discouraged by other people's negative reactions to his or her good intentions, and by his or her own frustrated desire to please.

Young Virgo needs to be taught to accent the positive side of his or her nature. Although reserved and modest, these children are naturally optimistic and progressive. They are also keenly intelligent. But the slightest antagonism and adversity tend to deflate them. They live on their nerves to a great extent. They are continually analyzing other people's motives and endeavoring to find a rationale for everything. The sheer impossibility of satisfying this desire explains their basic problem.

The Virgo child loves order and method. Once these are established at home or in school, he or she will settle down emotionally and seldom be any trouble. But in a disorganized system where people are uncertain, Virgo becomes disoriented. That's why it's often a traumatic experience for a Virgo child—or a Virgo adult for that matter—to move to a new home, school or job. One astrologer has even claimed you can cause great agitation in a Virgo cat by relocating its saucer!

Schoolwork itself, however, is seldom much of a problem for the Virgo youngster. Along with Gemini, Virgo is one of the easiest types in the Zodiac to teach. Virgo has an inquiring and logical mind, which is always trying to make practical sense out of the information received. Naturally, school lessons make sense to these boys and girls. They often take a special interest in science and mathematics. They are also quite inventive and enjoy devising new methods of doing things.

Young Virgo makes friends cautiously. He's not a sentimental or emotional character and prefers to judge people on their actions and achievements rather than their words. He is an idealist and at heart a perfectionist who wants to see everything in its proper place and logical order. When he discerns that a person is not being honest with himself or true to his type (his intellectual acuity is first rate), he will say so, not with the desire to hurt, but to help. This trait is naturally often misinterpreted, and his playmates may resent his remarks and attitude and ostracize him for them.

The Virgo child needs a good education so that he doesn't feel inferior to others. He doesn't, as a rule, enjoy close physical contact—in fact, he may feel that cuddling and caressing are unnecessary and embarrassing. His finer feelings have to be handled delicately and with understanding to prevent fussiness and queasiness from becoming fixed in his character.

Virgo children are apt to be faddish about certain foods and instantly dislike some kinds. They may refuse to eat in a place they feel is dirty, although they are unable to give a conscious reason for this attitude.

These children are very quick to learn about cleanliness and hygiene, but the subjects should not be overemphasized.

The Libra Child

The Libra child is a delicate flower because he or she is a meeting point of intellect and emotion and these two don't integrate easily. The child is usually very intelligent and bright but unsure of how to handle his or her feelings.

Libras crave love yet are reserved and shy about reaching out for it. Consequently, they may cling and yet be unable to give in return. They are constantly weighing up what to do in their relationships, which way to go, what is best. The result is they don't appear to have much initiative, and unless guided and directed by an understanding parent or teacher, may grow up unable to make positive use of their many potential talents.

Young Libras don't seem to have much willpower, mainly for the reasons given above. They become excited by an idea, plunge into action with enthusiasm—and then lose interest and look around for something new. If they can't find something special, they may lapse into apathy. These children have very little urge to develop their capabilities; ambition is something they have to learn. They prefer to depend on others without exerting themselves. They need to develop the habit of working along methodical lines—games and hobbies can be used for this. If their interest is not maintained—by the parent acting as a sort of partner—they will quickly get into mischief.

The wise parent of a Libra youngster will realize right from the start that his or her child is artistically inclined and that a harsh, uncongenial, severe or ugly environment will inhibit natural expression. In such an environment, the child is likely to become highly nervous and a constant problem for the parent. But once the innate Libra love of beauty and harmony is acknowledged and cultivated, the prospects of steady development and accomplishment are much improved. For these reasons, it is advisable for the parent to observe the child's proclivities in the formative years and coax him along in the right direction.

A Libra child is much more likely to become a successful dancer, actor, singer, writer, painter, interior decorator, architect or beauty specialist than shine in a cutthroat commercial occupation.

Moodiness and jealousy are often a problem. These children want desperately to be liked, but their attitude often suggests indifference to their playmates. They may be happy and gay one moment, and inexplicably depressed and silent the next. The more they are left alone, the more temperamental and introspective they become. If this is allowed to continue, the child may grow up with few friends and unreasonable possessiveness may cause great unhappiness in his or her future love life.

Libra children are usually well formed and attractive. They have a magnetic appeal that makes other children want to be with them, but they seem unable to maintain the initial attraction. This confuses them. The parents' task is to teach the Libra child, with love and understanding, to integrate his or her emotional and mental activities and express them in unselfish ways such as in art and social endeavors.

The Scorpio Child

The Scorpio child is a tight concentration of intense energy and the direction of his or her development will depend largely on the influence parents or guardians bring to bear.

Young Scorpio is particularly strong-willed. He or she also possesses abundant capabilities that bode success in future life as a surgeon, dentist, psychiatrist, scientist, occult investigator, researcher, lawyer, detective or military person.

If you can interest this youngster in constructive and productive activities, there is not much he or she is incapable of achieving. Once this child fixes a goal, he will pursue it relentlessly. And his capacity for hard work and endurance is unequaled by any of the other Signs of the Zodiac.

The problem is that Scorpio can go from one extreme to the other; that is, he or she can be very good and very bad. If early training is neglected or haphazard, or if the child happens to fall into bad company, he may grow up to be a selfish and tyrannical adult.

Young Scorpio has a keen and penetrating mind and cannot long be entertained by frivolous and pointless games and pastimes. At every stage, Scorpios enjoy grappling with sturdy problems that are not so easy for others of their age or experience to solve. Everything they attempt, they do with zest and relish—provided they are genuinely interested.

Schoolwork comes easy to Scorpio children. Trouble occurs when they can't find sufficiently satisfying outlets for their tremendous vitality.

It is wise for the parents of a Scorpio child to be honest and straightforward with him or her from the beginning because these children possess an almost mystical ability to detect lies and attempts to deceive them. Also, the negative side of a Scorpio nature is less likely to assert itself in an atmosphere of frank and open commitment. The habitual faults of the Scorpio character include brooding resentment, secretiveness and jealousy. These have less opportunity to fester in a young personality used to candid and truthful parents.

Young Scorpio is fiercely independent but surprisingly tractable if handled with subtlety and sensitivity. He or she resents being ordered about, and may react violently and willfully to this sort of treatment. Parents who reason with their Scorpio children and deal with them in an adult fashion will get the best results.

The shrewdness and comprehension of these youngsters may develop into an infuriating air of superiority when they are with less mentally acute adults. Their self-confidence is enormous. Their vanity is a weak spot.

The Scorpio child is sometimes so bent on getting his own way that when opposed by young playmates, he may resort to underhanded methods. He can be vindictive, and in extreme cases, exact cruel reprisals. If the negative qualities are strong in these boys and girls, they may plot revenge while pretending to be sorry.

The Sagittarius Child

The Sagittarius child is not a fast developer. He or she is cheerful, trusting, optimistic and a very congenial little person to have around, if you can tolerate some changeable and unpredictable ways. Sagittarius sometimes retains these childlike qualities well into adulthood, and in some cases, for his entrie life. His trust and faith in humanity is one of his most admirable traits. Yet, as many parents are pained to find out, this faith is often violated and imposed upon.

Still, not to worry—little Sagittarius certainly doesn't. He loves to play, to roam far afield, to visit people, to go on "adventures." These boys and girls are too interested in being on the move and experiencing life as it actually is to have much time for reading and study. However, they are mentally eager, bright and quick to learn, though lacking in concentration.

Sagittarius is passionately fond of animals. If he can get hold of a horse and ride it on his explorations and adventures, he is in his element. The parents of a Sagittarius child can expect to have around the house a menagerie of pets on which their youngster will lavish considerable affection. He may sometimes in his haste forget to feed the animals and afterward cry inconsolably with remorse. He is so genuine in his affection and sincere in his intentions that it is not wise to make a fuss over this kind of neglect.

Young Sagittarius tends to think everyone is good. He himself is truthful, spontaneous and honest. He doesn't have a selfish or vindictive bone in his body. He has to be taught, though, that there is such a thing as deceit and that he must practice putting his inherently good judgment to full use.

The Sagittarius child is not possessive. Emotionally, he or she loves to have a home, family (and pets) to return to. But these children can't stand the thought of being tied down to a confined or regimented existence. Their sense of freedom is essential to their continued and broadening development.

Here, a parent must exercise great care, striking a balance between the child's need to be restrained and taught responsibility and his or her fundamental urge to learn. The most effective way of securing this child's cooperation and interest, as well as this objective, is to treat him or her like a buddy and not try to dictate. Sagittarius is built for companionship and affection rather than for possessive love. He makes one of the finest friends of all.

Young Sagittarius must be guided toward a more responsible attitude to life. He thinks he can look after himself, but rarely can unless his parents have managed to cultivate in him the judgment that curbs impatience, restlessness, recklessness, extravagance and all that goes with a personality trying to throw off authority and its controls.

When it comes to a career, the Sagittarius youth is ambitious and resourceful. But he is inclined to jump from one job to another because he just can't stand the tedium of waiting for normal advancement.

The Capricorn Child

The Capricorn child is often far too serious for his or her own good. And frequently, it is the fault of one of the parents. This child needs mature but cheerful and happy handling that makes a point of not overstressing duty, responsibility and restriction. There are enough of these sobering elements in the Capricorn temperament already. Exaggeration will only create further problems for the youngster as he or she grows up.

Young Capricorn needs a great deal of praise and affection. These boys and girls often feel afraid and deeply dissatisfied with themselves. Criticism wounds them deeply, not because they resent it, but because they unwittingly believe it to be true. Obviously, these little people require a very special parental technique to help them develop a balanced and buoyant personality.

Never nag this child. Criticism should be leveled so that the positive alternative appears as the ideal solution. Every effort to instruct should be made optimistically and encouragingly.

With this Sign, the positions of the other planets in the child's horoscope are extremely important. If there are sunnier and more easygoing influences such as Jupiter in Leo, in Sagittarius or in Aries, the youngster's disposition will be correspondingly less grave. These other planetary configurations can be checked out in the Capricorn book of *AstroAnalysis*.

The true Capricorn child is very self-conscious. He wants to make friends, but is uneasy in the presence of others, especially strangers. Being withdrawn and a rather solitary figure, he doesn't attract the usual number of playmates. Without friends to help draw him out, he is inclined to become distrustful and wary of personal relationships, thus isolating himself even more.

Young Capricorn is very good at schoolwork and a willing little helper around the house. He enjoys running errands and completing small tasks for elders who display trust in him. He is extremely conscientious and wants to please. He usually enjoys study and reading and has a great capacity for sorting out detail and cataloging data. He is well suited for all kinds of hobbies connected with sciences such as chemistry, biology, astronomy, and the like where he can apply his considerable reasoning abilities.

The longer his education can be continued, the better, especially from the social angle. He needs to be in the company of people his own age to help overcome his shyness.

As Capricorn has a distinct talent for practical pursuits, he or she will generally feel more confident with an education along these lines rather than one that is strictly academic.

People of this Sign are born leaders and vaultingly ambitious. When young Capricorn does get around to organizing young friends, he or she is enterprising and frequently bossy.

The Aquarius Child

The Aquarius child is often precocious in a shy and rather retiring way. Juvenile pastimes and games don't hold his or her interest for as long in the formative years as they do other children's. Aquarius kids grow up mentally very quickly and often prefer the company of elders when they should be out playing. Sometimes they are called old-fashioned because of their adult ways, but these are only a reflection of the advanced understanding of life which is peculiar to Aquarius.

The Aquarius child is naturally affectionate and very obedient if parents or teachers are reasonable. He or she enjoys a position of trust and is particular about honoring obligations. The cooperation of these children can't be secured by threat or force. They are highly intellectual and demand to know from a very early age why they should or should not do certain things.

The most effective parental policy is to treat an Aquarius youngster as a mental equal, to confide in him or her and encourage confidences in return—in other words, to regard the child as an intelligent companion.

Although young Aquarius is a loving child with a sweet and kind disposition, he is noticeably impersonal in the way he shows affection. He doesn't cling to people in sentimental ways and is more likely to be adult and friendly.

These boys and girls are not great students and need to be encouraged and helped with their schoolwork. They find routine book learning and formal concentration arduous. Their independent minds tend to reject attempts to condition their thinking. However, if they can be convinced that education is a means to a personally desirable end, they will apply themselves and work conscientiously. They need to know there is progressive development for them in whatever they tackle. To accumulate indiscriminate knowledge is just not their style.

The Aquarius child is uniquely lacking in self-centered drive. Basically, he or she wants to be of use to the community. Material possessions are not all that important, and over the years this indifference becomes more and more evident. A strong humanitarian tendency is apt to appear.

Finally, Aquarius will probably choose a career in science or medicine, one connected with large welfare projects or social reform where they can satisfy their urge to serve on a wide scale. They are not so concerned with the individual as they are with the masses, which accounts for their sometimes detached attitude.

Young Aquarius often has a great love of animals. Here, he or she begins to demonstrate a deep protective instinct.

This child sometimes has the potential of brilliance—even genius—but not necessarily in conventional forms. His or her inclinations need to be closely observed so that any unusual aptitude can be cultivated and guided.

The Pisces Child

The true Pisces child is very intelligent but emotionally unstable. He or she is born believing that everything and everyone are good. Thus the Pisces life seems to be a progression of disillusionment.

Faced with an unacceptable reality, Pisces children retreat into a dream world where all is as perfect as they originally thought. The problem for the parent is to coax these little people back without smashing their dreams, to teach them it's not so bad after all and that every human being has within them the power to cope.

These children are essentially artistic and often show a talent for dancing, painting, music and writing—especially poetry. They are terribly self-conscious and need to be encouraged at every step with love, praise and admiration.

They are very critical of their own efforts and never seem to reach the standard of perfection their nature calls for. In despair, they will tear up what they've written or drawn, even though by normal standards it might be excellent. Or, more likely as they grow up, they will decide not to try at all anymore, that indolence is better than the pain of failure.

Young Pisces have no confidence in their own ability. They are great actors and can put on a show of indifference and self-assurance, for a short time. But then they are likely to go away on their own and cry until they sink into the delicious world of their own vivid imaginings. These boys and girls are generally timid, shy, secretive and very loving. But they also possess a strong spiritual quality.

A Pisces child has to be taught that harsh self-judgment is damaging to his or her attempts to be productive and expressive. These boys and girls must be led to understand that they are highly artistic, and that even their compassion for others (stronger in them than in any other Sign) is an act of love and creation—sublime artistry—that most others are not capable of. On the practical side, they must learn to allow those who are competent to judge their efforts to do so, since no one will be as cruelly critical of their work as they are themselves.

These boys and girls must be given a sense of proportion so that they understand every success means "failure" for someone. The important thing is to instill in the child a desire to perform, and especially to compete, for the sake of the work itself, without encouraging a competitive spirit or even acknowledging that it is necessary.

CHAPTER TWELVE

Ascendant: The Rising Sign

Your Ascendant—the Sign rising on the eastern horizon at the time of your birth—is a major influence in the formation of your personality. It shows, among other things, how you appear to other people.

It is interesting to touch on Astrology's rationale for the existence and significance of the Ascendant, the Rising Sign. To begin with, what exactly is it?

The Ascendant is your Earth point. At the moment of your birth the Sign in line with the Earth—as demarcated by the eastern horizon at your birth place—is called the Ascendant Sign, most usually called the Rising Sign. The Rising Sign changes approximately every two hours over the course of a day.

As the Earth is rotating at a constant speed and the 12 zodiacal signs seem "fixed" in a circular field in space, one of the Signs is always ascending—rising—on the eastern horizon at any time, at any place on Earth, just as the Sun at every moment is appearing to rise somewhere.

Each Sign measures 30 degrees across and takes approximately two hours (sometimes more, sometimes less depending on season) to clear the horizon. So every 24 hours, as the Earth makes a complete rotation, each Sign rises again.

At the moment of your birth, you inherit your fate—your genetic future, your hereditary limitations, the circumstances of your home and family. Your fate is what you can't avoid—until the Rising Sign starts to act on your personality. And the Rising Signs starts to act the moment you are born, and continues to be operative as you live and grow.

The Ascendant is a most significant part of the horoscope. It ties together on Earth the outward-going characteristics of the Sun and the unconscious emotional responses of the Moon. The Sun is heavenly, the Moon is sentimental, the Ascendant is worldly. The Sun reminds you of the present and allows you to identify yourself immediately as a conscious being. The Moon reminds you of the past, shows you habit patterns, memories and subjective feelings. The Ascendant reveals the means you will use to arrive at the future.

It is quite possible to have the same Ascendant and Sun Sign. For instance, a person with Pisces Sun and Pisces Rising would be a "double" Pisces, in whom the warm, dreamy, and timid characteristics of that Sign are powerfully reemphasized. But a Pisces with Libra Rising would be more artistic. A Pisces with Virgo Rising would be a more earthy and analytical personality all around.

That is why you might come across people who don't seem to conform to the characteristics of their Sun Sign. Their Rising Sign, combined with the placings of the planets in their horoscope, may be the stronger influence, and consequently modify or distort the basic character. But this is rare. The Sun Sign invariably shines through, even though, because of adverse aspects, it may take a negative form. You have to observe the person concerned more closely, or if it is yourself, more honestly than previously.

AstroAnalysis provides in the next chapter an in-depth study of the 12 zodiacal signs as Rising Sign personalities. Here are insights to help you evaluate how each Rising Sign modifies the Sun Sign personality.

All this is the fascination and fun of AstroAnalysis. It is a test of your skill to synthesize, to blend the various dominant and subtle influences described in this book so that you perceive an individual as he or she actually is and not just the public persona. In a way, it's like looking through three or four different-colored eyeglasses simultaneously. As you become more adept, the final image appears in its true color.

CHAPTER THIRTEEN

Ascendant Personalities: Rising Sign Types

The Ascendant Sign, or Rising Sign, represents your adjustment and immediate response to the world outside yourself. It is your business face, your social face, the various conscious and unconscious poses that you adopt in cultivating the sophistication that acts to hide your true Sun Sign self from other people, but not necessarily from yourself.

It is how you appear to other people, but not necessarily how you are deep down. It is the persona or mask that you present to the world. To fashion this mask, you draw, consciously or unconsciously, on the personality type of your Rising Sign, adapted, of course, to your particular circumstances. This chapter describes the 12 personality types defined by each of the zodiacal signs.

Aries Rising

You who were born with Aries Rising are lovers of action. You want to be out in front. You are the pioneering impulse of mankind. As soon as you get a good idea, you immediately try to put it into action. Since you are so impulsive, you will spend some time licking your wounds because you failed to make a thorough evaluation of the opposition or obstacles. But you are not easily discouraged from beginning again. You are at your best when you can lay down a plan of action for yourself and others to follow. Your mode of operation is to move on to greener pastures before the task is finished, leaving others to press on or clean up.

You enjoy a position of command. You have the ability to guide, control and govern yourself as well as others. You are an admirer of scientific thought and have some distinct philosophical leanings. You

are a lover of independence who doesn't like sharing your secrets or revealing your plans. You prefer to demonstrate your tactical inspiration in activity rather than talk about what you intend to do. Like a good general (Mars is the ruler of Aries), you don't like to risk having your plans fall into enemy hands.

You possess strong and penetrating willpower. You are quite versatile, able to change from one action to another without losing a beat as long as your interest is sustained. You sometimes miss out on the rewards of your considerable efforts because you moved before they were handed out. You are enterprising and ambitious and usually headstrong. You reach out eagerly for what you want, but are easily put off by complicated situations that might slow your progress. You react indignantly if imposed upon or abused, and are apt to speak out and let others know quickly that they have offended you. Your temper can be quite fiery, but you don't hold grudges for long. You prefer to settle differences quickly and get your battles over in a hurry, whichever way the result may go. You are brimful of initiative and make an able executive, though you may lack persistence. Quite often you are interested in physical sports and your physique reflects this. You will do best in a vocation that requires instant decisions and action.

Possessions and Personal Security

You are likely to be very good at acquiring property, especially land and buildings. You don't allow cash to lie idle in the bank; you would rather invest it in bricks and mortar. Tangible assets that give you a solid hold on the earth are what you like most. In business, where you are also prone to be impulsive you are likely to drive a hard bargain. You are more conservative in financial matters than in most others. You spend money to increase the value of your property. You don't allow anything you own to fall into disrepair, and that includes your body. You are health conscious and very aware of the need to keep your body fit.

Communication, Learning, Language

You are apt to scramble your words at times because your tongue can't keep up with the speed of your thought. Your expressive Aries speech may develop a stammer when you are excited or intense. You may be accused of opportunism because you can genuinely see the validity of several people's points of view at once. You tend to be hasty or explosive in speech when defending yourself. The unguarded word may give you cause for regret. You are restless and impatient, eager for new meetings. Your ingenious ideas impress those you work for. You are on the move a lot and may be inclined to stumble or knock things over.

Home, Family, Tradition

You are very sentimental about your family. Your mother or another close elder has a special place in your heart. Your home means a great deal to you. If you have not yet settled down, you long to do so and often think about it. You think a lot about the past. You are an admirer of tradition and the good old days. You are fond of reading about history and archeological subjects; you may also display this interest in a physical way by visiting museums and even taking part in digs at old ruins. You may make numerous changes of residence before finding the home you are looking for. You work hard at making your home a comfortable place to live in.

Self-Expression, Love Life, Entertainment

You have a longing to be noticed and applauded. Your Aries aggressiveness may cause others to accuse you of being bossy or dictatorial. You take satisfaction in dramatizing your efforts, in producing spectacular effects. Your accomplishments are impressive. Your head can be turned by flattery and glamour. An impatience to fulfill your ambitions may drive you into taking risks, although you usually hedge your bets so as to preserve your basic security. You enjoy a good time. Your love affairs are largely ego

trips. You need to be proud of your children and revel in situations where you can show them (at least the successful ones) off.

Work and Health

You are a steady worker, though no one would describe you as a plodder. You toil with deft dedication. You can separate the chaff from the wheat with great ease whether you are dealing with people or detail. You are efficient and disciplined in your personal life. You are keenly conscious of hygiene and sometimes can be finicky. You enjoy delicacies but seldom eat or drink to excess. You take more than average care of your body because good health means you can continue to be active. Sickness irritates you, makes you nervous and snappish. At times you are too quick to find fault with co-workers; but however annoying, your criticisms are very often right on the mark.

Partnerships and Marriage

In this department, the Aries is not an independent loner. You need to share your life with others, especially a love partner. You expect the admiration of your mate, and at times, adoring attention. You try to get along with your partners. Harmony is intensely important to you, but you don't always find it. Your directness and sometimes rugged manner may offend even your own finer sensibilities. You feel the pull of inner extremes and are constantly striving to restore your inner balance. You usually marry early after a romantic adolescence. Marriage to a compatible and charming person is important to you. You can be adamant, but at heart you are a peacemaker.

Shared Resources, Legacies, Sex

Secretive about your deeper feelings, you seldom engage in intimate discussions with outsiders. In your love life, you are sensual rather than sentimental. You have numerous secrets. You feel a need to rise above the temptations of your lower nature, although this may be neither easy nor personally desirable. You are a powerhouse of emotional energy that needs to be properly harnessed. Sometimes strenuous physical activity will work off your excess energy. By sublimating your deeper drives, you can reach towering heights of attainment. You are a realist. You understand human failings. You don't like pretense. You can be torn by jealousy.

Higher Learning and Travel

You have an interesting religious or philosophic outlook, although not really unconventional. You seek new vistas of the mind. You are highly intelligent and sometimes astound your acquaintances with your penetrative powers of perception. You are an expansive personality, forever trying to widen your horizons. You like to travel afar to absorb new cultures, meet different types of people and encounter fresh situations. You often do things on the spur of the moment through sheer inspiration. Your optimistic, frank and generous nature helps you to attract companions who have something out of the ordinary to offer.

Public Standing, Career, Prestige

Your Aries talent as an organizer in this position fits you for big business. You are sure to rise in your field, especially in later life. You are responsible and ambitious, though your methods may be conservative. You want to be recognized as an authority because you don't like to take orders. You are capable of great and enduring effort; persistence here is your long suit. You like to assume responsibility for others. You appear somewhat aloof and unfriendly, but this is just your customary manner when important matters have to be attended to. You are happier in charge of the big scene than coping with details, which you prefer to leave to others.

Friends, Groups, Hopes, Wishes

Your Aries love of independence may be overemphasized here. You may kick up your heels, break with some traditions and choose friends who do the same. But your business companions will be more conventional; you have the knack of coping well with the two extremes. You are a bit of a revolutionary, more intellectual than sentimental. Your advanced ideas may attract some odd-bods. You need to be able to express your broader views freely, and the bohemian types of this world are the most receptive listeners. You are tolerant of others' eccentricities. Your flair for originality is exceptional; you shine in group activities.

Hidden Motives, Selfless Service, Psychic Feelings

You are instinctively able to decide the right thing to do. Although you may be impulsive, your actions will probably turn out for the best. You have a very tender side to your nature, which you may unconsciously repress. Any excessively sympathetic responses you manage to control in one way will erupt into compulsive action in another. You may have difficulty understanding some of your own emotional reactions. The plight of your suffering fellow man is apt to move you to actions of self-denial. You may feel a need for solitude and introspection, but seldom be able to find the time for either. Your intuition is acute.

Taurus Rising

You who were born with Taurus Rising are self-reliant people capable of working hard for long periods to accomplish the goals you set for yourself. You are also extremely good at working for others. You are an ideal person to have on the payroll; you have a flair for earning money for whoever employs you.

You usually possess a pleasing or attractively distinctive voice. You give an impression of grace and compact movement, even though some of you may be on the chubby side. You like gold—literally. You strive to amass money so you can convert it into solid assets. Nothing would please you more than to own a gold mine, for the sheer, deliciously secure feeling of it. You don't like taking risks with what you own. You would rather depend on your practical capacity for dogged effort than take a big win-or-lose chance.

You are a gentle person at heart and don't go looking for trouble. You are not easy to provoke to anger, but once stirred, your rage can be formidable. When opposed, you can display an extraordinary stubbornness. It is this unyielding quality that allows you to hang on like a bulldog to tasks and causes that would daunt any other type in the Zodiac. Once you make up your mind, that is the end of it; you stick to your decision through thick and thin. There is a great deal of latent energy behind your powers of endurance. But if it is misplaced, you can be overly sensual, too dependent on comfort and indolent. You are sincere, reliable and trustworthy. You have a good deal of common sense. You make a very loyal friend. You have a flair for financial manipulation and considerable organizing ability, which will be helpful in your career.

You need time to think things over, to weigh all the pros and cons before reaching a decision, and for this reason, others sometimes regard you as ponderous and slow. You have a compelling need to get everything on a firm basis before proceeding. You are rather secretive and reserved concerning your personal affairs. Although usually of a quiet disposition, you can be surprisingly dogmatic. You are deeply influenced by sympathy. You love beauty in nature, music, literature or art. You are also fond of pleasure and the comforts of this world. You are keen to surround yourself with beautiful things. Good food and the refinements of entertaining that go with it are important to you. You are a most relaxed person and can have a calming and beneficial effect on those who are nervous or irritable. Although affectionate and loving, you can be exasperatingly unreasonable and prejudiced.

Possessions and Personal Security

You set your mind to making money. You think about different schemes, testing them with your considerable powers of imagination to make sure they work before putting them into action. You are very likely to take on an extra job to augment your income. You use wit and intelligence to diversify your financial interests so that your security is never really vulnerable. Money usually comes to you through various channels. You like to cultivate the friendship of people with wealth and material possessions. Since you also like to give the impression that you are doing well yourself, you don't mind spending money on gifts, traveling and other communications.

Communication, Learning, Language

You are in regular touch with your closest relatives. You have an urgent need to know that all is well with those who love you and with those to whom you feel related. You are sensitive to your surroundings, particularly to the neighborhood in which you live. If your home is not in a desirable area, you are unhappy. Although you are unsettled by the thought of a major change, you will probably move house more than once to find the right surroundings. Uninterfering neighbors can be a big consideration. Just as Taurus children learn much faster if the subject is given emotional meaning, you absorb knowledge slowly but surely, once the "feeling" is right.

Home, Family, Tradition

Your home is your castle, and you leave no doubt in anyone's mind that you want to be the lord or lady of it. Domestic life probably revolves around your preferences, even though there may be others to consider. You like to dispense hospitality from a well-stocked larder and an impressive wine cellar (or rack). You are an entertaining and gracious host with a flair for providing lavish and glamorous flourishes. If you can manage it, you'll buy yourself a mansion, fill it with luxurious things and arrange an endless parade of admiring guests. If "home" is only a cave, you can be depended upon to make it comfortable, impressive and homelike.

Self-Expression, Love Life, Entertainment

You enjoy love affairs but they don't obsess your thinking. You aren't partial to romantic daydreaming or to coloring your relationships with imagination. You believe in having everything in its right place, and that includes your emotions. You may be a bit prudish and critical of contemporary permissiveness. You select a love mate with great caution, but once having made your commitment, you like to get on with what happens next—so that you'll always *know* what's happening next. You are a bit too methodical for spontaneous gamesmanship. A stimulating discussion or an activity highlighting food is often your idea of entertainment. Strenuous games or sports don't appeal to you.

Work and Health

You need to work in harmonious conditions. Any degree of discord will throw you off balance and send you running for the exit or the escapist's bottle. Your health depends very much on your being able to maintain an amicable and agreeable atmosphere around you. You work very well with others. You are cooperative, good-natured and cheerful. Tact and diplomacy are your special qualities. You are prepared to work as one of a team and can frequently manage to bring together warring factions. Peace at almost any price is your slogan. But sometimes your exactitude irritates co-workers. Your work is often in fields that require the artistic touch.

Partnerships and Marriage

You are probably a quite demanding marriage partner, because you pour the considerable intensity of your emotions into your closest relationships. Jealousy and possessiveness can make life miserable at times for you both. You are much happier if you enjoy a satisfactory sexual relationship with your marriage partner. Disloyalty by the other person may have deep psychological repercussions. Partnerships for you are a serious business and you don't shirk from sharing your material wealth and means with those you live with. Your intuition acts like a sixth sense where partners are concerned. Although you are strongly physical, you need someone with intellectual qualities as well.

Shared Resources, Legacies, Sex

You are apt to benefit from an inheritance of money, property or title. The ending of a partnership could be particularly rewarding in material terms. Big business settlements may suddenly affect you and coincide with an abrupt change in your way of life. You have a strong social conscience about the way people handle the reproductive instinct and the effect of this on the community. You believe in the moral law, and this is reflected in your lofty ethics regarding sex. Whatever freedoms you may seem to take in sexual activity, you still observe strict principles of your own. You have faith in a life hereafter.

Higher Learning and Travel

Although your religious beliefs tend to be conventional, you have the intensity to inspire others to an enlightenment possibly greater than your own. You are conservative and rather orthodox in your opinions about the deeper questions of life. You are prepared to accept or live with doctrines handed down from the past until some authority proves they are wrong or lays down an alternative. You don't enjoy speculating about philosophic possibilities and you are a bit suspicious of those who do. Like the lawyer (a profession in which you should shine), you want concrete evidence before committing yourself. Travel doesn't usually hold special appeal unless it is connected with commerce.

Public Standing, Career, Prestige

You feel more secure and happy in a profession where you work with a group. You have much to contribute, being both a cohesive and persistent influence as well as an original thinker. You like to feel you are doing a good job and are pulling your weight. Emotionally, you are more involved with the cause than with the people concerned. Your ideas are often ingenious. You could be an able inventor. Science may provide a field where you can work with satisfaction and renown toward solving mankind's graver problems. You are prepared to sacrifice much for the greater cause. You are a tireless worker for the species rather than for the individual.

Friends, Groups, Hopes, Wishes

You have true friends, the kind who don't forget you even though you may seldom meet. You sincerely want to understand all your friends, but you are particular about who gets really close to you. You get along well with people. You are prepared to listen to their problems without trying to introduce your own. You have a deep reservoir of sympathy for your fellow man, especially for the underdog, the underprivileged and the sick. You depend on your companions a great deal to fill your need for emotional sharing. You are more easily hurt than most if you feel your friends are neglecting you. You identify with suffering people and are not beyond a grand but unostentatious gesture of self-denial on their behalf.

Hidden Motives, Selfless Service, Psychic Feelings

You initiate as many moves as you can behind the scenes. You don't announce what you are up to until you have to. The facade you present to the public sometimes bears little resemblance to the person inside. A sympathetic, vigorous and often secret imagination plots the course for your compelling actions. You feel sometimes that your decisions are made for you. This is the dynamic point in the Zodiac from where all your Taurus activity stems. The position gives you the power to repress impatience and to be rather long-suffering. Once your anger flares, it can become a self-paralyzing fury that explodes within you, causing debilitating results more harmful than suppressing your anger.

Gemini Rising

With Gemini Rising you must be constantly busy to be happy. You crave change and diversity; deprive you of these, and life loses its meaning. You live a mental existence. Your world is the world of ideas. You unrealistically expect your physical environment to move at the same pace as your mind; hence, you are frequently bored and restless.

You are ambitious and curious. You aim to develop an inquiring mind and a quick wit: these are the implements you use to get ahead and to defend yourself the moment trouble looms. You are not a very physical entity. You use your body as you use your mind, sometimes driving it to a state of near exhaustion. "Jack be nimble, Jack be quick, Jack jump over the candlestick"—is you! A usually slender and agile frame allows you to move with speed and flowing precision.

With Gemini Rising you are sensitive, quick to pick up the thoughts and attitudes of others. Your lucid perception is often mistaken for intuition, but you are essentially an intellectual creature. Being naturally idealistic, you often feel you can solve the problems of the world—in your head. You are not beyond helping a good cause in a practical way, especially if you can take on the job of whipping up enthusiasm and support with letters, telephone calls and the personal power of your rhetoric.

You like pleasure and adventure. Your fertile imagination is always at work, trying to introduce novelty into your activities. You enjoy all kinds of mental recreation, including brain-teaser games. You are interested in experimentation and investigation. Education in its wider sense attracts you, and you will often take up a study to amuse yourself or just to stay well informed. You are attracted by scientific subjects because they are concerned with facts and these are more important to you, basically, than opinions. You are extremely adaptable and can tailor your conversation and language to suit any company you happen to be in. You like to chat. To others, you seem to have an extraordinary zest for living and your acquaintances are often amazed at how you retain your youthful looks and outlook. Like Peter Pan, you don't seem to grow old as ordinary mortals do. As long as you are fired by enthusiasm's vital spark, you seem to be able to go on forever, dancing from project to project, never appearing to weary of incessant diversity.

At times, you become anxious, restless and indecisive. You can also be mentally timid. When inactive, you become impatient and irritable. Your high-strung nature makes you extremely excitable. You possess inherent literary ability and are fond of reading and writing. You are quick to learn and either admire or enjoy music, painting, drawing, languages, travel and most forms of innovation and invention. You are capable of doing several things at once and are very good at carrying on an intelligent conversation and deftly using your hands at the same time.

Possessions and Personal Security

You are best at increasing your income and building up assets in situations where you can appeal to people's emotions, particularly in their homes. You can be successful in this way through television, magazines, newspapers, books and radio. You could also be a con artist. You have a keen sense of values. You can prosper in trade and commerce, especially in the role of agent or middleman. You try to conserve your resources and don't throw your money around, except sometimes when you are chasing pleasure. You like to make your home comfortable and to provide well for your family. In doing this, you sometimes appear to be extravagant.

Communication, Learning, Language

You have a great talent for expressing yourself, for commanding the attention of others with a dash of showmanship. You are not just a fluent talker and writer; you have a style and presence that come through however you choose to communicate. Writing and speaking, to you, are arts that exist not only for persuading others but also for gaining their admiration and respect. You are the journalist who not only gets the scoop but who also feelingly conveys the atmosphere; the amusing storyteller, the entertaining public speaker, the absorbing lecturer. Sometimes you get carried away and in your enthusiasm, exaggerate, present fiction as fact, and also say the wrong thing.

Home, Family, Tradition

You are a tidy person and your home reflects this. You like orderliness and cleanliness. You would prefer to earn your living by working at home, and this thought is often in your head as you methodically strive to better yourself. You feel it is important to your health to live in peaceful surroundings where you can recuperate quickly and quietly from the rigors of your constant communication with the outside world. The country will often suit you as long as you have easy access to the brighter lights. You are a much deeper person than your flippant conversation sometimes suggests. You can be quite sharp for their own good with family members who step out of line.

Self-Expression, Love Life, Entertainment

You like a good balance to your activities and manage to mix sociability, creativity and working with considerable dexterity. It's not beyond you to go to work, give a party and produce something of artistic merit in the same day. You intend to behave in socially acceptable ways but it is not unknown for you to occasionally go off the wall when your spontaneity and enthusiasm get the better of you. You enjoy the company of artistic people and possess a flair for dressing well or stylishly either in traditional or modern mode. You are popular with children and have a gift for talking *with* them rather than *at* them. In your love life, you are basically a roamer and may have two or three affairs going at once.

Work and Health

You have a fine talent for ferreting out facts and you do well in any profession or field that demands this ability. You are well suited for laboratory work, scientific research programs, psychiatry, psychology and investigative journalism. You are able to cut through trivia with razor-sharp keenness and expose the reality that lies behind. In your work, you are able to overcome your natural Gemini flippancy and become deeply involved. Dedicated effort is not beyond you. You are often revitalized by unremitting endeavor. Co-workers who provoke you may feel the sting of your tongue.

Partnerships and Marriage

You marry more for mental than physical reasons. You are happiest with a companion who is intellectually bright and able to share your ideas. Sex is secondary to your need to be understood by your partner, to feel that your mental boundaries are being continually pushed back by the close contact between two intelligent people. You won't be nagged and you won't be imprisoned; you would rather be single. You want a mate who can handle your affairs and provide the sense of purpose you require, without limiting your freedom and scope for self-expression. It's a tall order. In turn, you offer a very adaptable, witty, communicative and hopeful personality.

Shared Resources, Legacies, Sex

Your sex life is fairly clear cut and you are able to keep it proportional to your other interests. You seldom have any serious hangups about sex; you are not a sentimental type and your approach is somewhat matter-of-fact. You usually have to wait until rather late in life to benefit from legacies. Settlements are often delayed. Your views on an afterlife are conservative and you have no great desire to speculate about death. Your interest in occult subjects, however, can be quite intense and you have a flair for digging out the truth. You enjoy exposing trickery.

Higher Learning and Travel

You are seldom a conformist in your religious beliefs. You think that the truths contained in traditional religions can be expressed in rational terms and require no mumbo-jumbo. You feel that the established churches should keep up with the times. You have a great urge to share your ideas with as many people as possible and to travel long distances. You like to disseminate information. You aim to understand other races, to visit and stay among them if you get the chance, to learn about other cultures firsthand. You are tolerant of other people's beliefs and don't set out to convert them to your own.

Public Standing, Career, Prestige

Your main problem in life is trying to make up your mind about what you want to do with it. The trouble is you can be successful in just about any career that appeals to you, which gives you little incentive to stick to one occupation. You never seem to find the occupation that can satisfy you for long. Once you know you can handle a job, you tend to move on. Often you use your versatility to follow more than one vocation simultaneously. You may switch from one job to another, looking for the golden one that will fulfill you. Some of you would rather be drifters than settle for a humdrum or mundane position. Your search for a dream may serve to reduce your immediate chances of recognition and renown.

Friends, Groups, Hopes, Wishes

Friendship is one of the most important spheres of your life. You have many friends and keep in regular touch. Friendship means variety, change, conversation, animation, movement, discussion—all the things you love most. As this department is the zodiacal point that gives rise to Gemini activity through enterprise, you are exceptionally good at making acquaintances. You get to know the right people, have a flair for enlisting cooperation and are particularly successful at initiating group activities. You join things to meet others, and once this is accomplished, often withdraw. You are apt to squander your energies marshaling support for too many projects at once and run out of steam before any are completed.

Hidden Motives, Selfless Service, Psychic Feelings

Although you may not show it, you are frequently shaken by feelings of material insecurity. You may try to affect a certain detachment from the things of this world, but underneath you worry about your bank account and try to put pennies aside for a rainy day. You are often a silent saver—busily, between other activities, stamping down the earth around your money chest. It is this vague anxiety about financial matters that accounts for much of your mercurial versatility. You reason unconsciously that the more talents you can develop and have at your disposal, the less chance there is of falling on hard times. Your methods are sometimes devious.

Cancer Rising

If the Sign of Cancer was ascending at the hour of your birth, you are a person of changing moods and emotions. You are extremely sensitive and of retiring disposition. You know what it's like to be hurt and you do your best to shield those you love, especially your family, from painful experiences. You are particularly solicitous of your mother or the matriarchal figures in your family. Although circumstances may force you to lose touch with these people, you are never really free of concern for them. You have strong memories of your childhood. Whether your recollections are happy or unhappy, you can't help reminiscing about the past.

You are sentimental, sympathetic and rather talkative. Your imagination is fertile and inventive. You feel first and think after; thought, to you, is almost unnecessary. Your ideas emerge as vivid "feeling" pictures, with which you can identify with great pain or pleasure. Although you are fond of your home, you are inclined to wander and may never really manage to settle down in one place. If you do set up a permanent residence, you are apt to pack up and move off again after two or three years.

You have a fine retentive memory, especially for family and historical events. You file away feelings rather than concepts. As you have a strong emotional attachment to the past, this probably accounts for your often phenomenal power of recall. You are fond of possessions and will work industriously to acquire them. Your personal needs are not great and you can be very economical, even frugal, with money. You like to travel and enjoy visiting people in their homes. You are especially likely to drop in on relatives. Novelty and change appeal to you in almost any form. Although you are careful with money, you are often imposed upon. Your sympathetic nature makes it difficult for you to refuse another person who appeals for help or appears to be

in need. But you have an extremely tenacious streak, which manifests itself in a variety of ways but is particularly vehement when you adopt a protective role.

You shy away from pressure. You can give the impression of hardy self-assurance and toughness and can cope with the best of them for a limited period. But then you must scuttle off to some warm and secure retreat where you can quietly restore your self-confidence. You fear criticism and ridicule and will go to great lengths to avoid either. This makes you rather conventional and very discreet. You are inclined to follow an occupation that will bring you in touch with the public. You enjoy praise and approbation; this, again, makes you exceedingly diplomatic. You are a lover of beauty and usually possess a psychic and mediumistic faculty.

Possessions and Personal Security

You like to do well so you can provide for your children with style. You are one of the real collectors of the Zodiac. You love to assemble objects of art, sets of beautiful things and relics of antiquity. You enjoy displaying these in your home for others to see. Your collections are often valuable, but this is not a prerequisite; you are just as capable of saving worthless objects with the same affection and pleasure because they give you a reassuring feeling of material security. You are painfully affected when anything you own is broken or destroyed. But no emotional scar hurts you for too long.

Communication, Learning, Language

You are rather apprehensive about the future so you tend to take refuge in the past. You think and talk a lot about the good old days. You feel that traditional attitudes are more desirable than contemporary ones. You like to quote precedents. You take pride in your patriotism. You are often critical of the ideas of others and try to put them on the right track. You like to feel that you and your associates are eating health-giving foods. You collect dietary books and articles to help all concerned. Your eye for descriptive detail is remarkable. You often exaggerate your problems to yourself and worry unnecessarily.

Home, Family, Tradition

You regard your home as the pivot of your life. As sentimental as you are about your family, you would rather have an empty house than disturb it with discord and disagreement. You aim to maintain harmony in your surroundings, and to achieve this, show tact and diplomacy to those with whom you live. If you fail to secure the balance you crave, you will leave the house temporarily or retire to the seclusion of your room. You spend much of your leisure time making your home a more attractive and congenial place to live. You like to feel that your family thinks and speaks well of you in your absence.

Self-Expression, Love Life, Entertainment

You are capable of producing work of superior artistic merit, but to do this, you have to overcome a curious self-repressive tendency, which is to be overly possessive of your loved ones, especially your children. You are inclined to play a watchdog role, continually guarding or brooding over them, and this introverted centering of your emotional forces reduces your creative fire and inspiration. In romance, you veer toward secret love affairs, finding excitement in the thought of tasting forbidden fruit and calculatedly ignoring the painful consequences that might be involved. You can suffer deeply through jealousy, which is often matched by an intensity of physical passion.

Work and Health

Your work as an employee is marked by an optimistic outlook that allows you to cope cheerfully with considerable detail. As long as you believe that what you are doing is useful and a step to bigger things in the future, you will apply yourself with diligence. You are an industrious worker. In organizing and planning, you use the lessons of the past with considerable discernment to get around the problems that lie ahead. As much as you dislike emotional scenes, you seem impelled to get involved in squabbles and arguments among co-workers. It is important to your health that you avoid eating while you are emotionally upset.

Partnerships and Marriage

You take marriage very seriously and often choose a partner who is helpless, lazy or unable to cope. Your inherent desire to nourish and protect induces you to accept responsibilities that others would find impossible. You are frequently the long-suffering husbands and wives of the Zodiac, although it is not in your character to complain. You are also ambitious for your mate to get on in the world and you do all in your power to encourage and to help it. The Cancer woman makes an excellent partner for men struggling to get to the top, particularly in oc-

cupations that depend on public support. The career woman could not have a more solid supporter than a Cancer husband.

Shared Resources, Legacies, Sex

You have advanced and original ideas about sex and the community. You are the type of person who is a leading advocate of enlightened approaches to abortion, homosexuality, birth control for teenagers and subjects once not discussed in polite gatherings. You may also hold forth with some independent thoughts about death and survival and participate in group inquiries into occult and metaphysical experiences. You have strong feelings about sharing with others and might visualize some sort of communal existence as a means of human regeneration.

Higher Learning and Travel

Experience of the higher consciousness is not uncommon among some of the more advanced Cancer types. You begin with as much zest, if not more, than the next person to fulfill your worldly ambitions, but eventually you discover that (as you've often suspected) your personal fulfillment lies in service and the surrender of egocentric desires. You have little time for orthodox religions and avoid discoursing with people who espouse dogma. You are a true meditator and spiritual pragmatist. Less evolved Cancer types are apt to lose themselves in dreaming, wishful thinking and regret.

Public Standing, Career, Prestige

You are a person who has to live with rhythm, the ebb and flow of a highly sensitive and in-drawn nature with an instinctive, outgoing urge. You are ambitious and more eager than some apparently less retiring types to get ahead. You are determined from the start to make a name for yourself, and the fact that you don't always succeed is no reflection on your efforts or tenacity. Your frequently aggressive drive helps to compensate for your lack of self-assurance and natural reserve. You often succeed in maritime occupations and those that offer the opportunity to travel, especially overseas.

Friends, Groups, Hopes, Wishes

Friendship is one of the mainstays of your life. Your friends are a buffer between you and the realities of the outside world. As you walk out of your home, you like to feel there are numerous other welcoming and comfortable places for you to go. You may stride into the thick of combative reality with an admirable display of aggression, but when the day is over, you heal your psychological wounds by contact with your friends. You enjoy helping your comrades and are the first to lend cash if you have it. You also like to spend money on friends. You tie yourself to your companions with deep bonds of affection and often form lifetime friendships. You are particularly loyal and caring. You enjoy the physical warmth of groups and the opportunity they provide to extend your sphere of influence by discussion.

Hidden Motives, Selfless Service, Psychic Feelings

Despite their overt need of friends, Cancer Rising people can be among the recluses of this life. The strength of your feelings, acting on a richly imaginative disposition, provides you with an inner life that often approaches self-sufficiency. You learn more from observing people and situations than from formal tuition. You have periods of soul-searching introspection. Your more abstract ideas clash with your sentimental nature, and while you are sorting out the contradictions, you can give the impression of moodiness. You have strong psychic powers and mediumistic ability. Intuition is more natural to you than thinking.

Leo Rising

You love power and distinction. You succeed most where you have authority. You usually occupy some high or responsible position in managing or executive work. You have the gift of inspiring others to great accomplishments—unless you become power-happy, in which case you can lead them to their ruin. You are ambitious, self-confident and fearless. Although high-strung and quick to anger, you are very forgiving and don't hold grudges for long.

You have great energy and are apt to pour it, without restraint, into any activity that arouses your sympathy or interest. Therefore you are always in danger of overdoing things (it is not unknown for a Leo-born person to work himself to death). Although you are usually strong, there is a distinct limit to how far you can push yourself before undermining your health. You have great hope and faith in the future. You are outgoing and magnanimous and scatter your goodwill in all directions while everything is going well. In adversity, you are easily troubled and may seem to withdraw from all other

pursuits to attend to one problem. You are not, in fact, neglecting any responsibility; your aim is to gather the sum of your forces to attack the problem that occupies you. You are impatient to come to grips with problems and to eliminate them. You have the fortitude to endure considerable discomfort and pain if it will lead to a peaceful life. Like the Lion, who is the symbol of this Sign, you are a great fighter, but you must also have your quiet hours lazing in the sun.

And again, like the King of Beasts, you are of noble disposition. You have dignity and integrity. You are philanthropic, charitable and loyal. You often receive favors as though they were your due and dispense them with much the same flourish. You are imperious and fond of command. You tend to dominate the social sphere in which you move. You are a physically attractive and vital person and gravitate to a position of leadership as though it were the most natural thing in the world. You are good-natured, generous and kindhearted. You are also independent, outspoken and at times brutally frank. Your aim, to grant freedom through your own ability to lead, sometimes degenerates into a power complex resulting in arrogant dictatorship. You enjoy nothing quite as much as an admiring audience.

Possessions and Personal Security

You are a bit of a paradox where money is concerned. You have quite extravagant tastes and yet your spending habits are conservative. You can put your pennies away with punctilious care and then blow the lot (well, almost the lot) on a night out or on some expensive luxury item. You enjoy manipulating money and balancing your accounts. You can teeter on the razor's edge between good living and bankruptcy with an adroitness that would make less confident types shudder. Usually, though, you know what you are doing and have calculated the extent of your resources and reserves down to the last coin. If you get into financial difficulty, you worry incessantly and this affects your health.

Communication, Learning, Language

Since you like people to agree with your ideas, it is fortunate that you are usually very good at the art of persuasion. You make, in fact, a fine salesperson. Articulate and polished in speech, you have the knack of communicating your enthusiasm through the vitality of your presentation. You are pleasing and tactful. Because you usually believe in whatever you recommend, you exude an air of sincerity. You are even prepared to risk an argument to make your point. On the other hand, if you don't have faith in what you are saying, the solar charisma tends to evaporate, making you fairly easy to see through. You strive to create harmony in your immediate environment, even to the extent of bringing like-minded or romantically inclined people together.

Home, Family, Tradition

You insist on being the master or mistress of your home. This is probably the reason why many leonine types do not enjoy a great amount of domestic happiness. You are imperious and extremely conscious of the dignity of a healthy family tree and the advantages of good breeding. If your ancestors are unknown quantities, you will set about establishing your own dynasty, however modest your circumstances may be. You are a proud descendant of admirable forebears, you prefer to ignore family skeletons and hope they'll go away. You run a tight (family) ship and expect the unquestioning loyalty and support of your dependents.

Self-Expression, Love Life, Entertainment

Your natural desire and flair for being noticed makes it possible for you to reach considerable heights of accomplishment. Although your compulsion to be recognized degenerates at times into sheer showmanship or showoffmanship, you are driven by the same forces to exploit your artistic and finer creative abilities. You will never rest content with what you attain; you will always have the conviction that far greater possibilities lie within you—and, for that matter, within others. You are especially capable of instilling exalted ideas in children and of awakening them to their potentialities. For this reason, you make an inspiring parent or teacher. You love to gamble—with money, love, skills . . . even your own destiny.

Work and Health

Your profound sense of responsibility for whatever job you take on makes you a most diligent and industrious employee. Your ability to work hard with creative inspiration, together with your innate leadership powers, usually ensures that you get to the top. Although ambitious, you are impelled mostly by the desire to do a job well for its own sake. The fact that you can then bask in the sunlight of other people's admiration is a hidden motivation. Your health can be affected by overwork, the most vulnerable areas being the heart and back. Self-confidence sometimes causes you to overestimate your powers of physical and mental endurance.

Partnerships and Marriage

You are not an easy person to be married to, although you can be devoted and disarmingly generous. You often choose the wrong type of partner. You have a strong streak of independence and a love of freedom, and if you choose a mate with similar characteristics—as you usually do—the result is fireworks. Your imperious nature makes it difficult for you to share authority in the home. You want a royal subject as well as a mate. You are often attracted to an artistic type, and this temperament is known more for rebellion than servitude. You need an intelligent partner who is keen and earnest enough to pay the relatively harmless doses of homage you require in exchange for royal munificence.

Shared Resources, Legacies, Sex

A degree of sacrifice and pain usually accompanies the Leo experience of sharing. To share with mankind is your greater purpose, befitting sons and daughters of the Sun's own Sign. You must learn to resist the natural urge to use up your energies and passion in satisfying personal desires and concupiscence. You are required, often after long suffering, to rise to compassionate heights where you can renew yourself in concern for your fellow man rather than for your own superficial self. You can do this by intense dedication to an artistic pursuit. Legacies are often surrounded by confused and disordered circumstances. There can be a long battle to win what you believe to be your rightful inheritance, whether it be property, title or the vindication of your family name. The Leo person usually succeeds in whatever he or she undertakes.

Higher Learning and Travel

Your deep-rooted optimism is based mainly on faith in yourself. And this, in turn, is frequently supported by the conviction that you are filling a destined role and being guided by inner forces you do not need to explain or understand. It is this faith, either consciously or unconsciously held, that enables you to assume a position of authority or rulership in practically any situation. The so-called divine right of kings is a postulate not hard for you to understand. You like to travel far afield, but you are not a rubberneck tourist type; you need to know that your journey has greater purpose than mere sightseeing to make it worth your while.

Public Standing, Career, Prestige

You are a lover of the vestments and tokens of office. If you become lord mayor or police chief, you want the 24-carat-gold chain around your neck, the big badge or the ivory-handled pistols. As soon as you can afford it, you surround yourself with status symbols. Apart from artistic considerations, all the objects you choose are usually workable, for you appreciate practicality as long as it doesn't cramp your style. Once in a position of power, you are often reluctant to step aside and may ferociously resist any order to step down. As a superior, you can be one of the boys as long as the boys remember you are the one. By learning to delegate, you can help protect your health.

Friends, Groups, Hopes, Wishes

You need a mixed group of people around you to stimulate your mind and to prevent you from becoming too fixed in your attitudes. You usually attract friends who, although they may be over-indulgent as an audience, are intelligent and vivacious. Many of your companions are young, clever and admiring, and in this company you allow others to shine beside you with an amused, paternal or maternal beneficence. You are generous to your friends and select the closest of them with care. Sometimes you ally yourself with humanitarian group efforts, usually on the organizational side. Philosophic movements and seminars also appeal to you, but only until you can formulate your own abstract ideas. Then you may well set up a "school" of your own.

Hidden Motives, Selfless Service, Psychic Feelings

You sometimes feel neglected and unappreciated and this causes you to retreat sulkily into yourself. Your towering pride won't allow you to disclose the reasons (such pettiness is rather unkingly, or is it?), so everyone in your vicinity feels a little bit uncomfortable without quite understanding why. Unless you have identified with a purpose in life, you are apt to drift off into glorious daydreams. You have considerable capacity for serving others selflessly, but sometimes spoil it by looking for applause and commendation. You will give up money and time, but

rarely the right to recognition or attention. You suffer most when these plaudits are not immediately forthcoming.

Virgo Rising

If Virgo is your Ascendant, you are a person who has an unusual amount of common sense. Basically, you are a very active thinker and you strive to implement your ideas rather than allow them to lie around in your head. You aim to tidy up your environment, to set things and people straight; therefore, you are sometimes perceived as fastidious or hypercritical. You possess a great aptitude for handling details, regarding them as the first essentials for establishing the order you love so much.

You are extremely good at work that requires precision and special skills. You can be counted on to have done your homework well and to possess a keen idea of sequences and procedures before you start. You learn readily and quickly and have impressive powers of endurance. You make a competent accountant, clerk, secretary and personal assistant. Your very practical way of looking at things also makes you an able worker in the service occupations such as foreman, housekeeper, institution orderly or aide and the like.

You are not easily contented. Although conservative in outlook, you have a speculative turn of mind and often become anxious about your affairs. You desire wealth and expend considerable effort building up your savings. You are economical and prudent. You don't enjoy making a scene about money, but you indicate clearly to others that you know what's going on. You are cautiously protective of your own interests and are not likely to plunge into financial ventures without thorough reflection. You can also be counted on to look after the interests of others, which makes you a trusted and valuable employee, guardian or companion.

You seek perfection, not so much in yourself, but in the outer world. You aim to put everything in its place and are extremely methodical and neat to this end. Your interest in order extends to your associates and you often endeavor to correct them by pointing out their faults. Despite your good intentions, this may be resented. If not controlled, your impulse to criticize can descend into trifling faultfinding. Otherwise, you prefer to remain in the background. You are a modest and rather nervous type, somewhat lacking in self-confidence. You like to dress neatly or well but not conspicuously. You are diplomatic, shrewd—and tactful when you want to be. A thoughtful person, you are much attracted to the study of diet and hygiene. You are frequently an enthusiastic cook, with a special bias toward foods and dishes that are regarded as contributing to good health.

Possessions and Personal Security

You prefer to earn your money through partnerships, through working with or for people. You dislike working alone. You are happiest making your living in a job or profession where you can follow a clear-cut course, using your great flair for selecting and filling in details as you go. You are very good at carrying out instructions. You would make an excellent number two to a top executive. You enjoy owning quality objects and would prefer to miss a bargain than to gamble on poor workmanship or inferior quality. You know you can be depended on to do a first-class job yourself, and you see no reason to settle for anything less from others. You are good at balancing budgets and take great care to try to save something out of everything you earn. The extravagance of others distresses you deeply if it upsets your own financial affairs.

Communication, Learning, Language

You are often cutting in your observations. You have a capacity for puncturing human vanity, but this ability to discern sham and self-delusion in others is not always appreciated. You would make an excellent media critic who could be counted on to start public controversy and debate. You are not particularly voluble and may refuse to explain or elaborate on your criticisms. You may be a little too fixed in your opinions. You possess a penetrating business mind and are capable of shrewd and subtle assessments. You can swiftly sort out confused situations and get down to the nitty-gritty.

Home, Family, Tradition

You are efficient at staying within a budget, paying bills on time and keeping the home spick and span. You enjoy supervising domestic and family affairs. You are deeply conscious of the importance of the family unit in maintaining a healthy, cohesive and well-ordered society. You have a keen sense of morality and would never aim to do anything that would harm or endanger the traditional family concept. You don't as a rule enjoy being away from your family for any extended period. And you are not so keen to travel long distances, except in connection with buying or moving into a grander or more spacious home.

Self-Expression, Love Life, Entertainment

Your approach to pleasurable activities is rather restrained, although you are not beyond breaking out on occasions. You tend to choose the safest or more socially acceptable course, and this can be inhibiting when it comes to romance and other exciting diversions. This reserve is not so pronounced in Virgo men as in women. The Virgo woman may appear frigid and politely unresponsive as a lover because she is never quite sure (nor anxious to find out) where her emotions will lead her. The man is more naturally responsive to his passionate desires. When face-to-face with his own spontaneous urges, the Virgo person usually manages to do the conventionally correct thing.

Work and Health

You are an able and persistent worker who will do his or her best to cooperate with fellow employees. You like being a member of a team. You share your ideas—often original and ingenious—without looking for special approbation. You excel in laboratory work. But whatever your occupation, you like to surround yourself with the very latest scientific equipment or tools designed for the job. You are acutely health conscious and have advanced views on food and diet. You are prone to overlook the fact that the strain of too much work can affect your highly sensitive nervous system.

Partnerships and Marriage

You need a mate who truly appreciates your unflagging efforts and endeavors to carry out your share of the bargain. You don't look so much for praise and admiration as for sympathetic understanding of your problems. Given the right treatment, you are easily soothed and prepared to go on serving and working with very little complaint. If your partner is not the placid and gentle type, you are apt to accept your lot with somewhat philosophic resignation. A Virgo person is often prepared to surrender his or her own personal desires to ensure an agreeable and workable union. Perhaps because of this, Virgo is not one of the Zodiac's most marrying types and sometimes makes an early and inflexible resolve to remain single.

Shared Resources, Legacies, Sex

Sharing is the department of your life that gives rise to activity through enterprise, so you yourself are continually involved with possessions, property and responsibilities belonging to other people. You are one of the great managers and caretakers of the Zodiac, as distinct from a principal or owner. In relation to sex, the Virgo person often regards his or her thoughts and longings as undesirable character elements and seeks to sublimate them in practical though sometimes obscure or complex ways. Virgo people are usually more concerned with sex than the chaste Virgo of tradition implies. Behind their controlled outward appearance may be a deep, though self-conscious, passion.

Higher Learning and Travel

You are inclined to be orthodox in your attitudes toward religion and metaphysical matters. You may also desire to teach in these fields. Although your vision of a particular religion may be wide and comprehensive, you will probably apply its tenets in recognized ways. Hence the Virgo person is often to be found conducting a bible study class, organizing a church bazaar or giving instruction at a Sunday school. You are keen to judge the merits of any philosophy or doctrinaire way of life on its practical results. Generalities irritate you because you think they are a way of ducking issues. Travel generally holds no great attraction except as a means of increasing material holdings or income.

Public Standing, Career, Prestige

It is said the Virgo people often become prominent because they are so inoffensive that no one opposes them! This is especially so in politics, which is frequently a game of nominating the compromise candidate to avoid a stalemate. But someone has to perform the myriad nonspectacular but necessary tasks of the world such as assembly-line work, clerking and machine operating, and no one is more efficient or better suited temperamentally to these occupations than Virgos. As computer and electronic technicians working on small and complex circuits, you are without a peer. You often acquire renown through an aptitude for words and therefore make able editors, journalists, broadcasters, commentators and critics. You also make good librarians, secretaries, record keepers and assistants in publishing firms.

Friends, Groups, Hopes, Wishes

You like to entertain your friends in an informal atmosphere—preferably at home—and you enjoy cooking for them. You are keenly solicitous of their welfare and health and spend a fair amount of time doing the rounds on the telephone and a little less in visiting them at their homes. You enjoy the company of homey people. You have an avid interest in the latest developments in domestic aids and appliances. You like to talk about decorating schemes, furniture and furnishings. You are not a great one for joining groups, but once you give your word, you are a dependable social worker, especially for deprived people, children and animals. You usually own one or two domestic pets, to which you are deeply attached. You are also likely to support societies whose aim is to preserve old homes, antiquities and community landmarks.

Hidden Motives, Selfless Service, Psychic Feelings

Individuals with Virgo Rising frequently move up to become a power behind the throne. Although outspoken and open, you are adept at organizing activity behind the scenes, at erecting and running little systems within the main power structure. You often fail to receive the recognition that your accomplishments entitle you to. It is this capacity of yours to perform thankless service for exceptionally long periods that fits you for many of the ennobling tasks of the world, such as caring for the sick, insane and underprivileged in conditions of obscurity and even penury. This characteristic self-sacrifice can produce a deeply religious state of mind that works for heavenly rewards and no others.

Libra Rising

You love balance and harmony. You are said to be the judges of the Zodiac, because of your constant attempts to restore equilibrium in a world where injustice is the norm. You admire neatness and order. Peace is not just a desire to you, but a deep-seated need. You can be quick to anger but are easily appeased. You love companionship and are usually pleasant, very courteous and agreeable.

You are extremely diplomatic and generally try to

please everyone at the same time. This calculated balancing of the Scales (the symbol of Libra) sometimes inclines you to vacillate. Not quite knowing what course to take next, you often sit on the fence, try to sense which way the wind is blowing, and then jump onto the nearest bandwagon. You are a person who relates to rather than initiates. You feel there are enough causes in the world without your starting up any new ones. You are fundamentally against aggravation and are aware of any aggressive move by you that will upset someone somewhere. This acute awareness often makes you mentally indecisive. You are better adapted to waiting placidly and agreeably for events to occur than to strike out assertively for yourself.

You admire beauty in most forms, especially nature, art, music and literature. You enjoy cultured and refined pleasures and amusements. You are a bright and congenial companion in social situations. You are usually endowed with remarkable grace and charm, which complements a well-formed body and symmetrical features. Your favorite companions are happy and cheerful types who frequently possess some artistic appreciation or talent. You are an admirer of courage and positive action in others. You are idealistic, adaptable, intuitive and constructive. A keen perception makes you very good at drawing comparisons. You are highly impressionable, and if your imagination is not curbed, it can soar to dizzy heights of daydreaming, wishful thinking, and impractical projects.

You are humane, sympathetic, modest and usually amorous. Although a very loving person, you are inclined to be changeable. You are ambitious, but dislike all discordant and unclean types of work. You enjoy getting out and about and have a feel for the social swing. You have good taste in clothes and furnishings and enjoy wearing expensive jewelry. Your love of fine things can lead to extravagance.

Possessions and Personal Security

You keep the details of your financial and property affairs fairly hidden. Although you may appear to be quite open and offhand about these matters, you seldom reveal the true situation. You can be secretly concerned about losing your possessions even though this fear has no actual foundation. You enjoy dealing in land if you get the chance and are very quick to see a potential bargain or to spot flaws in the sales talk. Most Libra-born people spend money freely and frequently live beyond their means. Financial strain can create an intensity in them that may erupt in greater extravagance! You enjoy the comfort of fine possessions and like to share this feeling by giving handsome gifts.

Communication, Learning, Language

Libra people often keep a diary about their travels or write long detailed letters to their family and friends. You also enjoy taking photographs of where you have been and distributing them to anyone who might be interested. You like to put your itinerary and plans neatly down on paper and have as many things as possible organized so there are no slipups. In conversation, you favor broader issues, but there is a danger here that you will focus on affairs that don't really concern you and neglect matters closer to home. Sometimes you waste your time and energy gathering and filing away useless details.

Home, Family, Tradition

You are admirably efficient and organized in the home. You enjoy having things arranged down to the last detail so there is a place for everything and a minimum of clutter. If things are disordered through no fault of your own, you will work hard and systematically to restore them to their original state, doing this over and over again if necessary. Your patience where your home and family are concerned can be quite remarkable. And you extend this quality by being a conscientious and law-abiding citizen. It is important to your sense of security to have a home of which you are proud; you seldom really settle down until this is achieved. You are usually interested in ancestral history, and if building or renovating a home, will often copy a tasteful feature from the past.

Self-Expression, Love Life, Entertainment

You are keen to express yourself through group efforts. You favor aims that are socially admired and, if possible, of notable and noticeable benefit to the community. Most Libras are deeply sympathetic to the needs of children—not necessarily just to their own offspring. They are frequently to be found taking an active part in parents' and teachers' associations as well as the Boy Scouts and Girl Scouts. In romance, they are usually guided by their head rather than their heart. They prefer to stay aloof from the untidy involvement that falling in love can mean.

They don't have great trust in the strength of their emotional detachment, though they like to pretend to the world that they do. Sometimes, though, Libras lose their cool in unusual love affairs that produce drastic changes.

Work and Health

Physical labor doesn't have much appeal for you. You also find it hard to apply yourself for any length of time to mundane or repetitive work. You try but . . . it just doesn't seem to come off. Anyway, you feel you are fitted for better things than being a cog in a series of wheels, though often you aren't sure just what these might be. You prefer to work in the background where you can do a little secret string pulling, manipulating those who perform the more menial tasks. If you have to, you can somehow muddle through in routine jobs, using your charm and affable disposition to conceal from others your painful feeling of failure. You often suffer physical disorders induced by an active imagination.

Partnerships and Marriage

You are usually better at introducing harmony into other people's relationships than into your own marital affairs. You have a flair for bringing similar-thinking individuals together, for combining the different idiosyncrasies of character into an agreeable unity. You are a tactful matchmaker and a dependable mediator. But your own marital relations can be tempestuous. By attempting to maintain a balanced atmosphere for yourself, you frequently manage to stir up aggression in your mate. You are a natural fighter for the rights of others, and if these can be identified with your own rights, you are indeed a formidable antagonist. You genuinely love peace, but not always at the price of surrender.

Shared Resources, Legacies, Sex

The Libra personality often attracts wealth and affluence without any great striving. In fact, the more these people struggle to acquire the possessions of this world, the less success they are apt to enjoy. Acting along preconceived lines of endeavor seems to push the object of their desire further away. Libras sometimes marry for money and almost inevitably regret it. Or they may resolve never again, and then repeat the experience with the same result. Despite your pleasant, easygoing manner, you have a good business mind. You can make money on the stock market and in corporate ventures. You also stand to gain through legacies. You usually reach mature age owning fairly substantial assets.

Higher Learning and Travel

You often develop a fully workable philosophy as you approach middle age. Although you have the ability to absorb abstract ideas, your style is to formulate them in concrete terms so they can be passed on to others. The more evolved Libra is often a respected and erudite pundit who may be found lecturing on philosophy or metaphysics at a university or for a quasi-religious organization. You are happy to study in other countries or to travel to spread your views; you may be just as happy at home, in the comfort of an armchair with a good book.

Public Standing, Career, Prestige

You Libra people feel a deep connection between your career and your home. You often show a preference for the professions that improve or beautify the residence, such as interior design, needlepoint, architecture and decorating. You like to work at or from your home. Your city office is frequently a streamlined version of it in decor, tasteful finishing touches. Your professional life is usually marked by a procession of ups and downs. You often make your reputation through activities involving the public. You make keen real estate and rental agents.

Friends, Groups, Hopes, Wishes

You are a lavish and extremely considerate host or hostess. Your friends are always given the royal treatment, irrespective of expense. You are basically high society in your social aspirations. If you can't afford to move in the best circles, you keep yourself informed through chic magazines and acquaintances of what the rich and famous are doing. You desire to mix and be seen in the company of socially important and influential people. You are usually renowned for superb taste in clothes. In group activities, you lean to enterprises where your flair for promotion, entertainment and decoration can be exploited. The grander events such as large charity balls and political convention benefits are your ideal scene. Your flair and enthusiasm usually guarantee you a leadership position in club affairs.

Hidden Motives, Selfless Service, Psychic Feelings

Libras often appear to lose interest and seem drained of energy. Some have to retire to the bedroom or another place of isolation to restore the psychological face they would present to the world, for they are periodically assailed by indefinable anxieties that sap their psychic forces. It is also not unusual for Libra women, despite naturally endowed beauty, to feel compelled to remake their faces frequently with new cosmetics and hairstyles. This is because of a largely hidden contradiction in the Libra personality: these people are continually suppressing a surprisingly virulent critical attitude toward all their relationships, which conflicts terribly with their deep-rooted longing for harmony.

Scorpio Rising

If Scorpio was ascending at the hour of your birth, you are one of the Zodiac's most steadfast and determined types. You possess true grit. You are an unflappable tower of strength in emergencies. You can be depended on to remain cool and practical while others are emotional and on the verge of panic. You can work under strain and pressure for remarkably sustained periods. You have unusual strength of will and will use subtlety and even force to achieve your purposes.

You are proud and reserved. You never allow others to get close enough to really know you. You seldom show your deeper feelings and you strive continually to repress your basic impulses. You are secretive and suspicious. Your habitual restraint can give you an air of inscrutability and poised intensity. You are the type of person one unconsciously likes to have on one's side.

You are quick in speech and action, often brusque, blunt and provoking. Your tongue can be venomous with a power to sting like the tail of the Scorpion, who symbolizes this Sign. Sudden and violent outbursts of rage mark the point where your self-enforced restraint ends. This, combined with a talent for quick-witted scalding retorts and sarcasm, makes you an enemy or opponent to be approached very warily. But as a friend, there are few more staunch or loyal.

You are enterprising, keen, shrewd and of acute judgment. You are fond of investigating mysteries and usually have a particular penchant for occult subjects. You are not easily influenced or imposed upon. You have a suspicious nature that on social occasions may manifest itself as good-humored mocking. Your views are bold and fixed, although your mind is exceedingly subtle. You are courageous and energetic and often possess a magnetic quality that suggests tremendous passion and power of conviction. You are fond of travel. Most Scorpios make good naval officers. Both men and women are attracted by scientific subjects, especially research. You have an innate mechanical skill, along with constructive, as well as pronounced destructive, capabilities. You are very practical and realistic and make a fine executive, businessman or woman, contractor or the like.

You have been described as the workhorses of the Zodiac, usually possessing a strong, stocky body, a robust constitution and an amazing capacity for seeing something through to the end. A quirk in your character is that you remain active as long as you are interested in what you are doing; at other times, you can be indolent and pleased to let the rest of the world go by.

Possessions and Personal Security

You are a person who fixes his or her financial goals clearly and well ahead, and then works with great energy toward them. You have a flair for discerning future trends; you can often put your finger on an area of profitable investment years in advance. You take the wider view. You have the patience and endurance to wait and work for long-term profits. You like to have money for the power and prestige it imparts, but you are not a greedy person. You enjoy having possessions around you, but prefer to put your spare cash into land and property. Your income is usually derived from business. (Sometimes you are drawn to mining investments. It is not unusual for you to earn money through travel.)

Communication, Learning, Language

You are one of the less communicative types of the Zodiac. You talk in facts or about things that are important to you personally, but you seldom engage in idle chat. Your lighter conversation usually has an ulterior motive; otherwise, you are inclined to be silent. You enjoy analyzing people as they talk, particularly the more intelligent ones. Your own speech is cautious and controlled. You aim to give little away. The early education of Scorpio people is sometimes disjointed and they may evince little interest in formal instruction. As they mature, however, they are often drawn to study and extensive reading as necessary aids to their ambitious drives.

Home, Family, Tradition

The home and family is an area where your views and attitudes are likely to be quite advanced and even unconventional. Usually inclined to be cautious and conservative, you like to equip your home with the very latest gadgets, especially electrical gear. You are original in your ideas about structural and decorative changes. You have a broad-minded approach to family matters, which may seem natural and modern to you, but which could strike others as radical or even odd. Although you are firm in your opinions while you hold them, you are willing to convert to more progressive ideas as often as your inner growth and development demand.

Self-Expression, Love Life, Entertainment

You love to imbue your activities with an aura of secrecy and your love life is usually indicative of this. This Sign has a reputation for sexual excess that is not always deserved because the Scorpio individual has strong self-repressive powers. However, there are often emotional perturbations that lead to secret love affairs, sometimes of great emotional intensity, and often with tragic or unhappy results. Your ability to sacrifice yourself to overcome the demands of your lower nature often produces a sublimation of energy that leads to soaring heights of creative attainment. You are often successful in the arts, especially in the entertainment professions.

Work and Health

You are the single-handed worker who could literally shift a mountian with a shovel, if you had the mind to. But fortunately for the rest of us, you like to throw your tremendous energies into projects that will make the world a better place to live in. You are accomplished in things requiring muscular skill and aggressive enterprise. You would make a fine industrial chemist. Because a job is rough or dirty doesn't put you off. You are excellent at solving pollution problems. You are often a specialist in drainage, sanitation and waste disposal. Medicine and scientific pursuits attract you. Because your nature is to take the initiative, you are better adapted to an executive position than an ordinary one.

Partnerships and Marriage

You are extremely cautious when it comes to choosing a marriage partner. You have very fixed ideas about what you want in a mate, and your expectations are frequently too exacting. Or, you may hesitate to take the plunge because of past hurts and experiences. You are old-fashioned in your ideas about marriage and are usually very possessive. Jealousy and suspicion can burn in you with volcanic fury. You are usually a loyal partner and will be inclined to see a marriage through even though it is unhappy. You often increase in wealth and influence through marriage.

Shared Resources, Legacies, Sex

Scorpio's supposed preoccupation with sex stems from a primitive urge to penetrate to the roots of life and uncover its mysteries. You are often just as curious about death and the afterlife or rebirth. Psychologically, you associate all three issues with your search for truth. You are intense about your sexual relationships but your approach is largely intellectual. You like variety and tend to flit from one sensual experience to another. You enjoy experimentation, so homosexuality is not uncommon among your type. As seething as your passions may be, they remain a vehicle for your incisive mind to probe deeper into all of life's inexplicable motivations. Often you are a shrewd investigator of psychic phenomena and mediumistic contact with the so-called dead. You may write or lecture on your findings.

Higher Learning and Travel

The evolution of the Scorpio individual depends largely upon extremes of experience. Just as you plunge into the depths of carnal enjoyment and gratification, so you are impelled to soar to the mental heights sometimes associated with mysticism. This is your essential ying and yang. The Scorpio person is a natural traveler who feels at home in any country. You often enjoy the feeling of seclusion and perverse distinction that you receive from living among foreigners. You take pleasure in voyages and like to settle near water. During your travels, you sometimes suffer from hurt and frustration in connection with your emotional needs.

Public Standing, Career, Prestige

You are intensely ambitious and usually achieve your objectives through sheer tenacity and an inordinate desire for personal power and prestige. You work according to a long-range plan whenever you can. You fix your sights on an influential position, and then toil toward it with single-minded determination. You use your amazing reserves of physical and mental energy to outflank the strongest opposition, sometimes endangering your health and even risking your life in the process. Your desire to make good is obsessive throughout your working life. You are not a notable egotistical type, but you expect due recognition for your accomplishments. You gravitate toward self-employment or a position where you can make the decisions without reference to others.

Friends, Groups, Hopes, Wishes

You must trust a person first to make him or her your friend; then he or she can join the chosen few you allow to gather around you. You have a magnetic quality that attracts a certain type of companion who will have respect as well as affection for you. It is your nature to keep one last barrier between you and all others, and this may be manifested as aloofness. You are staunch in friendship and will work unstintingly on behalf of your comrades if necessary. Being a loner, you are not at your best in groups and don't extend yourself with any great enthusiasm. However, you appreciate the commonsense advantages of the democratic vote and are prepared to go along with majority decisions.

Hidden Motives, Selfless Service, Psychic Feelings

Partnerships are not very fortunate for you (outside of material gains) and often result in deception and bitter disappointment. You seem to sense this intuitively; hence your cautious approach to partnership and your basic motivation to go-it-alone. The law courts can be particularly unlucky for you. You are likely to find that in disputed wills and the like you will fare better by settling out of court, even though it may mean accepting a smaller sum than you feel you deserve. The Scorpio person often fails to profit from the lessons of the past and may repeat the same painful error several times.

Sagittarius Rising

You are a lover of personal liberty and freedom. Although it is your nature to be jovial and good-humored, you don't take kindly to being ordered about. You like to be able to come and go as you please and will eventually gravitate to an occupation that provides this opportunity. You try to choose a love partner who respects your need for independence; if he or she doesn't, you are likely to rebel and go your own way.

You are bright, optimistic, generous and charitable. You are a consistent good friend, neighbor and relative. You have a strong sense of honor and fair play, which you do your best to live up to. Your manner is open, frank and helpful. Combining these qualities with a cheery and easygoing breeziness, you are never short of companions or a cordial welcome.

You are an expansive thinker. You like the big scene and the horizons that extend beyond. You enjoy visiting foreign countries and meeting people of differing backgrounds and cultures. You are drawn to big business and large financial deals. There is very little that is restrictive or narrow in your makeup.

You are the sports people of the Zodiac. There is hardly a sporting activity in which Sagittarius does not shine or lead the field. Movement, freedom, opportunity to display your energy and physical prowess and the possbility of travel—all these make sports a compelling attraction. If you happen not to be an athlete or performer on the playing field, then you are likely to be a sportscaster or sportswriter such is your love for the occupation.

You have a strong feeling for religion, law, medicine and sometimes philosophy. You make a capable teacher where moral guidance is required, but have to guard against a tendency to sermonize or lay down the law.

You are intuitive and prophetic and quick to arrive at conclusions. Though you sometimes appear blunt and abrupt, your observations are often uncannily on the mark. You are fearless, demonstrative and outspoken—and often restless. You are also impulsive and frequently too anxious to be on the move again to develop the concentration of which you are capable.

You are ambitious and quick to take advantage of opportunities. You make a good promoter or public relations expert. But, easily carried away by your own exuberance, you incline toward making super-optimistic predictions that have very little hope of fulfillment. Your interest and enthusiasm are quickly aroused by innovation, novelty and all that is ingenious. In commercial life, you have to restrain yourself from jumping from one promising new activity to another. You are a sympathetic and humane type of person who sincerely does what he can to help others. You have a soft spot for animals.

Possessions and Personal Security

You have a deep-seated interest in security that belies your offhand manner. You aim from the start to acquire wealth and possessions. And you usually succeed, provided you overcome the speculative and less dependable side of your nature. This is attracted to gambling and dabbling in get-rich-quick schemes. You are fortunate in business—big business and big connections. You prefer to invest your funds in gilt-edged securities and government-guaranteed bonds. You like to feel that you can spend your income freely while keeping the principal intact. You take pride in owning luxuries that imply status and have a special liking for expensive cars, yachts and other prestigious conveyances.

Communication, Learning, Language

You are extremely good at carrying on a knowledgeable conversation without knowing too much about the topic. You have a rare flair for putting snippets of information together so that they make sense and carry conviction. You are ingenious, inventive and original when you talk and write. Your ideas are often visionary, even though you may not have given the subject any great thought. You will go to some trouble to encourage others to learn and to pass on information that will be helpful to them. You have a great respect for education in its broadest sense and belive that its value lies in enabling all people to develop a moral ethic true to themselves.

Home, Family, Tradition

You are deeply sentimental about your home and family. You need to feel that wherever you may roam, you have a secluded place with people you care to return to. You are prepared to make sacrifices for the happiness and welfare of your loved ones, though you sometimes doubt that your self-denying actions are sufficient. You seldom communicate your personal doubts and fears to anyone. You can be rather fixed and assertive in your opinions around the house, although you do your best to create an atmosphere of freedom and liberal thinking. As much as you love your family, you don't let them tie you down. Your idealism can go to extremes.

Self-Expression, Love Life, Entertainment

You are a lover of all pleasures and entertainments that keep you on the move. You aren't the kind of person who enjoys staying in one place for long unless there is plenty of action. Activity is your standard for amusement. You are positive and forceful in your love affairs; the waiting game is not for you. Competitive sports and physical exercise are your particular strong points. Here you can show your personal skill and fine coordination, inspiring others, especially children, to emulate you. You combine physical prowess with a noble sense of sportsmanship that often makes you the captain of a team, a star player

with a big following or a respected coach. In later years, you may channel your energy into the study of philosophic subjects, and again show a flair for teaching.

Work and Health

You are a very conscientious person once you take on a job. You like to have a sure and steady income so you can indulge your many interests without having to worry about basic expenses. This is why many Sagittarius are found in solid jobs like the teaching profession. You may appear offhand in your attitude to work, but this is purely a reflection of your unfailing confidence in life. You are intent on establishing yourself. Once the vision of what you want to do becomes fixed in your mind, you can produce the energy and staying power to make it materialize. You are vividly aware of your dependence on good health for worldly accomplishment. You are usually diet-conscious and not only an advocate of physical fitness, you practice it.

Partnerships and Marriage

With Sagittarius Rising, you can be rather casual about marriage and more permanent emotional relationships. Basically you have a great need for mental stimulation, and only meetings with numerous people of different types can satisfy it. Although these contacts may be quite innocent, they can monopolize your time and make life miserable for a devoted partner who doesn't understand your motivations. Sagittarius frequently marry more than once. You look for someone to share your diverse interests with rather than a partner with whom you can plunge into exclusive intimacy. You are a pretty basic physical lover. Sometimes you find it easier to stay wedded to your work and mental pursuits.

Shared Resources, Legacies, Sex

An individual with Sagittarius Rising can be highly sensuous in his or her sexual relationships. Your deeper feelings may occasionally be excited to the degree of licentiousness. Sexual relations provide an opportunity to probe deeper into your nature than you are normally prepared to go. On these occasions you may discover you are two people—breezy and amicable on the surface, brooding and unsure inside. Death and the afterlife concern you more than you are prepared to admit. You often have vague intuitive feelings that you are not prepared to conceptualize except in uncomplicated conventional terms. Sagittarius frequently share in legacies.

Higher Learning and Travel

To you, life is a university and the obvious way to prepare for graduation is to travel. Visits to other countries you find particularly informative and interesting. You are absorbed not only by what new acquaintances have to say, but also in airing your own ideas. You take considerable pleasure and pride in these. Religion and topics with moral overtones are often your favorites. Although you are an abstract thinker, you tend to identify your conclusions with one of the traditional faiths. You are more an idealist than a realist. And your zeal at times suggests dogmatism.

Public Standing, Career, Prestige

Your professional aspirations are conventional in a way. You like to be close to big business or linked with a large umbrella organization where you will feel fairly safe and secure. Given this protection, you then feel free to spread your wings and show your intellectual inventiveness and capacity. You would do well in a public relations or advertising firm handling several large company accounts. You like to occupy a position where you can guide or enlighten others—the church or an educational situation would be ideal for this. You possess a keen critical faculty and writing ability. You excel in implementing detailed programs and grand strategies.

Friends, Groups, Hopes, Wishes

Your special ability is bringing people of different points of view together. In group activities, and especially in business, this can be of inestimable value. You often find yourself playing the role of arbitrator, negotiator, chairperson and common friend. You are, in fact, never short of friends, probably because you go out of your way to be diplomatic and seldom lose your affability. Group discussions in which you usually shine give you great pleasure. In club activities, you sometimes get carried away with enthusiasm and advocate an exciting but impractical idea. You are a stickler for a fair deal for all, even though your own interests may be affected.

Hidden Motives, Selfless Service, Psychic Feelings

You are often not altogether honest with yourself when it comes to your deeper feelings. You are in-clined to run away from mystical insights because you find them fundamentally upsetting and in severe contrast to your innately expansive and outward-going nature. All that is formless and vague you tend to reject; or you convert it to ideologies and beliefs that are socially tenable. You are suspicious of the occult; the closer it gets to the truth, the more uncomfortable you become. You prefer to take refuge in safe concepts. And yet, you possess the intellectual and emotional equipment to make an outstanding occultist.

Capricorn Rising

You are basically a serious and thoughtful person with an unusually high regard for dignity. You have a tendency to look out for yourself most times, but your self-esteem usually ensures that your actions are not easily reproachable. You are cautious and practical and seldom act without due consideration. You are prudent and economical and capable of depriving yourself of life's comforts in order to realize your goals.

Often you are more ambitious for prestige and position than for actual wealth and possessions. You are capable of hard and enduring effort wherever there is the slightest opportunity of making good, especially in business. Your powers of concentration seem indefatigable, and you can exhaust the strongest opposition with your persistence. You possess great organizing ability, along with a cautious, calculating and (when appropriate) conniving mind. Thus you are extremely well fitted for planning and carring out the schemes of large corporations and conglomerates. Your aim is to become a recognized authority in your chosen field. You want to be looked up to and sought out for the stream of wisdom that you feel you have to impart to the world. Even when you become rich and famous, you are apt to live frugally, in modest style.

You are not a demonstrative type of person. You don't show sympathy readily. You prefer to be judged on your actions (if anyone dare judge you) and to evaluate others' effectiveness in the same way. Words and promises don't have much significance for you. Your disposition is somewhat cold. You suffer from bouts of despondency. You are secretive, reserved, self-willed—and very responsible.

You have a scientific turn of mind that is drawn to investigate, dig out facts, make notes, file away, arrange in logical order. You succeed by determined and steady action rather than by bursts of effort.

In youth, you often look older than your years, and in maturity, you look younger. Some Capricorns have a difficult childhood; your education may be interrupted and your health indifferent. This is usually more pronounced if in youth you tried to subordinate your innately serious nature. In adulthood, you generally grow steadily tougher and wirier and seldom run to fat.

Possessions and Personal Security

The best outlet for your talents and the most lucrative is usually one connected with the sciences. Your unusual type of mind makes it possible for you to make money through commercializing the discoveries of science, particularly on a national or international scale. Your thinking is advanced and original. You are the distributor or wholesaler of the life-saving drug or the new smelting process. You are the industrial chemist who revolutionizes a technology through an inspired discovery. You are also a key member of any team that is engaged in global projects and research of too vast a magnitude for individual effort. You shine where you can establish authority, in drawing up systems and in working for the benefit of the community.

Communication, Learning, Language

You don't use words lightly. You like to say what you mean or remain silent, mostly out of a desire to avoid being misunderstood. You are not quick to communicate with all and sundry. People have to prove serious and trustworthy before you confide in them. Then you can be quite vocal. You perceive more in others' conversation than the words they use; you are aware of hidden connections, and whenever others speak, you are looking for subtle implications (what is not said also comes into your calculations). You can have a profound appreciation of music since it does not depend on words to convey meaning. To you, music is the embodiment of an otherworldliness you can readily understand.

Home, Family, Tradition

You take a keen interest in the day-to-day running of your home. You feel you know what is best for all concerned and you insist on having your ideas adhered to. Anyone who does not conform is likely to be urgently rebuked. Domestic rebellions are not rare these days in the Capricorn-dominated household. But you will rarely go to any extreme that might threaten family solidarity. Many of you with Capricorn Rising have had to overcome a lack of self-confidence in childhood, frequently with the assistance of an ambitious maternal influence. You feel that a solidly secure home life is a desirable base from which to confront life's ambitious struggle.

Self-Expression, Love Life, Entertainment

You find your amusements in rather conservative ways. You are not a party lover or given to rash or reckless escapades, but you do enjoy entertaining in a quiet and dignified way, particularly if it allows you to display your affluence or influence. You are more likely to give a dinner party to create an impression than to enjoy social warmth and conviviality, although this could never be inferred from the quality of your hospitality. Despite their reserved manner, Capricorn men are reputed to be exceedingly sensual. Women are more inclined to express their creative drives in artistic endeavors. Both enjoy physical warmth and a comfortable home.

Work and Health

You can be depended on to do an excellent job at work because you are conscientious and persevering. You also have the gift of clear and straightforward written expression, and since you are often drawn to scientific occupations, you can produce a lucid and compact technical report from a bewildering collection of data. You aim at versatility in your job and often develop new methods and techniques that are very profitable for your employers. Your logical mind prefers to deal in facts. You don't waste time or effort on fantasy. You are admirably suited for work in financial institutions, businesses and all kinds of research establishments. Your nerves are sometimes affected by overwork, but generally you have the good sense to take care of your body, particularly through diet.

Partnerships and Marriage

Capricorns are avidly sentimental about marriage. Men require a partner who will be almost motherly in her attentions. Capricorn women will put a protective ring of affection around their husbands and do all they can to make them comfortable and secure at home. Both sexes have a great desire to keep the family intact, for this is the taproot through which they cling to the earth and from which they reach up and out into the competitive world. Those of you with Capricorn Rising will repeatedly give way to your mate and even endure an unhappy marriage for the sake of your family. Your partnerships mature and become more binding with time.

Shared Resources, Legacies, Sex

To realize your full potential, you need to direct your creative energies along purposeful paths. If you squander your vital drive and look for self-renewal in sex, you are likely to miss the point as well as the boat and become lost in your own frustrated ambitions. If you are the advanced type of Capricorn, you have the ability to share in large-scale business and financial operations; through these you have a great chance of becoming a respected force in the power game, which so intrigues you. You can succeed with natural ease in mastering the intricacies and complex problems of giant conglomerates and combines; you and the computers will be among the few who grasp and understand the total picture. And the rewards can be enormous. The dedicated Capricorn in later years usually obtains the recognition which he or she craves.

Higher Learning and Travel

You are a stickler for the letter of the law, a sturdy pillar of society and a weighty influence on the side of rules and regulations. But in philosophic and higher-minded matters, you are not easily convinced. You don't have much time for abstractions and subtleties. Your approach is critical and analytical. You want proven systems and tidy thoughts that fit without any leftovers. If an idea can't be slotted into a definite place in your experience, then you will discount it. Your preoccupation with practical values can make you rigid and dogmatic, and if carried too far can give you a closed mind.

Public Standing, Career, Prestige

You often make a name for yourself in businesses and professions that require a partner. Numerous Capricorns are respected and influential partners in law firms. You are also likely to make your mark in fields that necessitate working in close collaboration with others and where your unemotional qualities can be exercised and developed. The administrative side of large institutions, the civil service and the sciences frequently offer appropriate opportunities. You also gravitate to dignified positions where your flair for arbitration and conciliation can be utilized.

Friends, Groups, Hopes, Wishes

Above all, you look for loyalty and steadfastness in the select group you choose to call friends. In return, you offer them the same earnest and staunch support. You have very few intimate associates. You don't have much time to spare for friendly gatherings with others. You prefer to devote yourself to the serious issues of life (you are proud you are not an escapist) and choose companions who share your stolidly realistic views. You are fond of meetings in old haunts and seldom alter your routines. Your band of cronies does not welcome newcomers easily. You are a bit suspicious of people who want to get too close too soon. You have a fondness for societies and movements that foster esoteric knowledge and teachings.

Hidden Motives, Selfless Service, Psychic Feelings

You have a talent for outscheming the best of the zodiacal schemers. Often you sum up a situation and decide on a series of moves before others have any idea of what's going on. You have the advantage of being extremely practical. You don't allow your nebulous feelings the luxury of useless daydreaming; you try to pare down each emotion with your practical intellect and make it work or discard it. When one does get past, you become despondent. Less evolved Capricorns live for their work and responsibilities; they seldom dwell on "significance." They can, indeed, be pretty drab people. Advanced types, although reticent about their beliefs, may leave a life trail blazed with words of wisdom.

Aquarius Rising

With Aquarius Rising at the hour of your birth, you are among the most humanitarian of mankind's zodiacal helpers. You are drawn to projects that will benefit the great majority rather than the individual. Your sentiment is to advance a cause. You are usually a leader in the search for truth, not as a philosophical exercise, but with the firm intention of applying it in practical ways. You often become a physician or a socialistic reformer.

Although you are pleasant and friendly, you are a person of strong likes and dislikes. You usually have a very large circle of acquaintances and friends, but your attitude toward them is somewhat detached. You are determined, sincere and fond of honor and dignity. Although sympathetic, you develop a dispassionate and reasoning outlook that fits you to be one of the progressive thinkers of the community. You have strong ideals and are attracted by all humanizing activities that lead to reform.

You are clear-minded and very capable of dealing with facts, your memory is extremely reliable and everything of a mental nature appeals to you. But you are an exceedingly independent person. Although keenly cooperative in a general sense, you retain a deep need for personal freedom. Unless this is appreciated by others, you can be badly misunderstood. Even though you are usually law-abiding, your impulse is to try to change things for the better. Your idea of "better" doesn't always agree with ruling opinion. You may be unorthodox and even revolutionary in your ideas. You put intense energy into a cause. An overzealous Aquarius always runs the risk of becoming so identified with his slogans that he veers away from the truth he is trying to propagate.

You are imaginative and broad-minded. Your capacity for originality can be quite electrifying. Your fertile mind makes you an inspired scientific worker. Inventive genius often appears in people born with Aquarius Rising.

You are unpredictable. You have a penchant for all that is unusual. You may on occasions be considered eccentric because of your freewheeling attitude. You can be a force in the artistic world. You enjoy literature, music, art and scenery.

Your disposition is unobtrusive, quiet and patient. You try to be faithful. It is necessary for you, both physically and mentally, to keep circulating so that you are well informed of what's going on and get sufficient exercise.

Possessions and Personal Security

You love possessions but can be quite impractical about them. Your ways of handling money may be hopelessly muddled. When you have money, you literally try to make your dreams come true—with some disillusioning results. You may receive income from unusual, and at times, quite unexpected, sources. You are a frequent recipient of gifts. Funds also are inclined to come from large institutions, sometimes in the form of grants and awards. Lack of money depresses you, makes you feel hamstrung. Sooner or later, most Aquarius have to go through the discomfort of loosening their attachment to material things. Or they may be forced by circumstances to arrange their financial affairs with a more conscious sense of proportion.

Communication, Learning, Language

You are vigorous and precise in your contacts. You like to have plenty of channels of communication open. You are seldom stuck for ideas or words or unsure of the next step to take. You have a clear and incisive way of expressing yourself. Often you propose remarkably original ideas that leave others wondering why the heck they didn't think of them. Your quiet manner belies the great intellectual strength and energy that powers your reasoning. Aquarius are often pioneers in the communications industry, particularly in electronics, radio and television. You don't hesitate to make public statements if you think you've got something important to say.

Home, Family, Tradition

You have a greater need for security than your unpredictable nature would suggest. You love your home for the reassuring substantiality it provides. You like it to be paid for, to hold the deed of ownership in your hands. You enjoy filling it with attractive furniture and furnishings as well as modern labor-saving devices. You dislike buying goods on credit but are sometimes forced to because there seems no other way to get what you want. You aren't fond of moving; once you're settled, you can be a bit of a stick-in-the-mud, so long as your mental activities are not restricted. You enjoy living in places where you can feel close to nature.

Self-Expression, Love Life, Entertainment

You enjoy variety in your love life. You are not a sentimentalist and are more inclined to have numerous casual romances than to fall deeply in love too quickly or too easily. Your approach to love is more intellectual than emotional; you personify the cool, calm and collected lover. As a parent, you foster intelligence in your children rather than sentiment. You find your entertainment mostly in mental ways: you enjoy conversing with different people in different places as often as possible. You can be a great traveler, preferring to move on when everyone else is just getting settled. You are deft and clever with your hands and often sew or make things in your spare time. You also write competently.

Work and Health

You usually choose a job where your efforts will directly or indirectly benefit others. You have an avid interest in the welfare and health of all humanity. This will often lead you into the laboratory or onto committees concerned with eliminating hunger in the world and alleviating other human suffering. When you find a satisfying job, you immerse yourself in it completely; you are the type who may even forget to go home! It is therefore not surprising that you try to make your office as homely as possible. You are a good employer, with an eye to efficiency, who likes his or her workers to feel they are one big happy family. You are aware of the need to keep fit, but may be too busy intellectually to get enough exercise. Many Aquarius manage to combine this critical intellectual faculty with talent for research and become renowned in professions requiring detailed discrimination. Some of the world's best detectives have been Aquarius. You also make able astrologers, psychologists and chemists. You possess a pronounced ability to keep professional secrets and to remain coolly detached in emotional situations.

Partnerships and Marriage

You usually take your time selecting a marriage partner. You marry for love but you also need someone whose accomplishments you can take pride in. You can be an easy person to live with and have a happy marriage provided you choose the right partner. Those Aquarius who select a bossy mate have little chance of domestic harmony; a clash of wills is almost certain. You have no great desire to seek glory for yourself; in fact, you are inclined to allow others to take credit that belongs to you. But you will not be dominated or dictated to. You must retain your independence in any partnership for it to work. Your ideal mate will be on the same mental wavelength, allowing an easy exchange of creative ideas.

Shared Resources, Legacies, Sex

You have a quite critical tendency, which can be off-putting. When this is restrained, you give out a coolness that can be inhibiting in your sex life. You are a mental creature and unless your intellectual interest is first stirred and then confirmed, you make no effort to encourage intimate relationships. Any legacies you receive are more likely to be in the form of numerous objects, possessions and small pieces of property and real estate rather than large, lump sums

and extensive holdings. Positions or jobs that are inherited—even when lucrative—may involve a fair amount of work and personal attention.

Higher Learning and Travel

Your admirable humanitarian instinct springs from a desire for universal justice and equality. To you, the individual is deserving of sympathy and consideration, but the urgently greater task is to eliminate the basic causes that afflict and degrade the human condition. You choose the broader outlook. Your impartiality allows you to listen to others and to make fair and practical assessments. You present your findings either as a scientist or humanitarian with honesty and forthrightness. You are a keen traveler, and if you get the chance, will often visit many countries in a short time.

Public Standing, Career, Prestige

You enjoy nothing quite as much as meeting a challenge. You make your way in the world, when you can, by embracing king-size tasks that for time and dedication would daunt most other types. You will toil for years to unlock nature's secrets as a medical researcher, engineer, physicist. Once committed, you will never quit halfway through a job. You have tremendous powers of concentration. Although you prefer mental activity, you are capable of considerable physical exertion if it is necessary for the success of a project or the attainment of your goals. Prestige does not mean as much to you as accomplishment; fortunately, both go together for you.

Friends, Groups, Hopes, Wishes

You have more acquaintances than friends. You are the type of person people find easy to talk to, a very intelligent and interesting conversationalist. You enjoy listening as much as talking. Since you need to range freely, exchanging views among a wide variety of people, you have neither the time nor the inclination to form deep friendships. You are more at home with groups of people, especially those who are not bound by conventional thinking. Your own views are advanced and frequently radical enough to split and disrupt groups and organizations if you press them hard enough. The strength of your ideas is a force to be reckoned with.

Hidden Motives, Selfless Service, Psychic Feelings

In this department of life, the typical Aquarius can be negatively disposed in one of two ways. He may make a lot of speeches about the need for progress and liberated thought, but when the time for action comes, he may be busily engaged elsewhere in strictly conservative pursuits. Or, he may be a truly inspired visionary who is so far ahead of his time that no one will listen to him. To be an effective force worthy of his brilliant ideas, Aquarius sometimes has to learn the discipline of frustrated desire. Most individuals with Aquarius Rising manage to conceal the great amount of energy they put into their enterprises so that their accomplishments seem rather effortless and natural.

Pisces Rising

If Pisces was ascending at the hour of your birth, you are among the most affectionate, sympathetic and trusting people of the Zodiac. You are also among the most modest and timid. This is not surprising when you consider that Pisces is the summation of the other 11 types. As Pisces stands at the "end" of the zodiacal wheel, so the individual stands at the end of his or her life with only the essential qualities of feeling—and much uncertainty.

You are kind and loving, easygoing, good-natured and charitable. You are very quick to understand. You have a strong and profound psychic faculty that you rely on to an immense degree: you "know" things most of the time without having to say or know what you know (a true Pisces will understand exactly what this means). You are skilled in detail, especially in putting the finishing touches to things. And paradoxically, though very orderly in manner, you are changeful in disposition—so you live a rather disjointed existence, leaving many things unfinished that were begun so well. You are quick to observe deficiencies in others; a lack of completeness in any thing or situation immediately catches your attention.

You are impressionable, emotional and imaginative. The intensity of your idealism can be quite painful to you at times, especially when you tune into others' sufferings and sorrows. You have a highly developed intuitive and inspirational faculty. Many of you with Pisces Rising are telepathetic and mediumistic.

You are courteous, confiding, affable and hospitable. You don't like to push yourself forward. You lack confidence and self-esteem. At times, you become overanxious, indecisive and disheartened, but in an emergency, your uncertainty seems to fall away, revealing a resolute, determined and very effective person.

You are extremely creative if you can discover the correct medium for your self-expression. You love music, good literature and all that is intrinsically beautiful. Your tastes are refined and at times impeccably subtle. You often write exquisite poetry. Your daydreams are very real to you and are an important part of your psychic processes. You are usually not very body conscious and can compensate for this by directing your vital energies into physical accomplishments—becoming an excellent dancer, gymnast or teacher of yoga and other disciplined postures and exercises.

You usually succeed in occupations where you are required to add the finer details to ensure completeness. Your hypersensitivity makes you a competent dramatic actor, an inspired painter or artist. You excel in situations where it is necessary to make the best of things and where discretion and understanding are required. You have a talent for publishing and social service. Many Pisces find an outlet for their humanitarian instincts by working in hospitals and institutions.

Possessions and Personal Security

You usually manage to have a fairly good income. You put considerable effort into your money-making activities and do a fair amount of scheming and manipulating behind the scenes. You work on the basis that if you have several enterprises going at once, you can afford a couple of failures. This often occurs and you accept it philosophically. You are a free spender, although not a particularly wise one. Unless you invest your funds in property, you will have a job holding on to them. You look for a quick turnover. You are frequently a successful promoter of onetime publishing ideas and pop culture events that appeal to the masses. The lucrative film industry attracts Pisces. Possessions, prestige and money help you maintain confidence in your own worth.

Communication, Learning, Language

Though you give the impression of flexibility, you can be surprisingly stubborn. You have a gift for dissolving your attitudes so that you remain receptive and open-minded most of the time, but once you get stuck on an idea, you will not relinquish it without a great deal of obstinate maneuvering. You are much more a feeling creature than a thinking one. You are continually picking up psychic sensations from your environment, then you act without conceptualizing them. Because the Pisces child finds it hard to relate to a formal education with its intellectual emphasis, he is sometimes thoughtlessly branded as a slow learner. If the child is approached through his feelings, which are acutely sensitive to beauty and emotional stimulus, he can understand a subject quickly and profoundly.

Home, Family, Tradition

You want your home and family relationships to be ideal. You look for story-book perfection, and when you don't find it, you are hurt, disappointed or disillusioned. You never really comprehend why things aren't as you imagine them. You are a mental creature where your loved ones and domestic life are concerned. Because it is not easy for you to adapt to the earthy realities of these relationships, you sometimes get in a muddle, unable to cope with the exigencies of children, mate and household duties all at the same time. You like to move often because this gives you a chance to make new and exciting starts— not to mention the opportunity to try yet again to materialize your dreams.

Self-Expression, Love Life, Entertainment

You enjoy parties at home but are not greatly attracted by noisy or boisterous amusements in public places. The more intimate types of recreation and pleasure appeal to your nature. You are happy visiting others in their homes. Pisces women welcome the opportunity to dress up. Their personal appearance is very important to them, and they will walk out of any function (or hide for hours in the background) rather than see it through inappropriately dressed. You have a strong sense of personal pride, which is easily dented. You get touchy if there is any criticism of your children or if they fail to come up to your expectations. You need continual praise and encouragement for your creative efforts. You have a romantic chocolate-box approach to love affairs and want to cherish and pet as well as be petted and cherished.

Work and Health

You have a compelling need to be proud of the job you do, so it is essential that you choose work you can perform well. If you don't, you will be mis-erable and downhearted most of your working hours. You like to be your own boss but you don't mind following instructions if you enjoy the work. Your talents are better suited to artistic occupations and to those that give you the chance to display something. You need to feel that your job carries prestige, or at least that it is glamorous enough to attract the interest and approval of your friends. Despite your retiring nature, you like to show off all your accomplishments. If you can't find an esteemed position, you may make out that lesser tasks are obviously unworthy of your talents and do nothing, but make gracious excuses.

Partnerships and Marriage

You aren't such the easy person to live with that your pliant nature suggests. You are intensely critical—of your partners as well as yourself. You have a way of projecting your inadequacies onto your mate and then paradoxically looking to him or her to provide the reassurance and confidence you can't find in yourself. You need to live with a reliable, methodical and efficient person who will serve you conscientiously. Being a sentimentalist at heart, you will work hard in your way to make the marriage conform to your dreams, but unless you choose the right mate, the psychological pressures may be too great for the union to stand. As much as you love the idea of romance, you may marry for security or even because you think it is the right thing to do. Pisces are sometimes happier and attain a greater self-sufficiency by remaining single.

Shared Resources, Legacies, Sex

Your fortunes largely depend on partners, but you can lose all through these people just as easily as gain. The balance of the scales of Pisces sharing are finely set. Partners can take you down to the depths or raise you to the heights. This applies in a sensual sense, as well as to spiritual and economic matters. You have a high expectation of others, which may be unjustified. You can seize greater control of your own destiny by becoming more balanced in yourself, by getting rid of ambivalence and psychological dependence on others, and by achieving a sense of purpose. Art and your love of beauty are the most powerful means of regeneration for you. You need to cultivate faith in yourself. When this is achieved, the Pisces Fishes swim purposefully in the same direction.

Higher Learning and Travel

You have the power to reach extraordinary heights of spirituality. Unfortunately, your dreams and illusions stand in the way. You have a fundamental longing to tear aside the veil, but this can only be done by coming to terms with your own past. For this reason, you are intolerant of formal religious paths and logical methods. You have faith only in direct experience—of yourself. It is not unusual for you to embrace the emotional side of orthodox religions, but the path always leads back to you. You are a spiritual pragmatist who relies on attunement with psychic and spiritual forces for eventual enlightenment. What others achieve by drugs, you achieve naturally. You are a spiritual mainliner who should understand that the induced experience, however vividly described, falls far short of your constant intuitions. You enjoy long voyages—both worldly and hallucinatory.

Public Standing, Career, Prestige

You are quite a lucky person. You often have only to think about something and hold the idea in your consciousness for it to happen. You aspire to greatness, or at least to a position of eminence or fame. You love to be popular. You choose to make your way in a profession that offers a wide scope; you like to be respected for your ethical rectitude. In business, your word is your bond. You are frequently required to travel in connection with your career. Pisces women often marry men whose occupations take them on journeys to distant places. You are basically a curious person who is well satisfied by the delights and novelty of travel. You aim high. You would rather lose than not try at all—for the biggest stakes.

Friends, Groups, Hopes, Wishes

Your friends are probably the most solid side of your life. You like to see in them the substance of your dreams. In fact, you are not beyond promoting someone to the highest pedestal of regard and then smashing his image to the ground with iconoclastic fervor. You would never hurt a friend, though you just grow out of them. You create and dissolve your friends with a rhythmic passion that leaves even you horrified at times. This makes you a bit hesitant to reach out, a bit of a loner. You are also cautious about joining in group activities. Quite often you may accept an invitation personally and then back out by letter or telegram. You relate to people through their emotions but tend to favor those who are tried and true. You admire people who are dashingly original, but finally settle for those who are reliable and dutiful.

Hidden Motives, Selfless Service, Psychic Feelings

Despite your sometimes vague otherworldliness, you have a practical and scientific approach to occult studies. It is as though this is *your* world, and in it you have all the confidence and authority you may lack in what others call "the world." Those of you with Pisces Rising are often a leading light in research into spiritualism, parapsychology and extrasensory perception. But you seldom achieve public admiration or recognition for your efforts; more likely, you devote years to a study only to have your findings annexed by another person or distorted for popular consumption. Pisces is the Sign of spiritual transcendance, which begins with the study and understanding of universal law and the sacrifice of egotistical impatience.

CHAPTER FOURTEEN

Planetary Influences

In Astrology, both the Sun and Moon are considered to be planets. Eight other planets of our solar system, together with the Sun and Moon, make up the 10 planets whose influence is studied in Astro-Analysis, The next two pages highlight the influences of the 10 planets.

You will recall that earlier chapters described the influence of the Sun. And the previous two chapters on the Ascendant described how our planet Earth is vital in constructing the individual profile. Each Ascendant, or Rising Sign, was covered in detail. The Ascendant, your Rising Sign, is your Earth point.

The following nine chapters describe in depth the influence of the Moon, Mercury, Mars, Venus, Jupiter, Saturn, Uranus, Neptune, and Pluto in the Signs of the Zodiac.

As you read about the planets, keep in mind that each Sign of the Zodiac is linked to a planet in a special way. Each Sign is ruled by one or more of the planets. No matter where the planets are located at any given moment, they still rule their respective Signs. And when they travel through the Signs they rule, they have special dignity and their effects are stronger.

Following is a list of the planets and the Signs they rule. After you construct your astro profile (page 210), glance back here. See if any of your planets are in a Sign they rule. If so, there is special dignity, or honor, in that planetary placement.

RULING PLANETS	SIGNS
Mars, Pluto	Aries
Venus	Taurus
Mercury	Gemini
Moon	Cancer
Sun	Leo
Mercury	Virgo
Venus	Libra
Pluto, Mars	Scorpio
Jupiter	Sagittarius
Saturn	Capricorn
Uranus, Saturn	Aquarius
Neptune, Jupiter	Pisces

Since there are the ten planets always radiating in particular Signs and Houses of the Zodiac, the result is fascinating diversity—or human experience as we know it. And it takes the skill and the art of AstroAnalysis to sort it out into patterns.

While the Sun, undeniably, is the center of our universe, the planets modify its influence according to their own special natures and energies. Each planet is highlighted here, then characterized in depth in the following nine chapters.

Sun ☉

Power, self-expression, individuality. The Sun is the constant, ever-shining source of life in the daytime. It symbolizes strength, vigor, ardor, generosity and the ability to fuction as a mature individual and a creative force. The Sun indicates the complete potential of every human being.

Moon ☽

Response, fluctuation, sensitivity, sympathy. The Moon rules our feelings, customs, habits and moods, and its position is an indicator of rapidly changing phases of behavior and personality. The Moon rules the female element in both women and men, the women in a man's life, fertility, food, health in general.

Mercury ☿

Communication, intellect, reasoning power, discernment. Mercury is the planet of the mind and the power of communication. Mercury has dominion over relatives, neighbors, students, messengers. Mercury rules speaking, language, mathematics, logic, drafting and design, short trips and, indeed, any profession in which the mind of man has wings.

Venus ♀

Attraction, unity, beauty, balance, valuation, assets. Venus symbolizes that rare and elusive harmony and radiance which is true beauty. Its ideal is the flame of spiritual love—Aphrodite, goddess of love. Venus indicates refinement, grace, delicacy, sensitivity, charm and the aesthetic sense. Venus rules the love of nature and pleasure, luck and wealth.

Mars ♂

Impulse, activity, self-assertion, initiative, enterprise. Mars is energy and drive, courage and daring. But Mars can be thoughtless and cruel, wild and angry. Mars symbolizes action and adventure—the frontier. Mars rules the military, surgeons, explorers, salespeople—any calling that requires pioneering spirit, bold skill, refined techniques and self-promotion.

Jupiter ♃

Expansion, optimism, foresight, fortune. Jupiter rules good luck and good cheer, health, wealth, happiness, success and joy. Jupiter is the symbol of opportunity, and is associated with gambling and games of chance. Jupiter rules acting, statecraft, publishing, philosophy, religion, sports and travel.

Saturn ♄

Limitation, restriction, obstacles, delay, discipline. Saturn creates limits and boundaries and shows the consequences of being human. Saturn rules time, old age and sobriety. Saturn symbolizes selfishness, reticence and depression, jealousy and greed. But Saturn can bring lasting rewards after long struggle.

Uranus ♅

Freedom, independence, originality, innovation. Uranus rules upheaval and revolution, and signifies sudden drastic change for good or evil. Uranus symbolizes intellectual genius and inventiveness. Uranus rules fashions, science, technology and electronic advances. Uranus influences humanity's great forward leaps.

Neptune ♆

Dreams, imagination, inspiration, spirituality, deception. As the planet of emotional genius, Neptune has dominance over many of the arts and inspirational thought. Neptune rules theater, sensationalism, poetry, music and transcendant modes of creativity. Neptune is also associated with all forms of escapism and delusion.

Pluto ♇

Resurrection, renewal, regeneration, resolution. Pluto symbolizes the capacity to change totally and forever one's lifestyle, thought and behavior. Pluto rules the forces of creation and destruction. As the planet of beginnings and endings, Pluto can effect total transformation. Pluto can also bring a lust for power with strong obsessions.

CHAPTER FIFTEEN

The Moon

This chapter on the Moon gives you some facts about its physical features, the myths and symbolism surrounding it, and an astrological account of its characteristics. Then follows a description of the Moon's influence in the various zodiacal signs.

The Planet

The Moon is the Earth's satellite. It is 238,000 miles away and is the only planet in the solar system that revolves around the Earth. The Moon is about a quarter of the size of the Earth, having a diameter of just over 2000 miles. It orbits the Earth in 27 days, 7 hours and 43 minutes. This is also the time it takes to rotate on its axis, so the same face is always kept toward us.

The Moon has no protective atmosphere. For eons of time, it has been exposed to every kind of cosmic influence, including solar radiation. Its surface is pockmarked from innumerable collisions with solid particles of all sizes.

All moonlight is a reflection of sunlight. But the Moon is a poor reflector and gives back only 7 percent of the light it receives.

On the Earth we see the Moon change from crescent shape to full and back again in 29½ days. From out in space, we would see that about half the moon is always lit up by the Sun and half is always in darkness, except during an eclipse. When the Moon is in a direct line between us and the Sun, we see only the dark side. When the Moon is on the other side of its orbit so that the Earth is in line between it and the Sun, we see the Moon's fully illuminated side and can watch it as a full Moon from sunset to the next sunrise. All the other stages (called phases of the Moon) are in between. When the Moon is a quarter of the way around its orbit, we still see half of its surface, but half of this half is dark and half is illuminated, giving us a quarter Moon.

Although the Moon is Earth's satellite, the Sun's pull on it is far greater; the Sun is the common center of gravity for both bodies. The Earth-Moon system is, in effect, a double planet.

The influence of the Moon (with the Sun) causes the tides. As the Earth rotates and the Moon revolves, most places receive alternating high and low tides. When the Sun and Moon both pull in line at new and full Moon, the tides are higher. When they pull at right angles and partly counteract one another, the tides are lower. Tide timetables can be prepared years ahead on the basis of the Moon's predicted movements. The tidal range is 3 to 10 feet, but in narrow bays, tides may rise to 50 feet.

Symbolism

In mythology, the Moon is personified as the goddess Luna, Selene, Artemis or Diana. She is the queen of the night, the twin sister of Apollo, the Sun. She is a huntress, the mistress of animals and goddess of the chase. She governs chastity as well as fertility.

As sister of Apollo, she shares many of his characteristics. She carries a bow and arrows and has the power to send plague and sudden death. She is also the protectress of children and young animals. Like Apollo, she is unmarried, a maiden goddess who severely punishes sexual lapses. As Artemis, she changed Acteon to a stag so that he was torn to pieces by his own hounds because he had seen her bathing. She was said to have killed the handsome Orion because of his unchastity. The hounds of Artemis also hunted down the nymph Callisto after she had been seduced by Zeus.

The poets and lyricists throughout the ages have sung praises to her beauty. She has been worshipped by the priests of all races. She waxes childlike, innocent, passive and receptive. She shines at her fullest as the glorious virgin wisdom of the Sun, inspiring us with fantastic dreams of attaining the unattainable.

She wanes with a wan, sad smile that luringly invites us to try again.

The ancient association of the Moon phases with fertility, growth and decay has been confirmed by science. It is now common knowledge that plant growth is influenced by the Moon, that the tidal rhythms depend upon her movements, that the female menstrual cycle corresponds to the sidereal lunar month.

Astrology

Astrologically, the Moon's influence is cold, moist, fruitful and feminine. Because its visual image alters daily, it characterizes changeability. Consequently, its influence is often unsettling. People born with the Moon prominent in their horoscopes (Cancer Sun Sign or Cancer Rising Sign, or Moon in Cancer) will be emotionally unsettled.

The Moon signifies the past. It rules all life-giving and life-sustaining liquids. In the fluids of brain and body, it accumulates and carries forward man's personal evolutionary history. Through the psychological and physical digestive actions, it transmutes experiences into the instinctive functions. It brings the past into the present, pleasing and paining man with his memories and subjective feelings. It cautions him to protect himself psychologically by forming habitual patterns that become predictable behavioral reactions and responses.

The Moon is the rhythm between now and then. It rules the ebb and flow of sensation and emotion, from the present to the past and from the past back to the present—that inner correspondence that allows man to revitalize his mind and thinking, to know inwardly where he stands today against yesterday, to separate both periods as concepts of time. As his being is revitalized in sleep by sinking into the deep pool of unconsciousness, so his waking imagination is revivified by the ebbing and flowing of his feelings between the past and the present.

The Sun is the conscious side and the Moon the unconscious side of the personality. The Sun indicates what a person is trying to become, whereas the Moon effects what he or she is trying to overcome. All that is instinctive and unconscious is in the Moon.

The Moon represents the mother and any strong matriarchal or family influence that has left a deep impression on the psyche. It often reveals itself in patriotism and a vivid awareness of traditional values and ancestral worth.

The Moon governs conception, pregnancy, birth and animal instinct. It rules the infant, most impressionable stage of a person.

Representing the weight of the past, the Moon acts like a brake on the progressive Sun and regulates our evolution toward cosmic consciousness. This, the Sun, in its unrestrained beneficence, would bestow prematurely with a mind-disintegrating flash.

The Moon is the regulator on the pendulum of time. It preserves—not the balance between past and present—but the essential *interaction* between the two, which is man's continual and gradual development. In so doing, it protects, nourishes and lovingly nurtures the spark of life wherever it appears.

The Moon's feeling nature is dual, but not erratic. It is changeable in that it swings from one side to the other, but it is constant in that the rhythm is measured and predictable (like the tidal phases). So the individual will fluctuate between painful and pleasurable emotions according to the pressure of time and circumstance.

The Moon rules the movement and volume of the sea but not the sea's nature. The Moon provides the raw and simple forms of life for consciousness to make the most of. It governs the public, the faceless masses and their combined emotional response, as distinct from the individual and the social order.

Physiologically, the Moon rules the digestive juices, the glandular secretions of the lymphatic system, the stomach, breasts, ovaries and the sympathetic nervous system. The last is intimately associated with the emotions, affections and desires. Hence the origin of the term *lunacy* to describe severe emotional disturbances.

Moon in Aries

Wham! Here is a head-on collision between the immovable cold of the Moon and the irresistible heat of Aries. Neither mixes with the other, and the result is a frenetic inner tension; either you handle it and accomplish much, or it handles you and converts your life into a constant nervous conflict.

You act instinctively. You have great faith in your senses. You don't wait to think, to weigh things, but accept them as you see them. Your assessments are instantaneous and often brilliant. You are at your best when working in an action atmosphere that requires moment-to-moment adjustments. You don't need to know where you are heading; you just follow the trail with greased-lightning speed and in so doing find an essential balance. When you stop, you lose your equilibrium and become restless, high-strung, edgy. You are easily provoked and upset. You flare up quickly, hit out blindly and say things you may later regret.

You are intensely emotional, always plugged in to what is happening around you. Success makes you even more excitable, sharper and prone to push yourself harder. You are extremely enthusiastic and ready to jump on any new bandwagon that may come along. On the surface, you may appear conventional, but you are always looking for a chance to take the initiative, to lead others, to strike out on your own. In no time at all, you'll be up there with the bandmaster's baton—playing your own tune. You are supremely sure of yourself and would rather depend on your own impressions than listen to the advice of others. This can be dangerous; you make mistakes in this way. You don't take kindly to people who try to tell you how to do things. You have a very independent mind. You are usually interested in occult studies. Your sense of sight is the most developed.

The dual nature of the Moon makes you inclined to fuss over trifles, but in major issues, you are swift and decisive. You seem to wear yourself out on lesser things and stumble around them with the persnicketiness of a mothering hen. Your talents are best suited for professions where success depends on quick decisions. The higher the stakes, the greater your satisfaction and competence. If you have a choice of jobs, you will often deliberately take the one that offers a risk, a gamble. You live to feel and to act without the necessity for pause. You are impulsive and quite often rash. But your enterprise and inventiveness make others, especially employers, tolerant of these lapses. You usually succeed by ending up in a position of authority.

You are fond of travel and are often employed in work connected with the public. You have a strongly persuasive manner; you can rally numbers to follow you and support your causes. You are acutely idealistic and apt to advocate changing conditions on a wide scale, but you may lack the perseverance and concentration to bring your crusading efforts to any notable success.

A man with Moon in Aries may have difficulty with the women in his life. He is apt to be inconstant, striding from one affair to another, never really ready to settle down. He is not a cozy domestic type. He will attract women who are passionate, headstrong and impractical. They may be highly intelligent but difficult. They certainly won't live under his thumb. Marriage for the Moon in Aries man may be a tempestuous and short-lived experience. But if the Moon is well aspected by other planets, women can be a great help to him in his career and professional life.

You may love your parents and family but there will always be tensions and conflict. It has been said that the Moon in Aries is like a rose in a fire. Usually you will prefer to communicate with older loved ones from a distance than to risk misunderstandings and arguments.

You may have strong memories of your mother's earlier ambitions for you and harbor some subconscious resentment about this.

Mothers with this Moon in Aries combination may try to run their children's lives even into adulthood. These same mothers may also lack the ability to cope with the practical side of life.

The Other Side of the Story

You may pour out vast amounts of energy in great spurts of enthusiasm and achieve nothing. You may be all show, all puff and wind. Your ideas are likely to be magnificently unworkable. You may start a project and drop it because you have lost interest, without a thought for any others involved. Your idealism may reach fanatical levels. You are likely to make indiscreet public statements and ruin your reputation through rash actions. Your temper may be uncontrollable and destructive. Your lack of inner stability may lead to a breakdown. You are likely to be a troublesome rebel without a cause. Your marital infidelities may cause unhappiness. You may be a thoughtless and dictatorial parent.

Moon in Taurus

This is an excellent position for the Moon, and it usually brings a fair amount of life's comforts and possessions. Here the Moon is exalted; here its emotional sensors find a compatible and fertile place in the Earth to put down deep and fruitful roots. The Moon in Taurus can be productive, not of change, but of constructive material activities.

You are a reliable person. You don't change your ideas easily or capriciously, and you don't intend to lose what you own in any silly sort of experimentation. You are a builder who likes to erect your estate on solid foundations.

You are intuitive and very impressionable. Your powers of concentration are good. You are attentive and know how to listen when you want to. You absorb the feeling of things to begin with rather than the idea of them. No instant decisions and reactions for you—you like to quietly and leisurely digest all your impressions before reaching a conclusion. But when you make up your mind, it's for keeps. You stick to your principles, come what may. And you proceed to implement them, working relentlessly toward your predetermined goals.

You love your family. There is something about the past, your childhood, that nothing that has happened since can displace. You are deeply nostalgic and these yearnings are satisfied by the constant stirrings of your memory. You often think about your home, your grandparents, ancestors and links with the past. You are ruminative and find delight in the fond recollection of bygone days. Your memory is tenacious.

You have a good feel for business and are not short of influential or affluent friends, even though you may not be wealthy yourself. You have a knack for making money and investing it wisely. Your funds usually grow, not overnight, but with an inexorable certainty that makes you a safe bet for being comfortable or well off one day. You have a developed sense of timing where public opinion and tastes are concerned. You can make money out of raw materials, and especially out of farm products; a sixth sense tells you the right time to buy and sell. Co-operative societies, wholesale associations and syndicates where you can pool your interests with others are usually fortunate. Restaurants, health food shops and other places that cater to the public taste are also likely to provide a lucrative living. Housing and land offer special opportunities, particularly large estates that attract small communities. Bricks and mortar are lucky for you.

You are courteous, affable and sympathetic. But you are not an adventurous type. Revolutionary fashions and fads are not for you. You enjoy the best of all that is established—the classical and the traditional. You don't mind at all having the old dressed up as the new as long as it is stylish and attractive. You have a strong attachment to the good things of life. You may overindulge your appetite for comfort, food and sex. Your senses of taste and touch are highly developed. You may be secretive about some of your activities. You gather friends easily and are a responsive host or hostess. You are romantic, and although innately cautious, attracted by the opposite sex. You are ambitious and eager to excel in whatever you undertake.

You are conservative and conventional, although your emotional life may at times seem to contradict this. You are not a great propounder of new ideas; more a renovator than an innovator, you are inclined to remold old ideas into attractive new shapes.

The women in a Moon in Taurus man's life are practical, affectionate and domestically inclined. He can count on their loyalty and unwavering support in difficult times and situations. But they may be emotional clinging vines, difficult to break away from once the decision to part is made. If you are a woman, you will observe these characteristics in your own makeup as well as in your female companions.

People with Moon in Taurus often have fine singing and speaking voices. They may choose occupa-tions connected with broadcasting, public speaking or recording.

The Other Side of the Story

You may be boringly conservative and totally lack originality. You are likely to be gluttonous and undermine your health through obesity. Your fondness for liquor may be a problem, especially for your family. You may mix with shady company or choose companions with dubious reputations and secretive or sly habits. You may be overly possessive toward your loved ones; your children may be driven to seek sympathy and understanding from others. You may marry too young and suffer for it. You are likely to stand by and watch others be unfairly treated rather than risk your own discomfort. You may pay lip service to your ideals but be too lazy or inept to take action.

Moon in Gemini

This is a restless combination. It imbues you with great intellectual ability, but indicates a tendency to skate on the surface of subjects, intent on covering a lot of ground rather than making any great or lasting impression. You have the ability but not much inclination to tackle fundamentals. You are very active both physically and mentally. You like to read, to study various topics at once and to visit other people, especially in their homes. You enjoy short trips, brisk walks, much chat. You often have a flair for math or science, and your literary ability can be quite impressive. Your sense perception is extraordinary. You pick up impressions with tremendous speed and are able to verbalize them with fascinating fluency or write them down in the form of poetry or prose. You then throw them away and forget them, just as though they had never existed in the first place.

You find most of your enjoyments in the mind, not in actual sensation. But you are sympathetic and humane. To you, the emotions are most valuable for the ideas they provoke, the opportunities they present for action and distraction, the contact and movement that flow from them. You have little time for sentiment; you will never wallow in your feelings. But you are very aware of what is happening in the family circle; you are acutely interested in what loved ones are doing and like to keep tabs on them through letters, phone calls and visits. You enjoy talking about the past but not with the nostalgic desire to repeat it. Your most serious moments relate to domestic and personal affairs.

You are instantly excitable and quickly propelled into new activities with a great display of enthusiasm. You are eager and quick to learn and a natural mimic.

You can file information away with the speed of a computer and retail it exactly wherever there is an attentive ear. But you seldom add anything of yourself to what you repeat; you are too busy communicating to reach down into your deeper feelings and come up with a seasoned package. With you, a half-baked loaf is better than no bread at all, it seems.

You have a keen sense of smell and an ear for music. Without continual mental stimulation and variety, your health is likely to suffer because you become nervous and irritable. You need to keep your imagination functioning vividly in full color. You are one of the few people who can half-read a book or story without any desire to finish it; it is not the satisfaction of endings or conclusions that you are after, but the opportunity to be able to start something fresh. You love to travel. You adore novelty.

You have a feel for language and languages. You prefer to tell people what they want to hear rather than be bothered trying to put your own point of view across. Or you may tell a lie because it will be better received than the truth. To you, the intellect is a cherished toy, something you never tire of playing with. It is this attitude that makes the Gemini temperament so suited to conning people. The compulsive need is to match wits, to change poses convincingly without losing a step, to trip unsuspected through the credulous minds of others. Material gains are only a bonus to you. It's the game that counts, not the petty satisfaction of winning some egotistical point.

You are not a malicious person, nor are you deliberately cruel, but sometimes you have to manufacture (or you might say, stir) your own intellectual sparring partners to keep your mind razor sharp.

You are capricious and likely to sweep your problems under the rug rather than face them. You detest disputes and quarreling—in fact, you'll run a mile (and enjoy the run) to avoid a scene. But you usually manage through indiscretion or lack of caution to land yourself in difficult and embarrassing situations.

You are inclined to change houses and jobs regularly. If you can settle down, you would make a good reporter, salesperson, writer, teacher or agent. A job that means contact with the masses is often lucrative for you.

For career women, this is a favorable position for the Moon. It creates no particular liking for domestic duties and no great emphasis on romance and love affairs. But the Moon does provide the necessary feminine vitality for these women to apply themselves to accomplishment with considerable fixity of purpose. Without a strong intellectual drive, the female mind in this position can be especially frivolous.

The women in the life of a man with the Moon in Gemini must have more brains than beauty to keep his interest and attention alive. They are seldom enthusiastic homemakers and may be fickle in love and avid seekers after novelty and excitement.

The Other Side of the Story

You may be a cheat and a plausible liar, incapable of concentrating for long on anything besides your own selfish interests. You may talk to hear the sound of your own voice and take pleasure in causing dissension among others. You think nothing of being inconsiderate, unsympathetic and shallowly calculating in order to bring about your own designs. Your mother and family may dislike you. You are apt to be unreliable, inconsistent and childish. What is expedient may be more important to you than what is fair or right. Your carefree and cheerful manner may be a subterfuge to hide a person who is undisciplined, immature and unwilling to face life on any terms.

Moon in Cancer

You are a true child of nature. You love beauty and your senses are keenly attuned to your surroundings and the people you mix with. You fit snugly into your environment and are prepared to go along with whatever is happening, provided there is sufficient harmony and a little tenderness exhibited.

Cancer is the Moon's own Sign and here the Moon is truly at home. Its positive qualities are emphasized and its negative aspects watered down. But there is the possibility that you are too comfortably inclined (mildness and placidity can be carried too far). With this combination, you may find it easy to sink into a state of drifting and effortless inertia.

You are less changeable and your temperament is a little warmer than those who have the Moon in other positions. You are extremely solicitous of the welfare of your family and offspring. You are vividly attached to the memories of your childhood, especially to your mother. The sorrows and joys of those early days occupy much of your thoughts. You love to think and reminisce about the past and sometimes brood over old disappointments and injustices. It is not unusual with this combination to have a mother complex. You may be unconsciously drawn to people you feel are protective and dependable. You also exhibit a strong nurturing instinct yourself and are inclined to fuss over your loved ones.

You make a loving parent and marriage partner. You lavish affection on your mate and all those who are emotionally dependent on you. You would prefer to work at or out of your home, and will actually accept a smaller income to do this if the opportunity comes along. You do all in your power to make your living quarters comfortable and homey. You like to have a few relics and antiques around. Your library usually includes quite a bit of historical matter.

You are extremely impressionable. Your mind is receptive rather than active—that is, you are more contemplative than cogitative. Thought to you is more a feeling than a mental image. Being hypersensitive to atmosphere, you absorb them instantaneously. But your reactions are slow and uncertain, and you take your time rendering a verdict. You don't like unsettled conditions or being disturbed yourself. You prefer to be left alone to ruminate and assimilate your impressions until you decide it's time to venture out into the world again and give it the benefit of your conclusions. By that time, though, it's often too late, the opportunity has slipped by. You will get nothing much done unless you push yourself to the limit or there are other energizing factors in your horoscope.

You may be too thorough in your reflections to be outstandingly creative. You have the raw material for brilliance but seldom the spontaneity. Languorous contentment and mental torpor are the obstacles.

You love ease and comfort and are at your best at home with congenial people. You also enjoy visiting and conversation. Since you have a penchant for good food and drink, weight can be a problem, especially if you get insufficient exercise. You are very adaptable to harmonious company and sensitive to the deeper feelings of others, so much so that you are easily swept out of your depth emotionally. Your enthusiasms come and go. Though you can fight with all your might for a worthy cause, a sudden change of mood will leave you high and dry without the will to go on.

Paradoxically, you have a way of projecting yourself into the public eye. Although you are reserved and your whole temperament recoils from this kind of thing, you get drawn into controversies and disputes that attract wide attention. Your own behavior is conspicuously erratic at times; you can blithely swing between two contradictory stands with the polished unconcern of a trapeze artist. Your extreme sensitivity often produces an awareness of psychic activity that is hidden to others. You "know" things without being told.

You are sentimental, sympathetic and humane. Although acutely aware of your senses, you don't allow them to plunge you into a great amount of physical activity. You infinitely prefer sensuous pleasures.

You make a good actor and mimic. You can call up emotion the way others call upon their memory.

You are usually fond of poetry, music, and the theater.

This placing of the Moon is not so favorable for women because it inclines them to be too much at the mercy of the men in their lives. Being passive and impressionable, they are easily influenced and often subjected to domineering and oppressive treatment. Almost all Moon in Cancer people run the risk of being imposed upon.

For men, this position usually means the women in their lives are the mothering type. Deeply affectionate and romantic, these females are apt to stick with the tenacity of limpets. Once committed, their loyalty is unquestionable.

The Other Side of the Story

You may be physically lazy and mentally inert. You are likely to be impressionable to the point of foolishness and have no mind of your own. An inordinate love of your mother or her memory may make you a difficult person to live with or be married to. You may be moody and morose—up one minute, down the next. Your changeability is apt to make others wary of your promises. You may blame "fate" for your weaknesses and failures and fail to develop a workable sense of responsibility. You are likely to be spoiled and feel you have a right to be looked after by society without exerting yourself. You may be excessively voluptuous and preoccupied with the search for sensuous gratification.

Moon in Leo

You are very sure of yourself and a great one for dramatizing situations. Although your mind is alert and quick, you are largely controlled by your emotions. Love and affection come first with you and unless you have them you become downhearted and retreat into yourself. You need desperately to be needed, appreciated, applauded. Fortunately, you have a warm and likable personality that attracts others, so you are rarely short of admirers, collaborators and pleasant companions whose presence shields you from the uncertainties that hover in the deeper recesses of your psyche.

You are intensely ambitious, have good business sense and are not afraid of responsibility. You intend to impress the world in some way or another. Sometimes this urge gets out of control, degenerating into flamboyance, ostentation and posturing conceit. You are a born actor whose wonderful emotional range of expression requires mature curbing.

Usually you are very popular with the opposite sex. In fact, your capacity to love might be called all-consuming. No matter how often you fall in love, you love each time with your entire being—which is flattering, comforting and reassuring to the other party. But after a while—if you still happen to be around—your affection may be regarded as somewhat smothering, and definitely overly protective.

You are self-sacrificing. If you give your word or your heart, you will see the obligation through. Though you may fret under the pressure of adversity, you will seldom go back on a promise. The exception is if the person concerned takes your loyalty and effort for granted. Then you break all ties in a sensational show of independence and indignation.

You are positive and decisive, optimistic and hopeful. The power to lead and to be followed inheres in you. Your initiative prevents you from acknowledging limitations; where there's a will there's definitely a way for those born with the Moon in Leo. But it takes something special to arouse your participation; you're not the type of person who goes looking for any old cause or crusade to invest your energies in. You are fairly fixed in your beliefs and emotions. Unless you are interested in a project or a subject there's no hope of its attracting your attention. You're not as curious as others, at least not intellectually. You require emotional stimulus to set you off. You're at peace lying in the sun with leonine ease. At least, until someone treads on your tail! Given the interest, you learn very quickly.

You are proud, honorable and generous, fond of your home and ambitious for your offspring. If a man, the women in your life might be a bit bossy and inclined to try to organize your activities for your own good. However, they will exert a strongly beneficial influence, especially in the mental and spiritual realms. Women with the Moon in Leo usually have more balanced personalities than the men. The men are that much more egotistical and tend to crunch ahead, ignoring people's feelings and contemptuously dismissing outside influences.

You are a neat type of person and take care with your appearance. You're almost certain to gravitate toward a position of prominence in your community. In many cases, people with this combination become public figures, especially in the entertainment world. You can usually count on the support of those in high places.

You are self-indulgent and very fond of pleasure. But somehow you choose your times for relaxation, entertainment and excess fairly judiciously and manage to prevent them from interfering with your work or reputation, both of which are of the utmost importance to you. You are seldom lucky in your love life; impulsive affairs with willing and coaxing playmates are extremely hard for you to resist.

Luxuries including jewelry, furs, expensive suits, and flashy cars may be a weakness. You enjoy music, art, literature and often are creative in these fields, and earn your living from them. Organized sport may appeal, either as a pastime or a business.

The Other Side of the Story

You may reduce yourself to a self-indulgent wreck. Your conceited and overbearing attitude may make you unpopular and propel you to constantly look out for new people to impress. Self-importance is probably a fetish with you. Although physically developed, you are apt to be mentally and emotionally immature. Your idea of love and affection may not go much further than permissiveness and voluptuousness. What you regard as sensitivity in yourself, others might see as self-pity and a complaining nature. Your striving for the limelight is apt to rebound—notoriety is more likely than fame. Scandal is a danger until you learn the necessary lesson of self-restraint.

Moon in Virgo

You are intelligent and practical—and probably the most efficient and uncomplaining worker in the zodiacal lineup. You can slice through a sea of detail like the prow of a cutter. You possess a special flair for devising more efficient ways of handling the work load, and you don't look for any special privileges or kudos. In many ways, you are the ideal employee—trustworthy, diligent, meticulous, practical and amazingly unassuming.

You are rather reserved and much less sure of yourself than you make out. This lack of confidence can often be traced to the influence of your mother or some maternal figure who had the habit of nagging you. Sympathetic warmth may have been lacking in your early family life. It is also possible that as a child you assumed emotional responsibility for another hard-pressed member of the family. Prejudices you picked up from the dominating figures of those days are probably still with you. An inability to come to terms with your own feelings makes it difficult for you to understand the emotions of others. You have your feelings very much under control, or so it seems. The danger is that you never really understand them.

You are basically an intellectual person, but you don't acquire knowledge just to be well informed, as your mercurial Gemini counterpart does. Everything you learn or absorb you try to put to practical use. You're a very steady, reliable, down-to-earth character.

You are fastidious about health and diet and a terror when it comes to hygiene. You know disease and illness are spread by germs, and you certainly don't intend to be immobilized in that way, if you can help it. You keep your body clean and your house spotless. You can't stand being sick—in fact, nothing is more nerve-racking to you than being laid up in bed.

You're a food faddist, usually enjoy the health-food kick and can't resist trying out exciting new recipes featuring plenty of fresh produce, fruit juices and possibly meat substitutes. Unless you take care with your diet, you are inclined to suffer from stomach disorders.

Left to your own devices, you're pretty easygoing. You're quietly ambitious and will do well working for a large organization.

Your memory is excellent and you learn easily. You have many talents, some of which your associates may not be aware of, because you are anything but egotistical. You put your views forward with clarity and candor but do not strive to impress people. Inadvertently you do, especially with your novel ideas and fresh approach to problems. You are unpretentious, disarmingly modest to the point of consistently underselling yourself. You like to know you're appreciated. You won't get uptight if someone makes a fortune out of one of your good ideas as long as he gives you a wave of recognition.

You're not greedy or avaricious with money. You don't expect any more than what's fair for your labor. You can be careful with the pennies and you're a very astute financial manager.

Women with the Moon in Virgo run the home like a well-oiled machine—everything in its place, working efficiently and contributing to comfort and serviceability—but their hearth is a bit cold. Perhaps this excessive efficiency implies an intolerance of human failings and disorder. It is in the area of personal relations that the Moon in Virgo person usually suffers most, basically because of an inability to identify with the feelings of others. Passion and romance are more mental concepts to these people than painful longings and ecstatic feelings. These women become intellectually rather than emotionally involved with their men. They have to be deeply soul-stirred, to begin to love in ordinary terms. Usually they learn in a negative fashion from an unhappy marriage or love affair, suffering secretly and silently.

You have an irritating way of instantly analyzing people and trying to correct their faults. Though you are basically well intentioned, too often the urge becomes compulsive and inevitably degenerates into carping criticism or wounding outspokenness.

You enjoy scientific studies and have more than a passing interest in the occult. Your own intuition often borders on clairvoyance.

The Other Side of the Story

You are acrimonious, bitterly critical and always complaining. You don't have a kind word for many people. In your family life, you use your clever mind to skim across the surface of problems and offer panaceas but seldom any real solutions. Your ceaseless peppering turns children and those you live with against you. You seem incapable of keeping your nose out of other people's affairs. You are boringly repetitive, superficial and fussy. You are quite likely a hypochondriac. Cleanliness and dietary fears may eventually be phobic.

Moon in Libra

You love companionship and are indeed a fine partner. Everything about you seems to fit into a pattern designed for attracting and pleasing others. You have a charisma that, even if you are not particularly striking to look at, makes even a brief encounter with you memorable. And on closer acquaintance you become even more interesting— as a possible lover, friend or trusted business partner.

Libra is the Sign of partnership and the Moon is the power of the senses. Together, as you may imagine, they add up to some heady connections with the opposite sex.

Emotionally, you are very easygoing. You accept others as you find them and are one of the most understanding types in the Zodiac. You don't want to reform others, educate them or correct them; you just want to enjoy their company. Not surprisingly, you are very popular. You are an excellent listener and can be depended on to make all the right noises at precisely the right time. When people tell you their troubles you are sympathetic, encouraging and terribly concerned. But though you express the most comforting sentiments, the chances of your doing anything practical about the problem are nil!

Not that you're two-faced or spurious. You just don't have much capacity for initiating action. You're not essentially a physical being. You're sensuous more than sensual. Your trouble is you are incredibly adaptable emotionally and respond idealistically to every feeling that others chuck at you. You give people exactly what they need to restore their emotional equilibrium. It might be concluded, then, that you have no genuine feelings of your own, but that's not true. Your fundamental desire is to restore emotional harmony wherever it is lacking.

Therefore, it's easy to understand why you are so

courteous and diplomatic—and why you are so sociable, visiting people in their homes, entertaining them at your place and generally being wherever groups are gathered together. It's your zodiacal function to bring people together in harmony, to build all the bridges you can over personally troubled waters.

But there is a kind of disharmony you'll run a mile from. That's any form of argument, coarseness or discord. You can't stand quarrels and fights. When you see one looming, you're off! In conversation, you'll adroitly skirt around controversial points. If anyone accuses you of dodging issues or vacillating you'll deny it with self-convincing fervor and disarming charm. Your wizardry at subtly producing red herrings is such that people will be put off the scent, giving you a chance to change the subject! Okay, this might be done unconsciously, but still, you are deluding yourself and eventually may be thought deceptive or devious by others.

Dirty, unpleasant and disharmonious surroundings upset you awfully. You become moody and unhappy in these conditions and can't perform.

Your finely developed senses heighten your natural proclivity to all that is aesthetically pleasing. Your appreciation of music, painting and the other fine arts often indicates a creative aptitude that could provide a satisfying and lucrative career, if exploited.

You are fond of smart and fashionable clothes. Your taste in most things is expensive. You have more chance of making a success of your life through partnerships than by trying to go it alone. You will probably marry young.

The women in the life of men born with the Moon in Libra are likely to be accomplished, detached, gentle, refined and undemandingly passionate. They may insist on living their own lives, even after marriage, which is also a characteristic of women born with this combination. The need to be accepted by others is crucial to happiness and makes you highly susceptible to flattery. What people say or think is probably more important to you than the truth. Attachment to social affairs and amusements tends to produce a frivolous personality.

The Other Side of the Story

You are likely to be a scatterbrained good-time gal or guy. You're very difficult to take seriously because you don't seem to have any permanent values. You are easily influenced and sometimes can't say "no" even for your own good. You are lazy, inclined to overeat and have no aim in life apart from being accepted by those with more money and superior status. Peace at any price may be a fixed attitude that costs you plenty—especially in self-respect.

Moon in Scorpio

There is something of the extremist, even the fanatic, in your nature. If you ever discover a cause to serve, you will never give it up, irrespective of the forces that oppose you. But if you never find a way to absorb this demolishing energy of yours, you'll have problems. For a start, there is likely to be a strong sensual bias in your makeup. The search for sexual gratification could lead you into tortuous and sometimes emotionally self-torturing paths. Erotic dreams and thoughts are likely to absorb you and stimulate your imagination to intense levels. There is much that is both creative and destructive in this sort of combination.

You are vigorously active, strong-willed and passionate. You don't confide your inner feelings or secret thoughts to anyone. When others are revealing their secrets in an affable exchange of confidences, you stay mum. Openness is not your style. You tend to tell people only what you want them to know. Although in many ways you are impulsive, you seldom allow a spontaneous disclosure of your inner feelings. Such self-repression leads to a tremendous buildup of energy that must have a constructive outlet.

The unevolved type of person with this combination is an out-and-out hedonist. The senses are used almost exclusively as mediums of pleasures; knowledge is regarded as an incidental by-product whose main function is to produce more opportunities for sensational excitation. These people can sink to terrible depths of perversion and often end up destroying themselves in one way or another. Drugs and drinking are likely to contribute to their misery. Having no real values to speak of, they are treacherous, vindictive and cruel. Revengeful hate is their automatic reaction to anyone who crosses them.

You are a loner with a great faith in your own abilities. When there's a job to be done, you rarely find it necessary to seek assistance. You much prefer to work in isolation, locked up in your office, away from co-workers' camaraderie. You are highly efficient, quick to eliminate unnecessary detail and capable of working incredibly long hours without tiring or losing your concentration. You will never be imposed upon. You are easily irritated but will remember a kindness with unsuspected tenderness. Your manner is abrupt and often blunt. You like to come straight to the point. You don't talk much unless discussing a pet subject. Then you can display voluble enthusiasm, discoursing in quick-fire sentences and leaving no doubt as to your mastery of the subject and perceptive insights. You have a special talent for grasping basic facts instantly.

You usually take an interest in scientific studies and are especially competent at extracting ideas and organizing them into an applicable pattern. The acuteness of your senses frequently gives you extraordinary powers of observation.

The women in your life are likely to be very determined and a little unscrupulous. They will know exactly what they want and be prepared to use deviously subtle means to get it. Time means nothing in the gaining of their ends. These women are intelligent, ambitious and courageous.

You don't like change and are fairly fixed in your opinions. When you do switch views or decide to support a particular line of action, you are capable of producing revolutionary changes. These may be quite unsettling and uncomfortable for others at the time, but in the end, they will probably be recognized as timely reforms or essential bits of surgery.

Mothers with the Moon in Scorpio should take care that their ambitions for their children do not stifle the youngsters' natural talents and creative urges. The willpower of people with this combination is so immense that even with the best of intentions they can overwhelm and misshape a developing personality.

The Other Side of the Story

You may be hopelessly corrupt, devoid of moral scruples and sexually degenerate. Addiction to drugs and alcohol may render you impossible to live with. You could betray your best friend to achieve your ends. You are likely to be utterly ruined by a woman or, going to the other extreme, be denied women's company for most of your life. Jealousy may destroy any chance of a happy marriage. Various perversions may be your idea of recreation. Your domineering and heartlessly ambitious plans for your children may produce carbon copies of yourself.

Moon in Sagittarius

You are an idealist and find it hard to obtain what you are looking for, which you probably can't even define. But you don't need an explicit end to push ahead; you often change your place of residence, more often your job, and are always on the move in one way or another toward a new horizon.

The important consideration at all times is for you to feel free. You don't object to discipline but you'll never cease testing its validity. You don't want to be tied down to other people's views or be limited by their beliefs. If there is any truth in this world—and you are certain there is—you are going to find it for yourself. You're a pretty volatile, free-wheeling package of good-humored energy.

You are extremely sociable and enjoy mixed company. You're passionate enough when it comes to sex but enjoy good companionship even more. You like listening to others' views about life and you filter these finely through your own experience. You are the wandering philosopher, always eager to absorb the meaning of things and not averse to holding forth in company with your own notions of what life is all about. You are as tolerant of others' viewpoints as you expect them to be of yours. Probably you had an early introduction to one-eyed beliefs by clashing with family members in your youth. You'll listen to anyone and form your own conclusions, but you won't stand for being told what to believe in.

You are seldom at rest either in mind or body. Usually you're considering some far-ranging scheme, which your incurable impatience insists on starting before the necessary preliminaries are completed. This is why you often make mistakes—you're inclined to overlook essential details. Optimism is almost an illness with you. You'll plunge into a venture with the confidence of a nine-year-old and then wonder what went wrong when you find yourself in over your head. You don't learn quickly from your rash errors. Even though you are usually cutting your losses in one way or another, you're still a sucker for a long shot.

Lady Luck smiles on you more than on most. Perhaps your generous, kindhearted and benevolent ways bring the same sort of treatment back to you. You get along very well with people in authority; they are more often likely to show favors than to refuse them. You also have a knack of exploiting your personal popularity so that, given the goods to sell or the creative talent to display, you can attract the attention of the crowd and go on to become famous. There is a danger that you will play on the public's emotions and tell them what they want to hear rather than the truth. Once you have success, you have a tendency to moral posturing and expedience.

Your easygoing attitude makes you a pleasant friend and associate but not such a good marital partner. You are not built for domestic happiness because you are too impersonal and unpossessive to make a go of it with other zodiacal people who need to be wanted. You're inclined to live and let live, and in love that means you go your own way when you feel like it. Any display of jealousy will usually send women with this influence racing off—probably straight into the arms of some temporarily interesting and very (temporarily) understanding gentleman.

You love the outdoor life and the feeling of freedom and independence it gives you. At times, you are quick-tempered, especially if someone—your lover, for instance—tries to order you about. You have the discomforting ability to see deep inside people and announce aloud piercing truths about their motives and attitudes. For this reason, you are often regarded as a terror, though more often than not the words come out of you with no deliberation and you just take the blame or the bows. Your disposition is open and frank.

You are genuinely solicitous of others' welfare and have an understanding relationship with all animals.

The Other Side of the Story

You are apt to be a swaggering braggard, wasting money in stupid and careless ways. You are usually prepared to back your inflated opinion of yourself with impossible promises. Your profligate and irresponsible habits may keep you constantly in debt; so that though you are recklessly open-handed with boon companions, you are unable to maintain a consistent standard of living for your dependents. You may live off your wits. A good time probably tops your list of priorities. You may be a narrow-minded bigot and bore behind a facade of righteousness.

Moon in Capricorn

This is not such a good position, especially for women. It tends to make both sexes cold, unresponsive and authoritarian, even though they may not wish to be this way. Circumstances, particularly in childhood, probably exposed you to the harsher side of life. Most people with this combination have unconsciously steeled themselves against being hurt again. Women have to make a special effort to keep their feminine charm. Both men and women feel, with some justification, that their lives will be austere and difficult.

Remember, though, other influences in the chart can mitigate these effects. The tendency toward discipline and restraint, with help elsewhere, can be turned to good account. Moon in Capricorn can be the makings of a most successful business tycoon. But you must expect some grinding hard work and isolating dedication to achieve this kind of success.

Moon in Capricorn dulls the responsiveness to human sentiment. The senses do not flow over into an impressionable plasmic sympathy; they are mainly carriers of information, which is used with astute efficiency in the individual's struggle for achievement and power. Ambition is the driving force. The capacity to persevere under oppressively daunting conditions is truly amazing. The sheer force of sustained exertion usually results in success, and quite commonly in fame or public renown.

There is also a chance of things going wrong—notoriety may be the reward of all this struggle. With such emphasis on ambition, a calculating mind and not a great deal of regard for other people's feelings, Moon in Capricorn people usually make enemies and generate ill will over a long period. When success does come, a secret or open foe often endeavors to destroy the person's reputation or influence.

You are extremely well suited to be a top administrator in situations where generalship and stern authority count. You are quite capable of inspiring confidence. Your ability to organize and to interest others in helping you to attain your particular objectives has to be respected. That you are aloof and somewhat standoffish helps to enhance your air of authority. Inside, you may be shy and uncertain, even fearful.

It is not unusual for a Moon in Capricorn child to be forced to take on responsibilities far beyond his or her years and to absorb the hardest lesson of all—that rewards come only to those who earn them. This isn't true, of course, but to a developing mind starved for love and sympathy, the lesson seems clear and final: when you excel, you are admired. So the will to succeed in concrete and unarguable terms consumes energies that might otherwise be more happily expended in tenderness and understanding.

If you are a man, the women in your life are apt to be upright, dependable, exacting and somewhat off-putting in their lack of warmth. If you are a woman, the men in your life will not be jealous of you, but very down-to-earth and practical. Incidentally, there will be no misunderstandings about your relationship, from which they are more likely to gain than you.

Men with Moon in Capricorn often marry older women or wed late in life. Their wives or lovers seldom bring them happiness and sometimes contribute to their downfall. Bachelorhood is not a difficult or unusual role for these males.

Mothers with this combination should go out of their way to give their children love and sympathy. They don't need to worry about being efficient in the home and providing practical instruction; these are disciplines they have naturally. Above any other duty to their offspring they should choose to show loving kindness and understanding. What will make a man or woman of their child in their eyes probably won't; it will merely make a crippled and thwarted adult.

The Other Side of the Story

You are ambitious but vague and uncertain about the direction in which you are heading. You never cease to worry. Given any form of authority, you are petty, critical, carping, whining and callous. You resent others who are popular or more productive and gifted than you. You are a snide character assassin, unable to give praise where it's due and never capable of a complimentary word for anyone. You lack creative ability. Desperate to attract attention, you are apt to toady to your bosses and tell tales. Frustration at being unable to materialize your desires often renders you a chronic depressive.

Moon in Aquarius

You are an interesting and nicely balanced person. As a pleasant companion, you're probably unbeatable, but as a serious romantic prospect, you're not such a good bet. You're too independent and unconventional to settle down for long with one partner. You're very loyal, mind you, and mean to keep your word, but you're really built for brotherhood and wider alliances. And when the call comes to circulate or serve some unusual cause, well, you gotta go when you've gotta go. You're not necessarily unfaithful to your mate during your peregrinations, but these sudden freedom jaunts can be very hard on the nerves and emotions of anyone who's attached to you.

Freedom is probably the key to your nature. And it's not just a physical impulse. You are mainly a mental creature, a creative idealist. You like to speak out. You not only believe passionately in freedom of thought, you practice it in constructive ways. You refuse to be inhibited by acceptable forms of thinking and custom. Your ideas are truly original, inventive, inspired. You have a rare gift for visualization and sometimes a touch of genius. The power of ideas to change and update society is frequently demonstrated through the individual with Moon in Aquarius.

Being out front like this incurs some risks. For one thing, you might be thought eccentric. This won't worry you unduly because you are aware you see things differently. You also possess an admirable tolerance for all points of view. In fact, your sympathies are as wide in scope as your power to visualize, and this makes you emotionally rather stable yet able to understand the fears and prejudices of others. Your conversation is always worth listening to, possibly because you've got some way-out ideas that make

sense when considered in the light of some of today's pressing problems.

You are agreeable, courteous and make a super collaborator. You are more comfortable working with groups than with individuals. Personal attachments make you feel hemmed in after a while. Your instincts are to serve humanity as a whole rather than to devote yourself to marriage or parenthood. This is not to say you can't enjoy a normal family life, but having to contend with a demanding and unimaginative partner or child can be awfully frustrating for you. Sooner or later you'll explode and do something quite unpredictable. Predictably, you could turn your back and walk out on any binding situation.

You are keenly interested in unusual subjects, especially those with a touch of mystery where you can employ your remarkable intuition. If you are a person living an ordinary kind of life without any great occupational opportunities for broad and original thinking, you have probably long ago dismissed the embryo signs described here as some sort of aberration peculiar to you. You could be hiding your creative potential under a bushel—and it's time the world had a look at it! It is the Aquarius Age that has given us marvelous electronic and mechanical aids. As with Moon in Aquarius, you share this inventive potential. It might be in scientific work, though you also have an aptitude for social work, politics and education. Moon in Aquarius usually gives a strong interest in occult matters and it is not unusual for the individual to possess some kind of ESP. Many of you have a very quick acceptance and understanding of Astrology, and sometimes a degree of clairvoyance. You seek knowledge, not for novelty or to impress, but to widen your understanding of universal principles.

With this combination, you are inclined to join clubs and associations having humanitarian or lofty aims. You possess a strong reforming instinct that desires to improve the lot of all human beings. When involved in a crusading venture, you do not go in for half-measures; you go all out to obtain public support. And you are not averse to making sensational announcements through the media aimed at surprising or shocking others into supporting your cause.

Friends and lovers are responsible for most of your sorrow and unhappiness.

The Other Side of the Story

You are likely to be a wanderer, moving from job to job and place to place, espousing ideas that never catch on. Your friends are probably dropouts and fruitless social rebels. Your anarchic views and erratic public behavior have probably led to a clash with the law or the Establishment. Notoriety and scandal may already have undercut any chance you had of success. Your attempts to show independence may cause unnecessary pain to others. Unexpected difficulties and sorrows are apt to make you bitter and quick to hurt others with thoughtless actions and a biting tongue.

Moon in Pisces

You are an amazing, baffling, surprising, intriguing and beguiling personality, difficult to live with, in fact, a headache at times for those who feel responsible for you. But as a person to be with occasionally, as a companion, a buddy, a confidant, you are superb. You are either good news or bad news, depending largely on how emotionally attached the other party is to you.

You live in a world of fantasy where there is no pressure and you are the hero or heroine. Money problems and dealing with disharmonious situations leave you exhausted and feeling unstable and insecure. In these times—especially if you are a woman—you rush to the dependable person you usually have tucked away someplace and make a soul-elevating confession of your failures and inability to cope. Then, nestled in the warmth of your confidant's comforting and loving presence, you talk your head off until the harsh reality (as far as you are concerned) is dissolved. When you return to earth (you've probably been relating a dream or a childhood happening), you will start afresh until the pressures mount again.

That person you have around, especially if you are a woman, is the most important in your life. If it's a man, he certainly loves you in an abounding way, for in these dark, terrifying moments of self-doubt, you can be comforted only by undemanding and unselfish love. It is not difficult, mind you, for a man or an older woman to love a Moon in Pisces individual, for you epitomize sweet, cuddly, dependent, innocent helplessness. When you're feeling low, that is.

At other times, when the world's not treating you so badly, you want lots of company and plenty of change and stimulation. No one guy or gal for you now—it's life and excitement you require and anyone who tries to leash you (yes, even that old anchor guy) will feel your teeth sink deep into his cautionary or restraining hand.

When emotionally high, you are extremely optimistic, hopeful, gay and apparently outgoing. When the wind changes (as is likely in a few hours), you don't just go down, you plummet—into depression, fear and phobias, and if you're really a tough case, into various stages of paranoia. But no matter how far you fall, you rise again. Like the tides the Moon controls, you're either running in or running out. You're never one thing for very long.

It's this ambivalence that makes you such a fascinating and maddening character. But, of course, there is a grave danger in such behavioral extremes, and even at the best of times, you refuse to see the world as it really is. You are an incurable romantic. You weave your own dreams and expect reality to conform. Not surprisingly, you suffer from numerous disappointments and a great deal of misfortune. In adversity you retreat further into the world of your imagination. Consequently, under stress and without a strong and benevolent hand, you are in danger of losing touch completely.

You are self-sacrificing, generous and fundamentally placid. Being impressionable and compliant in worldly affairs, you are at the mercy of the unscrupulous and are often misused. Because of the Moon's position, you have a great emotional attachment to sensation, which sometimes leads to sexual promiscuity. In afflicted cases, there may be a recourse to drugs and alcohol to fortify the imaginative powers and make withdrawal from the world more complete. Most people with this combination have a compulsive need to be alone, usually after a period of excitation and fraternizing.

You love beauty and harmonious people. Art in all its forms appeals to you. Usually you have a particular creative talent for literature, poetry, dancing or acting. This may lie dormant unless you make a special effort to overcome the innate inertia, sometimes mistaken for laziness, that typifies this combination. Your unconscious tendency to reflect complementary emotions for the benefit of the people you are with makes you quite an unpredictable package. But it does ensure harmony in your casual relationships, which is terribly important to you. It is also your way of guaranteeing that people will like you—in you, often a desperate longing. You are highly psychic and sometimes have bad trips in dreams.

Women and men with Moon in Pisces enjoy a heightened sensitivity and natural responsiveness. The Moon controls the sensibilities, the total emotional response to that which excites or pleases the senses whether it is love or beauty or the range of expressions in between. Whether you have a love of art or a love of love, the Moon's fluctuating influence affects your moods and makes you changeable in your affections. The Moon, which governs the tides, finds a receptive ally in the intuitive, impressionable, psychic, water Sign of Pisces. The combination of Moon in Pisces is extremely significant and effective.

The Other Side of the Story

You may be a self-indulgent escapist, addicted to narcotics, drink and the search for sexual gratification. Chances are you will be a follower of some extremist sect or personality. Distorted emotionalism may render you vulnerable to dangerous practices such as trying to commune with disincarnate energies and even devil worship. You may be lazy, slovenly, indiscriminate and incapable of earning your own living in a conventional way. Prison, hospitals and mental institutions may figure prominently in your life. Your body may run to fat.

CHAPTER SIXTEEN

Mercury

This chapter on Mercury gives you some facts about the planet's physical features, the myths and symbolism surrounding it, and an astrological account of its characteristics. Then follows a description of Mercury in the various zodiacal signs.

The Planet

Mercury is the smallest planet in the solar system and the nearest to the Sun. Its diameter is 3000 miles against the Earth's 8000. It is 36 million miles from the Sun, whereas the Earth is 96 million miles.

At times, Mercury can be seen just before sunrise, in the east, if you know where to look, and in the west, just after sunset. The planet revolves around the Sun just as the Moon revolves around the Earth. Its orbit is so close to the Sun that when it can be seen, it disappears from gaze beneath the horizon shortly after the Sun. The main problem spotting it with the naked eye (apart from glare) is its size. Mercury, relatively, is the size of a pea compared to the Sun's huge 54-inch-diameter sphere, and appears as a tiny black disc on the corona or halo of the solar giant.

Mercury has no atmosphere. If it had, the Sun's rays would be refracted and we would see a ring of light around the planet.

It is a planet of tremendous heat and cold. Because it takes the same time to rotate once on its axis as it does to complete a revolution of the Sun, one side is always exposed to the solar heat and light while the other remains in perpetual night and intense cold (as the Moon does in relation to the Earth).

Mercury's year—the time it takes to orbit the Sun—is only 88 Earth days. In keeping with its other mercurial qualities, the planet's speed is a dashing 95,000 miles per hour compared with the Earth's ambling 25,000 mph.

Symbolism

Mercury, or Hermes as it was known to the ancients, was the herald of Zeus, the ruler of heaven and the supreme god. Since this planet is the closest to the solar lord by observation from the Earth, and since it appears to precede or follow the Sun (they are never more than 28 degrees apart), Mercury is said to represent the wisdom of the creator and the vital intelligence in man.

If thought is a linking process based on the mind's reflection on memory and experience, then Mercury is the flash of inspirational brilliance that gives thought new and meaningful connections with man's practical needs and developing consciousness.

The progress and evolution of the species depend on Mercury's analytical genius and its power to discriminate. It is pure intelligence that transcends time and place and appears in the consciousness from nowhere.

Symbolically, the planet's dual aspect—one side in perpetual sunlight and the other in perpetual shadow—denotes the constant and necessary distinction between the conscious and unconscious in man.

Mercury can explain the most complex ideas, formulate dazzling concepts. As the bridge between spirit, mind and matter, he has no preference of his own but provides the channel of immediacy. He will serve the basest desire and the most sublime aspiration.

He is the inventor of the lyre (having fashioned it by stringing a tortoise shell with cow gut). All music, art and science are of his devising. Magicians owe their skills to him. Those who would commune with the supreme intelligence in silence and solitude are dependent on his mediation. Mercury represents the power of man to study his inner world of thought and feeling without losing sight of external nature.

Through his patronage, man discovered the correspondence between macrocosm and microcosm. "As above, so below," was the voice of Mercury.

To the ancients, he was the god of prudence and cunning as well as theft. To him is attributed the invention of astronomy, weights and measures, the musical scale and the arts of boxing and gymnastics. He was said to preside over games of dice. He was also regarded as the god of eloquence: in the Acts of the Apostles, the crowds of Lystra mistook St. Paul for Mercury "because he was the chief speaker." And because heralds promote peace and therefore trade, he was regarded as the god of peaceful commerce.

Mercury is usually depicted as a youth wearing a petasos (a traveling hat with wings)—or winged sandals, and carrying a caduceus or herald's staff made of olive wood, the ribbons of which were later changed to serpents, a traditional symbol of wisdom.

Astrology

As a boy, Mercury is mischievous, a puckish prankster. He has little sense of responsibility or concentration. He is a cheery, cheeky messenger boy whose capers make even the sternest of the gods smile.

Mercury's cleverness requires positive direction, for he can just as easily turn into a confidence trickster and cheat as into a brilliant scientific investigator. Pure mercurial intellect needs to be humanized, to connect with something worthwhile and significant, to discover lofty purpose; otherwise it may lose itself in the enjoyment of its own unemotional efficiency.

Mercury rules Gemini, the airy third Sign of the Zodiac, and Virgo, the earthy sixth Sign of the Zodiac. In both Signs, Mercury arouses a sharp curiosity and a respect for knowledge. Gemini does not have much tolerance for mysteries or the mysterious, while Virgo is impelled to solve all the complex riddles of life.

Mercury loves to pause briefly, and pass on. It is difficult for him to see things through, to build to last, because he is ever curious, always in motion. His task is to communicate his knowledge to others, and if he can't find one fulfilling way of doing this or a fertile field in which to work, he will either fritter away his fantastic intellectual energy in superficial activities or use his considerable persuasive powers to cast needless doubt, build up false hopes or undermine. His urge is to instruct in mental processes—regardless of content!

Mercury has a high-strung, volatile and restless disposition. Like his metallic namesake, his moods rise and fall with the temperature of his surroundings, which includes the company he is in. He needs a fraternal hand on his shoulder, not so much to restrict as to guide him—a warm sagelike hand like that of the judicious and moral Jupiter, who has the good of all humanity in mind and is not beyond rebuking or chastising the errant boy when he needs it; or the steadying influence of Saturn, who can introduce Mercury to wisdom and curb his frivolity and vanity. The pleasure-loving Venus may overwhelm and distract Mercury further with her plethora of attractions. Mercury will never be short of good companions, but he needs to be careful of the impulsive element of Mars, the inconstancy and changeability of the Moon, and the excessive stimulation of the Sun.

Mercury, as the emissary of the Sun, allows us to discriminate beyond the confines of instinct. He is himself amoral, a connecting force between the essential being and our own individual propensities. He is the lightning in the pitch black sky of discursive thought that reveals the living earth to us in the reflection of our senses.

Without the flash of mercurial intellect, the center of light and life—the Sun—would remain an incomprehensible mass. For this reason, Mercury, physiologically, is associated with the central nervous system, the brain and all sense perception and the sensory organs. It relates the exterior world to our own unique nature. It is the link between inner and outer, the interaction between objective and subjective realities.

Mercury in Aries

You are a prolific and enthusiastic producer of new ideas, some of them quite brilliant. You are quick-witted, the dismay of slow thinkers, the pride of the office think tank. You are not afraid to suggest way-out ideas and have no trouble justifying them at a moment's notice with a superb display of mental gymnastics. Whether some of your ideas are practicable is doubtful, but few will be intrepid enough to challenge you to a public debate on that score. Repartee is like a rapier in your hand with which you thrust and parry with consummate skill. If your rivals or opponents suggest that you put your own plans to work, you may run for cover behind a convincing smoke screen of excuses.

You would normally make a first-class administrator, magistrate or governor because you are able to analyze and sum up situations swiftly. Your ability to think on your feet and to give orders off the top of your head makes you good at directing others; your precise instructions in an emergency are most impressive.

Although you are very original, you are incapable of sustained interest in one idea without the continual stimulus of twist, change and novelty. Your concentration is erratic and dissolves easily under the strain of repetition and forced effort. You can tell others, brilliantly, how something should be done, but you are incapable of following your own instructions to the end.

You are a lover of literature; you like to read, write and discuss subjects for hours on end when you meet a knowledgeable person. Writers and other literary people appreciate your ability to see the same situation from different angles. You can offer good commonsense advice, even though you may be unable to follow it yourself. You rely on your mind to control your supporters; if you want to be, you are the supreme demagogue.

You are not a stereotyped conversationalist. You like to put forward new opinions, some of which you have not considered until you utter them with all the panache of a deeply ruminative thinker. You are the loquacious life of the party socially, and can usually manage to keep even the dullest company amused provided you feel you are receiving sufficient attention. You may exaggerate and enjoy the sound of your own voice. As a raconteur who can switch topics to suit the audience you have few equals. People come to you because you will listen keenly to their problems without attempting to moralize or to judge them. Your intellectual energy is quite amazing. You are a fast communicator. Words can flow from your mouth or pen with riveting impact or persuasive charm.

If your Sun is in Pisces, you have a gift for describing human emotions with subtlety and deep understanding; if in Aries, you are passionately identified with your ideas, sometimes to the point of recklessness; if in Taurus, you possess an unerring instinct for business and financial manipulation.

With Mercury in Aries, the pioneering instinct of the Sign gives your intellectual activities an adventurous touch. You are prepared to experiment intellectually when most others would be daunted by fear of ridicule or failure. You are the propounder of the new theory, the first to express or approve a new style whether it is in writing, composing, thinking

or inventing. Your mind, because it is so active and responsive, can be a wonderful servant or an oppressive master.

The Other Side of the Story

You are apt to want your own way immediately and be very impatient of opposition. As an employer, you may insist that your orders and instructions be carried out with an alacrity that borders on dictatorship. You are likely to lack method, order and perseverance, and skip from one thing to another. Some of you may suffer from fits of passion and anger that leave you physically exhausted; persistent and acute headaches may follow these temperamental outbursts. You may be perverse and willful, which could spoil your innate ability to lead.

You may lay down the law when compromise is essential, or be cruelly direct when tact is called for. You may be oblivious of your own power to hurt. In debate, you may see only your side of the argument, mistake cleverness for profundity, play to the gallery instead of playing the game. If others do not follow your rules, you may become peevish, critical, sardonic and quarrelsome. You may be quick to give an opinion on any subject but loath to listen to others. If you regard speech as your lifebuoy in any emergency, you may find that others are not as gullible as you thought. Those whom you think you have converted to your ideas are likely to turn against you in the end.

Mercury in Taurus

The plodding and methodical influence of Taurus brings your mercurial qualities down to earth. You use your mind and considerable intellect to amass a greater share of material things. You are practical, you look before you leap and your ideas are not insubstantial. You are a deep thinker, or a true conservative or both. If you work in a scientific field, you are in your element, cautiously applying your well thought out theories, diligently observing and recording the results. You don't jump to conclusions. You are patient, solid, constructive. Your goal is to hold onto what you have, and if possible without running any extra risks, garner a great deal more. You are often obstinate and resist change. You like the old and proven ideas. In a position of power, you will see to it that progress is by cautious evolution, not revolution.

Historically, people born with Mercury in Taurus have made a great impact on their times, but their contribution usually came out of an unyielding self-repression that prepared the way for new eras of luminous advance. This position often confers political acumen, but not the spectacular kind. Politicians with this combination tend to come to power in times of chaos, when a return to solid and traditional methods is necessary to restore confidence and order. They lead their followers back to fundamentals such as responsibility, perseverance, patience and economy. (Some might say now is a time for a Mercury in Taurus statesman or stateswoman to appear on the world scene.) It's not the creative achievement of these people that is impressive, but rather their ability to establish a firm basis others can use to go on to glorious accomplishment and discovery.

You stick to your opinions with great stubbornness. It may take you some time to decide what you want out of life, but when you make up your mind, you are usually unshakeable. You will pursue your objectives with almost slavish application. Once an idea becomes fixed in your mind, you usually set about gathering large amounts of information to augment it.

With this planetary lineup, you have a fine chance of making money, as Mercury's usually capricious and flighty tendencies here are given direction. The acquisitiveness of Taurus and the mental wizardry of Mercury together often produce wealth. You have the intellect to read and absorb facts, but you are a pragmatist who prefers to learn your lessons from life rather than from teachers, schools and books. As much as you respect theory, you realize it must be backed up by experience. You will never undertake a venture until you have carefully studied the ground and accumulated the necessary knowledge. You don't favor leaving success to chance, and you do believe in taking precautions. You like to build a solid framework and then patiently and doggedly fill in the panels. You are not easily distracted from your purpose. Slowly but surely, you wear down the opposition just as the sea erodes the coastline. You are the personification of the war of attrition.

You would make a sound banker because of your grasp of financial matters and your adherence to orthodox procedures and conservative policies. You are a good manager of both your own and other people's money. You are sociable, friendly and affectionate. Music, poetry and art often have more than the usual appeal. You have an innate appreciation of beautiful things and are often very knowledgeable about collecting objects of art. You enjoy the company of the opposite sex. You have enough intellectual pursuits to make you an interesting person to meet, and you are well aware of your ability to charm your way out of situations.

It is not unusual for people with this combination to acquire wealth, possessions or status through marriage. They tend to gravitate to more elevated social circles than their own. A pleasant, happy and relaxed disposition helps them gain acceptance where others would be considered rank interlopers.

Many famous popular singers have Mercury in Taurus. Music and dancing are also activities in which you may excel.

The Other Side of the Story

You may sink into a mental rut out of your dislike of change. If your ambitions are too earthy, you may not be able to make the best use of the abstractions and subtleties that Mercury has to offer. You may have the strength and massive solidarity of the Bull; but without the refining influence of the airy and volatile planet, your views will be fixed and repetitious. You may be excessively habitual, a bit of a bore. You can have lapses of uncontrollable rage and intense irritation. You may live for money or position. Your mind may rule your heart. Cash, possessions and the social life could be your ultimate objectives.

Mercury in Gemini

Life is not the puzzle to you that it is to others. You see things in a superrational way and are convinced that to you most problems can be sorted out intellectually. Because you believe logic is the simple answer to everything, you don't rely very much on feeling, even though you are naturally sympathetic. You think life should be lived intelligently, with reason as the guiding principle.

You are apt to generalize and skip over important considerations. At times your mind reaches great heights of lucidity. You are then fluent, clever, inquisitive and become irritated with others who do not see the facts as clearly as you do, although your facts are probably mere abstractions to them. You may win an argument by the sheer power of your logic, but leave the practical problem that provoked it just as far from solution. You are a master of superficial thought. You can dart here and there with a rapidity that leaves your weightier opponents continually on the wrong foot.

You often make a fine public speaker who gains

support by considering only popular ideas. You are on a wavelength with the common type of curiosity that requires interesting information but not necessarily the truth. You sometimes appear foolish, but never stupid or dull. Because you live in a mental world, your behavior at times may seem silly to more down-to-earth associates.

You are ideally suited to journalism because you can report or interpret quickly without concerning yourself with practical consequences, and have the knack of clarifying issues and stringing ideas together in natural sequences. You are not actually as intuitive or instinctive as you may appear. Your real intellectual strength is in constant awareness, the ability to look two ways at once, both inwardly and outwardly. For you, everything must have a causal explanation and your mind works like a scanner, noting sequences and looking for flaws and gaps in the logical order.

You don't like mysteries; they exist for you to solve. You are contemptuous of people who believe blindly and impatient with those who allow sentiment and emotion to distort their thinking. You do not try much to communicate with those who live conventional and sluggish lives. You are polite, but you look for compatible company, people who grasp concepts quickly without the need for punctuation. You need to circulate, to travel, to exchange ideas. A change of environment can set you off in a totally new direction. You are easily influenced and distracted and won't concentrate on one idea for long. You are more versatile than profound. You long to be free and unbound by concepts or surroundings. You can make an excellent linguist. Your superb sense of humor helps you to communicate ideas in pleasing form. Your mind is machinelike in its precision. You are well informed, ingenious and resourceful. You are very seldom prejudiced and have a great many interests.

In manual occupations, you should shine where dexterity is required. You would make an able carpenter, painter, stenographer, dressmaker or magician. You are fond of speculation, novelty, literature and science. You may be attracted to the study of occult subjects with considerable success. You enjoy acquiring obscure knowledge.

Your personality may be distinguished by a cold intellectual quality. This can be quite impressive in business or a position of authority, but in other circumstances, it may intimidate or repel others. You have a particular talent for seeing things as they are without allowing emotional considerations to distort your judgment. You may make unpopular decisions that are disputed, not because of their faulty logic, but because they disregard ordinary human feelings.

You're not a sentimentalist. But your mercurial wit and humor communicate a warmth that others can't help but respond to. Many actors and comedians are born with Mercury in Gemini.

The Other Side of the Story

You may live too much on the mental plane and consequently lack human warmth. It may be hard for you to communicate at a serious level with ordinary people; gossip may be your main pastime. Nervous breakdowns are likely because of anxiety and overwork. Restlessness may make it impossible for you to settle down. Enduring accomplishment may always elude you. You are apt to imitate rather than originate. Nervous excitement may cause sleeplessness.

Mercury in Cancer

Your mind is passive and receptive. You have an uncommon capacity for absorbing facts, particularly about the past. You are often a student of history, a collector of antiquities, an antique dealer, a scholar. You are discreet, tactful and bend over backward to please people. You would make a first-class diplomat. In your eagerness to create a favorable impression, you are apt to ignore your own convictions and say what you think others want to hear. You are likely to lose yourself in whatever happens to take your attention. You are often a bookworm, a dedicated librarian. Any literary efforts will tend toward histories about races and families and sensitive biographies of famous figures of the past.

You are not particularly original, in fact, you depend a lot on precedent for your opinions and judgments. You would rather obey a rule than struggle with alternatives. You often find your self-expression in the backwaters of human activity where there is not a great deal of competition or stress. You are extremely sensitive. Your intuition amazes others, while to you it is an essential faculty. Labored explanations are not necessary for you; you get the point very quickly by intuitive transference, and frequently grasp a whole argument before the speaker has finished the preamble. You may know things without being told them, but not know how you know.

You can't stand being in the company of people who are out of harmony with you. You will withdraw quietly from discordant situations without offering an explanation, and preferably without making a scene. You can resent people who argue with you, but you are wonderfully sympathetic and understanding and your compassion is easily aroused. Pain and suffering in any living thing disturb you. You are quite intense in your likes and dislikes, but you are extremely tolerant of the opinions and beliefs of others. You like to live and let live.

You are a natural psychologist. You can stare deeply into the past (or into another person's mind) without a ruffle and without taking sides. Your appreciation of symbolism and fantasy exceeds the understanding that is normally ascribed to your type. You apprehend subtleties that at times are beyond the rational. For this reason, you sometimes find yourself accused of being illogical.

You have a way of winning the confidence and trust of others so that they often confide in you. You won't betray another's confidence and frequently offer advice that helps those in distress to carry on.

Your memory is often extraordinary but may deteriorate in old age. You are impressionable, sometimes too easily persuaded. You are creative and artistic. Your sense of rhythm can make you a competent dancer, gymnast or athlete, or a poet, musician or graceful writer. You are often successful in the entertainment field. You are inclined to have a close link with your mother or her side of the family. You are excited by travel, particularly when it means crossing water. You are a quietly social person, a good and generous friend to those whom you select. You are discreet and faithful. You like to be appreciated by your friends and are easily influenced by kindness. An appeal to the senses will have much more effect on you than an appeal to logic. Praise will make you try harder.

Your outlook on affairs is broad and comprehensive. Your intellect may not be as outstanding as that of those born with other Mercury combinations, but your humanity and respect for people's feelings, particularly their anxieties, make you a very special kind of person.

Your imagination is extremely vivid and can cause you actual pain. You are inclined to become despondent through excess of sympathetic feeling. When you hear of a disaster, you visualize the scene with great and moving compassion for those affected. You are very aware of the needs of your family and will go to great lengths to protect and provide for them. Your children can be an especially tender spot.

You look to your family for admiration. A greater faith in your own reasoning power is often needed. You have a genuine desire to help others.

The Other Side of the Story

You are likely to drift like a rudderless ship. You may live in a world of fantasy or bore everyone stiff with tales about the past, particularly your childhood. You may lack discrimination. You may resort to telling lies to secure approval and recognition. You are likely to become a creature of habit in an attempt to avoid asserting yourself. You may run from one worthy cause to another without achieving anything of permanent value. Your unusually impressionable nature makes you an easy victim of circumstance. You are too easily swayed by the opinions of others. You are likely to embrace an erroneous view briefly, turn away and immediately become attached to another false idea. Your mind may become inactive. You may be dishonest with yourself in trying to please others. Your need of approbation may turn you into a bit of a trickster. You could be narrow-minded.

Mercury in Leo

You believe in your ideas with all your heart and soul. You feel you have something to say and you want the world to know it—and usually, you are well worth listening to. This is one of the best positions for the Mercury influence; here it responds well to the steadying dignity of the Sun, which rules Leo. You have a warm personality and usually considerable presence. Your words convey a personal conviction that seldom fails to excite interest. Your audience may not agree with what you say, but it will be quick to respect the articulate and impressive manner in which you present your case.

You don't take kindly to disagreement, which you regard as a personal slight. This is a terrible reflection on your power to discriminate between fact and fiction, the pertinent and impertinent. You are a direct and positive thinker. There is seldom any malice in your reactions—when faced with a doubting Thomas, you are likely to be astonished that he could possibly question your judgment or suggest there may be another way of looking at things. Believing yours is the only admissible point of view, you may surround yourself with yes-men.

You are ambitious and will probably get to the top in your field. You have a flair for management and organization and should make a topflight company director. The communications industry could be especially favorable for you. You can issue orders quickly and cogently. You are progressive, persistent, determined. Your personality emanates vitality and assurance. You have the human touch, derived from the blending of a fine intellect (Mercury) with the sympathetic warmth of the Sun. You are intuitive. You like people. You like to help them with advice and give them the benefit of your experience. You are not the intellectual type who sits in an ivory tower devising fanciful schemes and handing them down for execution. You are a doer. If you can't do something yourself, you won't ask another to do it. You demand loyalty from both subordinates and those who love you. You have a lot of heart and a lot of brain: you combine the perceptive and emotional qualities in a rare balance of harmonious action and response. You are fond of children and pets, music, fine arts and the opposite sex. You are pleasure-loving and inclined to self-indulgence.

Usually you occupy a position of authority. You want your own way, mostly because you sincerely believe that your ideas are best for the common good. For yourself, you want recognition, admiration, respect. If these are forthcoming, your other needs are not great. You can be extraordinarily magnanimous, and selfless. As a born leader, you react very sharply to any form of disobedience. Your anger is explosive but it doesn't last long. You don't hold grudges. You seldom stoop to low actions. You are often flamboyant and ostentatious. You love to impress others with your accomplishments. You enjoy glamorous situations and the company of glamorous people. You think on a grand scale.

This combination often allows the exemplar of genius close contact with the masses. Not everyone with Mercury in Leo is a genius, but with this combination, even the most ordinary person projects ideas and influence beyond his or her immediate circle. Some of the greatest (and most infamous) empire builders of history were born with Mercury in this position. So were numerous thinkers whose bold ideas have helped to enlighten society on religion, Astrology, literature and other means of mass communication. There is frequently a strong element of physical courage in these people; they are not afraid to risk their reputations or even their lives for their beliefs. They are often distinguished by personal charisma.

You are likely to possess a good singing voice or some other quality that entertains and draws people to you. In proper circumstances, your speeches may seize the public imagination and carry you forward to a position of power. You may be popular in the acting or writing professions. You can sell your ideas as long as you believe in them. You aren't the best of demagogues or charlatans. In whatever you do, you are looking over your shoulder at a potential audience. Above all, you thrive on applause, which is why you will never seek obscurity. You will always do a good job, not only because of the nobility in your makeup, but also because the fire in you is fed by the adulation and love of others.

The Other Side of the Story

You may be conceited and overbearing. You are likely to be on a continuous ego trip that demands rather than deserves. You may be a snob. Your opinions could be too fixed. Your great sense of pride and authority may degenerate into tiresome boasting. You may be a showoff who upsets others with your patronizing attitude, your pomposity. You may proffer advice where it is not wanted and display an intolerance and critical enthusiasm that alienate the very people who could be the most help to you. You may be an intellectual bully. Your urge for power may drive you to destruction; what you love most you may destroy out of misplaced sense of justice, zeal or a feeling of omnipotence. You may use alcohol and drugs to excess. Overindulgence is a danger for you in all pleasures.

Mercury in Virgo

This is a very strong intellectual position for Mercury. The planet both rules and is exalted in Virgo, which means its powers are greatly enhanced here. You have a finely discriminating mind. You can dissect issues with great detail and precision. Your approach is by pure reason; you don't, as a rule, allow emotional considerations to override the mental. You are inclined to overlook or be intolerant of human failure—in fact, nothing annoys you more than the blind stupidity of others. Some of your associates may regard you as altogether too exacting and computerlike in your thinking.

You are skeptical, critical and analytical. Your greatest satisfaction is to set everything neatly in its place, and you try to accomplish this in every department of your life. Mercury here confers the Virgo quality that tries unconsciously to tidy up the household of the world. Considering the vast amount of disorder in this world, you are incessantly busy making mental assessments, endeavoring to compensate, rearrange and correct. In anyone less fitted for unrewarding effort, it would be an exhausting business, but you can cope, though the effort keeps you in a high-strung state and your intentions are sometimes misinterpreted. You find it hard to understand why everyone is not as aware as you are of the desirability of method and order. Frequently you are disappointed and frustrated by people's lackadaisical responses to your urgings. You are seldom contented. Unless you can direct your discriminative faculties into a worthwhile occupation you are apt to focus them on your associates and gain a reputation for being overly critical, interfering and fussy.

You are a down-to-earth person, devoid of the diffusiveness that characterizes Mercury in Gemini, the planet's other Sign. Your character is disciplined, strictly practical, no-nonsense. You give the brilliant but unpredictable Mercury force stability. You apply your mental powers to practical affairs rather than abstract ends. You are ideally suited to scholarly research, because you are a master of detailed evaluation. You like to grind the particles down, sift, assimilate and digest the essential facts. Laboratory work, scientific inquiry, mathematics, accounting— any pursuit that requires a disciplined and controlled mind is one you will shine in. You enjoy activities that require involved planning and ingenuity. Crossword puzzles are child's play—or did you get stuck on a clue this morning? You are happier dealing with a multitude of details than with having to wrestle with the broader picture. You can be a great contributor to human knowledge through your ability to make painstaking studies and investigations. You are more adaptive than you are innovative. Exceedingly quick to learn, you are so quick that you may not concentrate enough to remember for long, though your power to memorize is unsurpassed if you wish to use it.

You aren't an easy person to convince; you insist on understanding a subject thoroughly before committing yourself. The way to appeal to you is through reason. With such concentrated intellectual power at your disposal, there is a danger you will overlook the human element in your calculations. You are apt to forget that though people often pay lip service to the power of reason, they more often run their lives according to a mixture of self-interest, prejudice and emotion.

You are naturally quiet and rather serious. You suffer from a painful lack of confidence, though you usually manage to disguise it. You try to avoid show-downs and taking strong stands on basic issues because you are so self-critical that you can't maintain a position of self-assertion for long.

You are interested in all intellectual pursuits, but you aren't showy or egotistical about these accomplishments. You would make an able linguist. Your powers of persuasion through the written and spoken word are considerable, though you have a tendency to go into too much detail and become tedious. You may also lack the warmth and fire of physical presence and thus fail to incite emotional fervor in others. You can make out an unarguable case why everyone should drink nothing but water, and the whole world will agree with you—and then go on drinking what they fancy.

Your love of solving mysteries sometimes inclines you to occult studies. You can write profusely on just about any subject that excites your interest and curiosity. You usually insist on having first-hand experience of things, and this enables you to give finely etched descriptions. Many writers with remarkable powers of observation have this combination. You usually endeavor to give others the benefit of your knowledge, although you are far from pushy (unless your Sun is in Leo).

You have a particular talent for devising special techniques for handling work. If there is a solution to a problem, you can be counted on to find it. Your discerning intellect will swiftly whittle away a mountain of conjecture into a molehill of fact and statistics.

Physical fitness especially interests you. Just as you strive to put details into place, so you endeavor to help people fit neatly and comfortably into their environment by staying healthy. You are a keen advocate of cleanliness and hygiene. You are strongly convinced of the healthiness of fresh and wholesome food, and try to set an example for others by keeping to a balanced and nutritious diet.

The Other Side of the Story

You are likely to ride roughshod over any opponent. Cold reason may be your god. The letter of the word may be so important to your judgments that any glow of human kindness is eclipsed. You may be too brittle, rigid and detached to deal effectively with practical affairs. You may be a harping critic, believing that only you know how things should be done. You are more likely to find fault than to praise, to quibble over unimportant details. You are probably selfish and sarcastic. You may be fanatical about health habits and inflict an unnecessary regimen on those you live with. Your penchant for neatness may become uncontrolled. You may be mean with money, and your reluctance to show love and feeling may eventually turn you into a dry, emotionless, unyielding individual. In a position of authority, you may be a trifling despot.

Mercury in Libra

This placing of Mercury makes you extremely broad-minded and intellectually capable. Your considered judgments are often impeccable for their justice and sheer logic, but in the rough and tumble of everyday living, you may be hesitant and indecisive. This can make life a bit difficult. An intuitive flash about how to go about something may be dissipated by an organized attempt to weigh all the pros and cons before proceeding. Thus are good opportunities lost. First thoughts are often best for you. It does not pay always to play safe. Remember, you can't hope to please everyone.

You are rather changeful. You sum up a situation admirably, decide on a course of action—and at the last second do something else. As refreshing as your openmindedness is, it does have certain drawbacks. For one, you are likely to be attracted to frivolous pursuits. Curiosity may lure you from one subject to another, preventing you from accomplishing any one thing that is really worthwhile.

You are ambitious for intellectual attainment. You will go to a lot of trouble to set up projects, discussing them with various people and assembling a large stack of reference material. But when the time comes for action, for disciplined effort, you may have flitted off (most gracefully) to some new interest. Therefore, you are apt to acquire voluminous knowledge about numerous topics but have little practical experience of anything in particular. You are not attracted to physical labor, though enjoy using your hands and can be quite deft and artistic with handicrafts and the like.

You have a charming way of saying the right thing. Quick to respond to the different factions in an audience, you have the knack of bringing them together or at least of convincing them all simultaneously that you understand their particular problem. You have a great eye for artistic detail and can fill a valuable role by putting the final touches to literary or artistic productions. You dot the i's as an artist, not as a pedant.

You have an air of authority, a suggestion of wisdom about you. You can combine the best of head and heart in your evaluations. If your Sun is also in Libra, you have an intellect of considerable polish and refinement. You are capable of expressing abstract ideas in a most interesting way. You are usually drawn to music, literature and public speaking.

With the Sun in Virgo, your outlook is more practical; you can be involved with the harsher side of life without bruising your finer sensibilities. With the Sun in Scorpio, you possess a flair for psychology that can be put to good use in business ventures.

Mercury in Libra should make you a well-balanced character, but equilibrium here, at the central Sign of the Zodiac, is so delicately poised that it can easily be upset by other aspects in the horoscope. No conclusions should be drawn until the other effects (indicated in the Pink and Blue Tables) are studied and weighed—an exercise that will appeal tremendously to the typical Mercury in Libra person.

Your choice of career will depend largely on the people most influential in your life at the time. As you change your companions, you are also likely to alter your views and this will usually be reflected in the quality or style of the work you do. It is important for young people with this combination to choose associates who will stimulate their flexible and facile minds in positive directions so that they are always moving forward in their field—and not sliding sideways.

You love friends and a good social life. You are extremely well suited to work with partners. In marriage, you require intellectual companionship more than physical presence. Sometimes this combination leads to an inferior marriage—socially or financially. It can also mean marriage to a distant relative. Your refined taste, smooth social manner and gift for sophisticated conversation make you an ideal host or hostess and a popular guest.

The Other Side of the Story

You may be weak-willed and too easily influenced. Your tactlessness and manner of expression may make you unpopular. You may be insincere and easy to see through, eventually even a social outcast. You are apt to be devious and depend on the clever use of words to paper over situations rather than genuinely try to heal them. You may be a glaring opportunist. You are likely to agree with everyone to save yourself from contention, and may give in to an argument even though you know you are right. You may be an escapist who lies your way out of situations rather than face the truth. You may prefer to live in a world of daydreams or spend your time gossiping and maligning others.

Mercury in Scorpio

Because the range of possibilities for good and evil is so extensive in this position and subject to modifications elsewhere in the horoscope, you must decide which traits apply to you personally in the following description. It is, by necessity, an analysis of extremes.

The typical person born with Mercury in Scorpio has a mind of almost unsurpassed clarity and intensity. You combine the heights of intellectual acuity with passionate fierceness of feelings. You can be most of what is best in humanity, and most of what is worst. Your reach is from heaven to hell. You are a visionary, able to see beyond the normal confines of the mind. Your perception is so shrewdly effective that it is almost impossible to deceive you. You can spot a phony a mile off.

You are hypercritical, highly suspicious and mistrustful. You have already observed in yourself all the inequities of which man is capable, so you recognize them instantly (though mostly subconsciously) in others. You are wary, cautious and possessed of a bitter intolerance that expresses itself eagerly in vitriolic condemnation. You are pitiless when opposed and will resort to any action or subterfuge likely to give you victory or revenge. Your capacity to hate and to wait patiently for vengeance can be diabolical. You are a vicious, ruthless and terrible enemy.

You are bold, reckless, ingenious and keen to demonstrate the penetrating swiftness of your mind. You enjoy the cat-and-mouse game, carefully baiting your unsuspecting opponent, skillfully maneuvering him or her into a vulnerable position. You strike to wound, not to kill; to ruin, not to destroy. You undermine by innuendo. Your insinuations are devilishly contrived. A sixth sense tells you exactly when and where to strike, when the psychological organism is at its weakest point.

You are secretive and cunningly protective of your personal interests. You hate committing yourself and refuse to take anyone into your confidence. But you like to listen to others' secrets, to hear their foolish, trusting statements. You are contemptuous of those who would oppose you and haughtily dismissive of the views of people you regard as your inferiors. You suffer many disappointments and have more trouble than most with relatives, neighbors and partners.

You would make a good undercover agent because you can keep up deception for an inordinate time. You are an inspired investigator of insurance frauds, conspiracies and complex financial swindles. You have great physical and nervous endurance. Your courage in the face of danger can be sublime. You enjoy pitting your wits against another, especially an adversary with a reputation. You are proud of your sharp mind and resourcefulness. You have a strong sexual drive and enjoy erotic reading and talk.

You are fascinated by mysteries and particularly enjoy solving those that have defied the ingenuity of others. You can be especially attracted to occult and metaphysical investigations. Your penetrative, subtle and intuitive mind allows you to be numbered among some of the most profound and inspirational mystics to have elevated the mind of man. Your bulldog tenacity and intellectual breadth fit you for a role in politics. You excel in a power struggle, especially if the in-fighting is rough and vicious. In a workshop, office or boardroom encounter, you don't expect sympathy or mercy and you certainly won't extend them. You have all the courage necessary to back up your convictions. Calmness under pressure is one of your most demoralizing weapons and you never fail to exhibit it.

The often pernicious effect of Mercury in Scorpio is softened if the Sun is in Libra. This personality is likely to be more yielding, less vitriolic, more given to satire than to straight-out ridicule or vindictive criticism. But still, there is a strong inclination to argue and oppose.

The Sun conjoined with Mercury in Scorpio confers a greater capacity for noble endurance and fortitude and heightens the perceptive and intuitive faculties. The Sun in Sagittarius combination gives the mind a broader and less introspective vision and heightens the interest in philosophic studies.

The Other Side of the Story

This is largely told above. It is possible for poorly evolved persons with this combination to engage in sadism. They can be deeply brooding and find partial relief for their resentments in starting scandalous and despicable rumors about rivals and opponents. Their jealousy can reach peaks of destructive fury that would not shrink from even self-immolation to even a score.

Mercury in Sagittarius

You are an extremely changeable person. Your mind is an open hotline that never ceases to receive and convey ideas. As one thought comes in, it quickly moves on and another takes its place. You are quite brilliant at times and can utter ideas and observations with the rapidity of a machine gun, hitting the target repeatedly with astounding accuracy. But your quick-fire thoughts lack depth and follow-through. You disappoint because your remarkable intuitions are never bolstered by digested knowledge and firsthand experience.

You enjoy being superactive physically as well as mentally and are apt to have one or two part-time jobs in addition to your main occupation. You are fond of doing several things at once. You love to talk to and meet people. You can scramble for hours, jumping from one topic to another, asking and answering questions, but remembering very little of consequence. Despite your brilliance, you talk off the top of your head and you often put your foot in things because you have neither the time nor the capacity to weigh a situation properly. Because your concentration is weak, you are bright but unwise and fail to consider the effect of your remarks.

Still, you are a sincere type of person, simple and honest. There is nothing underhanded about you. Unlike those with Mercury in Scorpio, you find it impossible to engage in deliberate cruelty. Such perversity would not even occur to you. If you tell a lie, it is on the spur of the moment. Since you lack malice, you are temperamentally unsuited to long drawn out feuds.

You love independence and are a strong and vociferous defender of free expression. You are impulsive and often rebellious, don't take kindly to authority and resent any overt display of its power. Because you can't stand injustice, you will often fight on the side of the underdog. You are ambitious and capable of surprising breadth of vision, but you seem unable to stick to one goal for any length of time and usually get diverted without noticing it.

Success often eludes you until late in life because you are inclined to move around too often to be there when the promotions are handed out. You live to live, not to work. You are interested in education, although you personally won't take it too seriously if it means being tied down in your early years. You enjoy traveling and probably wish to visit other countries, although you are very happy making numerous short trips, dropping in on people and cultivating contacts.

You often have a strong desire to understand life and its mysteries. You have great faith in the redemptive power of the moral law. You also respect science and religion and enjoy philosophic discussions. You imagine yourself, rightly or wrongly, to be well informed on these subjects.

A talent for writing and lecturing, which may lead to long-distance travel and unusual experiences, is indicated if your Sun is also in Sagittarius. Sun in Capricorn indicates a much more solid citizen, imbued with the ability to lay down the law and see that it is carried out. (The "law" in this case is usually a socio-moral concept the person enforces on his or her family or community.) Sun in Scorpio often turns the Mercury in Sagittarius vision inward, yielding great self-knowledge and a talent for sociology and psychology.

The Other Side of the Story

You may be incapable of reconciling your ideas with the facts of life, lacking in mature judgment and unable to weigh one idea against another—an absurd nonrealist. You may make an impressive show of urging others toward a greater life goal, while you yourself run around in foolish circles, patently achieving nothing. You may be tactless and carelessly hurtful, quick to make promises and slow to keep them. Your impatience and restlessness may prevent you from finishing anything worthwhile.

Mercury in Capricorn

This is a desirable position for Mercury. The brilliant and erratic planet has no chance of going off the rails here. It blends easily and advantageously with the Sign Capricorn, which epitomizes the cool, calculating and severe mentality, the mind that is rationalizing, disciplined and exacting. The result is a person of dignity, good sense, practicality, earnestness and prudence.

You seldom engage in frivolous or silly talk. You have an air of purposefulness. When you open your mouth, you are worth listening to. You can be counted on to have put your ideas through the strict acid test of reason. And if they are wrong or unacceptable, it will be because of an error in judgment, not because of any neglect of detail or thorough investigation.

You have an excellent memory, which you don't

bother to clutter with gossip and superficial information. The only details you decide to memorize are those you know will be useful. Your powers of concentration are likewise extraordinary. You have the knack of focusing your perceptive powers with unwavering intensity on the problem of the moment. Because your mind is usually engaged in some weighty consideration (the world is filled with problems for those who look for them), you may be intolerant of people who are interested in the lighter side of life. You may lack a sense of humor and find it hard to adapt to a purely social atmosphere.

You possess a great determination to succeed; Mercury ensures that you have the necessary wit and intelligence. You are very steady and sincere and tactfully curious about anything affecting your own ambitious interests. Your mind can attend to the smallest detail without losing sight for a second of the overall plan. You accept responsibility. You command respect even when you are wrong. Your deliberative seriousness gives you an air of wisdom.

You are reserved, cautious and suspicious. You have a moralistic outlook that may be too rigid to win many friends. Unless this Mercury in Capricorn combination is softened by other influences, you may tend to cut yourself off from people and make a cold and narrow intellectual world only you can live in.

You are often consulted by others for your wise advice. You enjoy the role of confidant and counselor, but it is one in which you take yourself too seriously.

You are always trying to develop your mind. You are keenly interested in science, chemistry, philosophy and business management. You may be discontented with the way things are run in this world, but your natural diplomacy and correctness of manner usually prevent others from taking offense. You are intensely conscious of your own dignity and will seldom forgive anyone who undercuts it.

You need to guard against depression. Although your mind is steady, your moods can be quite changeable. You may swing violently from one extreme to another, and this innate ability to adapt quickly at the emotional level may leave you temporarily insecure and tormented by vague and unreasonable fears. Your mature and painstaking examination of the human condition can produce a pessimistic outlook. This may be countered by cultivating a more cheerful and elastic attitude.

If your Sun is in Sagittarius, you have a warm and expansive mind and your attention is less minutely concentrated. Your curiosity goes beyond the immediate task and your own self-centered interests. You may then see hope in religion and feel the glow of optimism. You may also use your wisdom to instruct others in practical, day-to-day matters.

If your Sun is in Aquarius, you are likely to fling yourself into organized research projects aimed at solving recognized scientific or social problems on a global scale. You are then more original and less restrictive in your perceptions. If both your Sun and Mercury are in Capricorn, you are a grave person who has great faith in his or her own opinions. If your ideas are correct, you may make a great contribution to human knowledge after struggling valiantly to overcome opposition. But if they are wrong, you may live a life of rigid isolation trapped in your own narrow thought world.

The Other Side of the Story

You may be a religious bigot. Your close-mindedness may make you cruel and tyrannical, a wet blanket who spoils everyone else's fun and spreads gloom and depression. Your judgments may be unnecessarily harsh. You may also be stingy and selfish, and an unyieldingly severe boss who becomes increasingly tyrannical as your authority grows. You may be sullen and sulk at imagined insults.

Mercury in Aquarius

You have a gift for understanding both sides of an argument and resist siding with either. This equanimity may cause misunderstandings among associates and family members, who in emotionally charged moments usually demand a show of partiality. But you are too independent-minded to fall for this unless the subject happens to be one of your pet concerns. Then you can be as one-eyed as anyone, going so far as to verge on the fanatical.

You have a fine, versatile and broad mind. The petty issues of life and its superficial curiosities don't appeal to you much. You acquire knowledge to put it to work where it will do the most good for the greatest number. Scientific inquiry has a special attraction for you. Your mind can range over complex issues and with remarkable intuition light on the weakest point. You are capable of offering solutions that may be quite breathtaking in their originality and scope.

You are often drawn to the communications industries, using them to disseminate your ideas and to draw attention to necessary reforms. Broadcasting, television, magazine, book or newspaper publishing usually figure prominently in this combination.

You are an excellent judge of human nature but very tolerant of what you find. As a rule, you are not the type who goes in for deep emotional attachments. Aquarius embody the inventive and humanitarian impulses and thus need to be objective to function at their best. Emotionalism with its accompanying biases is something you try to exclude from your private life, too, so when it comes to love affairs, you're a bit too offhand and casual for the usual partner. You need a special kind of person who won't pester you with demands for devotion you are incapable of fulfilling. The exception to this may occur if your Sun happens to be in Pisces.

You are happier with groups where you can be friendly to everyone and get on with the business in hand. This business usually has some worthwhile objective, which may range from a plan for feeding the starving millions to a program for getting public support for a charity endeavor. You often join clubs, associations and movements connected with welfare.

You are a great mixer and enjoy conversing with people who have new and stimulating ideas like your own. Being intellectually bright, you enjoy the challenge and excitement of a controversial discussion. Sometimes you may go so far as to propound a proposition that you don't really believe in—purely for the satisfaction of sharpening your wits on an opponent.

Your social conscience is probably far more developed than that of your family and their friends. Your efforts to awaken in others an interest in the larger issues of life may earn you a reputation for heterodoxy or eccentricity.

If your Sun is also in Aquarius, the characteristics described above are more pronounced and you desire more effective expression. With this combination, you better appreciate the ramifications of what you are attempting and can see even greater possibilities in your mind. For the scientific thinker, deep theoretical speculation and inspired insights lead to inventions and innovations beyond those originally visualized. The artistic temperament is stronger.

With the Sun in Capricorn and Mercury in Aquarius, the emphasis is on action. Ideas are looked at more closely for their immediate practical application. There is a tendency to reject the more speculative and experimental propositions. Artistry is not so important. Words are used with clarity but in a down-to-earth style.

With the Sun in Pisces and Mercury in Aquarius, the person is supersensitive and capable of communicating his or her feelings and ideas in artistic ways. The humanitarian instincts are heightened and the desire to help others is much more personalized and emotional.

The Other Side of the Story

Your thought processes are erratic and confusing. Just when you have captured your audience, you dart off at a tangent, make some silly inappropriate observation or lose your train of thought. You probably find it hard to string three ideas together without being distracted. Your mind is curiously alert, flitting from one incidental happening to another, but incapable of sustaining one-track momentum. You choose friends who are your intellectual inferiors. When criticized or opposed in argument, you probably stutter or become spitefully indignant.

Mercury in Pisces

You're no great scientific mind. Your powers of reasoning are not conspicuous. But by golly, you've got tremendous understanding of people; and you know many things beyond the ken of others. It's not that you aren't intelligent. Far from it. It's just that the Pisces influence compels you to dispense largely with logical processes and rely mainly on instinct and intuition for your guidance.

You have a wonderful memory, especially for your childhood days. You spend much of your time wandering through these cerebral labyrinths, reflecting on this and that, and catching glimpses of astounding truths associated with past events. Whereas others grow brainier by absorbing great masses of useless information (much of which is only handy for watching television quiz shows), you educate yourself through the medium of inner feelings and emotions—that is, through self-knowledge. This is pretty powerful medicine. And that's why, on many occasions, you mentally poleax those who worship the god of reason by making uncanny prophecies that come true. You're a deep one, all right. And although you're pretty moody and exasperatingly vague at times, you prove consistently that there's something more profound in this wonderful life than a reasonable and clever mind!

You've got a lot of common sense, too. And when it comes to getting your own way by pretending, you'll win an Oscar every time. You absorb quickly and respond spontaneously. A tremendous capacity for showing sympathy to others and for understanding their intimate problems ensures a continual procession of friends. These people may not stay very long in your life, but they will certainly never forget you.

It is not unusual for Mercury in Pisces individuals to be employed in hospitals and other institutions where they can express their compassion in practical caring. Mind you, unless you are satisfying your urge for self-sacrifice, you will be easily upset by uncongenial environments. To everyone else, a place might seem cheery and harmonious, but you will pick up the discordant psychic impressions of previous occupants and events. Emotional turmoil and even physical illness can follow. Buying a house with a Mercury in Pisces person can be a long process of elimination by intangibles.

You are fond of pleasure and variety and enjoy exciting company until the urge for seclusion inevitably returns.

You tend to avoid responsibility and to project your troubles onto the one who's nearest and dearest. You are assailed by feelings of unworthiness and may long to extirpate a vague guilt. You are not built to cope with sustained mental pressure, and if forced to, may suffer a nervous breakdown. You are capable of describing occult and mystical matters with great insight and fluidity.

If your Sun is also in Pisces, you may have im-paired concentration and substitute an imaginative world for harsh reality. You are easily offended, supra-impressionable and so frequently misunderstood that you make as few social contacts as possible. Your inspiration is heightened by the Sun in this position, and you probably write poetry only a very few people will ever be allowed to read.

With the Sun in Aquarius, the urge to participate in large-scale humanitarian ventures may be irresistible, even to the point of interrupting an established career. You will probably travel to unusual places and absorb yourself at some time in trying to solve a mystery.

With the Sun in Aries, you are more positive and much less likely to be imposed upon or to delude yourself with fantasies. In this position, inspiration has a good chance of being translated into action. Revealing psychic insights may be written down and given to the world.

The Other Side of the Story

Your idealistic and wordy notions of how humanity can be saved are nothing more than gas-bagging. You'll talk about the past for hours, but when the time for action arrives, you'll disappear or blame someone or something for your slackness. You meet opposition with abject surrender and are incapable of facing up to your obligations. You are likely to live off others by stirring their sympathies with lying stories about your misfortunes. Doubts about your own mental health may exacerbate a fairly miserable and pathetic existence.

CHAPTER SEVENTEEN

Venus

This chapter on Venus gives you some facts about the planet's physical features, the myths and symbolism surrounding it, and an astrological account of its characteristics. Then follows a description of Venus in the various zodiacal signs.

The Planet

Venus is the brightest of all the planets. It orbits the Sun between Mercury and the Earth. It is the nearest planet to us and approaches to within 25 million miles.

Venus' size is roughly the same as the Earth's—7600 miles in diameter. The Venusian year is 225 Earth days. The planet's orbit is almost circular, so there is little variation in its 67-million-mile distance from the Sun.

In common with the other planets, Venus moves around the Sun in the same direction as the Earth. But it is the only one that rotates on its axis in the opposite direction.

Venus is often called the morning or evening star, depending on when it is visible, which varies with the time of the year. Observed from the Earth, the planet is never more than 48 degrees away from the Sun. When it is the evening star, we can see it for 3 hours and 12 minutes after sunset. At its brightest, Venus is 6 times as bright as Jupiter and 15 times as bright as Sirius, the brightest star in the sky.

In 1962, U.S. Mariner 2 recorded the surface temperature of Venus as 800° F. In 1967, the Russians soft-landed an instrumented canister on the planet from their Venus 4 research spacecraft. The data showed a very hostile environment of high atmospheric pressure and an atmosphere of almost pure carbon dioxide. Twin landings by Venus 5 and Venus 6 in 1969 provided information about the planet's mysterious veil of white clouds which account for its relatively high reflecting power.

The density of the planet is closest to the Earth's, being 5.23 times greater than water compared with the Earth's 5.52 times.

Symbolism

Venus or Aphrodite is the goddess of attraction, desire and eternal love. She was associated by the ancients with the spring, femininity and all things beautiful. She is said to have sprung from the seed of Uranus and to have risen naked from the sea, as in Botticelli's well-known painting, "The Birth of Venus."

According to Homer, Venus was unfaithful to her husband Vulcan and in love with Aries, or Mars, the god of war. Venus had many other lovers and several children. Her love for the mortal Adonis is the theme of Shakespeare's *Venus and Adonis*. Homer tells of her passion for Anchises, to whom she bore Aeneas, the hero of Virgil's epic poem.

Venus is a compelling figure in lore. She possesses a magic girdle that confers irresistible loveliness upon its wearer. Many flowers are named after Venus. Doves, symbol of peace, and sparrows, inveterate songbirds, are sacred to her. Everything graceful and fine comes from . . . one touch of Venus.

Astrology

Venus in the horoscope indicates a person's love life, the pleasures and luxuries he or she enjoys, social adjustment and the refinements that lead to gracious behavior and artistic expression.

It also represents ease, beauty, indolence and pleasure seeking. If Venus is in a strong position in your birth chart, you can be rather superficial and a light thinker. You enjoy the perfumed distractions of life and ignore the essences, make charming but inconsequential conversation, are nice to everyone and extremely popular in the best of social circles. You can be the host or hostess with the mostest, possessing all the delightful attributes that make relationships amiable and satisfying as long as the harsher and sterner realities of existence can be held at bay.

Venus is essentially fruitful and feminine like the Moon. Both rule the gentler and finer emotions of men and women. On their own, they are inclined to be vacillating and lacking in direction and discipline. But given the support of more positive and purposeful influences in the horoscope, the Venus accomplishments are often splendid and always artistically pleasing or uplifting. Much depends on the Sign in which the planet is placed and the aspects it receives from the other planets in the horoscope.

Venus is known as the "lesser benefic" or "lesser fortune." Jupiter, the giant of our solar system deemed to be the dignified, moralistic planet, is known as the "greater fortune." The influence of Venus is more material, more physical. It gives earthly happiness to man and woman through mating. It is the finer part of lovemaking. It rules the clothes, the plumage, the colors, the dance, the song and the alluring gestures that are inseparable from the mating game. It keeps the lovers tantalizingly but exquisitely apart, insisting on the proprieties and gentle play before the consummating act of union. Venus is desire, never gross, salacious appetite. Any coarseness or "venal" influence comes from another source.

Venus rules the magnetic quality of beauty, which includes symmetry and proportion. It is the genius of the arts and the inspiration of the artistic. Venus personifies partnership, generosity, mutual giving, agreeableness, good humor—and most of all, harmony.

Venus rules two zodiacal Signs—Taurus and Libra. Taurus is an earth Sign and represents possessions, money, security, the sense of values—all that symbolizes unity by gathering in and attaching to oneself. Libra is an air Sign and represents the desire to bring together, to unify by an outward-going effort, to bring relationships into harmony, to balance circumstances, to equate so that all is at rest as one.

A Venus that is not unfavorably aspected invariably bestows remarkable quality of beauty. This may not be "handsomeness" or "prettiness" in the usual sense, but an etheric fineness of form, a feature, a curve—that certain something in a person that arrests the inner eye. Venus also endows a man or woman with good taste, an appreciation of clothes and grooming and a refinement of manner that is reflected in the way the home is furnished and decorated.

Venus people are usually very popular, especially with the opposite sex. As their role is to smooth out the rough and discordant by harmonizing relationships, they are extremely polite and charming people as a general rule and very agreeable company. They are sympathetic, pleasing, lovable and affectionate. Consequently, they are usually in demand as companions and receive many gifts, invitations and compliments. Sometimes they are showered with luxuries. All this ill equips them to deal with physical adversity. Poverty, squalor and deprivation usually leave them wilting on the vine.

Venus often shows a very determined and percussive streak. If you hit the detonator in the right place, it will explode in your face. The Taurus person will absorb a tremendous amount of provocation before putting his head down and charging with all the fury of an enraged Bull. The Libra person will bend over backward to placate and conciliate, but if he feels an injustice is being done, his eyes will flash and he'll hit out with an impulsive and aggressive indignation that springs from Venus' zodiacal lover and opposite number—none other than the fiery and impetuous Mars!

Look for your Venus placement in the tables or from your astro profile and completed horoscope chart. With good aspects, the positive values of Venus are pronounced in accordance with the Signs where it appears. Venus is at home in Taurus and in Libra. That means Venus is in the Signs it rules. Venus is exalted in the Sign of Pisces. Here the influence of Venus is accentuated to a great extent. Venus in Pisces represents the most idealistic expression of universal love and platonic love, and gives rise to the most exquisite expressions of art and poetry and music.

With bad aspects, Venus can be out of sync with the surroundings, and it will not be such a comfortable placement. In Scorpio and in Aries, the Mars-ruled Signs opposite Taurus and Libra respectively, Venus loses its harmony. Here there is conflict. In the Sign of Virgo, Venus is comparatively weak giving rise to reserve or coldness or possibly just inhibition.

Venus people have a fondness for poetry, music, good food, soft lights and genteel conversation. They often paint, sculpt or sing. They have a flair for interior design, architecture and sometimes flower arranging. They are often connected with the professional side of providing high-class furnishings for homes and offices.

Physiologically, Venus (not surprisingly) rules the venous circulation, the afferent nerves and the return phase of the bodily cycles to their respective centers. Eating, the assimilation of food, the feeling of satisfaction that this produces, and all the other gratifying processes, are the domain of Venus. So also are the throat and kidneys (throat, Taurus; kidneys, Libra).

Venus in Aries

You are a passionate, restless and sexually attractive person. You have a roving eye that is quick to spot a possible conquest; and you act with alacrity and a great deal of impetuous charm. You are forever chasing the beautiful in life, whether it is a woman, a man, an experience or a possession—but it always seems to elude you. Although you are never satisfied, you will never give up the search.

You are exciting and brilliant. You flash from one activity to another. You are usually artistic and gifted, though you seldom manage to realize your full potential of creative expression because you have neither the time nor the patience. You direct your artistic drive into a bewildering variety of forms, some of them extremely energetic. You enjoy displaying your physical artistry and are often a stylish dancer, figure skater, gymnast or the like. Your prowess can also extend to the basketball court or the baseball field, but here you are not so much a combative type as a pure artist who keeps the crowd on its feet with your superb displays of skill.

You are an intense person but your emotions run along the surface. You are capable of great ardor but it quickly evaporates. You are an idealist and your conceptions of love and life very seldom match reality. You are searching for a perfection that can never be possessed. To your companions you seem fickle. No affair lasts for very long because your partners have very little hope of conforming to your abstract standards. To you, love is a mental thing that hides behind, but not in, the feelings. It waves enticingly—and off you dash, plunging impulsively into the stormy sea of emotion. You are single-minded in your pursuit because you are ruled by the head and not the heart. You fluctuate between ardent fire and cool detachment so that your loved ones are never quite sure of where they will stand from one hour to the next. If you do choose to settle down, you will aggressively fight off all rivals and contenders. You won't play second fiddle.

You are likely to marry early in life when your idealized conceptions lack the tempering of experience. Thus you may wed more than once. You may be woefully disappointed, but the scars won't last. Like that ancient Scottish King and the spider, you will try, try and try again. You need to love and to be loved, but you are not very good at going about it. You can be in love with the idea of love—and miss out on the real thing. Without love, you feel lost and sink into a brooding depression. You are a contradiction—an incurable romanticist and a sensationalist. You lose yourself in the glamour of the chase.

Venus in Aries is not a very good combination for a woman. The soft, feminine Venus is burned up in the aggressive masculinity of Aries, which, of course, is ruled by Mars. The Venus side of the nature gets no scope to charm, to gracefully arrange things into attractive patterns, to luxuriate. The love nature becomes demanding, impetuous, even ruthless—although always giving. Dashing Aries is more the knight in shining armor who races in quickly and rides off alone into the sunset as soon as it's over. For the feminine side of a person, which craves the stability of home and children, this is a disadvantage. Sometimes these people see themselves as their own persecutors. They have a need to be dominated, a factor which can resolve their basic problem.

You long for the security of love, but when you find it you tend to resent and rebel against the restrictions it imposes upon your freedom.

You are not a domesticated person. But you are far from hardhearted. You respond quickly to any appeal for help. Open-handed generosity can be almost a fault. You will give time and money to a person in need or to a worthy cause. Your sympathies lie very close to the surface and are easily touched. Quite often you accept people and situations as they appear, and are deceived.

The Other Side of the Story

You may be all head and no finer feelings, a heartless, roaming seducer. You are likely to be a promiscuous hedonist always on the lookout for sensation and gratification. You may use your artistic inclinations as a screen for your shallow intentions and excesses. You are likely to be ruthless and cruel. Your impulsive, thoughtless and inconsiderate actions may make life a torture for those who love you or live with you. You are apt to react violently when others fail to meet your impossible emotional demands. You may try to buy people and believe that money and gifts are a fair exchange for love and devotion. You may be discontented, frustrated and self-torturing. Bitterness and inner emptiness are likely to make growing old a travail.

Venus in Taurus

You have a very simple and direct approach to love. To you, to love another person is to love them physically and with your heart. And if you can do this, and at the same time make your life more comfortable—for instance, by marrying into money—you will probably live happily ever after. Incidentally, this may be a universal dream of mortals, though with most others it usually remains just a dream. However, realization of this dream is almost a characteristic of the Venus in Taurus combination, all other things being equal.

Here, the planet that symbolizes romance, beauty and love of comfort is in her own Sign. Like the charming, affectionate and gracious woman she represents, she is at home. Taurus is the Sign of money and possessions. Between them, they usually have a ball.

You are practical and uncomplicated in your love life. You don't like making the best of things. You realize you have an innate longing for comfort and security and that it is much easier for you to be affectionate and loving in a pleasing environment. You are prepared to wait for these things—and (as often happens) for the right person to come along and provide them. This is one reason why people born with Venus in Taurus are usually late developers sexually. They seem to know subconsciously they may have a long wait for the right marriage partner so they reject the risks and possible complications of premature sex. Other aspects in the birth chart must, of course, be considered.

Meanwhile, you work diligently toward providing yourself with all the comforts you long for. Seldom prepared to sit back and be idle, you know what you want and will work with great patience and determination to get it. You like to surround yourself with possessions because they ensure that you won't be victimized by harsh necessity, the thought of which appalls you. You also want what you own to be elegant and beautiful as possible. You regard your body as your first possession—and you make a point

of keeping it attractively healthy and well groomed. You have a flair for tasteful and appropriate dressing.

You furnish your home with the same artistic discrimination—and your office, as well, if your position allows it. You enjoy good companionship and mixing at the highest social level you can command. You pursue pleasure in a leisurely but determined way. You are an amiable and friendly person; people warm to you quickly and are pleased to be in your company. You are fond of giving gifts—you relish the feeling of pleasure that others receive from them. One reason you desire wealth is that it will permit you to entertain and share the luxury of your home. You need to possess psychologically so that you can unite the act of giving and receiving into one delicious feeling of having harmonized two opposites.

You have a penchant for creating pleasing effects. You are an admirer of natural beauty. In sex, you are modest and decorous but quite straightforward and unashamed of nakedness and your body. Sex is the most natural thing in the world to you—once you have decided to yield to it. You are an emotional and feeling creature. Idealistic love, platonic love mean very little to you. You are either attuned to someone or you aren't, but you are always aware of your personal magnetism and the subtle power of your physical presence and body movements. You give the impression of great passion and the capacity to love and be loved. And it is so . . . but not until it suits you. Then, and only then, are you capable of all that Venus promises.

You are likely to inherit money. You can be successful in business partnerships. Artistic pursuits offer you the chance of greatest satisfaction, but unless there are other favorable influences in the horoscope, you are probably not strikingly original. You are basically conservative and would rather put your trust in tried and proven methods than take risks experimenting.

Men with this combination have an intuitive understanding of women and are very attractive to them. They enjoy the domestic life and are good providers. Venus in Taurus women similarly appreciate masculine qualities and needs. They seldom remain single.

The Other Side of the Story

You may be a sucker—too quickly convinced, too easily taken in. You are likely to be ruled by your emotions and be incapable of mature, rational judgment. You can be horribly artificial, pretentious, affected in speech and mannerisms—an empty-headed social climber who is satisfied with basking in the reflected glory of the rich and famous. You may be mixed up, confused and unable to approach life's problems and joys simply and directly. The prospect of growing old is likely to horrify you. You can be inordinately susceptible to physical attractions and have little control over your sexual urges.

Venus in Gemini

You are not a passionate person in the normal sense. Your sexual contacts are made with enthusiasm but not much fire. You are a bright spark but no glowing ember. The earthy, emotional Venus is at a disadvantage in the airy, heady, intellectual atmosphere of Gemini. Here she loses much of her physical warmth and devotional power. Instead of judging and valuing experience through the feelings, she rationalizes. This is the Sign of intellect, the world of thought, reason and cold logic. The loving Venus lives here in the mind and very little in the body.

You are a mental lover. You engage in affairs for the idea of love and are frequently disappointed. You dream up images and situations that people can't measure up to and circumstances won't allow. You idealize your attractions. You work yourself into a mental state of desire that is electrifying but short-lived. You can't maintain a passionate relationship for long—your love affairs have to be continually revitalized by the power of your imagination, for your energy is of restless, nervous origin and lives off the conflict and contrast of ideas.

You understand love—you can write about it, talk about it with extraordinary insight—but you don't feel love to the depths of its wonderful profundity as ordinary long-suffering and tormented lovers do. You experience a fleeting, superficial sensation. At times, you are even intensely jealous. But always it is an attachment of the mind, and it wanes as soon as you know the person sufficiently or a substitute new source of knowledge is available.

You enjoy having admirers and you usually manage to attract quite a few at a time. You are extremely interesting and amusing company. You can debate just about any subject. Venus gives you the artistic verve and panache to impress the most sophisticated audiences.

She refines your mind, makes it lyrical, poetical, imaginative. You can detach yourself from the human scene in a way others can't. As a writer, actor or entertainer reporting or miming the weaknesses and absurdities of the passing parade, you are peerless.

You enjoy attention and diversity. You love to flirt. Because your emotional anchors are short-tied and seldom get hooked on the bottom, you are capable of keeping several love affairs going at once. Though these dalliances often cause you a fair amount of trouble, you revel in the fun, excitement and danger of multiple affairs and slip in and out of romantic snares with a will o' the wisp dexterity. You don't really fancy the obligations of married life. If you do marry, you often marry twice. Rarely do you find the man or woman you are looking for, but by one of the foibles of human nature that you can lampoon so amusingly, you insist on fidelity in your romantic entourage. Venus in Gemini people love to have a harem of vivacious and intelligent men or women whom they can visit or call up at any hour of the day or night.

You entice the opposite sex in an indefinably subtle way with a suggestion of promise, a floating seductiveness, an aura of refined and mysterious intimacy that when reached for, just isn't there. You delight. You disappoint. You delight again.

You are fond of traveling. You don't like hard physical work or the seamy side of life. You are attracted to quasi-artistic occupations where you can demonstrate your talents for original ideas and invention. Music, drama, teaching and writing also appeal, but sometimes you are hampered by a lack of formal education due to restlessness in your youth.

The Venus in Gemini woman has a rather material outlook where love is concerned. She is likely to use her wits and sex appeal to extract money and gifts from her beguiled admirers.

This combination gives a flair for trickery in both the male and the female, and an adroitness at providing remarkably plausible cover stories.

The Other Side of the Story

You may be a loquacious freeloader, eating and drinking off your friends, battening on any new acquaintances who happen to come along. You are likely to be immature and completely lacking in ambition. You may lie and cheat rather than go to work. You will probably get mixed up in some sort of fraud, possibly associated with fine arts, antiques, paintings or the like. You may be a bigamist. You are likely to use your charm and gift of gab to extort money and possessions from others, especially if they show a liking for you. You may indifferently betray those who have put their faith in you and blithely leave your responsibilities for others to cope with. You may be a barfly. Loneliness among the crowd may be your cross.

Venus in Cancer

Though you have a great need to love and be loved, you are not the type to go chasing after love or the companions whose company you enjoy. You prefer to sit and wait—knowing love will come. You will never say it hasn't come because tomorrow is another day. You have an abiding faith—a little too much at times—in the eternal life process that is said to provide everything with what it needs eventually. This probably explains why you find it so hard to resist the sensuous advances of another person. You need love, it is offered, you accept. Your propensity to take love as though it were the open-handed gift of destiny lands you in considerable trouble sometimes.

Venus is the planet of attraction and Cancer is the Sign of growth; together they make seductive melodies. But the love songs are not just those of physical attraction. You are deeply loving and sentimental about your family. Venus takes on a very maternal quality here, even in men. You are mothering and protective toward your near ones. You work to make the nest as comfortable, as soft and warm as humanly possible. You nourish, pet and cherish. You also want to be appreciated and fussed over yourself. To you, the home is the reassuring emotional center where you like to rest contented and undisturbed with all you love safe around you—and loving and admiring you in return for your good qualities. Given this, you are a loyal and nurturing partner.

But you are a bit too soft. Venus here makes you vulnerable to the machinations of loved ones who want to take advantage of you. You can be easily imposed upon—aggressive personalities can tear you to emotional shreds, even though you may not show your hurt. You may brood, become unhappy, sink into despondency. You may have a mother complex. There are likely to be obstacles to marriage. Your love life seldom runs smooth.

You need a positive outlet for your emotions. To bottle them up inside is like taking a dose of poison—it affects you physically. You are likely to suffer from digestive troubles and stomach complaints that are difficult to diagnose. To have something to love and serve is a kind of panacea—it keeps you fit psychologically, emotionally and physically.

If you can't lavish your affections on your family or another person, you are apt to turn your attention to the needs of humanity and serve some cause with slavish devotion. Sometimes you may devote your life to religion. Martyrdom is not beyond you.

Secret love affairs are very likely with this combination. Your receptive, sympathetic and loving nature is extremely attractive to married people disillusioned by their partners. More than one marriage is likely. Someone much older or younger than yourself is apt to figure prominently in your love life. As well as a strong sharing of passion, there may be a deep mutual attachment to metaphysical or occult matters. You have a profound appreciation of spiritual and mystical things that goes far deeper than orthodox religious beliefs. You enjoy the mysterious side of life. You are psychic, even though you may not publicize the fact.

You are charitable, sincere and kindhearted. You enjoy talking and listening to people and would make an excellent teacher or nurse; others sense your understanding and are encouraged by it. Your love of the home makes you a competent cook and able housekeeper. You may sometimes choose an occupation that others regard as inferior to your talents or station. Your associates can be of a lower social status, and you are not averse to now and again befriending people down on their luck and taking them in.

Although naturally reserved, you may become a popular public figure. You can usually make money dealing in liquids. Land and houses can also be profitable.

You love beauty and are attracted to music, literature and art. You have a secret longing for the splendor and elegant living (and loving) of the past.

The Other Side of the Story

You may be exceedingly sensual, unable to say no. You are apt to attract notoriety through your permissive behavior. You may be an emotional wreck, torn between simultaneous different passions and loves. You are likely to be ridiculously shy and self-conscious. Your hysterically emotional scenes may be the dread of your family and all who associate with you. You can be so unstable that you feel you have no permanent identity. On the other hand, you may be a social stick-in-the-mud. Your narrow possessiveness may make loved ones unhappy. You are likely to be absurdly responsive to flattery.

Venus in Leo

You can't help but attract the attention of the opposite sex. You love to be admired, and you're very good at dramatizing your entrances and timing your moves. You are always aware of who's looking and who's not but who ought to be. You are positive in speech and fluidly graceful in movement—the epitomy of an actor or actress who knows how to please an audience. You're Daniel or Danielle in the Lion's Den, and they're waiting to eat out of your hand.

You enjoy entertaining, particularly in luxurious surroundings. The most influential and glamorous people in town attend your parties. You are never awed or outshone. Your innate gift of showmanship ensures that you receive the Lion's share of attention, even in the most celebrated of company—and usually, not without merit. Your talent for self-expression is quite splendid to behold. The more personally demanding a social situation, the better you perform. Your art is the art of attraction: the result, understandably, is popularity.

You are often a pacesetter in fashions and fads. Venus gives you the capacity to combine color and form into universally pleasing patterns, and Leo provides the magic touch for projecting them as styles worth emulating. The thin line between a trend setter and an eccentric is often no more than the expressive flair this combination is able to bestow.

You are immensely warmhearted and kind, though on the proud side about receiving due respect. Although your gestures may be extravagant and at times ostentatious, your sincerity is unquestionable. You are out to impress, to be admired, there's no doubt about that, but you are conscious of people's deeper feelings. You have a loathing for all that is petty, spiteful, mean and unfair. You enjoy sharing your good fortune with others; an opportunity to do someone an unexpected good turn delights you.

You love excitement in all its sensual forms. Romance is something you can't live without, though it is often a source of disillusionment and sorrow. You love with your heart—each affair is the love of your life. You are generous to a fault with your emotions and possessions and tireless in your attempts to please the one you love. In return, you expect similar treatment and devotion. Not surprisingly, you are frequently disappointed and suffer bottomless despair. Nothing makes you more miserable than to discover your mate was only human after all and subject to the same frailties you sometimes turn a blind eye to in yourself. Until you learn that your great capacity to love has an altruistic function beyond individual desire, you go on loving, serving and being hurt, time after time.

You usually earn a living through a creative activity, especially writing and entertainment. In rarer instances, this combination can produce, through love, a saintliness that seeks to serve mankind without any attempt at personal aggrandizement.

If your social life becomes too absorbing, there is the danger your personality will become lost in superficialities. The need to be admired and talked about may induce an inordinate preoccupation with clothes, hairdressers, frivolous relationships, gossip and the like. The need to impress may lead to extreme forms of affectation, including speech. Overindulgence in food, drink and the party life may affect your health.

You have a knack of knowing a good investment when you see one and are quite likely to be a successful gambler or speculator as long as you refrain from acting until you know you are onto a good thing. Young people are good for you and often bring you luck. Most of your friends are probably junior to you in age. You stand to gain from an inheritance, sooner or later.

The Other Side of the Story

You frequently fall in love with people who don't reciprocate your affections or who betray you. You have experienced some fearful heartbreaks in your love life. You are bombastic, conceited and a show-off. Although you crave love, your manner attracts those who are incapable of giving it. You may mistake lust for love. After you gain another's affection, you ruin things by being domineering and possessive. If you don't receive sufficient attention (one might almost say worship), you sulk, find fault and try to pick arguments. Your taste in clothes is garish and gaudy. If a woman, you overdo the perfume, jewelry and makeup. Your taste in artistic things is showy and vulgar; everything essentially fine in its appeal is overstressed.

Venus in Virgo

Let's face it, you are not a spontaneous lover. In fact, you distribute your affections with deliberative care. You never really fall hopelessly in love, throwing discretion to the winds and passionately sharing your body and your being. No sir. You love in a very different way. You love—with service and with your mind. You seldom manage to express exactly what you feel. The world owes a lot to your type, although you are frequently misunderstood. You epitomize the goodness of supreme usefulness. You do not, as a rule, waste your energies in erotic or sentimental flights—or falls. You can be distraught, but rarely hysterical.

With this combination, the influences in the rest of the horoscope are exceedingly important. This description applies only to your Venus being placed in Virgo. On its own, it is a suppressed and intellectual position for the planet of love and beauty. Warmth elsewhere in the chart will soften the effects defined. The Sun in Libra or Leo, for instance, will help.

Above everything else, you are practical. You know you have to live in this world and make a go of it. You select your lovers to the best of your ability, always bearing in mind the possibility of marriage or a permanent association. You find it difficult to understand people who contract marriages based on passionate impulse when there are so many other things to be considered. You like to feel that you can help your mate by giving him or her the benefit of your experience—you want to improve your lover. Once you've found a reasonable partner to settle down with, you make the most of it. Even where there is contention and discord, you'll plug along rather than break up.

You are very sensitive and extremely aware of imperfections. Your impulse is to help, to serve, to improve, to reform, so when you spot weaknesses in people, you speak out. Though your intentions are the best, you often earn yourself a reputation for being hypercritical and outspokenly rude. The fact that what you say is usually true doesn't help you to hold friends. But that's you. And perhaps its one reason why you encourage acquaintances but are very wary of allowing close relationships. This reserve can attract people who admire cool indifference and self-possession.

Actually, you possess an acute desire to be appreciated and respected. You are not egotistical, but you want desperately to be needed. Once you are, the way is clear for you to serve diligently—and without question—and you are at your happiest.

If you are incapable of strongly expressing the emotion of love, you are certainly more capable than most of the labors of love. There is no end to your dutiful devotion as an employee, husband, wife or parent.

You will make a comfortable home for your mate

or family. Or you will serve a cause in the most menial way with selfless dedication. Quite often your inability to find personal love means that the world as a whole benefits. As a physician or nurse, you are capable of showing the utmost tenderness and care, tempered with an intelligent regard for the patient's good. Where others may indulge and harm someone out of pity, you have the strength and wit to withhold out of kindness.

If other influences are favorable, you can often gain materially through your partner. But this combination is not notable for happiness through the opposite sex. You are inclined to get involved with lovers who turn out to be materialistic, cold or callous. Secret romances that can never be revealed, delays in marriage and love affairs with people who are chronically ill or socially "inferior" are not uncommon.

The Other Side of the Story

Every attempt to express your emotions is probably misinterpreted and leads to sorrow. While you long to be loved, your fastidiousness and faultfinding rebuff and repel. You are apt to be all head and no heart, capable of deliberate mental cruelty. The absence of any real sympathy in yourself may make you ride roughshod over the feelings of others. In extreme cases, money may be made from drug pushing or other activities that show a pitiless disregard for human misery and suffering. Scandal is likely through associating with petty criminals and other similarly undesirable characters.

Venus in Libra

Beauty and harmony are essential for your enjoyment of life. This applies not only to your surroundings but also to your associates, right down to their attitudes, mannerisms and speech. Anything clumsy, jarring, coarse, blatant, uncouth or basically inelegant is distasteful to you. With this wondrously idealistic discriminating faculty functioning for you in a world more noted for its gaucheries than its graces, one would expect you to have a fairly rough ride, your sensibilities continually bruised. But not so. You're a subtle one. You weave, not a web like the spider, but in and out of the spider's web. You are adroit and entirely successful at building your own little private world of relative peace and harmony.

You have your bad moments and disappointments, of course, but they don't last long. If you can't harmonize a situation with your ineffable charm, you'll just take off.

You are a social creature above everything else. You adore dressing up in fine clothes, going to parties, entertaining, welcoming, greeting, conversing—all on a refined level. When the going gets too boisterous, you prefer to retreat to a comfortable armchair and discuss the weather or the latest in topic with a like-minded companion while amusedly viewing the action. You love cultured pastimes and dignified novelty.

Nothing pleases Venus in Libra more than to be with people in the higher strata of society—the wealthy and the influential (which often includes yourself). Your associates and friends are usually artistic and philosophical types and one or two of them are apt to be famous in their fields. You have a great fondness for painting, poetry, music and singing and could distinguish yourself in one of these areas. Your innate love of beauty and harmony is reflected in your extremely fine taste. You are probably capable of earning your living through one of the beautifying professions or industries such as interior decorating, cosmetics, fashion apparel, hair styling and architecture.

You possess strong magnetism, both physical and emotional. You unconsciously attract the people who appeal to you. In the old days, people would have said you were something of a sorcerer or sorceress. You beguile, emitting a promise so subtle that it exists only in the other party's awakened curiosity. You are sympathetic, kind and conciliatory, always ready with the oil at the first sign of troubled waters. You thrive on attention. You delight in the game of being nice, courteous, obliging, diplomatic—and tantalizingly unknowable. No one realizes better than you that familiarity breeds contempt. And as long as you can conceal your real self, you know that the magic is intact.

But love changes all this. In love, you give yourself totally with mind and spirit. Sometimes you are more in love with love than with the individual. You are blinded by the emotion. You tend to put your lovers on a level impossible of attainment by human nature. This is because you are more idealistic than physical in your rich love nature. Few people can live up to the consuming perfection demanded by this combination. So Venus in Libra folk sometimes garner a reputation for changing partners more frequently than others.

You love all the refinements of courtship, the flowers, phone calls, pretty words, chocolates, expensive note paper—and the full formal preliminaries. Sir Walter Raleigh, who threw his cloak on the muddy ground for Elizabeth to walk across, personifies the gracious sophistication that you adore as a woman and applaud as a man.

The ritual of love often means more to you than its consummation. Partnerships usually bring luck and money.

The Other Side of the Story

You are perversely cruel to those who love you, always changing your mind, flighty as a woman, inconstant as a man, flitting off and coming back with brand new promises you won't keep. You are lazy and play on the emotions of others to get what you want. You put on airs and graces about your artistic talents and tastes, which are quite mediocre. You have a deep longing for a refinement you can't find in yourself. Your social-climbing antics are a joke. You may be immoral and in constant danger of exposure. Partners defraud, disappoint and steal from you. You are extravagant and seldom out of debt. Witchcraft and secret cults where sex rites are practiced may attract you. Your domestic life is probably very unhappy.

Venus in Scorpio

This is not a good position for Venus, the impulse of love and beauty. She becomes sluttish, waspish and heavy-handed. Love turns to lust and possessiveness. Violence, hatred and the desire for revenge creep in. Passion becomes a dreadful force that must be gratified . . . or else. The feelings, instead of being rounded and subtly persuasive, work with the efficiency of a stone ax. Not much that is worthwhile will endure in a romance or marriage with a person having this combination.

But wait! That's the worst of it. It may not be a description of you or your life. There are numerous modifications in the horoscope that must be considered. Important though it is, this is but one isolated factor in your birth chart. For instance, if your Sun and Mercury are in Libra or Sagittarius, this will mollify the pure effects of Venus in Scorpio. You should also remember that the circumstances of your upbringing and education will also have an effect. If you are an evolved type who has learned the lessons of self-control—and Scorpio gives tremendous potential for this—these disturbing characteristics may never surface. You will feel their pressure, no doubt, but it can be directed into meaningful and productive activity. Otherwise, what follows will be evident in your life.

The opposite sex usually means trouble for you. Although you are a passionate and exciting lover, you overdo things. Only surfeit seems to suffice. You demand more and more. You want to possess body and soul. You are self-willed and absolutely determined to have your way. Your raging and tyrannical jealousy is likely to make married life a wretched misery. Your partner may be a nervous wreck imprisoned by your suspicion, distrust and cruelty. Violence, bitter quarreling, vindictiveness are all part of this depressing scene. You may marry for money and scheme in diabolical ways to benefit from inheritances. There is not much concerning the opposite sex that some people with this combination won't exploit for their own selfish enjoyment or profit.

From the social viewpoint, there is a tendency to gravitate to a low life, where sexual perversity can be indulged without question or risk of detection. The criminal class, with its passion for secrecy and attraction for violence, may have an irresistible appeal. Scandal and mayhem follow you like a long shadow.

You love pleasure, luxury and sensation. You are quite solicitous of the welfare of the person you love most and quick to demonstrate your affection. You share what you own with your mate. You are generous with friends and a lavish spender. Although you stand to inherit money or property sometime in your life, there will probably be a long delay before they are handed over. Partnerships are apt to be lucky only amid very great upheavals. Material gains are most likely to come to fruition when sorrow and pain are at their peak.

You are continually suppressing intense emotions, which makes you frustrated, irritable, restless and dissatisfied. Your energy buildup is often at the boiling point, and you may either explode into self-destructive actions or contain them. You can literally go to heaven or to hell. The peak of mystical and religious experience is within the scope of this combination, if you can harness your incredible passion and intense purposefulness.

You are not particularly artistic but you are efficient and practical. Your mind is sharp and penetrative, so you are very good at getting to the bottom of mysteries. Occult and mystical matters may fascinate you. At some time in your life you may be moved to sublimate your emotions with an extraordinary display of willpower and devote yourself en-

tirely to some regenerative purpose. Then you will probably attract a powerful, disruptive but helpful personality.

The Other Side of the Story

Individuals with this combination can reach unnatural depths of depravity. They are also likely to commit despicably cruel acts. To satisfy their voracious emotional appetites, they may participate in all kinds of weird experiments, some of which may involve blood spilling and sexual excitation through involuntary physical pain. Dissipation may be so complete that the individual finds it impossible to pursue an ordinary livelihood. Death of the husband or wife is likely. Drunkenness and drug addiction are not uncommon. Tragedy and betrayal may lead to violent changes in lifestyle.

Venus in Sagittarius

You are an idealistic lover and a bit of a disappointment when it comes to sensual delight. Oh, you emit an aura of promise, all right. You shine like a star in any company; as a woman, you are vivacious and seductive, as a man, masculine and sexy. But between the sheets, your light may be like a neon sign—less than lukewarm to the touch.

Your affections and passions are really too broadly based to be requited by any individual. You can't bring your mind to concentrate for long on one body and one other person's desires. Carnal passions are for release, you believe, not to be lingered over. Your gaze is forever returning to the horizon. You aspire toward the unknown. You wish, through your mind, to transcend the limitations of your body. And that means you need to keep moving, meeting new people and discovering fresh interests.

A single relationship very rarely transports you to fulfillment. If it does, you are very lucky indeed. Your basic need is for a partner who will help you to develop personally, share your love of refined pleasures—and give you plenty of free rein in the bargain!

You make a far better friend than lover. You are built for camaraderie, for the brief good-natured encounter, for fun and games—and the next happy meeting. With the opposite sex, you're a bit of a tease. You love change. You adore travel. You find it very difficult to settle down to domestic routine. Although you love your children, your mind is usually concerned with the possibility of getting away from them for a while, of being freed from your responsibilities just long enough to see what is over the horizon—and then to return. You are a less reliable wife or husband. Although your intentions are loyal, you find it very difficult to go through the rigmarole of establishing and running a home.

You feel you have something special to give to the world—but you're not sure what it is. It could be a kind of universal concern that you express in philosophic or religious ideals, or perhaps by dedicating yourself to some socially desirable project. Or maybe for you the secret lies in the simple act of giving your friendship to as many people among as many races and cultures as possible. Fundamentally, you would rather serve a cause than an individual.

You love the outdoors and have a refined sense of beauty. Nature delights you. Partnership is lucky for you and usually leads to material gain. It is not at all uncommon for people having this combination to marry for money or advancement.

Romantic partners seldom live up to your high expectations. One disappointment is enough to put you off. Habitual coarseness or indelicacy will kill the affair stone dead.

You are emotionally impulsive, fickle in your affections and likely to wed two or three times. You would rather flirt than have a deep affair. Frequently the love affairs of people with Venus in Sagittarius become so complicated that the only alternative they can see is to walk out. Once they do, they only set about entangling themselves in a similar situation all over again. Because there is such a wide gap between the inner profundity of these people and their superficial behavior, they seem to take a long time to learn from their mistakes.

With Venus in Sagittarius, there is an odd attraction to foreigners. The emotions are intensified and passionate affairs are likely while traveling in other countries. The sense of freedom that goes with being in unusual and unfamiliar environments seems to intoxicate these people.

The Other Side of the Story

Your emotional irresponsibility has probably ruined your chances of happiness. You go on making the same errors over and over again, to your own and others' despair. Your friends are frequently people of ill repute whom you can't seem to shake off. You are apt to have an unhappy affair with a neighbor or a relative. You are cold to those who love you and all over those you think can help. As a parent, you will prefer to put your children into board-ing school rather than make a home for them, making some excuse about its being good for them. You are wrapped up in your own selfish enjoyments. You are quite capable of two or three simultaneous affairs, while convincing each individual he or she is your only lover.

Venus in Capricorn

In love, caution is your catchword. You do not rush into permanent liaisons, and you certainly do not risk rebuff or reprimand by making premature advances. Love is generally a separate compartment in your life that you attend to when other more important matters such as work, income and position have been satisfactorily organized. But life seldom allows such tidy scheduling—as you've no doubt discovered!

This combination produces a higher and lower type of individual. The lower type is very earthy and saturnine in the dictionary sense of the word—heavy, gloomy and dull. The constrictive planet Saturn is the ruler of Capricorn. In immature people, it literally squeezes the life out of Venus, the planet of love and beauty. These individuals make love by numbers, being incapable of spontaneous response and expression. Every action is thought out, calculated against their own self-interest. The temptation to play on the sentiments of others where there is a possibility of material gain is usually irresistible. These people are mostly hurt through their wallets. They frequently marry for money or to improve their career chances.

But the goodies with this combination are far different. Although extremely ambitious and fascinated by power and position, you don't need to tread on heads to get to the top. You attract attention through your serious and responsible attitude to life. You work extremely hard and have a rare gift for organization. You epitomize willpower, concentration and enterprise in your chosen field. People in authority trust you instinctively and usually are quick to elevate you to an executive position.

You have an inordinate desire to be respected and esteemed. You will do nothing to risk your social status or business reputation. You are diplomatic, prudent, reserved and get along well with coworkers, associates and superiors. Elders can usually be depended on to help you.

Venus in Capricorn is often a slow developer sexually. The later you marry, the better your chances of making a go of it. In the beginning, you may find it difficult to settle down in double harness. Your mate will have to get used to your reluctance to demonstrate your affections, particularly in company. You may be jealous and rather demanding in love. Jealousy in you is a compensation for feelings of insecurity, which overwhelm your normally steady mind at times. Usually there is no real justification for these fears. When you do finally settle down with a person or into any situation, you identify with it completely. Your marriage will be for keeps, as far as you are concerned. You won't be interested in cheating on your mate.

You are apt to marry someone much older or younger than yourself. Domestic happiness can't be taken for granted; with this combination, you'll have to work hard at it. Sorrow and love are never far apart. The warm and fertile Venus can't really blossom in the cold and rocky domain of the Capricorn Mountain Goat. The danger is that either you or your partner will settle into a routine dedicated to outside interests that results in mutual alienation, indifference, coldness and finally rejection.

Your relentless drives are apt to make you wealthy and influential in later years. You may possess a fine house but not a home. You may tend to starve the emotions of your nearest ones, including your children. Too many practical considerations are likely to remove any chance of a normal, happy family life. You are not the type to gad about socially. When you can take a bit of time off from work, you're more likely to sit down by the fire with an informative book or watch an instructive program on TV.

You don't possess a great eye for beauty and seldom have any special aptitude for art. But you do respect proper conduct. Steadfastness, loyalty and all the qualities that contribute to moral rectitude are deemed by you the highest good.

You are easily slighted, and like the elephant, will never forget.

The Other Side of the Story

The human side of your development may be woefully lacking, leaving you a calculating, grasping and rather pathetically isolated creature. You probably have no friends to speak of. Your marriage was probably called off, or you are unhappily tied to a partner who is cold, exacting and indifferent. You live only to possess what you desire. Any finer emotions you once had have been blunted by selfishness and acquisitiveness. Your business chances are likely to be ruined by treacherous associates. You are apt to indulge a power complex by lording it over people in inferior positions or fraternizing with socially undesirable characters.

Venus in Aquarius

You love everyone, just about. Not sexually, of course. Sexually, you are fairly choosy, with a penchant for exciting, provocative and rather unconventional playmates. For most people, love usually ends in marriage or cohabitation, but Venus makes you crave much more than that. Love to you is more an idea than an emotion. You visualize it as a broad, sweeping, exciting, reforming, universal force—which it seldom is in ordinary relationships. You want a perpetuation of the romance, the novelty, the excitement—and sooner or later, you realize this is possible only by loving humanity as a whole.

You're a strange one in many ways, nowhere near as open and shut as you seem. You are one of fate's chosen victims. Odd things happen to you, out of the blue. As much as you try to be open and sincere, you are usually forced into secret love affairs at some time or other. You are no stranger to astounding and even bizarre happenings in connection with love affairs. These experiences can change your lifestyle virtually overnight, and even put you on the other side of the globe.

You have an extraordinary capability for discerning character. Your intuition cuts through the poses of personality right into the heart of the individual. As an artist—say, a painter or a writer—you can present vivid impressions of people that are unmistakable in character, though indefinably abstract. Attempts are often made to impose on you but this remarkable instinctive faculty usually provides an insight into the other's motives. However, you will go along with a mild deception without protest, as though unconsciously aware you must not misuse your gift. Music enjoyed with others probably provides your greatest relaxation. Apart from your acute appreciation of sound, you also have a strong sense of rhythm.

You delight in meeting people and make friends very easily. You probably have a wider circle of acquaintances than anyone else in your family, apart from those with the Sun in Aquarius. You enjoy chatting to strangers, too, and will arrive home occasionally with some poor guy or gal who needs a bed for the night. This open-house attitude may disturb other members of the household. You often attract bohemian and arty types of friends whose ideas may not jell with society's. Your own views are somewhat unconventional and ahead of the times, and you delight in discussing them with similar minded individuals. You are admirably tolerant of all beliefs. Even if these conflict with your own, you are genuinely interested in understanding the attitudes of their adherents and can listen without interrupting. You really prefer to have a lot of friends than one deep personal attachment.

At heart, you are a rambler and a traveler. Your independence and freedom mean more to you than you realize—until you lose either. Then you are constantly looking over your shoulder for a means of escape. In an effort to retain your sense of liberty, you may not marry until the second half of your life (if this is a second marriage, you felt fettered by the first, which was a youthful impulse).

You enjoy platonic relationships and have a cultured and intellectual approach that appeals to deep thinkers. You are almost fanatically sincere in some of your convictions and are not afraid to stick your neck out for your friends. Before you retire from active work, you will probably realize most of your earlier hopes and wishes.

Financially, you do best working with partners, societies, associations, cooperative concerns and public enterprises.

The Other Side of the Story

You're a drifter, an advocate of hopeless causes and a friend of the lunatic fringe. Women have been responsible for much of your unhappiness. You have no respect for marriage and other cohesive social conventions. You sleep with anyone, any time, not because you are highly sexed, but because you wish to dramatize your own cravings for freedom and expression. You are likely to support anarchy and lawlessness as a means of destroying detested authority, but have no clear idea of what should be substituted.

Venus in Pisces

You spend much of your life looking for love—real love. You may find it, you may not. If you don't, you will never feel you have fulfilled your earthly purpose. If you do, you will experience an ecstatic devotional completeness. But can it last? Is it forever? Chances are, you'll discover it is not. But you will have the satisfaction of knowing you have loved more profoundly and consumingly than most others even dream of.

Venus in Pisces is at her most idealistic, emotional and loving best. Here the goddess of love and beauty is searching for something that may not be attainable in this world. But that won't stop her from trying.

You are kind, generous, sensitive and extremely compassionate. Self-sacrifice in love is natural to you—in fact, you are inclined to be too willing to surrender yourself to another, too eager to worship your beloved. Wherever your tender feelings are aroused, you can't resist the role of selfless comforter or bemused, adoring lover. Of course, other strengthening influences in the horoscope can make you more practical and self-preserving, assuming that these qualities are to be preferred. Sun in Aries or Capricorn, for instance, will bestow a more urgent sense of self.

On its own, Venus in Pisces is a cherishing and self-abnegating impulse. At the same time, it helps to make you fickle. In the search for love, you are likely to spread your net of gentle affections over a very wide area. Quite unconsciously, you drag in a lot of odd fish, as well as the occasional real prospect. If it is not the real thing, you tire very quickly and move on. The idol you are seeking is the person who conforms to your peculiar ideals, some of which have no relation to human nature. But you are willing to plug the holes in the characters you find with your incredible plastic imagination. Consequently, you are frequently disillusioned or heartbroken.

Personal love is not the only string on your emotional violin. You are also passionately responsive to any form of human sorrow or suffering. You will pick up any tragic stray who catches your attention and minister to him or her with melting concern. As some of these people are not always victims of circumstances but suffering rather from an overdose of self-inflicted maladjustment, you often emerge badly mauled here, too. You have an unfortunate habit of attracting individuals who play on your placid, yielding sympathy.

Venus in Pisces can be very badly misused by rogues and opportunists. However, if you manage to fall in love with a genuinely helpless or underprivileged, dependent person, you can really have a ball. But the pressure of worldly responsibility, finding the money and paying the bills, has to be be left to someone else. You are a poor battler when it comes to coping with cruel reality. Loving—even dying—is easy for you; but living is hard. Venus in Pisces is fulfilled by the exquisite sensation of yielding all to another.

Trust is intrinsic to your nature. You don't hold

grudges and are far too forgiving and understanding to make enemies.

Although sociable, cheerful, hospitable and fond of mixing with the opposite sex, you are more romantic than voluptuous. However, you may marry more than once. You enjoy ease and comfort and sincerely wish that the whole world could be at peace. As much as you love your family, you will not necessarily give them priority over a stranger you believe requires your help. People with this combination often take up voluntary work or are employed in hospitals and similar institutions.

The business of earning a living, which others take in their stride, may distress you. Unless your sympathies are aroused, you don't have much staying power. The need to be needed is paramount, and then your energies are formidable. Unneeded, you lose interest and retreat into a world of romantic daydreams.

You possess a deep appreciation of all that is beautiful in art and nature and are particularly fond of music. As a composer, dancer, writer, artist or poet, you have great inspiration.

The Other Side of the Story

You are devious, secretive and unable to face facts. You retreat from the slightest challenge. You are devoid of ambition and purpose and are prepared to drift along in a dream world, depending on your friends and family for subsistence. You are hysterically impressionable and emotional, putty in the hands of anyone who is prepared to tell you what to do. You may be so afraid of failure and criticism that you attempt very little outside of menial tasks. You are apt to lose money through deception and fraud or your own muddleheaded thinking. Your love life may contain numerous illicit affairs, as well as weird and shattering experiences.

CHAPTER EIGHTEEN

Mars

This chapter on Mars gives you some facts about the planet's physical features, the myths and symbolism surrounding it, and an astrological account of its characteristics. Then follows a description of Mars in the various zodiacal signs.

The Planet

Mars is the first and nearest of the outer planets to the Earth. On the Sun side of us is Venus, on the other side is Mars. The mean distance between the Sun and the Earth is 93 million miles; between the Sun and Mars, it is 141 million miles.

The Martian year—the time it takes the planet to circle the Sun—is 687 days, just under two Earth years. Being an outer planet, Mars can never appear between the Earth and the Sun, as the Moon, Mercury and Venus do. Mars is smaller than the Earth. Its diameter is 4200 miles—just double that of the Moon. The planet rotates on its axis in 24 hours 37 minutes 23 seconds. Its mass is one-tenth that of the Earth.

Mars is reddish in color and can be seen at night as a brilliant ruddy dot. Every 15 years it is at its closest distance to us—36 million miles, when it shines with the brilliance of Sirius, the brightest star. This proximity will be reached again in 2014.

The U.S. Mariner 9 space probe carried out an extensive study of Mars in 1971–1972, covering 85 percent of the surface in great detail. Earlier probes by Mariner 6 and Mariner 7 had indicated that Mars was a dead and featureless planet, but Mariner 9 showed it had extremely interesting and distinct characteristics, some of which raised new questions. Important new findings were that water played an active role in Mars's evolution. Photographs revealed four major geological regions: a polar region with terrace-like formations and deep grooves; an equa-torial plateau scarred by deep canyons, with evidence of water erosion; a volcanic region; and a large cratered terrain like the Moon's. The Russians have also sent spaceships to Mars.

Mars has two small moons—Phobos and Deimos, each about 10 miles in diameter. Phobos revolves so incredibly fast that it rises and sets three times a day.

Symbolism

Aries or Mars, as he was known to the Romans, was the god of war and one of the 12 great Olympian deities. He was the son of Zeus (Jupiter), the supreme god, and Hera (Juno), the Great Goddess of the pre-Hellenic matriarchal society. He was a divinity of Thracian origin, representing dispute, destruction and war. Mars was said to delight in battle for its own sake. He was not popular with the Greeks, who disliked purposeless war and despised those (like the Thracians) who enjoyed it. The Greek myths about Mars reflect this hostile attitude.

According to legend, he was hated by all the other deities except three. One of these was Aphrodite or Venus. Mars was her lover and they were caught together by her husband in an invisible net and exposed to ridicule among the gods.

Mars was not invincible in war. The other gods wounded and conquered him many times. Once he was imprisoned for 13 months until Mercury freed him.

It is not surprising that the god of war was held in high esteem and honored in the Roman Empire. Mars ruled the first month of the Roman year (March—Aries) and was associated with the eighth month of the Roman year (October—Libra, which is ruled by Venus). Certain days in those months were given over to Martian ceremonies. Mars had two temples in Rome. One was an altar, the other a gate through which the army marched.

Astrology

Mars is dry, fiery and masculine. In the horoscope, it represents the outgoing physical force. It is significant of energy, both constructive and destructive, depending on its position and aspects in the horoscope. Mars is closely associated with ambition and desire. It symbolizes the senses and rules over the animal instinct in man.

Mars is said to be a malefic planet, but if it is well aspected and allowed to express itself positively, it represents courage, endurance, strength, self-confidence and the driving impulse that all ventures, including deeds of heroism, require.

Other attributes are initiative, combativeness, sharp wit, the ability to argue, independence, imposing determination, the ambition to be successful in material matters against all odds, force of character—and above all, leadership.

Mars also endows a person with extraordinary muscular strength, the power of practical execution and great organizing ability in an active rather than armchair way. Without Mars, it would be impossible to make use of what the other planets offer. Mars is resourceful and ingenious and provides the wherewithal to reach just about any material goal desired. Like a good soldier, Mars knows when to strike and when to withdraw. He is not a person to tackle lightly.

The developed Mars person combines physical delight with spiritual well-being. But the negative side of Mars is dreadful. When the planet is at a bad angle to the Earth, violence erupts. Murders, accidents, fires, rapes and mayhem break loose. When it is afflicted in a horoscope, the person is rash, violent, contentious, quick-tempered and foolhardy. He wants to quarrel and can't resist a fight. According to the influence, he may be weak and cowardly, himself a victim of aggression. (Not enough Mars is as bad as an exaggerated amount of him.) Or he may be a ruthless bully, always spoiling for a fight but frequently losing it because he brings out the worst sort of animal fury in others. He may submit to drink. Where there is a difference of opinion, he will rely on brute force instead of reasoned argument. He will act first, think later, lash out, collide, stumble, trip over. He is accident-prone, careless, takes unnecessary chances, reacts pugnaciously and aggressively. In one way or another, he releases his excessive energy so as to bring disaster or some kind of trouble down on himself.

A well-aspected Mars produces a vigorous, forceful and well-knit character. These people usually succeed in what they undertake. They don't give in to superior forces but they don't take a blind smack at them either; they have a "feel" for combat and they understand the necessity for timing. They are busy clearing away obstacles that lie in the way of practical accomplishment. The role of these people is to win, to conquer. And all things being considered, they can do this in a strong and enterprising way that is socially acceptable. During times of war, these are the men who win the battles, brush aside the mediocrity of inherited command, claw and fight their way up from the ranks to leadership, victory and glory.

In love, Mars is responsible for the best and the worst. As the Earth stands between the orbits of Venus and Mars, so man is the collision point between love and force. Neither is complete without the other: they come together as a passionate, potent power. The worst type of sexuality is governed by Mars. These people will satisfy their sexual hunger without any thought for the pain they cause their partners or others. On the other hand, Mars and Venus together provide the sort of love that will sacrifice anything, even life, to save another. There is no one truer in a practical way than a Mars friend.

As a lover, Mars is filled with exuberance and creative energy. He is impulsive, simple and direct. He has a red-blooded need of sex. Until he has free and regular expression of this compulsive basic drive, he can't devote himself fully to his practical activities because thoughts about sex will distract him. These gnawing thoughts can only be disintegrated in one great percussive act of union with Venus.

Mars rules Aries and is the co-ruler of Scorpio. Aries is the fiery first Sign of the Zodiac and typifies the initial thrust of energy into the world, the beginning, the pulsing seed, the body, the power, and the impulse; it also signifies initiative, enterprise, leadership, courage, independence and the pioneering, indomitable and adventurous spirit.

Scorpio is the watery, healing, mysterious eighth Sign, the powerhouse of repressed energy, intense emotion that unconsciously seeks to reunite itself with the source through the sexual function. It is subtle, secretive, purposeful, penetrating—the focal point of death and regeneration. It is the phoenix of immortality that waits in everyone to rise from the burned-out ashes of the self.

Physiologically, Mars is the body's resistance and attacking factor against invading disease and foreign bodies. Fevers and inflammations are the signs of this power at work. Mars also controls the elimination of waste products. As Venus governs the in-gathering forces of the body, so Mars rules the outgoing; the eliminating of waste as urine, the discharge of the male sperm from the testes, the shedding of eggs from the female ovaries and the release of sweat.

Mars is associated with the muscular system, the sympathetic nervous system and the red corpuscles of the blood. Where Mars is strongly emphasized, the person is prone to burns, fevers, cuts, accidents, scalds and inflammations. Mars is the physical side of sex—passion, lust. Venus provides the attraction, Mars supplies the phallic apparatus and the sensual stimulus.

Mars in Aries

You are iron-willed. You don't bend from your purpose. You may switch to something else before you finish a job—but only because it suits you to do so. You won't be dictated to. You are independent. You'll fight any opposition to the death if necessary, or you'll labor without help or encouragement until you drop to carry out your plans. Mars has always been associated with iron—it is the plowshare and the sword. In your hands, both get results.

In this position, the mighty Mars is in its own Sign so it is doubly strong and fiery. Whether what you undertake is for good or bad—and this will depend on the other influences in your horoscope—you will perform with great vigor and urgency. Aries and Mars represent the body, the dynamic principle of action. Here, the prime consideration is "me first." You are not so much naturally individualistic as a go-getter, an adventurer who is in it for himself or herself.

But you are not mean or selfish with money and worldly goods. You give freely, generously, often without thought. You crave excitement and freedom, not the deadening weight of accumulation. You'll leave everything behind on an impulse if you envision a new world to conquer. You'll upend your whole bag of goods for all to see and take what they want, so long as you can get where the action is. And you won't care if the prize is withheld—so long as you win.

You are open, frank and direct. There are no back doors to your nature. You march boldly through the main gate for all to see, with the sure-footed confidence of a soldier. You have nothing to hide. You are what you are. The fact that you might accidentally knock down a brick or two as you make your bustling entrance does not concern you.

Mars in this position gives brilliance and leadership. It is excellent for a man or woman of action. It provides determination and the practical ability to succeed in life, whether it be in the tug of war of business or the rough and tumble of politics. You are a good propagandist—you know how to make an idea popular. Your work as a writer, musician or artist can gain wide acceptance. You are original and ingenious, a real pioneer in whatever field you choose. But when it comes to conspiracies or scheming, you are likely to be the odd one out. You are too impulsive and impatient to be successful in endeavors demanding diplomacy and tact. You would rather throw down the gauntlet and let whoever dares pick it up. However, if the enemy fails to come forward, you are stymied.

You are quick-tempered and easily irritated. Unless you cultivate self-control, your rages are likely to be quite violent. You like to clear the air quickly and you don't hold grudges. You are prone to accidental injury. People with this combination usually have a scar on their head or face from some old wound. You may also need to wear spectacles earlier than usual or sunglasses as a therapeutic aid.

Your manner is sometimes blunt and aggressive. You sincerely believe you are the master of your own destiny and you don't intend to be caught napping. You aim at continual accomplishment, but sometimes you get so caught up in the action that you lose sight of the desired end. You need to use your willpower to see things through, to resist turning your attention to some fresh challenge before the old one has been satisfactorily concluded. You don't like detail. When the time for cleaning up arrives, you will probably vanish. People who object to noise and bustle do not like having you around. Steady plodding and patient cooperation are not your metier, and routine work nearly drives you mad. Even if you don't have to hurry a job, you'll put a time limit on yourself . . . and needle everyone else along at the same gallop.

You have a strong sexual urge and a tremendous amount of energy to get rid of. It is important to your health that you release your feelings and desires because you require free expression as well as self-control. You need a partner who is physically compatible and who understands the simplicity of your mental processes. You are an idealist. When you identify with a person, cause or principle, you go all the way.

You love active sports. You are physically tough. You do all in your power to keep your body healthy and fit.

The Other Side of the Story

You are likely to be oversexed and preoccupied with satisfying that basic urge. An extremely violent and uncontrollable temper may make you dangerous to life and limb. Recklessness and impatience can make it difficult for you to hold down a job. You may be brusque and bullying. Your language and manner of speaking may be vulgar and provoking. You are apt to be insensitive to other people's feelings as well as tactless and argumentative. An overly optimistic outlook may distort your judgment. Your hatred of detail may make you a slapdash planner.

Mars in Taurus

Mars here is in a bit of a quandary. He can't be outgoing, as in Aries, scattering his fiery brilliance and originality with scant regard for economy. Here he must hold onto what he owns and continually gather what he wants. He must be more material, more set on acquiring, on possessing—altogether more set—than his forceful, action-loving nature is comfortable with. Here in Taurus, the Sign of money and worldly goods, Mars is in his detriment. His driving energy turns to obstinacy. But despite his discomfort, this can be a good combination. Mars in Taurus means toil—but usually a substantial share of the world's comforts as well.

You want to make money. You are down to earth about it. You know the peace of mind that security confers, and you aim to get it. You are not interested in moralizing stories or philosophic theorizing about what methods should or should not be employed for success. When you see the chance for action, you move. And you keep moving with a dogged determination that won't admit defeat until the end is reached.

Though you are usually successful over the long haul, the climb may be painful and slowed by obstacles. (Sometimes—halfway up the summit—you may look back and wonder if it has been worthwhile.) You are likely to create difficulties by rushing ahead and grappling with problems before they emerge. You are a practical person. You know that, above all, you have to hang onto what you win.

But, paradoxically, after all your efforts to secure the prize, you are likely to let it slip away at the last minute. It is almost as though you are willing to surrender to the object desired, but never to the obstacles that would keep you from it. You stop. You change. You take a rest. And then you resume your efforts with the same tenacity. You tend sometimes to swing from one extreme to another—peacefully compliant, then obstinately aggressive; self-indulgent, then ascetic; open-handed, then grasping. In many ways, you are a living contradiction, ill-harmonized within yourself.

You are strongly sexual. The physical side of love is likely to dominate your thoughts and affections. The normal refinements of this Venus Sign are apt to be consumed in sensual desire. Obstacles to your gratification may send you into a mood of fury or smoldering resentment, depending on the other influences in the chart. Your compulsion to retain possessions can extend to the people you love; you may be cruelly jealous—a suspicious, snarling guard dog. A well-aspected Mars in Taurus makes you a competent and satisfying lover who is usually very popular with the opposite sex. But there is a danger that the stability of your character may be undermined if you route too much of your energy into these relationships. Marriage may be a stormy and troublesome passage.

You are a conservative person who can be depended on to follow instructions and do a job well. You prefer, though, to be in a position where you can make decisions for yourself within an overall plan. With Mars in Taurus, the Sign of nature, the man is likely to be a capable engineer, bridge builder or construction worker, using his talents to change the look of the landscape. Formerly, a woman with this combination was usually employed or engaged in some sort of activity that called for stamina and perseverance—even if only in coping with an unruly family. Today, women are trained in these occupations and are equally capable of handling the same job.

You make a good executive with a talent for organizing and directing. You can visualize a goal with uncanny accuracy and make it materialize. You are most successful where there is a high element of self-interest.

You can be a successful writer or artist with a pronounced flair for expression that is sensual, rounded, voluptuous; the style is more earthy and classic than brilliantly stimulating, like that of Mars in Aries.

A vivid awareness of physical power, graceful movement and muscular coordination can produce fine ballet dancers, gymnasts, figure skaters and the like.

Although you are intent on acquiring money and assets, you can be a lavish spender when it comes to pleasure and the things you enjoy.

The Other Side of the Story

You may be stubborn and unable to see another person's point of view. Worries may come through property and sudden money crises. You are likely to steamroller your opposition, and with a little bit of authority, punish the innocent with the guilty just because they were on the wrong side. You may have a power complex that leads you to insist that antagonists be punished as well as vanquished. You can be fiercely jealous and unreasonably possessive. Your appreciation of beauty and refinement may be confined to the things you own or can control. You may have legal difficulties and lose a legacy. Your arrogance may make you an overweening boss and an insensitive parent. You may be vicious in sex and a callous materialist in your aims. Any cruel means may justify the end.

Mars in Gemini

You get some really great ideas—at times you are even inspired—and you have no difficulty spurring others into action. You make an excellent politician, a convincing salesperson, a provocative writer and lecturer, a clever personal assistant or top secretary and an aggressive or rapier tongued debater or lawyer. You not only are brilliant at putting an argument across, but you also arouse vital enthusiasm in an audience. You are forceful and blunt when you want to be, dancingly light and lacerating with your wit and sarcasm when it suits you. You are a rabble rouser, a morale booster, an ideologist who can tell people how to do the impossible.

But you are lacking in full-blooded physical energy. You do your best to avoid heavy work. Yours is a nervous energy that activates the mind. Here in Gemini—the Sign of intellect—the potent power of Mars expresses itself in an effusion of ideas and concepts. You are an energetic thinker. Your mind is always busy, restless. You want to change things—mostly to suit yourself—and you use other people to do it. You are the brains of the outfit, the master

mind. You want action. You build verbal bridges for others to cross between the conceptual plane and the concrete world. Your ideas can literally set the world on fire. You are the type of person who proposes an ideology that the next generation might fight or die for.

If you are a Mars in Gemini thinker in a small world, you are just as effective; your friends, co-workers and acquaintances are equally impressed. You are talkative, an impulsive debater and disputant, but you seldom talk nonsense, unless there are upsetting influences in the horoscope. You are practical and speak in order to produce effective action. The fact that you might never take action is incidental. Your role is to show the way. You make an idealistic plan sound feasible and desirable.

You have mechanical aptitude. Although you may not be moved to dismantle a machine, you understand what needs to be done. You are deft with your hands. You are inventive, sometimes marvelously ingenious. There are very few situations you can't deal with. You like to look through handbooks, to glance at plans to see whether you can improve on them.

You have many interests. You are continually running around, meeting people, making contacts, living largely off your nerves. You are high-strung and very excitable. You are also easily irritated. You sometimes show a remarkable inconsistency in your beliefs; you can take an opposite stand to one you've already advocated with magnificent aplomb.

You may have a love affair with a relative. Two marriages are common. You frequently have two affairs current.

You are not averse to exaggerating and telling untruths if it helps your cause—or the impact of your story. Physical violence is something you prefer to avoid. Your weapons are words and the influence they have on people and events. You can quickly cut an opponent down to size with the edge of your tongue. You verbally fence with the enemy to find his weak spot so you can puncture him, swiftly and neatly.

You enjoy reading and are drawn to educational activities. You would like to teach, to lecture. You are fond of travel, science and chemistry. You have great deductive ability and your conclusions usually make good sense and are extremely workable.

Your main fault is that you lack follow-through. Though your ideas are sound and wonderful, they must be carried forward by others. What you do seems to depend on the energy at your disposal, which is erratic and siphoned off by a variety of pursuits rather than one dearly held objective. You participate for the sake of the action, the excitement, the mental stimulus, more than for the result. Although your insight and perception are needle-sharp, you are easily distracted and need to cultivate concentration.

You are physically agile but don't possess the stamina to shine in strenuous competitive sports. You are sometimes accident-prone and are likely to injure your shoulder, arms or hands. There is also a possibility you will suffer from nervous prostration.

The Other Side of the Story

You are likely to be disagreeable in your speech and tiresomely faultfinding. You may use your quick wit to embarrass and discomfort others unnecessarily, particularly in company. Neighbors, relatives and those who work for you may cause you trouble. Brothers and sisters are likely to create special problems; or there could be painful separations or estrangements. Your education may have been neglected, making it hard for you to get ahead. You are likely to become an excessivily heavy smoker or drug user in an attempt to calm your nerves. Your lungs may give you pain. You are apt to be indecisive and possess a stutter or some other irritating speech impediment.

Mars in Cancer

This is the combination that signifies the true artist, whether he or she be a painter, writer, sculptor, philosopher, musician—or gentle humanitarian. The fiery and energetic Mars, when immersed in Cancer, the deep receptive water Sign of the Moon, seems to bring out an unsuspected magical quality. Here are the men and women who serve the idea of art and not the fashion, the people who reveal its universal oneness and timelessness, those whose egos perish but whose essences linger on: Shakespeare, Michelangelo, Dante, Petrarch, Byron, Balzac, Kant, Copernicus. You, too, have some of this magic.

You are ambitious and industrious; you are also changeable and lacking in continuity. But you can wait for the things you really want. A master of the war of attrition, you can wear away the opposition as the sea erodes the hardest rocks. Mars stirs you at your deepest levels; you churn to the surface; you have sudden outbursts of temper and irritation. You

are rebellious and refuse to be hemmed in and ordered about. Authority and its poses annoy you.

You want security, the security of the law as well as of the home. But you don't particularly like other people's ideas of security; you want things your way. The law in many ways fails the public, sets up power centers that restrict rather than resolve, pamper rather than protect, punish rather than prevent—and this is the source of your revolt and protest. You are often misunderstood and thought to be a sniping dissenter rather than a person with positive ideals. You would like to see the world run on home and family lines—with love—but you are enough of a realist (and sufficiently seasoned in domestic experience) to understand the odds against this becoming reality.

You are original, independent and enterprising. You love your home, and especially the family ideal, but your home life is often disturbed from inside as well as outside. You constantly have to deal with interference and never seem to be able to settle down for long.

You have an emotional approach to action rather than a reasoning one. Your instinctive knowledge is quite amazing and you have learned to rely on it. Because of this, the usual Mars impulsiveness is less rash and reckless in this position, drawing as it does on the deep subconscious knowledge of human experience stored in the profound reservoir of Cancer.

You are often in a ferment inside and this disturbs your stomach and digestive processes. Unless frustration and irritation are brought under control and a calmer temperament cultivated, you are apt to suffer from stomach ulcers and other intestinal disorders. A sense of humor can provide some release. If these self-destructive forces are channeled into a single effort, astonishing progress can be made; if not used constructively, these energies are pernicious.

You are easily offended and hold grudges. You resent, repress and smolder. You are inclined to depend on alcohol, tobacco or drugs. Probably you clashed with your mother in younger years, and this may have left an unconscious traumatic scar. There is a possibility that death or separation occurred during childhood. Mars gives you a capacity for objective, no-nonsense self-analysis, which, if utilized, can release the emotional pressures you have allowed to build up through ignoring or rejecting issues.

You are likely to be involved in work requiring enterprise and initiative. A job that takes you abroad frequently or on long cross-country journeys can be profitable. Professions associated with children, houses, food and the sea may also lead to success. Some strenuous physical work is indicated, and here the rigorous demands of looking after a home and family can't be excluded.

You are likely to have to move home abruptly—several times. Unforeseen circumstances may involve you in sudden changes in numerous departments of your life.

The Other Side of the Story

Unhappy childhood experiences may still discolor your outlook on life. You are likely to be depressed by sad and sorrowful memories; when you try to snap out of it (as you continually do), you are irritable and psychologically ill at ease. You may have little in common with your marriage partner or the person you live with. Your home may be an arena of worries, difficulties and troubles. You are likely to be unfortunate where property and legacies are concerned. Accidents, thefts, fires, storms and danger through water are all possible causes of loss and injury. You may have eye trouble.

Mars in Leo

You're a powerhouse of energy and vitality and know exactly where you're going—to the top, of course! It's not the pot of gold at the end of the rainbow that interests you, but the power and the glory—especially the glory. You're a showman, and you know it. You dramatize every emotion and action whenever someone is around to see. You never cease playing to the gallery. You are entertaining, enterprising and exciting. Your detractors might say you're proud and egotistical, but it must be admitted that you seldom fail to give the audience their money's worth.

You are a warmhearted, generous and passionate character. In love, you take over completely and in return give everything you've got. You are wildly emotional, recklessly romantic and inclined to make promises in the ardor of the moment that would be more wisely left unmade. Acutely conscientious—and as your critics say, proud—you endeavor never to go back on your word. Naturally, when your passion has cooled, you find yourself burdened with some tricky and irritating obligations.

Still, you're a man or woman of action. You get more done in a day than many others accomplish in a week. You work largely from intuition and are guided by your heart. When a challenge looms, you seem to know without deliberation what has to be done and fearlessly go on the attack. You have an extraordinary faith in life—not just in survival—that seldom measures the risk to yourself. If you bother to attempt something, you feel it has to be worthwhile. So why hang around? You have no time for timidity or hesitation. It's in or out. Opportunities are seldom wasted on you with Mars in Leo.

But it's not all plain sailing, as you've probably noticed. You're a demon for going that little bit too far—which, to others, is overboard. Extremes have a fatal attraction for you. In love, as has been mentioned, you are frequently overhasty and impulsive, contemptuous of indecision and disdainful of consequences. Your love of pleasure and the party life costs you a packet. You're a bit ingenuous and foolishly trusting. Sometimes cunning types penetrate your guard. You're surprisingly easy to deceive with flattery and praise, and a personal compliment, no matter how outrageously extravagant, seldom seems inappropriate to you.

You are a born leader who invariably enjoys the trust and confidence of those in authority. Power and command pass to you with a natural affinity. You have a passion for justice and fair play and will defend the case of the underdog or any minority as though it were your own. Sometimes you are overassertive to the point of dogmatism. The result is you stir up unnecessary opposition and enmity. For instance, you may go too far when presenting arguments to superiors; although they are usually on your side, you are not averse to pushing them to the extremity of their tolerance. It is easy for you to earn a reputation for defiance and aggression. Rashness and recklessness can lead to your downfall.

Although rather fixed in your opinions, you are willing to listen to what others have to say. This willingness never prevents you from arguing your own ideas readily and forcefully. You are a resourceful debater and inclined to present fiction as fact if you think you can get away with it. Whatever your field, you will rise to an executive position. It is in your own interests to curb excessive zeal and to resist becoming exclusively identified with a particular idea or belief. Fanaticism lurks in this particular combination, especially where political and social crusades are concerned.

You are apt to be most successful in occupations connected with the government, stock exchange and entertainment industry. A musical ability is often latent with Mars in Leo.

You are fond of exercise and competitive sports. Although sometimes accident-prone, you enjoy speed and taking risks.

The Other Side of the Story

You are power mad but lack the positive qualities of leadership. Your dictatorial and belligerent manner makes you more enemies than friends—you even antagonize those you believe you are helping. Your love life has probably been marred by tragedy, most of your romantic affairs ending in disappointment or sorrow. Gambling and reckless extravagance keep you poor and worried. People in authority trust you to begin with, but soon lose confidence. You are brash and a braggart, clumsy, irritable and prone to blame others for your misfortunes. When opposed, you are bullheaded, threatening and violent.

Mars in Virgo

It may not be easy, but you'll probably attain your goals in the end. Mars makes you a little impatient, too eager to move on to something else when you should be persevering in what you have already begun. The fiery, energetic planet produces peculiar setbacks and reversals, but once you have settled on a particular aim—really settled on it—not much can thwart you. The secret is to know what you want.

In your job, you are a born specialist. You have a particular talent for organizing work into formularized systems. Your ideas are original and extremely practical, and you are sure to stand out in any profession or trade you follow. Science often provides a fertile field for your inventive and analytical mind. You are keenly interested in medicine, hygiene, foodstuffs and diet—in any of these fields, you could succeed. Your ability to handle vast amounts of detail without losing concentration or interest fits you admirably for research projects. You should also be able to make your mark as a medical technician, a mechanic or engineer.

You are not a passionate person. All your feelings are well and truly under control. To some of your acquaintances, you may appear a bit coldblooded. Emotional and excitable types find you difficult to understand and may not be prepared to try very hard. You're a handy person to have around in emergencies because your detachment allows you to take an impersonal view. Sometimes, though, you act out emotions you don't feel—this happens particularly

when loved ones are upset or being demanding. It is this facility for acting that often leads Mars in Virgo people to a successful stage or film career.

You possess a lot more energy than you display. Because you are inclined to be conservative, you go about your work in a quiet and methodical manner. Even when pressures reach the screaming point, you manage to keep your cool and carry on efficiently as though nothing unusual were happening. You are strong-willed, shrewd and ambitious in a subdued way. Setbacks don't affect your work; you are quite prepared to start all over again. In many ways, Mars in Virgo produces the "perfect" employee.

Being inclined to worry and determined not to show it, you suffer from nerves that may affect your digestion. Otherwise, through close attention to hygiene and diet, you manage to keep fairly fit and healthy.

You don't go out of your way to look for love affairs. You enjoy the company of the opposite sex, like to talk about romantic matters and sometimes flirt a little, but when it comes down to the nitty-gritty, you'd rather avoid the emotional turmoil love invariably means. You are more intellectual than sensual. You enjoy talking and love to gossip.

You are rather puritanical in your beliefs, favoring the old-fashioned values that have stood the test of time. If you become fixed on a moral idea or ethic, you can espouse it with a degree of conviction that may verge on sermonizing.

You believe in a fair day's work for a fair day's pay, and that much current talk about individual freedom is merely an excuse to avoid responsibility. You are acquisitive but not money hungry. Economy is natural to you.

You enjoy the social life and are a pleasant and efficient host or hostess. You don't believe in being lavish nor are you particularly attracted by luxuries. Comfort, a clean house and everything in good working order are your most important domestic priorities. You are not the type to intrude on others and will wait for an invitation rather than drop in. You are tactful, modest and a lot less self-assured than your detached and "professional" manner would suggest.

You are a careful planner and seldom initiate an action without having calculated that the odds are in your favor. Although bold and enterprising in your approach to working problems, you have very little stomach for risks or venturesome activitity in your personal life.

The Other Side of the Story

You are a cold fish with haughty contempt for the emotions of ordinary people. You are proud, obstinate, irritable and terribly lonely in your aloofness. Unless constantly encouraged in your work, you lose heart. You make many starts and few finishes. Your nerves are continually on edge, even though you may present a controlled facade. You remember slights and will take revenge at the first opportunity. Loss comes through friends, co-workers, subordinates, strikes and labor troubles. You are sarcastic and argumentative, capable of thinking one way, then doing the other.

Mars in Libra

You possess a strong social conscience. You are very much aware of the inequalities and injustices imposed on your fellow man—sometimes you seethe with resentment on their behalf. Though you truly don't enjoy violence, you can understand why many of the champions of humanity in the past have had to resort to force to rid the world of an evil. You might be tempted to do the same yourself, given the right circumstances. War to stop war! Can it ever really work! This is the conflict that you must learn to live with—or resolve—in yourself.

Mars, the god of war, is not too comfortable here. Libra is ruled by Venus, the goddess of love and harmony. Love and war are an uneasy mixture, but that's your chemistry. In sex, the soldier Mars and the beautiful goddess Venus fall together in a wild embrace of passion and ecstasy. But when it comes to cohabitation, they fight with the fury of cat and dog.

You usually marry early in life and probably more than once. Disappointment invariably follows each attempt to establish a permanent love relationship. Quarrels, accusations and unhappiness are the rule, not the exception. The opposite sex has a great influence on your life. Even the direction of your work or career seems to be affected by these relationships.

You are a rash and impulsive lover. As a man, you dazzle your women with suavity and charm and then sweep them up with thrilling red-blooded ardor. As a woman, you satisfy with a mind-blowing carburetion of feminity and pure animalism. Inevitably, it ends in love and war—or at its worst, a snarling truce.

The person with Mars in Libra needs a goal in life, not just for his or her own sake, but because the individual has something tangible to contribute to society. This position endows you with keen judgment and a discerning eye, backed by a determination to see your decisions through to the bitter end. You can view a situation from both sides without becoming emotionally committed. Others listen to your advice. You are realistic and refined, and given the opportunity, may become a popular public figure or prominent in your particular set.

Your gift for presenting the sword edge with a firm and gentle gesture makes you an impressive diplomatist and a formidable opponent in the political arena. You would make a wily statesman, a top-ranking military man or a reforming lawyer. A steady mind as well as a steady hand when there is a delicate job to do also fits you for the role of surgeon. You are an idealist who observes life closely and, too often for your own good, becomes upset by the injustice of what you see. Despite the controlling power of your reason, you occasionally flare up in anger and righteous indignation and involve yourself in conflicts and discord that have an amazing habit of spreading. One inflammatory word or action by you seems enough to start a chain reaction among innumerable people. Frequently you have to overcome your own ground swell before getting started. You are no stranger to obstacles, enmity and determined opposition.

You have strong artistic leanings, especially toward poetry, painting and music. Whatever you produce of a creative nature has an urgency and unmistakable vitality to it. You have many friends, most of whom are in the professions. You enjoy getting together with them over drinks and dinner and having a free-ranging discussion that may go on until the early hours. You are a night owl and come to life with great vigor when the dancing starts. You enjoy animated speculation about philosophic and religious matters. Your views on politics are interesting and usually sound.

Your main problem is trying to balance the disharmonious and irritating elements you feel. If you attempt to correct the wrongs outside without resolving the belligerence in your own peace-aspiring nature, you will have trouble finding happiness. The key is to realize the means does *not* justify the end; the means *is* the end.

The Other Side of the Story

You have to battle for everything you get. Nothing comes easy. If it does, it soon disappears or is destroyed. You are unfortunate in love. Vindictive women have cost you much. You quarrel easily with friends and partners and are often unreasonable. Bad luck and open hostility have prevented you from achieving your most treasured ambitions. You often feel cheated by a cruel fate. You rise to an occasion with a tremendous show of energy and enthusiasm, but soon lose heart or burn yourself out. You are a flash in the pan. Jealous associates make a habit of undercutting you. Your own faulty judgment can be seen as the cause of most of your troubles.

Mars in Scorpio

Good or evil? Call it what you like, the choice is yours. Nowhere else in the Zodiac does such a tremendous reservoir of energy await direction than when Mars, the planet of energy and force, pulsates in Scorpio, the Sign of repressed or hidden power. Energy and repressed or hidden power? There's a three-letter word for it: *sex*. The sex drive starts here.

This should not be interpreted as meaning that everyone with Mars in Scorpio is a sexual maniac. Far from it. These people have access to a mighty energy at its very source, deep in the nonphysical unconscious. True, it takes some handling as it surfaces through the senses into the mind. True, the propensity of such a fundamental, assertive force is toward some kind of violent, willful and piercing expression. That could be sexual gratification, cruelty for its own sake or a ruthless quest for power. Or this force could just as easily be used to root out iniquity from the world in one dedicated through rigid self-discipline to altruistic aims.

Not surprisingly, this combination gives a steel-nerved capacity for self-control and unswerving determination—once the individual has decided which course he or she is to take. All people with Mars in Scorpio discover early in life that they live on an emotional volcano. They develop a repressive temperament that appears to others as a cool, calculating shrewdness and total self-sufficiency.

You are practical, hardheaded and one of the most hardworking types in the Zodiac. To attain your goals, you are capable of toiling under the most punishing conditions with almost superhuman endurance. Once committed, you never give up. But the aim must be personally desirable. No one on earth can make you perform against your will, although you'll go through the actions out of economic necessity, if it pleases you. Sometimes you are thought to be lazy, by those who don't understand that you

are one of nature's self-starters. It is not unusual for you to have to sacrifice physical comfort and happiness to achieve your ambitions.

You are a hard-driving, relentless individual who cannot be placated with half-measures and good intentions. Give you an inch and you'll take a foot and immediately make a stand for more from there. You are unstoppable. At the same time, you are diplomatic, urbane if it suits you. You realize the importance of social formalities in achieving cooperation, though when off your guard, you can be rather blunt.

Your mind is quick and penetrating. You have a knack of getting to the bottom of things. You can probe another person's mind with the same impersonal precision that a Mars in Scorpio brain surgeon uses to excise a tumor. This combination is found in people who earn their living through various forms of analysis in mining, psychotherapy and science. They also enjoy solving mysteries and may be attracted to occult and psychic investigations. Sometimes a profound flash of mystical insight changes their entire lifestyle. Frequently, people with Mars in Scorpio possess an innate mechanical ability. Being quite physically strong themselves, they enjoy the feel of using powerful machines.

You are not an adaptable person. Your opinions are fixed. You prefer to have one clear aim and stick to it through thick and thin. This way, you are never confused. In fluid situations where you are denied predetermined references, you suffer considerable inner strain, though you may never show it. Uncertainty you regard as your worst enemy. Fortunately, you rarely feel it.

You find danger attractive and are prone to taking physical risks. With this combination, there is always the chance of a violent and unexpected death. Without softening influences elsewhere in the horoscope, you will be selfish and think nothing of riding roughshod over others.

Secretiveness, a liking for revenge and a mute awareness of their own erotic thought patterns characterize Mars in Scorpio people.

The Other Side of the Story

You have no respect for the rights of others. You take as much as you can of what you want whenever you see it. You are contemptuous of ordinary people and use them outrageously to indulge your sensual and other selfish desires. You are despotic and tyrannical, quarrelsome, sarcastic, vitriolic and revengeful. You are oversexed, obsessed with luridly erotic thoughts, cruel, unscrupulous, violent and probably sexually deviate. Or you may be the victim of others with the same traits. Troubles come through those who work for you; a secret affair with one of these individuals is likely to end tragically. Major operations and serious accidents are likely.

Mars in Sagittarius

Given the chance, you'd love to be a rolling stone. You're fond of travel, adore adventure, make friends instantly and have a pounding lust for life. But above all, you're independent. You are in love with liberty—the freedom to go where you like, when you like, as you like, and to say what you like. Obviously, you're not a very safe bet as a marriage partner. But despite your transitory habits and inclinations, you often manage to acquire a substantial place in the community.

You're a good sport, popular and have immense vitality. Not many people can keep up as you whisk from one situation to another, intrigued by novelty, fascinated by experiment and exploration, and dauntless when it comes to physical danger. In a risky situation, you're certainly foolhardy.

Yet you're not a stayer, a sticker. When it comes to perseverance and tenacity, you don't want even to be consulted. You're a sportsman in heart and soul, a kind of light-footed pugilist, one might say. Your style is to prance into the fray, knock 'em down, drag 'em out, bleed like fury if you have to, and then move on smartly to the next contest or tournament. Although Mars is a warrior, he has no stamina for the war of attrition or lackluster siege.

Your mind is sharp, active and original, your thinking supremely optimistic and futuristic. You're constantly questioning and seeking, but seldom stay around long enough to make enough use of the answers. Tomorrow and not today seems to be your main interest. Over the horizon is the promise this moment lacks. When you can manage to apply yourself, you are often brilliant, but your concentration soon ebbs, leaving you chasing that end of the rainbow where you know it's all happening.

You do well in any occupation where your natural urges can be expressed. Any other kind of job will seem drudgery. You would make a fine traveling sales representative, itinerant lecturer or teacher, crusading politician, adventure writer, military com-

mander or space explorer. If you can set your mind on a single objective and marshal all your energetic and intellectual resources, there's no limit to how far you can go. The vital point is to know what you want and to deal with the problems as they occur instead of rushing out to meet them.

You have a keen interest in social, philosophic and religious matters. Although you hesitate to reject outright the orthodox dogmas, you are impatient with the restrictions they impose on the individual's thinking. Frequently you are drawn into good-humored arguments and express your views in an articulate and forceful manner. Your opinions are often at variance with those of the Establishment. Your style of speaking is open and candid, and combined with your strong views on morality and justice, usually guarantees you a hearing in any company. Sometimes you upset others with personal observations that are remarkable for their accuracy, if not for their tact.

You love company and have many boon companions. Most exciting outdoor sports and games appeal to you. You're a lucky and impulsive gambler and seem to have a sixth sense. If you lose, you have a happy knack of being able to forget it and plunge into the next adventure with the same optimism and high spirits.

Simplicity in all its forms appeals to you. You dislike insincerity and affectation and can be depended on to give an honest opinion at all times. You are particularly critical of people in high places who put on airs and graces, and are not afraid to publicly say so. You will never allow the fear of what others may think to inhibit your free speech.

You stand to gain financially through marriage and may wed more than once. Money may also come through legacies and social position.

The Other Side of the Story

Court actions are likely to go against you with ruinous results. You lack a sense of proportion and create unnecessary difficulties and hardship for yourself through rash and careless actions. You exaggerate to impress others and make impossible promises. Neighbors, brothers, sisters and other relatives are unlucky. The death of one of these people may have a profound effect on your life. Your religious beliefs, unorthodox ideas and skepticism are likely to wreck your career or social status. You might foolishly risk all on what amounts to the throw of the (probably loaded) dice.

Mars in Capricorn

This is the best position in the horoscope for the fiery energy of Mars. Here the planet's wonderful driving force links up with the astute organizing ability of Capricorn and produces you—a person who commands respect in whatever field you choose and who is certain (other influences in the chart being equal) to rise to the position of executive or chief.

Your work or career is the most important thing in your life. You are aggressively ambitious and determined to make a name for yourself. No amount of responsibility deters you—on the contrary, you thrive on it. You are even prepared to shoulder the responsibilities of others if you feel it's necessary. You possess remarkable persistence and, as a tactic, patience. You will work day and night to achieve your goals and are not afraid to get out the sledgehammer and deliver a few well-aimed blows when the obstacle or opposition gets too tough. It's an exceptional man or woman who can stand against you. Fortunately, few wish to try.

Your progress is generally smooth because you have a talent for marshaling all available forces into one mighty continuing effort, with you very active as the guiding and cohesive spirit. This stratagem eliminates much of the need for struggle, which so often wears out the subject before the object. Like an old sailing master, you use the crosswinds to drive you forward. This strategy may cost a few miles, but the going is easier for all, and the end result more productive.

Your personality is magnetic and commanding. You are able to inspire others from the workshop floor to top management. People enjoy working with you and for you; above all they respect you. And nothing makes you feel happier or nobler than being esteemed for your practical qualities and wisdom.

You are severe and stern when necessary. You insist on obedience from subordinates and have the happy knack of getting it without confrontations. You are precise, know exactly what you want and can usually do any job you ask of another. Austerity is no hardship for you. You have supreme confidence in your own ability, but your impressive acumen and expertise may inhibit initiative in your associates.

Financially powerful people can usually be counted on to give you assistance. You're what's regarded in business circles as a good bet. You're also prepared to take a chance, to grab an opportunity boldly when others might hesitate. It is your style to know exactly what is going on in all departments of your organization and to keep informed of market developments and trends. So although you delight in a bit of venturous plunging, it's rarely that much of a gamble!

This astuteness and assiduous concern for responsibility may not be so evident in the youth of a person born with Mars in Capricorn. Sometimes these young people may seem to have an intractable love of pleasure and appear quite undisciplined. This, however, is a development phase. Capricorn usually affects the circumstances so that the youth enjoys himself but only by surmounting constant difficulties and setbacks. The underlying seriousness and gravity in the character can usually be discerned, even though the glimpse may be fleeting.

Now, what of love for the mature person born with this combination? Here is a guy or gal who responds to only real affection. It pierces the tough layer of inhibitions that protects their love nature from hurt, and stirs the intense sensual longings throbbing there. But love has got to be for real. Let someone love them truly and they'll be loyal forevermore. Lovers with this combination are easily offended, and if rejected, suffer excruciatingly.

There's always a chance you will blow your top. Although you can take a tremendous amount of sustained mental and physical effort, it must be justified by progress. Prolonged delays and irritations cause a buildup of frustration that's finally released in a violent way.

The Other Side of the Story

You have an atrocious temper, which is a danger to life and limb. None of your affairs ever seems to advance smoothly; you are usually the victim of delays, mistakes, inefficiency and other people's nastiness. Even at this moment, a project important to you is probably held up for unaccountable reasons. You may have the best of plans but be incapable of stirring the interest of those whose cooperation is necessary. You have a habit of wasting time on detail and ill-conceived projects. A love affair early in life with a person much older or in an inferior position probably proved disastrous in more ways than one.

Mars in Aquarius

You probably want to change the world with your ideas and make it a better place to live in. The trouble is, you're in a terrible hurry and in your rush you'll probably succeed only in turning everything upside down—and making us all unhappy and very uncomfortable.

Slow down, be patient and keep up the good work. You have flair and imagination. You're the type of person who gives the world some of its best reforming ideas. You are a genuine intellectual with the good of humanity at heart. You discern the hairline cracks in society long before they open into fissures of political clamor and discontent. You are visionary. You demand action. Your mind is sharp, incisive and dynamic. Your unique and original thinking puts you out in front—sometimes so far out that you are a voice crying in the wilderness.

You are very convincing in your arguments. Your reasoning power is impeccable. You are fearless in debate and will say exactly what you think. But you do occasionally get overexcited. At these times, you are impulsive, self-willed and rash in speech. Overall, with Mars in Aquarius, you are susceptible to acting in spurts and spasms. Your opinions are fairly fixed and you don't like to water them down.

You are more a thinker than a doer, equipped to whip others into action with your galvanizing presence and slogans. You enjoy a free and easy life. Restrictions imposed by job or family irritate you. You are much happier with groups of people than in an emotional entanglement with one or two others. Bohemian types attract you most; you enjoy their informality and uninhibited ways, which are very similar to your own. These characters are inclined to be enthusiastic about your more revolutionary views and make you feel less eccentric than misunderstood.

Mars in Aquarius usually confers an ability to write as well as a wide-ranging interest in literature. You are apt to use your pen or a worldwide web site to propagate your advanced ideas or to secure public support for a pet project. You are never content with results. You must move forward. When one project ends, you immediately pick up another with the same enthusiasm and idealistic fervor. Whatever your circumstances, you manage in some way or other to stand out from the crowd—even if through a simple gesture such as affecting an unusual style in clothes.

It is not uncommon for people with this combination to win public acclaim. They are often connected with international welfare organizations and groups dedicated to the eradication of disease, hunger and poverty, as well as the protection of human rights.

Mars in Aquarius is a catalyst that produces unusual events and lightning changes around the people born with this combination. Even in quiet and private conversations, their unusual ideas may set others in motion with far-reaching and even violent repercussions. They typify the revolutionary spirit and the release of ideological forces that ignite mass emotions long suppressed by injustice and inequality.

You are well suited for a career in medicine, welfare, social work, politics, psychiatry or science. Solving problems connected with electronic communications and with space travel should appeal to your enterprising and inventive mind. You may also make a competent lecturer in psi (parapsychic sensitivity) subjects and have a talent for experimental work in these fields.

In all your activities, you will be more effective if you exert a constant pressure on yourself rather than work by fits and starts.

The Other Side of the Story

You are too independent to be taken seriously. Your blunt and insensitive manner turns off people who might otherwise support you and your views. You're all talk and hopelessly ineffective when dealing with practical problems. Inwardly, you are a mass of nervous tension and project an image of instability and restrained hysteria. If you lose your temper, you are apt to go berserk. You are unreliable, reckless and fanatical. You may be betrayed by friends and separated quite early in life from a parent.

Mars in Pisces

You are frequently tortured by your own thoughts and frustrated by your inability to put your plans across. You know precisely what you mean—in your imagination you can visualize every detail—but when it comes to tangible expression, you often flop. There are exceptions to this, powerful ones, because Mars is the planet of force and energy. If well aspected, Mars confers the necessary strength to overcome the debilitating effect. Even so, you will always have difficulties to surmount in practical endeavors. Pisces is self-sacrificing, sensitive, goodhearted and psychic. These qualities reflect the very antithesis of the Mars warriorlike aggression and rambunctiousness. This is probably the most difficult position in the whole Zodiac for fiery Mars.

You are most likely to be successful in occupations that depend on tuning in to other people's emotions, or in those in which you can express yourself in abstract and subtle ways so as to arouse the finer feelings of others. As an actor or actress, you can communicate to your audience on a very satisfying but indefinable wavelength. Mars provides the vigor for physical action, Pisces restrains it. The result may be an intriguingly languid movement, exciting in its suggestion, even sexy, but exasperatingly elusive. This combination could produce a first rate dancer.

You could also be successful as a writer or an artist, again arousing emotions and even passions with an insinuative style, rather than an explicit one. The power to switch emotions quickly is extremely evident in people with this combination. But as beneficent as this trait may be in creative expression, it can cause great internal confusion. These people's constant ambivalences make them wary of their own moods. They are subject to depression because of the hopeless feeling that they'll never be as normal as they imagine those around them to be. What they fail to realize is that the normalcy they covet so much in despairing moments would destroy their wonderful artistic potential.

You have a great desire to be liked, to be popular, but circumstances usually work against this, particularly where the larger public is concerned. In any case, no matter how highly regarded you are—by the world or only by your own friends—you'll never feel satisfied. It is not that you want more acclaim. It's that in your dreams where you act out much of your life before it happens, the feeling of success and acceptance is different.

You are courageous in the face of misfortune, and this often comes through love affairs. You adore excitement and mystery and can fall head-over-heels in love with those you feel project these qualities. But unless it's the real thing—which is very rare with Mars in Pisces—your affections quickly fade. Ordinary personalities, no matter how attractive, don't possess the depth of character to stand up to your intuitive scrutiny, which is actually searching for Love Everlasting! You revel in other people and read them like books—and the "paperback" types take no time at all to get through.

You are extremely impressionable and sometimes easily led. You'd rather comply than resist if there is no great issue at stake. You can't be bothered raising objections just to have your own voice heard. Your egotism is far deeper than that—you like to manipulate people and situations quietly and unobtrusively, and a compliant and receptive nature (as you know only too well) is ideal for this.

The Other Side of the Story

You suffer deeply from your own indecision and vacillating moods. Your friends learn to be cautious of you, knowing you are likely to be pleasant and obliging one moment and bitterly resentful the next. Marriage is likely to be delayed. You may be deserted by lovers or plunged into scandal through an illicit affair. Because of your inability to cope with normal life, you are apt to seek escape in drink or drugs. You are probably promiscuous and permissive but unable to satisfy your sexual cravings. You are lazy, easily depressed and cannot seem to remain in one job for very long.

CHAPTER NINETEEN

Jupiter

This chapter on Jupiter gives you some facts about the planet's physical features, the myths and symbolism surrounding it, and an astrological account of its characteristics. Then follows a description of Jupiter in the various zodiacal signs.

The Planet

Jupiter is the largest planet in the solar system. After Venus, it is the brightest. Its diameter is 88,000 miles compared with the Earth's 8000 miles. Jupiter is nearly 500 million miles out from the Sun, and is never closer than 367 million miles to the Earth.

The huge "empty" space between Mars and Jupiter—an inconceivable 342 million miles—is littered with cosmic rubble. This is called the asteroid belt.

Jupiter takes a little over 12 Earth years to circle the Zodiac. Jupiter's transit through each of the Signs takes about 12 to 14 months, not always the same amount of time in each Sign.

Despite the planet's tremendous size, Jupiter rotates in less than 10 hours, against the Earth's 24. The sections near the poles are not completely solidified, so the period of rotation for all parts of Jupiter is not uniform. Because of the planet's lack of density and its speed of rotation, its poles have a pronounced flattened appearance.

The striking features of the planet's atmosphere are light- and dark-colored belts paralleling the equator, which slowly change, and the Great Red Spot. This "spot" is 20,000 miles long, and although fading, appears to be more permanent than the belts.

In January 1610, Galileo made history by discovering Jupiter's satellites. He named them the Medician planets after his patron Cosimo Medici. These can easily be seen through good binoculars. They have diameters of 2300 to 3200 miles and revolve around Jupiter in 2 to 17 days. There are eight other Jovian moons, all of which are less than 100 miles in diameter. One, very close to the planet, revolves at a speed of over 1000 miles a minute.

Jupiter is largely or entirely composed of gases. Hydrogen, methane and ammonia have been detected in its atmosphere. Pioneer 10 passed within 81,000 miles of the planet in December 1973 and sent back color pictures and information as it flew out of the solar system.

Symbolism

Zeus or Jupiter, as he was called by the Romans, was the greatest of the Olympian divinities. He was the omnipotent ruler of the ancient Greek gods who lived on the summit of Mount Olympus. He was regarded as the father of men and thought possibly to be even the master of fate. The Romans considered him the guardian of the law, protector of justice and virtue, and defender of the truth.

Jupiter was the son of Cronus who, fearing he would be deposed by his sons, swallowed them one by one at birth. But his wife, Rhea, gave Cronus a stone to swallow when Jupiter was born, and the young god was brought up in a cave in Crete. In 1900, archeologists explored this reputed "birth cave" and found votive offerings to Jupiter believed to have been there since the year 2000 B.C. It was said that Rhea's priests clashed their weapons in the cave to drown the infant Jupiter's cries and that a goat acted as his nurse. The goat was rewarded by being placed among the stars as Capricorn. (The Goat is, of course, the symbol of the Sign Capricorn.)

Jupiter fathered four Olympian deities by mortal women: Mercury, Artemis or Diana (the Moon), Apollo (god of prophesy) and Dionysus (god of wine).

Jupiter was called the Thunderer and his chief weapon was the thunderbolt. Sacred to him were the oak, the eagle and mountain summits. His sacrifices were usually goats, cows and bulls. He sometimes wore a wreath of oak or olive leaves. The rustling of oak leaves was said to be his voice.

Jupiter's attributes were the scepter, a thunderbolt, an eagle and a figure of victory held in the hand.

Astrology

Jupiter is fiery, noble, benevolent, fruitful and masculine. It typifies all that is jovial, optimistic, expansive, buoyant, positive and dignified in man. It is the good provider, the respecter and upholder of the law, the generous and genial helper.

Jupiter rules Sagittarius, the ninth Sign of the Zodiac, which is associated with long journeys both metaphysical and geographical and with higher studies. Jupiter also has co-rulership, with Uranus, of Pisces, the twelfth Sign of the Zodiac, which is disposed to long journeys, life in a foreign place and acute religious or spiritual insight.

Jupiter is well aspected in the Sign of Cancer. Here Jupiter is exalted, which means that its influence is more powerful than in other zodiacal signs. In Capricorn, however, the Sign opposite Cancer, Jupiter loses some of its strength and so its influence is comparatively weak.

Jupiter in Astrology is called the "greater benefic," or "greater fortune." (Venus is called the "lesser benefic" or "lesser fortune.") Jupiter not only brings an abundance of material benefits, but is also the source of philosophical wisdom. It teaches frequently by coming to the rescue at the last minute, when all hope seems lost. Saturn is also a great teacher, but teaches by restriction, denial and adversity without any (immediately apparent) saving grace. Jupiter's nature is to fulfill; it delivers the goods at the end of the lesson. Jupiter is the strength that allows us to endure trials with philosophic steadiness in the knowledge that we are growing in wisdom and experience. It is the happy ending, the great protector. The only danger from a well-placed Jupiter is that you may fail to see or take full advantage of the opportunities it offers.

People with Jupiter prominent in their horoscope are generous and candid. They have a good intellect and astute judgment. Their observations are often uncannily on the mark. They show a greater understanding of morality and religious ideals and have a deep respect for law and order. Their conscience continually reminds them that in the final analysis, justice and decency depend on the individual. These men and women are broad-minded, logical, determined and extremely self-confident.

Jupiter makes for a happy, outgoing, sociable and likable person. He or she enjoys a good time, is hospitable and has many friends. These people often display an interest in the law and enjoy philosophic and religious studies. They have a penchant for foreign travel, and until they can make such a journey, will read and talk avidly about the places they want to visit.

The influence of Jupiter is expansive, creative and prosperous. Unless the planet is ill placed, it invariably bestows a great amount of what appears to be good luck. The person is either born with money, is provided with an income or becomes well off later in life. These men and women usually display great faith in their good fortune by being lavishly generous when economy is indicated, or exceedingly easygoing about their possessions. Easy come, easy go is often their attitude.

Jupiter is associated with organized sports, and its influence extends to gambling and games of chance— indeed any activity in which a wager can be made for fun or for profit. Compulsive gambling can become a problem if Jupiter is badly aspected in an individual's horoscope.

Jupiter people love activity and physical exercise. They usually develop a strong, muscular frame and in later years become stout or fat. Since Jupiter is the planet of expansion, such people are readily susceptible to middle-age spread even though they like to move about freely, the farther the better. The means and the freedom to travel are very important as a consequence of Jupiter's influence.

Jupiter governs travel and long journeys, foreign countries and international affairs. People far away, in-laws, distant relatives, experts and professionals come under the sway of Jupiter.

Education is also a keyword for Jupiter's domain. This means education in the sense of developing the higher faculties of mind in contrast to short-term training, basic learning or knowledge gained by experience. Such higher learning includes philosophy, religion, ethics, justice and the law.

A fortunate Jupiter placement in an individual's horoscope can lead to honorable involvement in the teaching professions. He or she makes a competent judge, lawyer, banker, broker or physician. These people are usually fitted for positions of dignity, trust or power in business or social circles. Large charities, religious foundations and philanthropic organizations often provide them with the scope they need for the exercise of their particular talents.

A badly placed Jupiter causes restlessness and uncertainty. The person may be an extremist in his or her views and become a religious or political fanatic. Excessive optimism and carelessness may mar judgment. Losses are likely through bad investments, gambling and extravagance. These people may run up debts, borrow money indiscriminately, fail to honor their obligations and generally lead a lazy, luxury-loving, shallow life devoid of any uplifting philosophic or religious thoughts.

Jupiter represents the power of uniform growth throughout the organism. The urge is to mature, to expand the consciousness through understanding what has been experienced rather than merely to accumulate knowledge. Jupiter strives to counterbalance our inadequacies and failures by developing compensation features elsewhere. The subconscious awareness of these weaknesses form the conscience. The conscience is the motivating factor in Jupiter people. They are continually reminded of the need for justice, morality, mercy and the law—both man-made and religious.

Physiologically, Jupiter rules the expansion of the body and is associated with the disposition of fats, the liver (the largest gland) and the pituitary gland, which regulates hormone production. Some problems arising due to Jupiter's influence are high blood pressure, hypertension, apoplexy, gout, overweight, and pleurisy.

Jupiter in Aries

You are a person with great and grand ambitions. You aim to get to the top in whatever field you choose. You are not content to follow in the footsteps of others. You consent to knuckle down to an apprenticeship for as short a time as possible out of sheer necessity, but as soon as you think you are qualified, you will be off into the wide blue yonder where you can display your originality, initiative and leadership—and do as you like.

You won't settle for second place in anything. This combination gives an aggressive determination to succeed for the good of all concerned and not just the self. You genuinely feel you have a mission in life. You don't have faith in the orthodox or the established. In fact, you are a bit of a skeptic where religious doctrines are concerned. But you believe wholeheartedly that forces deep within you are pushing you toward a predestined point.

You are intent on broadening your mind. You love to travel, to do big things on the spur of the moment. You detest detail, and routine jobs you avoid like the plague. You have a flair for organization, for handling numbers of people and big concerns. You are a born leader. Men make excellent military chiefs. Women are just as gifted in military fields. Both sexes have an impelling desire to establish a reputation. If this can be done with dash and a flourish of heroics, you will be delighted. You can burst into politics—enrich and enliven the scene with outrageous policies that catch the popular imagination and leave the diehards standing flatfooted. Your ideas are likely to be so original that at first they may seem impractical. But you have the ability to put your point of view across forcefully and intelligently. You are at your best when defending an idea that is under attack from reactionary and conservative forces.

You don't like working under others and you usually succeed finally to a position of independence and authority. People respect you because you always seem to know where you are heading. You have tremendous enthusiasm and energy—sometimes you get carried away by your own optimism and self-confidence and make promises you can't keep. Your generosity and desire to be helpful also get the better of you. You say you will do things and then find you can't.

You have a natural aptitude for literature, science and the law. You are generally lucky with speculative investments, though this depends specifically on other influences in your chart. Gambling can be your making or ruin. Young people usually play a prominent and fortunate role in your affairs. You often make a successful marriage that brings you money or raises your social standing. Otherwise, you make your mark in the world through your own qualifications and unremitting effort.

You are likely to change your career at some time in your life. Your business interests may be widely diversified so that you have to be on the move to keep a check on what's going on because you are known for your open-handed habits; you have plenty of company when ever you want it. You prefer the congenial, intellectual type of friend with whom you can discuss a wide range of topics. You enjoy nothing better than new places and new faces. You are keenly interested in expanding your experience of life; you want to feel that you have tried everything at least once. You develop a definite philosophy that is pragmatic rather than idealistic, but once your views are formed, they may become fixed and dogmatic. You may enjoy laying down the law and arguing with people. You love sports and displaying your excellent physical coordination, but you are not much of a spectator.

The Other Side of the Story

You may expect too much from life and be constantly disappointed. Gambling is likely to be a compulsive and ruinous disease. You may be a big talker, promising anything to anybody to get attention, and avoiding people you have let down. You are likely to be unrealistic and count on luck when common sense warns otherwise. Your desire for experience may degenerate into a bustling search for sensual gratification.

Jupiter in Taurus

You have a great love of pleasure and home comforts. Money seems to come easily (you are lucky that way) but you are also prepared to work hard for what you want. The combination of the abundant Jupiter in Taurus, the Sign of material acquisition and income, makes you a naturally favored individual.

You are warmhearted, generous, reserved and affectionate. You love beauty in all its forms. You may not be an artist yourself, but you could easily be a connoisseur or collector. You like to fill your home with elegant and beautiful things that others will admire. Apart from aesthetics, you also enjoy the feeling of security derived from owning valuable objects. You usually possess a fine collection of books, many of them to do with religion, metaphysics and philosophy.

You go all out to make money and to build up your estate. You have a flair for making money earn money. Whether you work for yourself or an employer, you can usually be counted on to turn a profit. You are especially able in fields connected with building, banking, the land and mining. With this combination, you are a potential tycoon. A wizard at building up businesses, you tend to rely on solid and proven methods and are reluctant to take unnecessary chances. But you spread your investments widely and wisely. You are determined; you work toward your planned objectives with untiring persistence. Your Midas touch often extends into the oil business, ranching, massive construction projects, agriculture and industry. Although your ideas are often advanced, even radical, you like to apply them in a systematical manner. The quicker you can reduce your procedures to a routine, the happier you are. At heart, you are cautious and conservative.

Your love of the good life is likely to make you extravagant. You enjoy reveling in luxury. You may run into debt supplying yourself with the best in food, drink, entertainment and accommodations. You can very easily go to extremes where sensual pleasures are concerned. You are strongly attracted to the opposite sex.

Although you enjoy reading and talking about other countries, you aren't a great one for traveling unless it is connected with business or education. If you do have to visit a foreign city, you enjoy it (provided you're traveling first class), but in your heart of hearts, you prefer the psychological comfort of familiar surroundings, particularly your own home. You are devoted to your family and like to feel you are a good provider. Sometimes you may have an exaggerated idea of what you are doing for loved ones; other times, you make lavish promises you have no hope of fulfilling. You take to domestic life like a duck to water: you enjoy sitting in your favorite chair, feeling the fine wood of your furniture, walking on quality carpets. You are fond of entertaining and showing off your possessions. You have a penchant for jewelry, paintings, miniatures, porcelain and fine hand-crafted objects.

You believe in helping people who help themselves, that is, you prefer to create opportunities for others to take advantage of rather than give them a straight handout. You are a fair and a generous employer but you won't tolerate gold-bricking. You want to see justice done on both sides. You can be very firm when the occasion demands it.

You have strong religious leanings but you don't allow them to interfere with your day-to-day activities. Your ethics are practical and straightforward: you believe that if you treat others fairly and justly in your worldly affairs, you are largely obeying all the religious tenets.

With Jupiter in Taurus, you may possess a good singing or speaking voice. Many talented actors and singers have the Jupiter in Taurus combination.

You are likely to gain financially through marriage, partnerships and legacies. Your children may give you reason to be proud of them.

The Other Side of the Story

Your love of luxury may wreck your health. You are likely to overeat and have a weight problem, overspend and always be in debt. Gambling may ruin your chances. Your children may fail to come up to your expectations. Your taste is such that you are likely to clutter your home with cheap and junky ornaments, believing them to be artistic and desirable. You may be an out-and-out materialist who lives only for the pleasure your possessions (including the people you love) give you. Your own ability to love may be as shallow as the platitudes you constantly spout. You are likely to be a hypocritical religionist. Your marriage or business partners may take you down. You may lose a legacy or an inheritance. You are likely to be easily fooled with promises. You may be lackadaisical and quick to give up.

Jupiter in Gemini

Your ideas are grandiose. Your mind can stretch beyond the normal horizons—out of this world, in fact. You are a master at seizing hold of abstract ideas and propounding them in ingenious ways. You are voluble, eloquent, amusing, intelligent, articulate, likable, knowledgeable and persuasive. But one question usually remains unanswered when you have finished holding forth: Will your scheme actually work? Frequently the answer is no.

In this position, the expansive, jovial and optimistic Jupiter combines with the nervous, restless intellectual and airy Sign of Gemini. The result is often insubstantial. Jupiter here is at its detriment. It is not that the planet is incompatible with Gemini; it is just that it can't manage to contribute its heavyweight qualities to this often scatterbrained Sign.

You are a person who has great faith in the mind's ability to solve all the world's problems. Your aim is to gather knowledge. You believe in higher education and would like to have at least one academic degree yourself. You want to travel as far afield as possible, to see things first hand, to meet people, talk, exchange ideas, correspond, to become a well-informed person.

You are not only a quiz kid but a whiz kid. You are constantly on the move. You love to make friends—to pop in on them, call them up. You scatter your views and opinions around with the abandon of someone throwing wheat to chickens. You are seldom around long enough to collect any eggs. You know a little about a great many subjects, but you lack the power to concentrate long and deeply on any single study. Actually, you are seldom at a disadvantage because your fine intellect and retentive memory enable you to ad-lib in most situations with an amazing show of erudition.

You aim to earn a living through mental pursuits. You are not a very practical person. Physical routine and manual labor are anathema to you. You are a theorist, a visionary. You have the brilliant answer in your mind; it is for others with an aptitude for detailed procedures to apply your solutions. You make an excellent diplomat, writer, teacher, lawyer, actor, linguist, banker, stockbroker, underwriter. You can be successful in air transport, broadcasting or television. With maturity, those of you who are writers may gravitate to the publishing field and enjoy considerable success. You probably play a musical instrument. If you try, you should be able to compose music and may even be able to earn a living from it.

You are an idealist who limits your chances of lasting accomplishment by jumping from one new activity to another. You scatter your energies, both mental and physical. You live for the satisfaction of the moment; the promises of tomorrow are just promises. Still, you build in a practical fashion despite yourself and are often fortunate and successful. Your instincts are strongly humanitarian. Although your approach to other people's problems is usually a reasoning one, you are kind and sympathetic.

You make friends very quickly and sometimes attract the wrong type—the go-getters and the schemers. You are so trusting and overconfident at times that you can be taken in by these people, especially in business matters. New ventures and propositions, especially the way-out kind, need to be vetted thoroughly.

You will probably marry twice. You are not the domestic type but will do your best to make your mate happy. You need a partner who is intellectual rather than emotional, one who understands your need to come and go much as you please. You are a rather disorganized person and your home sometimes reflects this. Travel, relatives and poor dependents are likely to cause marital problems. You may even marry a relative or a close associate.

You show a pronounced flair for philosophic reasoning. Your ideas in this field are sometimes provocative and original. You are worth listening to, but your appeal is principally to the intellect and fails to satisfy deeper human longings that depend on faith rather than reason.

The Other Side of the Story

Your writings and beliefs may stir others up against you. Sudden difficulties can make it impossible for you to continue in your profession or job. You may be forced by circumstances to keep traveling and be unable to settle down when you wish to. Your marriage is likely to break up and divorce or separation may involve you in considerable expense. You may have to work to support another person and have very little money for yourself. Differences and separations from relatives are likely to occur in distressing circumstances. A publishing venture may flop. Your best ideas or plans may be stolen. You are likely to talk your way into jobs and then out of them. You may be a compulsive gossip.

Jupiter in Cancer

This is a most auspicious placing for Jupiter. It generally means roses all the way. The person is charitable, popular, enterprising and good-humored. Circumstances are usually fortunate and fulfilling. Jupiter, the influence of good fortune and growth, is at its strongest in Cancer.

You are a person whose sympathies are easily aroused. You will put yourself out to help another in a practical way and genuinely endeavor to understand people's problems. You combine thought and feeling in a rare balance, which makes you a kind, benevolent and well-integrated human being.

You have a great attachment to your home and family. You are fiercely protective of your loved ones and will do all in your power to help them get on in the world, even if they don't deserve your aid. You try very successfully to live up to the traditions of elegance and good living you have assimilated. You don't deny yourself any comforts. You aim at being surrounded in your home with all the things you admire. These include not only objects that are pleasing to the eye but also those redolent of the past. You have a penchant for antiques, relics and memorabilia. You are likely to keep a family bible, handed down from generation to generation, in a special place. Your furnishings or decor will reflect your admiration of classical lines and historical form. There will be no shortage of sentimental bric-a-brac. Old photographs, letters, a family coat of arms and well-worn leather-bound books, if not displayed, will be tucked away with loving care.

You enjoy traveling, especially over the sea or to places by the water. You may travel for education or business purposes but are not averse to making a trip just for pleasure. While you are away, you think about your home, and vice versa. You often manage to get away once or twice a year, and this helps you appreciate both your home and your love of travel.

Your financial judgment is extremely good. More often than not, you are helped by good luck. You enjoy making money, but no more than you delight in spending it. You are a very self-possessed person; you have it all together in a natural and unaffected way. The influence of a stable and happy childhood usually creates a deep inner sense of security in people born with Jupiter in Cancer. An understanding and provident mother is also characteristic of this group, other things being equal. The image you present to the world is one of restrained optimism and confidence. This suggests—quite rightly—that you are able to handle your affairs more than capably. Women with this combination can take good care of themselves if anything happens to their male providers. All of you tend to share in inheritances or legacies at some time in your life and to receive money without having to work for it. The men frequently benefit materially from the women in their lives.

You are a gracious host or hostess. You enjoy the domestic life. You love to serve the best of food and drink. Your fondness for food and good living can create a weight problem, which will have to be dealt with eventually to safeguard your health. You enjoy a good time. By pouring too much energy into pleasurable activities, you risk stultifying your deeper development.

You are patriotic and very interested in public and national affairs. You like to keep yourself well informed of what is happening in the world. You are intuitive about the needs of people and your political views are well worth heeding.

You are suited for a wide variety of occupations. Usually you are most successful in fields requiring an assessment of the public mood and tastes, or in providing the masses with life's necessities. These include politics, the manufacturing industries, wholesale distribution, shipping and large-scale ventures connected with liquids and refreshments. Women with Jupiter in Cancer frequently marry prominent public figures. They also make exceptional nurses.

Your religious views are usually carried forward

from your childhood. You are apt to be a staunch supporter of the church or to espouse a homespun philosophy that stresses the basic interdependence of social groups and the moral law expressed through the family unit.

The Other Side of the Story

Blind extravagance is likely to lead to all kinds of complications and unhappiness if this combination is badly influenced by other factors. Excesses such as overindulgence in sex, food and drink are likely trouble starters. Your health may suffer through gluttonous habits and obesity. Inner misery brought about by an inability to cope with the conflict between intellect and emotions may make you seek relief in drugs or liquor.

Jupiter in Leo

Everything about you is expansive—and probably expensive, if you reflect the full potential of this very fortunate zodiacal placing. In some cases, it is a little too good and the person concerned becomes a slave of his own grandiose ambitions to be the wealthiest, best-dressed, most popular or influential guy or gal in town. Thus he or she misses out on the enjoyment money and position can give in moderation. Jupiter unrestrained tends toward excess; Leo often means a double dose.

Still, the fact remains that with Jupiter in regal Leo you have the capacity and the luck to raise yourself to a position of prominence in your particular community. Whether you spoil it by going to extremes is your decision.

As a mature person with this combination, you are generous, warmhearted and very keen on seeing justice done for your fellow man. You intend to make an impact for good on the world and to be remembered with genuine affection. Your ambitions are unlimited (everything you attempt is on a grand scale), but your lofty aspirations are supported by a magnanimous, dignified and noble temperament.

Although you enjoy comfort and luxury and are basically extravagant, you tend to accept these boons as your right while they are available. A sincere and honest type, you possess an innate sense of purpose, a feeling of being directed by powers greater than yourself—why should you dispute with a benevolent fate? Others may think you're a little too grand at times.

You inevitably rise to a position of authority and revel in all the honors and privileges it confers. You possess excellent executive ability and are particularly well suited for high government office and work in large well-established public companies. You have dash, loads of self-confidence, good humor and a splendid sense of the dramatic. Employees respect and admire you. You inspire loyalty and even hero-worship, which may arouse the jealousy of superiors.

You are ideally suited for heading a public relations or advertising firm. You would make an excellent figurehead, ready to step in and do the lesser tasks if necessary, but prepared to enjoy the lavish living and entertainment if not. The film-making industry may also be a suitable medium for your talents, and maybe the promotion and organizing of tours by international celebrities. You are quite likely to rise to fame yourself.

You are a proud and passionate lover—as a man, masterful, as a woman, utterly yielding to the guy who can demonstrate (to your satisfaction) that he is worthy of you. You love being pursued. The center of attention in any company you feel is reserved for you. Social popularity means so much that you spend much of your income (or expense account) on entertaining to keep up your position. You make a wonderful host or hostess.

You possess a flair for art as well as a genuine love of it. Your artistic preferences, whether they take the form of color, sound or shape, reflect either the flamboyant and spectacular or the richly conservative—nothing in between. You know precisely what you like and don't like. You are seldom confused or undecided. You lean toward philosophic subjects and literature and may try your hand at writing a book sometime.

You have exceptional judgment in business and financial matters, and usually acquire a reputation for wisdom and foresight in regard to everyday affairs. You are unusually lucky with speculative investments.

The Other Side of the Story

You may hog all the glory and conveniently forget to give credit where credit is due. You are puffed up with your own importance, boastful, domineering and an incorrigible spendthrift. Your health is poorer than you think because you won't exercise, you overeat and you drink too much. You are always in debt and constantly borrow from friends. You are a social climber and a poseur, blinded by appearances and affectation. You choose the wrong friends nearly every time. Your love of glamour and all that is gawdy, ostentatious and phony makes you easy to deceive. Your love life is a procession of disappointments and arguments over money and possessions.

Jupiter in Virgo

Yours is a mind ideally suited for coping with the frenzied activity and pace of modern business. You are not the tycoon type who sits in his or her ivory tower controlling or figureheading a vast organization. Your aim is to be down where the day-to-day and job-to-job action is, where you can have a hand in the actual production, distribution and on-the-spot management. You're not an empire builder; you are, rather, the type who keeps commercial enterprises growing at the grassroots level.

Expansion, based on impeccably sound, prudent and practical reasoning, is your theme. You never overlook the little things. You have an instinct for turning the simplest ideas into paying propositions. Any hobby of yours can usually earn money. Detail intrigues you—your acute discriminative powers help you to isolate the smallest essentials so they can be applied in proper sequence. You know that with a mind as analytical as yours, attention to detail leads to practical solutions—minute atoms strung together make up the world of matter, after all!

You are an intricate planner, and if allowed too much latitude, are likely to get bogged down in materialistic considerations. Under your capable direction, all systems providing for efficiency, order and creature comforts are likely to be go. But where does this lead ultimately? To you, the question may have no relevance; but to others, who know that human happiness is not based on a well-paid 35-hour week, a smooth production line or a personal computer, it's not that simple. To put it bluntly, you're excessively intellectual and, unless there are other mitigating influences in the chart, emotionally undeveloped. The quality of life does not depend on what can be weighed or measured.

Personally, you are inclined to be unbending and stereotyped, not lacking in imagination by any means, but short on spontaneity and the ability to relax in company. Your reserve and formal manner put a damper on your social life. You don't make friends easily and are inclined to choose those who share your intellectual interests rather than look for empathetic connections.

Scientific subjects have a fascination for you. You love probing possibilities such as whether there is life on the other planets. Philosophic speculation also appeals to you. You possess an innate talent for technological research. People with Jupiter in Virgo are frequently found working with computers and other highly advanced electronic devices used in modern industry and experimental laboratories. You have a very special interest in diet and hygiene and busy yourself in one way or another with propagating your discoveries and views on these subjects.

You are likely to make business trips to foreign countries and possibly marry someone you meet there. Chances are your wife or husband will not be as well off or as intellectually advanced as you. The circumstances in which you marry could be peculiar. In middle life, you will probably enjoy a more comfortable and sophisticated existence than people would have predicted in your earlier years.

You have a gift for writing and speaking clearly and are equipped to produce books about your travels as well as manuals and textbooks dealing with your particular line of work. You would also make a capable lecturer or teacher.

You get along well with co-workers and employees. Your honesty and openness are attractive. Superiors trust you. Sometimes you are overly critical and this upsets others. You are also rather skeptical about religious matters, and if outspoken in this regard, can sound intolerant. You believe that if people were to do the right thing in their daily lives, there would be no call for dogmatic reminders.

The Other Side of the Story

Your ideas lack depth and betray an inability to see life as it really is. Your proposals usually paper over problems rather than provide solutions. You lack concentration and rely on quick-witted cunning to get you through. You write and speak for effect. You exaggerate the simplest situations and have a reputation for wasting your own and other people's time with trivia. Your ambitions far exceed your capabilities. You are unlucky in love. Marriage is likely to lead to irritating restrictions and lost chances. You read avidly but learn very little of consequence.

Jupiter in Libra

Once upon a time there was a kind, obliging and gentle person who saw more good than evil in everyone, who sincerely tried to promote peace wherever he went and who consistently denied his own self-interest to see justice done to others. Recognize him or her? It's you—provided there are no spoilers among the rest of the influences in your horoscope.

This combination confers a breadth of vision that exceeds the limited ego and embraces the aspirations of humanity as a whole. As a pure reflection of Jupiter in Libra, you would rather serve than be served—not in menial ways, mind you, for it is not in physical effort that your gifts and abilities lie. You are an intellectual and aesthetic being. You possess a rare balance of most that is refined or admirable in man. You embody the spirit of fair play. Being just, you can judge.

Now, everyone with Jupiter in Libra can't be a saint or sit on the Supreme Court. But the basic principle holds true and expresses itself through the individual irrespective of how ordinary or seemingly undistinguished his or her life may be.

You need an occupation that allows you to express these basic urges. Being a sensitive soul, you are not going to be happy in disharmonious and squalid surroundings or where people are coarse and aggressive. (If these are your present working conditions, then Jupiter is probably badly aspected.) You will be most contented in work that has a light artistic element or a profound humanistic value. You shine where you can employ your superlative judgment, which is not restricted to a judiciary role. You may just as easily receive satisfaction from employment in the chemical industry, weighing one ingredient against another to produce a better cosmetic, synthetic material or pleasing dye color, or as a jeweler or fine-metal worker. An appreciation or talent for writing, poetry and singing is natural to this pleasant combination. But it is in expressing your social conscience as a lawyer and judge, or in your devotional insight as a prophet, mystic or religious leader, that you seem to fulfill your highest potential. You may also be successful as a banker, broker, engineer, electrician, architect or designer. You do not adapt well to the harsh competition and methods of the business world.

Although you can often manage to sort out other people's affairs, you are not so good at managing your own. You are inclined to let financial matters slide and to get yourself into a muddle. You are very fond of entertaining and mixing in higher social circles. This and a predilection for beautiful and expensive things, including fashionable clothes, makes you an extravagant spender—when you have the money.

You are tormented by what could be described as a pernicious desire to be liked and accepted by your associates. As long as any doubt on this score remains in your mind, you will suffer painfully and go to extraordinary lengths to win people over with courtesy and hospitality. You are so addicted to the need to make a good impression that you will sometimes even neglect old friends for a casual acquaintance.

Friends are usually lucky for you, both financially and socially.

You are often on close terms with influential people in the community. Money and social position often come through partners. You are lucky in love and generally enjoy a happy marriage. Children of people with Jupiter in Libra are usually very bright.

The Other Side of the Story

The women in your life are vindictive, extravagant and two-faced. You are frequently disappointed and let down by friends and associates. As much as you try, you can't seem to break into the right social circles. People are put off by your unctious manner and obvious insincerity. You have a weight problem, or you dress in an ostentatious and gaudy style. You are affected, boastful and can't adjust to your position in life. You are always trying to go one better than the other person. Lawsuits and lawyers are unlucky for you. You are often confronted with hostile people who refuse to see your point of view.

Jupiter in Scorpio

Mysteries, secrets and other people's confidences are usually prominent in the lives of people born with Jupiter in Scorpio.

You have a strange attraction for those who are looking for someone to confide in, and often the information imparted is serious enough to give you a hold of sorts over the other party. In normal circumstances (depending on other influences in the chart), you would never betray another. But that doesn't alter the fact that you have a knack of conveying you know more than you are telling so that you can "induce" others to make "confessions." Not surprisingly, this combination is often found in the horoscopes of spies, detectives, private investigators, psychiatrists—and religious extremists!

You are an emotionally charged person, but very capable of concealing your feelings. You can go to extremes, dangerous extremes, but seldom do you allow others to detect any sign of weakness that may impair their faith in you as a person who knows exactly what he or she is doing at all times. It is this tremendous capacity for self-control that makes you such an asset in an emergency. You don't crack under pressure, or doubt your own ability to eventually get the upper hand. You are basically the steel-nerved type who would make a competent surgeon, dentist or military commander.

One of your problems is you tend to make the same serious mistakes more than once. It's as though you are attracted to the same situations and mesmerized, by your sheer faith in yourself, into believing that this time you can overcome. Unfortunately, you seldom do. Few people are better able to endure difficulties and physical discomfort than you. You possess an iron will; once you've fixed your goal, you won't be deflected from it under any circumstances.

You are enthusiastic and shrewd, absorbingly ambitious and have a great yearning for power. Once this is achieved, you usually attempt to change conditions so fundamentally that they can never be reversed; thus do you irrevocably destroy the old order. "Destroy" is a word most appropriate to this combination: these people can be powerful agents for destruction (or construction). They enjoy handling and manipulating masses of people, equipment or construction materials. The religiously inclined can become fanatical and, given the opportunity, cause drastic upheavals in the immediate community.

Jupiter in Scorpio people are often engineers engaged in large-scale building projects, especially dams, as well as huge drainage and sewerage schemes. High government jobs also attract them. But, as usual, wherever Scorpio is involved, the danger exists that the person may misuse power for his or her own selfish ends. In public life, this combination permits unlimited lawlessness and tyrannical behavior.

You are proud—sometimes haughty—but not egotistical. Your mind is extremely subtle and capable of the most abstruse analytical reasoning. If there are two ways of approaching a problem, you can be counted on to try the most indirect first. You believe in gentle persuasion and deft tactics, but if these fail, you do not hesitate to crack the whip or, given the right circumstances, use force.

You usually manage to move in circles where power and authority are exercised. Your ability to sense money-making opportunities is quite phenomenal. You have a way of quietly noting significant but small signs or changes and waiting with astounding patience for the right time to make your move. Timing is your specialty in most things. You have an intuitive capability for spotting investments that will pay off later on.

There is a danger that younger people with this combination will be tempted to experiment with drugs out of a desire to penetrate deeper into experience. The addictive perils involved are completely overlooked.

The Other Side of the Story

Your judgment has proved to be unsound, but still you persist with speculative investments and go on losing. Your love life is unhappy and has probably landed you in more than one legal tangle. Arguments, hostility and jealousy are apt to mar your professional progress. Your so-called friends are unreliable and more than once have sold you out. Your bitter envy of someone in a more powerful position is likely to provoke his or her enmity and spoil your own chances. Any money gained from legacies will probably be lost or absorbed in legal costs. Sex may well be a major problem area.

Jupiter in Sagittarius

This is a lucky combination. Genial Jupiter, said to be the planet of greater fortune and success, is in its own Sign and therefore strong. Sagittarius itself stands for activities not normally associated with the hard grind of earning a living—travel, philosophy, religion and outdoor sports. The result is an active, independent and good-humored person—you.

You've probably noticed that you attract money or the things you need in life. Not that you necessarily have an overabundance, but sufficient amounts of what you require to proceed with the job at hand seem to be provided (as long as you don't worry excessively). That's the first phenomenon that often accompanies this combination. The second is a caveat: you're only lucky so long as you don't lose faith in your luck! In other words, if you have money, you've got to spend it, not try to hold onto it. As a general rule, as long as you spend, it keeps coming. When you stop, the fountain shuts off.

Not surprisingly, you are incurably optimistic. And your optimism—along with your free and easy manner—makes you popular with your associates and a welcome visitor. You enjoy conversation and mixing with as many different types of people as you can. You're a very acute observer of others and this emerges as an interest in their problems and a desire to help as much as possible. You have a broadminded interest in most topics, especially science, serious literature, law and animals. You are remarkably candid and at times your comments to people about themselves are so accurate that they offend. But your open and patently sincere manner usually guarantees that any ill feeling will evaporate immediately. You also possess a lively sense of humor and a love of fun, which enables you to win friends quickly.

Your mind is sharp and clear and particularly adroit at producing ideas for making money. You rely a great deal on your intuition and because of it are quite successful at gambling and speculation. A sixth sense warns you when others are lying or situations are dangerous. You are the type who can walk out of a crowded public building seconds before the roof collapses just because you "felt it was the best thing to do."

You love to entertain and visit others at their homes, and are generous both as a guest and as a host or hostess. Whatever you do in the way of entertainment, you do lavishly with a touch of panache. Your parties are probably very popular events. You also enjoy night life.

You possess a great sense of humor and try to be kind and considerate. You won't knowingly hurt or deceive another person. Your conscience, literally, is your guide, and if ever you should feel remorseful, you will go well out of your way to make amends with a generous gesture and heart-felt apologies. You are tolerant of other people's weaknesses and it is natural for you to sympathize and offer help. You are generally high-minded, just and farseeing.

Although contemptuous of bureaucractic restrictions and many outdated traditions, you can be quite orthodox in your approach to religious matters. You usually feel that it is the moral code espoused by the great religions that prevents society from collapsing under undue contemporary stresses and strains. You tend to favor reforms that are acceptable to a majority of thinking people like yourself rather than subscribe to revolutionary ideas and tactics.

You are keenly interested in education but have doubts about the usefulness of some of the knowledge taught in classrooms. You are more likely to support an education system that puts the emphasis on practical experience and participation. You also believe that travel is one of the finest teachers.

It should be remembered that this combination can produce a person whose views on life are serious and profound, as befitting a basically metaphysical Sign. This outlook may curb much of the outward-going joviality. The personality may be kind and pleasant, but reserved and ponderous.

The Other Side of the Story

Parties, entertainment and other social affairs have a habit of ending unfortunately. Quarrels and misunderstandings are frequent. Your efforts to please others seldom work out. Love partners complicate your life and saddle you with many unnecessary expenses. Although you probably enjoy sports, you may have had some trouble or bad luck through them. You are sometimes a lucky gambler, but in the long run, you are a loser and this might be an incurably compulsive habit. Travel abroad usually leads to loss or aggravation of some kind.

Jupiter in Capricorn

There is not much doubt that you will work your way steadily to the top in the occupation of your choice. You have an abiding sense of responsibility, a flair for financial manipulation, good business sense and a powerful urge to succeed. You may take longer than is actually necessary to attain your goals, for you are very thorough and don't enjoy taking risks.

Jupiter in Capricorn people often feel pulled in two directions at once. Jupiter is the planet of optimism and expansion; Capricorn is the Sign of caution, restraint and deliberation. The combination creates some stresses and strains in the personality, which are often alleviated by understanding the basic causes.

For instance, you are inclined to be conservative and thrifty when dealing in small amounts of money. But where large sums are concerned, and especially if your reputation or business image is involved, you will spend as though the sky's the limit. This is not a bad trait. It permits you to build up your savings and make a good start at something, and it prevents you from squandering your money to make an impression. Clear and astute thinking always lies behind your financial actions. You may lay out four dollars to earn one, but it's a safe bet you are not taking that much of a gamble. However, you can be rather glib at justifying your mistakes and occasional excesses.

You are also a mixture of enthusiasm and caution. When you have a bright idea—which is quite often—you are likely to get carried away with the possibilities for success, only to be assailed at the last moment (or when the first obstacle is encountered) by sudden doubts and indecision. This also is not a bad trait. Your natural restraint will force you to thoroughly examine facts that you might have skated over in the first wave of optimism. Of course, hesitation means you will sometimes miss out on good opportunities, but once you learn to handle this paradoxical part of your nature, you will generally make solid progress.

People with Jupiter in Capricorn are natural leaders, usually on the business scene where weighty and sound achievement counts most. They are extremely well suited to executive positions where practical experience has to be augmented with the power to command and organize. The larger the business and the responsibility, the more likely these people will distinguish themselves. They possess a serious approach that impresses their superiors and engenders the respect and obedience (or cooperation) of employees. A high government post or a career culminating in heading a large public foundation or financial institution is likely to eventuate for those who have the opportunities. These people are also capable of running international conglomerates where the interests are widely diversified and complex.

You are inventive and occasionally unorthodox, especially when it comes to self-education in mature years. You enjoy reading and study, and probably have some practical connection with politics, science and even a religious organization. Your personal philosophy is well worth listening to if you can be persuaded to disclose it.

You have far less self-confidence than your manner suggests. In truth, you suffer severely from insecurity, even though it may be unjustified. To compensate, you do all in your power to preserve your reputation and good name. The respect and esteem of others, particularly those in authority, are enormously important to you. You are deeply pained by criticism, especially if it is delivered in public. Your fear of what others might think can be quite self-torturing. To be made a fool of in company is excruciating—and you will never really forgive the person responsible for your mortification.

You have a great capacity for handling detail and for devising economical and efficient measures. Occupations connected with the land, such as farming, mining and real estate, are likely to attract you. You should also be successful in the manufacturing industries or as a wholesaler or merchandiser. Wherever there is a need for perseverance, planning and prudence, with a dash of style, you should do well.

The Other Side of the Story

You plunge into projects with great enthusiasm, then back out for no apparent reason. Inside, you may be nearly a nervous wreck, afraid to attempt anything really constructive for fear of failing. Your fears of what others think of you may be almost phobic. Excessive worry could lead to stomach disorders. You may be mean and miserly. You are unnecessarily critical and severe with those who work for you and kowtow to those in authority. Sexual perversity and a coarse sense of humor are sometimes associated with the negative side of this combination. Friends are likely to be a source of trouble. You may be forced to pay for others' mistakes.

Jupiter in Aquarius

Your capacity for doing good in the world is considerable. Others may be more practical and possess greater stamina to serve in a physical sense, but you are, literally, the "brains of the outfit." You are supremely idealistic, a visionary in your way, a person who can see beyond obvious effects to the causes that need eliminating or remedying. You are sometimes called unrealistic by the more down-to-earth characters, who would prefer to give a starving man another bowl of soup than try to eradicate the conditions responsible for his poverty.

Aquarius is the Sign associated with the latest electronic inventions that have taken much of the drudgery out of our lives, especially in the modern home. Jupiter is the planet of material fortune and wisdom. Sign and planet blend naturally together here to produce a person who not only wishes to help his fellow man in practical and lasting ways, but frequently does so through new and novel means.

You are ideally suited for social, scientific and charitable work. You would make an excellent sociologist or union leader. You have a breadth of vision that allows you to visualize and plan large-scale humanitarian projects such as international medical relief and global campaigns against hunger. You have a flair for administration, for handling group funds and for distributing resources in complex conditions, particularly at the international level. You usually excel working abroad.

In ordinary business, you may be casual about your own best interests and inclined to put the welfare of employees and others before profitability—with predictable results. Your type of person is not particularly materialistic in his or her ambitions. You are usually better off working for an organization where your energies are not drained by accounting problems. In a nutshell, you are not so much an acquisitive type as a dedicated one.

In the professions, the independence and originality conferred by Jupiter in Aquarius makes you particularly creative in a social sense, so that through architecture, medicine, banking, politics, education, town planning and the like, you can implement reforms and lay down sweeping new lines, styles and patterns for the next generation to follow.

You enjoy unusual work of the kind that constantly tests your ingenuity, imagination and inventiveness. An ordinary nine-to-five routine job would drive you mad. Commercial businesses do not have any great appeal, unless they offer opportunities to satisfy and exhibit your innate unconventionality.

You make friends very easily and can harmonize with just about any type. You're not a sentimental person and are sometimes perceived as detached and cool in your affections. This is largely true—but not because you don't care. You see beyond the confines of limited personal attachments and realize that these can obstruct the grand principle of brotherhood and the breaking down of social barriers—principles you feel are so worthwhile.

You stand to gain in various ways through your friends and acquaintances. You do well in just about any group situation. You don't want power for its own sake, but you do respect it as a means for achieving reform. Friends often involve you in peculiar situations. Your life is subject to sudden and dramatic changes. You have a fondness for reading about ESP and other psychic experiences. Your intuition is first-rate.

The Other Side of the Story

You are alarmingly unpredictable and erratic. You can't be depended on from one moment to the next. You possess extraordinary ideas about politics and social reform, some of which are so far-fetched that no one will listen to them. Though you constantly advocate changes or some kind of revolution, you never seem to do anything concrete yourself. Oddballs, misfits and others belonging to the lunatic fringe of society are numbered among your friends. You don't remain long enough in one job to get anywhere. You have very little chance of making a success of marriage. Love affairs invariably end in separation. You are far too easily influenced by the opinions and ideals of others.

Jupiter in Pisces

People can't help but like you. You go straight to their hearts. Others can probably tell better stories, make more scintillating conversation and appear more clever and intellectual. Yours is a more simple appeal, a soul appeal. You care about people, all people, and frequently suffer personally when you see them sorrowful or in pain. With Jupiter in Pisces, you can often touch and stir in others emotions they didn't realize lay within them.

You need work that is not intellectual. There's not much doubt you will find what you are looking for—in the end—but for some time you are likely to go from job to job. You will never stay where you are unhappy. You cannot endure work that involves pressure and concentrated thought. Your ability to charm and get along with employers and co-workers does not satisfy you—you must have a function you consider worthwhile. You want to be of use to humanity in some way. If you understand this peculiar need, you should be able to save yourself a lot of time and aggravation the next time you have to change positions or go looking for satisfaction elsewhere.

Many of you can find sufficient contentment in an artistic occupation, especially acting or dancing. This type of activity allows you to communicate directly to an audience and to feel their emotional response. Without the stimulus of emotional exchange, your life is very empty. The intellectual type of person has very little appeal for you. Unless you can reach empathetic union with your companion, you become bored, restless and unhappy.

You are kind, sympathetic and unbelievably idealistic. Your love of humanity and sympathy for the downtrodden, poor, and sick is very moving in a world that doesn't exactly overflow with compassion. You will work with selfless devotion to help people in prison, sanitariums, hospitals and the like, provided they possess that tiny spark you know lingers in nearly every human breast but is sometimes obscured by worldliness and sophistication. When you don't find this in an individual, you quietly move on. Often, people with Jupiter in Pisces receive public honors and recognition for their humanitarian work. Unfortunately, not all are able to find the correct means to serve, and suffer considerable frustration and despair.

You are acutely sensitive, psychic and spiritual. Hardly a night passes that you don't have some kind of prophetic dream or peculiar experience. You are often clairvoyant and probably have had some visions. Sometimes it is difficult for people with Jupiter in Pisces to distinguish between reality and their daydreams, mainly because so many of these seem to come true.

It is important for you to have a friend or lover who understands your feelings of otherworldliness and to whom you can confide your dreams and secret wishes. Before you allow intimate relationships of this nature, the person must demonstrate deep love, loyalty and understanding. You are more discriminating, as a rule, in your choice of confidants than you are in ordinary love affairs. Because you don't possess the keen body consciousness of most people, you tend to ignore physical pain and even ill treatment. In illness, you often feel you can heal yourself—but only after you've suffered a sufficient amount of discomfort. You don't complain.

As much as you enjoy lively company, you need regular periods of seclusion. Without these, you become irritable, depressed and fiercely self-critical. Communion with nature restores your spirits. Music soothes or stimulates you, according to your mood. The sea and the forest can provide idyllic delight.

You have to be careful not to lose interest in worldly affairs and retreat into a personal dream world. This is most likely if you can't find a means of expressing your altruistic urges, or if you are forced to work or live in a highly competitive or disharmonious environment.

The Other Side of the Story

Members of the opposite sex may take advantage of your cooperative, kind and placid nature. You are likely to be easily deceived and imposed upon. You may prefer to drift aimlessly without ambition rather than to make a place for yourself in the world. You probably never feel settled or contented. Although anxious to succeed and be respected, you are not prepared to make the necessary effort. You may be lazy, indecisive, moody—and self-hating. Some people with Jupiter in Pisces are inveterate liars who can't help exaggerating even the simplest statement. They may resort to fraud to live in comfort and peace.

CHAPTER TWENTY

Saturn

This chapter on Saturn gives you some facts about the planet's physical features, the myths and symbolism surrounding it, and an astrological account of its characteristics. Then follows a description of Saturn in the various zodiacal signs.

The Planet

Saturn is said to be the most visually beautiful planet in the solar system. It appears as a bright "star" to the unaided eye, but the unique system of rings that surround the planet and its lustrous, contrasting colors can be clearly seen through a telescope. It appears as a blue ball with three yellow rings against the velvet black of deep outer space.

Saturn is the sixth planet out from the Sun and the second largest (after Jupiter). Its diameter is 75,000 miles, more than nine times that of the Earth. It spins once every 10¼ hours, an enormous rate for such an immense sphere. Its volume is 736 times that of the Earth, but its mass or weight is only 95 times greater.

Saturn is 886 million miles from the Sun. The closest it gets to the Earth is 745 million miles. Its orbit takes nearly 29½ years, which means it spends a leisurely 2½ years in each Sign of the Zodiac.

Like Jupiter, the planet is covered with banded clouds. The bands are not as clear as Jupiter's, but seem more nearly permanent. Bright spots occasionally appear in them.

Saturn rings were discovered in 1655 by telescope. They are composed of myriads of tiny satellites or cosmic dust particles. The first is a dull outer ring, next to a dark area, and the second is the widest, brightest ring. Inside this is a thin dark space and then the third ring, which is described as the crepe ring because it resembles the texture of the dress material.

The total width across the three rings is 41,000 miles. The outer ring is 10,000 miles wide, the second about 16,000 miles and the crepe ring about 11,000 miles. The crepe ring begins about 7000 miles above the surface of the planet.

Outside the rings, Saturn has at least ten moons. One of these, Titan, with a diameter of around 4000 miles, is one of the largest satellites in the solar system.

Symbolism

Saturnus, or Cronus as the Greeks called him, was the god of agriculture and the founder of civilization and social order. He was the rebellious son of Uranus, the first supreme god. Armed with a flint and a sickle, Saturn overthrew his father, who cursed him predicting that Saturn himself would in turn be deposed by his own son. To forestall this, Saturn swallowed each of his children at birth. But when Zeus (Jupiter), the youngest was born, his mother deceived Saturn by giving him a stone to swallow instead. The young god was brought up secretly in a cave. In a war that lasted ten years, Jupiter overthrew Saturn. The old man, still with his sickle or scythe, became Father Time, a bitter, decrepit figure whose eyes looked meaningfully from the hour-glass in his hand to all that was new and young in the world.

Astrology

Saturn's influence is heavy, restrictive and long-lasting. It is melancholy, cold, dry, barren, constant, defensive, hard, secretive, nervous, binding and masculine. It is ponderous, slow-moving, serious and has an extremely powerful and important effect on the horoscope.

Saturn is called "the lawgiver." It is the last of the personal planets. Beyond its orbit, the three remaining known planets—Uranus, Neptune and Pluto—take so long to go around the Sun that their effects are more generalized and gradual.

As Saturn stands in space, so it stands in relation to individual man. It is the periphery. It represents the time man has on Earth—and the end of it. It is the boundary no one can cross over in physical form. Saturn keeps man and life within specific bounds. As such, it represents the law that governs human behavior; the self-discipline that allows man to govern himself; the sense of duty that permits responsible action; the patience and perseverance that make accomplishment possible; and the practical reflection that gives rise to self-consciousness, including the inevitable realization of separateness from other beings, of isolation and aloneness.

Saturn is the ruler of Capricorn, the tenth Sign of the Zodiac. Capricorn represents the individual's social status, accruing from responsibility and self-discipline. Saturn is the co-ruler, with Uranus, of the eleventh Sign, Aquarius.

Saturn stands for the skin and the skeleton. As the skin, it restricts and yet protects—from without. As the skeleton, it gives form and hardness and protects—from within. Between the two lie the vital functions and organs.

From the above it is not difficult to conclude that Saturn is the planet of restriction, hardship and delay. Its influence gives a hard time. By imposing inherited burdens, uncontrollable events and the consequences of errors arising from the past, Saturn represents the distance between man and his goals. Saturn's law is supremely just. Every man gets exactly what he deserves, whether he thinks so or not. Saturn's law gives at the same time it exacts—by ensuring that an individual faces in circumstantial form the weaknesses flawing his or her character. These must be overcome before the person can finally enjoy that which lies beyond skin, skeleton and all limitation: the freedom to be himself or herself.

Saturn squanders the individual's time, halts his progress despite redoubled efforts, wastes his resources, uses others to impede, disappoint and frustrate. However, once Saturn's discipline is accepted and the lessons are learned, "the law-giver" reveals its true nature and rewards in full.

Saturn will sometimes delay things that are promised by the other planets in the horoscope. As master of time, it can do this. Its function is to see that no one receives anything of lasting value that is not deserved. At other times, Saturn will not deny—and the individual will suffer as a result of boons and abundance because he was not ready to cope with them.

A well-aspected Saturn has an ennobling and dignifying effect. The person is conscientious and industrious. He or she may choose the hard way to go about things, but this is often out of thoroughness

and a tendency to equate patience and painstaking care with responsibility. This person can always be depended on to do a job to the best of his or her ability. These men and women also have a sense of moral rectitude that compels them to do the right thing. They are discreet and can be relied on to keep a secret. They can get to the bottom of a problem, put it in its correct perspective and suggest practical solutions. Their advice is objective, realistic, always down to earth. They are conservative, tread warily in new territory. Under attack, they are nervously aware but show restraint and self-control. Under pressure, they are superbly in command. Their approach to life is serious and cautious. They do not waste money and can account at any time for all their resources. They are thrifty but not stingy.

A badly aspected Saturn produces a person who is inclined to complain and moan a lot. He or she has bad luck, misses opportunities, is slow off the mark. The tendency is to be selfish, gloomy, given to self-pity and censorous of those who enjoy themselves. This person is mean, stingy, unpopular. Either he has a hard time earning money or is too miserly to spend it on normal comforts and pleasures. He is fearful and usually suffers from prolonged obscure and often depressing illnesses.

Physiologically, Saturn controls the bone and skin systems, the crystallization and constriction of the body's growth. As time, it gives shape to form, imposing the necessary limitations on growth; and then the drying and ossifying constrictions of age. Saturn is also associated with the spleen, gallbladder, knees, teeth, inner ear and anterior lobe of the pituitary gland, which promotes masculinity as well as regulating the sex glands.

Toothache and colds are among the most common Saturn ailments.

Saturn in Aries

Although you are ambitious, the way up is extremely hard. You have to work for everything you get. This is a hard-slog combination. Saturn here sits on the strong and impulsive shoulder of Aries like a ton of bricks. It is difficult to move. To move with speed and flourish, as you so often try to do, is impossible.

Despite these severe limitations, you are determined to succeed. The first half of your life is usually the worst, but this is the time when you are likely to develop the strength of character that will eventually bring success. Saturn will see you are tested by plenty of obstacles and adversity.

Your best chance of making a name for yourself—

which is what you most long to do—is through ventures that appeal to the public imagination. You are probably more capable of building a reputation than of becoming a millionaire. As you have a great desire for respect and esteem, this order of things will probably appeal to you. Your capacity to persevere in the face of seemingly overwhelming odds makes you an excellent pioneer type. You are the sort who could disappear into the hostile wilderness for years, undergo dreadful privations, and finally emerge with the holy grail to immense public acclaim.

You are not a person who gets along very well with others. You are more a loner, a toiler; some might say (in the beginning) a loser. You continually feel frustrated. The pace of your life never seems to synchronize with your lofty ambitions. You miss out on the big chance—arrive too early, too late or just don't hear about it. You are sometimes envious of others who seem to get all the breaks. You are easily irritated. You build up heat inside slowly, like a pile of lawn clippings, and suddenly flare into an angry outburst. Then the iron hand of self-discipline comes down and you quickly get a grip on your emotions. And the cycle of spontaneous combustion starts again.

You make a good military type because you are a disciplinarian. Seldom do you show your feelings except in a corrective, critical way. You know the value to authority of clipped aloofness. If you do not try to relax your self-imposed constrictions, you will become overbearing. As a parent, you can be too strict; as a human being, too intent on maintaining your position against whatever the odds.

A happy marriage is seldom your luck. Your mate may be jealous or project his or her feelings of insecurity onto you. Your reluctance to join in the usual social activities does not help. You may be grumpy in lighthearted company, quick to find fault and plunge into an argument. At heart, you prefer to be alone or with a crony who shares your rather jaded views on life. Underneath, you are somewhat distrustful of people and inclined to be selfish.

You have good reasoning ability, though your mind may not possess the depth your manner and mien suggest. However, when left alone, you can be quietly contemplative and this helps to stabilize your emotions. You are quite sure of yourself when dealing with practical matters. It is the inner stresses and strains that you have the most difficulty coping with.

You are diplomatic when you want to be and quite impressive. Your reserved and austere manner suggests hidden strength, capability and wisdom. You would like to occupy a position of power in a large organization. You want to be admired for your accomplishments, particularly for your sense of responsibility. You yearn to transform your outer show of these qualities into an inner reality.

You may suffer from chronic health problems that make it difficult to compete with others on even terms. But you have the fortitude to bear up and not allow physical impediments to get the better of you. In moments of despondency or depression, it may help you to remember that Saturn, the lawgiver whose influence is afflicting you, pays off in full measure at the end.

The Other Side of the Story

You may be a puritanical despot, the terror of your home, office or community. You are likely to be lonely and friendless. Your depression and whining complaints may get on everybody's nerves. The only lesson you may have learned from a domineering father is how to be even more oppressive and severe as a parent or boss. You may try to reform others for their own good and make their lives a misery. You could be a typical zealous missionary who sets out to "save" an uncivilized people but succeeds only in destroying their culture and self-respect. You may be tortured by feelings of personal inadequacy. You are likely to suffer from severe headaches, toothache, deafness or eye trouble.

Saturn in Taurus

You are too intent on holding onto your worldly goods to really enjoy them. Possessions and money come to you so slowly and laboriously that you are in constant dread of losing them to some capricious act of fate. But you won't give up what you own without a grim struggle—any more than you will surrender your impelling ambition to acquire more and more. You know that with wealth comes status, prestige, respect—and these mean just about as much to you as the security you crave.

You are thoughtful and kind. You are not given to rash actions, although you will lose your temper suddenly if badgered enough. As much as you are able to, you lead a steady sort of existence. You prefer to think long about things before making any moves because you like to know in advance exactly where you are going. You fix your goals well ahead, and because all the pros and cons have been considered (you hope!), you seldom see any need to change your plans or to listen to others' advice. You plow on, regardless. The unexpected unnerves you. You find it hard to make sudden adjustments. You are not adaptive. You really prefer to work for someone else or under the auspices of a large organization where you can express your authority without having to worry about security.

Your greatest strength is the ability to persevere and overcome obstacles. Your determination is prodigious. The things you strive for in life do not come easily. You are not a lucky individual. But your dogged persistence often gets you there in the end. You are frugal with money, and can go without luxuries, although you enjoy life's comforts once you feel you can afford them. You try hard to save but it is a slow and daunting process: something usually drains off your accumulated funds. Many of your problems come through relatives, especially elders. You may have to support or care for a parent over a long period. Other unfortunate domestic experiences may bring loss and sorrow. There may be ill feeling between you and your neighbors.

Most of your anxieties stem from money and love. You are indecisive and seldom able to strike when the iron is hot. You lack confidence in your own timing: you hesitate. In love, when you eventually do act, it is often at the wrong moment, or with the wrong person. You may become quite depressed at the topsy-turvy way your personal relations seem to operate compared with the experiences of others. You keep your emotions too much to yourself. You need to give your feelings and deeper thoughts an airing, to open up to another person. Your continual reserve and restraint lead to brooding, a kind of emotional in-breeding that gives rise to fear, imagined slights and seething resentment. You don't forgive or forget easily.

You acquire money through judicious investments. You play it safe. You know all about the hazards of get-rich-quick schemes, the nailbiting and sleepless nights when things go wrong. They are not for you. You are an excellent person to have on the payroll to keep costs down because you know how to economize and can explain economical moves to others diplomatically. In your personal affairs, you are prudent and thrifty. You can be trusted implicitly with other people's money. You will do nothing that might undercut your reputation or cause others to be disrespectful. You have a high sense of moral duty. Despite your nervous disposition, you are dependable under pressure and can help others overcome their panic and hysteria.

You possess a love of natural beauty. The order and precision of nature fascinate you. You are often drawn to scientific studies or occupations associated with horticulture, stock breeding and botany.

The Other Side of the Story

You may be pitifully self-conscious and incapable of mixing socially. Your fear of insecurity may make you miserly and avaricious. You are likely to worry yourself into a nervous breakdown. Your home may be an unhappy place. You are likely to begrudge showing others simple kindnesses. You can be unresponsive in love and have no feeling for beauty. All your thoughts may be calculated to bring about materialistic ends.

Saturn in Gemini

You are a person with great intellectual capacities. You can write and think with depth and inspiration. You would make an excellent mathematician, theoretical or practical scientist, penetrating lecturer, wise teacher or impressive lawyer. You would also do well in commerce as a merchant, a publisher, printer or broker. In even the most humble walks of life, you will be noted for the astuteness of your views and the nimbleness of your mind.

In this position, the effervescent intellectual Sign of Gemini receives the steadying influence of the wise and experienced Saturn. It is a sound and fruitful alliance.

You are intensely aware of all that is going on around you. You are continually picking up information but holding only onto that which will be of some practical use later on. You have the ability to forget the inconsequential and remember the profound. Still, you can tell a droll story with an admirable turn of wit.

You are inclined to study a number of subjects at one time. Although you move quickly from one topic to another, it is not in a superficial way. You absorb in depth; you understand; you don't just study to accumulate a lot of useless information. You are an intellectual being. It is essential to your health and well-being that you keep your mind engaged. Other more earthy temperaments would wilt and verge on a nervous breakdown under the constant cerebral activity, but you are in your element.

You are urbane and sophisticated. Given the proper circumstances, you would make a fine diplomat, elder statesman, head of state, titular president. You are deeply serious and yet retain a refreshing, youthful sense of humor, a naiveté that makes you rather lovable, especially in later years. You are capable of great literary effort. You possess extraordinary powers of observation and have the mental equipment to describe what you see in graphic and moving language. Your comprehension is quite remarkable.

You are usually plagued with difficulties, trials and

sorrows brought about by relatives, especially brothers and sisters. Responsibilities impinging on you from this direction may restrict your freedom and independence. False accusations are likely to be made against you. Court proceedings you institute may fail or succeed only after long drawn out delays. In the end, charges against you may be dismissed, but the damage to your reputation will never quite be repaired. There is also the possibility that some period of your life may have to be spent in another country in a form of exile. Travel is likely to be unfortunate for you. Words written or spoken in haste or anger may result in libel or slander actions. Neighbors may also be a cause of aggravation.

The above experiences, plus the strong intellectual nature of Saturn in Gemini, can make you rather bitter and cynical. Without other good aspects, there may be an absence of warmth in your personality. You could be a bit too hard and exacting. A deviousness and lack of candor may also creep in.

As a general rule, Saturn in Gemini produces a person with lofty ideals. You have a fine sense of the correct way to do things and practice what you preach. You are responsible and serious-minded, but sometimes trust the wrong people and are therefore let down. Disillusionment usually leads to depression. The imagination sometimes colors the judgment and you see situations, especially adverse ones, as you would like them to be. Disappointment is then inevitable. A philosophic approach helps to allay your natural nervousness and apprehension.

This combination frequently means that early education is interrupted or delayed. It is then difficult to get a start in a chosen field. Or you may lack direction, certainty about what you want to do for a living. Early hardships are more than likely. You may have trouble with your chest and lungs.

The Other Side of the Story

Depression may lead to suicidal thoughts. You are likely to yearn for love, but do nothing about attracting it. You may be an incorrigible pessimist living under the delusion that you are a realist. You are likely to be offensively critical of others. Opportunities may be missed through fear of failure; nothing is ventured, nothing is gained. Your thinking is likely to be dull and ponderous, your manner of speaking irritatingly halting and slow. An obstinate and pigheaded attitude may make you a monologuist. You are likely to be illogical and a bit scatterbrained.

Saturn in Cancer

You are an inveterate worrier. You worry about your mother, your family, your home, your future,
your childhood, your children, your past. You seldom throw off the feeling of insecurity and personal inadequacy—except when you plunge into the delights of sensual gratification through sex, food, liquor and the like. Afterward you go back to worrying again.

Saturn in Cancer is like dipping bread in water. The bread loses its consistency, falls to pieces. Saturn is in its detriment here, almost at its weakest. Its discipline, morality and persistence are largely dissolved.

But there remains a possibility of outstanding accomplishment. When Saturn in Cancer people apply themselves to a job—whether it be a profession, an artistic venture or a business pursuit—they rally the best of both the Saturn and Cancer qualities, with extraordinary results. But when the work is over, they sink back into inertia, laziness or dissipation.

You are supersensitive. Your emotions, which were tuned so finely by your surroundings when you were a child, still dictate your responses. You either had too much love or not enough of it. If you had an excess, you miss it now, long for it, feel deprived, insecure. If you were starved for love, you still miss it, long for it, feel deprived, insecure. You are a prisoner of the past who is too plastic, fearful and lacking in self-confidence to break away.

You don't like making new moves. The pioneering and competitive urges disturb you. You think about being original and stepping out on your own, but you quickly dismiss the idea. You prefer to stick to what you know you can do, what's been proved, what's been accepted by your associates and especially those you love. You are confined by the limitations imposed by your childhood. Usually your background includes sorrow or suffering connected with your mother or home. You may have seen your mother coping in difficult circumstances and had to share her troubles or shoulder her burdens. Sometimes there is a history of harsh maternal discipline, which conditions adult responses. Sometimes the mother died at an early age. Any of these produce a complex, a vacuum of uncertainty and insecurity. Your usual defense is to take no risks, do nothing—which makes you appear lax or lazy. You fall back on the things you know you can trust and enjoy—your own senses, sensual pleasure—or you throw yourself into work you love, if you have been fortunate enough to find it.

Saturn, unless very favorably aspected, deprives the child of many comforts and normal enjoyments. Or it denies the person in later years, ruining his or her career or inflicting an impoverished or lonely old age—or both. This combination also causes distressing illnesses usually associated with the stomach and women's breasts. Wasting diseases or obstructions such as ulcers and tumors—and obesity—are common.

People born with Saturn in Cancer desperately need to justify their existence. This is their main problem. In the attempt to justify themselves, they constantly look for admiration from their loved ones, and sulk when they don't get it. They may pose as martyrs to the rest of the family, overstressing their slavish and thankless devotion as homemaker or breadwinner. They may strive desperately to win the approval and the nod of approbation from their boss, the police chief, the society leader—any figure of authority. They even enjoy passing a policeman in the street to feel the satisfaction of being law-abiding, on the law's side. They want to be told over and over: "You are doing well. Your existence is justified." Then they are happy—for a while.

People born with this combination can couple the protective urge of Cancer with Saturn's discipline, and at the same time satisfy their inner longings, by fighting at the authority level for the rights of the sick, the distressed, the needy and the underprivileged.

The Other Side of the Story

You may be insufferably moody, changeful and unreliable. The more promiscuous you are sexually, the more depressed and dissatisfied you will become. Overeating may make you fat, sloppy and miserable. A dependence on drugs could be disastrous. People may laugh behind your back at the excuses you make to justify your excesses; or you may be an object of pity. You are likely to have a punishing mother or father complex. Your unhappiness may be largely due to the lies you tell yourself.

Saturn in Leo

Situations involving leadership or love are likely to make great personal demands on you and culminate in disappointment or heartache. You are a born leader, but in many ways a severe one. You're not the congenial leonine type who steps down off his thrown to mix freely with his subjects. You're a saturnine Leo. Although suited to rule, you are too aware of the dignity and distinction of your position. These, you believe implicitly, can only be maintained if you yourself remain aloof and isolated.

Leo is a warm, human and generous Sign; Saturn is the planet of weighty responsibility and cold constriction. It is an odd combination and often leads to power and enviable success in worldly affairs, but rarely results in personal satisfaction or real happiness.

You are a stickler for hard work and doing your duty. Although you may be drawn to the entertainment industry or be occupied in a profession that gives pleasure to others, you seldom let your hair down and actually join in the fun. This sort of behavior, you feel, would demean you. You may be extremely good at your job and gifted at pleasing the masses, but it's always only a job, never an expression of your true feelings.

What your true feelings are is a bit of a mystery even to yourself. Like everyone, you want love. And deep down inside, you have a vast quantity of it that groans and strains to be released and shared. But with Saturn in Leo, this is not to be. You have great difficulty expressing your emotions. Often when you try, the result is awkward, inappropriate, inadequate. People with this combination frequently resolve early in life not to bother trying to demonstrate their affections anymore. As a protection, they adopt an aloof and self-contained attitude that discourages other from reaching out to them emotionally. They settle comfortably into this armor-plated style and very rarely manage to break out of it again.

Sometimes saturnine Leos find a release for their emotions by engaging in love affairs with socially inferior people. In these situations, they feel their actually being with the person is sufficient expression of their affection or regard and that no further demonstrations are necessary. It doesn't always work out so smoothly, however; bitterness and scandal are too often the outcome.

You an excellent organizer, cool in an emergency and able to handle large groups of people with an authority that others seldom think to question. You are constructive, practical, impressive and, given the opportunity, should have no difficulty rising to a powerful position in government or politics. Your talent for diplomacy is quite remarkable.

In business and employment, you are the ideal company man or woman. You put the organization first, your personal concerns second. Obviously, you are soon singled out for promotion by discerning and progressive management.

In your personal life, your mode of living usually reflects extremes of austerity and splendor. If wealthy, you may surround yourself with all the creature comforts and yet have no one to share them with. In ordinary circumstances, you may treat yourself now and again to the best meal in town—and eat alone. Splendid isolation may be your way.

You are bold in action when committed, but cautious in reaching your conclusions. It is not easy to deflect you from a course; you can be counted on to have weighed all the pros and cons well in advance. You are seldom persuaded by appeals to sentiment.

Justice and logic carry much more power of conviction for you.

The Other Side of the Story

You are a rigid disciplinarian and fixed in your views, which are largely out of date. You desire to move with the times but an inner mistrust and reserve hold you back. With children, you are apt to be far too strict and unbending. Some unhappiness has probably come to you through youngsters. You believe your way is the only way. Subordinates and members of the opposite sex enjoying less social status than you are likely to cause serious trouble. Secret enemies may work against you. You sometimes suffer from mental depression and vague aches and pains. Your love life has always been a source of problems, misunderstandings and sorrow. You endanger your health by working far too hard.

Saturn in Virgo

You are capable of considerable accomplishment. Your mind is sharp, original, practical and disciplined. You can be depended on to do a job properly and to work without slacking for as long as necessary. You are a person of your word, an excellent employee and ideally suited for a position of authority in one of the professions, especially where there is a tutorial element.

But you are a worrier. Hardly a day goes by that you don't feel a vague uneasiness. Gloom and depression descend on you without warning. Your mind remains clear and able during these times as far as work is concerned, but your personal relationships suffer. Others may find your moods melancholy and difficult to put up with. The fact that often there is no real justification for them makes your associates even less tolerant.

You enjoy work for work's sake. Nothing pleases you more than to be tucked away in an office grappling with a difficult problem that requires prolonged concentration. You are especially interested in scientific inquiry. Your analytical mind can sift detail with amazing precision. All types of research and laboratory work are apt to appeal to you. You should excel as a university professor.

People with Saturn in Virgo often distinguish themselves in work connected with diet, health and hygiene. They pay strict attention to these disciplines in their personal life and sometimes become food faddists and hypochondriacs. They are often competent speakers and writers and may turn to lecturing or writing books or articles about their pet subjects. Efficiency and order have tremendous appeal for them. Their studies are usually aimed at improving

something or someone (very seldom themselves). Because of this, they seem to be uncommonly critical and fussy individuals and tend to alienate the more lighthearted and less discriminating types who are content to live and let live.

You are a little suspicious of your fellow man and very distrustful of new situations. You are extremely observant and rather prudish about the relaxation of moral restraints in modern society. Your views are traditional and orthodox and you seldom find any reason for changing them. You don't make friends easily, although you do enjoy conversing with people who share your intellectual interests. Your manner is quiet, serious, reserved. You prefer to remain in the background and to observe life from there. You are courteous, diplomatic and discreet.

With money, you are conservative and sometimes a bit stingy. You feel less vulnerable when there is cash in the bank. You tend to live a frugal life. It would never occur to you to throw your money around on lavish entertainment. Other people's extravagance irritates you.

You derive most of your relaxation and pleasure from simple pursuits that are usually not far removed from your working habitat. Many people born with this combination spend considerable time with hobbies. Sometimes these are developed to such a high standard that they become commercially viable.

Your ability to work for long periods without distraction usually enables you to forge to the forefront of your field eventually. The middle years are generally the most successful and productive. Your early life is apt to have been difficult at home and in school. You will probably end up in a comfortable financial position as a result of steady effort and careful investment.

The somber, dour and somewhat pessimistic outlook of people born with Saturn in Virgo does not help them to be happy in marriage. They may also have difficulty with teenage children, who are likely to resent minor tyrannies.

The Other Side of the Story

Marital and business partnerships are likely to be most unfortunate. Your constant criticism of others makes you irritating company. You are also too quick to condemn your own shortcomings without making positive endeavors to correct them. Negative thinking can be a form of illness with this combination. You are unnecessarily stingy with money and have probably lost the art of spontaneous giving. Your early years may have been marked by ill health and sorrow. Memories you can't erase may still prey on your mind. Unless you adopt a more optimistic frame of mind and stop worrying about trivial matters, you may be heading for a nervous breakdown.

Saturn in Libra

Here is the artist who triumphs after years of obscure and dedicated effort. Here is the wisest judge. Here, also, is the honest, clever but frustrated politician who must watch the corrupt and inefficient rule of others while awaiting the call that may never come.

Saturn is the eternal taskmaster—he makes things hard wherever he appears. And yet, if the job has been well done with discipline and selflessness, he usually distributes the rewards with impeccable fairness. Our own opinion of how we've worked pulls no weight with Saturn; he considers himself the only judge. In Libra, Saturn is in the Sign of balance. If you've balanced your accounts, you're okay. If you haven't . . . watch out!

You are an artistic and high-minded person who gets most of his or her pleasure through relating to others. You have many friends and social acquaintances. Because art and entertainment are good means of reaching others, these activities appeal to you. In the back of your mind, you always aim to bring people closer together, to eliminate their differences and harmonize their positive qualities, with you at the center.

You believe in moderation in everything—in reserved and refined behavior, manners, tastes, and most of all, in goodwill and peace. But as much as you strive to stay on this middle path, you are constantly swept from one side to the other like an emotional pendulum. Where you work for order, you usually get turmoil. Yet your extraordinary tact and good judgment frequently save the day.

In marriage, much depends on whether Saturn is badly aspected. But Libra is ruled by Venus, the planet of love.

Generally, people born with Saturn in Libra benefit from the stabilizing influence of a partner. Libra is the Sign of partnership but Saturn makes severe demands, which, if not met in the right spirit, create obstacles and difficult circumstances. Partnerships often contain deep flaws (undiscernible in the beginning) that cause sorrow and unhappiness.

Both business and marital relationships may continue in harassing conditions for several years, or be quickly terminated and new ones begun with exactly the same results. People with Saturn in Libra frequently marry more than once. They seldom achieve their romantic ideals, although these persist right to the end. They never let what is make them lose sight of what might be.

Women are generally unfortunate for people with this combination. If you are a woman, the women in your life are likely to stir up trouble behind your back, to undermine your position or reputation in some way. Lifelong feuds are a distinct possibility. If you are a man, you have probably suffered considerable loss or psychological pain through the open enmity or indifference of a woman. Early heartbreak that will never really be repaired is likely. Separations in the midst of happiness and the reemergence of old love problems long forgotten are to be expected. Women are also apt to cause you employment difficulties.

You are intelligent, eminently suited for scientific work or for distinguishing yourself in medicine or law. In art, your success depends largely on your mastery of fundamental techniques. If you attempt to short-cut experience or training, you will probably fail at a distant future point when success seems crucial to your career.

Although you naturally shrink from contentious situations, you frequently become involved in arguments and sharp exchanges. You find it necessary to correct wrong assumptions, especially when another person is being unfairly criticized. The underdog has a particular place in your heart and you will risk a great deal on his or her behalf.

The Other Side of the Story

Loss is likely through broken contracts, lawsuits and the dishonesty of partners. Your love life is probably remarkable for the number of affairs that end unhappily. Marriage will probably be delayed. Sometimes with this combination, the person achieves wide success and influence and suddenly is discredited or falls from favor. The faults and weaknesses most prominent in your own nature will probably be encountered in your closest associates. Until you learn to live with these and assimilate the right lessons, you have little chance of overcoming your frustrations.

Saturn in Scorpio

You are a very forceful character, though you mightn't show it, for you are shrewd and know precisely when an agreeable and pleasant facade will create the desired effect. In most of the relationships you encourage, you usually have an ulterior motive. Basically, you are a loner, so when you reach out to others, they can be fairly sure you have more in mind than friendship.

You are serious, painstaking and secretive. Much goes on inside of you that no one on earth ever hears about. You suppress your emotions deliberately, control yourself with rigorous persistence, so that most of your true self is concealed and you appear something of an enigma to others. Your basic drive is for power, and you are more dangerous than the average power seeker because you have learned the crucial secret of achieving power, which is to first gain power over oneself.

In people with this combination, emotion burns with a suppressed fury. Scorpio is the Sign of sexual energy, which must be released in one way or another. And Saturn, the cold, heavy, restrictive planet, sits on it here like a giant stopper. As the pressure builds up, the need to express the creative Scorpio force becomes intense and the person is propelled toward art, domination, mystical achievement, lawlessness or sexual gratification. Fortunately, Saturn dampens the destructive potential of this energy and generally allows it to be harnessed in dynamic but socially acceptable ways.

You favor working behind the scenes. Your subtle and penetrative mind is ideally suited for manipulating others and for solving all kinds of mysteries. In the sciences, you can apply this faculty as a geologist or archeologist, probing the secrets of the past; or as an astronomer, probing time and space. You may also excel in microscopic research or psychiatry. Mysticism and the occult also intrigue you because you like to penetrate the depths of the mind and emotions. Training is essential so you can marshal your innate capacities into an effective method.

In love, you are extremely passionate and likely to suffer excruciating jealousy. You are true to your loved ones and expect their fidelity in return. When betrayed in love, you hit out cruelly, wait patiently to take revenge, or withdraw into yourself and suffer in searing but dignified silence. You are proud but not arrogant, haughty but not vain, fiercely determined once decided, and fixed in your attitudes.

People with this combination make first-rate spies, undercover agents and insurance investigators. They have a knack of getting results by indirect or backdoor methods. Being naturally suspicious and distrustful, they are seldom surprised by any human foible or weakness. They are capable of enduring incredible deprivation, physical hardship and mental harassment to achieve their ends. They can also be supremely selfish and despotic.

You have a violent temper but usually manage to keep it under control, provided Saturn is not badly aspected. You regard your independence as inviolable and can react viciously if someone attempts to curtail it.

You are seldom as cool, calm and collected as you appear. Sometimes, in fact, you are swamped by feelings of failure and insecurity, though you usually manage to conquer these by the sheer power of your will.

The Other Side of the Story

Health may be indifferent in the early years, but once maturity is reached, physical stamina may be exceptional. However, unless the energies at your disposal are directed toward higher aims, sex may be a problem and lead to health difficulties. Someone's sudden death is likely to bring about major changes in your lifestyle. You have probably made the same serious mistakes in your life more than once. Complexes about wealth, sex and power are apt to create serious personality difficulties.

Saturn in Sagittarius

This is a favorable position for several reasons. It means you have high ideals, a strong desire to help humanity, and that you are prepared to do something practical about your beliefs rather than just engage in enthusiastic discussions. You are, in your way, a driving force for good. However, since Saturn, the planet of restriction and delay, is posited in Sagittarius, the Sign of bounding optimism, you can expect some hard going, including tedious and infuriating detours. But there's not much doubt that by persisting you will finally win through.

You have a strong social conscience. You would make a first-rate politician, writer, lecturer or minister who uses his or her knowledge and position to draw attention to the ills of the community. You possess the energy, vision and administrative ability to organize crusades at the grass-roots level, where continual contact with the public gives you the opportunity to mold opinion.

Not everyone, of course, can be a shining light in this world, but this combination gives you the capacity to display these talents to some degree in whatever walk of life you choose. Half the battle is to realize that your inner urges to be committed to a worthwhile cause are not aberrations. They are real, valuable, and you are capable of taking the initiative.

You are a wise and philosophic person, particularly after you have reached your middle years. You learn from adversity and setbacks. The more you are required to struggle while maintaining a confident and good-natured outlook, the wiser you will become. Your opinion is highly regarded by your friends and associates. You don't act or speak lightly, although you always manage to convey a cheerful and independent attitude. You believe in looking behind the obvious—in meditating on your problems but not worrying about them. You depend a lot on your intuition, which throws up solutions without a great amount of deliberation.

In business, you are down to earth and straightforward, unafraid to call a spade a spade. You are open and fair in your dealings and don't like fools or crooks. You have a flair for seeing possibilities a long way off and are almost certain to make money out of projects anticipating future trends. You can afford to play your hunches because you know from experience that they are reliable. You can't explain this because it is derived from the prophetic nature of the metaphysical Sign Sagittarius. The presence of Saturn, the planet of business and administration, introduces the commercial angle.

Your feelings are easily hurt. They are also easily touched by the sorrow and unhappiness of another. You are kind, obliging and compassionate. But criticism cuts you to the bone. You feel you don't really deserve this kind of treatment; you don't dish it out nor do you try to hurt others unnecessarily. In fact, you are very wary about doing anything that may cause people to lose their respect for you.

You want to be liked, and sometimes this desire conflicts with your innate urge to be frank and honest, causing uncertainty and pangs of conscience. One of the drawbacks of this combination is that despite your high regard for ethical and moral rectitude, your own methods or motives may be publicly questioned sometime during your life. Considerable anguish may result. You may be perfectly innocent but be forced to carry the blame for someone else. In one way or another, your honor and reputation are likely to suffer.

You are also a bit like the elephant and slow to forget a slight. When censured by superiors, you are apt to overreact and be too outspoken for your own good. Promotion and advancement may be delayed as a consequence. If you can learn to curb and control this rather irrational resentment, your positive qualities such as persistence, responsibility and creative thinking should bring you quickly to the notice of those who count.

The Other Side of the Story

You may think that sermonizing is a practical way of helping others. Your outdated ideas may have little application to today's conditions. You probably have very little grasp of modern economic trends; your investments may be safe but yield very little profit. Your judgment is poor, basically because you're not prepared to take any risks—except with your reputation, which you endanger through odd personal alliances and indiscreet moves. Scandal is likely to hurt your family and associates. Slander and libel suits are possible. If you have known success, you will probably be deprived of it. Health and nervous strains in the latter part of your life may lead to progressive depression.

Saturn in Capricorn

Saturn in Capricorn produces a very worldly and materialistic outlook. It is an exceedingly good placing for the achievement of ambitions and for the rise to power. But without softening influences elsewhere in the horoscope, this personality may be too harsh, disciplined, self-centered and grasping to achieve the happiness that normally comes from a relaxed state of mind. Here life is a very serious business, and work with its concrete rewards may represent the beginning and end of all aspirations.

You are fiercely determined to succeed. You wish to build a reputation so that others will respect and esteem you. You are very reliable and hardworking. You will never let a superior down—or anyone else, for that matter, who may be able to help you in attaining your goals. You make a point of quietly cultivating people in authority, believing you can't have too many contacts for future success. You are suavely tactful, persuasively diplomatic and incurably conservative—and you persevere.

When it comes to making friends and selecting lovers, you are very choosy. The thought of deep emotional involvement makes you uneasy. You are not nearly as composed and in command of your feelings as you like to make out. You are actually terrified of being hurt, or ridiculed. You would rather venture nothing in the way of love or friendship than risk a rebuff.

Yet you often seem to draw unhappy experiences to you. Friends frequently fail you in one way or another. In love, you are also apt to be unlucky. Perhaps it is your unnatural wariness. You try so hard to play it safe all the time that you end up making impossible compromises in your personal relationships. Unless your Venus, Sun or Jupiter are in Virgo or Taurus, or—to a lesser degree—in Pisces or Scorpio, your marital affairs will probably be wearyingly depressing. Whether married or living with your parents, you have little chance of avoiding unhappiness and worry. People with this combination frequently end up living alone—or living only for their work. Their chronic anxieties may cause illness and sometimes mental problems.

Not without justification, you have great faith in your own abilities. Your intellect is sharp and your reasoning powers well above average. You can strip a business proposition down to the rawest details and expose its flaws with consummate brevity. At the same time, you can plan the largest venture without overlooking a single important detail—and then set up the organization to handle it. Given the circumstances, you can pull yourself up to just about any commercial height. Fundamentally, you are tycoon material, but you may have to pay a price in isolation from human sentiment.

You have a flair for writing, even though this may not yet have occurred to you. You can express abstract ideas clearly and put the most complex data into simple, cogent language. You are also suited for scientific work where the object is to crystallize facts and formulate workable theories. As a teacher, you should shine. But it is probably in running your own business (if you get the chance) that you will be able to make the best use of your talents and at the same time satisfy your strong desire for independence.

Despite your immense persistence, you are likely to become depressed and melancholy. The progress you make is seldom sufficient to satisfy your ambition. You also seem to run into more than your share of obstacles and hindrances. Opposition sometimes infuriates you, breaks down your reserve—and you lose your temper. In a position of authority, you are quite capable of throwing your weight around and insisting that others fulfill their obligations to the letter of the law. When treasured goals are threatened, you may become ruthless.

With this combination, you should try to remember that success is likely to come only after perseverance in the face of prolonged difficulty and aggravation.

The Other Side of the Story

You may marry to escape an unhappy family life only to experience even greater sorrow. Your love partners are apt to be unfaithful, your friends unreliable. You are suspicious and distrustful of others, and this makes them avoid your company. You are probably lonely and unhappy, weighed down by worries emanating from your own selfishness. In the home, you may be a tyrant and unnecessarily severe on children. You will probably become attached to someone intellectually inferior. You usually choose the hard way to do things rather than take normal risks. You are obstinate and refuse to listen to good advice.

Saturn in Aquarius

This is a fine position for Saturn, possibly the best in the horoscope. It makes you an outgoing and very responsible person. You sincerely care about your fellow man. You are keenly aware of the limitations imposed on him, but are convinced half are unnecessary and can be gradually thrown off by more liberal and enlightened thinking. You realize that political and social ills can't be remedied overnight. In this, you are not a radical like some Sun Sign Aquarius. You believe in evolution rather than revolution. But you are willing to take an active part in giving things a kick in the right direction.

You have a great deal of common sense, the product of an observant mind that learns from every experience. Your policies are down to earth. You are at your best working in a job where the team spirit is essential. You understand the value of cooperation and have a talent for bringing together in working harmony totally different personalities. You don't play one person against the other. Although you may show some autocratic tendencies at times, you respect the individual's longing for freedom and independence. Your style is to inspire unity of effort that allows everyone to do his or her own thing, preferably under your direction. Authority comes easily to you and others don't seem to question it. This makes you an ideal group leader. Many people with Saturn in Aquarius are occupied in research laboratories where numbers of scientists combine to find a single solution.

You are likely to enjoy an unusual, but lasting, marriage or love attachment. You may be parted from this person on numerous occasions, but separation never severs the deep link that binds you together. You are not the type to form frivolous liaisons. You won't play around with another's affections. You are true and faithful. Whatever you undertake, you approach with a serious and responsible attitude. You have many social acquaintances and a very wide range of contacts in your field.

You are probably an authority on your work, or will be in later life. In your early years, the particular direction of your career may be uncertain. Seemingly insuperable difficulties may discourage you from pursuing the occupation of your choice. But eventually, people with Saturn in Aquarius usually win through on the merit of their fine intellects, perseverance (when they are interested in a project) and ability to get along with others.

You are friendly and considerate, courteous and well meaning. If something needs to be done, you take direct action. You enjoy study, especially in maturity, and regard it as a means of keeping your mind fresh and vital. You are a deep thinker, drawn to subjects that others consider profound and abstract. You are often accomplished in refined artistic expressions that verge on the mathematical, such as musical composition and modernistic stage routines and body rhythmics. Games and gadgets employing odd magnetic and electronic phenomena are apt to originate in the mind of someone with Saturn in Aquarius. These people are also responsible for bringing into the home exciting technical advances and inventions which they use to decorate or entertain. They originated psychedelic colors and effects.

You are extremely able at putting your ideas into words. As a lecturer, you can make the dullest subject vibrate. You have a knack of pleasing an audience. Any work that brings you into contact with the public or depends on public support is likely to project you into prominence.

Quite often you are prepared to play a backstage role and allow others to receive the acknowledgment that is rightly due you. This is because you are not egotistical; you value the work more than the recognition. The esteem of your colleagues generally means more to you than public plaudits.

Saturn in Aquarius individuals often show great interest in occult subjects, especially in the practical aspects of such studies.

The Other Side of the Story

Your high-handed attitude makes you an unpopular teammate. You always seem to want to go in the opposite direction to everyone else. You are a troublemaker; you talk too much about topics you don't understand and provoke others to complain. You can't stand being told what to do without retaliating in some way. You are apt to hold extreme political views that may be offensively autocratic or communistic. But you don't have the courage of your convictions; excuses are your subtitute for action. Your radical opinions may arouse public hostility and lead to your being ostracized. Or you may be regarded as a crank and have no impact whatever. Trouble with the law is indicated.

Saturn in Pisces

You are a person with unique qualities, some of which may not have surfaced yet. You are basically creative, artistic and refined. What you have to give to the world comes through your ability to tap the nature of things—the universal spirit, if you like, or the plane of psychic causes. This is a bit confusing—especially for you who has to live the strange in-between existence that epitomizes Pisces, the watery final Sign of the Zodiac. The presence of Saturn, the earthy and practical planet, makes it a little easier for you to express in concrete terms the extraordinary things that go on in your mind.

Many inventors, philosophers, poets and sensitive writers have this combination. At its best, it enables them to pluck inspiration out of the nebulous mass of impressions they feel, project it through the saturnine spirit in their mind and, like magic, the world-shaking discovery or classical masterpiece materializes!

Saturn brings Pisces, the Sign of mysticism and self-sacrifice, down to earth, in more ways than one. It usually exposes these supersensitive people to the full rigors of worldly struggle. Frequently, especially if the planet is badly aspected, they undergo considerable physical hardship and for a long time may be denied the material success and recognition they deserve. Their friends and acquaintances are often their worst enemies, or so it seems.

Saturn in Pisces individuals must remain hopeful and resolute in the face of obstacles. A tendency is to give up at the first sign of opposition—to throw in the towel before any blows are even struck. However, these individuals are acutely sympathetic, and if their emotions can be sufficiently aroused, they are capable of great achievement. The humanitarian fields attract them particularly, and they are often found working in hospitals, prisons and other institutions for the destitute, underprivileged and crippled. Sometimes they are widely acclaimed for their devotion and dedication. These people really understand that there are others worse off than themselves, so they suffer their own disabilities and misfortunes with saintly silence.

You are not so materialistic as many others. Still, you would like to get ahead and be popular and respected. Your difficulty is in summoning up the will-power to stick to something long enough to achieve results. You can't help wondering if worldly ambition is worth such a struggle, especially since the fruits of your efforts will all disappear one day. You understand serving others, you enjoy comfort and ease, but you don't comprehend the need for acquisitiveness and the sacrifice of peace of mind required to succeed in the material sense.

When you do reach a position of honor and prestige, it is very difficult for you to hang onto it. You can't perform as others expect you to; you don't have the same solid and convenient values as the masses. When the chips are down, money doesn't matter that much to you beyond its power to provide the necessities of life. Sometimes people with Saturn in Pisces can even get satisfaction out of the martyrdom of destitution.

However, you are well equipped mentally to deal with worldly affairs because you are ingenious, can spot opportunities instantly and have a rare gift for assessing character at first meetings.

Many people with this combination are intensely interested in mysticism, the occult and parapsychology. Their emotional receptivity confers firsthand knowledge and experience of these matters. If they are unable to make a career in connection with their psi gifts, they are apt to use them in seclusion, often with results that may be unstabilizing. Visionary flashes, if confused, misunderstood, or criticized, can lead to distressing psychic conditions. These people can suffer the frustration of longing to help humanity but being rebuffed or ridiculed for their mystical powers.

The taskmaster planet Saturn in the karmic Sign of Pisces can be regarded, astrologically speaking, as either the end or the beginning of a cycle of reason, responsibility, spiritual uplift and inspiration. Individuals with this combination of Saturn in Pisces have hidden resources often, if ever, not tapped until the middle or later years in life.

A complete transit of planet Saturn through all 12 zodiacal signs takes about 29 to 30 years. If one begins with Saturn in Pisces, the Saturn return to Pisces would take about 32 years. This is why people with Saturn in Pisces often are late developers, only beginning to feel and know their depths during the middle years.

The persevering power of Saturn combined with the emotional genius of Pisces can help bring unfulfilled dreams, the creative potential of individuals with this combination, to fruition. Here also these people's sympathies are stirred so deeply that they are not beyond making sacrifices on behalf of others who are in need, confined or isolated in some way.

Your obligation to help people in your profession as well as your own dependents and loved ones who are sick or upon hard times can be the very thing that halts your progress.

The Other Side of the Story

You are badgered by hard luck and misfortune. Your love life is filled with sorrow and disappointment. You tend to link up with people who are so dominant that they take over your entire life and give you very little freedom. Or you choose weak but unscrupulous partners who exploit you, ill treat you, defraud you or misuse you. You have probably suffered more than your share of sadness, even tragedy. Much of your unhappiness and frustration is probably owing to your own pessimistic outlook, dependence and lackadaisical habits.

CHAPTER TWENTY-ONE

Uranus

This chapter on Uranus gives you some facts about the planet's physical features, the myths and symbolism surrounding it, and an astrological account of its characteristics. Then follows a description of Uranus in the various zodiacal signs.

The Planet

Uranus is the seventh planet out from the Sun, after Saturn. Its diameter is 32,000 miles, four times that of the Earth. It is 1782 million miles from the Sun, takes 84 years to complete one orbit and rotates on its axis in 10 hours 48 minutes.

Uranus is an "eccentric" planet—it has eccentric bands around it and its axis is tilted a unique 98 degrees (compared with the Earth's 23.5 degrees). This means that the planet lies virtually on its side, and that at opposite ends of its orbit, the Sun seems to stand directly over one of its poles. When this is the North Pole, the Southern Hemisphere lies in total darkness—for 20 years at a time. At the other end of the planet's orbit, the Northern Hemisphere has its 20-year "night."

Uranus was officially discovered in 1781. The discovery is attributed to William Herschel (1738–1822), a professional musician whose hobby was astronomy. But actually it had been seen and recorded on several occasions almost a century before by John Flamsteed, the first English Astronomer Royal. Flamsteed (1646–1719) was the astrologer for whom Charles II built the Observatory at Greenwich. He timed the laying of the foundation stone from astrological data, and the horoscope he cast for the Observatory is still on view today.

Uranus is the last of the planets that can be seen with the naked eye. But an observer on Uranus would not be able to see the Earth. Planet Uranus is so far out in space that the Earth would appear to be about 3 degrees away from the Sun, making observation from Uranus impossible.

Uranus has five satellites, all named after characters created by William Shakespeare and Alexander Pope.

For more than 100 years, the planet was called Herschel after its discoverer, although a famous contemporary astronomer, Johann Bode (1747–1826), had suggested the name Uranus. Bode was the man who discovered the intriguing proportions in the distances of the planets from the Sun—Bode's Law. It is little wonder that the name Herschel did not stick when the symbolic and astrological significance of the planet is taken into account.

Symbolism

Mythologically, Uranus was the first of the gods. He was the son of Earth, or Ge, who sprang from the original empty space, known as Chaos. He was the father of Saturn, the grandfather of Jupiter and the great-grandfather of Mars and Mercury. Urania is the muse of astronomy.

Astrology

In accord with the extraordinary consistency of the evolution of astrological knowledge, Uranus was not discovered until the human mind was ready to cope with its influences in a constructive way. Prior to that, its strange and eccentric potencies affected only the unconscious; Uranus was part of the sum of life's forces, one of the vagaries of existence that just had to be borne, as contrasted with a positive power that could be harnessed for the betterment of man and the deepening of human knowledge.

The discovery of Uranus coincided with the scientific epoch (Age of Reason) and ushered in the sudden and shattering events and upheavals of the Age of Revolution. The Uranus epoch encompassed the American Revolution, the French Revolution, the Napoleonic Wars. Uranus ushered in an era seeing the abolition of the slave trade and the struggle for women's rights. The Uranus influence led to the first experiments with electricity and electromagnetism and to such inventions as the locomotive, airplane, television. Fashion industries for the average individual, not for just the aristocracy or privileged, were associated with Uranus.

Uranus is the first of the three planets beyond Saturn. They are considered to be more general than personal in their effects. Since Uranus spends seven years in each Sign, it affects large groups of people in the same basic way. Uranus is said to produce the differences in outlook, attitude and tastes that so clearly distinguish one generation from another. It is the generation gap.

Uranus is the planet of genius that goes beyond the intellect. It includes the power of intuition, ESP, Astrology, warning dreams, clairvoyance, clairaudience, visions, electricity, magnetism, inventions.

It is regarded as a strange and malefic planet. It acts without premeditation. It is the force nature employs to disrupt established patterns, societies and civilizations so that entirely new orders and cycles can begin. It is the power behind new political certainties that sweep away the old, often with devastating destruction and misery. It was the power behind the social and political revolutions of the last two centuries. And it will be the power that overthrows these when they become effete, stagnant or sterile.

Uranus is disruption, originality, inventiveness, rebellion, freedom, fanaticism, shock, separation. It is independent, electrifying, unconventional, unexpected, virulent, drastic, radioactive, modern. It represents divorce, bombing, explosives, adventure, gas, astrologers, automobiles, microscopes, electrical goods, alloys, electrons, astronomy, spaceships.

It is reform, creative inspiration, anarchy—and free and illicit sexual behavior.

Uranus is the main ruler (with Saturn) of Aquarius, the eleventh Sign of the Zodiac.

The Uranus influence makes a person prophetic and able to predict the outcome of business and scientific matters with great accuracy. These people have a "feel" for knowing, outside the normal reasoning process. They are quick to act on their insights. Because they can see far ahead of their times, they are frequently branded eccentric by conventional minds. Their imagination is extremely constructive and strong; they can find a way to improve on just about anything. And they are always convinced they are right.

The Uranus individual loves electronic gadgets, especially radios, tape recorders and all electrically operated musical instruments and appliances. He or she delights in the cyclic rhythms of music and usually likes loud sounds.

These men and women have a great number of friends and acquaintances and mix with ease. But they are not emotional, and feel more affinity with groups than with individuals. They cultivate companions who appreciate their way-out ideas and who are intellectually supple enough to discuss them. They enjoy listening to the unorthodox views and opinions of others and are remarkably free of prejudice. They attract odd kinds of people who (like themselves) are sometimes regarded as the lunatic fringe of society. In reality, these people are the vanguard of new social customs and political ideas. The flower children, hippies, and dropouts of the 1960s were eruptions of the Uranus soul wave. Not all succeeded in revolutionizing society or becoming permanent fixtures, but they left their mark in one way or another.

The Uranus individual is a great humanitarian. He fervently believes in freedom for all. And he understands that the individual must suffer, even perish, to bring about the new order. His realistic approach to change makes him appear dispassionate and detached by sentimental standards. Sometimes he gets carried away with his progressive aims and becomes autocratic, even despotic, a megalomaniac. The imagined good of the whole prevents any consideration for the part. The individual is expendable. This person, out of obsession for a cause, can deviate from his own lofty ideals and become a cheating, lying propagandist.

The Uranus influence prompts people to act erratically. Unexpected things happen to them and around them. Sudden changes, new situations, fateful meetings, unexpected partings—all are the work of Uranus. It is hopeless to cling to the past or the old. To be free of Uranus, or united with its power, requires a willingness to move on without looking back.

Physiologically, Uranus is associated with the pathetic nervous system. It is said to cause sudden nervous breakdowns, spasms, fits and paralysis, all kinds of convulsive and violent mental disorders, hysteria and freak growth.

Uranus in Aries

You are exceedingly impatient to tell and show the world what you can do. Your ideas are often brilliant and your flair for originality well known among your associates. But you are frequently in too much of a hurry. You go off half-cocked without thinking your moves through. You start off wonderfully, then lose direction. You make superb suggestions, propose instantaneous solutions—and drop some terrible clangers. You are unpredictable and impetuous, but you are never a bore.

You have an almost obsessional love of freedom and independence. You won't accept any situation that ties you down. A nine-to-five existence drives you mad. Unless a job or profession allows you to show your initiative and originality, you will quit. You are resourceful and inventive, extremely well suited to work connected with scientific discovery and development. You are the ideal space-age technician. You have a special affinity for electronics, and on the human side, social reforms. You have the kind of mind that in a flash can solve problems that may have been delaying progress in a whole technology. You are inspirational and intuitive. You enjoy improving on things, employing new and advanced ideas. You have a lively interest in education and a firm belief that children should be taught in liberal and up-to-date ways.

You possess a flair for attracting attention to yourself. If you move in public circles, your name is often in the newspapers. The publicity you receive is not always favorable. You are too much of a free thinker to conform to a comfortable public image. Your fiery and headstrong temperament often rubs people the wrong way. Uranus in Aries can mean notoriety. You are sometimes brusque and tactless. You always want to get things moving and sometimes steamroller over those patient, plodding people who like to think first. You have great intellectual vigor and insight; you are often intolerant of slower minds, particularly when they fail to grasp your radical ideas. You frequently despair that the Establishment will ever understand what you are trying to do. You may be just too advanced for the times.

Your enthusiasm is formidable. You are a live wire—continually turned on. You spend most of your leisure time contacting a wide circle of acquaintances. You frequently fall out with your associates but quickly find new companions. You are argumentative and erratic. You lose interest suddenly in people and ventures. You have the irritating habit of changing horses in midstream, switching from one contradictory course to another with the dexterous unconcern of a pony express rider. You are "for this" today and "for that" tomorrow. And you seldom appreciate your own inconsistencies.

You have trouble with your love life. Partners find it difficult to put up with your way of living. After you have your cake, you want to eat it too. You desire a mate, but you want to be able to come and go as you please. Because of your unusual vitality and personal magnetism you have no difficulty attracting the opposite sex. Your ideas about liberty and equality are terribly appealing. Your way of life is exciting; you seem to promise so much. But when it's time for sharing, you lack heart. Generosity isn't enough.

Disputes, separations and divorce are not uncommon for this combination. Being self-willed and headstrong, you are often careless and lacking in self-control. You do silly, upsetting things, speak out of turn and unintentionally offend others with your bluntness. You also tend to be reckless and somewhat accident-prone.

You are a compulsive traveler. You like to roam unimpeded, meeting different groups, sampling other cultures, spreading your ideas, living as much as possible from day to day. You tire quickly of the same suburban environment and move quite often.

The Other Side of the Story

You may have a reckless disregard for safety and often endanger your own life and that of others. You should be extremely careful when handling explosives, firearms and electricity. As a driver, you can be a menace. You are likely to be a mental bully, making life miserable for subordinates and those not as bright as yourself. You may reject good advice and fail or suffer as a result. Any form of restraint can make you uncontrollably violent. You may be a misfit who has no respect for authority. If your revolutionary urges get out of hand, there may be trouble with the law. Justice to you may be anything you manage to get away with. You are too easily bored to build consistently.

Uranus in Taurus

You are the type who can build an empire—and lose it overnight. You have probably noticed long before this that your financial and business fortunes are subject to extraordinary ups and downs when compared with other people's. You are always running into unexpected reverses. Yet you gain or things fall happily into place with the same abrupt tempo. This is the result of the rather incongruous alliance between Uranus and Taurus.

Taurus is the Sign of income, possessions and landed property—the solid, earthly comforts. Uranus is the force of startling and electrifying change bringing a new order. Together they make some strange music.

You are best fitted to acquire money and possessions in unorthodox ways. Although yours may be a traditional job or profession, you can spot new and novel possibilities. You see opportunities long before others. And when you act on your intuitions, you are usually successful. You are especially good with financial and property investments; here you are usually the first one in. You are the type who may start a new fashion or cycle in commercial enterprise. You are ingenious, inventive.

You are at your best when working as a member of a group or in a loose kind of partnership. You are too independent to be tied down by hard and fast rules and binding agreements with others. But if you strike the happy balance in your cooperative efforts, you can be a catalyst, producing the ideas and energy for all concerned to benefit from. The biggest threat to your material security and advancement is your inability to accept advice. You either think you know it all or pigheadedly stick to your plans because you don't like the idea of changing them. In this way, you court loss and disaster. Some would say Napoleon, who was born with Uranus in Taurus, was defeated because he ignored the advice of his friends.

You attract numerous people to you in both business and personal life. But when successful, you are inclined to gather an entourage of hangers-on who aim to separate you from your money or to use your influence. You need to be cautious about whom you trust and to make sure that the schemes and people you support are sound. Your money-making ideas are also likely to be stolen by these types.

You have remarkable willpower and determination to succeed. You can push ahead against great odds as long as you have confidence in what you are doing. But you tend to have several goals at once. Since you can't give each the attention it needs, you work in fits and starts, pushing this activity and then that activity. Although you seem to pour yourself out in a continual stream of energy, you get a bit bored doing one thing at a time. You have a one-pointed aim to succeed, but you choose a dispersive way of going about it.

You possess considerable artistic ability. This may be expressed through music or literature. Being born with Uranus in Taurus also gives an impressive quality to the voice; many prominent singers and actors have this combination in their horoscopes. If Uranus is poorly aspected, you may have trouble with your throat or generative organs.

Your love life is not likely to run smoothly, although you can gain financially through your mate. Your free-wheeling ways and popularity are likely to antagonize your lovers. Your partner's jealousy, suspicion and attempts to make you conform to accepted patterns of married life may make it impossible for you to settle down. These negative effects can be largely offset by good aspects in the horoscope; a congenial and prosperous marriage is then possible. The influence of the Moon, Jupiter and Venus, as given in the Pink Tables, must be considered.

The Other Side of the Story

You may have poor taste in colors or dress badly or in an old-fashioned way. You are likely to be absurdly obstinate, refusing to listen to the good advice of others and pushing ahead with unpopular and unfortunate plans. Your artistic efforts may lack the necessary refinement and show a garish style. In financial matters, you are likely to take foolish risks; a lack of discretion and judgment may make you a poor money manager. Conflicting desires for security and freedom may cause nervousness and uncertainty. You are likely to have cruel and vindictive ways toward those who oppose you. In group activities, you may be a destructive element, proposing radical ideas that undermine harmony and cohesion.

Uranus in Gemini

You are a superactive and inspired thinker. Your mind is especially suited for advanced scientific studies. You can understand the most abstract ideas, from atomic fission to the intricacies of the computer. But that is not all. You have the potential to expand these fields of knowledge by contributing new and original notions. You would make an excellent logician, a first-rate theorist in any branch of science or a facile and interesting writer.

But you are not the kind of person who can get much done physically. You prefer to work in your mind, at lightning speed. Ideas flash into your consciousness like X rays, giving you insights and solutions to all sorts of problems, some of which don't even concern you at the time. You have an extraordinarily penetrative vision that keeps producing advanced and novel thoughts.

Unless you can find a suitable profession or occupation to hitch your ideas to, you may get a reputation for being a bit odd. Your views may be too radical, revolutionary, ultramodern for normal minds to accept. Your written or spoken opinions on sex education in schools, abortion and other controversial subjects may shock and cause resentment. Success and association with publicly recognized endeavors give your wilder or more advanced ideas greater credence and acceptance.

It is not unusual for people born with Uranus in Gemini to be considered eccentric. They also have unusual ways of expressing themselves. They are sharp, often too frank without meaning to cause offense. They can appreciate several points of view simultaneously, and in disputes, quickly perceive an acceptable compromise. Writing offers an excellent field of expression. It enables them to get their ideas across in logical form and to anticipate and answer conservative opinion, which usually opposes them.

With Uranus in Gemini, you have an undoubted capacity for psi and ESP and, given the chance, can write on these subjects. Whether you know it or not, you are an expert in one way or another at the art of communication. You merely have to find the role that suits you. Your versatile and clever mind can convey ideas in ingenious and interesting ways. You would make a fine teacher, musician, secretary, lawyer, public speaker, lecturer or popular commentator on scientific subjects. You have a flair for languages and would be a capable interpreter. The probability of travel, which this field offers, would make it doubly attractive.

You enjoy travel and meeting people. You usually gravitate toward the intelligentsia and number among your associates those with radical and extreme views. Literary and scientific people are among your closest friends. You have a sympathetic understanding of reformers. Most out-of-the-ordinary subjects attract your attention sooner or later.

You have probably had to adapt to a number of abrupt changes in your life. Many moves of residence disrupted your formal education, or circumstances may have prevented you from making a normal start in a profession or occupation. Your strong desire to study and learn may only be fulfilled in adult years. You may find that although you are intellectually superior to your rivals, you can't secure the recognition you deserve because of educational drawbacks. Your professional advancement will probably be jeopardized by this deficiency.

Some of the above problems may have been caused by relatives. Uranus in Gemini signifies problems with and estrangements from relatives, especially brothers and sisters. Neighbors can also be a source of trouble and unhappiness. Letters, telephone calls and gossip may produce unfortunate effects.

The Other Side of the Story

You may be so lacking in vital force and energy that you seldom manage to get your own way. You are likely to be the victim of scurrilous talk and be unable to vindicate yourself. Friendship with dubious people may damage your reputation. Unexpected difficulties, including loss of baggage, may beset you whenever you travel. Happiness at home may always elude you. You may be forced to change your profession or bring yourself up to date in your field in later years. You are likely to be disorganized in your thoughts and unable to sustain a logical argument for long.

Uranus in Cancer

You can catch the imagination of the public if you care to develop your talents and act positively. You have great sensitivity. You are reserved and most times prefer to retire rather than advance. You are ambitious and would like to make a name for yourself, but when the time comes for action, you feel it is too much effort. Uranus in Cancer gives you the chance to make your mark, not in a rip-roaring way (which would only unsettle you), but pervasively (which better suits your placid disposition).

You can be successful in the arts. You possess a keen sense of beauty and a deep inner longing for completeness that enable you to contribute a unique flavor to any creative line you develop. You can be a superior artist, writer, sculptor—or humanitarian—bringing to these activites the Uranus verve and originality without its usual jarring effects. You bring evolution, not revolution. But first of all, you have to overcome your passivity.

You may also be successful in an unaggressive way in politics, advertising, literature or publishing. You are a gentle persuader. In a business, your innate ability to sense what the public does and does not want gives you an advantage to be exploited. You have a fine magnetic quality that attracts groups of people. They will listen to what you have to say, read your works or patronize your enterprises. You can do well as a quality restaurateur, a gourmet, a connoisseur or a supplier of food and drinks. Your penchant for custom and things of the past makes you a natural collector of antiques. This combination produces the popular radio and TV personality who, with Old World charm and urbanity, gives his or her views on the important social and community issues of the moment.

You are more likely to obey your feelings and intuitions than your reason. You are acutely sensitive to your environment, especially to the deeper emotions of the people around you. You are strongly motivated by your subconscious and often do things without quite knowing why. The sorrow of other human beings and the sufferings of animals can distress you profoundly. Injustice—either against yourself or others—arouses your anger and indignation.

You are intensely psychic. If you wish, you can use this faculty to help others who are troubled. Because you are so high-strung and your emotions so easily moved, you are susceptible to sudden nervous disorders; hysteria and palpitations may be problems. You are also prone to stomach disorders, ulcers and cramps.

Your domestic life may be very unsettled. As much as you may love your home and family, it may be impossible to keep familial relations on an even keel. Upheavals and sudden departures may result in long absences from the people you love most. You may no sooner be reunited than another separation is forced on you. In love, you may be unpredictable and too fond of other company and parties to forge a strong marriage tie. You may find temporary escape from your sorrows and disappointments by having love affairs with whoever happens to come along at the time. Legal proceedings concerning your home or property are likely to cause loss, worry and illness. The childhood influence of an eccentric parent may still inhibit you and color your views on life.

You are ardently patriotic and may take an active part in a political organization, especially in a national crisis. Your views may not be consistent enough for political loyalty, but you like to feel that this is because you keep an open mind. Your heart is with your country. Your main political concern is to maintain national unity so that the traditions and values of the past are not lost.

The Other Side of the Story

You may be restless, changeable, unreliable and a stranger to your own mind. Your behavior may seem odd to friends and co-workers. Your radical and peculiar views may be publicly criticized. You are likely to be oversensitive to what other people say and quick to take offense. Being alone may hold a special horror for you. You are likely to be irritable, cranky, sulky and impatient when you fail to get your own way or sufficient attention. If a man, your reputation may be destroyed by a woman. If a woman, you may have been severely and erratically disciplined by an eccentric mother. You may suffer from obsessional fears. Nervous indigestion and ulcers of the stomach are possible.

Uranus in Leo

You have a great desire for freedom and independence, and yet are likely to deny them to others. You believe in yourself. You feel—with some justification—that you are the leader of any group you happen to be in. You think you know what is best for others, and when you appear bossy or domineering, it is usually because you genuinely feel you have the other party's interests at heart.

That's all very well. You do have a lot of positive qualities. But you're a trifle too erratic and excitable to instill great confidence in those you want to follow you.

Leo is the royal Sign of monarchy and rulers; Uranus is the planet of the unusual and unexpected, the abrupt and jarring change. These two hardly go hand in hand, but the combination often produces brilliant ideas (sometimes approaching genius), original schemes and thrilling scientific discoveries.

You are a person whose life is punctuated by remarkable changes. You don't seem to be able to keep on one course for very long not because your mind is changeable or because you are unable to concentrate (far from it), but rather because circumstances seem to seize you and fling you in the opposite direction. Hence, you don't get much chance to follow through on things. Making plans for the future can be a nightmare.

Still, you have an exciting life. You won't settle for a humdrum existence. You insist on being that little bit different.

You are apt to be attracted to the entertainment

and leisure industries. Filmmaking could easily be the field in which you will shine. You enjoy glamorous situations and everything that contributes to spectacle. As a stuntman or stuntwoman, an originator of special effects or a public relations or advertising executive specializing in gimmickry, the Uranus in Leo type is without a peer. You enjoy being in the limelight, adore a personal audience and can be counted on to take just about any kind of risk for the sake of applause or hero-worship.

You are attracted to odd types of people and frequently clash with those who support the Establishment.

Your love life is turbulent, often tempestuous. You reach the peaks of happiness and the depths of despair. It is difficult for you to stay on one emotional level for long. You have frequent love affairs—or none at all for long stretches. If married, it is not easy to avoid separations and estrangements. Strange and sudden eventualities are just as likely to part you from a loved one as to bring you together. Not a great deal that is routine or pedestrian happens where your affections are involved.

Your views often verge on the eccentric. You frequently upset co-workers, associates and even superiors with your unconventional actions and unorthodox methods. You will deliberately try a different way of doing something rather than use a tried and trusted procedure. Anything can be improved on, is your motto. You will only be happy in a job where you may experiment and test your ideas in practical and dynamic ways.

It's not surprising that such an independent and often rebellious character has difficulty taking orders. Unless you are handled carefully, or respect the person in charge, you will walk out at the first sign of high-handedness. You won't tolerate being told what to do. But if you are in a position of authority yourself, you won't brook contradiction.

You are beaverishly industrious and will give a project all you've got. You wish to change the world with your ideas and you make no secret of the fact that you want to be noticed while you're doing it. People with this combination are inclined to draw attention to themselves by dressing in unusual ways, affecting way-out hairstyles or driving flashy cars.

The Other Side of the Story

Your father may have been an eccentric and caused family hardship through his unreliable habits. The sudden death of a dear one may have left you deeply grieved. You are probably a troublemaker, a bit of a showoff and a braggart. People resent your dogmatic attitude. You have inordinately strong likes and dislikes that border on the irrational. You are dangerously headstrong and impulsive. Your recklessness and disregard for convention make you a poor example for younger people. Loss and sadness are likely through children. You have violent outbursts of temper, which, although not long-lasting, may distress those near to you. If you are a woman, the men in your life are probably erratic and very difficult to live with.

Uranus in Virgo

You can turn your hand and your mind to a great many occupations, with a good chance of success in all of them. You are not particularly ambitious for yourself but are intent on producing a good article or performing a worthwhile job. You prefer to be engaged in work where you can employ your flair for devising novel methods and inventing helpful gadgets. If there's a bottleneck anywhere in the production line, you can be depended on to come up with a simple solution. Whether in the professions or at the workbench, you are solidly effective.

You have to avoid working in spurts to be at your happiest. Your need is for a job you can get your teeth into, such as solving mechanical problems, teaching groups of people practical subjects or generally overseeing continuous work.

Your specialty is scientific research, if you can manage to get started in it. Your mind is brilliantly analytical and ideally suited for sifting large amounts of detail without losing concentration or interest.

People with this combination are often in the forefront of laboratory work connected with the chemical industries. They are intensely interested in the latest attempts to control air, water and soil pollution. They are intrigued by all aspects of diet and are often able to devise new formulas for slimming as well as for improving the vitamin effectiveness of staple foods in developing countries. Their contribution to the fields of hygiene, biology and particularly sophisticated electronics have won many of them world renown.

You are generally quiet and reserved in manner but fearfully obstinate when you believe you are right. You tend to affect an unruffled exterior even when your emotions are undergoing intense turmoil. This happens quite frequently. Unless people with this combination learn to relax, to laugh, not to take themselves too seriously and to confide more in others, they are apt to become introverted and eccentric in their behavior.

Uranus in Virgo epitomizes the absentminded professor who is so identified with his overriding interest that he merely goes through the motions in his other relationships. This can be undesirable here. Pent-up pressure should be released in adequate social activity and not in odd habit patterns. The longer the electric energy of Uranus is suppressed in Virgo, the greater is the chance of mental instability.

You have an inquisitive mind. You are continually questioning the environment and trying to put the pieces together in a new and original way. You want your achievements to be of practical benefit to as many people as possible.

You would do well working in a government or municipal department where your advanced ideas would be of direct assistance to the public. Another good area for you is the manufacturing industries, where mass production techniques help to make life easier for everyone. You should be able to write books about your work or make a living from lecturing. You can be an entertaining speaker, explaining your pet subjects, and are seldom stuck for a clever or humorous phrase.

The Other Side of the Story

Your manner is abrupt and unsettling. You seldom get along well with co-workers or subordinates. Your management or executive skills seem to consist chiefly of carping and bullying. Trenchant criticism is your long suit. As a boss, your success is marred by labor troubles, noncooperation, excessive rule enforcement and ill will. You lack concentration; your brain works in spurts and spasms. You are fanatical in your ideas about food and hygiene, though inconsistent in practicing them. You are unreliable and prone to forget where you are at times. Nerves and mental aberrations are common among immature people born with Uranus in Virgo.

Uranus in Libra

Your personal and social life undergoes numerous jarring fluctuations. For a while, you get along swimmingly with people. Then suddenly a violent change occurs, either in the other person, yourself or circumstances. And nothing is ever quite the same again. It's annoying, exciting, exasperating, amusing. But one thing is certain: it's not as boring.

This on-off electric impulse is due to Uranus, the planet that activates everything it touches—briefly. Libra is the Sign of balance, a state achieved by putting a little more or less on either side of the scales. When Uranus steps in (or on), balance fluctuates wildly. You therefore are kept very busy trying to maintain the harmony you crave in your relationships.

Friends are a great help. They have been responsible for much of your success in life as well as for providing the pleasure and intellectual stimulus your expansive mentality requires. Work and social acquaintances usually become your buddies, and many of them are influential. You have a way of attracting the people who appeal to you, and are usually surrounded by more companions than the average person. But there is a constantly changing scene. As new friends arrive, others move on—and not always in peace! Uranus turns friends into enemies. Sharp and heated exchanges frequently shatter your dreams of idyllic friendship.

The same problems afflict your love life. And yet you enjoy intense moments of happiness—sometimes even physical ecstasy—as the scale rises to heights others may never experience. The lows, of course, can be shatteringly disruptive. But as people with this combination mature and learn to live with their fluctuating emotions, they find sufficient compensations to make it all very much worthwhile. Were Uranus badly aspected, however, there would be a considerable disproportion of discord and unhappiness.

You are an artistic type of person with a special interest in music, painting or literature. People with a knowledge of these subjects are among your closest confidants. You are fascinated by the latest scientific discoveries and enjoy discussing developments in electronics and space research, as well as trendy pseudosciences. The possibilities of Astrology excite you, and although you may not have time for practical study, you are likely to be an avid reader of the latest books. Your own ideas on the topics that interest you are often original and advanced. Given the opportunity through an appropriate career, you have the capacity for making a unique contribution in your field.

Your ideas are often considered ahead of the times, perhaps even a little eccentric. Because of this, you tend to choose unconventional companions who are prepared to listen to you. Aside from being a good audience, these people appeal to you because they are intellectually flexible and creative and therefore better company. Your living habits are somewhat bohemian. You like to dress in noticeably different styles or furnish your home modernistically. You are restless and enjoy change. Your temper is volatile but brief.

People with Uranus in Libra often marry suddenly, sometimes very young or in astonishing circumstances. Eventualities in their love life often shock their families and conventional-minded associates. Partnerships, both marital and business, have a way of turning upside down—not necessarily for either bad or good—but usually to the amazement or consternation of others.

The Other Side of the Story

The sudden death of a loved one or friend may leave a vacuum in your life. You have many enemies and rivals. Friendship can seldom stand the strain of your violent temper and abrupt changes of mood. You lose your best friends and keep those who indulge your liking for luxury and pleasure. Marriage is apt to end in divorce or death. The unpredictable conduct of a partner may result in scandal and ridicule. You arouse people's hostility and antagonism, and never seem to attract understanding or sympathy even when these are well deserved.

Uranus in Scorpio

This is an extremely powerful position. The possibilities for material success and making an impact on society are tremendous. But so are the chances of failure. It depends, to a great extent, on the aspects to Uranus. Theoretically, there are three paths for those with this combination to choose from: first, a career in science, medicine or another constructive occupation where their penetrating intellect and love of investigation can be used for the benefit of all; second, treachery, cunning and lawlessness, at which the Uranus in Scorpio person unfortunately can excel; third, uncontrolled passion and sensuality, which can enslave the underdeveloped person with this combination. In any of these three paths, the person will show relentless dedication.

You are determined to succeed. You like to fix a goal well in advance and work persistently toward it. Circumstances often change suddenly and force you to make detours, but your faith in yourself and your ultimate victory never falters. You are one of the most self-willed types of the Zodiac. You never give in either to opposition or obstacles.

Your methods are novel and unconventional and frequently arouse the admiration of associates. You have a knack of visualizing future eventualities, and with your shrewd mind and diplomatic artfulness can manipulate people into making the moves your strategy requires. However, your tactfulness is usually limited to situations where you feel some advantage can be gained. Otherwise, your manner is rather blunt and aggressive. You have a stinging tongue when you want to use it and are likely to withdraw your cooperation abruptly at any time.

In many ways, you are erratic and unpredictable—one moment bold and adventurous, the next conservative and cautious. As a rule, you are secretive and for no apparent reason may withhold even unimportant information from your associates. You prefer to work alone, within a group. You understand the value of cooperation, but will not involve yourself in any scheme that does not have a solid and practical objective. Light chat is not your scene. Hen parties don't interest you.

When working, you believe in using the most modern equipment available. You are quite mechanically minded yourself and often enjoy tinkering with machines and electronic gadgets or reading articles about inventions in these fields.

You have an explosive temper. Your family, co-workers and especially subordinates have probably learned never to push you too far. You tend to rub others the wrong way, to be haughtily dogmatic and dictatorial. But at the same time, you have a magnetic appeal so that people tend to see your strong and positive qualities rather than your flaws. Weaker types, although apprehensive in your company, draw strength from you. Few who know you would ever try to provoke your animosity or endeavor to outfox you.

You deride many of society's most respected values and would like to see them replaced with your own. The fact that you are in a minority does not deter your enthusiasm or forcefulness.

You are a sensual and passionate lover, though your relations with the opposite sex seldom run smooth. Marriage is usually marked by violent arguments, tempestuous emotional scenes and lusty reconciliations.

If your energies are properly directed, you possess great artistic and creative powers. These are sometimes manifested in exceptional mystical insight. Uranus in Scorpio has produced some of the finest musicians, painters and writers—artists who reveal rather than merely relate. It also endows exceptional potential for surgical medicine, psychiatry, invention, philosophy and just plain moneymaking.

The Other Side of the Story

You are likely to be crude, coarse, bad-tempered, violent, brooding, cruel, vindictive and revengeful. Your love life is apt to be devoid of romance. Your relations with the opposite sex may end in tragedy or scandal. Lower types with this combination are bewilderingly erratic and unreliable. They may be preoccupied with the search for sexual gratification. Their perverse ways usually bring them into contact with shady and underworld types.

Uranus in Sagittarius

People with this combination are often instrumental in reforming and refining public opinion. They have a sense of identity with the common man that explodes limited material desires and opens up brave new worlds of thought and accomplishment for him.

You believe in freedom and independence for everyone. You realize that man often imprisons himself in worn-out dogmas and automatic support of discredited authority. You want to do away with these fetters—not by rebellion and physical violence, but by reeducation and enlightened thinking.

So out of Uranus in Sagittarius comes a new message, giving a more realistic meaning to religion, philosophy, morals, ethics, education and the law. And at the more mundane level, people with this combination are likely to be the initiators and innovators of new methods of long-distance travel, technical advances that speed up communications between nations, and scientific discoveries that help eliminate poverty and suffering. The end of their activities is to bring humanity as a whole closer to the concept of universal dignity.

You are an adventurer at heart. If you can't get away to visit other countries or participate in daring exploits, you manage to travel in your mind. You are an avid reader and listener. Progressive and helpful ideas crackle through your brain day and night. Whatever your line of work, you have something valuable to contribute. Broad-minded visionary is an appropriate description of this combination at its best. If you get the chance, you will be daring, courageous and quite contemptuous of physical danger. You would make a wonderful space explorer and an eager wanderer in cyber space.

You change your views often and abruptly, but generally in a progressive direction. You are continually replacing old ideas with new ones. To you, to live means to experience, so one should keep one's mind moving with the times. Since deep inside you are mainly interested in the truth and universal principles, you are not weighed down by many opinions. You know personal opinions are notoriously unreliable and depend largely on individual conditioning and circumstances. You'd much prefer to stick to facts. That's probably why you would favor any system of education based on actual experiencing. You are suspicious of classroom learning and academic certainties. Life itself and an observant and responsive mind, you believe, are the ideal teachers. But then, most of your beliefs are ahead of the times. Occasionally they land you in hot water with those who esteem conservative and traditional values.

You are not a character who can be browbeaten into silence. You believe vehemently in free speech. Frequently you offend others with your candid remarks, though your spontaneous and sincere nature usually softens the blow of these telling barbs.

Generosity is your second nature. You give without a thought to anyone in need. (Few even have to ask.) You place great value on comradeship. You are not so keen on emotional attachments because you see them as restrictions on your freedom.

You are acutely intuitive and have powerful hunches. Your dreams can be prophetic. People with this combination sometimes have visions.

The Other Side of the Story

You are constantly on the move but never succeed in doing anything worthwhile. Your reckless nature and inability to concentrate make you unreliable and forgetful—though you always come up with a good excuse for your chronic unpunctuality. You like to imagine yourself a sage or leader, but run at the first sign of responsibility. You are a big and impulsive spender, especially of money that doesn't belong to you. You can't resist a bet and will gamble wildly against hopeless odds. You depend on a glib tongue to get you out of most of your troubles. Long journeys are unlucky. Difficulties come through partners and their relatives.

Uranus in Capricorn

You are intensely ambitious and very capable—a force to be reckoned with. Not much can stand against your indomitable will. It is important with this combination to know where you are going, what you want out of life, for there is very little doubt—given favorable aspects to Uranus—that you will reach your goal eventually. It would be a pity to waste power and ability on inconsequential activities.

Despite the seriousness and discipline of this combination, it is possible for you to dart off in a totally different direction without apparent rhyme or reason. This is because of the dual effect of Uranus on Capricorn. Capricorn is the Sign that literally means business. It stands for responsibility, restraint, prudence and perseverance. Uranus, on the other hand, is the planet of abrupt changes, the unexpected, which strikes like an electric shock. Uranus takes a lot of the heaviness and dullness out of Capricorn and reinforces its resourcefulness.

But Uranus is upset at times by the movements of other planets in the heavens, and on these occasions those inexplicable inconsistencies that you must have noticed in your temperament come to the fore. And you, along with your colleagues, are often amazed at the change. You become suddenly restless and even a bit eccentric. In yourself, you feel uneasy and not so sure of the direction you are heading in. At these times, you are likely to espouse quite radical views and want to see the established order changed abruptly. You may act impulsively, and unwisely, and obstinately refuse to consider other people's viewpoints.

However, Uranus in Capricorn generally makes you a first-rate business person and executive. Your mind is quick and penetrating, and yet profound in its ability to reason in practical terms. Your business methods are novel and progressive. You are determined to get to the top, and as you climb higher, you update the system and organization under your control. You admire broad-minded and creative people and gather this type around you. You have no time for fogies and old-fashioned ideas.

You work very hard and have a special talent for getting the best out of your employees. They and your colleagues are pleased to cooperate because they know you are capable and usually successful in whatever you undertake. You are particularly adapted to take charge of a large organization, especially municipal and public works. You gravitate to positions of trust and those that require exceptional responsibleness.

You respect the independence of the individual and will always listen to the protests, objections and arguments of others—even though you may not agree with them. You have an acute sense of fair play. You won't ask someone to go against his or her principles, if you believe in this person. Although somewhat conservative, you do believe in taking the initiative. The bold enterprise that offers a challenge but not a gamble will attract you every time.

You have a flair for making accurate long-range assessments. Your logic, vision and developed social conscience all fit you for a role in politics and government.

You are also capable of writing and speaking in a revealing way, particularly when drawing attention to social ills. You seldom speak unless you have something to say. Satire is a field in which you may excel.

The Other Side of the Story

Your early home life may have been unhappy, possibly because of the death of or separation from your father or another patriarchal figure. People in authority may tend to treat you unjustly and be responsible for financial loss and anxiety. You have probably had to start a new career or been forced by circumstances beyond your control to change jobs frequently. Promotion may depend on one person who hinders or dislikes you. This combination often involves public criticism or false accusations by superiors, when the person is of the negative type. It also makes the individual weak-willed, changeable and erratic.

Uranus in Aquarius

You probably run into difficulty at work and around the home through your inability to appreciate the points of view of others. Some people might call you perverse—you invariably want to go the other way to accepted opinion. This is most admirable when you take up a worthy cause and try to institute reform in the face of unyielding authority, but at the personal level it can be quite annoying.

Still, the irritation that Uranus in Aquarius may cause other individuals is often downtrodden society's gain. For people with this combination, even in ordinary life, have a deep concern for their fellow man. They genuinely desire to see him emancipated, and they will do all they can at their own level to help, whether it is by spreading propaganda in conversation and in letters to newspapers, or by organizing their own little quasi-political groups of agitators, activists and protesters.

It's the Age of Aquarius remember, and since it

has dawned by the new millennium, never in history have so many monarchs, rulers, despots and tin-god authorities been deposed and discarded.

You are a high-minded, well-intentioned freedom lover. You love peace, but not at the price of surrender. Although your views may be unconventional or a bit ahead of the times, people respect your ebullience and sincerity. You are popular among a very wide circle of casual acquaintances. Whatever line of work you follow, you soon build up a long list of helpful contacts. Your informal, friendly and easygoing manner, together with your bright and interesting conversation, combine to make you very pleasant and entertaining company.

You are exceptionally loyal to your friends. You don't form deep emotional attachments but find your link at the intellectual level through sisterhood and brotherhood, which is a rapport you feel with most people. You like to move around a lot, circulating among club or society friends. You are interested in odd and unusual subjects, and this brings you into contact with similarly minded companions. Quite often Uranus Aquarius people and their friends are bohemian types who dress differently and have little in common with established society.

In your love life, you are faithful to the partner of the moment. You won't double-cross that guy or gal as long as it's understood that you're a twosome. But you must have a constant change of scene, not for sensual reasons, but because you're basically a mental creature and depend on different viewpoints to spark your ideas. The partner who does not understand this and tries to restrain you will lose you.

You are ideally suited for working with teams and groups or in large organizations whose aims are humanistic. Science has a special attraction. You prefer to be associated with some kind of advanced technology such as that encountered in space programs, electronics, radiation research and the like.

Uranus in Aquarius produces a person whose mind is particularly quick and ingenious. A highly developed intuition gives you flashing brilliance. Your capacity for original thinking and invention can approach the genius level. Sometimes your mind and imagination expand so fast that an otherworldliness creeps in and you appear odd.

When politically inclined, an individual with this combination is likely to get carried away with his or her own enthusiasm and slogans to the point of losing sight of the original aim. In these cases, excessive zeal may become fanaticism. Taken to an extreme, a worthy humanitarian effort may degenerate into a dictatorial rampage.

The Other Side of the Story

You may be violently antisocial, believing that all that is customary is wrong. Friends and partners may desert or betray you. Those in authority may loose a vendetta against you. You are apt to suffer from sudden falls and injuries and may be physically assaulted by a mob. You could be rude, tactless and lacking in principles. Friends may be used for your own power-grasping ends. You are probably erratic, unruly and fanatical.

Uranus in Pisces

This is not a particularly strong position from the materialistic point of view. It's something like immersing a red-hot poker in a pail of water. Clouds of obscuring steam are the result rather than dynamic power.

The power you possess is an inner one. It is expressed in a refinement, a sensitivity, a gravitation to art and a deep appreciation and understanding of the pain and suffering that exist throughout the world.

You are also profoundly psychic. You are likely to hear voices, see visions and sense atmospheres that others in the same room are oblivious of. You also have weird and peculiar dreams, some of which are amazingly prophetic. You sometimes wake up startled in the middle of the night for no apparent reason. You are apt to take a pessimistic view of your psychic experiences. Sometimes they depress you for days.

Uranus in Pisces is the conjunction of two exceptionally intuitive forces. Uranus is flashing and outward; Pisces is subdued and intuitive. If the rest of the horoscope is favorable, the person will have the strength to utilize his or her extreme sensitivity in probing and understanding the unseen forces that regulate much of our lives. In this way, he or she can fulfill the basic urge to be of service and to help mankind by describing in rational terms what is experienced.

This combination with its affinity for art and creative expression often produces singularly talented writers whose work is notable for its subtlety and finesse. Their own love of the unusual ensures that the topic will not be trite or dull.

Uranus in Pisces individuals are also likely to be proficient students of Astrology and active in other occult investigations. They can be a great personal comfort to others who may have lost loved ones.

If positive use is not made of their psychic gifts, these people are likely to become overly introspective and slip into a world of daydreams and delusion.

A career associated with hospitals, orphanages and similar public institutions often appeals to people with this combination. In the medical and welfare fields, especially, they are able to put their splendid inventive minds to work and make life easier for the sick and the handicapped. Their innovations and success in these fields may not always be featured in the newspapers, for public recognition does not come easily with the Uranus in Pisces lineup, and if achieved, may be transient. But these people will receive delicious personal satisfaction from the knowledge that they are serving those less privileged than themselves.

Pisces is a self-sacrificing Sign and, despite its spasmodic ambitious urges, is more attracted by the achievement of good than the prospect of fame. These people radiate a sympathetic aura that communicates at the unconscious level. Others recognize their innate kindness and concern and are inclined to go out of their way to help them without being aware of it. It's as though the forces of good in these individuals attract a similar response from the people around them. A sick person served by a Uranus in Pisces individual may be moved to extreme expressions of gratitude and deep-felt love.

The Other Side of the Story

You are constantly disillusioned by life, mainly because it seldom measures up to your self-deluding dreams. Although you possess the highest ideals, you lack the willpower and resolution to act on them. You are depressed by your own failures and yearn constantly for a chance to start anew, which seldom materializes. You change accommodations frequently. Unexpected reversals and difficulties often make you despair. Progress in your job or career is slow. Friends are unreliable, superiors hostile and lovers unsympathetic. You are usually separated from the people you enjoy being with most. Scandal and notoriety may be hard to avoid.

CHAPTER TWENTY-TWO

Neptune

This chapter on Neptune gives you some facts about the planet's physical features, the myths and symbolism surrounding it, and an astrological account of its characteristics. Then follows a description of Neptune in the various zodiacal signs.

The Planet

Mysterious Neptune is the eighth and second most distant planet in the solar system. It was discovered less than 180 years ago. It is so far out from the Sun (2793 million miles) that it appears as no more than a disc through the most powerful Earthbound telescopes. No markings are visible.

Neptune is another large planet. With a diameter of 27,700 miles, it is about four times the size of Earth. Although very slightly oblate, it is the most perfectly spherical of all the planets. Neptune, like the other outer giants, spins quite rapidly, having a day of 15 hours 48 minutes.

Neptune takes 165 years to orbit the Sun. It has not completed one round since its discovery, and won't have done so until the year 2011. This means the planet spends nearly 14 years in each Sign of the Zodiac.

Interesting circumstances surrounded the discovery of Neptune on September 23, 1846. For years, astronomers had been speculating and calculating, trying to account for the increasing deviation of Uranus from its regular path. It was suspected that another large cosmic body was in the vicinity, exerting a pull on Uranus—but where was it? The French astronomer Urbain Jean Joseph Leverrier postulated the position of the hypothetical planet by mathematical reckoning. A few months later, Johann Gottfried Galle, a German astronomer, spotted Neptune through a telescope—within 1 degree of the position Leverrier had calculated!

Neptune has two moons, Triton and Nereids. Triton, discovered in 1846, is the largest known satellite in the solar system. With a diameter of nearly 5000 miles, it is larger than the planets Mars and Venus. Triton orbits Neptune at 219,000 miles, which is closer than our Moon is to the Earth. Nereids, discovered in 1949, has an orbit that takes it 3 to 5 million miles away from Neptune.

Symbolism

Neptune, called Poseidon by the Greeks, was the eldest son of Saturn. After Saturn was deposed, Neptune and his brothers, Jupiter and Hades, cast lots for sovereignty and Neptune won the sea. He lived in an underwater palace. Neptune's symbol of power was the trident, thought to have originally been a lightning bolt, with which he could shake the Earth or subdue the waves.

Astrology

Neptune is associated with formlessness and refinement through dissolution, immateriality and subtlety. It is the force behind the appearance of things, the deceiver and the revealer. It is the psychic as opposed to the physical, the spirit as opposed to the flesh. It represents escape from the mundane world through the awakening of supersensitive perceptive faculties. It is the mystical link between the planes of inspiration and genius and the artists and visionaries who give the world the finest music, poetry, literature, form, uplifting spiritual truths and melting compassion. It is the medium for good or evil between man and his highest aspirations, whatever they may be.

Neptune is a higher octave of Venus, the planet of love and beauty. Neptune idealizes these emotions into one potent and discerning force, scalding but intangible and nebulous, which pervades rather than persists, flounders rather than floats, redeems rather than reforms. It is the mysterious and unknowable force that releases man from matter and reveals to him what does and does not signify. It is terribly personal. It is the path through the body and the ego mechanism to high consciousness. It is matter attuned to its own finest vibrations.

Neptune links man with the deceptive forces of his subconscious. With Neptune, things are seldom what they seem. It produces queer and indefinable feelings, sensations and emotions. It is the psychic power behind spiritual mediums, the hypnotist and the hypnotized. It creates impressionability, mystical experience, daydreaming and all that is associated with the supernatural. It raises the sensitivity to such a pitch that the feelings of others—even the feelings others impress by their presence on inanimate objects—are discerned and emotionally identified without making use of the reasoning process. This psychometric faculty is a refined extension of the Venus-ruled sense of touch.

If you are strongly influenced by Neptune in your horoscope, the total number of good and adverse aspects between Neptune and the other planets will exceed neutral aspects. To make an accurate determination, you will have to read the detailed descriptions that follow. You can then draw your own conclusions.

Neptune well aspected means you are a gentle and unassuming person. You are receptive, subtle and visionary. Since you are ultra-sensitive and impressionable, your emotions are very close to the surface and easily disturbed. You have a great need of silence and solitude at times to restore your psychic balance. Unless your companions understand this, they will not understand you. You appear extremely charming and gracious, but this is largely a persona or mask, and although you are compelled by your nature to don it, you are aware it is illusory. You have strong and vivid spiritual insights, which can produce vague yearnings to burst through to understanding through renunciation. You find it very difficult to stand up to pressure for long; you sag, and without respite are likely to suffer a nervous breakdown.

A badly aspected Neptune can produce an escapist who retreats into his or her own dream world rather than try to improve or change the environment. This type is irresponsible and will turn to drugs and liquor to sustain a hallucinatory existence. Psychosomatic illnesses are very common among these people; they have an extraordinary capacity for producing symptoms of particular illnesses with a thought. Given the environmental stimulus they want (or their own way), they can snap back into glowing health in a moment. Negative Neptune people use their considerable charm to deceive others in business and personal life. They make the most plausible villains and confidence tricksters. They are also capable of being promiscuously permissive with their bodies.

Neptune rules Pisces, the twelfth and last zodiacal sign, and is at its strongest in Cancer. Both are water Signs. The planet controls the sea, oil, chemicals and other liquids. Its discovery coincided with distinct new human trends that correlate with its nature: mesmerism (later to lead to hypnotism) swept Europe; the famous Rochester Rappings in the United States gave birth to modern spiritualism in America and England; anesthetics began to be used in surgery; and so on.

Neptune is in each Sign of the Zodiac for about 14 years. Its effects are more visible in generations than in individuals. It has much to do with influencing the unconscious actions and modes of thought that, although expressed through individuals, become what might be called collective characteristics of that time. Neptune's influence works through all the individuals born during that time as an expression of their generation. The planet's effect is more pervasive than direct, more motivating than activating. It is a powerful force moving behind the scenes, manifesting in individuals as mood and attitude.

Because the planet spends nearly 14 years in a Sign, its effects are less specific on the individual than those of the personal planets and even Uranus (7 years). However, these effects will be expressed through the characteristics of the Sign Neptune occupied at birth. Neptune is not the precise generation gap typified by Uranus; it represents the hidden undercurrents in the collective psyche that work partially in the minds of men and women and guide each generation haltingly to a point from which the next can step up in consciousness.

To Neptune, war and peace, famine and plenty, are virtually irrelevant externals, the province of other planetary forces. Neptune is concerned with the *inner* changes these events work. The Neptune influence, like the lightning bolt the old god used to shake the earth and quell the sea, shatters the inner temples of materialistic values that individuals and generations would put their faith in.

The planet's energy is a transmuting force that, for the want of a better or more scientific word, is called spiritual. The spirit, like Neptune, can never really be defined but its effects are unmistakable. Whereas the revolutions of Uranus occur outside of man, Neptune revolutionizes from within. Neptune's mists seem to drift in confusion, but the nebulousness is part of the transmutation process.

The materialist who is ready for the next evolutionary step up in his consciousness will be pitilessly driven by Neptune until confusion dissolves his certainty. The person already moving toward spiritual awareness and truer values will be inwardly elevated and exalted in his feelings by the same force.

Neptune, compared with the planets out to Saturn, is an otherworld force. Its power relates to a period longer than a lifetime and to a life purpose that is intangible. It gives no real inklings, no promises—just more stirrings to go on. The Neptune impulse is to share, so the Neptune individual (or true Pisces) is passionately, impassionately and compassionately involved in humanity's progress. This personal commitment to the elevation of a species can be deluding, enlightening, confusing, inspiring, misguiding, sublime, divine or chaotic—depending on the individual.

Physiologically, Neptune is associated with the optic and hearing nerves, the spinal canal and the nervous and mental processes generally. When afflicted, it causes deep-seated neuroses, several emotional and mental disturbances and incurable insanity.

Neptune in Cancer (1902—1916)

You are a person who has experienced some very unusual happenings connected with your family or home. Your childhood was not what it appears to others to have been. You may have had reason to keep secret some of the circumstances of your earlier years, or perhaps you were deceived by a family member and the memory and its associations are still clear in your mind.

You were born at a time when the world was making traumatic adjustments. Your generation was raised by people who experienced the rigors of war on a world scale for the first time. Yours was the task of trying to build a viable modern society on the shaky ground of inherited mistakes and uncertainty. You are a generation of transitions, and you are never too sure that what you have accomplished is essentially better than what went before.

You are inclined to be too passive and allow things to slide. You are not disposed to determined and positive actions. With Neptune in Cancer, you feel your way ahead very carefully; the grand and sweeping gesture is not in your repertoire. You are somewhat negative in your approach to problems. People, especially your family or children, may tend to take you for granted, to walk over you in a sense. You are too sympathetic and affectionate. You have known many disappointments in the past.

You love to travel and have probably made at least one ocean cruise. You would prefer to travel by ship than by air, but have to do the modern thing to save time and expense. You don't like being away from home for long. You are a person who was probably overindulgent as a parent. Discipline was never your strong point; you preferred to bring up your children in a relaxed and homely atmosphere. Some of your ideas about domestic affairs may have been regarded as a bit odd. But you probably found that no matter how much you tried to guide your children with love and affection, they seldom responded as you would have expected. You may feel at times that you were not and will not be really appreciated by your dear ones. But this does not prevent you from continuing to care and concern yourself deeply with family affairs.

You have always possessed a psychic faculty, which probably first revealed itself in childhood. You are extremely sensitive to other people's moods, and without their saying a word, you know exactly what they are feeling. You also have deep spiritual insights. Although you may not speak about these very often, they help you to cope with daily affairs and to understand life better. Sometimes you have premonitions that are amazingly accurate.

You are idealistic, refined and love nature. You are exceedingly sentimental and enjoy all contact with the past. You remember the good old days with a great deal of nostalgia. You surround yourself with antiques and other relics of the periods you admire most, especially objects and souvenirs handed down by older family members. Your love for your mother was moving and profound. She had a great influence on you as a child, and may have helped to develop your psychic powers or encouraged you spiritually.

You really love your country. Although normally reserved, you can display fervent patriotism in a national crisis or political emergency. Other times, you take an active interest in what is going on by keeping yourself informed through newspapers and magazines. You are a loyal supporter of whichever political party you feel stands for the preservation of standards.

The Other Side of the Story

You are restless, discontented and rarely able to settle in one place for long. Your impressionability makes you neurotic and a difficult person to live with. Peculiar and even weird experiences in your childhood have probably left deep scars on your mind, which have never really healed. Your domestic life may be complicated and unhappy. You may suffer from nervousness and anxiety. A pessimistic and gloomy frame of mind may repel others and reduce you to loneliness. You are likely to suffer from chronic indigestion or stomach ulcers. You may have to engage in some sort of deception in connection with your home or family. Your political views may be extreme and you may be thought a little eccentric.

Neptune in Leo (1916—1929)

This is an excellent position for Neptune. It gives an innate desire and ability to serve the world and your fellow man in practical ways. You want to throw over the old and help bring on the new. But whether your objectives are worthwhile or worthless depends largely on how Neptune is aspected in your horoscope. You may be a source of hope or a source of trouble. In between, stands misguided optimism.

Many of the world's most effective revolutionaries were born when Neptune was in Leo. The leading lights of the American Revolution and many of the fighting men had this combination. So did numerous figures in the French Revolution, including Robespierre, Danton—and Marie Antoinette. Although on the other side, she believed (misguided optimism?) in what she stood for and did try to negotiate with the revolutionaries before losing her head.

Another example of opposing forces, both fighting for their idea of freedom, were the leaders John Kennedy and Fidel Castro, who brought the world to the brink of nuclear war when Russia moved atomic missiles into Cuba. Both were born with Neptune in Leo. So was Oliver Cromwell (nearly four hundred years earlier) who led the Puritan Rebellion against the English monarchy, and so was Christopher Columbus, who proved revolutionary theory—the Earth was not flat.

You are ambitious, conscientious and considerate. You are spiritually inclined and are moved to improve conditions rather than allow them to continue as they are. You have a keen intellect and sensitive emotions. You can interpret the feelings of the masses and express yourself in artistic and entertaining ways, which are received with acclaim. You are the product of the generation that gave the world the motion picture industry. Through this make-believe medium, glamour, romance and movie-star adoration were introduced into the otherwise prosaic lives of vast numbers of people. Neptune in Leo often bestows the charisma of irresistible charm and popularity that reaches the level of hero-worship. Many of the modern superstars of politics, screen, medicine and philosophy and psychology have this combination.

Neptune in Leo makes you social-minded and a lover of pleasure and the outdoors. You have a special way with children; you can guide them toward a less materialistic outlook without destroying their natural ambitions. You encourage the artistic and creative urge in others because you sincerely want them to develop to their highest potential. Your own interests include poetry, music, painting and drama. You can be a capable author, playwright, actor, actress or entertainer.

At times, you have peculiar feelings and intuitions, some of which are indescribable. Usually you know what you must do without any great thought about it. You trust your emotions and sympathies a little more than you do your reason. But you insist on being rational in your relationships and channel your energies into practical and purposeful endeavors. Art, spirituality and reform, to you, are not just topics to be talked about; they require action, determination and dedication—qualities you inspire in others by your own example.

Your love life is unsettled. Over the years you have had quite a few crushing disappointments. Love as a personal expression or selfish need does not have much chance of success where you are concerned. You may be deceived or suffer heartbreak through separation from the great love of your life. You are never short of individuals to love or to love you, but circumstances usually intervene after a while and force you apart, either physically or psychologically. The inner drive of Neptune is toward a more detached and pervasive love, which sacrifices egotistical satisfaction for the universal good. You need to find a humanitarian cause big enough and worthy enough to absorb the love and devotion you have to give.

The Other Side of the Story

You may live for pleasure and thus undermine your health and chances. You may go from one love affair to another, never finding satisfaction. Your search for physical gratification may lead to gluttony and drunkenness. Your father may have taught you low principles. You may attract degenerate company. You are likely to be a slave to your feelings and emotions and lack reasonable restraint. You can spend money as quickly as you get it on lavish living and entertainment. You may make a show of generosity in an attempt to win attention and applause. You are likely to be self-centered, boastful and loud. You may have been poorly educated and forced to fabricate qualifications. You are likely to be weak, cowardly, lazy or bullying. Your closest companions may be yes-men.

Neptune in Virgo (1929—1943)

You are a gentle and patient individual, particularly when dealing with what are often thought to be the less important things in life. You give the smallest detail its correct place in the scheme of things, and this attention extends to animal and plant life. You are compassionate for the little creatures—the grasshoppers, fish, worms, birds, wild flowers, small animals, shrubs—and assume the bigger things are capable of looking after themselves.

You are also drawn to help people who can't help themselves—the sick, the aged and children who are poor or underprivileged. You don't have such sympathy for others; ordinary people you find necessary, but not easy to love. In fact, you are quite reserved and even shy in a social sense. You enjoy company and conversation, but your emotions are not easily aroused; you give the impression of being animated but lukewarm. You would make an excellent nurse or horticulturalist, zoologist or agriculturalist. Scientific matters relating to health intrigue you. You would find it easy and satisfying to make a living from medicine, chemistry, pharmacy. You have some unusual views about diet, which you put into practice with lively enthusiasm until you discard them for even better (or more peculiar) nutritional ideas. You enjoy writing about health and food and are not averse to sending off letters to friends or a newspaper detailing your latest theories and discoveries. You are a quite competent cook. You are acutely conscious of the necessity for hygiene and may go to extremes with perpetual handwashing and the like.

You have definite views about labor conditions and the plight of the workers. You want to improve the lot of those who are exploited, but you are inclined to overlook the shortcomings of some of the individuals in these conditions. If Neptune is badly aspected, you may be confused in your judgments and mistake laziness for lack of opportunity. You are keenly interested in education generally; you want to see everyone educated to the hilt, zealously ignoring the fact that those who find it hard to learn would be very unhappy under your prescription.

You possess exceptional psychic powers, which allow you to predict situations with amazing accuracy. You can visualize a set of circumstances and immediately see the flaws and advantages that events will present. Napoleon had this occult insight. He knew men. He could gauge what they would do. In matters of state, he could look years ahead and erect a detailed conceptual structure of what the future would require. Parts of his Code Napoleon, which reformed the French legal system, are still in use. Posterity is continually reminded of him by the ideas he projected.

The general tendency with Neptune in Virgo is to allow psychic vision to take the place of spiritual insight, to be caught up in the desire to leave things in good order without harmonizing inner conditions. Material considerations, including man-made laws and wisdom, become paramount values (this, no doubt, is what finally led to Napoleon's downfall).

Your psychic perception makes you an especially capable researcher into occult fields. You also possess the literary ability to describe your findings in clear and logical language. Many astrologers are born with this combination.

You have an affinity for city and suburban life. Even if you live in the country, you will work in a more populated area and visit the city regularly. You have a talent for architectural work and draftmanship. You can conceive schemes for vast building projects—industrial complexes, shopping centers, new towns—and either construct them or design them down to the last quantitative detail.

The Other Side of the Story

You may be a cold fish who doesn't care for anyone. You may live a life of fastidious and efficient selfishness and not be averse to keeping up a long deception to get your own way. You are likely to be a hypochondriac with a special weakness for drugs and liquor. You may feel the world owes you a living and exist on the dole, handouts and your own cunning. You may be perverse in your sexual appetites. In employment, you may seldom contribute a fair day's work if it can be avoided by cheating or falsifying. You may use your talents for writing and public speaking to extract or extort money from others. You have a sharp, destructively critical tongue that causes much pain to others.

Neptune in Libra (1943–1956)

You people of the 1940s and 1950s have been called the "love generation" because you tried to introduce this concept to the world. You did it quietly and passively with love and sit-ins. But if you were successful, it is a reforming impulse that has now sunk deep into the human psyche. The effects are superficially obscured by the fundamental drives of the generation that followed yours—those born with Neptune in Scorpio. As an individual, you still believe in love, peace and equality. But your generation, which produced the extraordinary era of the flower and love cults, petered out as a reigning world force when Neptune left Libra and entered Scorpio.

You are an idealist and a humanitarian. Your mind is continually considering how man's lot can be improved. Libra is the Sign of art, love, beauty and justice; Neptune is the planet of pervasive, reforming spiritual power. So your higher aspirations are even more refined than is normally the case in the creative and humanistic worlds. This makes you an individual who is filled with idealism but lacking in force. Although your convictions about the rights of man are firmly entrenched, you don't have much power to change the order of things. Because the reforms you want to make are dependent on inner workings, you won't see any great evidence of the lasting effects of your efforts.

You are refined in your tastes and behavior. You are more intellectual than physical. You have an extremely active imagination that likes to soar beyond mundane problems to the realm of lofty ideals and magnificent aspirations. When it comes down to everyday lick-and-polish activity, you are easily discouraged. You don't wish to be involved in the drab tasks of life and you make no secret of your distaste. You desire elegant living, gracious forms, gentle manners and peaceful and pleasant surroundings, as well as the company of artistic and sophisticated people. You are drawn to art, music, philosophy, literature and social reform.

You love love, you tend to idealize it, and in the hands of harsh reality, your illusions are often destroyed. But you invariably manage to create another ethereal vision. This is because you believe in love, not as it is practiced by a cynical society through hypocritical conventions, but as you know it can be. Your dream of love allows you to hang on to the ultrareality, to believe that it will one day be realized on Earth.

You are popular and much in demand socially. You have a tender spot for the underdog and will go out of your way to befriend neighbors and others who are unhappy or worse off economically than yourself. Your compassion, understanding, charm and love of harmony make you a desirable and pleasing companion. As a lover you are tender and affectionate. But if Neptune is badly aspected, you are likely to be overly emotional, changeable and sexually promiscuous. Your love affairs often lead to peculiar situations and frequently result in mutually unwanted separations.

You are very firm in your views about the need for justice in the world. You can be quite forceful and aggressive when debating this subject. But Neptune is inclined to cloud your judgment when you identify with a cause, and you need to listen to advice or you may ruin the very thing you are trying to promote.

Mystical, mysterious and magical subjects hold a fascination for you. You are extremely interested in the occult. But you need the encouragement or in-spiration of another person or a group to become active in this field. You have a special liking for good films and television. You love dancing and music. Scientific discoveries, especially space explorations, excite you.

The Other Side of the Story

If a woman, you may be a crybaby, a hysterical person who is likely to break into tears at any moment for no apparent reason. If a man, you may be emotionally unstable and unable to discuss a contentious subject without feeling under personal attack. Your love life may be a succession of disasters that lead to broken homes. You may be oversexed and unable to resist any opportunity to gratify your appetite. You may aim at promoting harmony between people and succeed only in stirring enmity, misunderstanding and anger. You are likely to be an interfering do-gooder who collapses at the first sign of hard work, opposition or pressure. You may run from responsibility. Your idea of social reform may extend no further than having your name published in the society columns.

Neptune in Scorpio (1956—1970)

Neptune was in Scorpio from approximately late 1956 to 1970. This was the time when those in a position to mold public opinion decided to bring sex out from under wraps and place it squarely in the public eye. There was fierce and outraged opposition to plays like *Oh, Calcutta!* and *Hair*, and the increasing permissiveness of the screen, but gradually the protests became a drone that few really heard.

Neptune is the planet of subtle revelation and Scorpio is the Sign of sex, secrets and the investigation of mysteries. Scorpio also is a harsh and perverse Sign, and anyone looking back on those times cannot help but notice the rash of entertaining but murderously slick spy stories and films, the ferocity and torment of the war in Vietnam, the assassinations of the Kennedy brothers and Martin Luther King, Jr. as well as the prominence of the drug scene with its Neptune delusions and Scorpio wretchedness.

But out of the agony and anguish came much that was regenerative in human thought. And those of you who were born with this influence will have the opportunity of showing exactly what that means when you begin sitting on the benches of power and authority at the end of the twentieth century and into the twenty-first century—the new millennium.

You can't stand hypocrisy and affectation. You want to see the world stripped of pretentiousness and insincerity. You believe in being honest—even if it hurts—though your methods sometimes make others suspect you believe the means justifies the end. But most of all, you believe in being honest with yourself. This can be a traumatic discipline not only for you, but also for those who have to live and work with you. You don't always measure up to your rigorous ideal, but you keep trying. You are intractably self-willed and have unshakable faith in your ultimate victory over all resistance.

You have a fierce temper, which you usually manage to keep under control; in fact, you don't like showing any of your feelings. Although your emotions are intense and quite often in a repressed state of turmoil, no one can tell this from your appearance. You are reserved and secretive, slow to make friends and rather doubting and suspicious. You have learned not to accept things at their face value.

You are fascinated by stories about the occult and have had numerous psychic experiences of your own, especially when you were young. Your dreams are often extremely vivid and sometimes symbolize events yet to come. People with this combination have visions at times of immense stress or just after a crisis.

You would do well in any occupation that requires a penetrative or inventive mind. Psychiatry, engineering, mechanics, investigation, chemistry, surgery or an army career could provide a field for your considerable talents.

One of the dangers of Neptune in Scorpio may be a tendency to drink excessively or to experiment with drugs. You have a deep attachment to all forms of sensation and a desire to expand your experience.

The Other Side of the Story

You are probably obsessed with some weird ideas that make life very difficult for those you live with. If this combination is afflicted by bad aspects, your nature is likely to be twisted with brutal urges to satisfy an insatiable lust for power over others and sexual gratification. In some cases, you are yourself the helpless victim of malicious and degenerate types. Bad luck may dog you at every step and cease only when there is nothing left to you in the material world. Some form of spiritual regeneration is possible in the midst of final despair.

Neptune in Sagittarius (1970—1984)

The Neptune in Sagittarius generation will be incurable idealists and incredibly optimistic about the future of mankind—if only other people will see things as they do. While they will recognize that there are many ills in the world, they will be inclined to fight them with words and ideas, by stirring up public opinion rather than by taking direct action to eliminate the causes. They will look to the future rather than to the present.

Their vision will be broad, sweeping and original. Demanding details of their expansive schemes would be like asking a millionaire exactly how much he's worth—it's irrelevant: he's a millionaire! Using a few broad brush strokes to show what they mean, they will leave the filling in to those of lesser inspiration and intellect.

This will work very well both in business and in humanitarian schemes, for they will undoubtedly manage to surround themselves with willing helpers before racing off to launch another idea somewhere else.

Their intuition will sometimes be astonishing. They will seem to be able to look down the line of time and conceive exactly what will be required to make the most of events yet to happen. They will go out on a limb to carry out their hunches and will even back them with money and reputation.

Their public-spiritedness will extend to a keen interest in education, especially the kind that makes minds receptive to loftier principles and ideas. In the realm of religion and metaphysics, they will probably have some very original notions. Neptune in Sagittarius tends to link mystical experience with some of the less explicable phenomena in today's psi experiments and occultism. They will be inclined to pull down the barriers and demonstrate how the golden rules of the old-time religions still hold true: they will require wider application, not necessarily wider interpretation. They may believe that ideas have the power to change human minds, and they will demonstrate that power in measurable ways. They will be against hidebound reasoning, but will believe in truth—and that every thought should begin afresh from there.

Just as they will like to let their minds run free, so will they love to keep their bodies on the move. They will crave the outdoor life and all sports and games. They will demand travel, as far and as often as possible, both through the spaces of their minds as well as to other countries.

The ability to express themselves will fit them for a career in journalism or as authors of travel books and articles. The more they are able to move around and explore, the happier and more productive they will be. They will be also competent or itinerant artists who refuse to be tied down by their many possessions. A career in science, which would allow them to explore exotic places or to live with other races and study comparative cultures, will also be enticing to these idealists.

Deep-seated emotions will sometimes reach fever

pitch and make them exceedingly restless in both mind and body. On these occasions, they may well act without thinking and then live to regret it.

Their dreams may sometimes be weirdly prophetic. A sense of humor will often be crucial in preventing lapses into vague depressions.

The Other Side of the Story

Long journeys and visits to other countries will probably end in odd experiences for these people. Foreigners may try to deceive them, especially those who pretend to be friendly. The political and religious views they hold will undoubtedly be criticized by those in important positions and public ridicule may result. Psychic experiences and terrifying dreams may make sleep itself a nightmare. Their concentration may be weak, their religious ideas misleading; these factors could result in torment and unhappiness for others.

Neptune in Capricorn (1984—1998)

These individuals born in the last two decades of the twentieth century will want to see greater order established on Earth in the new millennium. They will show that the resources of the world can be better organized. They will feel strongly that efficient—and possibly global—political and bureaucratic control can be the only answer to man's age-old struggles for supremacy. They will prove that, if given the chance, they can make life much easier for everyone—if they are free to put their ideas into play. The biggest problem will be their inclination to concentrate on man's material needs, ignoring the intense human longing for aesthetic fulfillment.

Neptune in Capricorn people will be brilliantly practical and painstakingly thorough. They will seldom make a move without considering every possibility. Their minds will seem almost inspired in their ability to gauge, weigh and measure. They will have the makings of gifted physicists, chemists, engineers; as top executives, they will run the largest organizations and can be counted on to increase profits and reduce costs.

As politicians, they may not be so popular, but will have the compensating virtue of delivering promised results. They may live by the letter of the law rather than its spirit. Those who support this group may hope, in a way, that they will fail. Their methods, although effective, may become quite wearying for all concerned after a time. While likely to awaken man's desire for a change—any sort of change—they will free him from the imposed sterility and regimen of security. In the face of opposition, they will show great courage and determination. Although naturally careful and cautious, they will be quite versatile and resilient when it comes to defending their position.

Their personal lives may very likely be rather unhappy, beginning with problems in the home during childhood. Married life is apt to be spoiled by the absence of warmth and spontaneity in either partner. What begins with high promise may well degenerate into impersonal compromises or total disregard.

This group will probably be connected with the entertainment industry through dancing, music or acting, but they will be more than likely to take an organizational or servicing role rather than an artistic one. Any artistic flair in this combination will undoubtedly be limited to qualitative excellence in the things produced, manufactured or supplied. For instance, a person with Neptune in Capricorn may be a printer of attractive packaging, reading matter, cards, sheet music and other high-class color work.

They will have a strong tendency to suffer from painful and vivid dreams in which they find themselves being publicly rebuked by someone in authority. In these dreams, they may be horrified by their own irresponsible actions or may have to face the reality of poverty in old age.

Insecurity, failure and the feeling that they are not respected may frequently depress them, even though these have no foundation in fact.

The Other Side of the Story

This group will be uncertain and vague and will tend to rely on others to make decisions for them. They will wait too long and will miss opportunities. They will be fearful worriers and their digestion will suffer as a result. They may resolve to be decisive and definite, but will fail as soon as any pressure is brought to bear. Family affairs will contain some peculiar situations; there will probably be a skeleton in the closet that will depress them; or a business scandal may leave their reputations in tatters and thus ruin their hopes. Family members will complicate their lives in unusual ways.

Neptune in Aquarius (1998—2012)

Near the end of the twentieth century Neptune made its first appearance in Aquarius, beginning its transit of that Sign in late January 1998. Neptune is in Aquarius approximately 14 years until early February 2012. For a few months in 1998 Neptune returned to Capricorn before moving again into Aquarius for its stay there. The Neptune in Aquarius placement influences the entire span of these 14 years.

Individuals born in this generation will have a

highly developed collective consciousness. They will often think first of the greater good, the common cause, before considering personal needs and desires. Private hopes and wishes will become identified with publicly stated goals for all humanity. Such a utopian mind set can lead to an extreme idealism that makes argument likely and compromise improbable.

Neptune in Aquarius bears the humanitarian vision. This planetary placement has the potential to put individuals on a path of enlightenment and service in the new millennium. Involvement in the larger global community will teach many lessons. Sympathy combined with action will be required to make the future safe and secure for all.

The creative potential of people born with Neptune in Aquarius will be tremendous. That creativity will be wide ranging, not restricted to one field or area of human endeavor. The Sign of Aquarius is associated with electricity, electronics, and electromagnetism. Here new inventions will be noteworthy.

The next visionaries of broadband communications networking, of optical networking, of refinements in all electronic messaging, will come from this generation. Speed will be a priority—in travel as well as communication. Neptune in Aquarius individuals will be inventing new media for the transmission of culture, improved means and machines for taking a journey. Space travel will be emphasized, due to the airy energy of Aquarius. Ocean and undersea transport, the sea being Neptune's doman, will begin reconfiguration.

The visionary magic of Neptune combined with the electric genius of Aquarius will illuminate avantgarde film, literature, music, fashion. The union of art and science will reach a new plateau. Here will be the power to create profoundly moving and satisfying forms that excite rather than soothe the senses.

Neptune's brilliant intuitions and impressionability are given form and practical significance in Aquarius. This generation will have depth and clarity of thought. Yet weird and mystical subjects will attract these men and women. Insights into the psychic world will be defined in precise and meaningful ways.

The often vague idealism of Neptune is given direction, in unusual ways, by the galvanizing force of Aquarius. Aquarius never loses sight of the fact that haumanity has to live in the material world. The scientific researcher knows that physics, astronomy, chemistry, biology, engineering are the rational and visible parts of the universe.

Neptune in Aquarius represents two sides of the coin of wisdom: inspiration and reason. Neptune in Aquarius stirs intellectual currents carrying a rich and varied harvest. It is a perfect breeding ground for idealistic aims as long as practical considerations are taken into account. Individuals must distinguish the oasis from the mirage. Only then will the visionary qualities conferred by this planetary placement find fertile soil.

The Other Side of the Story

Nervous hypertension can make these individuals appear otherwordly, eccentric, erratic, nebulous, self-deluding and uselessly self-sacrificing. Financial affairs can be a mess, a constant worry. Discredit or scandal can visit these individuals. Friendships, group associations, marriage, romance will be complicated. Too much will be expected of others, too little responsibility taken by the individual. The possibilities for deception and delusion will run high. The capacity for disruption and upheaval will lie in this generation. A tendency to act without due deliberation, an urge to rebel against established patterns, the wish to sweep away the old will drive these individuals.

Neptune in Pisces (2012—2026)

Neptune in Pisces is at home, a placement in dignity. Neptune rules Pisces, sharing rulership with benevolent planet Jupiter. Neptune enters Pisces on April 4, 2011, goes back to Aquarius for several months, then returns to Pisces February 4, 2012 and resides in Pisces until 2026. The generation born with Neptune in Pisces over these 14 years will be striving for universal understanding, universal love, universal generosity, universal forgiveness.

Neptune in Pisces can represent the fruition of a two-century old struggle to achieve the noblest aims: universal human rights and liberation from all forms of tyranny. To say that Neptune in Pisces is a transcendental or sublime placement would be to understate its pervasive influence in changing people's consciousness of the here and now—and in stirring people to act in the here and now. To illuminate and to inspire will be the work of Neptune in Pisces.

Nothing is written in stone, as only a Neptune in Pisces individual would know. As the ocean waves and the tides change, so does human consciousness. Imagination and vision will be key. This generation will make fabulous strides in art, science, politics, sports, religion, spirituality, philosophy. And it will be this generation's imperative that *everyone* be given the chance to participate in the here and now, not just as part of a group but as an individual.

Dreamed of, undreamed of, breakthroughs will come in oceanography, biology, medicine—all endeavors connected to the sea or to fluids within living organisms. The challenge of regenerating parts of living organisms will be met by Neptune in Pisces men and women. Exploration and development of the oceans and seas, Neptune's domain, will lead to boons for civilization.

Neptune in Pisces individuals will possess a powerful, vivid imagination. Self-expression through music, poetry, literature, dance, sculpture, painting—all the theater, entertainment, performance arts—will come rhythmically, pleasingly. Capable of psychic experiences, including visions, these men and women will pour illumination into their art.

Neptune in Pisces individuals will be drawn to mysticism and the occult. Ritual, theatrical, devotional sides of religion or a faith will appeal. Yet faith may derive more from the natural world of living organisms—the flora, the fauna, the fish, all the sea creatures as well as the living saints and martyrs who struggle in the here and now—than from the unseen world of gods and goddesses.

This generation will prefer to develop spiritual principles outside the realm of orthodox and traditional religions. Dogma will be anathema to these people who believe in universal concert and cooperation. As long as the principles remain open, capable of interpretation and reinterpretation, and available to all, the Neptune in Pisces generation will progress beyond the closed systems of past centuries.

Two sides of the Neptune in Pisces character will be prominent, often intertwined in harmony yet sometimes opposing each other—like the Pisces Fishes swimming together or swimming in opposite directions. The swimmer, the explorer will visit every venue of human endeavor and illuminate it with the vision of a finer world. To reach a frontier, to scout it out, to settle it will be the impulse of the Neptune in Pisces generation.

The Other Side of the Story

Neptune, the revealer, is also the deceiver playing tricks on the mind and imagination. Too much introspection can block effective action. All that is favorable can be turned into delusion, lost chance, trouble or hardship. The danger of fantasy overriding reason is great. Excuses may be found for treachery, moral degradation, addiction, dropoutism. Fanaticism in beliefs can lead to isolation or emotional disturbances. Physical health may suffer, mental outlook may be distorted by secret sorrows and self-condemnation.

CHAPTER TWENTY-THREE

Pluto

This chapter on Pluto gives you some facts about the planet's physical features, the myths and symbolism surrounding it, and an astrological account of its characteristics. Then follows a description of Pluto in the various zodiacal signs.

The Planet

Pluto was discovered less than 75 years ago. It is the last-known planet out from the Sun. Like Neptune, the planet's presence was suspected before it was located. Around the turn of the century, astronomers noted that Neptune's orbit was being increasingly disturbed by a body that seemed to be farther out in space. In an attempt to find the new planet, Dr. Percival Lowell built an observatory at Flagstaff, Arizona. He installed a 13-inch telescope—quite a sizable apparatus for those days—but was unsuccessful in his search. Then, in 1930, at the same Lowell Observatory, a student astronomer, C. W. Tombaugh, spotted the planet and photographed it.

This was quite a feat. Pluto is only about half the size of the Earth—3650 miles in diameter—and it is an inconceivable 3600 million miles out in space—about 39 times the distance of the Earth from the Sun.

Pluto takes the longest time of all the planets to complete its orbit around the Sun—248 years—and its movement is highly irregular. While all the other planets move within degrees of the Sun's path (called the ecliptic), Pluto moves within 17 degrees. It spends an average of 24 years in each zodiacal Sign, but because of its irregular movements, this period can vary from 13 to 32 years.

Symbolism

Pluto, or Hades as he was known to the Greeks, was the ruler of the dead and the underworld. He was the son of Saturn and brother of Jupiter and Neptune. When Saturn was deposed by his sons, the three divided the government of the world by lot. Pluto won the underworld. The ancients associated Pluto with wealth because gold and precious stones in their raw form and buried treasure were said to be in his custody. Hence the word "plutocracy": government by the wealthy.

Pluto's most treasured possessions were the helmet of darkness, a two-forked scepter and the staff with which he drove the ghosts or shades of men. He ruled with his queen, Persephone, whom he had forcibly abducted from the upper world. She was forced to spend half the year with Pluto and the other half on the surface of the Earth. Pluto was usually accompanied by Cerberus, the dog-monster of Hades that had three heads, a serpent's tail and a mane of snakes. Pluto was not depicted as a tempter of men, like the Christian devil. He was certainly a physical seducer of women, but not a psychological one. Mostly he was the custodian of the dead, the ruler of the house of the dead, who had to be stern and pitiless, but only in those roles.

Astrology

When a planet is discovered, its basic characteristics coincide with the trends and events then beginning to show in human affairs. Invariably, it seems, the broad mythological connotations apply. Pluto's discovery in 1930 coincided with the rise of gangsterism, the rule by those of the underworld who enslave, rob and kill for money and power. It marked the rise to power of Hitler and his attempt to produce a super-race through exterminating those he deemed "subhuman"—Jews, Poles, Slavs. It was the era of racketeers, the mob and machine-gun justice; the Mister Bigs with massive psychoses and paranoic drives, who liked to remain mysteriously respectable while pulling villainous strings behind the scenes. It was the buildup period to the most devastating war in history, beginning with the worst financial depression ever known.

The task for astrologers was to decide which Sign of the Zodiac was Pluto's. All the planets rule a Sign—that is, there is one Sign (sometimes two) that has a characteristic affinity with the life principle or force each planet represents. In the case of Pluto, the Sign was never really in doubt, although the surmise had to be verified by events. This has taken many decades, but there are few serious astrologers today who dispute that Pluto rules Scorpio.

Until the discovery of Pluto, the rulership of Scorpio was attributed to Mars, which is still regarded as co-ruler. Over the centuries to come, the Mars influence over Scorpio will gradually give way to the Pluto influence for Scorpio. Scorpio is the Sign of death, and such other things as redemption, secrecy, elimination, repression, suspicion, legacies, inheritances, penetration, intensity, investigation, sewage disposal—and sex.

Other Signs and planets affect a person's love life, but Scorpio and Pluto relate to the sex act devoid of the desire for progeny, love or the finer emotions. It is the act of sex as the power to penetrate into the very origins of being, beyond conscious motive; the urge to concentrate the libidinal force into a point so intense that it sears through the obstruction of desire to reach release, self-forgetfulness and unity with one's source.

Pluto represents the power of money and sex, but not as universal currencies that confer some sort of preference or privilege when exchanged. In Pluto, money and sex represent the two root drives that every human being sooner or later must learn to control in himself, and in so doing convert force—the personal need of preference or privilege—into the wealth and power of individual self-sufficiency.

The time it takes for Pluto to transit a Sign varies widely. Pluto can spend over 25 years in a Sign or as little as 11 years. Pluto controls the mass movements of change in each generation. It is constructive and destructive. It is the principle that gave us the blessings of nuclear power and the horror of the atom bomb. It is soothing psychology, healing psychiatry, the bludgeoning of brainwashing and the debasement of propaganda. It is the benefits of mass communication through newspapers and broadcasting, and the mass hysteria generated by the same media. It is a contradiction: a transformer and an annihilator.

Wherever Pluto appears in your horoscope, you will find contradictions in yourself. You can be forceful and strong, but suffer from nerves. You can know intense dislike and consuming love. You may be acquisitive, and yet be indifferent to possessions once they are yours.

Pluto is the last of the three known "spiritual" planets. All its effects on the individual are designed to change the physical habits that have straitjacketed the psychological being. It upsets established patterns and order. It destroys suddenly, then teaches the individual to build again, not as things were before, but with the exhilarating and creative freedom to make a fresh start while remembering the mistakes of the past.

Pluto splits opinion, usually on issues that involve masses of people. It divides tidy, close-knit groups, setting one faction against the other, so that hard-won reform must itself yield to progressive thought and perhaps revolution. Pluto stands for automation. It makes human labor obsolete compared to machines so that man must create new thresholds of activity that machines cannot duplicate—for a while. Pluto represents endless repetition and reproduction. It is the spirit of mass production. It has set the marveldogs of modern science howling after man's necessity so that he must work ceaselessly at learning and developing new skills to stay out in front.

Pluto gives a person a dual view so that his or her personality ranges from one extreme to the other. When well aspected, the person is able to contain these opposites within himself and pour out the resultant energy in progressive, positive ways. Pluto provides a talent for medicine and science, particularly for theoretical work that grapples with the problems standing in the way of progress. Radical political action arises in Pluto. Pluto endows spiritual insight leading to popular new philosophies like those expounded by the Beatles and subsequent pop heroes, gradually idealizing the crass and hysterical emotions of each generation.

Badly aspected, Pluto makes a person a victim of his or her own extremes. Thus the individual can be an evil genius, a magnificent scoundrel, a cruel dictator, a vicious gangster—or suffer under these types.

Physiologically, Pluto is associated with the sex glands and their influence on the mind and will. It is the force of renewal through elimination, and this applies to the psychological as well as the physical. Pluto forces to the surface the unconscious blockages in the psyche; neurotic causes must be eliminated by being faced or lived through. If the planet is afflicted, this process may be difficult and lead to nervous and mental disorders. In extremes, violence, viciousness and self-destruction are likely.

Pluto in Gemini (1882–1914)

You are a person who always likes to speak your mind. You have firm views on many subjects and you are not constrained by other people's feelings from expressing them. You say what you think is true or needs to be said. You don't have much time for people with narrow and closed minds, nor do you like conversing with those who cling to obsolete ideas. Although you are of mature age and have many memories to reflect on, you do not stick to old-fashioned ideas for sentiment's sake. The values you prize today are those you consider have stood the test of time. You are unsure of some contemporary standards and are especially doubtful of the values espoused by current world political leaders.

You take an active interest in all that is going on around you. You enjoy reading the newspapers, watching the news on television and keeping abreast of the times. In your way, you have achieved recognition of your talents. Even if you have never been a public figure, you have made sufficient impact in your field to give you a fair amount of personal satisfaction.

You are an individual used to many changes in your personal life. Nothing shocks you much now; you are prepared for just about anything. You have followed several vocations, probably changed your career entirely at least once and maybe had a great variety of jobs. You have a good mind for figures and have probably managed to earn quite a lot of money in your time, even though you may not have held on to much of it.

You are a bit of an extremist and inclined to be self-contradictory at times. You suffer from sharp changes of mood and sometimes feel dejected or negative about life. You can be inspiringly positive and depressingly gloomy. But you soon swing back onto a progressive course. You can usually hold your own in any sort of debate and are pretty clever when it comes to covering up your mistakes or concealing your weaknesses. You sum up situations quickly and are an excellent judge of character. No one fools you for very long.

You have an inventive turn of mind. You are always looking for ways of improving on things. You never feel that the ultimate has been reached. It is second nature for you to believe in life after death. You know there is always something else to be discovered.

You have always shown a talent for handling or dealing with groups of people, for being able to sway and convince them with the force of your logic. You would make a capable teacher, textbook writer, designer, theoretician. You enjoy sweeping the board clean of old ideas and laying down new easy-reference criteria that help people to do and produce things quickly and efficiently.

You are highly sensitive and nervously alert. You have always enjoyed a psychic ability, which gives you an acute understanding of occult matters. You also have spiritual depths, which can help you to appreciate the reasons for any personal failure.

The Other Side of the Story

You may never have really made a success of anything. Your inability to concentrate on one activity and to control your sudden mood changes have probably left you little to show for your working life. If a woman, you are likely to have married several times and still not found what you are searching for. You may have a perverse sense of humor that gets satisfaction out of teasing and lampooning others. Or you may be cruelly critical, tormenting or a vicious scandalmonger. You may judge others by harsh standards that you fail dismally to live up to yourself. You may be a cheat, capable of defrauding your friends in games or business with the same detachment with which you would embezzle from a corporation.

Pluto in Cancer (1915–1938)

Your nature reflects a generation that threw off many of the traditional yokes, especially in relation to the home and family. You were not prepared to be a slave to outmoded ideas. You were the first of the modern moderns, particularly where the emancipation of women was concerned. For a start, your generation started the kitchen revolution. Out went the dark old drudgery equipment and in came the bright new stoves, refrigerators, washing machines, sinks and so many other time-saving gadgets that women were able to start functioning outside the home. They kicked up their skirts and raised their hemlines to unheard of levels. They discovered that there is comfort, style and femininity in simple, lightweight gear.

But you didn't discard all of the past. That is not your nature. In fact, you have found that the greatest satisfaction comes from improving on what went before. And this is what you aim to do in most departments of your life. You like to develop new standards based on what has already been proved by experience. You have endeavored to bring up your family along these lines. You probably would not have gone as far as today's permissive society. But you try to keep an open mind because you appreciate the necessity for trial and error.

You have profound inner feelings. You draw most of your strength and understanding from your emotions—reasoning and intellectual considerations seem to come second. You have a highly developed sense of knowing what is right for you without having to think about it a great deal. Your convictions seem to rise up from your subconscious mind. You enjoy spreading new ideas. You are determined to give others the benefit of your experience. You have a talent for getting the things you recommend accepted by the majority. Once an idea has your imprimatur, it seems to become acceptable and popular.

Your memory is phenomenal. You can recall the most obscure details about your personal life with amazing clarity. You can tell anecdotes galore. You have a keen interest in archeology; historical topics never bore you. You especially enjoy reading biographies of people who were responsible for significant social changes.

You are often able to tune in to what others are thinking or feeling. This gives you an uncanny ability to anticipate what people will do, especially in an emergency or crisis. You also have an affinity with the earth that often creates an interest in geological studies. Sometimes people born with Pluto in Cancer have a sixth-sense knowledge of where certain minerals can be found. This makes them particularly suited for mining careers.

As Pluto is often responsible for reversing situations, it is not uncommon for mothers or wives to go out to work and for husbands to take over some or all of the usual housekeeping duties.

Many of you have found careers in the entertainment world. You are also likely to be successful in advertising. Careers where there is intense competition are most likely to attract you. Television and radio can have special appeal. The manufacture of frozen and prepared foods, as well as packaging and the production of lines of products, are also areas in which people with this combination can shine.

The Other Side of the Story

You may cut yourself off from others and live a lonely, introverted and reclusive existence. Or, you may be insufferably domineering, especially toward relatives and friends. You are likely to be an ambitious egotist who never really achieves anything because you are so busy telling others what they should do or trying to deprecate their efforts. If a woman, you may neglect your children or family to further a career. You may be bored by the trivialities of home life and spend your time and money looking for diversions.

Pluto in Leo (1939—1957)

Everything you do or want to do is on a grand scale. You are artistic and creative. You want to give all and sundry the benefit of your talents. There are no half-measures about you. You possess tremendous energy and drive, which you apply to whatever you undertake. You would be an excellent actor, entertainer or creative artist: you are keen on making a public impression. You are also likely to be drawn to one of the sciences, where you may make some timely discoveries. Whatever line you are in, you will tend to attract public attention and generate an aura of glamour and showmanship.

You and your generation think you can do better—and you have, in many ways. Yours was the age that swept away a record number of the world's kings and started the syndrome of 30-day governments. You insisted that the old regime must go. But no one—including yourselves—seems quite sure of what to erect in its place. But you did get rid of many of the old heavy hands. This is your nature—to try to improve conditions, often by taking the opposite course.

Yours was the era that turned the spotlight on the young people of the world. Teenagers discovered their massive vocal strength; and what a noise they made! They also realized they had formidable economic power; from then on manufacturers who wanted their support had to do things their way. Television came and boomed. Everyone had more money. Entertainment was paramount. Sex lost a couple more of its seven veils.

You and your generation have been taking control of the world. In the new century, in every country and society, you will be challenged to improve politics, science, medicine, law and the arts. You can be counted on to make many changes. And you will have your chance to deal with the problems that were born with your own generation and that will, by then, have matured along with you. The elder statesmen and the custodians of the obsolescent will have to give way to sit on the sidelines and watch you battle with the dragon of your own times. You like an audience. Well, here's your chance.

You are a leader. You have never liked the idea of making the best of things. You want to make things better. You have new ideas for art, entertainment and the theater. You intend to overhaul education, and some of your proposals will be unconventional and highly contentious. But you will introduce them, nevertheless. Every Lion must have his day.

You are adventurous and the thought of taking

responsibility for the future doesn't daunt you. You prefer that affairs be in your hands rather than anyone else's. You know that at least you have the good of the majority at heart. You won't flinch in the face of difficulties or danger; you have a natural daring and a deep faith in your own mission in life. Your generation will do more with space than travel to the Moon. You will explore new places. This will include expeditions into the field of parapsychology. The world of unseen forces—clairvoyance, clairaudience and the etheric double—waits to be mapped, a challenge beyond the capabilities of yesterday's materialists.

The Other Side of the Story

You may be a racist who tries to spread his or her ideas with hatred and violence. Bloodshed, force and revolution may be your chosen methods of bringing about change. You are likely to be a troublemaker, a glory seeker who leaps on any popular bandwagon. Your only aim may be to build a reputation for yourself, good or bad. You are likely to be a dictator at heart who rules his or her family and subordinates with fear and threats of reprisals. You may be sexually promiscuous and perverse.

Pluto in Virgo (1957–1971)

Yours is the age that brought great changes in the practice of medicine and in the use of chemicals. Attempts were made to clean up the earth and improve on the chemistry of the human body. Virgo is the Sign that rules health; Pluto is the force of rejuvenation, death and rebirth, often through reversed procedures. So it was your era that pioneered the heart transplant and went on to develop even more refined techniques of spare-parts surgery. The use of drugs to induce mind-blowing experiences became widespread. The psychedelic age dawned and human beings, under the influence of hallucinogens, tried to take off like birds—from buildings.

The Pluto in Virgo mind is incisive and penetrating in the extreme. There is a natural talent for psychoanalysis. This influence can temporarily rid the mind of its inhibitions and conditioning in order to perceive the hidden emotions working in another. Pluto can throw off the Virgo tendency to worry, and so ease nervous tensions. With this planetary placement you are able to reason from new angles and get refreshing results.

Virgo also is concerned with food, and this was the age of awareness of contamination. For the first time, the public became conscious that the excessive use of insecticides, preservatives and hormones was slowly poisoning them, and that the industrial wastes being discharged into the water and atmosphere were killing us just as effectively. Ecology was a science receiving widespread attention. Pollution of the environment had to be stopped. Governments passed all sorts of laws in a feeble attempt to prevent the oceans, the rivers, the lakes and the air from accumulating more poisons.

When this generation sat in the seats of power at the end of the twentieth century and the beginning of the new millennium, there was a revival of fears and anxieties about more virulent forms of environmental poisons—chemical and biological agents of war. Here is the chance on behalf of humanity to find a solution that threatens not just the individual in a particular part of the world but the global village at large.

Virgo also stands for work and workers. Pluto's passage through the Sign saw the beginning of the end of exploitation: employees began to feel their power, flex their industrial muscles, demand, picket, strike. Servants disappeared. And the Third World nations forged their way onto the international scene, determined to secure recognition and equal opportunity, even if it took force and disruption.

The Other Side of the Story

You may use a keen mind to harass or tyrannize others and take advantage of their weaknesses. A teasing yet sarcastic and potentially vitriolic personality is about to explode. Nerves are continually on edge, and perverse ways can be chosen to ease the strain. You can be secretive and scheming. If there is no restraining influence in the rest of the horoscope, you can be capable of using the written or spoken word, innuendo or rumor to destroy another's reputation. In accord with Pluto's extreme nature, lawlessness in pernicious ways such as skyjacking, international kidnapping, parapolitical violence and murder, campus revolutions, police brutality, drug dealing, built-in obsolescence all made a bewildered world wonder what comes next.

Pluto in Libra (1971–1983)

Pluto in Libra individuals are ardent and enthusiastic about close relationships. You may marry very young or suddenly. Your thoughts range from the lustily erotic to the spiritually profound. You may have many lovers, then suddenly become celibate. Love life may be marked by violent changes that, oddly, produce favorable results in the end.

Partnership matters seldom run as planned. Disclosures and exposures may force new starts. You become attached to people and situations, then often have to give them up. Once you make a change, something inside you prevents you from going back. You can be somewhat of a fatalist.

You appreciate art in all its forms, especially when it has practical application. You will try to put creative plans into the most pleasing combination. Individuals from this generation are likely to be drawn into careers of architecture, sculpture, engraving or engineering concerned with balance and shapes. With a fine head for business, you can earn money better than you can hold on to it.

This generation was born at a time when the world's haves and have-nots confronted each other in surprisingly reversed situations—a typical Pluto effect. Pluto is the planet of beginnings and endings. Two globally significant and eruptive examples of its influence, as the planet became established in Libra, were the beginning of the oil embargo and the ending of the Vietnam War during the years 1973 and 1974.

Libra is the Sign of balance; its symbol is the Scales; it stands for justice through equality. It is the Sign of peace, but also the Sign of war and aggression, which are often thought necessary to correct injustice and restore a workable harmony.

Pluto is the planet of violent extremes marking the end of one phase and the beginning of another. It rules the underworld, the depths of the earth, the source of gold (finance) and oil. Through Libra, without taking sides, Pluto naturally strives to correct the balance by using the wealth tokens under its control.

The generation of children born with Pluto in Libra embody the characteristic urge to restore equality wherever they may find it lacking. This will have a profound impact at the national and international levels when their generation assumes positions of power and influence in the world beginning as early as the first decade of the twenty-first century.

This generation will face tremendous problems to preserve peace, protect international law and promote harmony. Pluto in Libra individuals must possess the consciousness to deal effectively with the consequences of crises that developed in their generation.

The Other Side of the Story

Shattering reversals are not uncommon in love affairs. Associations can end unpleasantly. Try as you may, you rarely succeed in putting the pieces back together. Attachments invariably result in wrenching unhappiness, or you have a habit of mistaking infat-

uation for love and then being disenchanted. Once entrenched, your desires are obsessive. Money may mean more to you than people. Sex can be a major problem. Divisive and unhappy experiences are repeated until the lessons are learned.

Pluto in Scorpio (1983—1995)

Pluto, the planet of transformation, is in its rightful home in the Sign of Scorpio, which it rules. Pluto in Scorpio is the powerhouse placement of the Zodiac. Uncompromising Pluto, seeker of truth, challenges all that is false and cowardly. Enduring Scorpio confers a lasting love for investigation. Here together in this 12-year span is the key to unlock riddles, expose cover-ups, unearth hidden treasures, penetrate walls of silence.

Individuals born with Pluto in Scorpio will be able to plumb the mysteries of life, to leap high in understanding and tolerance. Emotional and spiritual values will underscore material considerations, ushering in widespread experimentation and change in all forms of human endeavor. A wish to rejuvenate, to recharge merely pleasing forms into powerful statements of conscience will mark this generation of men and women.

This planetary placement might cause disintegrating upheavals that nevertheless turn out for the best in the end. Painful endings forced by circumstance can miraculously become bright new beginnings. Pluto in Scorpio bestows a protective influence on health and well-being, operating to remove confusion and stress. Individuals born into this generation will have splendid recuperative powers and can bounce back into action, with tremendous energy, after a setback.

Pluto in Scorpio men and women will enjoy power, stepping in to take command in nearly hopeless situations. Combative and unsentimental, this generation will not dwell on the past. Power and power alone may be the driver toward the future, as the struggle for ultimate victory is waged against any odds and at any price. With Pluto, the planet of extremes and brand-new beginnings after sudden endings, the results cannot be foreseen—yet the truths behind all struggle will be laid bare.

Scorpio is a magnetic, creative Sign. It stands for people's ability, through courageous self-discipline, to gain power over themselves. It is the Sign of the loftiest aspirations, as well as the lowest. Here alone can the soul soar through self-mastery to fantastic levels of consciousness, which may bring humanity to the start of the long-awaited Golden Age.

Pluto has the right transforming energy for this

process. It is the planet of regeneration. Its extremes include death and rebirth. It also represents money and all the untapped resources lying deep in the earth, perhaps even a new source of energy from the Earth's molten core.

With maturity of consciousness, Pluto in Scorpio can provide humanity with all the material means to bring about undreamed of social and economic reforms on a global scale. Then, perhaps, peace and goodwill on Earth may be more than a beautiful concept.

Young women and men born with Pluto in Scorpio have the potential to reach such heights of consciousness. They will begin taking their places in the seats of power around the year 2020. Their generation will be equipped in one way or another to deal with the aftermath of the crises born into the world with them.

The Other Side of the Story

Explosive change may force you to face new conditions. As soon as you throw yourself into a challenge, it mysteriously takes an abrupt or violent new turn. Although you endeavor to cling to situations, you are compelled to let go. You possess a strong, aggressive yet self-tormenting drive that impels you to speak cruelly and vindictively, then deeply regret it. Happiness and fulfillment always seem to beckon on the other side of a fight. Your combative nature may continually get the better of you no matter how often you resolve to cool it.

Pluto in Sagittarius (1995–2008)

Pluto in Sagittarius marks a new journey of exploration and learning. As the cycle of Pluto in Scorpio came to an end, the pieces of a puzzling past fit into place. The generation of men and women born with Pluto in Sagittarius will experience an awakening on intellectual and artistic levels.

Pluto has the transforming power to change an individual's identity, lifestyle, modes of self-expression—the whole persona. Uncovering the real you will be the work of Pluto, leading to the kind of understanding and meaningful communication that can bond diverse communities. Pluto in Sagittarius can be the guiding light illuminating the first decade of the twenty-first century. With this planetary placement good luck is riding on the waves of change.

Sagittarius, the Sign of travel and exploration, of study and play, of sports and gambling, likes to be free to roam wherever heart or mind leads without being bound by duty or conscience. Pluto in Sagit-tarius increases a person's optimism, giving renewed hope and vigor. The horizon seems to expand endlessly, promising abundant good fortune. Never leap before you look, it is said. Foresight will be vital with this position of Pluto.

The buoyant influence of Sagittarius will run free in social and professional life. It will seem possible to create a new design for living. In business there will always be a chance to go for the brass ring. Gain through study and knowledge will be the preferred route. Yet as the stakes mount, the temptation to gamble will grow. Speculation can become wild, rampant. Undaunted idealism and irrational exuberance can lead to recklessness. Blind faith in speculation can be ruinous. Pluto's imperative here will be to assess the risks versus the rewards.

Men and women born with Pluto in Sagittarius may suddenly become famous or prominent. Rapid progress will be based on discarding old methods, on breaking contacts with the past. These men and women will be resourceful, never really stuck for a way in or a way out. As competent business executives, capable of controlling international and multinational corporations, they will expand the Internet and all broadband communications networks.

This generation will have deep insights into character and will evoke courage and enthusiasm from people in the face of danger and adversity. Broadminded and tolerant, Pluto in Sagittarius individuals will be concerned about the root problems of the world, and they will be prepared to act concretely on their beliefs. Helping others who help themselves will be a truly altruistic motive that can attain the noble end sought.

The Other Side of the Story

You can be a rabble-rousing revolutionary who destroys your chances through impatience. A desire for violent change may be more important than any transforming principles involved. Yet the so-called freedoms gained from violent action can be more binding than the old order that was swept away. Out of a compulsion to escape duty, obligation, restrictions of any kind, you may wander a solitary, fruitless life. Greed and ambition, a lust for power, can be the driving force. Or, in the name of a cause or ideal, there can be marked cruelty toward others. Yet you may suffer through your own extreme actions, always in danger of damaging your health by working or playing too hard. Compulsive gambling may keep you in debt, evading creditors and wasting your family's resources. Difficulty through long journeys and distant places or contacts is foreseen. Broken contracts and deception may add to your troubles.

Pluto in Capricorn (2008—2024)

Pluto enters the earthy Sign of Capricorn in 2008 for a 15-year stay. Pluto in Capricorn demands reason, responsibility, discipline, diligence, depth—on the positive side. On the negative side will be obstacles, delay, pessimism, selfishness, greed, ruthlessness. The transforming energy of Pluto and the persevering power of Capricorn will teach lessons in adversity, and the lessons will be learned.

Pluto in Capricorn will bring focus and cohesion to the disparate and diverse creative and inventive forms flowing in communities around the world. Pluto in Capricorn is fruitful, with the potential to change the landscape and the humanscape permanently—or at least until new cycles take root and grow.

Privacy and safety will be concerns for the business and work environments, especially in global communications networking. Standards and ethics will be questioned. A narrow mentality may confront radical modes of expression. Pluto in Capricorn investigative skills will give depth to the attack. Inventive, efficient, systematic, resourceful, individuals born with this combination must not let limitations to thinking halt an ability to face and to solve divisive issues.

You will be prepared to cut old ties and begin anew. As avenging politician or law enforcement officer, you will be bent on uprooting corruption from high places. You will delight in rebuilding after the old has been discarded. You must free yourself from rigid notions and situations in order to make your new edifice strong, steady and enduring.

You will be indomitable, combining transformative energy with dogged persistence. There is little you cannot accomplish—in time. Defeat will not deter you. You will strive and strive again, rising to a position of prominence and esteem. You will cope with emotional stress and strain by releasing it through work.

Pluto in Capricorn men and women will become excellent top executives, money managers, research scientists, engineering wizards capable of great achievement. Your problem-solving ability and flair for organization will be in demand. If you are not chosen as the head, you will break away and set up in opposition—alone. You will not mind a solitary life if you are brewing and building for the future.

As a leader you will have exceptional ability for maintaining control of a project, even an empire. Yet two inimical qualities within yourself—freedom and limitation—are in conflict, pulling and tugging at your conscience. Harmony and closure can be achieved, but at what expense, at what price?

Young people born with Pluto in Capricorn can expect a hard time from parents and other adult authority figures. Lack of affection and sympathy on both sides will mark a real generation gap. Trouble may manifest in manipulation, ego struggles and power plays. A seat of power, the very place you want to reach, is an uneasy seat, the people there distrusted and often despised. This generation's dilemma will be that what they want they do not like.

The Other Side of the Story

You can be lawless and vengeful, grindingly patient in exacting what you believe is yours. You may stop at nothing to impose your ideas. Callous and ruthless, you may use people with no regard for their feelings and welfare. Battling for territory, you resent opposition and will be cruel in meting out punishment to rivals and pretenders. Cynical, selfish, stern, harsh, you will not engender love. Partnerships suffer from your cold silent treatment or your overbearing power and sex drive. You want to throw off all limitations but are held back by peer pressure, fear of ridicule and scorn. Self-destructive tendencies may result in injury from blows, collisions, falls, or in long and incurable illness.

CHAPTER TWENTY-FOUR

Your Planets and What They Signify

If you read the chapters on Scorpio, no doubt you recognized your basic self in those descriptions. There were probably areas where your personality and character did not conform. Naturally! Although you are a Scorpio, you are also an individual. You share many common traits with your Scorpio kin. But in behavior and lifestyle there are distinct, special, unique traits that make you what you are.

How does Astrology and AstroAnalysis account for all this? By "reading" the positions of planets other than the Sun on the day of your birth. The Sun is only one influence, though by far the most important one. There is your Ascendant, the Rising Sign, which is the second most significant part of your horoscope. And there are nine other planets whose positions in the horoscope affect and modify the basic Sun Sign personality.

As a Scorpio, you may wonder where your ruling planet Pluto was at the time of your birth. Where was your co-ruler Mars and where was Venus, planets that impact sexual energy and affectionate desire? And where were the Moon and Mercury, planets that can bridge the gap between sentiment and logic—or create a conflict there?

And what about Jupiter and Saturn, the largest of the planets, on the day you were born? Suppose Jupiter or Saturn or both planets together were in Taurus, the Sign exactly opposite your Scorpio Sun Sign? What effects would these planets in your opposite Sign have on your conscious and subconscious mind?

The colored planet tables in this section contain all the information you need to find where the planets were when you were born. You can enter that information in your astro profile record on the next page. Then you can construct your own horoscope chart quickly. In fact, you can construct a horoscope chart for anyone whose Sun Sign is Scorpio.

First, use the Blue Ascendant Tables provided on pages 216–218. Find your Rising Sign, then enter it in your astro profile record, using either the name of the Sign or the symbol for the Sign.

Next, use the Pink Planet Tables (pages 219–271). Here the positions of the other nine planets in the Signs are given for the years 1910–2015. Select your birth year and birth date. There you can see exactly where each planet was when you were born. Enter each planet's position (Sign placement) in your astro profile record.

See the world time zone map and suggestions for using the tables (pages 212–215) if there is uncertainty about when the Moon entered a Sign for a specific time zone, or geographical location. Also, you may have to adjust for daylight saving time if that applies to your date of birth.

After you have completed your astro profile record, you will be able to construct your own horoscope chart in a way professional astrologers do. The flat horoscope chart, or natural wheel, that astrologers use is pictured for your use on page 211.

Even if you do not want to create a horoscope chart, you can use your astro profile as a guide to your overall personality. Refer again to the descriptions of the planets in the various zodiacal signs. Read yours!

As you progress, you will be amazed at how many facets of your own personality reveal themselves to you. You may discover hidden strengths and weaknesses—you may have suspected their existence before but never quite put them into words. You will be astounded as your AstroAnalysis helps you on your voyage of self-discovery and, as the mystery unfolds, you'll be startled to see just how Astrology is zeroing in on your character.

CHAPTER TWENTY-FIVE

Your Astro Profile and Horoscope Chart

The Blue and Pink Tables in this section show the positions of the planets for your birth date. Use the Blue Tables to find your Ascendant, your Rising Sign. Use the Pink Tables to find the Sign occupied by each of the other planets.

Then fill in your astro profile. Your astro profile can serve as a permanent record and also as the basis for establishing your own horoscope chart on the next page. Astro symbols for the zodiacal signs and the planets are shown below.

At the Time of My Birth . . .

My Ascendant, the Rising Sign, is: _____

My Sun is in the Sign of: _____

My Moon is in the Sign of: _____

My Mercury is in the Sign of: _____

My Venus is in the Sign of: _____

My Mars is in the Sign of: _____

My Jupiter is in the Sign of: _____

My Saturn is in the Sign of : _____

My Uranus is in the Sign of: _____

My Neptune is in the Sign of: _____

My Pluto is in the Sign of: _____

SIGNS & SYMBOLS			
Aries	♈	Libra	♎
Taurus	♉	Scorpio	♏
Gemini	♊	Sagittarius	♐
Cancer	♋	Capricorn	♑
Leo	♌	Aquarius	♒
Virgo	♍	Pisces	♓

PLANETS & SYMBOLS			
Sun	☉	Jupiter	♃
Moon	☽	Saturn	♄
Mercury	☿	Uranus	♅
Venus	♀	Neptune	♆
Mars	♂	Pluto	♇

Construct Your Own Horoscope Chart

Now you are ready to construct your own horoscope chart. The illustration below shows the flat chart, or natural wheel, that a professional astrologer uses. The inner circle of the wheel is labeled 1 through 12. These 12 divisions are known as the Houses of the Zodiac, and they were discussed in Chapter 1 of AstroAnalysis.

The 1st House always starts from the position on the left (the "9 o'clock" position), which corresponds to the eastern horizon. The remaining Houses 2 through 12 follow around in a "counterclockwise" direction, as the illustration shows. The point where each House starts is known as a cusp, or edge.

The cusp, or edge, of the 1st House is where you will place your Ascendant, your Rising Sign. You can write the Sign name or use the astro symbol for the Sign, as shown on the opposite page.

Once your Ascendant has been placed on the cusp of the 1st House, you are ready to label the remaining Houses—from 2 through 12—with the Signs that follow in natural zodiacal order. For your quick ref- erence the Signs in natural zodiacal order are listed on the opposite page.

Here is an example. Suppose your Ascendant is Virgo. You would label the cusp of the 1st House Virgo. Then you would label House 2 Libra, House 3 Scorpio, and so on until you come to House 12, which would be Leo.

Now suppose that your Sun is also in Virgo. Put the Sun in the 1st House. But suppose your Sun is in Pisces. Then put the Sun in the 7th House because Pisces is on the cusp of the 7th House.

Do the rest of the planets—Moon through Pluto—in a similar manner. Now you have constructed a horoscope chart for your birth date.

If you want to construct a chart for a friend, draw the astro wheel as the illustration suggests, create an astro profile using the relevant *AstroAnalysis* book for the person's Sun Sign, and fill in the wheel following the steps above.

Have fun and inspiration constructing astro profiles and horoscope charts for significant others.

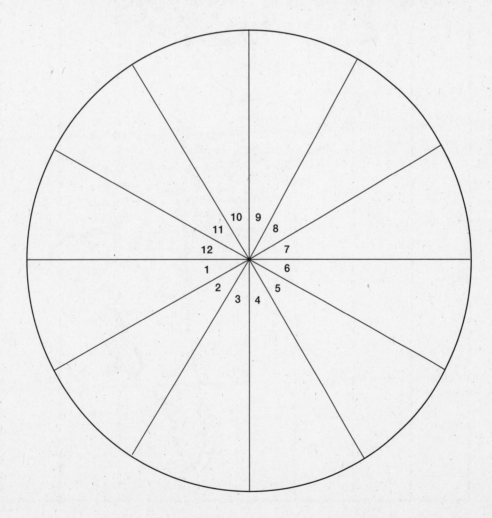

World Time

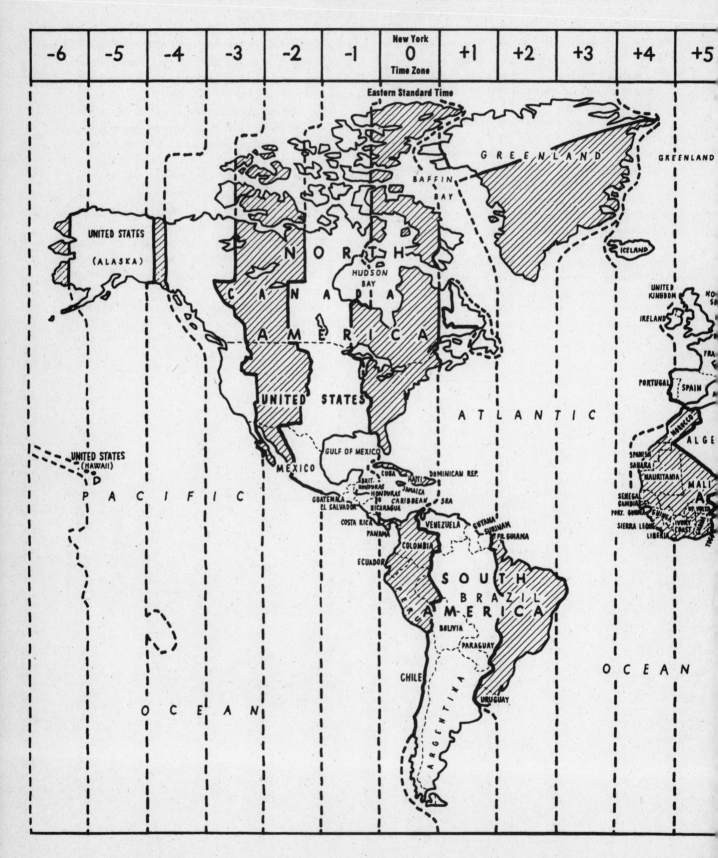

-6	-5	-4	-3	-2	-1	New York 0 Time Zone	+1	+2	+3	+4	+5

Zone Map

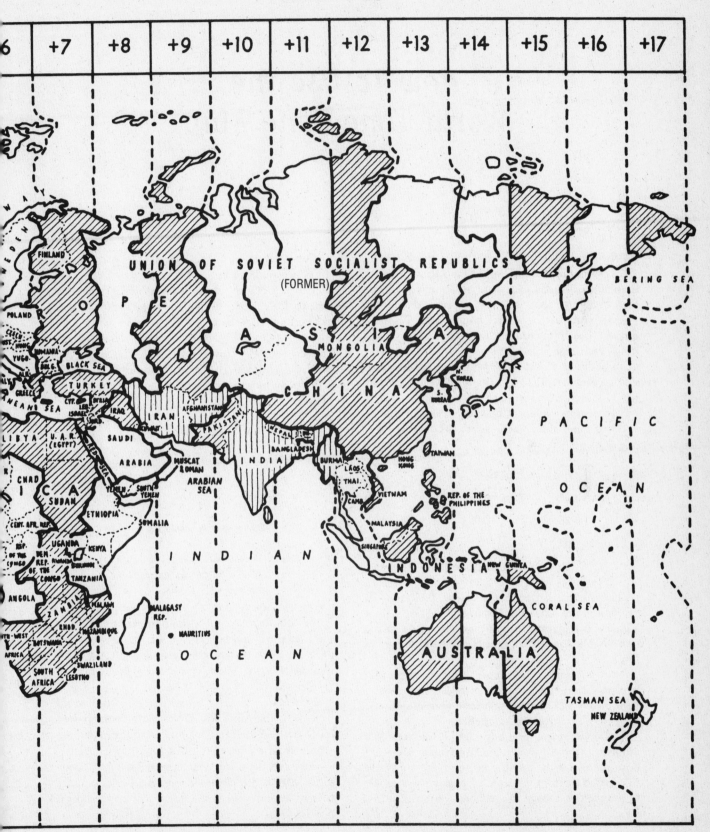

For explanation of Time Zone Map, see next page.

How To Use the
World Time Zone Map

The actual time of your birth is important when considering the position of the Moon. You see in the Pink Planet Tables that the Moon moves from Sign to Sign in about two and a quarter days, often several hours less or several hours more. Within a month, the Moon changes Sign 13 or 14 times, "visiting" each Sign at least once.

In addition to showing what Sign the Moon is visiting each day, the Pink Tables tell you what time the Moon enters a new Sign.

Moon times in the tables are based on eastern standard time, often called New York time.

For example:

	MOON
March 22	7:56 PM Virgo
23	
24	
25	6:45 AM Libra

This means that at 7:56 in New York, on the evening of the 22nd, the Moon entered the Sign of Virgo and remained in that Sign until 6:45 in the morning of March 25th, when it entered the Sign of Libra.

You will notice that the map on the preceding two pages is divided into zones. Locate the place of your birth on the map. If you were born in the zone marked 0, no calculation is needed.

However, if you were born outside this zone, the number at the top of the zone in which you were born represents the number of hours you must add to or subtract from the time of your birth in order to use the times given in the tables (eastern standard time).

For example:

You were born in San Francisco on March 25 at 6:30 AM. Since the time in the tables is applicable only to those people born in the zone marked 0, look at the number at the top of the zone in which California is found. The number is −3. Therefore, to convert to New York 0 time, going eastward, you must add 3 hours to the time of your birth. The result is 9:30 AM, indicating that the Moon was in Libra at the time of your birth.

	MOON
March 22	7:56 PM Virgo
23	
24	
25	6:45 AM Libra
26	
27	7:06 PM Scorpio

On the other hand, if you were born on March 25 in London at 9:30 AM, the number at the top of the zone is +5. Subtracting 5 hours, going westward to New York 0 time, the result is 4:30 AM. This indicates that the Moon was in Virgo at the time of your birth.

In certain years and certain places of the world daylight saving time was in effect. If your hour of birth was recorded in daylight saving time, subtract 1 hour from it and consult that hour in the tables.

For example, if you were born at 7 AM DST, consult 6 AM in the tables—even before you convert Moon time to your time zone if that conversion is necessary.

How To Use the Tables

When you use the tables, you will be drawing on the skills of a group of experienced international astrologers. It took over two years to reduce the complex calculations of all the planets' movements to an easy-to-read, easy-to-follow format. It uses only words—no symbols—and numerals for the day and time you were born.

Blue Ascendant Tables

In the Blue Ascendant Tables (pages 216–218) your Rising Sign, the Ascendant, is clearly worked out for every day of the Scorpio Sun Sign period during October and November.

Time of birth is a factor in finding your Rising Sign, at least within two hours. In the tables, under the day of the month you were born, refer to the hour of your birth to see which Sign was rising (ascending) at that time. Standard time is used, so remember to adjust for daylight saving time if it applies to you.

If you don't know your birth time, try to contact someone who might help, as the Rising Sign is the starting point of the horoscope. If that fails, try to guess guided by the descriptions of Rising Sign types in Chapter 13. Choose the one most like you. You will discover what well may be an explanation of the hidden or unsuspected in your makeup.

Year of birth is not a factor in finding your Rising Sign. It is determined only by the time of birth. You can see from the tables that the Rising Sign changes within every two hours or so.

Place of birth is not a factor either, except for the southern hemisphere. See the conversion below.

Ascendant Conversion for the Southern Hemisphere

Here is a simple way to find your Rising Sign if you live south of the equator. Just add twelve hours to your birth time, then look in the Blue Tables for that time. When you locate the appropriate Sign, refer to the list below to determine your Rising Sign south of the equator.

SIGN FROM TABLES	YOUR RISING SIGN
Aries	Libra
Taurus	Scorpio
Gemini	Sagittarius
Cancer	Capricorn
Leo	Aquarius
Virgo	Pisces
Libra	Aries
Scorpio	Taurus
Sagittarius	Gemini
Capricorn	Cancer
Aquarius	Leo
Pisces	Virgo

Pink Planet Tables

From the Pink Planet Tables (pages 219–271) select your birth year and birth date. Under your birth date use a ruler or pointer, or draw a pencil line across the page. Now you can see exactly where the nine planets were when you were born.

Starting with the Moon on the left, read which Sign the Moon was in. For Moon time in your geographical area, see the world time zone map and how to use it (opposite page). Remember to adjust for daylight saving time if it applied to you.

Then, proceeding from left to right, read which Sign Mercury was in on your birth date. Do the same across the page for all the other planets—Venus, Mars, Jupiter, Saturn, Uranus, Neptune, Pluto.

It will be fun to create your astro profile and to construct your horoscope chart once you have found where your planets are. Get set to AstroAnalyze yourself and embark on a voyage of discovery.

SCORPIO
YOUR ASCENDANT

	OCTOBER 22-23	OCTOBER 24-25	OCTOBER 26	OCTOBER 27	OCTOBER 28
MIDNIGHT	LEO	LEO	LEO	LEO	LEO
1 AM	LEO	LEO	LEO	LEO	LEO
2 AM	VIRGO	VIRGO	VIRGO	VIRGO	VIRGO
3 AM	VIRGO	VIRGO	VIRGO	VIRGO	VIRGO
4 AM	LIBRA	LIBRA	LIBRA	LIBRA	LIBRA
5 AM	LIBRA	LIBRA	LIBRA	LIBRA	LIBRA
6 AM	LIBRA	LIBRA	LIBRA	LIBRA	LIBRA
7 AM	SCORPIO	SCORPIO	SCORPIO	SCORPIO	SCORPIO
8 AM	SCORPIO	SCORPIO	SCORPIO	SCORPIO	SCORPIO
9 AM	SAGITTARIUS	SAGITTARIUS	SAGITTARIUS	SAGITTARIUS	SAGITTARIUS
10 AM	SAGITTARIUS	SAGITTARIUS	SAGITTARIUS	SAGITTARIUS	SAGITTARIUS
11 AM	SAGITTARIUS	SAGITTARIUS	SAGITTARIUS	CAPRICORN	CAPRICORN
NOON	CAPRICORN	CAPRICORN	CAPRICORN	CAPRICORN	CAPRICORN
1 PM	CAPRICORN	CAPRICORN	AQUARIUS	AQUARIUS	AQUARIUS
2 PM	AQUARIUS	AQUARIUS	AQUARIUS	AQUARIUS	AQUARIUS
3 PM	PISCES	PISCES	PISCES	PISCES	PISCES
4 PM	ARIES	ARIES	ARIES	ARIES	ARIES
5 PM	ARIES	ARIES	TAURUS	TAURUS	TAURUS
6 PM	TAURUS	TAURUS	TAURUS	TAURUS	TAURUS
7 PM	GEMINI	GEMINI	GEMINI	GEMINI	GEMINI
8 PM	GEMINI	GEMINI	GEMINI	GEMINI	GEMINI
9 PM	CANCER	CANCER	CANCER	CANCER	CANCER
10 PM	CANCER	CANCER	CANCER	CANCER	CANCER
11 PM	LEO	LEO	LEO	LEO	LEO

	OCTOBER 29	OCTOBER 30	OCTOBER 31	NOVEMBER 1	NOVEMBER 2
MIDNIGHT	LEO	LEO	LEO	LEO	LEO
1 AM	LEO	VIRGO	VIRGO	VIRGO	VIRGO
2 AM	VIRGO	VIRGO	VIRGO	VIRGO	VIRGO
3 AM	VIRGO	VIRGO	VIRGO	VIRGO	VIRGO
4 AM	LIBRA	LIBRA	LIBRA	LIBRA	LIBRA
5 AM	LIBRA	LIBRA	LIBRA	LIBRA	LIBRA
6 AM	LIBRA	SCORPIO	SCORPIO	SCORPIO	SCORPIO
7 AM	SCORPIO	SCORPIO	SCORPIO	SCORPIO	SCORPIO
8 AM	SCORPIO	SCORPIO	SCORPIO	SCORPIO	SCORPIO
9 AM	SAGITTARIUS	SAGITTARIUS	SAGITTARIUS	SAGITTARIUS	SAGITTARIUS
10 AM	SAGITTARIUS	SAGITTARIUS	SAGITTARIUS	SAGITTARIUS	SAGITTARIUS
11 AM	CAPRICORN	CAPRICORN	CAPRICORN	CAPRICORN	CAPRICORN
NOON	CAPRICORN	CAPRICORN	CAPRICORN	CAPRICORN	CAPRICORN
1 PM	AQUARIUS	AQUARIUS	AQUARIUS	AQUARIUS	AQUARIUS
2 PM	AQUARIUS	AQUARIUS	AQUARIUS	AQUARIUS	PISCES
3 PM	PISCES	PISCES	PISCES	PISCES	PISCES
4 PM	ARIES	ARIES	ARIES	ARIES	ARIES
5 PM	TAURUS	TAURUS	TAURUS	TAURUS	TAURUS
6 PM	TAURUS	TAURUS	TAURUS	TAURUS	GEMINI
7 PM	GEMINI	GEMINI	GEMINI	GEMINI	GEMINI
8 PM	GEMINI	GEMINI	GEMINI	CANCER	CANCER
9 PM	CANCER	CANCER	CANCER	CANCER	CANCER
10 PM	CANCER	CANCER	CANCER	CANCER	CANCER
11 PM	LEO	LEO	LEO	LEO	LEO

SCORPIO
YOUR ASCENDANT

	NOVEMBER 3	NOVEMBER 4	NOVEMBER 5	NOVEMBER 6	NOVEMBER 7
MIDNIGHT	LEO	LEO	LEO	LEO	LEO
1 AM	VIRGO	VIRGO	VIRGO	VIRGO	VIRGO
2 AM	VIRGO	VIRGO	VIRGO	VIRGO	VIRGO
3 AM	VIRGO	VIRGO	LIBRA	LIBRA	LIBRA
4 AM	LIBRA	LIBRA	LIBRA	LIBRA	LIBRA
5 AM	LIBRA	LIBRA	LIBRA	LIBRA	LIBRA
6 AM	SCORPIO	SCORPIO	SCORPIO	SCORPIO	SCORPIO
7 AM	SCORPIO	SCORPIO	SCORPIO	SCORPIO	SCORPIO
8 AM	SCORPIO	SCORPIO	SCORPIO	SAGITTARIUS	SAGITTARIUS
9 AM	SAGITTARIUS	SAGITTARIUS	SAGITTARIUS	SAGITTARIUS	SAGITTARIUS
10 AM	SAGITTARIUS	SAGITTARIUS	SAGITTARIUS	SAGITTARIUS	SAGITTARIUS
11 AM	CAPRICORN	CAPRICORN	CAPRICORN	CAPRICORN	CAPRICORN
NOON	CAPRICORN	CAPRICORN	CAPRICORN	CAPRICORN	CAPRICORN
1 PM	AQUARIUS	AQUARIUS	AQUARIUS	AQUARIUS	AQUARIUS
2 PM	PISCES	PISCES	PISCES	PISCES	PISCES
3 PM	PISCES	PISCES	ARIES	ARIES	ARIES
4 PM	ARIES	ARIES	ARIES	ARIES	ARIES
5 PM	TAURUS	TAURUS	TAURUS	TAURUS	TAURUS
6 PM	GEMINI	GEMINI	GEMINI	GEMINI	GEMINI
7 PM	GEMINI	GEMINI	GEMINI	GEMINI	GEMINI
8 PM	CANCER	CANCER	CANCER	CANCER	CANCER
9 PM	CANCER	CANCER	CANCER	CANCER	CANCER
10 PM	CANCER	CANCER	CANCER	CANCER	LEO
11 PM	LEO	LEO	LEO	LEO	LEO

	NOVEMBER 8	NOVEMBER 9	NOVEMBER 10	NOVEMBER 11	NOVEMBER 12
MIDNIGHT	LEO	LEO	LEO	LEO	LEO
1 AM	VIRGO	VIRGO	VIRGO	VIRGO	VIRGO
2 AM	VIRGO	VIRGO	VIRGO	VIRGO	VIRGO
3 AM	LIBRA	LIBRA	LIBRA	LIBRA	LIBRA
4 AM	LIBRA	LIBRA	LIBRA	LIBRA	LIBRA
5 AM	LIBRA	LIBRA	LIBRA	LIBRA	LIBRA
6 AM	SCORPIO	SCORPIO	SCORPIO	SCORPIO	SCORPIO
7 AM	SCORPIO	SCORPIO	SCORPIO	SCORPIO	SCORPIO
8 AM	SAGITTARIUS	SAGITTARIUS	SAGITTARIUS	SAGITTARIUS	SAGITTARIUS
9 AM	SAGITTARIUS	SAGITTARIUS	SAGITTARIUS	SAGITTARIUS	SAGITTARIUS
10 AM	SAGITTARIUS	SAGITTARIUS	SAGITTARIUS	CAPRICORN	CAPRICORN
11 AM	CAPRICORN	CAPRICORN	CAPRICORN	CAPRICORN	CAPRICORN
NOON	CAPRICORN	CAPRICORN	AQUARIUS	AQUARIUS	AQUARIUS
1 PM	AQUARIUS	AQUARIUS	AQUARIUS	AQUARIUS	AQUARIUS
2 PM	PISCES	PISCES	PISCES	PISCES	PISCES
3 PM	ARIES	ARIES	ARIES	ARIES	ARIES
4 PM	ARIES	ARIES	ARIES	TAURUS	TAURUS
5 PM	TAURUS	TAURUS	TAURUS	TAURUS	TAURUS
6 PM	GEMINI	GEMINI	GEMINI	GEMINI	GEMINI
7 PM	GEMINI	GEMINI	GEMINI	GEMINI	GEMINI
8 PM	CANCER	CANCER	CANCER	CANCER	CANCER
9 PM	CANCER	CANCER	CANCER	CANCER	CANCER
10 PM	LEO	LEO	LEO	LEO	LEO
11 PM	LEO	LEO	LEO	LEO	LEO

SCORPIO
YOUR ASCENDANT

	NOVEMBER 13	NOVEMBER 14	NOVEMBER 15	NOVEMBER 16	NOVEMBER 17
MIDNIGHT	LEO	LEO	VIRGO	VIRGO	VIRGO
1 AM	VIRGO	VIRGO	VIRGO	VIRGO	VIRGO
2 AM	VIRGO	VIRGO	VIRGO	VIRGO	VIRGO
3 AM	LIBRA	LIBRA	LIBRA	LIBRA	LIBRA
4 AM	LIBRA	LIBRA	LIBRA	LIBRA	LIBRA
5 AM	LIBRA	SCORPIO	SCORPIO	SCORPIO	SCORPIO
6 AM	SCORPIO	SCORPIO	SCORPIO	SCORPIO	SCORPIO
7 AM	SCORPIO	SCORPIO	SCORPIO	SCORPIO	SCORPIO
8 AM	SAGITTARIUS	SAGITTARIUS	SAGITTARIUS	SAGITTARIUS	SAGITTARIUS
9 AM	SAGITTARIUS	SAGITTARIUS	SAGITTARIUS	SAGITTARIUS	SAGITTARIUS
10 AM	CAPRICORN	CAPRICORN	CAPRICORN	CAPRICORN	CAPRICORN
11 AM	CAPRICORN	CAPRICORN	CAPRICORN	CAPRICORN	CAPRICORN
NOON	AQUARIUS	AQUARIUS	AQUARIUS	AQUARIUS	AQUARIUS
1 PM	AQUARIUS	AQUARIUS	AQUARIUS	AQUARIUS	PISCES
2 PM	PISCES	PISCES	PISCES	PISCES	PISCES
3 PM	ARIES	ARIES	ARIES	ARIES	ARIES
4 PM	TAURUS	TAURUS	TAURUS	TAURUS	TAURUS
5 PM	TAURUS	TAURUS	TAURUS	TAURUS	GEMINI
6 PM	GEMINI	GEMINI	GEMINI	GEMINI	GEMINI
7 PM	GEMINI	GEMINI	GEMINI	CANCER	CANCER
8 PM	CANCER	CANCER	CANCER	CANCER	CANCER
9 PM	CANCER	CANCER	CANCER	CANCER	CANCER
10 PM	LEO	LEO	LEO	LEO	LEO
11 PM	LEO	LEO	LEO	LEO	LEO

	NOVEMBER 18	NOVEMBER 19	NOVEMBER 20	NOVEMBER 21	NOVEMBER 22	NOVEMBER 23
MIDNIGHT	VIRGO	VIRGO	VIRGO	VIRGO	VIRGO	VIRGO
1 AM	VIRGO	VIRGO	VIRGO	VIRGO	VIRGO	VIRGO
2 AM	VIRGO	VIRGO	VIRGO	LIBRA	LIBRA	LIBRA
3 AM	LIBRA	LIBRA	LIBRA	LIBRA	LIBRA	LIBRA
4 AM	LIBRA	LIBRA	LIBRA	LIBRA	LIBRA	LIBRA
5 AM	SCORPIO	SCORPIO	SCORPIO	SCORPIO	SCORPIO	SCORPIO
6 AM	SCORPIO	SCORPIO	SCORPIO	SCORPIO	SCORPIO	SCORPIO
7 AM	SCORPIO	SCORPIO	SCORPIO	SAGITTARIUS	SAGITTARIUS	SAGITTARIUS
8 AM	SAGITTARIUS	SAGITTARIUS	SAGITTARIUS	SAGITTARIUS	SAGITTARIUS	SAGITTARIUS
9 AM	SAGITTARIUS	SAGITTARIUS	SAGITTARIUS	SAGITTARIUS	SAGITTARIUS	SAGITTARIUS
10 AM	CAPRICORN	CAPRICORN	CAPRICORN	CAPRICORN	CAPRICORN	CAPRICORN
11 AM	CAPRICORN	CAPRICORN	CAPRICORN	CAPRICORN	CAPRICORN	CAPRICORN
NOON	AQUARIUS	AQUARIUS	AQUARIUS	AQUARIUS	AQUARIUS	AQUARIUS
1 PM	PISCES	PISCES	PISCES	PISCES	PISCES	PISCES
2 PM	PISCES	PISCES	PISCES	ARIES	ARIES	ARIES
3 PM	ARIES	ARIES	ARIES	ARIES	ARIES	ARIES
4 PM	TAURUS	TAURUS	TAURUS	TAURUS	TAURUS	TAURUS
5 PM	GEMINI	GEMINI	GEMINI	GEMINI	GEMINI	GEMINI
6 PM	GEMINI	GEMINI	GEMINI	GEMINI	GEMINI	GEMINI
7 PM	CANCER	CANCER	CANCER	CANCER	CANCER	CANCER
8 PM	CANCER	CANCER	CANCER	CANCER	CANCER	CANCER
9 PM	CANCER	CANCER	CANCER	CANCER	LEO	LEO
10 PM	LEO	LEO	LEO	LEO	LEO	LEO
11 PM	LEO	LEO	LEO	LEO	LEO	LEO

1910 SCORPIO

DATE	MOON FROM IN	MERCURY	VENUS	MARS	JUPITER	SATURN	URANUS	NEPTUNE	PLUTO
OCT.									
24	11:07 PM LEO	LIBRA	LIBRA	LIBRA	LIBRA	TAURUS	CAPRICORN	CANCER	GEMINI
25		LIBRA	LIBRA	LIBRA	LIBRA	TAURUS	CAPRICORN	CANCER	GEMINI
26		LIBRA	LIBRA	LIBRA	LIBRA	TAURUS	CAPRICORN	CANCER	GEMINI
27	5:53 AM VIRGO	LIBRA	LIBRA	LIBRA	LIBRA	TAURUS	CAPRICORN	CANCER	GEMINI
28		LIBRA	LIBRA	LIBRA	LIBRA	TAURUS	CAPRICORN	CANCER	GEMINI
29	3:29 PM LIBRA	LIBRA	LIBRA	LIBRA	LIBRA	TAURUS	CAPRICORN	CANCER	GEMINI
30		LIBRA	LIBRA	LIBRA	LIBRA	TAURUS	CAPRICORN	CANCER	GEMINI
31		LIBRA	SCORPIO	LIBRA	LIBRA	TAURUS	CAPRICORN	CANCER	GEMINI
NOV.									
1	3:11 AM SCORPIO	SCORPIO	SCORPIO	LIBRA	LIBRA	TAURUS	CAPRICORN	CANCER	GEMINI
2		SCORPIO	SCORPIO	LIBRA	LIBRA	TAURUS	CAPRICORN	CANCER	GEMINI
3	4:06 PM SAGITTARIUS	SCORPIO	SCORPIO	LIBRA	LIBRA	TAURUS	CAPRICORN	CANCER	GEMINI
4		SCORPIO	SCORPIO	LIBRA	LIBRA	TAURUS	CAPRICORN	CANCER	GEMINI
5		SCORPIO	SCORPIO	LIBRA	LIBRA	TAURUS	CAPRICORN	CANCER	GEMINI
6	5:00 AM CAPRICORN	SCORPIO	SCORPIO	LIBRA	LIBRA	TAURUS	CAPRICORN	CANCER	GEMINI
7		SCORPIO	SCORPIO	SCORPIO	LIBRA	TAURUS	CAPRICORN	CANCER	GEMINI
8	4:18 PM AQUARIUS	SCORPIO	SCORPIO	SCORPIO	LIBRA	TAURUS	CAPRICORN	CANCER	GEMINI
9		SCORPIO	SCORPIO	SCORPIO	LIBRA	TAURUS	CAPRICORN	CANCER	GEMINI
10		SCORPIO	SCORPIO	SCORPIO	LIBRA	TAURUS	CAPRICORN	CANCER	GEMINI
11	0:25 AM PISCES	SCORPIO	SCORPIO	SCORPIO	LIBRA	TAURUS	CAPRICORN	CANCER	GEMINI
12		SCORPIO	SCORPIO	SCORPIO	SCORPIO	TAURUS	CAPRICORN	CANCER	GEMINI
13	4:42 AM ARIES	SCORPIO	SCORPIO	SCORPIO	SCORPIO	TAURUS	CAPRICORN	CANCER	GEMINI
14		SCORPIO	SCORPIO	SCORPIO	SCORPIO	TAURUS	CAPRICORN	CANCER	GEMINI
15	5:46 AM TAURUS	SCORPIO	SCORPIO	SCORPIO	SCORPIO	TAURUS	CAPRICORN	CANCER	GEMINI
16		SCORPIO	SCORPIO	SCORPIO	SCORPIO	TAURUS	CAPRICORN	CANCER	GEMINI
17	5:11 AM GEMINI	SCORPIO	SCORPIO	SCORPIO	SCORPIO	TAURUS	CAPRICORN	CANCER	GEMINI
18		SCORPIO	SCORPIO	SCORPIO	SCORPIO	TAURUS	CAPRICORN	CANCER	GEMINI
19	4:52 AM CANCER	SAGITTARIUS	SCORPIO	SCORPIO	SCORPIO	TAURUS	CAPRICORN	CANCER	GEMINI
20		SAGITTARIUS	SCORPIO	SCORPIO	SCORPIO	TAURUS	CAPRICORN	CANCER	GEMINI
21	5:41 AM LEO	SAGITTARIUS	SCORPIO	SCORPIO	SCORPIO	TAURUS	CAPRICORN	CANCER	GEMINI
22		SAGITTARIUS	SCORPIO	SCORPIO	SCORPIO	TAURUS	CAPRICORN	CANCER	GEMINI

1911

DATE	MOON FROM IN	MERCURY	VENUS	MARS	JUPITER	SATURN	URANUS	NEPTUNE	PLUTO
OCT.									
25		SCORPIO	VIRGO	GEMINI	SCORPIO	TAURUS	CAPRICORN	CANCER	GEMINI
26		SCORPIO	VIRGO	GEMINI	SCORPIO	TAURUS	CAPRICORN	CANCER	GEMINI
27	1:36 AM CAPRICORN	SCORPIO	VIRGO	GEMINI	SCORPIO	TAURUS	CAPRICORN	CANCER	GEMINI
28		SCORPIO	VIRGO	GEMINI	SCORPIO	TAURUS	CAPRICORN	CANCER	GEMINI
29	2:13 PM AQUARIUS	SCORPIO	VIRGO	GEMINI	SCORPIO	TAURUS	CAPRICORN	CANCER	GEMINI
30		SCORPIO	VIRGO	GEMINI	SCORPIO	TAURUS	CAPRICORN	CANCER	GEMINI
31		SCORPIO	VIRGO	GEMINI	SCORPIO	TAURUS	CAPRICORN	CANCER	GEMINI
NOV.									
1	1:10 AM PISCES	SCORPIO	VIRGO	GEMINI	SCORPIO	TAURUS	CAPRICORN	CANCER	GEMINI
2		SCORPIO	VIRGO	GEMINI	SCORPIO	TAURUS	CAPRICORN	CANCER	GEMINI
3	8:48 AM ARIES	SCORPIO	VIRGO	GEMINI	SCORPIO	TAURUS	CAPRICORN	CANCER	GEMINI
4		SCORPIO	VIRGO	GEMINI	SCORPIO	TAURUS	CAPRICORN	CANCER	GEMINI
5	12:52 PM TAURUS	SCORPIO	VIRGO	GEMINI	SCORPIO	TAURUS	CAPRICORN	CANCER	GEMINI
6		SCORPIO	VIRGO	GEMINI	SCORPIO	TAURUS	CAPRICORN	CANCER	GEMINI
7	2:27 PM GEMINI	SCORPIO	VIRGO	GEMINI	SCORPIO	TAURUS	CAPRICORN	CANCER	GEMINI
8		SCORPIO	VIRGO	GEMINI	SCORPIO	TAURUS	CAPRICORN	CANCER	GEMINI
9	3:10 PM CANCER	SCORPIO	LIBRA	GEMINI	SCORPIO	TAURUS	CAPRICORN	CANCER	GEMINI
10		SCORPIO	LIBRA	GEMINI	SCORPIO	TAURUS	CAPRICORN	CANCER	GEMINI
11	4:38 PM LEO	SCORPIO	LIBRA	GEMINI	SCORPIO	TAURUS	CAPRICORN	CANCER	GEMINI
12		SAGITTARIUS	LIBRA	GEMINI	SCORPIO	TAURUS	CAPRICORN	CANCER	GEMINI
13	8:05 PM VIRGO	SAGITTARIUS	LIBRA	GEMINI	SCORPIO	TAURUS	CAPRICORN	CANCER	GEMINI
14		SAGITTARIUS	LIBRA	GEMINI	SCORPIO	TAURUS	CAPRICORN	CANCER	GEMINI
15		SAGITTARIUS	LIBRA	GEMINI	SCORPIO	TAURUS	CAPRICORN	CANCER	GEMINI
16	2:04 AM LIBRA	SAGITTARIUS	LIBRA	GEMINI	SCORPIO	TAURUS	CAPRICORN	CANCER	GEMINI
17		SAGITTARIUS	LIBRA	GEMINI	SCORPIO	TAURUS	CAPRICORN	CANCER	GEMINI
18	10:27 AM SCORPIO	SAGITTARIUS	LIBRA	GEMINI	SCORPIO	TAURUS	CAPRICORN	CANCER	GEMINI
19		SAGITTARIUS	LIBRA	GEMINI	SCORPIO	TAURUS	CAPRICORN	CANCER	GEMINI
20	8:57 PM SAGITTARIUS	SAGITTARIUS	LIBRA	GEMINI	SCORPIO	TAURUS	CAPRICORN	CANCER	GEMINI
21		SAGITTARIUS	LIBRA	GEMINI	SCORPIO	TAURUS	CAPRICORN	CANCER	GEMINI
22		SAGITTARIUS	LIBRA	GEMINI	SCORPIO	TAURUS	CAPRICORN	CANCER	GEMINI

1912   SCORPIO

OCT.	MOON FROM	IN	MERCURY	VENUS	MARS	JUPITER	SATURN	URANUS	NEPTUNE	PLUTO
24			SCORPIO	SCORPIO	SCORPIO	SAGITTARIUS	GEMINI	CAPRICORN	CANCER	GEMINI
25	5:13 PM	TAURUS	SCORPIO	SAGITTARIUS	SCORPIO	SAGITTARIUS	GEMINI	CAPRICORN	CANCER	GEMINI
26			SCORPIO	SAGITTARIUS	SCORPIO	SAGITTARIUS	GEMINI	CAPRICORN	CANCER	GEMINI
27	11:21 PM	GEMINI	SCORPIO	SAGITTARIUS	SCORPIO	SAGITTARIUS	GEMINI	CAPRICORN	CANCER	GEMINI
28			SCORPIO	SAGITTARIUS	SCORPIO	SAGITTARIUS	GEMINI	CAPRICORN	CANCER	GEMINI
29			SCORPIO	SAGITTARIUS	SCORPIO	SAGITTARIUS	GEMINI	CAPRICORN	CANCER	GEMINI
30	3:34 PM	CANCER	SCORPIO	SAGITTARIUS	SCORPIO	SAGITTARIUS	GEMINI	CAPRICORN	CANCER	GEMINI
31			SCORPIO	SAGITTARIUS	SCORPIO	SAGITTARIUS	GEMINI	CAPRICORN	CANCER	GEMINI
NOV.										
1	6:45 AM	LEO	SCORPIO	SAGITTARIUS	SCORPIO	SAGITTARIUS	GEMINI	CAPRICORN	CANCER	GEMINI
2			SCORPIO	SAGITTARIUS	SCORPIO	SAGITTARIUS	GEMINI	CAPRICORN	CANCER	GEMINI
3	9:33 AM	VIRGO	SCORPIO	SAGITTARIUS	SCORPIO	SAGITTARIUS	GEMINI	CAPRICORN	CANCER	GEMINI
4			SCORPIO	SAGITTARIUS	SCORPIO	SAGITTARIUS	GEMINI	CAPRICORN	CANCER	GEMINI
5	12:31 PM	LIBRA	SAGITTARIUS	SAGITTARIUS	SCORPIO	SAGITTARIUS	GEMINI	CAPRICORN	CANCER	GEMINI
6			SAGITTARIUS	SAGITTARIUS	SCORPIO	SAGITTARIUS	GEMINI	CAPRICORN	CANCER	GEMINI
7	4:12 PM	SCORPIO	SAGITTARIUS	SAGITTARIUS	SCORPIO	SAGITTARIUS	GEMINI	CAPRICORN	CANCER	GEMINI
8			SAGITTARIUS	SAGITTARIUS	SCORPIO	SAGITTARIUS	GEMINI	CAPRICORN	CANCER	GEMINI
9	9:44 PM	SAGITTARIUS	SAGITTARIUS	SAGITTARIUS	SCORPIO	SAGITTARIUS	GEMINI	CAPRICORN	CANCER	GEMINI
10			SAGITTARIUS	SAGITTARIUS	SCORPIO	SAGITTARIUS	GEMINI	CAPRICORN	CANCER	GEMINI
11			SAGITTARIUS	SAGITTARIUS	SCORPIO	SAGITTARIUS	GEMINI	CAPRICORN	CANCER	GEMINI
12	5:47 AM	CAPRICORN	SAGITTARIUS	SAGITTARIUS	SCORPIO	SAGITTARIUS	GEMINI	AQUARIUS	CANCER	GEMINI
13			SAGITTARIUS	SAGITTARIUS	SCORPIO	SAGITTARIUS	GEMINI	AQUARIUS	CANCER	GEMINI
14	4:45 PM	AQUARIUS	SAGITTARIUS	SAGITTARIUS	SCORPIO	SAGITTARIUS	GEMINI	AQUARIUS	CANCER	GEMINI
15			SAGITTARIUS	SAGITTARIUS	SCORPIO	SAGITTARIUS	GEMINI	AQUARIUS	CANCER	GEMINI
16			SAGITTARIUS	SAGITTARIUS	SCORPIO	SAGITTARIUS	GEMINI	AQUARIUS	CANCER	GEMINI
17	5:23 AM	PISCES	SAGITTARIUS	SAGITTARIUS	SCORPIO	SAGITTARIUS	GEMINI	AQUARIUS	CANCER	GEMINI
18			SAGITTARIUS	CAPRICORN	SCORPIO	SAGITTARIUS	GEMINI	AQUARIUS	CANCER	GEMINI
19	5:16 PM	ARIES	SAGITTARIUS	CAPRICORN	SCORPIO	SAGITTARIUS	GEMINI	AQUARIUS	CANCER	GEMINI
20			SAGITTARIUS	CAPRICORN	SCORPIO	SAGITTARIUS	GEMINI	AQUARIUS	CANCER	GEMINI
21			SAGITTARIUS	CAPRICORN	SCORPIO	SAGITTARIUS	GEMINI	AQUARIUS	CANCER	GEMINI
22	2:11 AM	TAURUS	SAGITTARIUS	CAPRICORN	SCORPIO	SAGITTARIUS	GEMINI	AQUARIUS	CANCER	GEMINI

1913

OCT.	MOON FROM	IN	MERCURY	VENUS	MARS	JUPITER	SATURN	URANUS	NEPTUNE	PLUTO
24	11:05 PM	VIRGO	SCORPIO	LIBRA	CANCER	CAPRICORN	GEMINI	AQUARIUS	CANCER	CANCER
25			SCORPIO	LIBRA	CANCER	CAPRICORN	GEMINI	AQUARIUS	CANCER	CANCER
26			SCORPIO	LIBRA	CANCER	CAPRICORN	GEMINI	AQUARIUS	CANCER	CANCER
27	0:16 AM	LIBRA	SCORPIO	LIBRA	CANCER	CAPRICORN	GEMINI	AQUARIUS	CANCER	CANCER
28			SCORPIO	LIBRA	CANCER	CAPRICORN	GEMINI	AQUARIUS	CANCER	CANCER
29	0:30 AM	SCORPIO	SCORPIO	LIBRA	CANCER	CAPRICORN	GEMINI	AQUARIUS	CANCER	CANCER
30			SCORPIO	LIBRA	CANCER	CAPRICORN	GEMINI	AQUARIUS	CANCER	CANCER
31	1:30 AM	SAGITTARIUS	SAGITTARIUS	LIBRA	CANCER	CAPRICORN	GEMINI	AQUARIUS	CANCER	CANCER
NOV.										
1			SAGITTARIUS	LIBRA	CANCER	CAPRICORN	GEMINI	AQUARIUS	CANCER	CANCER
2	5:08 AM	CAPRICORN	SAGITTARIUS	LIBRA	CANCER	CAPRICORN	GEMINI	AQUARIUS	CANCER	CANCER
3			SAGITTARIUS	LIBRA	CANCER	CAPRICORN	GEMINI	AQUARIUS	CANCER	CANCER
4	12:44 PM	AQUARIUS	SAGITTARIUS	LIBRA	CANCER	CAPRICORN	GEMINI	AQUARIUS	CANCER	CANCER
5			SAGITTARIUS	LIBRA	CANCER	CAPRICORN	GEMINI	AQUARIUS	CANCER	CANCER
6			SAGITTARIUS	LIBRA	CANCER	CAPRICORN	GEMINI	AQUARIUS	CANCER	CANCER
7	0:01 AM	PISCES	SAGITTARIUS	LIBRA	CANCER	CAPRICORN	GEMINI	AQUARIUS	CANCER	CANCER
8			SAGITTARIUS	LIBRA	CANCER	CAPRICORN	GEMINI	AQUARIUS	CANCER	CANCER
9	1:01 PM	ARIES	SAGITTARIUS	LIBRA	CANCER	CAPRICORN	GEMINI	AQUARIUS	CANCER	CANCER
10			SAGITTARIUS	LIBRA	CANCER	CAPRICORN	GEMINI	AQUARIUS	CANCER	CANCER
11			SAGITTARIUS	LIBRA	CANCER	CAPRICORN	GEMINI	AQUARIUS	CANCER	CANCER
12	1:15 AM	TAURUS	SAGITTARIUS	LIBRA	CANCER	CAPRICORN	GEMINI	AQUARIUS	CANCER	CANCER
13			SAGITTARIUS	LIBRA	CANCER	CAPRICORN	GEMINI	AQUARIUS	CANCER	CANCER
14	11:23 AM	GEMINI	SAGITTARIUS	SCORPIO	CANCER	CAPRICORN	GEMINI	AQUARIUS	CANCER	CANCER
15			SAGITTARIUS	SCORPIO	CANCER	CAPRICORN	GEMINI	AQUARIUS	CANCER	CANCER
16	7:16 PM	CANCER	SAGITTARIUS	SCORPIO	CANCER	CAPRICORN	GEMINI	AQUARIUS	CANCER	CANCER
17			SAGITTARIUS	SCORPIO	CANCER	CAPRICORN	GEMINI	AQUARIUS	CANCER	CANCER
18			SAGITTARIUS	SCORPIO	CANCER	CAPRICORN	GEMINI	AQUARIUS	CANCER	CANCER
19	1:15 AM	LEO	SAGITTARIUS	SCORPIO	CANCER	CAPRICORN	GEMINI	AQUARIUS	CANCER	CANCER
20			SAGITTARIUS	SCORPIO	CANCER	CAPRICORN	GEMINI	AQUARIUS	CANCER	CANCER
21	5:39 AM	VIRGO	SAGITTARIUS	SCORPIO	CANCER	CAPRICORN	GEMINI	AQUARIUS	CANCER	CANCER
22			SAGITTARIUS	SCORPIO	CANCER	CAPRICORN	GEMINI	AQUARIUS	CANCER	CANCER

1914   SCORPIO

OCT.	MOON FROM	IN	MERCURY	VENUS	MARS	JUPITER	SATURN	URANUS	NEPTUNE	PLUTO
24			SCORPIO	SAGITTARIUS	SCORPIO	AQUARIUS	CANCER	AQUARIUS	LEO	CANCER
25	2:40 PM	AQUARIUS	SCORPIO	SAGITTARIUS	SCORPIO	AQUARIUS	CANCER	AQUARIUS	LEO	CANCER
26			SCORPIO	SAGITTARIUS	SCORPIO	AQUARIUS	CANCER	AQUARIUS	LEO	CANCER
27	11:13 PM	PISCES	SCORPIO	SAGITTARIUS	SCORPIO	AQUARIUS	CANCER	AQUARIUS	LEO	CANCER
28			SCORPIO	SAGITTARIUS	SCORPIO	AQUARIUS	CANCER	AQUARIUS	LEO	CANCER
29			SCORPIO	SAGITTARIUS	SCORPIO	AQUARIUS	CANCER	AQUARIUS	LEO	CANCER
30	10:34 AM	ARIES	SCORPIO	SAGITTARIUS	SCORPIO	AQUARIUS	CANCER	AQUARIUS	LEO	CANCER
31			SCORPIO	SAGITTARIUS	SCORPIO	AQUARIUS	CANCER	AQUARIUS	LEO	CANCER
NOV.										
1	11:09 PM	TAURUS	SCORPIO	SAGITTARIUS	SCORPIO	AQUARIUS	CANCER	AQUARIUS	LEO	CANCER
2			SCORPIO	SAGITTARIUS	SCORPIO	AQUARIUS	CANCER	AQUARIUS	LEO	CANCER
3			SCORPIO	SAGITTARIUS	SCORPIO	AQUARIUS	CANCER	AQUARIUS	LEO	CANCER
4	11:43 AM	GEMINI	SCORPIO	SAGITTARIUS	SCORPIO	AQUARIUS	CANCER	AQUARIUS	LEO	CANCER
5			SCORPIO	SAGITTARIUS	SCORPIO	AQUARIUS	CANCER	AQUARIUS	LEO	CANCER
6	11:32 PM	CANCER	SCORPIO	SAGITTARIUS	SCORPIO	AQUARIUS	CANCER	AQUARIUS	LEO	CANCER
7			SCORPIO	SAGITTARIUS	SCORPIO	AQUARIUS	CANCER	AQUARIUS	LEO	CANCER
8			SCORPIO	SAGITTARIUS	SCORPIO	AQUARIUS	CANCER	AQUARIUS	LEO	CANCER
9	9:35 AM	LEO	SCORPIO	SAGITTARIUS	SCORPIO	AQUARIUS	CANCER	AQUARIUS	LEO	CANCER
10			SCORPIO	SAGITTARIUS	SCORPIO	AQUARIUS	CANCER	AQUARIUS	LEO	CANCER
11	4:40 PM	VIRGO	SCORPIO	SAGITTARIUS	SAGITTARIUS	AQUARIUS	CANCER	AQUARIUS	LEO	CANCER
12			SCORPIO	SAGITTARIUS	SAGITTARIUS	AQUARIUS	CANCER	AQUARIUS	LEO	CANCER
13	8:09 PM	LIBRA	SCORPIO	SAGITTARIUS	SAGITTARIUS	AQUARIUS	CANCER	AQUARIUS	LEO	CANCER
14			SCORPIO	SAGITTARIUS	SAGITTARIUS	AQUARIUS	CANCER	AQUARIUS	LEO	CANCER
15	8:35	SCORPIO	SCORPIO	SAGITTARIUS	SAGITTARIUS	AQUARIUS	CANCER	AQUARIUS	LEO	CANCER
16			SCORPIO	SAGITTARIUS	SAGITTARIUS	AQUARIUS	CANCER	AQUARIUS	LEO	CANCER
17	7:42 PM	SAGITTARIUS	SCORPIO	SAGITTARIUS	SAGITTARIUS	AQUARIUS	CANCER	AQUARIUS	LEO	CANCER
18			SCORPIO	SAGITTARIUS	SAGITTARIUS	AQUARIUS	CANCER	AQUARIUS	LEO	CANCER
19	7:42 PM	CAPRICORN	SCORPIO	SAGITTARIUS	SAGITTARIUS	AQUARIUS	CANCER	AQUARIUS	LEO	CANCER
20			SCORPIO	SAGITTARIUS	SAGITTARIUS	AQUARIUS	CANCER	AQUARIUS	LEO	CANCER
21	10:43 PM	AQUARIUS	SCORPIO	SAGITTARIUS	SAGITTARIUS	AQUARIUS	CANCER	AQUARIUS	LEO	CANCER
22			SCORPIO	SAGITTARIUS	SAGITTARIUS	AQUARIUS	CANCER	AQUARIUS	LEO	CANCER

1915

OCT.	MOON FROM	IN	MERCURY	VENUS	MARS	JUPITER	SATURN	URANUS	NEPTUNE	PLUTO
25	9:16 AM	GEMINI	LIBRA	SCORPIO	LEO	PISCES	CANCER	AQUARIUS	LEO	CANCER
26			LIBRA	SCORPIO	LEO	PISCES	CANCER	AQUARIUS	LEO	CANCER
27	9:53 PM	CANCER	LIBRA	SCORPIO	LEO	PISCES	CANCER	AQUARIUS	LEO	CANCER
28			LIBRA	SCORPIO	LEO	PISCES	CANCER	AQUARIUS	LEO	CANCER
29			LIBRA	SCORPIO	LEO	PISCES	CANCER	AQUARIUS	LEO	CANCER
30	10:26 AM	LEO	LIBRA	SCORPIO	LEO	PISCES	CANCER	AQUARIUS	LEO	CANCER
31			LIBRA	SCORPIO	LEO	PISCES	CANCER	AQUARIUS	LEO	CANCER
NOV.										
1	8:30 PM	VIRGO	LIBRA	SCORPIO	LEO	PISCES	CANCER	AQUARIUS	LEO	CANCER
2			LIBRA	SCORPIO	LEO	PISCES	CANCER	AQUARIUS	LEO	CANCER
3			LIBRA	SCORPIO	LEO	PISCES	CANCER	AQUARIUS	LEO	CANCER
4	2:28 AM	LIBRA	LIBRA	SCORPIO	LEO	PISCES	CANCER	AQUARIUS	LEO	CANCER
5			LIBRA	SCORPIO	LEO	PISCES	CANCER	AQUARIUS	LEO	CANCER
6	4:37 AM	SCORPIO	LIBRA	SCORPIO	LEO	PISCES	CANCER	AQUARIUS	LEO	CANCER
7			LIBRA	SCORPIO	LEO	PISCES	CANCER	AQUARIUS	LEO	CANCER
8	4:36 AM	SAGITTARIUS	LIBRA	SCORPIO	LEO	PISCES	CANCER	AQUARIUS	LEO	CANCER
9			LIBRA	SAGITTARIUS	LEO	PISCES	CANCER	AQUARIUS	LEO	CANCER
10	4:34 AM	CAPRICORN	LIBRA	SAGITTARIUS	LEO	PISCES	CANCER	AQUARIUS	LEO	CANCER
11			LIBRA	SAGITTARIUS	LEO	PISCES	CANCER	AQUARIUS	LEO	CANCER
12	6:23 AM	AQUARIUS	SCORPIO	SAGITTARIUS	LEO	PISCES	CANCER	AQUARIUS	LEO	CANCER
13			SCORPIO	SAGITTARIUS	LEO	PISCES	CANCER	AQUARIUS	LEO	CANCER
14	11:06 AM	PISCES	SCORPIO	SAGITTARIUS	LEO	PISCES	CANCER	AQUARIUS	LEO	CANCER
15			SCORPIO	SAGITTARIUS	LEO	PISCES	CANCER	AQUARIUS	LEO	CANCER
16	6:40 PM	ARIES	SCORPIO	SAGITTARIUS	LEO	PISCES	CANCER	AQUARIUS	LEO	CANCER
17			SCORPIO	SAGITTARIUS	LEO	PISCES	CANCER	AQUARIUS	LEO	CANCER
18			SCORPIO	SAGITTARIUS	LEO	PISCES	CANCER	AQUARIUS	LEO	CANCER
19	4:30 AM	TAURUS	SCORPIO	SAGITTARIUS	LEO	PISCES	CANCER	AQUARIUS	LEO	CANCER
20			SCORPIO	SAGITTARIUS	LEO	PISCES	CANCER	AQUARIUS	LEO	CANCER
21	3:57 PM	GEMINI	SCORPIO	SAGITTARIUS	LEO	PISCES	CANCER	AQUARIUS	LEO	CANCER
22			SCORPIO	SAGITTARIUS	LEO	PISCES	CANCER	AQUARIUS	LEO	CANCER

SCORPIO

	MOON FROM	IN	MERCURY	VENUS	MARS	JUPITER	SATURN	URANUS	NEPTUNE	PLUTO
OCT.										
24	3:45 AM	LIBRA	LIBRA	VIRGO	SAGITTARIUS	TAURUS	LEO	AQUARIUS	LEO	CANCER
25			LIBRA	VIRGO	SAGITTARIUS	TAURUS	LEO	AQUARIUS	LEO	CANCER
26	10:08 AM	SCORPIO	LIBRA	VIRGO	SAGITTARIUS	TAURUS	LEO	AQUARIUS	LEO	CANCER
27			LIBRA	VIRGO	SAGITTARIUS	ARIES	LEO	AQUARIUS	LEO	CANCER
28	2:07 PM	SAGITTARIUS	LIBRA	VIRGO	SAGITTARIUS	ARIES	LEO	AQUARIUS	LEO	CANCER
29			LIBRA	VIRGO	SAGITTARIUS	ARIES	LEO	AQUARIUS	LEO	CANCER
30	5:01 PM	CAPRICORN	LIBRA	VIRGO	SAGITTARIUS	ARIES	LEO	AQUARIUS	LEO	CANCER
31			LIBRA	VIRGO	SAGITTARIUS	ARIES	LEO	AQUARIUS	LEO	CANCER
NOV.										
1	7:50 PM	AQUARIUS	LIBRA	VIRGO	SAGITTARIUS	ARIES	LEO	AQUARIUS	LEO	CANCER
2			LIBRA	VIRGO	SAGITTARIUS	ARIES	LEO	AQUARIUS	LEO	CANCER
3	11:05 PM	PISCES	LIBRA	LIBRA	SAGITTARIUS	ARIES	LEO	AQUARIUS	LEO	CANCER
4			LIBRA	LIBRA	SAGITTARIUS	ARIES	LEO	AQUARIUS	LEO	CANCER
5			SCORPIO	LIBRA	SAGITTARIUS	ARIES	LEO	AQUARIUS	LEO	CANCER
6	3:00 AM	ARIES	SCORPIO	LIBRA	SAGITTARIUS	ARIES	LEO	AQUARIUS	LEO	CANCER
7			SCORPIO	LIBRA	SAGITTARIUS	ARIES	LEO	AQUARIUS	LEO	CANCER
8	8:07 AM	TAURUS	SCORPIO	LIBRA	SAGITTARIUS	ARIES	LEO	AQUARIUS	LEO	CANCER
9			SCORPIO	LIBRA	SAGITTARIUS	ARIES	LEO	AQUARIUS	LEO	CANCER
10	3:20 PM	GEMINI	SCORPIO	LIBRA	SAGITTARIUS	ARIES	LEO	AQUARIUS	LEO	CANCER
11			SCORPIO	LIBRA	SAGITTARIUS	ARIES	LEO	AQUARIUS	LEO	CANCER
12			SCORPIO	LIBRA	SAGITTARIUS	ARIES	LEO	AQUARIUS	LEO	CANCER
13	1:20 AM	CANCER	SCORPIO	LIBRA	SAGITTARIUS	ARIES	LEO	AQUARIUS	LEO	CANCER
14			SCORPIO	LIBRA	SAGITTARIUS	ARIES	LEO	AQUARIUS	LEO	CANCER
15	1:45 PM	LEO	SCORPIO	LIBRA	SAGITTARIUS	ARIES	LEO	AQUARIUS	LEO	CANCER
16			SCORPIO	LIBRA	SAGITTARIUS	ARIES	LEO	AQUARIUS	LEO	CANCER
17			SCORPIO	LIBRA	SAGITTARIUS	ARIES	LEO	AQUARIUS	LEO	CANCER
18	2:33 AM	VIRGO	SCORPIO	LIBRA	SAGITTARIUS	ARIES	LEO	AQUARIUS	LEO	CANCER
19			SCORPIO	LIBRA	SAGITTARIUS	ARIES	LEO	AQUARIUS	LEO	CANCER
20	1:02 PM	LIBRA	SCORPIO	LIBRA	SAGITTARIUS	ARIES	LEO	AQUARIUS	LEO	CANCER
21			SCORPIO	LIBRA	SAGITTARIUS	ARIES	LEO	AQUARIUS	LEO	CANCER
22	7:48 PM	SCORPIO	SCORPIO	LIBRA	SAGITTARIUS	ARIES	LEO	AQUARIUS	LEO	CANCER

1917

	MOON FROM	IN	MERCURY	VENUS	MARS	JUPITER	SATURN	URANUS	NEPTUNE	PLUTO
OCT.										
24			LIBRA	SAGITTARIUS	LEO	GEMINI	LEO	AQUARIUS	LEO	CANCER
25	1:02 PM	PISCES	LIBRA	SAGITTARIUS	LEO	GEMINI	LEO	AQUARIUS	LEO	CANCER
26			LIBRA	SAGITTARIUS	LEO	GEMINI	LEO	AQUARIUS	LEO	CANCER
27	2:09 PM	ARIES	LIBRA	SAGITTARIUS	LEO	GEMINI	LEO	AQUARIUS	LEO	CANCER
28			SCORPIO	SAGITTARIUS	LEO	GEMINI	LEO	AQUARIUS	LEO	CANCER
29	3:00 PM	TAURUS	SCORPIO	SAGITTARIUS	LEO	GEMINI	LEO	AQUARIUS	LEO	CANCER
30			SCORPIO	SAGITTARIUS	LEO	GEMINI	LEO	AQUARIUS	LEO	CANCER
31	5:27 PM	GEMINI	SCORPIO	SAGITTARIUS	LEO	GEMINI	LEO	AQUARIUS	LEO	CANCER
NOV.										
1			SCORPIO	SAGITTARIUS	LEO	GEMINI	LEO	AQUARIUS	LEO	CANCER
2	11:10 PM	CANCER	SCORPIO	SAGITTARIUS	VIRGO	GEMINI	LEO	AQUARIUS	LEO	CANCER
3			SCORPIO	SAGITTARIUS	VIRGO	GEMINI	LEO	AQUARIUS	LEO	CANCER
4			SCORPIO	SAGITTARIUS	VIRGO	GEMINI	LEO	AQUARIUS	LEO	CANCER
5	8:43 AM	LEO	SCORPIO	SAGITTARIUS	VIRGO	GEMINI	LEO	AQUARIUS	LEO	CANCER
6			SCORPIO	SAGITTARIUS	VIRGO	GEMINI	LEO	AQUARIUS	LEO	CANCER
7	8:57 PM	VIRGO	SCORPIO	CAPRICORN	VIRGO	GEMINI	LEO	AQUARIUS	LEO	CANCER
8			SCORPIO	CAPRICORN	VIRGO	GEMINI	LEO	AQUARIUS	LEO	CANCER
9			SCORPIO	CAPRICORN	VIRGO	GEMINI	LEO	AQUARIUS	LEO	CANCER
10	9:26 AM	LIBRA	SCORPIO	CAPRICORN	VIRGO	GEMINI	LEO	AQUARIUS	LEO	CANCER
11			SCORPIO	CAPRICORN	VIRGO	GEMINI	LEO	AQUARIUS	LEO	CANCER
12	8:13 PM	SCORPIO	SCORPIO	CAPRICORN	VIRGO	GEMINI	LEO	AQUARIUS	LEO	CANCER
13			SCORPIO	CAPRICORN	VIRGO	GEMINI	LEO	AQUARIUS	LEO	CANCER
14			SCORPIO	CAPRICORN	VIRGO	GEMINI	LEO	AQUARIUS	LEO	CANCER
15	4:36 AM	SAGITTARIUS	SCORPIO	CAPRICORN	VIRGO	GEMINI	LEO	AQUARIUS	LEO	CANCER
16			SAGITTARIUS	CAPRICORN	VIRGO	GEMINI	LEO	AQUARIUS	LEO	CANCER
17	10:55 AM	CAPRICORN	SAGITTARIUS	CAPRICORN	VIRGO	GEMINI	LEO	AQUARIUS	LEO	CANCER
18			SAGITTARIUS	CAPRICORN	VIRGO	GEMINI	LEO	AQUARIUS	LEO	CANCER
19	3:38 PM	AQUARIUS	SAGITTARIUS	CAPRICORN	VIRGO	GEMINI	LEO	AQUARIUS	LEO	CANCER
20			SAGITTARIUS	CAPRICORN	VIRGO	GEMINI	LEO	AQUARIUS	LEO	CANCER
21	7:04 PM	PISCES	SAGITTARIUS	CAPRICORN	VIRGO	GEMINI	LEO	AQUARIUS	LEO	CANCER
22			SAGITTARIUS	CAPRICORN	VIRGO	GEMINI	LEO	AQUARIUS	LEO	CANCER

1918

SCORPIO

	MOON									
	FROM	IN	MERCURY	VENUS	MARS	JUPITER	SATURN	URANUS	NEPTUNE	PLUTO
OCT.										
24	1:42 AM	CANCER	SCORPIO	LIBRA	SAGITTARIUS	CANCER	LEO	AQUARIUS	LEO	CANCER
25			SCORPIO	LIBRA	SAGITTARIUS	CANCER	LEO	AQUARIUS	LEO	CANCER
26	7:55 AM	LEO	SCORPIO	LIBRA	SAGITTARIUS	CANCER	LEO	AQUARIUS	LEO	CANCER
27			SCORPIO	LIBRA	SAGITTARIUS	CANCER	LEO	AQUARIUS	LEO	CANCER
28	5:43 PM	VIRGO	SCORPIO	LIBRA	SAGITTARIUS	CANCER	LEO	AQUARIUS	LEO	CANCER
29			SCORPIO	LIBRA	SAGITTARIUS	CANCER	LEO	AQUARIUS	LEO	CANCER
30			SCORPIO	SCORPIO	SAGITTARIUS	CANCER	LEO	AQUARIUS	LEO	CANCER
31	5:45 AM	LIBRA	SCORPIO	SCORPIO	SAGITTARIUS	CANCER	LEO	AQUARIUS	LEO	CANCER
NOV.										
1			SCORPIO	SCORPIO	SAGITTARIUS	CANCER	LEO	AQUARIUS	LEO	CANCER
2	6:32 PM	SCORPIO	SCORPIO	SCORPIO	SAGITTARIUS	CANCER	LEO	AQUARIUS	LEO	CANCER
3			SCORPIO	SCORPIO	SAGITTARIUS	CANCER	LEO	AQUARIUS	LEO	CANCER
4			SCORPIO	SCORPIO	SAGITTARIUS	CANCER	LEO	AQUARIUS	LEO	CANCER
5	6:52 AM	SAGITTARIUS	SCORPIO	SCORPIO	SAGITTARIUS	CANCER	LEO	AQUARIUS	LEO	CANCER
6			SCORPIO	SCORPIO	SAGITTARIUS	CANCER	LEO	AQUARIUS	LEO	CANCER
7	5:50 PM	CAPRICORN	SCORPIO	SCORPIO	SAGITTARIUS	CANCER	LEO	AQUARIUS	LEO	CANCER
8			SCORPIO	SCORPIO	SAGITTARIUS	CANCER	LEO	AQUARIUS	LEO	CANCER
9			SAGITTARIUS	SCORPIO	SAGITTARIUS	CANCER	LEO	AQUARIUS	LEO	CANCER
10	2:25 AM	AQUARIUS	SAGITTARIUS	SCORPIO	SAGITTARIUS	CANCER	LEO	AQUARIUS	LEO	CANCER
11			SAGITTARIUS	SCORPIO	CAPRICORN	CANCER	LEO	AQUARIUS	LEO	CANCER
12	7:52 AM	PISCES	SAGITTARIUS	SCORPIO	CAPRICORN	CANCER	LEO	AQUARIUS	LEO	CANCER
13			SAGITTARIUS	SCORPIO	CAPRICORN	CANCER	LEO	AQUARIUS	LEO	CANCER
14	10:11 AM	ARIES	SAGITTARIUS	SCORPIO	CAPRICORN	CANCER	LEO	AQUARIUS	LEO	CANCER
15			SAGITTARIUS	SCORPIO	CAPRICORN	CANCER	LEO	AQUARIUS	LEO	CANCER
16	10:27 AM	TAURUS	SAGITTARIUS	SCORPIO	CAPRICORN	CANCER	LEO	AQUARIUS	LEO	CANCER
17			SAGITTARIUS	SCORPIO	CAPRICORN	CANCER	LEO	AQUARIUS	LEO	CANCER
18	10:21 AM	GEMINI	SAGITTARIUS	SCORPIO	CAPRICORN	CANCER	LEO	AQUARIUS	LEO	CANCER
19			SAGITTARIUS	SCORPIO	CAPRICORN	CANCER	LEO	AQUARIUS	LEO	CANCER
20	11:48 AM	CANCER	SAGITTARIUS	SCORPIO	CAPRICORN	CANCER	LEO	AQUARIUS	LEO	CANCER
21			SAGITTARIUS	SCORPIO	CAPRICORN	CANCER	LEO	AQUARIUS	LEO	CANCER
22	4:24 PM	LEO	SAGITTARIUS	SCORPIO	CAPRICORN	CANCER	LEO	AQUARIUS	LEO	CANCER

1919

	MOON									
	FROM	IN	MERCURY	VENUS	MARS	JUPITER	SATURN	URANUS	NEPTUNE	PLUTO
OCT.										
24			SCORPIO	VIRGO	VIRGO	LEO	VIRGO	AQUARIUS	LEO	CANCER
25			SCORPIO	VIRGO	VIRGO	LEO	VIRGO	AQUARIUS	LEO	CANCER
26	5:31 AM	SAGITTARIUS	SCORPIO	VIRGO	VIRGO	LEO	VIRGO	AQUARIUS	LEO	CANCER
27			SCORPIO	VIRGO	VIRGO	LEO	VIRGO	AQUARIUS	LEO	CANCER
28	6:35 PM	CAPRICORN	SCORPIO	VIRGO	VIRGO	LEO	VIRGO	AQUARIUS	LEO	CANCER
29			SCORPIO	VIRGO	VIRGO	LEO	VIRGO	AQUARIUS	LEO	CANCER
30			SCORPIO	VIRGO	VIRGO	LEO	VIRGO	AQUARIUS	LEO	CANCER
31	6:08 AM	AQUARIUS	SCORPIO	VIRGO	VIRGO	LEO	VIRGO	AQUARIUS	LEO	CANCER
NOV.										
1			SCORPIO	VIRGO	VIRGO	LEO	VIRGO	AQUARIUS	LEO	CANCER
2	2:18 PM	PISCES	SCORPIO	VIRGO	VIRGO	LEO	VIRGO	AQUARIUS	LEO	CANCER
3			SAGITTARIUS	VIRGO	VIRGO	LEO	VIRGO	AQUARIUS	LEO	CANCER
4	6:30 PM	ARIES	SAGITTARIUS	VIRGO	VIRGO	LEO	VIRGO	AQUARIUS	LEO	CANCER
5			SAGITTARIUS	VIRGO	VIRGO	LEO	VIRGO	AQUARIUS	LEO	CANCER
6	7:31 PM	TAURUS	SAGITTARIUS	VIRGO	VIRGO	LEO	VIRGO	AQUARIUS	LEO	CANCER
7			SAGITTARIUS	VIRGO	VIRGO	LEO	VIRGO	AQUARIUS	LEO	CANCER
8	7:03 PM	GEMINI	SAGITTARIUS	VIRGO	VIRGO	LEO	VIRGO	AQUARIUS	LEO	CANCER
9			SAGITTARIUS	LIBRA	VIRGO	LEO	VIRGO	AQUARIUS	LEO	CANCER
10	7:03 PM	CANCER	SAGITTARIUS	LIBRA	VIRGO	LEO	VIRGO	AQUARIUS	LEO	CANCER
11			SAGITTARIUS	LIBRA	VIRGO	LEO	VIRGO	AQUARIUS	LEO	CANCER
12	9:15 PM	LEO	SAGITTARIUS	LIBRA	VIRGO	LEO	VIRGO	AQUARIUS	LEO	CANCER
13			SAGITTARIUS	LIBRA	VIRGO	LEO	VIRGO	AQUARIUS	LEO	CANCER
14			SAGITTARIUS	LIBRA	VIRGO	LEO	VIRGO	AQUARIUS	LEO	CANCER
15	2:42 AM	VIRGO	SAGITTARIUS	LIBRA	VIRGO	LEO	VIRGO	AQUARIUS	LEO	CANCER
16			SAGITTARIUS	LIBRA	VIRGO	LEO	VIRGO	AQUARIUS	LEO	CANCER
17	11:27 AM	LIBRA	SAGITTARIUS	LIBRA	VIRGO	LEO	VIRGO	AQUARIUS	LEO	CANCER
18			SAGITTARIUS	LIBRA	VIRGO	LEO	VIRGO	AQUARIUS	LEO	CANCER
19	10:59 PM	SCORPIO	SAGITTARIUS	LIBRA	VIRGO	LEO	VIRGO	AQUARIUS	LEO	CANCER
20			SAGITTARIUS	LIBRA	VIRGO	LEO	VIRGO	AQUARIUS	LEO	CANCER
21			SAGITTARIUS	LIBRA	VIRGO	LEO	VIRGO	AQUARIUS	LEO	CANCER
22	11:48 AM	SAGITTARIUS	SAGITTARIUS	LIBRA	VIRGO	LEO	VIRGO	AQUARIUS	LEO	CANCER

SCORPIO

OCT.	MOON FROM	IN	MERCURY	VENUS	MARS	JUPITER	SATURN	URANUS	NEPTUNE	PLUTO
24	7:52 PM	ARIES	SCORPIO	SAGITTARIUS	CAPRICORN	VIRGO	VIRGO	PISCES	LEO	CANCER
25			SCORPIO	SAGITTARIUS	CAPRICORN	VIRGO	VIRGO	PISCES	LEO	CANCER
26			SCORPIO	SAGITTARIUS	CAPRICORN	VIRGO	VIRGO	PISCES	LEO	CANCER
27	2:33 AM	TAURUS	SCORPIO	SAGITTARIUS	CAPRICORN	VIRGO	VIRGO	PISCES	LEO	CANCER
28			SCORPIO	SAGITTARIUS	CAPRICORN	VIRGO	VIRGO	PISCES	LEO	CANCER
29	4:59 AM	GEMINI	SCORPIO	SAGITTARIUS	CAPRICORN	VIRGO	VIRGO	PISCES	LEO	CANCER
30			SCORPIO	SAGITTARIUS	CAPRICORN	VIRGO	VIRGO	PISCES	LEO	CANCER
31	6:35 AM	CANCER	SAGITTARIUS	SAGITTARIUS	CAPRICORN	VIRGO	VIRGO	PISCES	LEO	CANCER
NOV.										
1			SAGITTARIUS	SAGITTARIUS	CAPRICORN	VIRGO	VIRGO	PISCES	LEO	CANCER
2	8:38 AM	LEO	SAGITTARIUS	SAGITTARIUS	CAPRICORN	VIRGO	VIRGO	PISCES	LEO	CANCER
3			SAGITTARIUS	SAGITTARIUS	CAPRICORN	VIRGO	VIRGO	PISCES	LEO	CANCER
4	12:04 PM	VIRGO	SAGITTARIUS	SAGITTARIUS	CAPRICORN	VIRGO	VIRGO	PISCES	LEO	CANCER
5			SAGITTARIUS	SAGITTARIUS	CAPRICORN	VIRGO	VIRGO	PISCES	LEO	CANCER
6	5:25 PM	LIBRA	SAGITTARIUS	SAGITTARIUS	CAPRICORN	VIRGO	VIRGO	PISCES	LEO	CANCER
7			SAGITTARIUS	SAGITTARIUS	CAPRICORN	VIRGO	VIRGO	PISCES	LEO	CANCER
8			SAGITTARIUS	SAGITTARIUS	CAPRICORN	VIRGO	VIRGO	PISCES	LEO	CANCER
9	0:51 AM	SCORPIO	SAGITTARIUS	SAGITTARIUS	CAPRICORN	VIRGO	VIRGO	PISCES	LEO	CANCER
10			SAGITTARIUS	SAGITTARIUS	CAPRICORN	VIRGO	VIRGO	PISCES	LEO	CANCER
11	10:27 AM	SAGITTARIUS	SCORPIO	SAGITTARIUS	CAPRICORN	VIRGO	VIRGO	PISCES	LEO	CANCER
12			SCORPIO	SAGITTARIUS	CAPRICORN	VIRGO	VIRGO	PISCES	LEO	CANCER
13	10:03 PM	CAPRICORN	SCORPIO	SAGITTARIUS	CAPRICORN	VIRGO	VIRGO	PISCES	LEO	CANCER
14			SCORPIO	SAGITTARIUS	CAPRICORN	VIRGO	VIRGO	PISCES	LEO	CANCER
15			SCORPIO	SAGITTARIUS	CAPRICORN	VIRGO	VIRGO	PISCES	LEO	CANCER
16	10:46 AM	AQUARIUS	SCORPIO	SAGITTARIUS	CAPRICORN	VIRGO	VIRGO	PISCES	LEO	CANCER
17			SCORPIO	SAGITTARIUS	CAPRICORN	VIRGO	VIRGO	PISCES	LEO	CANCER
18	10:37 PM	PISCES	SCORPIO	CAPRICORN	CAPRICORN	VIRGO	VIRGO	PISCES	LEO	CANCER
19			SCORPIO	CAPRICORN	CAPRICORN	VIRGO	VIRGO	PISCES	LEO	CANCER
20			SCORPIO	CAPRICORN	CAPRICORN	VIRGO	VIRGO	PISCES	LEO	CANCER
21	7:45 AM	ARIES	SCORPIO	CAPRICORN	CAPRICORN	VIRGO	VIRGO	PISCES	LEO	CANCER
22			SCORPIO	CAPRICORN	CAPRICORN	VIRGO	VIRGO	PISCES	LEO	CANCER

OCT.	MOON FROM	IN	MERCURY	VENUS	MARS	JUPITER	SATURN	URANUS	NEPTUNE	PLUTO
24			SCORPIO	LIBRA	VIRGO	LIBRA	LIBRA	PISCES	LEO	CANCER
25			SCORPIO	LIBRA	VIRGO	LIBRA	LIBRA	PISCES	LEO	CANCER
26	1:40 AM	VIRGO	SCORPIO	LIBRA	VIRGO	LIBRA	LIBRA	PISCES	LEO	CANCER
27			SCORPIO	LIBRA	VIRGO	LIBRA	LIBRA	PISCES	LEO	CANCER
28	3:49 AM	LIBRA	SCORPIO	LIBRA	VIRGO	LIBRA	LIBRA	PISCES	LEO	CANCER
29			SCORPIO	LIBRA	VIRGO	LIBRA	LIBRA	PISCES	LEO	CANCER
30	6:34 AM	SCORPIO	SCORPIO	LIBRA	VIRGO	LIBRA	LIBRA	PISCES	LEO	CANCER
31			SCORPIO	LIBRA	VIRGO	LIBRA	LIBRA	PISCES	LEO	CANCER
NOV.										
1	11:09 AM	SAGITTARIUS	SCORPIO	LIBRA	VIRGO	LIBRA	LIBRA	PISCES	LEO	CANCER
2			SCORPIO	LIBRA	VIRGO	LIBRA	LIBRA	PISCES	LEO	CANCER
3	6:38 PM	CAPRICORN	SCORPIO	LIBRA	VIRGO	LIBRA	LIBRA	PISCES	LEO	CANCER
4			SCORPIO	LIBRA	VIRGO	LIBRA	LIBRA	PISCES	LEO	CANCER
5			SCORPIO	LIBRA	VIRGO	LIBRA	LIBRA	PISCES	LEO	CANCER
6	5:18 AM	AQUARIUS	SCORPIO	LIBRA	VIRGO	LIBRA	LIBRA	PISCES	LEO	CANCER
7			SCORPIO	LIBRA	LIBRA	LIBRA	LIBRA	PISCES	LEO	CANCER
8	5:51 PM	PISCES	SCORPIO	LIBRA	LIBRA	LIBRA	LIBRA	PISCES	LEO	CANCER
9			SCORPIO	LIBRA	LIBRA	LIBRA	LIBRA	PISCES	LEO	CANCER
10			SCORPIO	LIBRA	LIBRA	LIBRA	LIBRA	PISCES	LEO	CANCER
11	5:52 AM	ARIES	SCORPIO	LIBRA	LIBRA	LIBRA	LIBRA	PISCES	LEO	CANCER
12			SCORPIO	LIBRA	LIBRA	LIBRA	LIBRA	PISCES	LEO	CANCER
13	3:19 PM	TAURUS	SCORPIO	LIBRA	LIBRA	LIBRA	LIBRA	PISCES	LEO	CANCER
14			SCORPIO	SCORPIO	LIBRA	LIBRA	LIBRA	PISCES	LEO	CANCER
15	9:40 PM	GEMINI	SCORPIO	SCORPIO	LIBRA	LIBRA	LIBRA	PISCES	LEO	CANCER
16			SCORPIO	SCORPIO	LIBRA	LIBRA	LIBRA	PISCES	LEO	CANCER
17			SCORPIO	SCORPIO	LIBRA	LIBRA	LIBRA	PISCES	LEO	CANCER
18	1:41 AM	CANCER	SCORPIO	SCORPIO	LIBRA	LIBRA	LIBRA	PISCES	LEO	CANCER
19			SCORPIO	SCORPIO	LIBRA	LIBRA	LIBRA	PISCES	LEO	CANCER
20	4:32 AM	LEO	SCORPIO	SCORPIO	LIBRA	LIBRA	LIBRA	PISCES	LEO	CANCER
21			SCORPIO	SCORPIO	LIBRA	LIBRA	LIBRA	PISCES	LEO	CANCER
22	7:17 AM	VIRGO	SCORPIO	SCORPIO	LIBRA	LIBRA	LIBRA	PISCES	LEO	CANCER

1922

SCORPIO

OCT.	MOON FROM	IN	MERCURY	VENUS	MARS	JUPITER	SATURN	URANUS	NEPTUNE	PLUTO
24	6:34 PM	CAPRICORN	LIBRA	SAGITTARIUS	CAPRICORN	LIBRA	LIBRA	PISCES	LEO	CANCER
25			LIBRA	SAGITTARIUS	CAPRICORN	LIBRA	LIBRA	PISCES	LEO	CANCER
26			LIBRA	SAGITTARIUS	CAPRICORN	LIBRA	LIBRA	PISCES	LEO	CANCER
27	2:01 AM	AQUARIUS	LIBRA	SAGITTARIUS	CAPRICORN	SCORPIO	LIBRA	PISCES	LEO	CANCER
28			LIBRA	SAGITTARIUS	CAPRICORN	SCORPIO	LIBRA	PISCES	LEO	CANCER
29	1:08 PM	PISCES	LIBRA	SAGITTARIUS	CAPRICORN	SCORPIO	LIBRA	PISCES	LEO	CANCER
30			LIBRA	SAGITTARIUS	CAPRICORN	SCORPIO	LIBRA	PISCES	LEO	CANCER
31			LIBRA	SAGITTARIUS	AQUARIUS	SCORPIO	LIBRA	PISCES	LEO	CANCER
NOV.										
1	2:04 AM	ARIES	LIBRA	SAGITTARIUS	AQUARIUS	SCORPIO	LIBRA	PISCES	LEO	CANCER
2			LIBRA	SAGITTARIUS	AQUARIUS	SCORPIO	LIBRA	PISCES	LEO	CANCER
3	2:39 PM	TAURUS	LIBRA	SAGITTARIUS	AQUARIUS	SCORPIO	LIBRA	PISCES	LEO	CANCER
4			LIBRA	SAGITTARIUS	AQUARIUS	SCORPIO	LIBRA	PISCES	LEO	CANCER
5			LIBRA	SAGITTARIUS	AQUARIUS	SCORPIO	LIBRA	PISCES	LEO	CANCER
6	1:33 AM	GEMINI	LIBRA	SAGITTARIUS	AQUARIUS	SCORPIO	LIBRA	PISCES	LEO	CANCER
7			LIBRA	SAGITTARIUS	AQUARIUS	SCORPIO	LIBRA	PISCES	LEO	CANCER
8	10:23 AM	CANCER	LIBRA	SAGITTARIUS	AQUARIUS	SCORPIO	LIBRA	PISCES	LEO	CANCER
9			SCORPIO	SAGITTARIUS	AQUARIUS	SCORPIO	LIBRA	PISCES	LEO	CANCER
10	5:05 PM	LEO	SCORPIO	SAGITTARIUS	AQUARIUS	SCORPIO	LIBRA	PISCES	LEO	CANCER
11			SCORPIO	SAGITTARIUS	AQUARIUS	SCORPIO	LIBRA	PISCES	LEO	CANCER
12	9:36 PM	VIRGO	SCORPIO	SAGITTARIUS	AQUARIUS	SCORPIO	LIBRA	PISCES	LEO	CANCER
13			SCORPIO	SAGITTARIUS	AQUARIUS	SCORPIO	LIBRA	PISCES	LEO	CANCER
14			SCORPIO	SAGITTARIUS	AQUARIUS	SCORPIO	LIBRA	PISCES	LEO	CANCER
15	0:01 AM	LIBRA	SCORPIO	SAGITTARIUS	AQUARIUS	SCORPIO	LIBRA	PISCES	LEO	CANCER
16			SCORPIO	SAGITTARIUS	AQUARIUS	SCORPIO	LIBRA	PISCES	LEO	CANCER
17	0:59 AM	SCORPIO	SCORPIO	SAGITTARIUS	AQUARIUS	SCORPIO	LIBRA	PISCES	LEO	CANCER
18			SCORPIO	SAGITTARIUS	AQUARIUS	SCORPIO	LIBRA	PISCES	LEO	CANCER
19	1:52 AM	SAGITTARIUS	SCORPIO	SAGITTARIUS	AQUARIUS	SCORPIO	LIBRA	PISCES	LEO	CANCER
20			SCORPIO	SAGITTARIUS	AQUARIUS	SCORPIO	LIBRA	PISCES	LEO	CANCER
21	3:20 AM	CAPRICORN	SCORPIO	SAGITTARIUS	AQUARIUS	SCORPIO	LIBRA	PISCES	LEO	CANCER
22			SCORPIO	SAGITTARIUS	AQUARIUS	SCORPIO	LIBRA	PISCES	LEO	CANCER

1923

OCT.	MOON FROM	IN	MERCURY	VENUS	MARS	JUPITER	SATURN	URANUS	NEPTUNE	PLUTO
24	12:48 PM	TAURUS	LIBRA	SCORPIO	LIBRA	SCORPIO	LIBRA	PISCES	LEO	CANCER
25			LIBRA	SCORPIO	LIBRA	SCORPIO	LIBRA	PISCES	LEO	CANCER
26			LIBRA	SCORPIO	LIBRA	SCORPIO	LIBRA	PISCES	LEO	CANCER
27	1:29 AM	GEMINI	LIBRA	SCORPIO	LIBRA	SCORPIO	LIBRA	PISCES	LEO	CANCER
28			LIBRA	SCORPIO	LIBRA	SCORPIO	LIBRA	PISCES	LEO	CANCER
29	1:39 PM	CANCER	LIBRA	SCORPIO	LIBRA	SCORPIO	LIBRA	PISCES	LEO	CANCER
30			LIBRA	SCORPIO	LIBRA	SCORPIO	LIBRA	PISCES	LEO	CANCER
31	11:59 PM	LEO	LIBRA	SCORPIO	LIBRA	SCORPIO	LIBRA	PISCES	LEO	CANCER
NOV.										
1			LIBRA	SCORPIO	LIBRA	SCORPIO	LIBRA	PISCES	LEO	CANCER
2			SCORPIO	SCORPIO	LIBRA	SCORPIO	LIBRA	PISCES	LEO	CANCER
3	7:07 AM	VIRGO	SCORPIO	SCORPIO	LIBRA	SCORPIO	LIBRA	PISCES	LEO	CANCER
4			SCORPIO	SCORPIO	LIBRA	SCORPIO	LIBRA	PISCES	LEO	CANCER
5	10:23 AM	LIBRA	SCORPIO	SCORPIO	LIBRA	SCORPIO	LIBRA	PISCES	LEO	CANCER
6			SCORPIO	SCORPIO	LIBRA	SCORPIO	LIBRA	PISCES	LEO	CANCER
7	10:37 AM	SCORPIO	SCORPIO	SCORPIO	LIBRA	SCORPIO	LIBRA	PISCES	LEO	CANCER
8			SCORPIO	SAGITTARIUS	LIBRA	SCORPIO	LIBRA	PISCES	LEO	CANCER
9	9:37 AM	SAGITTARIUS	SCORPIO	SAGITTARIUS	LIBRA	SCORPIO	LIBRA	PISCES	LEO	CANCER
10			SCORPIO	SAGITTARIUS	LIBRA	SCORPIO	LIBRA	PISCES	LEO	CANCER
11	9:38 AM	CAPRICORN	SCORPIO	SAGITTARIUS	LIBRA	SCORPIO	LIBRA	PISCES	LEO	CANCER
12			SCORPIO	SAGITTARIUS	LIBRA	SCORPIO	LIBRA	PISCES	LEO	CANCER
13	12:41 PM	AQUARIUS	SCORPIO	SAGITTARIUS	LIBRA	SCORPIO	LIBRA	PISCES	LEO	CANCER
14			SCORPIO	SAGITTARIUS	LIBRA	SCORPIO	LIBRA	PISCES	LEO	CANCER
15	7:47 PM	PISCES	SCORPIO	SAGITTARIUS	LIBRA	SCORPIO	LIBRA	PISCES	LEO	CANCER
16			SCORPIO	SAGITTARIUS	LIBRA	SCORPIO	LIBRA	PISCES	LEO	CANCER
17			SCORPIO	SAGITTARIUS	LIBRA	SCORPIO	LIBRA	PISCES	LEO	CANCER
18	6:25 AM	ARIES	SCORPIO	SAGITTARIUS	LIBRA	SCORPIO	LIBRA	PISCES	LEO	CANCER
19			SCORPIO	SAGITTARIUS	LIBRA	SCORPIO	LIBRA	PISCES	LEO	CANCER
20	6:35 PM	TAURUS	SCORPIO	SAGITTARIUS	LIBRA	SCORPIO	LIBRA	PISCES	LEO	CANCER
21			SAGITTARIUS	SAGITTARIUS	LIBRA	SCORPIO	LIBRA	PISCES	LEO	CANCER
22			SAGITTARIUS	SAGITTARIUS	LIBRA	SCORPIO	LIBRA	PISCES	LEO	CANCER

SCORPIO

OCT.	MOON FROM	IN	MERCURY	VENUS	MARS	JUPITER	SATURN	URANUS	NEPTUNE	PLUTO
24			LIBRA	VIRGO	PISCES	SAGITTARIUS	SCORPIO	PISCES	LEO	CANCER
25	3:48 PM	LIBRA	SCORPIO	VIRGO	PISCES	SAGITTARIUS	SCORPIO	PISCES	LEO	CANCER
26			SCORPIO	VIRGO	PISCES	SAGITTARIUS	SCORPIO	PISCES	LEO	CANCER
27	6:26 PM	SCORPIO	SCORPIO	VIRGO	PISCES	SAGITTARIUS	SCORPIO	PISCES	LEO	CANCER
28			SCORPIO	VIRGO	PISCES	SAGITTARIUS	SCORPIO	PISCES	LEO	CANCER
29	7:03 PM	SAGITTARIUS	SCORPIO	VIRGO	PISCES	SAGITTARIUS	SCORPIO	PISCES	LEO	CANCER
30			SCORPIO	VIRGO	PISCES	SAGITTARIUS	SCORPIO	PISCES	LEO	CANCER
31	7:39 PM	CAPRICORN	SCORPIO	VIRGO	PISCES	SAGITTARIUS	SCORPIO	PISCES	LEO	CANCER
NOV.										
1			SCORPIO	VIRGO	PISCES	SAGITTARIUS	SCORPIO	PISCES	LEO	CANCER
2	9:54 PM	AQUARIUS	SCORPIO	VIRGO	PISCES	SAGITTARIUS	SCORPIO	PISCES	LEO	CANCER
3			SCORPIO	LIBRA	PISCES	SAGITTARIUS	SCORPIO	PISCES	LEO	CANCER
4			SCORPIO	LIBRA	PISCES	SAGITTARIUS	SCORPIO	PISCES	LEO	CANCER
5	2:35 AM	PISCES	SCORPIO	LIBRA	PISCES	SAGITTARIUS	SCORPIO	PISCES	LEO	CANCER
6			SCORPIO	LIBRA	PISCES	SAGITTARIUS	SCORPIO	PISCES	LEO	CANCER
7	9:40 AM	ARIES	SCORPIO	LIBRA	PISCES	SAGITTARIUS	SCORPIO	PISCES	LEO	CANCER
8			SCORPIO	LIBRA	PISCES	SAGITTARIUS	SCORPIO	PISCES	LEO	CANCER
9	6:44 PM	TAURUS	SCORPIO	LIBRA	PISCES	SAGITTARIUS	SCORPIO	PISCES	LEO	CANCER
10			SCORPIO	LIBRA	PISCES	SAGITTARIUS	SCORPIO	PISCES	LEO	CANCER
11			SCORPIO	LIBRA	PISCES	SAGITTARIUS	SCORPIO	PISCES	LEO	CANCER
12	5:35 AM	GEMINI	SAGITTARIUS	LIBRA	PISCES	SAGITTARIUS	SCORPIO	PISCES	LEO	CANCER
13			SAGITTARIUS	LIBRA	PISCES	SAGITTARIUS	SCORPIO	PISCES	LEO	CANCER
14	5:57 PM	CANCER	SAGITTARIUS	LIBRA	PISCES	SAGITTARIUS	SCORPIO	PISCES	LEO	CANCER
15			SAGITTARIUS	LIBRA	PISCES	SAGITTARIUS	SCORPIO	PISCES	LEO	CANCER
16			SAGITTARIUS	LIBRA	PISCES	SAGITTARIUS	SCORPIO	PISCES	LEO	CANCER
17	6:51 AM	LEO	SAGITTARIUS	LIBRA	PISCES	SAGITTARIUS	SCORPIO	PISCES	LEO	CANCER
18			SAGITTARIUS	LIBRA	PISCES	SAGITTARIUS	SCORPIO	PISCES	LEO	CANCER
19	6:11 PM	VIRGO	SAGITTARIUS	LIBRA	PISCES	SAGITTARIUS	SCORPIO	PISCES	LEO	CANCER
20			SAGITTARIUS	LIBRA	PISCES	SAGITTARIUS	SCORPIO	PISCES	LEO	CANCER
21			SAGITTARIUS	LIBRA	PISCES	SAGITTARIUS	SCORPIO	PISCES	LEO	CANCER
22	1:50 AM	LIBRA	SAGITTARIUS	LIBRA	PISCES	SAGITTARIUS	SCORPIO	PISCES	LEO	CANCER

1925

OCT.	MOON FROM	IN	MERCURY	VENUS	MARS	JUPITER	SATURN	URANUS	NEPTUNE	PLUTO
24	12:12 PM	AQUARIUS	SCORPIO	SAGITTARIUS	LIBRA	CAPRICORN	SCORPIO	PISCES	LEO	CANCER
25			SCORPIO	SAGITTARIUS	LIBRA	CAPRICORN	SCORPIO	PISCES	LEO	CANCER
26	3:14 PM	PISCES	SCORPIO	SAGITTARIUS	LIBRA	CAPRICORN	SCORPIO	PISCES	LEO	CANCER
27			SCORPIO	SAGITTARIUS	LIBRA	CAPRICORN	SCORPIO	PISCES	LEO	CANCER
28	6:24 PM	ARIES	SCORPIO	SAGITTARIUS	LIBRA	CAPRICORN	SCORPIO	PISCES	LEO	CANCER
29			SCORPIO	SAGITTARIUS	LIBRA	CAPRICORN	SCORPIO	PISCES	LEO	CANCER
30	10:30 PM	TAURUS	SCORPIO	SAGITTARIUS	LIBRA	CAPRICORN	SCORPIO	PISCES	LEO	CANCER
31			SCORPIO	SAGITTARIUS	LIBRA	CAPRICORN	SCORPIO	PISCES	LEO	CANCER
NOV.										
1			SCORPIO	SAGITTARIUS	LIBRA	CAPRICORN	SCORPIO	PISCES	LEO	CANCER
2	4:45 AM	GEMINI	SCORPIO	SAGITTARIUS	LIBRA	CAPRICORN	SCORPIO	PISCES	LEO	CANCER
3			SCORPIO	SAGITTARIUS	LIBRA	CAPRICORN	SCORPIO	PISCES	LEO	CANCER
4	2:07 PM	CANCER	SCORPIO	SAGITTARIUS	LIBRA	CAPRICORN	SCORPIO	PISCES	LEO	CANCER
5			SCORPIO	SAGITTARIUS	LIBRA	CAPRICORN	SCORPIO	PISCES	LEO	CANCER
6			SAGITTARIUS	SAGITTARIUS	LIBRA	CAPRICORN	SCORPIO	PISCES	LEO	CANCER
7	2:16 AM	LEO	SAGITTARIUS	CAPRICORN	LIBRA	CAPRICORN	SCORPIO	PISCES	LEO	CANCER
8			SAGITTARIUS	CAPRICORN	LIBRA	CAPRICORN	SCORPIO	PISCES	LEO	CANCER
9	3:06 PM	VIRGO	SAGITTARIUS	CAPRICORN	LIBRA	CAPRICORN	SCORPIO	PISCES	LEO	CANCER
10			SAGITTARIUS	CAPRICORN	LIBRA	CAPRICORN	SCORPIO	PISCES	LEO	CANCER
11			SAGITTARIUS	CAPRICORN	LIBRA	CAPRICORN	SCORPIO	PISCES	LEO	CANCER
12	1:51 AM	LIBRA	SAGITTARIUS	CAPRICORN	LIBRA	CAPRICORN	SCORPIO	PISCES	LEO	CANCER
13			SAGITTARIUS	CAPRICORN	LIBRA	CAPRICORN	SCORPIO	PISCES	LEO	CANCER
14	9:05 AM	SCORPIO	SAGITTARIUS	CAPRICORN	SCORPIO	CAPRICORN	SCORPIO	PISCES	LEO	CANCER
15			SAGITTARIUS	CAPRICORN	SCORPIO	CAPRICORN	SCORPIO	PISCES	LEO	CANCER
16	1:12 PM	SAGITTARIUS	SAGITTARIUS	CAPRICORN	SCORPIO	CAPRICORN	SCORPIO	PISCES	LEO	CANCER
17			SAGITTARIUS	CAPRICORN	SCORPIO	CAPRICORN	SCORPIO	PISCES	LEO	CANCER
18	3:38 PM	CAPRICORN	SAGITTARIUS	CAPRICORN	SCORPIO	CAPRICORN	SCORPIO	PISCES	LEO	CANCER
19			SAGITTARIUS	CAPRICORN	SCORPIO	CAPRICORN	SCORPIO	PISCES	LEO	CANCER
20	5:48 PM	AQUARIUS	SAGITTARIUS	CAPRICORN	SCORPIO	CAPRICORN	SCORPIO	PISCES	LEO	CANCER
21			SAGITTARIUS	CAPRICORN	SCORPIO	CAPRICORN	SCORPIO	PISCES	LEO	CANCER
22	8:38 PM	PISCES	SAGITTARIUS	CAPRICORN	SCORPIO	CAPRICORN	SCORPIO	PISCES	LEO	CANCER

SCORPIO

MOON FROM IN	MERCURY	VENUS	MARS	JUPITER	SATURN	URANUS	NEPTUNE	PLUTO
OCT.								
24		SCORPIO	LIBRA	TAURUS	AQUARIUS	SCORPIO	PISCES	LEO	CANCER
25 12:10 PM CANCER	SCORPIO	LIBRA	TAURUS	AQUARIUS	SCORPIO	PISCES	LEO	CANCER
26	SCORPIO	LIBRA	TAURUS	AQUARIUS	SCORPIO	PISCES	LEO	CANCER
27 9:31 PM LEO	SCORPIO	LIBRA	TAURUS	AQUARIUS	SCORPIO	PISCES	LEO	CANCER
28	SCORPIO	LIBRA	TAURUS	AQUARIUS	SCORPIO	PISCES	LEO	CANCER
29	SCORPIO	LIBRA	TAURUS	AQUARIUS	SCORPIO	PISCES	LEO	CANCER
30 9:43 AM VIRGO	SCORPIO	SCORPIO	TAURUS	AQUARIUS	SCORPIO	PISCES	LEO	CANCER
31	SAGITTARIUS	SCORPIO	TAURUS	AQUARIUS	SCORPIO	PISCES	LEO	CANCER
NOV.								
1 10:22 PM LIBRA	SAGITTARIUS	SCORPIO	TAURUS	AQUARIUS	SCORPIO	PISCES	LEO	CANCER
2	SAGITTARIUS	SCORPIO	TAURUS	AQUARIUS	SCORPIO	PISCES	LEO	CANCER
3	SAGITTARIUS	SCORPIO	TAURUS	AQUARIUS	SCORPIO	PISCES	LEO	CANCER
4 9:37 AM SCORPIO	SAGITTARIUS	SCORPIO	TAURUS	AQUARIUS	SCORPIO	PISCES	LEO	CANCER
5	SAGITTARIUS	SCORPIO	TAURUS	AQUARIUS	SCORPIO	PISCES	LEO	CANCER
6 6:51 PM SAGITTARIUS	SAGITTARIUS	SCORPIO	TAURUS	AQUARIUS	SCORPIO	PISCES	LEO	CANCER
7	SAGITTARIUS	SCORPIO	TAURUS	AQUARIUS	SCORPIO	PISCES	LEO	CANCER
8	SAGITTARIUS	SCORPIO	TAURUS	AQUARIUS	SCORPIO	PISCES	LEO	CANCER
9 2:10 AM CAPRICORN	SAGITTARIUS	SCORPIO	TAURUS	AQUARIUS	SCORPIO	PISCES	LEO	CANCER
10	SAGITTARIUS	SCORPIO	TAURUS	AQUARIUS	SCORPIO	PISCES	LEO	CANCER
11 7:42 AM AQUARIUS	SAGITTARIUS	SCORPIO	TAURUS	AQUARIUS	SCORPIO	PISCES	LEO	CANCER
12	SAGITTARIUS	SCORPIO	TAURUS	AQUARIUS	SCORPIO	PISCES	LEO	CANCER
13 11:21 AM PISCES	SAGITTARIUS	SCORPIO	TAURUS	AQUARIUS	SCORPIO	PISCES	LEO	CANCER
14	SAGITTARIUS	SCORPIO	TAURUS	AQUARIUS	SCORPIO	PISCES	LEO	CANCER
15 1:28 PM ARIES	SAGITTARIUS	SCORPIO	TAURUS	AQUARIUS	SCORPIO	PISCES	LEO	CANCER
16	SAGITTARIUS	SCORPIO	TAURUS	AQUARIUS	SCORPIO	PISCES	LEO	CANCER
17 2:54 PM TAURUS	SAGITTARIUS	SCORPIO	TAURUS	AQUARIUS	SCORPIO	PISCES	LEO	CANCER
18	SAGITTARIUS	SCORPIO	TAURUS	AQUARIUS	SCORPIO	PISCES	LEO	CANCER
19 5:11 PM GEMINI	SAGITTARIUS	SCORPIO	TAURUS	AQUARIUS	SCORPIO	PISCES	LEO	CANCER
20	SAGITTARIUS	SCORPIO	TAURUS	AQUARIUS	SCORPIO	PISCES	LEO	CANCER
21 9:55 PM CANCER	SAGITTARIUS	SCORPIO	TAURUS	AQUARIUS	SCORPIO	PISCES	LEO	CANCER
22	SAGITTARIUS	SCORPIO	TAURUS	AQUARIUS	SCORPIO	PISCES	LEO	CANCER

1927

MOON FROM IN	MERCURY	VENUS	MARS	JUPITER	SATURN	URANUS	NEPTUNE	PLUTO
OCT.								
24		SCORPIO	VIRGO	LIBRA	PISCES	SAGITTARIUS	ARIES	LEO	CANCER
25 8:08 AM SCORPIO	SCORPIO	VIRGO	LIBRA	PISCES	SAGITTARIUS	ARIES	LEO	CANCER
26	SCORPIO	VIRGO	SCORPIO	PISCES	SAGITTARIUS	ARIES	LEO	CANCER
27 8:48 PM SAGITTARIUS	SCORPIO	VIRGO	SCORPIO	PISCES	SAGITTARIUS	ARIES	LEO	CANCER
28	SCORPIO	VIRGO	SCORPIO	PISCES	SAGITTARIUS	ARIES	LEO	CANCER
29	SCORPIO	VIRGO	SCORPIO	PISCES	SAGITTARIUS	ARIES	LEO	CANCER
30 8:22 AM CAPRICORN	SCORPIO	VIRGO	SCORPIO	PISCES	SAGITTARIUS	ARIES	LEO	CANCER
31	SCORPIO	VIRGO	SCORPIO	PISCES	SAGITTARIUS	ARIES	LEO	CANCER
NOV.								
1 5:26 PM AQUARIUS	SCORPIO	VIRGO	SCORPIO	PISCES	SAGITTARIUS	ARIES	LEO	CANCER
2	SCORPIO	VIRGO	SCORPIO	PISCES	SAGITTARIUS	ARIES	LEO	CANCER
3 10:55 PM PISCES	SCORPIO	VIRGO	SCORPIO	PISCES	SAGITTARIUS	ARIES	LEO	CANCER
4	SCORPIO	VIRGO	SCORPIO	PISCES	SAGITTARIUS	ARIES	LEO	CANCER
5	SCORPIO	VIRGO	SCORPIO	PISCES	SAGITTARIUS	PISCES	LEO	CANCER
6 0:53 AM ARIES	SCORPIO	VIRGO	SCORPIO	PISCES	SAGITTARIUS	PISCES	LEO	CANCER
7	SCORPIO	VIRGO	SCORPIO	PISCES	SAGITTARIUS	PISCES	LEO	CANCER
8 0:37 AM TAURUS	SCORPIO	VIRGO	SCORPIO	PISCES	SAGITTARIUS	PISCES	LEO	CANCER
9	SCORPIO	VIRGO	SCORPIO	PISCES	SAGITTARIUS	PISCES	LEO	CANCER
10 0:04 AM GEMINI	SCORPIO	LIBRA	SCORPIO	PISCES	SAGITTARIUS	PISCES	LEO	CANCER
11	SCORPIO	LIBRA	SCORPIO	PISCES	SAGITTARIUS	PISCES	LEO	CANCER
12 1:17 AM CANCER	SCORPIO	LIBRA	SCORPIO	PISCES	SAGITTARIUS	PISCES	LEO	CANCER
13	SCORPIO	LIBRA	SCORPIO	PISCES	SAGITTARIUS	PISCES	LEO	CANCER
14 5:49 AM LEO	SCORPIO	LIBRA	SCORPIO	PISCES	SAGITTARIUS	PISCES	LEO	CANCER
15	SCORPIO	LIBRA	SCORPIO	PISCES	SAGITTARIUS	PISCES	LEO	CANCER
16 2:15 PM VIRGO	SCORPIO	LIBRA	SCORPIO	PISCES	SAGITTARIUS	PISCES	LEO	CANCER
17	SCORPIO	LIBRA	SCORPIO	PISCES	SAGITTARIUS	PISCES	LEO	CANCER
18	SCORPIO	LIBRA	SCORPIO	PISCES	SAGITTARIUS	PISCES	LEO	CANCER
19 1:41 AM LIBRA	SCORPIO	LIBRA	SCORPIO	PISCES	SAGITTARIUS	PISCES	LEO	CANCER
20	SCORPIO	LIBRA	SCORPIO	PISCES	SAGITTARIUS	PISCES	LEO	CANCER
21 2:27 PM SCORPIO	SCORPIO	LIBRA	SCORPIO	PISCES	SAGITTARIUS	PISCES	LEO	CANCER
22	SCORPIO	LIBRA	SCORPIO	PISCES	SAGITTARIUS	PISCES	LEO	CANCER

1928

MOON FROM IN	MERCURY	VENUS	MARS	JUPITER	SATURN	URANUS	NEPTUNE	PLUTO
OCT.								
24 3:49 AM PISCES	SCORPIO	SAGITTARIUS	CANCER	TAURUS	SAGITTARIUS	ARIES	VIRGO	CANCER
25	LIBRA	SAGITTARIUS	CANCER	TAURUS	SAGITTARIUS	ARIES	VIRGO	CANCER
26 8:04 AM ARIES	LIBRA	SAGITTARIUS	CANCER	TAURUS	SAGITTARIUS	ARIES	VIRGO	CANCER
27	LIBRA	SAGITTARIUS	CANCER	TAURUS	SAGITTARIUS	ARIES	VIRGO	CANCER
28 9:16 AM TAURUS	LIBRA	SAGITTARIUS	CANCER	TAURUS	SAGITTARIUS	ARIES	VIRGO	CANCER
29	LIBRA	SAGITTARIUS	CANCER	TAURUS	SAGITTARIUS	ARIES	VIRGO	CANCER
30 9:11 AM GEMINI	LIBRA	SAGITTARIUS	CANCER	TAURUS	SAGITTARIUS	ARIES	VIRGO	CANCER
31	LIBRA	SAGITTARIUS	CANCER	TAURUS	SAGITTARIUS	ARIES	VIRGO	CANCER
NOV.								
1 9:41 AM CANCER	LIBRA	SAGITTARIUS	CANCER	TAURUS	SAGITTARIUS	ARIES	VIRGO	CANCER
2	LIBRA	SAGITTARIUS	CANCER	TAURUS	SAGITTARIUS	ARIES	VIRGO	CANCER
3 12:15 PM LEO	LIBRA	SAGITTARIUS	CANCER	TAURUS	SAGITTARIUS	ARIES	VIRGO	CANCER
4	LIBRA	SAGITTARIUS	CANCER	TAURUS	SAGITTARIUS	ARIES	VIRGO	CANCER
5 5:42 PM VIRGO	LIBRA	SAGITTARIUS	CANCER	TAURUS	SAGITTARIUS	ARIES	VIRGO	CANCER
6	LIBRA	SAGITTARIUS	CANCER	TAURUS	SAGITTARIUS	ARIES	VIRGO	CANCER
7	LIBRA	SAGITTARIUS	CANCER	TAURUS	SAGITTARIUS	ARIES	VIRGO	CANCER
8 2:06 AM LIBRA	LIBRA	SAGITTARIUS	CANCER	TAURUS	SAGITTARIUS	ARIES	VIRGO	CANCER
9	LIBRA	SAGITTARIUS	CANCER	TAURUS	SAGITTARIUS	ARIES	VIRGO	CANCER
10 12:54 PM SCORPIO	LIBRA	SAGITTARIUS	CANCER	TAURUS	SAGITTARIUS	ARIES	VIRGO	CANCER
11	SCORPIO	SAGITTARIUS	CANCER	TAURUS	SAGITTARIUS	ARIES	VIRGO	CANCER
12	SCORPIO	SAGITTARIUS	CANCER	TAURUS	SAGITTARIUS	ARIES	VIRGO	CANCER
13 1:20 AM SAGITTARIUS	SCORPIO	SAGITTARIUS	CANCER	TAURUS	SAGITTARIUS	ARIES	VIRGO	CANCER
14	SCORPIO	SAGITTARIUS	CANCER	TAURUS	SAGITTARIUS	ARIES	VIRGO	CANCER
15 2:25 PM CAPRICORN	SCORPIO	SAGITTARIUS	CANCER	TAURUS	SAGITTARIUS	ARIES	VIRGO	CANCER
16	SCORPIO	SAGITTARIUS	CANCER	TAURUS	SAGITTARIUS	ARIES	VIRGO	CANCER
17	SCORPIO	CAPRICORN	CANCER	TAURUS	SAGITTARIUS	ARIES	VIRGO	CANCER
18 1:39 AM AQUARIUS	SCORPIO	CAPRICORN	CANCER	TAURUS	SAGITTARIUS	ARIES	VIRGO	CANCER
19	SCORPIO	CAPRICORN	CANCER	TAURUS	SAGITTARIUS	ARIES	VIRGO	CANCER
20 12:18 PM PISCES	SCORPIO	CAPRICORN	CANCER	TAURUS	SAGITTARIUS	ARIES	VIRGO	CANCER
21	SCORPIO	CAPRICORN	CANCER	TAURUS	SAGITTARIUS	ARIES	VIRGO	CANCER
22 6:14 PM ARIES	SCORPIO	CAPRICORN	CANCER	TAURUS	SAGITTARIUS	ARIES	VIRGO	CANCER

1929

MOON FROM IN	MERCURY	VENUS	MARS	JUPITER	SATURN	URANUS	NEPTUNE	PLUTO
OCT.								
24	LIBRA	LIBRA	SCORPIO	GEMINI	SAGITTARIUS	ARIES	VIRGO	CANCER
25 0:55 AM LEO	LIBRA	LIBRA	SCORPIO	GEMINI	SAGITTARIUS	ARIES	VIRGO	CANCER
26	LIBRA	LIBRA	SCORPIO	GEMINI	SAGITTARIUS	ARIES	VIRGO	CANCER
27 4:09 AM VIRGO	LIBRA	LIBRA	SCORPIO	GEMINI	SAGITTARIUS	ARIES	VIRGO	CANCER
28	LIBRA	LIBRA	SCORPIO	GEMINI	SAGITTARIUS	ARIES	VIRGO	CANCER
29 8:39 AM LIBRA	LIBRA	LIBRA	SCORPIO	GEMINI	SAGITTARIUS	ARIES	VIRGO	CANCER
30	LIBRA	LIBRA	SCORPIO	GEMINI	SAGITTARIUS	ARIES	VIRGO	CANCER
31 3:02 PM SCORPIO	LIBRA	LIBRA	SCORPIO	GEMINI	SAGITTARIUS	ARIES	VIRGO	CANCER
NOV.								
1	LIBRA	LIBRA	SCORPIO	GEMINI	SAGITTARIUS	ARIES	VIRGO	CANCER
2 11:47 PM SAGITTARIUS	LIBRA	LIBRA	SCORPIO	GEMINI	SAGITTARIUS	ARIES	VIRGO	CANCER
3	LIBRA	SAGITTARIUS	SCORPIO	GEMINI	SAGITTARIUS	ARIES	VIRGO	CANCER
4	LIBRA	LIBRA	SCORPIO	GEMINI	SAGITTARIUS	ARIES	VIRGO	CANCER
5 10:57 AM CAPRICORN	LIBRA	LIBRA	SCORPIO	GEMINI	SAGITTARIUS	ARIES	VIRGO	CANCER
6	SCORPIO	LIBRA	SCORPIO	GEMINI	SAGITTARIUS	ARIES	VIRGO	CANCER
7 11:33 PM AQUARIUS	SCORPIO	LIBRA	SCORPIO	GEMINI	SAGITTARIUS	ARIES	VIRGO	CANCER
8	SCORPIO	LIBRA	SCORPIO	GEMINI	SAGITTARIUS	ARIES	VIRGO	CANCER
9	SCORPIO	LIBRA	SCORPIO	GEMINI	SAGITTARIUS	ARIES	VIRGO	CANCER
10 11:30 AM PISCES	SCORPIO	LIBRA	SCORPIO	GEMINI	SAGITTARIUS	ARIES	VIRGO	CANCER
11	SCORPIO	LIBRA	SCORPIO	GEMINI	SAGITTARIUS	ARIES	VIRGO	CANCER
12 8:43 PM ARIES	SCORPIO	LIBRA	SCORPIO	GEMINI	SAGITTARIUS	ARIES	VIRGO	CANCER
13	SCORPIO	SCORPIO	SCORPIO	GEMINI	SAGITTARIUS	ARIES	VIRGO	CANCER
14	SCORPIO	SCORPIO	SCORPIO	GEMINI	SAGITTARIUS	ARIES	VIRGO	CANCER
15 2:19 AM TAURUS	SCORPIO	SCORPIO	SCORPIO	GEMINI	SAGITTARIUS	ARIES	VIRGO	CANCER
16	SCORPIO	SCORPIO	SCORPIO	GEMINI	SAGITTARIUS	ARIES	VIRGO	CANCER
17 4:53 AM GEMINI	SCORPIO	SCORPIO	SCORPIO	GEMINI	SAGITTARIUS	ARIES	VIRGO	CANCER
18	SCORPIO	SCORPIO	SCORPIO	GEMINI	SAGITTARIUS	ARIES	VIRGO	CANCER
19 5:53 AM CANCER	SCORPIO	SCORPIO	SAGITTARIUS	GEMINI	SAGITTARIUS	ARIES	VIRGO	CANCER
20	SCORPIO	SCORPIO	SAGITTARIUS	GEMINI	SAGITTARIUS	ARIES	VIRGO	CANCER
21 6:58 AM LEO	SCORPIO	SCORPIO	SAGITTARIUS	GEMINI	SAGITTARIUS	ARIES	VIRGO	CANCER
22	SCORPIO	SCORPIO	SAGITTARIUS	GEMINI	SAGITTARIUS	ARIES	VIRGO	CANCER

1930 SCORPIO

DATE	MOON FROM IN	MERCURY	VENUS	MARS	JUPITER	SATURN	URANUS	NEPTUNE	PLUTO
OCT.									
24	0:25 AM SAGITTARIUS	LIBRA	SAGITTARIUS	LEO	CANCER	CAPRICORN	ARIES	VIRGO	CANCER
25		LIBRA	SAGITTARIUS	LEO	CANCER	CAPRICORN	ARIES	VIRGO	CANCER
26	7:27 AM CAPRICORN	LIBRA	SAGITTARIUS	LEO	CANCER	CAPRICORN	ARIES	VIRGO	CANCER
27		LIBRA	SAGITTARIUS	LEO	CANCER	CAPRICORN	ARIES	VIRGO	CANCER
28	5:54 PM AQUARIUS	LIBRA	SAGITTARIUS	LEO	CANCER	CAPRICORN	ARIES	VIRGO	CANCER
29		LIBRA	SAGITTARIUS	LEO	CANCER	CAPRICORN	ARIES	VIRGO	CANCER
30		SCORPIO	SAGITTARIUS	LEO	CANCER	CAPRICORN	ARIES	VIRGO	CANCER
31	6:23 AM PISCES	SCORPIO	SAGITTARIUS	LEO	CANCER	CAPRICORN	ARIES	VIRGO	CANCER
NOV.									
1		SCORPIO	SAGITTARIUS	LEO	CANCER	CAPRICORN	ARIES	VIRGO	CANCER
2	6:35 PM ARIES	SCORPIO	SAGITTARIUS	LEO	CANCER	CAPRICORN	ARIES	VIRGO	CANCER
3		SCORPIO	SAGITTARIUS	LEO	CANCER	CAPRICORN	ARIES	VIRGO	CANCER
4		SCORPIO	SAGITTARIUS	LEO	CANCER	CAPRICORN	ARIES	VIRGO	CANCER
5	4:37 AM TAURUS	SCORPIO	SAGITTARIUS	LEO	CANCER	CAPRICORN	ARIES	VIRGO	CANCER
6		SCORPIO	SAGITTARIUS	LEO	CANCER	CAPRICORN	ARIES	VIRGO	CANCER
7	11:58 AM GEMINI	SCORPIO	SAGITTARIUS	LEO	CANCER	CAPRICORN	ARIES	VIRGO	CANCER
8		SCORPIO	SAGITTARIUS	LEO	CANCER	CAPRICORN	ARIES	VIRGO	CANCER
9	5:05 PM CANCER	SCORPIO	SAGITTARIUS	LEO	CANCER	CAPRICORN	ARIES	VIRGO	CANCER
10		SCORPIO	SAGITTARIUS	LEO	CANCER	CAPRICORN	ARIES	VIRGO	CANCER
11	8:45 PM LEO	SCORPIO	SAGITTARIUS	LEO	CANCER	CAPRICORN	ARIES	VIRGO	CANCER
12		SCORPIO	SAGITTARIUS	LEO	CANCER	CAPRICORN	ARIES	VIRGO	CANCER
13	11:41 PM VIRGO	SCORPIO	SAGITTARIUS	LEO	CANCER	CAPRICORN	ARIES	VIRGO	CANCER
14		SCORPIO	SAGITTARIUS	LEO	CANCER	CAPRICORN	ARIES	VIRGO	CANCER
15		SCORPIO	SAGITTARIUS	LEO	CANCER	CAPRICORN	ARIES	VIRGO	CANCER
16	2:27 AM LIBRA	SCORPIO	SAGITTARIUS	LEO	CANCER	CAPRICORN	ARIES	VIRGO	CANCER
17		SAGITTARIUS	SAGITTARIUS	LEO	CANCER	CAPRICORN	ARIES	VIRGO	CANCER
18	5:37 AM SCORPIO	SAGITTARIUS	SAGITTARIUS	LEO	CANCER	CAPRICORN	ARIES	VIRGO	CANCER
19		SAGITTARIUS	SAGITTARIUS	LEO	CANCER	CAPRICORN	ARIES	VIRGO	CANCER
20	10:01 AM SAGITTARIUS	SAGITTARIUS	SAGITTARIUS	LEO	CANCER	CAPRICORN	ARIES	VIRGO	CANCER
21		SAGITTARIUS	SAGITTARIUS	LEO	CANCER	CAPRICORN	ARIES	VIRGO	CANCER
22	4:43 PM CAPRICORN	SAGITTARIUS	SCORPIO	LEO	CANCER	CAPRICORN	ARIES	VIRGO	CANCER

1931

DATE	MOON FROM IN	MERCURY	VENUS	MARS	JUPITER	SATURN	URANUS	NEPTUNE	PLUTO
OCT.									
24		SCORPIO	SCORPIO	SCORPIO	LEO	CAPRICORN	ARIES	VIRGO	CANCER
25		SCORPIO	SCORPIO	SCORPIO	LEO	CAPRICORN	ARIES	VIRGO	CANCER
26	4:12 AM TAURUS	SCORPIO	SCORPIO	SCORPIO	LEO	CAPRICORN	ARIES	VIRGO	CANCER
27		SCORPIO	SCORPIO	SCORPIO	LEO	CAPRICORN	ARIES	VIRGO	CANCER
28	3:47 PM GEMINI	SCORPIO	SCORPIO	SCORPIO	LEO	CAPRICORN	ARIES	VIRGO	CANCER
29		SCORPIO	SCORPIO	SCORPIO	LEO	CAPRICORN	ARIES	VIRGO	CANCER
30		SCORPIO	SCORPIO	SCORPIO	LEO	CAPRICORN	ARIES	VIRGO	CANCER
31	1:26 AM CANCER	SCORPIO	SCORPIO	SAGITTARIUS	LEO	CAPRICORN	ARIES	VIRGO	CANCER
NOV.									
1		SCORPIO	SCORPIO	SAGITTARIUS	LEO	CAPRICORN	ARIES	VIRGO	CANCER
2	8:38 AM LEO	SCORPIO	SCORPIO	SAGITTARIUS	LEO	CAPRICORN	ARIES	VIRGO	CANCER
3		SCORPIO	SCORPIO	SAGITTARIUS	LEO	CAPRICORN	ARIES	VIRGO	CANCER
4	1:07 PM VIRGO	SCORPIO	SCORPIO	SAGITTARIUS	LEO	CAPRICORN	ARIES	VIRGO	CANCER
5		SCORPIO	SCORPIO	SAGITTARIUS	LEO	CAPRICORN	ARIES	VIRGO	CANCER
6	3:02 PM LIBRA	SCORPIO	SCORPIO	SAGITTARIUS	LEO	CAPRICORN	ARIES	VIRGO	CANCER
7		SCORPIO	SCORPIO	SAGITTARIUS	LEO	CAPRICORN	ARIES	VIRGO	CANCER
8	3:21 PM SCORPIO	SCORPIO	SAGITTARIUS	SAGITTARIUS	LEO	CAPRICORN	ARIES	VIRGO	CANCER
9		SCORPIO	SAGITTARIUS	SAGITTARIUS	LEO	CAPRICORN	ARIES	VIRGO	CANCER
10	3:39 PM SAGITTARIUS	SAGITTARIUS	SAGITTARIUS	SAGITTARIUS	LEO	CAPRICORN	ARIES	VIRGO	CANCER
11		SAGITTARIUS	SAGITTARIUS	SAGITTARIUS	LEO	CAPRICORN	ARIES	VIRGO	CANCER
12	5:53 PM CAPRICORN	SAGITTARIUS	SAGITTARIUS	SAGITTARIUS	LEO	CAPRICORN	ARIES	VIRGO	CANCER
13		SAGITTARIUS	SAGITTARIUS	SAGITTARIUS	LEO	CAPRICORN	ARIES	VIRGO	CANCER
14	11:42 PM AQUARIUS	SAGITTARIUS	SAGITTARIUS	SAGITTARIUS	LEO	CAPRICORN	ARIES	VIRGO	CANCER
15		SAGITTARIUS	SAGITTARIUS	SAGITTARIUS	LEO	CAPRICORN	ARIES	VIRGO	CANCER
16		SAGITTARIUS	SAGITTARIUS	SAGITTARIUS	LEO	CAPRICORN	ARIES	VIRGO	CANCER
17	9:33 AM PISCES	SAGITTARIUS	SAGITTARIUS	SAGITTARIUS	LEO	CAPRICORN	ARIES	VIRGO	CANCER
18		SAGITTARIUS	SAGITTARIUS	SAGITTARIUS	LEO	CAPRICORN	ARIES	VIRGO	CANCER
19	10:09 PM ARIES	SAGITTARIUS	SAGITTARIUS	SAGITTARIUS	LEO	CAPRICORN	ARIES	VIRGO	CANCER
20		SAGITTARIUS	SAGITTARIUS	SAGITTARIUS	LEO	CAPRICORN	ARIES	VIRGO	CANCER
21		SAGITTARIUS	SAGITTARIUS	SAGITTARIUS	LEO	CAPRICORN	ARIES	VIRGO	CANCER
22	10:59 AM TAURUS	SAGITTARIUS	SAGITTARIUS	SAGITTARIUS	LEO	CAPRICORN	ARIES	VIRGO	CANCER

SCORPIO

OCT.	MOON FROM	IN	MERCURY	VENUS	MARS	JUPITER	SATURN	URANUS	NEPTUNE	PLUTO
24	9:03 PM	VIRGO	SCORPIO	VIRGO	LEO	VIRGO	CAPRICORN	ARIES	VIRGO	CANCER
25			SCORPIO	VIRGO	LEO	VIRGO	CAPRICORN	ARIES	VIRGO	CANCER
26			SCORPIO	VIRGO	LEO	VIRGO	CAPRICORN	ARIES	VIRGO	CANCER
27	0:16 AM	LIBRA	SCORPIO	VIRGO	LEO	VIRGO	CAPRICORN	ARIES	VIRGO	CANCER
28			SCORPIO	VIRGO	LEO	VIRGO	CAPRICORN	ARIES	VIRGO	CANCER
29	0:31 AM	SCORPIO	SCORPIO	VIRGO	LEO	VIRGO	CAPRICORN	ARIES	VIRGO	CANCER
30	11:40 PM	SAGITTARIUS	SCORPIO	VIRGO	LEO	VIRGO	CAPRICORN	ARIES	VIRGO	CANCER
31			SCORPIO	VIRGO	LEO	VIRGO	CAPRICORN	ARIES	VIRGO	CANCER
NOV.										
1	11:55 PM	CAPRICORN	SCORPIO	VIRGO	LEO	VIRGO	CAPRICORN	ARIES	VIRGO	CANCER
2			SCORPIO	LIBRA	LEO	VIRGO	CAPRICORN	ARIES	VIRGO	CANCER
3			SAGITTARIUS	LIBRA	LEO	VIRGO	CAPRICORN	ARIES	VIRGO	CANCER
4	3:06 AM	AQUARIUS	SAGITTARIUS	LIBRA	LEO	VIRGO	CAPRICORN	ARIES	VIRGO	CANCER
5			SAGITTARIUS	LIBRA	LEO	VIRGO	CAPRICORN	ARIES	VIRGO	CANCER
6	10:07 AM	PISCES	SAGITTARIUS	LIBRA	LEO	VIRGO	CAPRICORN	ARIES	VIRGO	CANCER
7			SAGITTARIUS	LIBRA	LEO	VIRGO	CAPRICORN	ARIES	VIRGO	CANCER
8	8:25 PM	ARIES	SAGITTARIUS	LIBRA	LEO	VIRGO	CAPRICORN	ARIES	VIRGO	CANCER
9			SAGITTARIUS	LIBRA	LEO	VIRGO	CAPRICORN	ARIES	VIRGO	CANCER
10			SAGITTARIUS	LIBRA	LEO	VIRGO	CAPRICORN	ARIES	VIRGO	CANCER
11	8:34 AM	TAURUS	SAGITTARIUS	LIBRA	LEO	VIRGO	CAPRICORN	ARIES	VIRGO	CANCER
12			SAGITTARIUS	LIBRA	LEO	VIRGO	CAPRICORN	ARIES	VIRGO	CANCER
13	9:13 PM	GEMINI	SAGITTARIUS	LIBRA	LEO	VIRGO	CAPRICORN	ARIES	VIRGO	CANCER
14			SAGITTARIUS	LIBRA	VIRGO	VIRGO	CAPRICORN	ARIES	VIRGO	CANCER
15			SAGITTARIUS	LIBRA	VIRGO	VIRGO	CAPRICORN	ARIES	VIRGO	CANCER
16	9:32 AM	CANCER	SAGITTARIUS	LIBRA	VIRGO	VIRGO	CAPRICORN	ARIES	VIRGO	CANCER
17			SAGITTARIUS	LIBRA	VIRGO	VIRGO	CAPRICORN	ARIES	VIRGO	CANCER
18	8:35 PM	LEO	SAGITTARIUS	LIBRA	VIRGO	VIRGO	CAPRICORN	ARIES	VIRGO	CANCER
19			SAGITTARIUS	LIBRA	VIRGO	VIRGO	CAPRICORN	ARIES	VIRGO	CANCER
20			SAGITTARIUS	LIBRA	VIRGO	VIRGO	AQUARIUS	ARIES	VIRGO	CANCER
21	5:05 AM	VIRGO	SAGITTARIUS	LIBRA	VIRGO	VIRGO	AQUARIUS	ARIES	VIRGO	CANCER
22			SAGITTARIUS	LIBRA	VIRGO	VIRGO	AQUARIUS	ARIES	VIRGO	CANCER

1933

OCT.	MOON FROM	IN	MERCURY	VENUS	MARS	JUPITER	SATURN	URANUS	NEPTUNE	PLUTO
24			SCORPIO	SAGITTARIUS	SAGITTARIUS	LIBRA	AQUARIUS	ARIES	VIRGO	CANCER
25	1:49 PM	AQUARIUS	SCORPIO	SAGITTARIUS	SAGITTARIUS	LIBRA	AQUARIUS	ARIES	VIRGO	CANCER
26			SCORPIO	SAGITTARIUS	SAGITTARIUS	LIBRA	AQUARIUS	ARIES	VIRGO	CANCER
27	6:17 PM	PISCES	SCORPIO	SAGITTARIUS	SAGITTARIUS	LIBRA	AQUARIUS	ARIES	VIRGO	CANCER
28			SCORPIO	SAGITTARIUS	SAGITTARIUS	LIBRA	AQUARIUS	ARIES	VIRGO	CANCER
29			SCORPIO	SAGITTARIUS	SAGITTARIUS	LIBRA	AQUARIUS	ARIES	VIRGO	CANCER
30	0:41 AM	ARIES	SAGITTARIUS	SAGITTARIUS	SAGITTARIUS	LIBRA	AQUARIUS	ARIES	VIRGO	CANCER
31			SAGITTARIUS	SAGITTARIUS	SAGITTARIUS	LIBRA	AQUARIUS	ARIES	VIRGO	CANCER
NOV.										
1	8:53 AM	TAURUS	SAGITTARIUS	SAGITTARIUS	SAGITTARIUS	LIBRA	AQUARIUS	ARIES	VIRGO	CANCER
2			SAGITTARIUS	SAGITTARIUS	SAGITTARIUS	LIBRA	AQUARIUS	ARIES	VIRGO	CANCER
3	7:02 PM	GEMINI	SAGITTARIUS	SAGITTARIUS	SAGITTARIUS	LIBRA	AQUARIUS	ARIES	VIRGO	CANCER
4			SAGITTARIUS	SAGITTARIUS	SAGITTARIUS	LIBRA	AQUARIUS	ARIES	VIRGO	CANCER
5			SAGITTARIUS	SAGITTARIUS	SAGITTARIUS	LIBRA	AQUARIUS	ARIES	VIRGO	CANCER
6	7:05 AM	CANCER	SAGITTARIUS	SAGITTARIUS	SAGITTARIUS	LIBRA	AQUARIUS	ARIES	VIRGO	CANCER
7			SAGITTARIUS	CAPRICORN	SAGITTARIUS	LIBRA	AQUARIUS	ARIES	VIRGO	CANCER
8	7:58 PM	LEO	SAGITTARIUS	CAPRICORN	SAGITTARIUS	LIBRA	AQUARIUS	ARIES	VIRGO	CANCER
9			SAGITTARIUS	CAPRICORN	SAGITTARIUS	LIBRA	AQUARIUS	ARIES	VIRGO	CANCER
10			SAGITTARIUS	CAPRICORN	SAGITTARIUS	LIBRA	AQUARIUS	ARIES	VIRGO	CANCER
11	7:24 AM	VIRGO	SAGITTARIUS	CAPRICORN	SAGITTARIUS	LIBRA	AQUARIUS	ARIES	VIRGO	CANCER
12			SAGITTARIUS	CAPRICORN	SAGITTARIUS	LIBRA	AQUARIUS	ARIES	VIRGO	CANCER
13	3:11 PM	LIBRA	SAGITTARIUS	CAPRICORN	SAGITTARIUS	LIBRA	AQUARIUS	ARIES	VIRGO	CANCER
14			SAGITTARIUS	CAPRICORN	SAGITTARIUS	LIBRA	AQUARIUS	ARIES	VIRGO	CANCER
15	6:52 PM	SCORPIO	SAGITTARIUS	CAPRICORN	SAGITTARIUS	LIBRA	AQUARIUS	ARIES	VIRGO	CANCER
16			SCORPIO	CAPRICORN	SAGITTARIUS	LIBRA	AQUARIUS	ARIES	VIRGO	CANCER
17	7:35 PM	SAGITTARIUS	SCORPIO	CAPRICORN	SAGITTARIUS	LIBRA	AQUARIUS	ARIES	VIRGO	CANCER
18			SCORPIO	CAPRICORN	SAGITTARIUS	LIBRA	AQUARIUS	ARIES	VIRGO	CANCER
19	7:24 PM	CAPRICORN	SCORPIO	CAPRICORN	CAPRICORN	LIBRA	AQUARIUS	ARIES	VIRGO	CANCER
20			SCORPIO	CAPRICORN	CAPRICORN	LIBRA	AQUARIUS	ARIES	VIRGO	CANCER
21	8:21 PM	AQUARIUS	SCORPIO	CAPRICORN	CAPRICORN	LIBRA	AQUARIUS	ARIES	VIRGO	CANCER
22			SCORPIO	CAPRICORN	CAPRICORN	LIBRA	AQUARIUS	ARIES	VIRGO	CANCER

1934 SCORPIO

	MOON FROM IN	MERCURY	VENUS	MARS	JUPITER	SATURN	URANUS	NEPTUNE	PLUTO
OCT.									
24	5:58 PM GEMINI	SCORPIO	LIBRA	VIRGO	SCORPIO	AQUARIUS	ARIES	VIRGO	CANCER
25		SCORPIO	LIBRA	VIRGO	SCORPIO	AQUARIUS	ARIES	VIRGO	CANCER
26		SCORPIO	LIBRA	VIRGO	SCORPIO	AQUARIUS	ARIES	VIRGO	CANCER
27	2:46 AM CANCER	SCORPIO	LIBRA	VIRGO	SCORPIO	AQUARIUS	ARIES	VIRGO	CANCER
28		SCORPIO	LIBRA	VIRGO	SCORPIO	AQUARIUS	ARIES	VIRGO	CANCER
29	2:43 PM LEO	SCORPIO	SCORPIO	VIRGO	SCORPIO	AQUARIUS	ARIES	VIRGO	CANCER
30		SCORPIO	SCORPIO	VIRGO	SCORPIO	AQUARIUS	ARIES	VIRGO	CANCER
31		SCORPIO	SCORPIO	VIRGO	SCORPIO	AQUARIUS	ARIES	VIRGO	CANCER
NOV.									
1	3:36 AM VIRGO	SCORPIO	SCORPIO	VIRGO	SCORPIO	AQUARIUS	ARIES	VIRGO	CANCER
2		SCORPIO	SCORPIO	VIRGO	SCORPIO	AQUARIUS	ARIES	VIRGO	CANCER
3	2:41 PM LIBRA	SCORPIO	SCORPIO	VIRGO	SCORPIO	AQUARIUS	ARIES	VIRGO	CANCER
4		SCORPIO	SCORPIO	VIRGO	SCORPIO	AQUARIUS	ARIES	VIRGO	CANCER
5	10:32 PM SCORPIO	SCORPIO	SCORPIO	VIRGO	SCORPIO	AQUARIUS	ARIES	VIRGO	CANCER
6		SCORPIO	SCORPIO	VIRGO	SCORPIO	AQUARIUS	ARIES	VIRGO	CANCER
7		SCORPIO	SCORPIO	VIRGO	SCORPIO	AQUARIUS	ARIES	VIRGO	CANCER
8	3:33 AM SAGITTARIUS	SCORPIO	SCORPIO	VIRGO	SCORPIO	AQUARIUS	ARIES	VIRGO	CANCER
9		SCORPIO	SCORPIO	VIRGO	SCORPIO	AQUARIUS	ARIES	VIRGO	CANCER
10	6:56 AM CAPRICORN	SCORPIO	SCORPIO	VIRGO	SCORPIO	AQUARIUS	ARIES	VIRGO	CANCER
11		SCORPIO	SCORPIO	VIRGO	SCORPIO	AQUARIUS	ARIES	VIRGO	CANCER
12	9:52 AM AQUARIUS	SCORPIO	SCORPIO	VIRGO	SCORPIO	AQUARIUS	ARIES	VIRGO	CANCER
13		SCORPIO	SCORPIO	VIRGO	SCORPIO	AQUARIUS	ARIES	VIRGO	CANCER
14	0:56 PM PISCES	SCORPIO	SCORPIO	VIRGO	SCORPIO	AQUARIUS	ARIES	VIRGO	CANCER
15		SCORPIO	SCORPIO	VIRGO	SCORPIO	AQUARIUS	ARIES	VIRGO	CANCER
16	4:26 PM ARIES	SCORPIO	SCORPIO	VIRGO	SCORPIO	AQUARIUS	ARIES	VIRGO	CANCER
17		SCORPIO	SCORPIO	VIRGO	SCORPIO	AQUARIUS	ARIES	VIRGO	CANCER
18	8:47 PM TAURUS	SCORPIO	SCORPIO	VIRGO	SCORPIO	AQUARIUS	ARIES	VIRGO	CANCER
19		SCORPIO	SCORPIO	VIRGO	SCORPIO	AQUARIUS	ARIES	VIRGO	CANCER
20		SCORPIO	SCORPIO	VIRGO	SCORPIO	AQUARIUS	ARIES	VIRGO	CANCER
21	2:47 AM GEMINI	SCORPIO	SCORPIO	VIRGO	SCORPIO	AQUARIUS	ARIES	VIRGO	CANCER
22		SCORPIO	SAGITTARIUS	VIRGO	SCORPIO	AQUARIUS	ARIES	VIRGO	CANCER

1935

	MOON FROM IN	MERCURY	VENUS	MARS	JUPITER	SATURN	URANUS	NEPTUNE	PLUTO
OCT.									
24	11:31 AM LIBRA	LIBRA	VIRGO	SAGITTARIUS	SCORPIO	PISCES	TAURUS	VIRGO	CANCER
25		LIBRA	VIRGO	SAGITTARIUS	SCORPIO	PISCES	TAURUS	VIRGO	CANCER
26	11:14 PM SCORPIO	LIBRA	VIRGO	SAGITTARIUS	SCORPIO	PISCES	TAURUS	VIRGO	CANCER
27		LIBRA	VIRGO	SAGITTARIUS	SCORPIO	PISCES	TAURUS	VIRGO	CANCER
28		LIBRA	VIRGO	SAGITTARIUS	SCORPIO	PISCES	TAURUS	VIRGO	CANCER
29	9:17 AM SAGITTARIUS	LIBRA	VIRGO	CAPRICORN	SCORPIO	PISCES	TAURUS	VIRGO	CANCER
30		LIBRA	VIRGO	CAPRICORN	SCORPIO	PISCES	TAURUS	VIRGO	CANCER
31	5:31 PM CAPRICORN	LIBRA	VIRGO	CAPRICORN	SCORPIO	PISCES	TAURUS	VIRGO	CANCER
NOV.									
1		LIBRA	VIRGO	CAPRICORN	SCORPIO	PISCES	TAURUS	VIRGO	CANCER
2	11:38 PM AQUARIUS	LIBRA	VIRGO	CAPRICORN	SCORPIO	PISCES	TAURUS	VIRGO	CANCER
3		LIBRA	VIRGO	CAPRICORN	SCORPIO	PISCES	TAURUS	VIRGO	CANCER
4		LIBRA	VIRGO	CAPRICORN	SCORPIO	PISCES	TAURUS	VIRGO	CANCER
5	3:20 AM PISCES	LIBRA	VIRGO	CAPRICORN	SCORPIO	PISCES	TAURUS	VIRGO	CANCER
6		LIBRA	VIRGO	CAPRICORN	SCORPIO	PISCES	TAURUS	VIRGO	CANCER
7	4:54 AM ARIES	LIBRA	VIRGO	CAPRICORN	SCORPIO	PISCES	TAURUS	VIRGO	CANCER
8		LIBRA	VIRGO	CAPRICORN	SCORPIO	PISCES	TAURUS	VIRGO	CANCER
9	5:29 AM TAURUS	LIBRA	VIRGO	CAPRICORN	SAGITTARIUS	PISCES	TAURUS	VIRGO	CANCER
10		SCORPIO	LIBRA	CAPRICORN	SAGITTARIUS	PISCES	TAURUS	VIRGO	CANCER
11	6:52 AM GEMINI	SCORPIO	LIBRA	CAPRICORN	SAGITTARIUS	PISCES	TAURUS	VIRGO	CANCER
12		SCORPIO	LIBRA	CAPRICORN	SAGITTARIUS	PISCES	TAURUS	VIRGO	CANCER
13	10:56 AM CANCER	SCORPIO	LIBRA	CAPRICORN	SAGITTARIUS	PISCES	TAURUS	VIRGO	CANCER
14		SCORPIO	LIBRA	CAPRICORN	SAGITTARIUS	PISCES	TAURUS	VIRGO	CANCER
15	6:51 PM LEO	SCORPIO	LIBRA	CAPRICORN	SAGITTARIUS	PISCES	TAURUS	VIRGO	CANCER
16		SCORPIO	LIBRA	CAPRICORN	SAGITTARIUS	PISCES	TAURUS	VIRGO	CANCER
17		SCORPIO	LIBRA	CAPRICORN	SAGITTARIUS	PISCES	TAURUS	VIRGO	CANCER
18	6:10 AM VIRGO	SCORPIO	LIBRA	CAPRICORN	SAGITTARIUS	PISCES	TAURUS	VIRGO	CANCER
19		SCORPIO	LIBRA	CAPRICORN	SAGITTARIUS	PISCES	TAURUS	VIRGO	CANCER
20	6:52 PM LIBRA	SCORPIO	LIBRA	CAPRICORN	SAGITTARIUS	PISCES	TAURUS	VIRGO	CANCER
21		SCORPIO	LIBRA	CAPRICORN	SAGITTARIUS	PISCES	TAURUS	VIRGO	CANCER
22		SCORPIO	LIBRA	CAPRICORN	SAGITTARIUS	PISCES	TAURUS	VIRGO	CANCER

SCORPIO

	MOON FROM	IN	MERCURY	VENUS	MARS	JUPITER	SATURN	URANUS	NEPTUNE	PLUTO
OCT.										
24			LIBRA	SAGITTARIUS	VIRGO	SAGITTARIUS	PISCES	TAURUS	VIRGO	CANCER
25	1:28 PM	PISCES	LIBRA	SAGITTARIUS	VIRGO	SAGITTARIUS	PISCES	TAURUS	VIRGO	CANCER
26			LIBRA	SAGITTARIUS	VIRGO	SAGITTARIUS	PISCES	TAURUS	VIRGO	CANCER
27	3:09 PM	ARIES	LIBRA	SAGITTARIUS	VIRGO	SAGITTARIUS	PISCES	TAURUS	VIRGO	CANCER
28			LIBRA	SAGITTARIUS	VIRGO	SAGITTARIUS	PISCES	TAURUS	VIRGO	CANCER
29	2:34 PM	TAURUS	LIBRA	SAGITTARIUS	VIRGO	SAGITTARIUS	PISCES	TAURUS	VIRGO	CANCER
30			LIBRA	SAGITTARIUS	VIRGO	SAGITTARIUS	PISCES	TAURUS	VIRGO	CANCER
31	1:49 PM	GEMINI	LIBRA	SAGITTARIUS	VIRGO	SAGITTARIUS	PISCES	TAURUS	VIRGO	CANCER
NOV.										
1			LIBRA	SAGITTARIUS	VIRGO	SAGITTARIUS	PISCES	TAURUS	VIRGO	CANCER
2	3:00 PM	CANCER	SCORPIO	SAGITTARIUS	VIRGO	SAGITTARIUS	PISCES	TAURUS	VIRGO	CANCER
3			SCORPIO	SAGITTARIUS	VIRGO	SAGITTARIUS	PISCES	TAURUS	VIRGO	CANCER
4	7:37 PM	LEO	SCORPIO	SAGITTARIUS	VIRGO	SAGITTARIUS	PISCES	TAURUS	VIRGO	CANCER
5			SCORPIO	SAGITTARIUS	VIRGO	SAGITTARIUS	PISCES	TAURUS	VIRGO	CANCER
6			SCORPIO	SAGITTARIUS	VIRGO	SAGITTARIUS	PISCES	TAURUS	VIRGO	CANCER
7	4:00 AM	VIRGO	SCORPIO	SAGITTARIUS	VIRGO	SAGITTARIUS	PISCES	TAURUS	VIRGO	CANCER
8			SCORPIO	SAGITTARIUS	VIRGO	SAGITTARIUS	PISCES	TAURUS	VIRGO	CANCER
9	3:15 PM	LIBRA	SCORPIO	SAGITTARIUS	VIRGO	SAGITTARIUS	PISCES	TAURUS	VIRGO	CANCER
10			SCORPIO	SAGITTARIUS	VIRGO	SAGITTARIUS	PISCES	TAURUS	VIRGO	CANCER
11			SCORPIO	SAGITTARIUS	VIRGO	SAGITTARIUS	PISCES	TAURUS	VIRGO	CANCER
12	3:52 AM	SCORPIO	SCORPIO	SAGITTARIUS	VIRGO	SAGITTARIUS	PISCES	TAURUS	VIRGO	CANCER
13			SCORPIO	SAGITTARIUS	VIRGO	SAGITTARIUS	PISCES	TAURUS	VIRGO	CANCER
14	4:34 PM	SAGITTARIUS	SCORPIO	SAGITTARIUS	VIRGO	SAGITTARIUS	PISCES	TAURUS	VIRGO	CANCER
15			SCORPIO	SAGITTARIUS	LIBRA	SAGITTARIUS	PISCES	TAURUS	VIRGO	CANCER
16			SCORPIO	SAGITTARIUS	LIBRA	SAGITTARIUS	PISCES	TAURUS	VIRGO	CANCER
17	4:20 AM	CAPRICORN	SCORPIO	CAPRICORN	LIBRA	SAGITTARIUS	PISCES	TAURUS	VIRGO	CANCER
18			SCORPIO	CAPRICORN	LIBRA	SAGITTARIUS	PISCES	TAURUS	VIRGO	CANCER
19	2:11 PM	AQUARIUS	SCORPIO	CAPRICORN	LIBRA	SAGITTARIUS	PISCES	TAURUS	VIRGO	CANCER
20			SCORPIO	CAPRICORN	LIBRA	SAGITTARIUS	PISCES	TAURUS	VIRGO	CANCER
21	9:04 PM	PISCES	SAGITTARIUS	CAPRICORN	LIBRA	SAGITTARIUS	PISCES	TAURUS	VIRGO	CANCER

1937

	MOON FROM	IN	MERCURY	VENUS	MARS	JUPITER	SATURN	URANUS	NEPTUNE	PLUTO
OCT.										
24	0:49 AM	CANCER	LIBRA	LIBRA	CAPRICORN	CAPRICORN	PISCES	TAURUS	VIRGO	LEO
25			LIBRA	LIBRA	CAPRICORN	CAPRICORN	PISCES	TAURUS	VIRGO	LEO
26	3:44 AM	LEO	SCORPIO	LIBRA	CAPRICORN	CAPRICORN	PISCES	TAURUS	VIRGO	LEO
27			SCORPIO	LIBRA	CAPRICORN	CAPRICORN	PISCES	TAURUS	VIRGO	LEO
28	9:03 AM	VIRGO	SCORPIO	LIBRA	CAPRICORN	CAPRICORN	PISCES	TAURUS	VIRGO	LEO
29			SCORPIO	LIBRA	CAPRICORN	CAPRICORN	PISCES	TAURUS	VIRGO	LEO
30	4:50 PM	LIBRA	SCORPIO	LIBRA	CAPRICORN	CAPRICORN	PISCES	TAURUS	VIRGO	LEO
31			SCORPIO	LIBRA	CAPRICORN	CAPRICORN	PISCES	TAURUS	VIRGO	LEO
NOV.										
1			SCORPIO	LIBRA	CAPRICORN	CAPRICORN	PISCES	TAURUS	VIRGO	LEO
2	2:49 AM	SCORPIO	SCORPIO	LIBRA	CAPRICORN	CAPRICORN	PISCES	TAURUS	VIRGO	LEO
3			SCORPIO	LIBRA	CAPRICORN	CAPRICORN	PISCES	TAURUS	VIRGO	LEO
4	2:48 PM	SAGITTARIUS	SCORPIO	LIBRA	CAPRICORN	CAPRICORN	PISCES	TAURUS	VIRGO	LEO
5			SCORPIO	LIBRA	CAPRICORN	CAPRICORN	PISCES	TAURUS	VIRGO	LEO
6			SCORPIO	LIBRA	CAPRICORN	CAPRICORN	PISCES	TAURUS	VIRGO	LEO
7	3:50 AM	CAPRICORN	SCORPIO	LIBRA	CAPRICORN	CAPRICORN	PISCES	TAURUS	VIRGO	LEO
8			SCORPIO	LIBRA	CAPRICORN	CAPRICORN	PISCES	TAURUS	VIRGO	LEO
9	4:16 PM	AQUARIUS	SCORPIO	LIBRA	CAPRICORN	CAPRICORN	PISCES	TAURUS	VIRGO	LEO
10			SCORPIO	LIBRA	CAPRICORN	CAPRICORN	PISCES	TAURUS	VIRGO	LEO
11			SCORPIO	LIBRA	CAPRICORN	CAPRICORN	PISCES	TAURUS	VIRGO	LEO
12	2:03 AM	PISCES	SCORPIO	LIBRA	AQUARIUS	CAPRICORN	PISCES	TAURUS	VIRGO	LEO
13			SCORPIO	SCORPIO	AQUARIUS	CAPRICORN	PISCES	TAURUS	VIRGO	LEO
14	7:58 AM	ARIES	SAGITTARIUS	SCORPIO	AQUARIUS	CAPRICORN	PISCES	TAURUS	VIRGO	LEO
15			SAGITTARIUS	SCORPIO	AQUARIUS	CAPRICORN	PISCES	TAURUS	VIRGO	LEO
16	10:10 AM	TAURUS	SAGITTARIUS	SCORPIO	AQUARIUS	CAPRICORN	PISCES	TAURUS	VIRGO	LEO
17			SAGITTARIUS	SCORPIO	AQUARIUS	CAPRICORN	PISCES	TAURUS	VIRGO	LEO
18	10:10 AM	GEMINI	SAGITTARIUS	SCORPIO	AQUARIUS	CAPRICORN	PISCES	TAURUS	VIRGO	LEO
19			SAGITTARIUS	SCORPIO	AQUARIUS	CAPRICORN	PISCES	TAURUS	VIRGO	LEO
20	9:48 AM	CANCER	SAGITTARIUS	SCORPIO	AQUARIUS	CAPRICORN	PISCES	TAURUS	VIRGO	LEO
21			SAGITTARIUS	SCORPIO	AQUARIUS	CAPRICORN	PISCES	TAURUS	VIRGO	LEO
22	10:57 AM	LEO	SAGITTARIUS	SCORPIO	AQUARIUS	CAPRICORN	PISCES	TAURUS	VIRGO	LEO

1938

SCORPIO

OCT.	MOON FROM IN	MERCURY	VENUS	MARS	JUPITER	SATURN	URANUS	NEPTUNE	PLUTO
24		SCORPIO	SAGITTARIUS	VIRGO	AQUARIUS	ARIES	TAURUS	VIRGO	LEO
25	12:58 PM SAGITTARIUS	SCORPIO	SAGITTARIUS	LIBRA	AQUARIUS	ARIES	TAURUS	VIRGO	LEO
26		SCORPIO	SAGITTARIUS	LIBRA	AQUARIUS	ARIES	TAURUS	VIRGO	LEO
27	11:40 PM CAPRICORN	SCORPIO	SAGITTARIUS	LIBRA	AQUARIUS	ARIES	TAURUS	VIRGO	LEO
28		SCORPIO	SAGITTARIUS	LIBRA	AQUARIUS	ARIES	TAURUS	VIRGO	LEO
29		SCORPIO	SAGITTARIUS	LIBRA	AQUARIUS	ARIES	TAURUS	VIRGO	LEO
30	12:07 PM AQUARIUS	SCORPIO	SAGITTARIUS	LIBRA	AQUARIUS	ARIES	TAURUS	VIRGO	LEO
31		SCORPIO	SAGITTARIUS	LIBRA	AQUARIUS	ARIES	TAURUS	VIRGO	LEO
NOV.									
1		SCORPIO	SAGITTARIUS	LIBRA	AQUARIUS	ARIES	TAURUS	VIRGO	LEO
2	0:05 AM PISCES	SCORPIO	SAGITTARIUS	LIBRA	AQUARIUS	ARIES	TAURUS	VIRGO	LEO
3		SCORPIO	SAGITTARIUS	LIBRA	AQUARIUS	ARIES	TAURUS	VIRGO	LEO
4	9:33 AM ARIES	SCORPIO	SAGITTARIUS	LIBRA	AQUARIUS	ARIES	TAURUS	VIRGO	LEO
5		SCORPIO	SAGITTARIUS	LIBRA	AQUARIUS	ARIES	TAURUS	VIRGO	LEO
6	3:37 PM TAURUS	SCORPIO	SAGITTARIUS	LIBRA	AQUARIUS	ARIES	TAURUS	VIRGO	LEO
7		SAGITTARIUS	SAGITTARIUS	LIBRA	AQUARIUS	ARIES	TAURUS	VIRGO	LEO
8	7:01 PM GEMINI	SAGITTARIUS	SAGITTARIUS	LIBRA	AQUARIUS	ARIES	TAURUS	VIRGO	LEO
9		SAGITTARIUS	SAGITTARIUS	LIBRA	AQUARIUS	ARIES	TAURUS	VIRGO	LEO
10	8:59 PM CANCER	SAGITTARIUS	SAGITTARIUS	LIBRA	AQUARIUS	ARIES	TAURUS	VIRGO	LEO
11		SAGITTARIUS	SAGITTARIUS	LIBRA	AQUARIUS	ARIES	TAURUS	VIRGO	LEO
12	10:51 PM LEO	SAGITTARIUS	SAGITTARIUS	LIBRA	AQUARIUS	ARIES	TAURUS	VIRGO	LEO
13		SAGITTARIUS	SAGITTARIUS	LIBRA	AQUARIUS	ARIES	TAURUS	VIRGO	LEO
14		SAGITTARIUS	SAGITTARIUS	LIBRA	AQUARIUS	ARIES	TAURUS	VIRGO	LEO
15	1:40 AM VIRGO	SAGITTARIUS	SAGITTARIUS	LIBRA	AQUARIUS	ARIES	TAURUS	VIRGO	LEO
16		SAGITTARIUS	SCORPIO	LIBRA	AQUARIUS	ARIES	TAURUS	VIRGO	LEO
17	6:03 AM LIBRA	SAGITTARIUS	SCORPIO	LIBRA	AQUARIUS	ARIES	TAURUS	VIRGO	LEO
18		SAGITTARIUS	SCORPIO	LIBRA	AQUARIUS	ARIES	TAURUS	VIRGO	LEO
19	12:28 PM SCORPIO	SAGITTARIUS	SCORPIO	LIBRA	AQUARIUS	ARIES	TAURUS	VIRGO	LEO
20		SAGITTARIUS	SCORPIO	LIBRA	AQUARIUS	ARIES	TAURUS	VIRGO	LEO
21	9:00 PM SAGITTARIUS	SAGITTARIUS	SCORPIO	LIBRA	AQUARIUS	ARIES	TAURUS	VIRGO	LEO
22		SAGITTARIUS	SCORPIO	LIBRA	AQUARIUS	ARIES	TAURUS	VIRGO	LEO

1939

OCT.	MOON FROM IN	MERCURY	VENUS	MARS	JUPITER	SATURN	URANUS	NEPTUNE	PLUTO
24		SCORPIO	SCORPIO	AQUARIUS	ARIES	ARIES	TAURUS	VIRGO	LEO
25	7:28 AM ARIES	SCORPIO	SCORPIO	AQUARIUS	ARIES	ARIES	TAURUS	VIRGO	LEO
26		SCORPIO	SCORPIO	AQUARIUS	ARIES	ARIES	TAURUS	VIRGO	LEO
27	6:05 PM TAURUS	SCORPIO	SCORPIO	AQUARIUS	ARIES	ARIES	TAURUS	VIRGO	LEO
28		SCORPIO	SCORPIO	AQUARIUS	ARIES	ARIES	TAURUS	VIRGO	LEO
29		SCORPIO	SCORPIO	AQUARIUS	ARIES	ARIES	TAURUS	VIRGO	LEO
30	2:30 AM GEMINI	SCORPIO	SCORPIO	AQUARIUS	PISCES	ARIES	TAURUS	VIRGO	LEO
31		SCORPIO	SCORPIO	AQUARIUS	PISCES	ARIES	TAURUS	VIRGO	LEO
NOV.									
1	8:47 AM CANCER	SAGITTARIUS	SCORPIO	AQUARIUS	PISCES	ARIES	TAURUS	VIRGO	PLUTO
2		SAGITTARIUS	SCORPIO	AQUARIUS	PISCES	ARIES	TAURUS	VIRGO	LEO
3	2:00 PM LEO	SAGITTARIUS	SCORPIO	AQUARIUS	PISCES	ARIES	TAURUS	VIRGO	LEO
4		SAGITTARIUS	SCORPIO	AQUARIUS	PISCES	ARIES	TAURUS	VIRGO	LEO
5	3:55 PM VIRGO	SAGITTARIUS	SCORPIO	AQUARIUS	PISCES	ARIES	TAURUS	VIRGO	LEO
6		SAGITTARIUS	SCORPIO	AQUARIUS	PISCES	ARIES	TAURUS	VIRGO	LEO
7	6:03 PM LIBRA	SAGITTARIUS	SAGITTARIUS	AQUARIUS	PISCES	ARIES	TAURUS	VIRGO	LEO
8		SAGITTARIUS	SAGITTARIUS	AQUARIUS	PISCES	ARIES	TAURUS	VIRGO	LEO
9	8:16 PM SCORPIO	SAGITTARIUS	SAGITTARIUS	AQUARIUS	PISCES	ARIES	TAURUS	VIRGO	LEO
10		SAGITTARIUS	SAGITTARIUS	AQUARIUS	PISCES	ARIES	TAURUS	VIRGO	LEO
11	11:44 PM SAGITTARIUS	SAGITTARIUS	SAGITTARIUS	AQUARIUS	PISCES	ARIES	TAURUS	VIRGO	LEO
12		SAGITTARIUS	SAGITTARIUS	AQUARIUS	PISCES	ARIES	TAURUS	VIRGO	LEO
13		SAGITTARIUS	SAGITTARIUS	AQUARIUS	PISCES	ARIES	TAURUS	VIRGO	LEO
14	5:43 AM CAPRICORN	SAGITTARIUS	SAGITTARIUS	AQUARIUS	PISCES	ARIES	TAURUS	VIRGO	LEO
15		SAGITTARIUS	SAGITTARIUS	AQUARIUS	PISCES	ARIES	TAURUS	VIRGO	LEO
16	3:03 PM AQUARIUS	SAGITTARIUS	SAGITTARIUS	AQUARIUS	PISCES	ARIES	TAURUS	VIRGO	LEO
17		SAGITTARIUS	SAGITTARIUS	AQUARIUS	PISCES	ARIES	TAURUS	VIRGO	LEO
18		SAGITTARIUS	SAGITTARIUS	AQUARIUS	PISCES	ARIES	TAURUS	VIRGO	LEO
19	5:00 AM PISCES	SAGITTARIUS	SAGITTARIUS	AQUARIUS	PISCES	ARIES	TAURUS	VIRGO	LEO
20		SAGITTARIUS	SAGITTARIUS	PISCES	PISCES	ARIES	TAURUS	VIRGO	LEO
21	3:33 PM ARIES	SAGITTARIUS	SAGITTARIUS	PISCES	PISCES	ARIES	TAURUS	VIRGO	LEO
22		SAGITTARIUS	SAGITTARIUS	PISCES	PISCES	ARIES	TAURUS	VIRGO	LEO

1940 — SCORPIO

OCT.	MOON FROM IN	MERCURY	VENUS	MARS	JUPITER	SATURN	URANUS	NEPTUNE	PLUTO
24	2:01 AM LEO	SCORPIO	VIRGO	LIBRA	TAURUS	TAURUS	TAURUS	VIRGO	LEO
25		SCORPIO	VIRGO	LIBRA	TAURUS	TAURUS	TAURUS	VIRGO	LEO
26	4:07 AM VIRGO	SCORPIO	VIRGO	LIBRA	TAURUS	TAURUS	TAURUS	VIRGO	LEO
27		SCORPIO	VIRGO	LIBRA	TAURUS	TAURUS	TAURUS	VIRGO	LEO
28	5:35 AM LIBRA	SCORPIO	VIRGO	LIBRA	TAURUS	TAURUS	TAURUS	VIRGO	LEO
29		SCORPIO	VIRGO	LIBRA	TAURUS	TAURUS	TAURUS	VIRGO	LEO
30	5:25 AM SCORPIO	SCORPIO	VIRGO	LIBRA	TAURUS	TAURUS	TAURUS	VIRGO	LEO
31		SCORPIO	VIRGO	LIBRA	TAURUS	TAURUS	TAURUS	VIRGO	LEO
NOV. 1	5:22 AM SAGITTARIUS	SCORPIO	VIRGO	LIBRA	TAURUS	TAURUS	TAURUS	VIRGO	LEO
2		SCORPIO	LIBRA	LIBRA	TAURUS	TAURUS	TAURUS	VIRGO	LEO
3	7:23 AM CAPRICORN	SCORPIO	LIBRA	LIBRA	TAURUS	TAURUS	TAURUS	VIRGO	LEO
4		SCORPIO	LIBRA	LIBRA	TAURUS	TAURUS	TAURUS	VIRGO	LEO
5	1:07 PM AQUARIUS	SCORPIO	LIBRA	LIBRA	TAURUS	TAURUS	TAURUS	VIRGO	LEO
6		SCORPIO	LIBRA	LIBRA	TAURUS	TAURUS	TAURUS	VIRGO	LEO
7	10:49 PM PISCES	SCORPIO	LIBRA	LIBRA	TAURUS	TAURUS	TAURUS	VIRGO	LEO
8		SCORPIO	LIBRA	LIBRA	TAURUS	TAURUS	TAURUS	VIRGO	LEO
9		SCORPIO	LIBRA	LIBRA	TAURUS	TAURUS	TAURUS	VIRGO	LEO
10	11:13 AM ARIES	SCORPIO	LIBRA	LIBRA	TAURUS	TAURUS	TAURUS	VIRGO	LEO
11		SCORPIO	LIBRA	LIBRA	TAURUS	TAURUS	TAURUS	VIRGO	LEO
12		SCORPIO	LIBRA	LIBRA	TAURUS	TAURUS	TAURUS	VIRGO	LEO
13	0:11 AM TAURUS	SCORPIO	LIBRA	LIBRA	TAURUS	TAURUS	TAURUS	VIRGO	LEO
14		SCORPIO	LIBRA	LIBRA	TAURUS	TAURUS	TAURUS	VIRGO	LEO
15	11:59 AM GEMINI	SCORPIO	LIBRA	LIBRA	TAURUS	TAURUS	TAURUS	VIRGO	LEO
16		SCORPIO	LIBRA	LIBRA	TAURUS	TAURUS	TAURUS	VIRGO	LEO
17	9:50 PM CANCER	SCORPIO	LIBRA	LIBRA	TAURUS	TAURUS	TAURUS	VIRGO	LEO
18		SCORPIO	LIBRA	LIBRA	TAURUS	TAURUS	TAURUS	VIRGO	LEO
19		SCORPIO	LIBRA	LIBRA	TAURUS	TAURUS	TAURUS	VIRGO	LEO
20	5:37 AM LEO	SCORPIO	LIBRA	LIBRA	TAURUS	TAURUS	TAURUS	VIRGO	LEO
21		SCORPIO	LIBRA	SCORPIO	TAURUS	TAURUS	TAURUS	VIRGO	LEO

1941

OCT.	MOON FROM IN	MERCURY	VENUS	MARS	JUPITER	SATURN	URANUS	NEPTUNE	PLUTO
24	2:44 PM CAPRICORN	SCORPIO	SAGITTARIUS	ARIES	GEMINI	TAURUS	TAURUS	VIRGO	LEO
25		SCORPIO	SAGITTARIUS	ARIES	GEMINI	TAURUS	TAURUS	VIRGO	LEO
26	6:08 PM AQUARIUS	SCORPIO	SAGITTARIUS	ARIES	GEMINI	TAURUS	TAURUS	VIRGO	LEO
27		SCORPIO	SAGITTARIUS	ARIES	GEMINI	TAURUS	TAURUS	VIRGO	LEO
28		SCORPIO	SAGITTARIUS	ARIES	GEMINI	TAURUS	TAURUS	VIRGO	LEO
29	0:53 AM PISCES	SCORPIO	SAGITTARIUS	ARIES	GEMINI	TAURUS	TAURUS	VIRGO	LEO
30		LIBRA	SAGITTARIUS	ARIES	GEMINI	TAURUS	TAURUS	VIRGO	LEO
31	10:39 AM ARIES	LIBRA	SAGITTARIUS	ARIES	GEMINI	TAURUS	TAURUS	VIRGO	LEO
NOV. 1		LIBRA	SAGITTARIUS	ARIES	GEMINI	TAURUS	TAURUS	VIRGO	LEO
2	10:20 PM TAURUS	LIBRA	SAGITTARIUS	ARIES	GEMINI	TAURUS	TAURUS	VIRGO	LEO
3		LIBRA	SAGITTARIUS	ARIES	GEMINI	TAURUS	TAURUS	VIRGO	LEO
4		LIBRA	SAGITTARIUS	ARIES	GEMINI	TAURUS	TAURUS	VIRGO	LEO
5	10:53 AM GEMINI	LIBRA	SAGITTARIUS	ARIES	GEMINI	TAURUS	TAURUS	VIRGO	LEO
6		LIBRA	CAPRICORN	ARIES	GEMINI	TAURUS	TAURUS	VIRGO	LEO
7	11:24 PM CANCER	LIBRA	CAPRICORN	ARIES	GEMINI	TAURUS	TAURUS	VIRGO	LEO
8		LIBRA	CAPRICORN	ARIES	GEMINI	TAURUS	TAURUS	VIRGO	LEO
9		LIBRA	CAPRICORN	ARIES	GEMINI	TAURUS	TAURUS	VIRGO	LEO
10	10:47 AM LEO	LIBRA	CAPRICORN	ARIES	GEMINI	TAURUS	TAURUS	VIRGO	LEO
11		LIBRA	CAPRICORN	ARIES	GEMINI	TAURUS	TAURUS	VIRGO	LEO
12	7:23 PM VIRGO	SCORPIO	CAPRICORN	ARIES	GEMINI	TAURUS	TAURUS	VIRGO	LEO
13		SCORPIO	CAPRICORN	ARIES	GEMINI	TAURUS	TAURUS	VIRGO	LEO
14		SCORPIO	CAPRICORN	ARIES	GEMINI	TAURUS	TAURUS	VIRGO	LEO
15	0:16 AM LIBRA	SCORPIO	CAPRICORN	ARIES	GEMINI	TAURUS	TAURUS	VIRGO	LEO
16		SCORPIO	CAPRICORN	ARIES	GEMINI	TAURUS	TAURUS	VIRGO	LEO
17	1:37 AM SCORPIO	SCORPIO	CAPRICORN	ARIES	GEMINI	TAURUS	TAURUS	VIRGO	LEO
18		SCORPIO	CAPRICORN	ARIES	GEMINI	TAURUS	TAURUS	VIRGO	LEO
19	0:53 AM SAGITTARIUS	SCORPIO	CAPRICORN	ARIES	GEMINI	TAURUS	TAURUS	VIRGO	LEO
20		SCORPIO	CAPRICORN	ARIES	GEMINI	TAURUS	TAURUS	VIRGO	LEO
21	0:14 AM CAPRICORN	SCORPIO	CAPRICORN	ARIES	GEMINI	TAURUS	TAURUS	VIRGO	LEO
22		SCORPIO	CAPRICORN	ARIES	GEMINI	TAURUS	TAURUS	VIRGO	LEO

SCORPIO

1942

MOON FROM	IN	MERCURY	VENUS	MARS	JUPITER	SATURN	URANUS	NEPTUNE	PLUTO
OCT.									
24		LIBRA	LIBRA	LIBRA	CANCER	GEMINI	GEMINI	LIBRA	LEO
25		LIBRA	LIBRA	LIBRA	CANCER	GEMINI	GEMINI	LIBRA	LEO
26	8:19 AM GEMINI	LIBRA	LIBRA	LIBRA	CANCER	GEMINI	GEMINI	LIBRA	LEO
27		LIBRA	LIBRA	LIBRA	CANCER	GEMINI	GEMINI	LIBRA	LEO
28	8:02 PM CANCER	LIBRA	LIBRA	LIBRA	CANCER	GEMINI	GEMINI	LIBRA	LEO
29		LIBRA	SCORPIO	LIBRA	CANCER	GEMINI	GEMINI	LIBRA	LEO
30		LIBRA	SCORPIO	LIBRA	CANCER	GEMINI	GEMINI	LIBRA	LEO
31	8:48 AM LEO	LIBRA	SCORPIO	LIBRA	CANCER	GEMINI	GEMINI	LIBRA	LEO
NOV.									
1		LIBRA	SCORPIO	LIBRA	CANCER	GEMINI	GEMINI	LIBRA	LEO
2	8:15 PM VIRGO	LIBRA	SCORPIO	SCORPIO	CANCER	GEMINI	GEMINI	LIBRA	LEO
3		LIBRA	SCORPIO	SCORPIO	CANCER	GEMINI	GEMINI	LIBRA	LEO
4		LIBRA	SCORPIO	SCORPIO	CANCER	GEMINI	GEMINI	LIBRA	LEO
5	4:19 AM LIBRA	LIBRA	SCORPIO	SCORPIO	CANCER	GEMINI	GEMINI	LIBRA	LEO
6		LIBRA	SCORPIO	SCORPIO	CANCER	GEMINI	GEMINI	LIBRA	LEO
7	8:26 AM SCORPIO	SCORPIO	SCORPIO	SCORPIO	CANCER	GEMINI	GEMINI	LIBRA	LEO
8		SCORPIO	SCORPIO	SCORPIO	CANCER	GEMINI	GEMINI	LIBRA	LEO
9	9:46 AM SAGITTARIUS	SCORPIO	SCORPIO	SCORPIO	CANCER	GEMINI	GEMINI	LIBRA	LEO
10		SCORPIO	SCORPIO	SCORPIO	CANCER	GEMINI	GEMINI	LIBRA	LEO
11	10:19 AM CAPRICORN	SCORPIO	SCORPIO	SCORPIO	CANCER	GEMINI	GEMINI	LIBRA	LEO
12		SCORPIO	SCORPIO	SCORPIO	CANCER	GEMINI	GEMINI	LIBRA	LEO
13	11:51 AM AQUARIUS	SCORPIO	SCORPIO	SCORPIO	CANCER	GEMINI	GEMINI	LIBRA	LEO
14		SCORPIO	SCORPIO	SCORPIO	CANCER	GEMINI	GEMINI	LIBRA	LEO
15	3:31 PM PISCES	SCORPIO	SCORPIO	SCORPIO	CANCER	GEMINI	GEMINI	LIBRA	LEO
16		SCORPIO	SCORPIO	SCORPIO	CANCER	GEMINI	GEMINI	LIBRA	LEO
17	9:33 PM ARIES	SCORPIO	SCORPIO	SCORPIO	CANCER	GEMINI	GEMINI	LIBRA	LEO
18		SCORPIO	SCORPIO	SCORPIO	CANCER	GEMINI	GEMINI	LIBRA	LEO
19		SCORPIO	SCORPIO	SCORPIO	CANCER	GEMINI	GEMINI	LIBRA	LEO
20	5:39 AM TAURUS	SCORPIO	SCORPIO	SCORPIO	CANCER	GEMINI	GEMINI	LIBRA	LEO
21		SCORPIO	SCORPIO	SCORPIO	CANCER	GEMINI	GEMINI	LIBRA	LEO
22	3:37 PM GEMINI	SCORPIO	SAGITTARIUS	SCORPIO	CANCER	GEMINI	GEMINI	LIBRA	LEO

1943

MOON FROM	IN	MERCURY	VENUS	MARS	JUPITER	SATURN	URANUS	NEPTUNE	PLUTO
OCT.									
24		LIBRA	VIRGO	GEMINI	LEO	GEMINI	GEMINI	LIBRA	LEO
25		LIBRA	VIRGO	GEMINI	LEO	GEMINI	GEMINI	LIBRA	LEO
26	3:35 AM LIBRA	LIBRA	VIRGO	GEMINI	LEO	GEMINI	GEMINI	LIBRA	LEO
27		LIBRA	VIRGO	GEMINI	LEO	GEMINI	GEMINI	LIBRA	LEO
28	12:12 PM SCORPIO	LIBRA	VIRGO	GEMINI	LEO	GEMINI	GEMINI	LIBRA	LEO
29		LIBRA	VIRGO	GEMINI	LEO	GEMINI	GEMINI	LIBRA	LEO
30	6:11 PM SAGITTARIUS	LIBRA	VIRGO	GEMINI	LEO	GEMINI	GEMINI	LIBRA	LEO
31		SCORPIO	VIRGO	GEMINI	LEO	GEMINI	GEMINI	LIBRA	LEO
NOV.									
1	10:34 PM CAPRICORN	SCORPIO	VIRGO	GEMINI	LEO	GEMINI	GEMINI	LIBRA	LEO
2		SCORPIO	VIRGO	GEMINI	LEO	GEMINI	GEMINI	LIBRA	LEO
3		SCORPIO	VIRGO	GEMINI	LEO	GEMINI	GEMINI	LIBRA	LEO
4	2:09 AM AQUARIUS	SCORPIO	VIRGO	GEMINI	LEO	GEMINI	GEMINI	LIBRA	LEO
5		SCORPIO	VIRGO	GEMINI	LEO	GEMINI	GEMINI	LIBRA	LEO
6	5:16 AM PISCES	SCORPIO	VIRGO	GEMINI	LEO	GEMINI	GEMINI	LIBRA	LEO
7		SCORPIO	VIRGO	GEMINI	LEO	GEMINI	GEMINI	LIBRA	LEO
8	8:10 AM ARIES	SCORPIO	VIRGO	GEMINI	LEO	GEMINI	GEMINI	LIBRA	LEO
9		SCORPIO	VIRGO	GEMINI	LEO	GEMINI	GEMINI	LIBRA	LEO
10	11:33 AM TAURUS	SCORPIO	LIBRA	GEMINI	LEO	GEMINI	GEMINI	LIBRA	LEO
11		SCORPIO	LIBRA	GEMINI	LEO	GEMINI	GEMINI	LIBRA	LEO
12	4:35 PM GEMINI	SCORPIO	LIBRA	GEMINI	LEO	GEMINI	GEMINI	LIBRA	LEO
13		SCORPIO	LIBRA	GEMINI	LEO	GEMINI	GEMINI	LIBRA	LEO
14		SCORPIO	LIBRA	GEMINI	LEO	GEMINI	GEMINI	LIBRA	LEO
15	0:26 AM CANCER	SCORPIO	LIBRA	GEMINI	LEO	GEMINI	GEMINI	LIBRA	LEO
16		SCORPIO	LIBRA	GEMINI	LEO	GEMINI	GEMINI	LIBRA	LEO
17	11:29 AM LEO	SCORPIO	LIBRA	GEMINI	LEO	GEMINI	GEMINI	LIBRA	LEO
18		SCORPIO	LIBRA	GEMINI	LEO	GEMINI	GEMINI	LIBRA	LEO
19		SAGITTARIUS	LIBRA	GEMINI	LEO	GEMINI	GEMINI	LIBRA	LEO
20	0:20 AM VIRGO	SAGITTARIUS	LIBRA	GEMINI	LEO	GEMINI	GEMINI	LIBRA	LEO
21		SAGITTARIUS	LIBRA	GEMINI	LEO	GEMINI	GEMINI	LIBRA	LEO
22	12:16 PM LIBRA	SAGITTARIUS	LIBRA	GEMINI	LEO	GEMINI	GEMINI	LIBRA	LEO

	MOON FROM IN	MERCURY	VENUS	MARS	JUPITER	SATURN	URANUS	NEPTUNE	PLUTO
OCT.									
24	3:15 PM AQUARIUS	SCORPIO	SAGITTARIUS	SCORPIO	VIRGO	CANCER	GEMINI	LIBRA	LEO
25		SCORPIO	SAGITTARIUS	SCORPIO	VIRGO	CANCER	GEMINI	LIBRA	LEO
26	6:48 PM PISCES	SCORPIO	SAGITTARIUS	SCORPIO	VIRGO	CANCER	GEMINI	LIBRA	LEO
27		SCORPIO	SAGITTARIUS	SCORPIO	VIRGO	CANCER	GEMINI	LIBRA	LEO
28	7:52 PM ARIES	SCORPIO	SAGITTARIUS	SCORPIO	VIRGO	CANCER	GEMINI	LIBRA	LEO
29		SCORPIO	SAGITTARIUS	SCORPIO	VIRGO	CANCER	GEMINI	LIBRA	LEO
30	7:47 PM TAURUS	SCORPIO	SAGITTARIUS	SCORPIO	VIRGO	CANCER	GEMINI	LIBRA	LEO
31		SCORPIO	SAGITTARIUS	SCORPIO	VIRGO	CANCER	GEMINI	LIBRA	LEO
NOV.									
1	8:33 PM GEMINI	SCORPIO	SAGITTARIUS	SCORPIO	VIRGO	CANCER	GEMINI	LIBRA	LEO
2		SCORPIO	SAGITTARIUS	SCORPIO	VIRGO	CANCER	GEMINI	LIBRA	LEO
3		SCORPIO	SAGITTARIUS	SCORPIO	VIRGO	CANCER	GEMINI	LIBRA	LEO
4	0:09 AM CANCER	SCORPIO	SAGITTARIUS	SCORPIO	VIRGO	CANCER	GEMINI	LIBRA	LEO
5		SCORPIO	SAGITTARIUS	SCORPIO	VIRGO	CANCER	GEMINI	LIBRA	LEO
6	7:45 AM LEO	SCORPIO	SAGITTARIUS	SCORPIO	VIRGO	CANCER	GEMINI	LIBRA	LEO
7		SCORPIO	SAGITTARIUS	SCORPIO	VIRGO	CANCER	GEMINI	LIBRA	LEO
8	7:01 PM VIRGO	SCORPIO	SAGITTARIUS	SCORPIO	VIRGO	CANCER	GEMINI	LIBRA	LEO
9		SCORPIO	SAGITTARIUS	SCORPIO	VIRGO	CANCER	GEMINI	LIBRA	LEO
10		SAGITTARIUS	SAGITTARIUS	SCORPIO	VIRGO	CANCER	GEMINI	LIBRA	LEO
11	7:44 AM LIBRA	SAGITTARIUS	SAGITTARIUS	SCORPIO	VIRGO	CANCER	GEMINI	LIBRA	LEO
12		SAGITTARIUS	SAGITTARIUS	SCORPIO	VIRGO	CANCER	GEMINI	LIBRA	LEO
13	7:45 PM SCORPIO	SAGITTARIUS	SAGITTARIUS	SCORPIO	VIRGO	CANCER	GEMINI	LIBRA	LEO
14		SAGITTARIUS	SAGITTARIUS	SCORPIO	VIRGO	CANCER	GEMINI	LIBRA	LEO
15		SAGITTARIUS	SAGITTARIUS	SCORPIO	VIRGO	CANCER	GEMINI	LIBRA	LEO
16	6:00 AM SAGITTARIUS	SAGITTARIUS	CAPRICORN	SCORPIO	VIRGO	CANCER	GEMINI	LIBRA	LEO
17		SAGITTARIUS	CAPRICORN	SCORPIO	VIRGO	CANCER	GEMINI	LIBRA	LEO
18	2:18 PM CAPRICORN	SAGITTARIUS	CAPRICORN	SCORPIO	VIRGO	CANCER	GEMINI	LIBRA	LEO
19		SAGITTARIUS	CAPRICORN	SCORPIO	VIRGO	CANCER	GEMINI	LIBRA	LEO
20	8:44 PM AQUARIUS	SAGITTARIUS	CAPRICORN	SCORPIO	VIRGO	CANCER	GEMINI	LIBRA	LEO
21		SAGITTARIUS	CAPRICORN	SCORPIO	VIRGO	CANCER	GEMINI	LIBRA	LEO

1945

	MOON FROM IN	MERCURY	VENUS	MARS	JUPITER	SATURN	URANUS	NEPTUNE	PLUTO
OCT.									
24		SCORPIO	LIBRA	CANCER	LIBRA	CANCER	GEMINI	LIBRA	LEO
25	5:13 AM CANCER	SCORPIO	LIBRA	CANCER	LIBRA	CANCER	GEMINI	LIBRA	LEO
26		SCORPIO	LIBRA	CANCER	LIBRA	CANCER	GEMINI	LIBRA	LEO
27	9:57 AM LEO	SCORPIO	LIBRA	CANCER	LIBRA	CANCER	GEMINI	LIBRA	LEO
28		SCORPIO	LIBRA	CANCER	LIBRA	CANCER	GEMINI	LIBRA	LEO
29	6:15 PM VIRGO	SCORPIO	LIBRA	CANCER	LIBRA	CANCER	GEMINI	LIBRA	LEO
30		SCORPIO	LIBRA	CANCER	LIBRA	CANCER	GEMINI	LIBRA	LEO
31		SCORPIO	LIBRA	CANCER	LIBRA	CANCER	GEMINI	LIBRA	LEO
NOV.									
1	5:09 AM LIBRA	SCORPIO	LIBRA	CANCER	LIBRA	CANCER	GEMINI	LIBRA	LEO
2		SCORPIO	LIBRA	CANCER	LIBRA	CANCER	GEMINI	LIBRA	LEO
3	5:30 PM SCORPIO	SCORPIO	LIBRA	CANCER	LIBRA	CANCER	GEMINI	LIBRA	LEO
4		SAGITTARIUS	LIBRA	CANCER	LIBRA	CANCER	GEMINI	LIBRA	LEO
5		SAGITTARIUS	LIBRA	CANCER	LIBRA	CANCER	GEMINI	LIBRA	LEO
6	6:18 AM SAGITTARIUS	SAGITTARIUS	LIBRA	CANCER	LIBRA	CANCER	GEMINI	LIBRA	LEO
7		SAGITTARIUS	LIBRA	CANCER	LIBRA	CANCER	GEMINI	LIBRA	LEO
8	6:33 PM CAPRICORN	SAGITTARIUS	LIBRA	CANCER	LIBRA	CANCER	GEMINI	LIBRA	LEO
9		SAGITTARIUS	LIBRA	CANCER	LIBRA	CANCER	GEMINI	LIBRA	LEO
10		SAGITTARIUS	LIBRA	CANCER	LIBRA	CANCER	GEMINI	LIBRA	LEO
11	4:57 AM AQUARIUS	SAGITTARIUS	LIBRA	CANCER	LIBRA	CANCER	GEMINI	LIBRA	LEO
12		SAGITTARIUS	SCORPIO	LEO	LIBRA	CANCER	GEMINI	LIBRA	LEO
13	12:01 PM PISCES	SAGITTARIUS	SCORPIO	LEO	LIBRA	CANCER	GEMINI	LIBRA	LEO
14		SAGITTARIUS	SCORPIO	LEO	LIBRA	CANCER	GEMINI	LIBRA	LEO
15	3:19 PM ARIES	SAGITTARIUS	SCORPIO	LEO	LIBRA	CANCER	GEMINI	LIBRA	LEO
16		SAGITTARIUS	SCORPIO	LEO	LIBRA	CANCER	GEMINI	LIBRA	LEO
17	3:46 PM TAURUS	SAGITTARIUS	SCORPIO	LEO	LIBRA	CANCER	GEMINI	LIBRA	LEO
18		SAGITTARIUS	SCORPIO	LEO	LIBRA	CANCER	GEMINI	LIBRA	LEO
19	3:04 PM GEMINI	SAGITTARIUS	SCORPIO	LEO	LIBRA	CANCER	GEMINI	LIBRA	LEO
20		SAGITTARIUS	SCORPIO	LEO	LIBRA	CANCER	GEMINI	LIBRA	LEO
21	3:19 PM CANCER	SAGITTARIUS	SCORPIO	LEO	LIBRA	CANCER	GEMINI	LIBRA	LEO
22		SAGITTARIUS	SCORPIO	LEO	LIBRA	CANCER	GEMINI	LIBRA	LEO

1946 SCORPIO

OCT.	MOON FROM	IN	MERCURY	VENUS	MARS	JUPITER	SATURN	URANUS	NEPTUNE	PLUTO
24	4:47 PM	SCORPIO	SCORPIO	SAGITTARIUS	SCORPIO	SCORPIO	LEO	GEMINI	LIBRA	LEO
25			SCORPIO	SAGITTARIUS	SCORPIO	SCORPIO	LEO	GEMINI	LIBRA	LEO
26			SCORPIO	SAGITTARIUS	SCORPIO	SCORPIO	LEO	GEMINI	LIBRA	LEO
27	4:05 AM	SAGITTARIUS	SCORPIO	SAGITTARIUS	SCORPIO	SCORPIO	LEO	GEMINI	LIBRA	LEO
28			SCORPIO	SAGITTARIUS	SCORPIO	SCORPIO	LEO	GEMINI	LIBRA	LEO
29	4:59 PM	CAPRICORN	SCORPIO	SAGITTARIUS	SCORPIO	SCORPIO	LEO	GEMINI	LIBRA	LEO
30			SAGITTARIUS	SAGITTARIUS	SCORPIO	SCORPIO	LEO	GEMINI	LIBRA	LEO
31			SAGITTARIUS	SAGITTARIUS	SCORPIO	SCORPIO	LEO	GEMINI	LIBRA	LEO
NOV.										
1	5:32 AM	AQUARIUS	SAGITTARIUS	SAGITTARIUS	SCORPIO	SCORPIO	LEO	GEMINI	LIBRA	LEO
2			SAGITTARIUS	SAGITTARIUS	SCORPIO	SCORPIO	LEO	GEMINI	LIBRA	LEO
3	3:22 PM	PISCES	SAGITTARIUS	SAGITTARIUS	SCORPIO	SCORPIO	LEO	GEMINI	LIBRA	LEO
4			SAGITTARIUS	SAGITTARIUS	SCORPIO	SCORPIO	LEO	GEMINI	LIBRA	LEO
5	9:18 PM	ARIES	SAGITTARIUS	SAGITTARIUS	SCORPIO	SCORPIO	LEO	GEMINI	LIBRA	LEO
6			SAGITTARIUS	SAGITTARIUS	SCORPIO	SCORPIO	LEO	GEMINI	LIBRA	LEO
7	11:42 PM	TAURUS	SAGITTARIUS	SAGITTARIUS	SAGITTARIUS	SCORPIO	LEO	GEMINI	LIBRA	LEO
8			SAGITTARIUS	SCORPIO	SAGITTARIUS	SCORPIO	LEO	GEMINI	LIBRA	LEO
9			SAGITTARIUS	SCORPIO	SAGITTARIUS	SCORPIO	LEO	GEMINI	LIBRA	LEO
10	0:07 AM	GEMINI	SAGITTARIUS	SCORPIO	SAGITTARIUS	SCORPIO	LEO	GEMINI	LIBRA	LEO
11			SAGITTARIUS	SCORPIO	SAGITTARIUS	SCORPIO	LEO	GEMINI	LIBRA	LEO
12	0:20 AM	CANCER	SAGITTARIUS	SCORPIO	SAGITTARIUS	SCORPIO	LEO	GEMINI	LIBRA	LEO
13			SAGITTARIUS	SCORPIO	SAGITTARIUS	SCORPIO	LEO	GEMINI	LIBRA	LEO
14	2:01 AM	LEO	SAGITTARIUS	SCORPIO	SAGITTARIUS	SCORPIO	LEO	GEMINI	LIBRA	LEO
15			SAGITTARIUS	SCORPIO	SAGITTARIUS	SCORPIO	LEO	GEMINI	LIBRA	LEO
16	6:10 AM	VIRGO	SAGITTARIUS	SCORPIO	SAGITTARIUS	SCORPIO	LEO	GEMINI	LIBRA	LEO
17			SAGITTARIUS	SCORPIO	SAGITTARIUS	SCORPIO	LEO	GEMINI	LIBRA	LEO
18	1:18 PM	LIBRA	SAGITTARIUS	SCORPIO	SAGITTARIUS	SCORPIO	LEO	GEMINI	LIBRA	LEO
19			SAGITTARIUS	SCORPIO	SAGITTARIUS	SCORPIO	LEO	GEMINI	LIBRA	LEO
20	11:03 PM	SCORPIO	SAGITTARIUS	SCORPIO	SAGITTARIUS	SCORPIO	LEO	GEMINI	LIBRA	LEO
21			SCORPIO	SCORPIO	SAGITTARIUS	SCORPIO	LEO	GEMINI	LIBRA	LEO
22			SCORPIO	SCORPIO	SAGITTARIUS	SCORPIO	LEO	GEMINI	LIBRA	LEO

1947

OCT.	MOON FROM	IN	MERCURY	VENUS	MARS	JUPITER	SATURN	URANUS	NEPTUNE	PLUTO
24	12:44 PM	PISCES	SCORPIO	SCORPIO	LEO	SAGITTARIUS	LEO	GEMINI	LIBRA	LEO
25			SCORPIO	SCORPIO	LEO	SAGITTARIUS	LEO	GEMINI	LIBRA	LEO
26	10:28 PM	ARIES	SCORPIO	SCORPIO	LEO	SAGITTARIUS	LEO	GEMINI	LIBRA	LEO
27			SCORPIO	SCORPIO	LEO	SAGITTARIUS	LEO	GEMINI	LIBRA	LEO
28			SCORPIO	SCORPIO	LEO	SAGITTARIUS	LEO	GEMINI	LIBRA	LEO
29	5:16 AM	TAURUS	SCORPIO	SCORPIO	LEO	SAGITTARIUS	LEO	GEMINI	LIBRA	LEO
30			SCORPIO	SCORPIO	LEO	SAGITTARIUS	LEO	GEMINI	LIBRA	LEO
31	9:36 AM	GEMINI	SCORPIO	SCORPIO	LEO	SAGITTARIUS	LEO	GEMINI	LIBRA	LEO
NOV.										
1			SCORPIO	SCORPIO	LEO	SAGITTARIUS	LEO	GEMINI	LIBRA	LEO
2	12:32 PM	CANCER	SCORPIO	SCORPIO	LEO	SAGITTARIUS	LEO	GEMINI	LIBRA	LEO
3			SCORPIO	SCORPIO	LEO	SAGITTARIUS	LEO	GEMINI	LIBRA	LEO
4	3:04 PM	LEO	SCORPIO	SCORPIO	LEO	SAGITTARIUS	LEO	GEMINI	LIBRA	LEO
5			SCORPIO	SCORPIO	LEO	SAGITTARIUS	LEO	GEMINI	LIBRA	LEO
6	5:58 PM	VIRGO	SCORPIO	SCORPIO	LEO	SAGITTARIUS	LEO	GEMINI	LIBRA	LEO
7			SCORPIO	SAGITTARIUS	LEO	SAGITTARIUS	LEO	GEMINI	LIBRA	LEO
8	9:45 PM	LIBRA	SCORPIO	SAGITTARIUS	LEO	SAGITTARIUS	LEO	GEMINI	LIBRA	LEO
9			SCORPIO	SAGITTARIUS	LEO	SAGITTARIUS	LEO	GEMINI	LIBRA	LEO
10			SCORPIO	SAGITTARIUS	LEO	SAGITTARIUS	LEO	GEMINI	LIBRA	LEO
11	3:06 AM	SCORPIO	SCORPIO	SAGITTARIUS	LEO	SAGITTARIUS	LEO	GEMINI	LIBRA	LEO
12			SCORPIO	SAGITTARIUS	LEO	SAGITTARIUS	LEO	GEMINI	LIBRA	LEO
13	10:35 AM	SAGITTARIUS	SCORPIO	SAGITTARIUS	LEO	SAGITTARIUS	LEO	GEMINI	LIBRA	LEO
14			SCORPIO	SAGITTARIUS	LEO	SAGITTARIUS	LEO	GEMINI	LIBRA	LEO
15	8:41 PM	CAPRICORN	SCORPIO	SAGITTARIUS	LEO	SAGITTARIUS	LEO	GEMINI	LIBRA	LEO
16			SCORPIO	SAGITTARIUS	LEO	SAGITTARIUS	LEO	GEMINI	LIBRA	LEO
17			SCORPIO	SAGITTARIUS	LEO	SAGITTARIUS	LEO	GEMINI	LIBRA	LEO
18	8:45 AM	AQUARIUS	SCORPIO	SAGITTARIUS	LEO	SAGITTARIUS	LEO	GEMINI	LIBRA	LEO
19			SCORPIO	SAGITTARIUS	LEO	SAGITTARIUS	LEO	GEMINI	LIBRA	LEO
20	9:15 PM	PISCES	SCORPIO	SAGITTARIUS	LEO	SAGITTARIUS	LEO	GEMINI	LIBRA	LEO
21			SCORPIO	SAGITTARIUS	LEO	SAGITTARIUS	LEO	GEMINI	LIBRA	LEO
22			SCORPIO	SAGITTARIUS	LEO	SAGITTARIUS	LEO	GEMINI	LIBRA	LEO

SCORPIO

OCT.	MOON FROM	IN	MERCURY	VENUS	MARS	JUPITER	SATURN	URANUS	NEPTUNE	PLUTO
24			LIBRA	VIRGO	SAGITTARIUS	SAGITTARIUS	VIRGO	CANCER	LIBRA	LEO
25	5:09 AM	LEO	LIBRA	VIRGO	SAGITTARIUS	SAGITTARIUS	VIRGO	CANCER	LIBRA	LEO
26			LIBRA	VIRGO	SAGITTARIUS	SAGITTARIUS	VIRGO	CANCER	LIBRA	LEO
27	7:53 AM	VIRGO	LIBRA	VIRGO	SAGITTARIUS	SAGITTARIUS	VIRGO	CANCER	LIBRA	LEO
28			LIBRA	VIRGO	SAGITTARIUS	SAGITTARIUS	VIRGO	CANCER	LIBRA	LEO
29	7:51 AM	LIBRA	LIBRA	VIRGO	SAGITTARIUS	SAGITTARIUS	VIRGO	CANCER	LIBRA	LEO
30			LIBRA	VIRGO	SAGITTARIUS	SAGITTARIUS	VIRGO	CANCER	LIBRA	LEO
31	10:33 AM	SCORPIO	LIBRA	VIRGO	SAGITTARIUS	SAGITTARIUS	VIRGO	CANCER	LIBRA	LEO
NOV.										
1			LIBRA	LIBRA	SAGITTARIUS	SAGITTARIUS	VIRGO	CANCER	LIBRA	LEO
2	1:50 PM	SAGITTARIUS	LIBRA	LIBRA	SAGITTARIUS	SAGITTARIUS	VIRGO	CANCER	LIBRA	LEO
3			LIBRA	LIBRA	SAGITTARIUS	SAGITTARIUS	VIRGO	CANCER	LIBRA	LEO
4	6:45 PM	CAPRICORN	LIBRA	LIBRA	SAGITTARIUS	SAGITTARIUS	VIRGO	CANCER	LIBRA	LEO
5			LIBRA	LIBRA	SAGITTARIUS	SAGITTARIUS	VIRGO	CANCER	LIBRA	LEO
6			LIBRA	LIBRA	SAGITTARIUS	SAGITTARIUS	VIRGO	CANCER	LIBRA	LEO
7	2:45 AM	AQUARIUS	LIBRA	LIBRA	SAGITTARIUS	SAGITTARIUS	VIRGO	CANCER	LIBRA	LEO
8			LIBRA	LIBRA	SAGITTARIUS	SAGITTARIUS	VIRGO	CANCER	LIBRA	LEO
9	3:34 PM	PISCES	LIBRA	LIBRA	SAGITTARIUS	SAGITTARIUS	VIRGO	CANCER	LIBRA	LEO
10			SCORPIO	LIBRA	SAGITTARIUS	SAGITTARIUS	VIRGO	CANCER	LIBRA	LEO
11			SCORPIO	LIBRA	SAGITTARIUS	SAGITTARIUS	VIRGO	CANCER	LIBRA	LEO
12	4:11 AM	ARIES	SCORPIO	LIBRA	SAGITTARIUS	SAGITTARIUS	VIRGO	CANCER	LIBRA	LEO
13			SCORPIO	LIBRA	SAGITTARIUS	SAGITTARIUS	VIRGO	GEMINI	LIBRA	LEO
14	3:21 PM	TAURUS	SCORPIO	LIBRA	SAGITTARIUS	SAGITTARIUS	VIRGO	GEMINI	LIBRA	LEO
15			SCORPIO	LIBRA	SAGITTARIUS	CAPRICORN	VIRGO	GEMINI	LIBRA	LEO
16	11:59 PM	GEMINI	SCORPIO	LIBRA	SAGITTARIUS	CAPRICORN	VIRGO	GEMINI	LIBRA	LEO
17			SCORPIO	LIBRA	SAGITTARIUS	CAPRICORN	VIRGO	GEMINI	LIBRA	LEO
18			SCORPIO	LIBRA	SAGITTARIUS	CAPRICORN	VIRGO	GEMINI	LIBRA	LEO
19	6:10 AM	CANCER	SCORPIO	LIBRA	SAGITTARIUS	CAPRICORN	VIRGO	GEMINI	LIBRA	LEO
20			SCORPIO	LIBRA	SAGITTARIUS	CAPRICORN	VIRGO	GEMINI	LIBRA	LEO
21	10:31 AM	LEO	SCORPIO	LIBRA	SAGITTARIUS	CAPRICORN	VIRGO	GEMINI	LIBRA	LEO

1949

OCT.	MOON FROM	IN	MERCURY	VENUS	MARS	JUPITER	SATURN	URANUS	NEPTUNE	PLUTO
24			LIBRA	SAGITTARIUS	LEO	CAPRICORN	VIRGO	CANCER	LIBRA	LEO
25	9:16 PM	CAPRICORN	LIBRA	SAGITTARIUS	LEO	CAPRICORN	VIRGO	CANCER	LIBRA	LEO
26			LIBRA	SAGITTARIUS	LEO	CAPRICORN	VIRGO	CANCER	LIBRA	LEO
27			LIBRA	SAGITTARIUS	VIRGO	CAPRICORN	VIRGO	CANCER	LIBRA	LEO
28	2:54 AM	AQUARIUS	LIBRA	SAGITTARIUS	VIRGO	CAPRICORN	VIRGO	CANCER	LIBRA	LEO
29			LIBRA	SAGITTARIUS	VIRGO	CAPRICORN	VIRGO	CANCER	LIBRA	LEO
30	12:23 PM	PISCES	LIBRA	SAGITTARIUS	VIRGO	CAPRICORN	VIRGO	CANCER	LIBRA	LEO
31			LIBRA	SAGITTARIUS	VIRGO	CAPRICORN	VIRGO	CANCER	LIBRA	LEO
NOV.										
1			LIBRA	SAGITTARIUS	VIRGO	CAPRICORN	VIRGO	CANCER	LIBRA	LEO
2	0:34 AM	ARIES	LIBRA	SAGITTARIUS	VIRGO	CAPRICORN	VIRGO	CANCER	LIBRA	LEO
3			LIBRA	SAGITTARIUS	VIRGO	CAPRICORN	VIRGO	CANCER	LIBRA	LEO
4	1:36 PM	TAURUS	SCORPIO	SAGITTARIUS	VIRGO	CAPRICORN	VIRGO	CANCER	LIBRA	LEO
5			SCORPIO	SAGITTARIUS	VIRGO	CAPRICORN	VIRGO	CANCER	LIBRA	LEO
6			SCORPIO	CAPRICORN	VIRGO	CAPRICORN	VIRGO	CANCER	LIBRA	LEO
7	1:53 AM	GEMINI	SCORPIO	CAPRICORN	VIRGO	CAPRICORN	VIRGO	CANCER	LIBRA	LEO
8			SCORPIO	CAPRICORN	VIRGO	CAPRICORN	VIRGO	CANCER	LIBRA	LEO
9	12:33 PM	CANCER	SCORPIO	CAPRICORN	VIRGO	CAPRICORN	VIRGO	CANCER	LIBRA	LEO
10			SCORPIO	CAPRICORN	VIRGO	CAPRICORN	VIRGO	CANCER	LIBRA	LEO
11	8:56 PM	LEO	SCORPIO	CAPRICORN	VIRGO	CAPRICORN	VIRGO	CANCER	LIBRA	LEO
12			SCORPIO	CAPRICORN	VIRGO	CAPRICORN	VIRGO	CANCER	LIBRA	LEO
13			SCORPIO	CAPRICORN	VIRGO	CAPRICORN	VIRGO	CANCER	LIBRA	LEO
14	2:40 AM	VIRGO	SCORPIO	CAPRICORN	VIRGO	CAPRICORN	VIRGO	CANCER	LIBRA	LEO
15			SCORPIO	CAPRICORN	VIRGO	CAPRICORN	VIRGO	CANCER	LIBRA	LEO
16	5:35 AM	LIBRA	SCORPIO	CAPRICORN	VIRGO	CAPRICORN	VIRGO	CANCER	LIBRA	LEO
17			SCORPIO	CAPRICORN	VIRGO	CAPRICORN	VIRGO	CANCER	LIBRA	LEO
18	6:18 AM	SCORPIO	SCORPIO	CAPRICORN	VIRGC	CAPRICORN	VIRGO	CANCER	LIBRA	LEO
19			SCORPIO	CAPRICORN	VIRGO	CAPRICORN	VIRGO	CANCER	LIBRA	LEO
20	6:15 AM	SAGITTARIUS	SCORPIO	CAPRICORN	VIRGO	CAPRICORN	VIRGO	CANCER	LIBRA	LEO
21			SCORPIO	CAPRICORN	VIRGO	CAPRICORN	VIRGO	CANCER	LIBRA	LEO
22	7:20 AM	CAPRICORN	SAGITTARIUS	CAPRICORN	VIRGO	CAPRICORN	VIRGO	CANCER	LIBRA	LEO

1950

	MOON FROM	IN	MERCURY	VENUS	MARS	JUPITER	SATURN	URANUS	NEPTUNE	PLUTO
OCT.										
24			LIBRA	LIBRA	SAGITTARIUS	AQUARIUS	VIRGO	CANCER	LIBRA	LEO
25	12:04 PM	TAURUS	LIBRA	LIBRA	SAGITTARIUS	AQUARIUS	VIRGO	CANCER	LIBRA	LEO
26			LIBRA	LIBRA	SAGITTARIUS	AQUARIUS	VIRGO	CANCER	LIBRA	LEO
27			SCORPIO	LIBRA	SAGITTARIUS	AQUARIUS	VIRGO	CANCER	LIBRA	LEO
28	0:22 AM	GEMINI	SCORPIO	SCORPIO	SAGITTARIUS	AQUARIUS	VIRGO	CANCER	LIBRA	LEO
29			SCORPIO	SCORPIO	SAGITTARIUS	AQUARIUS	VIRGO	CANCER	LIBRA	LEO
30	1:02 PM	CANCER	SCORPIO	SCORPIO	SAGITTARIUS	AQUARIUS	VIRGO	CANCER	LIBRA	LEO
31			SCORPIO	SCORPIO	SAGITTARIUS	AQUARIUS	VIRGO	CANCER	LIBRA	LEO
NOV.										
1			SCORPIO	SCORPIO	SAGITTARIUS	AQUARIUS	VIRGO	CANCER	LIBRA	LEO
2	0:34 AM	LEO	SCORPIO	SCORPIO	SAGITTARIUS	AQUARIUS	VIRGO	CANCER	LIBRA	LEO
3			SCORPIO	SCORPIO	SAGITTARIUS	AQUARIUS	VIRGO	CANCER	LIBRA	LEO
4	9:19 AM	VIRGO	SCORPIO	SCORPIO	SAGITTARIUS	AQUARIUS	VIRGO	CANCER	LIBRA	LEO
5			SCORPIO	SCORPIO	SAGITTARIUS	AQUARIUS	VIRGO	CANCER	LIBRA	LEO
6	2:05 PM	LIBRA	SCORPIO	SCORPIO	CAPRICORN	AQUARIUS	VIRGO	CANCER	LIBRA	LEO
7			SCORPIO	SCORPIO	CAPRICORN	AQUARIUS	VIRGO	CANCER	LIBRA	LEO
8	3:26 PM	SCORPIO	SCORPIO	SCORPIO	CAPRICORN	AQUARIUS	VIRGO	CANCER	LIBRA	LEO
9			SCORPIO	SCORPIO	CAPRICORN	AQUARIUS	VIRGO	CANCER	LIBRA	LEO
10	2:52 PM	SAGITTARIUS	SCORPIO	SCORPIO	CAPRICORN	AQUARIUS	VIRGO	CANCER	LIBRA	LEO
11			SCORPIO	SCORPIO	CAPRICORN	AQUARIUS	VIRGO	CANCER	LIBRA	LEO
12	2:29 PM	CAPRICORN	SCORPIO	SCORPIO	CAPRICORN	AQUARIUS	VIRGO	CANCER	LIBRA	LEO
13			SCORPIO	SCORPIO	CAPRICORN	AQUARIUS	VIRGO	CANCER	LIBRA	LEO
14	4:20 PM	AQUARIUS	SCORPIO	SCORPIO	CAPRICORN	AQUARIUS	VIRGO	CANCER	LIBRA	LEO
15			SAGITTARIUS	SCORPIO	CAPRICORN	AQUARIUS	VIRGO	CANCER	LIBRA	LEO
16	9:44 PM	PISCES	SAGITTARIUS	SCORPIO	CAPRICORN	AQUARIUS	VIRGO	CANCER	LIBRA	LEO
17			SAGITTARIUS	SCORPIO	CAPRICORN	AQUARIUS	VIRGO	CANCER	LIBRA	LEO
18			SAGITTARIUS	SCORPIO	CAPRICORN	AQUARIUS	VIRGO	CANCER	LIBRA	LEO
19	6:39 AM	ARIES	SAGITTARIUS	SCORPIO	CAPRICORN	AQUARIUS	VIRGO	CANCER	LIBRA	LEO
20			SAGITTARIUS	SCORPIO	CAPRICORN	AQUARIUS	VIRGO	CANCER	LIBRA	LEO
21	6:09 PM	TAURUS	SAGITTARIUS	SAGITTARIUS	CAPRICORN	AQUARIUS	LIBRA	CANCER	LIBRA	LEO
22			SAGITTARIUS	SAGITTARIUS	CAPRICORN	AQUARIUS	LIBRA	CANCER	LIBRA	LEO

1951

	MOON FROM	IN	MERCURY	VENUS	MARS	JUPITER	SATURN	URANUS	NEPTUNE	PLUTO
OCT.										
25	8:59 AM	VIRGO	SCORPIO	VIRGO	VIRGO	ARIES	LIBRA	CANCER	LIBRA	LEO
26			SCORPIO	VIRGO	VIRGO	ARIES	LIBRA	CANCER	LIBRA	LEO
27	5:20 PM	LIBRA	SCORPIO	VIRGO	VIRGO	ARIES	LIBRA	CANCER	LIBRA	LEO
28			SCORPIO	VIRGO	VIRGO	ARIES	LIBRA	CANCER	LIBRA	LEO
29	10:06 PM	SCORPIO	SCORPIO	VIRGO	VIRGO	ARIES	LIBRA	CANCER	LIBRA	LEO
30			SCORPIO	VIRGO	VIRGO	ARIES	LIBRA	CANCER	LIBRA	LEO
31			SCORPIO	VIRGO	VIRGO	ARIES	LIBRA	CANCER	LIBRA	LEO
NOV.										
1	0:18 AM	SAGITTARIUS	SCORPIO	VIRGO	VIRGO	ARIES	LIBRA	CANCER	LIBRA	LEO
2			SCORPIO	VIRGO	VIRGO	ARIES	LIBRA	CANCER	LIBRA	LEO
3	1:40 AM	CAPRICORN	SCORPIO	VIRGO	VIRGO	ARIES	LIBRA	CANCER	LIBRA	LEO
4			SCORPIO	VIRGO	VIRGO	ARIES	LIBRA	CANCER	LIBRA	LEO
5	3:45 AM	AQUARIUS	SCORPIO	VIRGO	VIRGO	ARIES	LIBRA	CANCER	LIBRA	LEO
6			SCORPIO	VIRGO	VIRGO	ARIES	LIBRA	CANCER	LIBRA	LEO
7	7:23 AM	PISCES	SCORPIO	VIRGO	VIRGO	ARIES	LIBRA	CANCER	LIBRA	LEO
8			SCORPIO	VIRGO	VIRGO	ARIES	LIBRA	CANCER	LIBRA	LEO
9	12:54 PM	ARIES	SAGITTARIUS	VIRGO	VIRGO	ARIES	LIBRA	CANCER	LIBRA	LEO
10			SAGITTARIUS	LIBRA	VIRGO	ARIES	LIBRA	CANCER	LIBRA	LEO
11	8:09 PM	TAURUS	SAGITTARIUS	LIBRA	VIRGO	ARIES	LIBRA	CANCER	LIBRA	LEO
12			SAGITTARIUS	LIBRA	VIRGO	ARIES	LIBRA	CANCER	LIBRA	LEO
13			SAGITTARIUS	LIBRA	VIRGO	ARIES	LIBRA	CANCER	LIBRA	LEO
14	5:16 AM	GEMINI	SAGITTARIUS	LIBRA	VIRGO	ARIES	LIBRA	CANCER	LIBRA	LEO
15			SAGITTARIUS	LIBRA	VIRGO	ARIES	LIBRA	CANCER	LIBRA	LEO
16	4:30 PM	CANCER	SAGITTARIUS	LIBRA	VIRGO	ARIES	LIBRA	CANCER	LIBRA	LEO
17			SAGITTARIUS	LIBRA	VIRGO	ARIES	LIBRA	CANCER	LIBRA	LEO
18			SAGITTARIUS	LIBRA	VIRGO	ARIES	LIBRA	CANCER	LIBRA	LEO
19	5:12 AM	LEO	SAGITTARIUS	LIBRA	VIRGO	ARIES	LIBRA	CANCER	LIBRA	LEO
20			SAGITTARIUS	LIBRA	VIRGO	ARIES	LIBRA	CANCER	LIBRA	LEO
21	5:32 PM	VIRGO	SAGITTARIUS	LIBRA	VIRGO	ARIES	LIBRA	CANCER	LIBRA	LEO
22			SAGITTARIUS	LIBRA	VIRGO	ARIES	LIBRA	CANCER	LIBRA	LEO
23			SAGITTARIUS	LIBRA	VIRGO	ARIES	LIBRA	CANCER	LIBRA	LEO

	MOON		MERCURY	VENUS	MARS	JUPITER	SATURN	URANUS	NEPTUNE	PLUTO
	FROM	IN								
OCT.										
24			SCORPIO	SAGITTARIUS	CAPRICORN	TAURUS	LIBRA	CANCER	LIBRA	LEO
25	7:17 PM	AQUARIUS	SCORPIO	SAGITTARIUS	CAPRICORN	TAURUS	LIBRA	CANCER	LIBRA	LEO
26			SCORPIO	SAGITTARIUS	CAPRICORN	TAURUS	LIBRA	CANCER	LIBRA	LEO
27	9:12 PM	PISCES	SCORPIO	SAGITTARIUS	CAPRICORN	TAURUS	LIBRA	CANCER	LIBRA	LEO
28			SCORPIO	SAGITTARIUS	CAPRICORN	TAURUS	LIBRA	CANCER	LIBRA	LEO
29	11:27 PM	ARIES	SCORPIO	SAGITTARIUS	CAPRICORN	TAURUS	LIBRA	CANCER	LIBRA	LEO
30			SCORPIO	SAGITTARIUS	CAPRICORN	TAURUS	LIBRA	CANCER	LIBRA	LEO
31			SCORPIO	SAGITTARIUS	CAPRICORN	TAURUS	LIBRA	CANCER	LIBRA	LEO
NOV.										
1	2:14 AM	TAURUS	SCORPIO	SAGITTARIUS	CAPRICORN	TAURUS	LIBRA	CANCER	LIBRA	LEO
2			SAGITTARIUS	SAGITTARIUS	CAPRICORN	TAURUS	LIBRA	CANCER	LIBRA	LEO
3	6:39 AM	GEMINI	SAGITTARIUS	SAGITTARIUS	CAPRICORN	TAURUS	LIBRA	CANCER	LIBRA	LEO
4			SAGITTARIUS	SAGITTARIUS	CAPRICORN	TAURUS	LIBRA	CANCER	LIBRA	LEO
5	1:28 PM	CANCER	SAGITTARIUS	SAGITTARIUS	CAPRICORN	TAURUS	LIBRA	CANCER	LIBRA	LEO
6			SAGITTARIUS	SAGITTARIUS	CAPRICORN	TAURUS	LIBRA	CANCER	LIBRA	LEO
7			SAGITTARIUS	SAGITTARIUS	CAPRICORN	TAURUS	LIBRA	CANCER	LIBRA	LEO
8	0:24 AM	LEO	SAGITTARIUS	SAGITTARIUS	CAPRICORN	TAURUS	LIBRA	CANCER	LIBRA	LEO
9			SAGITTARIUS	SAGITTARIUS	CAPRICORN	TAURUS	LIBRA	CANCER	LIBRA	LEO
10	10:42 AM	VIRGO	SAGITTARIUS	SAGITTARIUS	CAPRICORN	TAURUS	LIBRA	CANCER	LIBRA	LEO
11			SAGITTARIUS	SAGITTARIUS	CAPRICORN	TAURUS	LIBRA	CANCER	LIBRA	LEO
12	10:53 PM	LIBRA	SAGITTARIUS	SAGITTARIUS	CAPRICORN	TAURUS	LIBRA	CANCER	LIBRA	LEO
13			SAGITTARIUS	SAGITTARIUS	CAPRICORN	TAURUS	LIBRA	CANCER	LIBRA	LEO
14			SAGITTARIUS	SAGITTARIUS	CAPRICORN	TAURUS	LIBRA	CANCER	LIBRA	LEO
15	8:37 AM	SCORPIO	SAGITTARIUS	SAGITTARIUS	CAPRICORN	TAURUS	LIBRA	CANCER	LIBRA	LEO
16			SAGITTARIUS	CAPRICORN	CAPRICORN	TAURUS	LIBRA	CANCER	LIBRA	LEO
17	4:53 PM	SAGITTARIUS	SAGITTARIUS	CAPRICORN	CAPRICORN	TAURUS	LIBRA	CANCER	LIBRA	LEO
18			SAGITTARIUS	CAPRICORN	CAPRICORN	TAURUS	LIBRA	CANCER	LIBRA	LEO
19	8:55 AM	CAPRICORN	SAGITTARIUS	CAPRICORN	CAPRICORN	TAURUS	LIBRA	CANCER	LIBRA	LEO
20			SAGITTARIUS	CAPRICORN	CAPRICORN	TAURUS	LIBRA	CANCER	LIBRA	LEO
21			SAGITTARIUS	CAPRICORN	CAPRICORN	TAURUS	LIBRA	CANCER	LIBRA	LEO
22	0:15 AM	AQUARIUS	SAGITTARIUS	CAPRICORN	AQUARIUS	TAURUS	LIBRA	CANCER	LIBRA	LEO

1953

	MOON		MERCURY	VENUS	MARS	JUPITER	SATURN	URANUS	NEPTUNE	PLUTO
	FROM	IN								
OCT.										
24	10:52 AM	GEMINI	SCORPIO	LIBRA	VIRGO	GEMINI	SCORPIO	CANCER	LIBRA	LEO
25			SCORPIO	LIBRA	VIRGO	GEMINI	SCORPIO	CANCER	LIBRA	LEO
26	1:55 PM	CANCER	SCORPIO	LIBRA	VIRGO	GEMINI	SCORPIO	CANCER	LIBRA	LEO
27			SCORPIO	LIBRA	VIRGO	GEMINI	SCORPIO	CANCER	LIBRA	LEO
28	9:14 PM	LEO	SCORPIO	LIBRA	VIRGO	GEMINI	SCORPIO	CANCER	LIBRA	LEO
29			SCORPIO	LIBRA	VIRGO	GEMINI	SCORPIO	CANCER	LIBRA	LEO
30			SCORPIO	LIBRA	VIRGO	GEMINI	SCORPIO	CANCER	LIBRA	LEO
31	8:01 AM	VIRGO	SCORPIO	LIBRA	VIRGO	GEMINI	SCORPIO	CANCER	LIBRA	LEO
NOV.										
1			SAGITTARIUS	LIBRA	VIRGO	GEMINI	SCORPIO	CANCER	LIBRA	LEO
2	9:02 PM	LIBRA	SAGITTARIUS	LIBRA	LIBRA	GEMINI	SCORPIO	CANCER	LIBRA	LEO
3			SAGITTARIUS	LIBRA	LIBRA	GEMINI	SCORPIO	CANCER	LIBRA	LEO
4			SAGITTARIUS	LIBRA	LIBRA	GEMINI	SCORPIO	CANCER	LIBRA	LEO
5	9:22 AM	SCORPIO	SAGITTARIUS	LIBRA	LIBRA	GEMINI	SCORPIO	CANCER	LIBRA	LEO
6			SAGITTARIUS	LIBRA	LIBRA	GEMINI	SCORPIO	CANCER	LIBRA	LEO
7	8:15 PM	SAGITTARIUS	SCORPIO	LIBRA	LIBRA	GEMINI	SCORPIO	CANCER	LIBRA	LEO
8			SCORPIO	LIBRA	LIBRA	GEMINI	SCORPIO	CANCER	LIBRA	LEO
9			SCORPIO	LIBRA	LIBRA	GEMINI	SCORPIO	CANCER	LIBRA	LEO
10	5:29 AM	CAPRICORN	SCORPIO	LIBRA	LIBRA	GEMINI	SCORPIO	CANCER	LIBRA	LEO
11			SCORPIO	LIBRA	LIBRA	GEMINI	SCORPIO	CANCER	LIBRA	LEO
12	12:23 PM	AQUARIUS	SCORPIO	SCORPIO	LIBRA	GEMINI	SCORPIO	CANCER	LIBRA	LEO
13			SCORPIO	SCORPIO	LIBRA	GEMINI	SCORPIO	CANCER	LIBRA	LEO
14	2:53 PM	PISCES	SCORPIO	SCORPIO	LIBRA	GEMINI	SCORPIO	CANCER	LIBRA	LEO
15			SCORPIO	SCORPIO	LIBRA	GEMINI	SCORPIO	CANCER	LIBRA	LEO
16	7:19 PM	ARIES	SCORPIO	SCORPIO	LIBRA	GEMINI	SCORPIO	CANCER	LIBRA	LEO
17			SCORPIO	SCORPIO	LIBRA	GEMINI	SCORPIO	CANCER	LIBRA	LEO
18	8:25 PM	TAURUS	SCORPIO	SCORPIO	LIBRA	GEMINI	SCORPIO	CANCER	LIBRA	LEO
19			SCORPIO	SCORPIO	LIBRA	GEMINI	SCORPIO	CANCER	LIBRA	LEO
20	9:18 PM	GEMINI	SCORPIO	SCORPIO	LIBRA	GEMINI	SCORPIO	CANCER	LIBRA	LEO
21			SCORPIO	SCORPIO	LIBRA	GEMINI	SCORPIO	CANCER	LIBRA	LEO
22	11:59 PM	CANCER	SCORPIO	SCORPIO	LIBRA	GEMINI	SCORPIO	CANCER	LIBRA	LEO

1954

SCORPIO

	MOON FROM	IN	MERCURY	VENUS	MARS	JUPITER	SATURN	URANUS	NEPTUNE	PLUTO
OCT.										
24			SCORPIO	SAGITTARIUS	AQUARIUS	CANCER	SCORPIO	CANCER	LIBRA	LEO
25			SCORPIO	SAGITTARIUS	AQUARIUS	CANCER	SCORPIO	CANCER	LIBRA	LEO
26	7:24 AM	SCORPIO	SCORPIO	SAGITTARIUS	AQUARIUS	CANCER	SCORPIO	CANCER	LIBRA	LEO
27			SCORPIO	SAGITTARIUS	AQUARIUS	CANCER	SCORPIO	CANCER	LIBRA	LEO
28	7:55 PM	SAGITTARIUS	SCORPIO	SCORPIO	AQUARIUS	CANCER	SCORPIO	CANCER	LIBRA	LEO
29			SCORPIO	SCORPIO	AQUARIUS	CANCER	SCORPIO	CANCER	LIBRA	LEO
30			SCORPIO	SCORPIO	AQUARIUS	CANCER	SCORPIO	CANCER	LIBRA	LEO
31	8:12 AM	CAPRICORN	SCORPIO	SCORPIO	AQUARIUS	CANCER	SCORPIO	CANCER	LIBRA	LEO
NOV.										
1			SCORPIO	SCORPIO	AQUARIUS	CANCER	SCORPIO	CANCER	LIBRA	LEO
2	7:00 PM	AQUARIUS	SCORPIO	SCORPIO	AQUARIUS	CANCER	SCORPIO	CANCER	LIBRA	LEO
3			SCORPIO	SCORPIO	AQUARIUS	CANCER	SCORPIO	CANCER	LIBRA	LEO
4			SCORPIO	SCORPIO	AQUARIUS	CANCER	SCORPIO	CANCER	LIBRA	LEO
5	0:24 AM	PISCES	LIBRA	SCORPIO	AQUARIUS	CANCER	SCORPIO	CANCER	LIBRA	LEO
6			LIBRA	SCORPIO	AQUARIUS	CANCER	SCORPIO	CANCER	LIBRA	LEO
7	5:58 AM	ARIES	LIBRA	SCORPIO	AQUARIUS	CANCER	SCORPIO	CANCER	LIBRA	LEO
8			LIBRA	SCORPIO	AQUARIUS	CANCER	SCORPIO	CANCER	LIBRA	LEO
9	6:04 AM	TAURUS	LIBRA	SCORPIO	AQUARIUS	CANCER	SCORPIO	CANCER	LIBRA	LEO
10			LIBRA	SCORPIO	AQUARIUS	CANCER	SCORPIO	CANCER	LIBRA	LEO
11	5:36 AM	GEMINI	LIBRA	SCORPIO	AQUARIUS	CANCER	SCORPIO	CANCER	LIBRA	LEO
12			SCORPIO	SCORPIO	AQUARIUS	CANCER	SCORPIO	CANCER	LIBRA	LEO
13	5:36 AM	CANCER	SCORPIO	SCORPIO	AQUARIUS	CANCER	SCORPIO	CANCER	LIBRA	LEO
14			SCORPIO	SCORPIO	AQUARIUS	CANCER	SCORPIO	CANCER	LIBRA	LEO
15	8:45 AM	LEO	SCORPIO	SCORPIO	AQUARIUS	CANCER	SCORPIO	CANCER	LIBRA	LEO
16			SCORPIO	SCORPIO	AQUARIUS	CANCER	SCORPIO	CANCER	LIBRA	LEO
17	2:50 PM	VIRGO	SCORPIO	SCORPIO	AQUARIUS	CANCER	SCORPIO	CANCER	LIBRA	LEO
18			SCORPIO	SCORPIO	AQUARIUS	CANCER	SCORPIO	CANCER	LIBRA	LEO
19			SCORPIO	SCORPIO	AQUARIUS	CANCER	SCORPIO	CANCER	LIBRA	LEO
20	1:13 AM	LIBRA	SCORPIO	SCORPIO	AQUARIUS	CANCER	SCORPIO	CANCER	LIBRA	LEO
21			SCORPIO	SCORPIO	AQUARIUS	CANCER	SCORPIO	CANCER	LIBRA	LEO
22	1:40 PM	SCORPIO	SCORPIO	SCORPIO	AQUARIUS	CANCER	SCORPIO	CANCER	LIBRA	LEO

1955

	MOON FROM	IN	MERCURY	VENUS	MARS	JUPITER	SATURN	URANUS	NEPTUNE	PLUTO
OCT.										
25			LIBRA	SCORPIO	LIBRA	LEO	SCORPIO	LEO	LIBRA	LEO
26	4:42 AM	PISCES	LIBRA	SCORPIO	LIBRA	LEO	SCORPIO	LEO	LIBRA	LEO
27			LIBRA	SCORPIO	LIBRA	LEO	SCORPIO	LEO	LIBRA	LEO
28	11:07 AM	ARIES	LIBRA	SCORPIO	LIBRA	LEO	SCORPIO	LEO	LIBRA	LEO
29			LIBRA	SCORPIO	LIBRA	LEO	SCORPIO	LEO	LIBRA	LEO
30	1:50 PM	TAURUS	LIBRA	SCORPIO	LIBRA	LEO	SCORPIO	LEO	LIBRA	LEO
31			LIBRA	SCORPIO	LIBRA	LEO	SCORPIO	LEO	LIBRA	LEO
NOV.										
1	2:53 PM	GEMINI	LIBRA	SCORPIO	LIBRA	LEO	SCORPIO	LEO	LIBRA	LEO
2			LIBRA	SCORPIO	LIBRA	LEO	SCORPIO	LEO	LIBRA	LEO
3	3:39 PM	CANCER	LIBRA	SCORPIO	LIBRA	LEO	SCORPIO	LEO	LIBRA	LEO
4			LIBRA	SCORPIO	LIBRA	LEO	SCORPIO	LEO	LIBRA	LEO
5	5:21 PM	LEO	LIBRA	SCORPIO	LIBRA	LEO	SCORPIO	LEO	LIBRA	LEO
6			LIBRA	SCORPIO	LIBRA	LEO	SCORPIO	LEO	LIBRA	LEO
7	9:39 PM	VIRGO	LIBRA	SAGITTARIUS	LIBRA	LEO	SCORPIO	LEO	LIBRA	LEO
8			LIBRA	SAGITTARIUS	LIBRA	LEO	SCORPIO	LEO	LIBRA	LEO
9			SCORPIO	SAGITTARIUS	LIBRA	LEO	SCORPIO	LEO	LIBRA	LEO
10	4:27 AM	LIBRA	SCORPIO	SAGITTARIUS	LIBRA	LEO	SCORPIO	LEO	LIBRA	LEO
11			SCORPIO	SAGITTARIUS	LIBRA	LEO	SCORPIO	LEO	LIBRA	LEO
12	1:28 PM	SCORPIO	SCORPIO	SAGITTARIUS	LIBRA	LEO	SCORPIO	LEO	LIBRA	LEO
13			SCORPIO	SAGITTARIUS	LIBRA	LEO	SCORPIO	LEO	LIBRA	LEO
14			SCORPIO	SAGITTARIUS	LIBRA	LEO	SCORPIO	LEO	LIBRA	LEO
15	0:37 AM	SAGITTARIUS	SCORPIO	SAGITTARIUS	LIBRA	LEO	SCORPIO	LEO	LIBRA	LEO
16			SCORPIO	SAGITTARIUS	LIBRA	LEO	SCORPIO	LEO	LIBRA	LEO
17	12:48 PM	CAPRICORN	SCORPIO	SAGITTARIUS	LIBRA	LEO	SCORPIO	LEO	LIBRA	LEO
18			SCORPIO	SAGITTARIUS	LIBRA	VIRGO	SCORPIO	LEO	LIBRA	LEO
19			SCORPIO	SAGITTARIUS	LIBRA	VIRGO	SCORPIO	LEO	LIBRA	LEO
20	1:21 AM	AQUARIUS	SCORPIO	SAGITTARIUS	LIBRA	VIRGO	SCORPIO	LEO	LIBRA	LEO
21			SCORPIO	SAGITTARIUS	LIBRA	VIRGO	SCORPIO	LEO	LIBRA	LEO
22	12:54 PM	PISCES	SCORPIO	SAGITTARIUS	LIBRA	VIRGO	SCORPIO	LEO	LIBRA	LEO
23			SCORPIO	SAGITTARIUS	LIBRA	VIRGO	SCORPIO	LEO	LIBRA	LEO

1956 SCORPIO

	MOON FROM IN	MERCURY	VENUS	MARS	JUPITER	SATURN	URANUS	NEPTUNE	PLUTO
OCT.									
24	4:31 AM CANCER	LIBRA	VIRGO	PISCES	VIRGO	SAGITTARIUS	LEO	SCORPIO	VIRGO
25		LIBRA	VIRGO	PISCES	VIRGO	SAGITTARIUS	LEO	SCORPIO	VIRGO
26	7:21 AM LEO	LIBRA	VIRGO	PISCES	VIRGO	SAGITTARIUS	LEO	SCORPIO	VIRGO
27		LIBRA	VIRGO	PISCES	VIRGO	SAGITTARIUS	LEO	SCORPIO	VIRGO
28	10:14 AM VIRGO	LIBRA	VIRGO	PISCES	VIRGO	SAGITTARIUS	LEO	SCORPIO	VIRGO
29		LIBRA	VIRGO	PISCES	VIRGO	SAGITTARIUS	LEO	SCORPIO	VIRGO
30	1:26 PM LIBRA	LIBRA	VIRGO	PISCES	VIRGO	SAGITTARIUS	LEO	SCORPIO	VIRGO
31		LIBRA	VIRGO	PISCES	VIRGO	SAGITTARIUS	LEO	SCORPIO	VIRGO
NOV.									
1	5:56 PM SCORPIO	SCORPIO	LIBRA	PISCES	VIRGO	SAGITTARIUS	LEO	SCORPIO	VIRGO
2		SCORPIO	LIBRA	PISCES	VIRGO	SAGITTARIUS	LEO	SCORPIO	VIRGO
3		SCORPIO	LIBRA	PISCES	VIRGO	SAGITTARIUS	LEO	SCORPIO	VIRGO
4	0:14 AM SAGITTARIUS	SCORPIO	LIBRA	PISCES	VIRGO	SAGITTARIUS	LEO	SCORPIO	VIRGO
5		SCORPIO	LIBRA	PISCES	VIRGO	SAGITTARIUS	LEO	SCORPIO	VIRGO
6	9:33 AM CAPRICORN	SCORPIO	LIBRA	PISCES	VIRGO	SAGITTARIUS	LEO	SCORPIO	VIRGO
7		SCORPIO	LIBRA	PISCES	VIRGO	SAGITTARIUS	LEO	SCORPIO	VIRGO
8	9:08 PM AQUARIUS	SCORPIO	LIBRA	PISCES	VIRGO	SAGITTARIUS	LEO	SCORPIO	VIRGO
9		SCORPIO	LIBRA	PISCES	VIRGO	SAGITTARIUS	LEO	SCORPIO	VIRGO
10		SCORPIO	LIBRA	PISCES	VIRGO	SAGITTARIUS	LEO	SCORPIO	VIRGO
11	10:11 AM PISCES	SCORPIO	LIBRA	PISCES	VIRGO	SAGITTARIUS	LEO	SCORPIO	VIRGO
12		SCORPIO	LIBRA	PISCES	VIRGO	SAGITTARIUS	LEO	SCORPIO	VIRGO
13	9:06 PM ARIES	SCORPIO	LIBRA	PISCES	VIRGO	SAGITTARIUS	LEO	SCORPIO	VIRGO
14		SCORPIO	LIBRA	PISCES	VIRGO	SAGITTARIUS	LEO	SCORPIO	VIRGO
15		SCORPIO	LIBRA	PISCES	VIRGO	SAGITTARIUS	LEO	SCORPIO	VIRGO
16	4:50 AM TAURUS	SCORPIO	LIBRA	PISCES	VIRGO	SAGITTARIUS	LEO	SCORPIO	VIRGO
17		SCORPIO	LIBRA	PISCES	VIRGO	SAGITTARIUS	LEO	SCORPIO	VIRGO
18	9:02 AM GEMINI	SCORPIO	LIBRA	PISCES	VIRGO	SAGITTARIUS	LEO	SCORPIO	VIRGO
19		SAGITTARIUS	LIBRA	PISCES	VIRGO	SAGITTARIUS	LEO	SCORPIO	VIRGO
20	11:36 AM CANCER	SAGITTARIUS	LIBRA	PISCES	VIRGO	SAGITTARIUS	LEO	SCORPIO	VIRGO
21		SAGITTARIUS	LIBRA	PISCES	VIRGO	SAGITTARIUS	LEO	SCORPIO	VIRGO
22	1:11 PM LEO	SAGITTARIUS	LIBRA	PISCES	VIRGO	SAGITTARIUS	LEO	SCORPIO	VIRGO

1957

	MOON FROM IN	MERCURY	VENUS	MARS	JUPITER	SATURN	URANUS	NEPTUNE	PLUTO
OCT.									
24		SCORPIO	SAGITTARIUS	LIBRA	LIBRA	SAGITTARIUS	LEO	SCORPIO	VIRGO
25	2:50 AM SAGITTARIUS	SCORPIO	SAGITTARIUS	LIBRA	LIBRA	SAGITTARIUS	LEO	SCORPIO	VIRGO
26		SCORPIO	SAGITTARIUS	LIBRA	LIBRA	SAGITTARIUS	LEO	SCORPIO	VIRGO
27	7:34 AM CAPRICORN	SCORPIO	SAGITTARIUS	LIBRA	LIBRA	SAGITTARIUS	LEO	SCORPIO	VIRGO
28		SCORPIO	SAGITTARIUS	LIBRA	LIBRA	SAGITTARIUS	LEO	SCORPIO	VIRGO
29	4:31 PM AQUARIUS	SCORPIO	SAGITTARIUS	LIBRA	LIBRA	SAGITTARIUS	LEO	SCORPIO	VIRGO
30		SCORPIO	SAGITTARIUS	LIBRA	LIBRA	SAGITTARIUS	LEO	SCORPIO	VIRGO
31		SCORPIO	SAGITTARIUS	LIBRA	LIBRA	SAGITTARIUS	LEO	SCORPIO	VIRGO
NOV.									
1	4:45 AM PISCES	SCORPIO	SAGITTARIUS	LIBRA	LIBRA	SAGITTARIUS	LEO	SCORPIO	VIRGO
2		SCORPIO	SAGITTARIUS	LIBRA	LIBRA	SAGITTARIUS	LEO	SCORPIO	VIRGO
3	5:30 PM ARIES	SCORPIO	SAGITTARIUS	LIBRA	LIBRA	SAGITTARIUS	LEO	SCORPIO	VIRGO
4		SCORPIO	SAGITTARIUS	LIBRA	LIBRA	SAGITTARIUS	LEO	SCORPIO	VIRGO
5		SCORPIO	SAGITTARIUS	LIBRA	LIBRA	SAGITTARIUS	LEO	SCORPIO	VIRGO
6	4:44 AM TAURUS	SCORPIO	CAPRICORN	LIBRA	LIBRA	SAGITTARIUS	LEO	SCORPIO	VIRGO
7		SCORPIO	CAPRICORN	LIBRA	LIBRA	SAGITTARIUS	LEO	SCORPIO	VIRGO
8	2:05 PM GEMINI	SCORPIO	CAPRICORN	LIBRA	LIBRA	SAGITTARIUS	LEO	SCORPIO	VIRGO
9		SCORPIO	CAPRICORN	SCORPIO	LIBRA	SAGITTARIUS	LEO	SCORPIO	VIRGO
10	9:23 PM CANCER	SCORPIO	CAPRICORN	SCORPIO	LIBRA	SAGITTARIUS	LEO	SCORPIO	VIRGO
11		SCORPIO	CAPRICORN	SCORPIO	LIBRA	SAGITTARIUS	LEO	SCORPIO	VIRGO
12		SAGITTARIUS	CAPRICORN	SCORPIO	LIBRA	SAGITTARIUS	LEO	SCORPIO	VIRGO
13	2:39 AM LEO	SAGITTARIUS	CAPRICORN	SCORPIO	LIBRA	SAGITTARIUS	LEO	SCORPIO	VIRGO
14		SAGITTARIUS	CAPRICORN	SCORPIO	LIBRA	SAGITTARIUS	LEO	SCORPIO	VIRGO
15	6:40 AM VIRGO	SAGITTARIUS	CAPRICORN	SCORPIO	LIBRA	SAGITTARIUS	LEO	SCORPIO	VIRGO
16		SAGITTARIUS	CAPRICORN	SCORPIO	LIBRA	SAGITTARIUS	LEO	SCORPIO	VIRGO
17	8:31 AM LIBRA	SAGITTARIUS	CAPRICORN	SCORPIO	LIBRA	SAGITTARIUS	LEO	SCORPIO	VIRGO
18		SAGITTARIUS	CAPRICORN	SCORPIO	LIBRA	SAGITTARIUS	LEO	SCORPIO	VIRGO
19	10:31 AM SCORPIO	SAGITTARIUS	CAPRICORN	SCORPIO	LIBRA	SAGITTARIUS	LEO	SCORPIO	VIRGO
20		SAGITTARIUS	CAPRICORN	SCORPIO	LIBRA	SAGITTARIUS	LEO	SCORPIO	VIRGO
21	1:11 PM SAGITTARIUS	SAGITTARIUS	CAPRICORN	SCORPIO	LIBRA	SAGITTARIUS	LEO	SCORPIO	VIRGO
22		SAGITTARIUS	CAPRICORN	SCORPIO	LIBRA	SAGITTARIUS	LEO	SCORPIO	VIRGO

1958

SCORPIO

OCT.	MOON FROM IN	MERCURY	VENUS	MARS	JUPITER	SATURN	URANUS	NEPTUNE	PLUTO
24	2:30 PM ARIES	SCORPIO	LIBRA	GEMINI	SCORPIO	SAGITTARIUS	LEO	SCORPIO	VIRGO
25		SCORPIO	LIBRA	GEMINI	SCORPIO	SAGITTARIUS	LEO	SCORPIO	VIRGO
26		SCORPIO	LIBRA	GEMINI	SCORPIO	SAGITTARIUS	LEO	SCORPIO	VIRGO
27	3:09 AM TAURUS	SCORPIO	LIBRA	GEMINI	SCORPIO	SAGITTARIUS	LEO	SCORPIO	VIRGO
28		SCORPIO	SCORPIO	GEMINI	SCORPIO	SAGITTARIUS	LEO	SCORPIO	VIRGO
29	3:20 PM GEMINI	SCORPIO	SCORPIO	TAURUS	SCORPIO	SAGITTARIUS	LEO	SCORPIO	VIRGO
30		SCORPIO	SCORPIO	TAURUS	SCORPIO	SAGITTARIUS	LEO	SCORPIO	VIRGO
31		SCORPIO	SCORPIO	TAURUS	SCORPIO	SAGITTARIUS	LEO	SCORPIO	VIRGO
NOV.									
1	2:43 AM CANCER	SCORPIO	SCORPIO	TAURUS	SCORPIO	SAGITTARIUS	LEO	SCORPIO	VIRGO
2		SCORPIO	SCORPIO	TAURUS	SCORPIO	SAGITTARIUS	LEO	SCORPIO	VIRGO
3	12:19 PM LEO	SCORPIO	SCORPIO	TAURUS	SCORPIO	SAGITTARIUS	LEO	SCORPIO	VIRGO
4		SCORPIO	SCORPIO	TAURUS	SCORPIO	SAGITTARIUS	LEO	SCORPIO	VIRGO
5	5:47 PM VIRGO	SCORPIO	SCORPIO	TAURUS	SCORPIO	SAGITTARIUS	LEO	SCORPIO	VIRGO
6		SAGITTARIUS	SCORPIO	TAURUS	SCORPIO	SAGITTARIUS	LEO	SCORPIO	VIRGO
7	8:33 PM LIBRA	SAGITTARIUS	SCORPIO	TAURUS	SCORPIO	SAGITTARIUS	LEO	SCORPIO	VIRGO
8		SAGITTARIUS	SCORPIO	TAURUS	SCORPIO	SAGITTARIUS	LEO	SCORPIO	VIRGO
9	8:39 PM SCORPIO	SAGITTARIUS	SCORPIO	TAURUS	SCORPIO	SAGITTARIUS	LEO	SCORPIO	VIRGO
10		SAGITTARIUS	SCORPIO	TAURUS	SCORPIO	SAGITTARIUS	LEO	SCORPIO	VIRGO
11	8:22 PM SAGITTARIUS	SAGITTARIUS	SCORPIO	TAURUS	SCORPIO	SAGITTARIUS	LEO	SCORPIO	VIRGO
12		SAGITTARIUS	SCORPIO	TAURUS	SCORPIO	SAGITTARIUS	LEO	SCORPIO	VIRGO
13	9:16 PM CAPRICORN	SAGITTARIUS	SCORPIO	TAURUS	SCORPIO	SAGITTARIUS	LEO	SCORPIO	VIRGO
14		SAGITTARIUS	SCORPIO	TAURUS	SCORPIO	SAGITTARIUS	LEO	SCORPIO	VIRGO
15		SAGITTARIUS	SCORPIO	TAURUS	SCORPIO	SAGITTARIUS	LEO	SCORPIO	VIRGO
16	1:18 AM AQUARIUS	SAGITTARIUS	SCORPIO	TAURUS	SCORPIO	SAGITTARIUS	LEO	SCORPIO	VIRGO
17		SAGITTARIUS	SCORPIO	TAURUS	SCORPIO	SAGITTARIUS	LEO	SCORPIO	VIRGO
18	8:57 AM PISCES	SAGITTARIUS	SCORPIO	TAURUS	SCORPIO	SAGITTARIUS	LEO	SCORPIO	VIRGO
19		SAGITTARIUS	SCORPIO	TAURUS	SCORPIO	SAGITTARIUS	LEO	SCORPIO	VIRGO
20	8:49 PM ARIES	SAGITTARIUS	SCORPIO	TAURUS	SCORPIO	SAGITTARIUS	LEO	SCORPIO	VIRGO
21		SAGITTARIUS	SAGITTARIUS	TAURUS	SCORPIO	SAGITTARIUS	LEO	SCORPIO	VIRGO
22		SAGITTARIUS	SAGITTARIUS	TAURUS	SCORPIO	SAGITTARIUS	LEO	SCORPIO	VIRGO

1959

OCT.	MOON FROM IN	MERCURY	VENUS	MARS	JUPITER	SATURN	URANUS	NEPTUNE	PLUTO
25		SCORPIO	VIRGO	SCORPIO	SAGITTARIUS	CAPRICORN	LEO	SCORPIO	VIRGO
26	10:57 PM VIRGO	SCORPIO	VIRGO	SCORPIO	SAGITTARIUS	CAPRICORN	LEO	SCORPIO	VIRGO
27		SCORPIO	VIRGO	SCORPIO	SAGITTARIUS	CAPRICORN	LEO	SCORPIO	VIRGO
28		SCORPIO	VIRGO	SCORPIO	SAGITTARIUS	CAPRICORN	LEO	SCORPIO	VIRGO
29	3:44 AM LIBRA	SCORPIO	VIRGO	SCORPIO	SAGITTARIUS	CAPRICORN	LEO	SCORPIO	VIRGO
30		SCORPIO	VIRGO	SCORPIO	SAGITTARIUS	CAPRICORN	LEO	SCORPIO	VIRGO
31	5:13 AM SCORPIO	SCORPIO	VIRGO	SCORPIO	SAGITTARIUS	CAPRICORN	LEO	SCORPIO	VIRGO
NOV.									
1		SAGITTARIUS	VIRGO	SCORPIO	SAGITTARIUS	CAPRICORN	LEO	SCORPIO	VIRGO
2	5:05 AM SAGITTARIUS	SAGITTARIUS	VIRGO	SCORPIO	SAGITTARIUS	CAPRICORN	LEO	SCORPIO	VIRGO
3		SAGITTARIUS	VIRGO	SCORPIO	SAGITTARIUS	CAPRICORN	LEO	SCORPIO	VIRGO
4	5:23 AM CAPRICORN	SAGITTARIUS	VIRGO	SCORPIO	SAGITTARIUS	CAPRICORN	LEO	SCORPIO	VIRGO
5		SAGITTARIUS	VIRGO	SCORPIO	SAGITTARIUS	CAPRICORN	LEO	SCORPIO	VIRGO
6	7:32 AM AQUARIUS	SAGITTARIUS	VIRGO	SCORPIO	SAGITTARIUS	CAPRICORN	LEO	SCORPIO	VIRGO
7		SAGITTARIUS	VIRGO	SCORPIO	SAGITTARIUS	CAPRICORN	LEO	SCORPIO	VIRGO
8	1:01 PM PISCES	SAGITTARIUS	VIRGO	SCORPIO	SAGITTARIUS	CAPRICORN	LEO	SCORPIO	VIRGO
9		SAGITTARIUS	VIRGO	SCORPIO	SAGITTARIUS	CAPRICORN	LEO	SCORPIO	VIRGO
10	9:18 PM ARIES	SAGITTARIUS	LIBRA	SCORPIO	SAGITTARIUS	CAPRICORN	LEO	SCORPIO	VIRGO
11		SAGITTARIUS	LIBRA	SCORPIO	SAGITTARIUS	CAPRICORN	LEO	SCORPIO	VIRGO
12		SAGITTARIUS	LIBRA	SCORPIO	SAGITTARIUS	CAPRICORN	LEO	SCORPIO	VIRGO
13	8:11 AM TAURUS	SAGITTARIUS	LIBRA	SCORPIO	SAGITTARIUS	CAPRICORN	LEO	SCORPIO	VIRGO
14		SAGITTARIUS	LIBRA	SCORPIO	SAGITTARIUS	CAPRICORN	LEO	SCORPIO	VIRGO
15	8:07 PM GEMINI	SAGITTARIUS	LIBRA	SCORPIO	SAGITTARIUS	CAPRICORN	LEO	SCORPIO	VIRGO
16		SAGITTARIUS	LIBRA	SCORPIO	SAGITTARIUS	CAPRICORN	LEO	SCORPIO	VIRGO
17		SAGITTARIUS	LIBRA	SCORPIO	SAGITTARIUS	CAPRICORN	LEO	SCORPIO	VIRGO
18	8:38 AM CANCER	SAGITTARIUS	LIBRA	SCORPIO	SAGITTARIUS	CAPRICORN	LEO	SCORPIO	VIRGO
19		SAGITTARIUS	LIBRA	SCORPIO	SAGITTARIUS	CAPRICORN	LEO	SCORPIO	VIRGO
20	9:10 PM LEO	SAGITTARIUS	LIBRA	SCORPIO	SAGITTARIUS	CAPRICORN	LEO	SCORPIO	VIRGO
21		SAGITTARIUS	LIBRA	SCORPIO	SAGITTARIUS	CAPRICORN	LEO	SCORPIO	VIRGO
22		SAGITTARIUS	LIBRA	SCORPIO	SAGITTARIUS	CAPRICORN	LEO	SCORPIO	VIRGO
23	7:11 AM VIRGO	SAGITTARIUS	LIBRA	SCORPIO	SAGITTARIUS	CAPRICORN	LEO	SCORPIO	VIRGO

SCORPIO

OCT.	MOON FROM	IN	MERCURY	VENUS	MARS	JUPITER	SATURN	URANUS	NEPTUNE	PLUTO
24	5:52 PM	CAPRICORN	SCORPIO	SAGITTARIUS	CANCER	SAGITTARIUS	CAPRICORN	LEO	SCORPIO	VIRGO
25			SCORPIO	SAGITTARIUS	CANCER	SAGITTARIUS	CAPRICORN	LEO	SCORPIO	VIRGO
26	8:06 PM	AQUARIUS	SCORPIO	SAGITTARIUS	CANCER	SAGITTARIUS	CAPRICORN	LEO	SCORPIO	VIRGO
27			SCORPIO	SAGITTARIUS	CANCER	CAPRICORN	CAPRICORN	LEO	SCORPIO	VIRGO
28	11:31 PM	PISCES	SCORPIO	SAGITTARIUS	CANCER	CAPRICORN	CAPRICORN	LEO	SCORPIO	VIRGO
29			SCORPIO	SAGITTARIUS	CANCER	CAPRICORN	CAPRICORN	LEO	SCORPIO	VIRGO
30			SCORPIO	SAGITTARIUS	CANCER	CAPRICORN	CAPRICORN	LEO	SCORPIO	VIRGO
31	4:04 AM	ARIES	SCORPIO	SAGITTARIUS	CANCER	CAPRICORN	CAPRICORN	LEO	SCORPIO	VIRGO
NOV.										
1			SCORPIO	SAGITTARIUS	CANCER	CAPRICORN	CAPRICORN	LEO	SCORPIO	VIRGO
2	8:22 AM	TAURUS	SCORPIO	SAGITTARIUS	CANCER	CAPRICORN	CAPRICORN	LEO	SCORPIO	VIRGO
3			SCORPIO	SAGITTARIUS	CANCER	CAPRICORN	CAPRICORN	LEO	SCORPIO	VIRGO
4	6:50 PM	GEMINI	SCORPIO	SAGITTARIUS	CANCER	CAPRICORN	CAPRICORN	LEO	SCORPIO	VIRGO
5			SCORPIO	SAGITTARIUS	CANCER	CAPRICORN	CAPRICORN	LEO	SCORPIO	VIRGO
6			SCORPIO	SAGITTARIUS	CANCER	CAPRICORN	CAPRICORN	LEO	SCORPIO	VIRGO
7	5:37 AM	CANCER	SCORPIO	SAGITTARIUS	CANCER	CAPRICORN	CAPRICORN	LEO	SCORPIO	VIRGO
8			SCORPIO	SAGITTARIUS	CANCER	CAPRICORN	CAPRICORN	LEO	SCORPIO	VIRGO
9	6:05 PM	LEO	SCORPIO	SAGITTARIUS	CANCER	CAPRICORN	CAPRICORN	LEO	SCORPIO	VIRGO
10			SCORPIO	SAGITTARIUS	CANCER	CAPRICORN	CAPRICORN	LEO	SCORPIO	VIRGO
11			SCORPIO	SAGITTARIUS	CANCER	CAPRICORN	CAPRICORN	LEO	SCORPIO	VIRGO
12	6:37 AM	VIRGO	SCORPIO	SAGITTARIUS	CANCER	CAPRICORN	CAPRICORN	LEO	SCORPIO	VIRGO
13			SCORPIO	SAGITTARIUS	CANCER	CAPRICORN	CAPRICORN	LEO	SCORPIO	VIRGO
14	4:17 PM	LIBRA	SCORPIO	SAGITTARIUS	CANCER	CAPRICORN	CAPRICORN	LEO	SCORPIO	VIRGO
15			SCORPIO	SAGITTARIUS	CANCER	CAPRICORN	CAPRICORN	LEO	SCORPIO	VIRGO
16	9:52 PM	SCORPIO	SCORPIO	CAPRICORN	CANCER	CAPRICORN	CAPRICORN	LEO	SCORPIO	VIRGO
17			SCORPIO	CAPRICORN	CANCER	CAPRICORN	CAPRICORN	LEO	SCORPIO	VIRGO
18			SCORPIO	CAPRICORN	CANCER	CAPRICORN	CAPRICORN	LEO	SCORPIO	VIRGO
19	0:27 AM	SAGITTARIUS	SCORPIO	CAPRICORN	CANCER	CAPRICORN	CAPRICORN	LEO	SCORPIO	VIRGO
20			SCORPIO	CAPRICORN	CANCER	CAPRICORN	CAPRICORN	LEO	SCORPIO	VIRGO
21	1:38 AM	CAPRICORN	SCORPIO	CAPRICORN	CANCER	CAPRICORN	CAPRICORN	LEO	SCORPIO	VIRGO
22			SCORPIO	CAPRICORN	CANCER	CAPRICORN	CAPRICORN	LEO	SCORPIO	VIRGO

1961

OCT.	MOON FROM	IN	MERCURY	VENUS	MARS	JUPITER	SATURN	URANUS	NEPTUNE	PLUTO
24			LIBRA	LIBRA	SCORPIO	CAPRICORN	CAPRICORN	LEO	SCORPIO	VIRGO
25	7:43 PM	GEMINI	LIBRA	LIBRA	SCORPIO	CAPRICORN	CAPRICORN	LEO	SCORPIO	VIRGO
26			LIBRA	LIBRA	SCORPIO	CAPRICORN	CAPRICORN	LEO	SCORPIO	VIRGO
27			LIBRA	LIBRA	SCORPIO	CAPRICORN	CAPRICORN	LEO	SCORPIO	VIRGO
28	2:21 AM	CANCER	LIBRA	LIBRA	SCORPIO	CAPRICORN	CAPRICORN	LEO	SCORPIO	VIRGO
29			LIBRA	LIBRA	SCORPIO	CAPRICORN	CAPRICORN	LEO	SCORPIO	VIRGO
30	12:48 PM	LEO	LIBRA	LIBRA	SCORPIO	CAPRICORN	CAPRICORN	LEO	SCORPIO	VIRGO
31			LIBRA	LIBRA	SCORPIO	CAPRICORN	CAPRICORN	LEO	SCORPIO	VIRGO
NOV.										
1			LIBRA	LIBRA	SCORPIO	CAPRICORN	CAPRICORN	LEO	SCORPIO	VIRGO
2	1:33 AM	VIRGO	LIBRA	LIBRA	SCORPIO	CAPRICORN	CAPRICORN	VIRGO	SCORPIO	VIRGO
3			LIBRA	LIBRA	SCORPIO	CAPRICORN	CAPRICORN	VIRGO	SCORPIO	VIRGO
4	1:38 PM	LIBRA	LIBRA	LIBRA	SCORPIO	CAPRICORN	CAPRICORN	VIRGO	SCORPIO	VIRGO
5			LIBRA	LIBRA	SCORPIO	AQUARIUS	CAPRICORN	VIRGO	SCORPIO	VIRGO
6	11:37 PM	SCORPIO	LIBRA	LIBRA	SCORPIO	AQUARIUS	CAPRICORN	VIRGO	SCORPIO	VIRGO
7			LIBRA	LIBRA	SCORPIO	AQUARIUS	CAPRICORN	VIRGO	SCORPIO	VIRGO
8			LIBRA	LIBRA	SCORPIO	AQUARIUS	CAPRICORN	VIRGO	SCORPIO	VIRGO
9	7:00 AM	SAGITTARIUS	LIBRA	LIBRA	SCORPIO	AQUARIUS	CAPRICORN	VIRGO	SCORPIO	VIRGO
10			LIBRA	LIBRA	SCORPIO	AQUARIUS	CAPRICORN	VIRGO	SCORPIO	VIRGO
11	12:15 PM	CAPRICORN	SCORPIO	LIBRA	SCORPIO	AQUARIUS	CAPRICORN	VIRGO	SCORPIO	VIRGO
12			SCORPIO	SCORPIO	SCORPIO	AQUARIUS	CAPRICORN	VIRGO	SCORPIO	VIRGO
13	4:03 PM	AQUARIUS	SCORPIO	SCORPIO	SCORPIO	AQUARIUS	CAPRICORN	VIRGO	SCORPIO	VIRGO
14			SCORPIO	SCORPIO	SAGITTARIUS	AQUARIUS	CAPRICORN	VIRGO	SCORPIO	VIRGO
15	7:11 PM	PISCES	SCORPIO	SCORPIO	SAGITTARIUS	AQUARIUS	CAPRICORN	VIRGO	SCORPIO	VIRGO
16			SCORPIO	SCORPIO	SAGITTARIUS	AQUARIUS	CAPRICORN	VIRGO	SCORPIO	VIRGO
17	10:03 PM	ARIES	SCORPIO	SCORPIO	SAGITTARIUS	AQUARIUS	CAPRICORN	VIRGO	SCORPIO	VIRGO
18			SCORPIO	SCORPIO	SAGITTARIUS	AQUARIUS	CAPRICORN	VIRGO	SCORPIO	VIRGO
19			SCORPIO	SCORPIO	SAGITTARIUS	AQUARIUS	CAPRICORN	VIRGO	SCORPIO	VIRGO
20	0:58 AM	TAURUS	SCORPIO	SCORPIO	SAGITTARIUS	AQUARIUS	CAPRICORN	VIRGO	SCORPIO	VIRGO
21			SCORPIO	SCORPIO	SAGITTARIUS	AQUARIUS	CAPRICORN	VIRGO	SCORPIO	VIRGO
22	5:05 AM	GEMINI	SCORPIO	SCORPIO	SAGITTARIUS	AQUARIUS	CAPRICORN	VIRGO	SCORPIO	VIRGO

1962

SCORPIO

	MOON		MERCURY	VENUS	MARS	JUPITER	SATURN	URANUS	NEPTUNE	PLUTO
	FROM	IN								
OCT.										
24			LIBRA	SCORPIO	LEO	PISCES	AQUARIUS	VIRGO	SCORPIO	VIRGO
25	10:26 AM	LIBRA	LIBRA	SCORPIO	LEO	PISCES	AQUARIUS	VIRGO	SCORPIO	VIRGO
26			LIBRA	SCORPIO	LEO	PISCES	AQUARIUS	VIRGO	SCORPIO	VIRGO
27	10:52 PM	SCORPIO	LIBRA	SCORPIO	LEO	PISCES	AQUARIUS	VIRGO	SCORPIO	VIRGO
28			LIBRA	SCORPIO	LEO	PISCES	AQUARIUS	VIRGO	SCORPIO	VIRGO
29			LIBRA	SCORPIO	LEO	PISCES	AQUARIUS	VIRGO	SCORPIO	VIRGO
30	10:10 AM	SAGITTARIUS	LIBRA	SCORPIO	LEO	PISCES	AQUARIUS	VIRGO	SCORPIO	VIRGO
31			LIBRA	SCORPIO	LEO	PISCES	AQUARIUS	VIRGO	SCORPIO	VIRGO
NOV.										
1	8:20 PM	CAPRICORN	LIBRA	SCORPIO	LEO	PISCES	AQUARIUS	VIRGO	SCORPIO	VIRGO
2			LIBRA	SCORPIO	LEO	PISCES	AQUARIUS	VIRGO	SCORPIO	VIRGO
3			LIBRA	SCORPIO	LEO	PISCES	AQUARIUS	VIRGO	SCORPIO	VIRGO
4	4:02 AM	AQUARIUS	LIBRA	SCORPIO	LEO	PISCES	AQUARIUS	VIRGO	SCORPIO	VIRGO
5			LIBRA	SCORPIO	LEO	PISCES	AQUARIUS	VIRGO	SCORPIO	VIRGO
6	8:40 AM	PISCES	SCORPIO	SCORPIO	LEO	PISCES	AQUARIUS	VIRGO	SCORPIO	VIRGO
7			SCORPIO	SCORPIO	LEO	PISCES	AQUARIUS	VIRGO	SCORPIO	VIRGO
8	10:27 AM	ARIES	SCORPIO	SCORPIO	LEO	PISCES	AQUARIUS	VIRGO	SCORPIO	VIRGO
9			SCORPIO	SCORPIO	LEO	PISCES	AQUARIUS	VIRGO	SCORPIO	VIRGO
10	10:51 AM	TAURUS	SCORPIO	SCORPIO	LEO	PISCES	AQUARIUS	VIRGO	SCORPIO	VIRGO
11			SCORPIO	SCORPIO	LEO	PISCES	AQUARIUS	VIRGO	SCORPIO	VIRGO
12	11:00 AM	GEMINI	SCORPIO	SCORPIO	LEO	PISCES	AQUARIUS	VIRGO	SCORPIO	VIRGO
13			SCORPIO	SCORPIO	LEO	PISCES	AQUARIUS	VIRGO	SCORPIO	VIRGO
14	1:23 PM	CANCER	SCORPIO	SCORPIO	LEO	PISCES	AQUARIUS	VIRGO	SCORPIO	VIRGO
15			SCORPIO	SCORPIO	LEO	PISCES	AQUARIUS	VIRGO	SCORPIO	VIRGO
16	7:10 PM	LEO	SCORPIO	SCORPIO	LEO	PISCES	AQUARIUS	VIRGO	SCORPIO	VIRGO
17			SCORPIO	SCORPIO	LEO	PISCES	AQUARIUS	VIRGO	SCORPIO	VIRGO
18			SCORPIO	SCORPIO	LEO	PISCES	AQUARIUS	VIRGO	SCORPIO	VIRGO
19	4:49 AM	VIRGO	SCORPIO	SCORPIO	LEO	PISCES	AQUARIUS	VIRGO	SCORPIO	VIRGO
20			SCORPIO	SCORPIO	LEO	PISCES	AQUARIUS	VIRGO	SCORPIO	VIRGO
21	5:11 PM	LIBRA	SCORPIO	SCORPIO	LEO	PISCES	AQUARIUS	VIRGO	SCORPIO	VIRGO
22			SCORPIO	SCORPIO	LEO	PISCES	AQUARIUS	VIRGO	SCORPIO	VIRGO

1963

	MOON		MERCURY	VENUS	MARS	JUPITER	SATURN	URANUS	NEPTUNE	PLUTO
	FROM	IN								
OCT.										
25	9:05 AM	AQUARIUS	LIBRA	SCORPIO	SCORPIO	ARIES	AQUARIUS	VIRGO	SCORPIO	VIRGO
26			LIBRA	SCORPIO	SAGITTARIUS	ARIES	AQUARIUS	VIRGO	SCORPIO	VIRGO
27	4:19 PM	PISCES	LIBRA	SCORPIO	SAGITTARIUS	ARIES	AQUARIUS	VIRGO	SCORPIO	VIRGO
28			LIBRA	SCORPIO	SAGITTARIUS	ARIES	AQUARIUS	VIRGO	SCORPIO	VIRGO
29	7:38 PM	ARIES	SCORPIO	SCORPIO	SAGITTARIUS	ARIES	AQUARIUS	VIRGO	SCORPIO	VIRGO
30			SCORPIO	SCORPIO	SAGITTARIUS	ARIES	AQUARIUS	VIRGO	SCORPIO	VIRGO
31	7:57 PM	TAURUS	SCORPIO	SCORPIO	SAGITTARIUS	ARIES	AQUARIUS	VIRGO	SCORPIO	VIRGO
NOV.										
1			SCORPIO	SCORPIO	SAGITTARIUS	ARIES	AQUARIUS	VIRGO	SCORPIO	VIRGO
2	7:43 PM	GEMINI	SCORPIO	SCORPIO	SAGITTARIUS	ARIES	AQUARIUS	VIRGO	SCORPIO	VIRGO
3			MERCURY	SCORPIO	SAGITTARIUS	ARIES	AQUARIUS	VIRGO	SCORPIO	VIRGO
4	7:58 PM	CANCER	SCORPIO	SCORPIO	SAGITTARIUS	ARIES	AQUARIUS	VIRGO	SCORPIO	VIRGO
5			SCORPIO	SCORPIO	SAGITTARIUS	ARIES	AQUARIUS	VIRGO	SCORPIO	VIRGO
6	10:46 PM	LEO	SCORPIO	SAGITTARIUS	SAGITTARIUS	ARIES	AQUARIUS	VIRGO	SCORPIO	VIRGO
7			SCORPIO	SAGITTARIUS	SAGITTARIUS	ARIES	AQUARIUS	VIRGO	SCORPIO	VIRGO
8			SCORPIO	SAGITTARIUS	SAGITTARIUS	ARIES	AQUARIUS	VIRGO	SCORPIO	VIRGO
9	5:10 AM	VIRGO	SCORPIO	SAGITTARIUS	SAGITTARIUS	ARIES	AQUARIUS	VIRGO	SCORPIO	VIRGO
10			SCORPIO	SAGITTARIUS	SAGITTARIUS	ARIES	AQUARIUS	VIRGO	SCORPIO	VIRGO
11	3:13 PM	LIBRA	SCORPIO	SAGITTARIUS	SAGITTARIUS	ARIES	AQUARIUS	VIRGO	SCORPIO	VIRGO
12			SCORPIO	SAGITTARIUS	SAGITTARIUS	ARIES	AQUARIUS	VIRGO	SCORPIO	VIRGO
13			SCORPIO	SAGITTARIUS	SAGITTARIUS	ARIES	AQUARIUS	VIRGO	SCORPIO	VIRGO
14	3:43 AM	SCORPIO	SCORPIO	SAGITTARIUS	SAGITTARIUS	ARIES	AQUARIUS	VIRGO	SCORPIO	VIRGO
15			SCORPIO	SAGITTARIUS	SAGITTARIUS	ARIES	AQUARIUS	VIRGO	SCORPIO	VIRGO
16	3:48 PM	SAGITTARIUS	SCORPIO	SAGITTARIUS	SAGITTARIUS	ARIES	AQUARIUS	VIRGO	SCORPIO	VIRGO
17			SAGITTARIUS	SAGITTARIUS	SAGITTARIUS	ARIES	AQUARIUS	VIRGO	SCORPIO	VIRGO
18			SAGITTARIUS	SAGITTARIUS	SAGITTARIUS	ARIES	AQUARIUS	VIRGO	SCORPIO	VIRGO
19	4:11 AM	CAPRICORN	SAGITTARIUS	SAGITTARIUS	SAGITTARIUS	ARIES	AQUARIUS	VIRGO	SCORPIO	VIRGO
20			SAGITTARIUS	SAGITTARIUS	SAGITTARIUS	ARIES	AQUARIUS	VIRGO	SCORPIO	VIRGO
21	3:37 PM	AQUARIUS	SAGITTARIUS	SAGITTARIUS	SAGITTARIUS	ARIES	AQUARIUS	VIRGO	SCORPIO	VIRGO
22			SAGITTARIUS	SAGITTARIUS	SAGITTARIUS	ARIES	AQUARIUS	VIRGO	SCORPIO	VIRGO
23			SAGITTARIUS	SAGITTARIUS	SAGITTARIUS	ARIES	AQUARIUS	VIRGO	SCORPIO	VIRGO

1964

OCT.	MOON FROM IN	MERCURY	VENUS	MARS	JUPITER	SATURN	URANUS	NEPTUNE	PLUTO
24		SCORPIO	VIRGO	LEO	TAURUS	AQUARIUS	VIRGO	SCORPIO	VIRGO
25	6:41 AM CANCER	SCORPIO	VIRGO	LEO	TAURUS	AQUARIUS	VIRGO	SCORPIO	VIRGO
26		SCORPIO	VIRGO	LEO	TAURUS	AQUARIUS	VIRGO	SCORPIO	VIRGO
27	9:04 AM LEO	SCORPIO	VIRGO	LEO	TAURUS	AQUARIUS	VIRGO	SCORPIO	VIRGO
28		SCORPIO	VIRGO	LEO	TAURUS	AQUARIUS	VIRGO	SCORPIO	VIRGO
29	1:16 PM VIRGO	SCORPIO	VIRGO	LEO	TAURUS	AQUARIUS	VIRGO	SCORPIO	VIRGO
30		SCORPIO	VIRGO	LEO	TAURUS	AQUARIUS	VIRGO	SCORPIO	VIRGO
31	7:23 PM LIBRA	SCORPIO	VIRGO	LEO	TAURUS	AQUARIUS	VIRGO	SCORPIO	VIRGO
NOV.									
1		SCORPIO	LIBRA	LEO	TAURUS	AQUARIUS	VIRGO	SCORPIO	VIRGO
2		SCORPIO	LIBRA	LEO	TAURUS	AQUARIUS	VIRGO	SCORPIO	VIRGO
3	3:46 AM SCORPIO	SCORPIO	LIBRA	LEO	TAURUS	AQUARIUS	VIRGO	SCORPIO	VIRGO
4		SCORPIO	LIBRA	LEO	TAURUS	AQUARIUS	VIRGO	SCORPIO	VIRGO
5	1:54 PM SAGITTARIUS	SCORPIO	LIBRA	LEO	TAURUS	AQUARIUS	VIRGO	SCORPIO	VIRGO
6		SCORPIO	LIBRA	LEO	TAURUS	AQUARIUS	VIRGO	SCORPIO	VIRGO
7		SCORPIO	LIBRA	VIRGO	TAURUS	AQUARIUS	VIRGO	SCORPIO	VIRGO
8	2:02 AM CAPRICORN	SCORPIO	LIBRA	VIRGO	TAURUS	AQUARIUS	VIRGO	SCORPIO	VIRGO
9		SAGITTARIUS	LIBRA	VIRGO	TAURUS	AQUARIUS	VIRGO	SCORPIO	VIRGO
10	2:47 PM AQUARIUS	SAGITTARIUS	LIBRA	VIRGO	TAURUS	AQUARIUS	VIRGO	SCORPIO	VIRGO
11		SAGITTARIUS	LIBRA	VIRGO	TAURUS	AQUARIUS	VIRGO	SCORPIO	VIRGO
12		SAGITTARIUS	LIBRA	VIRGO	TAURUS	AQUARIUS	VIRGO	SCORPIO	VIRGO
13	2:18 AM PISCES	SAGITTARIUS	LIBRA	VIRGO	TAURUS	AQUARIUS	VIRGO	SCORPIO	VIRGO
14		SAGITTARIUS	LIBRA	VIRGO	TAURUS	AQUARIUS	VIRGO	SCORPIO	VIRGO
15	10:24 AM ARIES	SAGITTARIUS	LIBRA	VIRGO	TAURUS	AQUARIUS	VIRGO	SCORPIO	VIRGO
16		SAGITTARIUS	LIBRA	VIRGO	TAURUS	AQUARIUS	VIRGO	SCORPIO	VIRGO
17	2:14 PM TAURUS	SAGITTARIUS	LIBRA	VIRGO	TAURUS	AQUARIUS	VIRGO	SCORPIO	VIRGO
18		SAGITTARIUS	LIBRA	VIRGO	TAURUS	AQUARIUS	VIRGO	SCORPIO	VIRGO
19	3:27 PM GEMINI	SAGITTARIUS	LIBRA	VIRGO	TAURUS	AQUARIUS	VIRGO	SCORPIO	VIRGO
20		SAGITTARIUS	LIBRA	VIRGO	TAURUS	AQUARIUS	VIRGO	SCORPIO	VIRGO
21	3:21 PM CANCER	SAGITTARIUS	LIBRA	VIRGO	TAURUS	AQUARIUS	VIRGO	SCORPIO	VIRGO
22		SAGITTARIUS	LIBRA	VIRGO	TAURUS	AQUARIUS	VIRGO	SCORPIO	VIRGO

1965

OCT.	MOON FROM IN	MERCURY	VENUS	MARS	JUPITER	SATURN	URANUS	NEPTUNE	PLUTO
24	8:14 AM SCORPIO	SCORPIO	SAGITTARIUS	SAGITTARIUS	CANCER	PISCES	VIRGO	SCORPIO	VIRGO
25		SCORPIO	SAGITTARIUS	SAGITTARIUS	CANCER	PISCES	VIRGO	SCORPIO	VIRGO
26	1:34 PM SAGITTARIUS	SCORPIO	SAGITTARIUS	SAGITTARIUS	CANCER	PISCES	VIRGO	SCORPIO	VIRGO
27		SCORPIO	SAGITTARIUS	SAGITTARIUS	CANCER	PISCES	VIRGO	SCORPIO	VIRGO
28	10:07 PM CAPRICORN	SCORPIO	SAGITTARIUS	SAGITTARIUS	CANCER	PISCES	VIRGO	SCORPIO	VIRGO
29		SCORPIO	SAGITTARIUS	SAGITTARIUS	CANCER	PISCES	VIRGO	SCORPIO	VIRGO
30		SCORPIO	SAGITTARIUS	SAGITTARIUS	CANCER	PISCES	VIRGO	SCORPIO	VIRGO
31	9:40 AM AQUARIUS	SCORPIO	SAGITTARIUS	SAGITTARIUS	CANCER	PISCES	VIRGO	SCORPIO	VIRGO
NOV.									
1		SCORPIO	SAGITTARIUS	SAGITTARIUS	CANCER	PISCES	VIRGO	SCORPIO	VIRGO
2	10:48 PM PISCES	SCORPIO	SAGITTARIUS	SAGITTARIUS	CANCER	PISCES	VIRGO	SCORPIO	VIRGO
3		SAGITTARIUS	SAGITTARIUS	SAGITTARIUS	CANCER	PISCES	VIRGO	SCORPIO	VIRGO
4		SAGITTARIUS	SAGITTARIUS	SAGITTARIUS	CANCER	PISCES	VIRGO	SCORPIO	VIRGO
5	9:51 AM ARIES	SAGITTARIUS	SAGITTARIUS	SAGITTARIUS	CANCER	PISCES	VIRGO	SCORPIO	VIRGO
6		SAGITTARIUS	CAPRICORN	SAGITTARIUS	CANCER	PISCES	VIRGO	SCORPIO	VIRGO
7	5:59 PM TAURUS	SAGITTARIUS	CAPRICORN	SAGITTARIUS	CANCER	PISCES	VIRGO	SCORPIO	VIRGO
8		SAGITTARIUS	CAPRICORN	SAGITTARIUS	CANCER	PISCES	VIRGO	SCORPIO	VIRGO
9	11:10 PM GEMINI	SAGITTARIUS	CAPRICORN	SAGITTARIUS	CANCER	PISCES	VIRGO	SCORPIO	VIRGO
10		SAGITTARIUS	CAPRICORN	SAGITTARIUS	CANCER	PISCES	VIRGO	SCORPIO	VIRGO
11		SAGITTARIUS	CAPRICORN	SAGITTARIUS	CANCER	PISCES	VIRGO	SCORPIO	VIRGO
12	2:43 AM CANCER	SAGITTARIUS	CAPRICORN	SAGITTARIUS	CANCER	PISCES	VIRGO	SCORPIO	VIRGO
13		SAGITTARIUS	CAPRICORN	SAGITTARIUS	CANCER	PISCES	VIRGO	SCORPIO	VIRGO
14	5:29 AM LEO	SAGITTARIUS	CAPRICORN	SAGITTARIUS	CANCER	PISCES	VIRGO	SCORPIO	VIRGO
15		SAGITTARIUS	CAPRICORN	CAPRICORN	CANCER	PISCES	VIRGO	SCORPIO	VIRGO
16	8:02 AM VIRGO	SAGITTARIUS	CAPRICORN	CAPRICORN	CANCER	PISCES	VIRGO	SCORPIO	VIRGO
17		SAGITTARIUS	CAPRICORN	CAPRICORN	CANCER	PISCES	VIRGO	SCORPIO	VIRGO
18	11:21 AM LIBRA	SAGITTARIUS	CAPRICORN	CAPRICORN	GEMINI	PISCES	VIRGO	SCORPIO	VIRGO
19		SAGITTARIUS	CAPRICORN	CAPRICORN	GEMINI	PISCES	VIRGO	SCORPIO	VIRGO
20	4:04 PM SCORPIO	SAGITTARIUS	CAPRICORN	CAPRICORN	GEMINI	PISCES	VIRGO	SCORPIO	VIRGO
21		SAGITTARIUS	CAPRICORN	CAPRICORN	GEMINI	PISCES	VIRGO	SCORPIO	VIRGO
22	10:18 PM SAGITTARIUS	SAGITTARIUS	CAPRICORN	CAPRICORN	GEMINI	PISCES	VIRGO	SCORPIO	VIRGO

1966

OCT.	MOON FROM IN	MERCURY	VENUS	MARS	JUPITER	SATURN	URANUS	NEPTUNE	PLUTO
24		SCORPIO	LIBRA	VIRGO	LEO	PISCES	VIRGO	SCORPIO	VIRGO
25		SCORPIO	LIBRA	VIRGO	LEO	PISCES	VIRGO	SCORPIO	VIRGO
26	6:36 AM ARIES	SCORPIO	LIBRA	VIRGO	LEO	PISCES	VIRGO	SCORPIO	VIRGO
27		SCORPIO	LIBRA	VIRGO	LEO	PISCES	VIRGO	SCORPIO	VIRGO
28	6:13 PM TAURUS	SCORPIO	SCORPIO	VIRGO	LEO	PISCES	VIRGO	SCORPIO	VIRGO
29		SCORPIO	SCORPIO	VIRGO	LEO	PISCES	VIRGO	SCORPIO	VIRGO
30		SCORPIO	SCORPIO	VIRGO	LEO	PISCES	VIRGO	SCORPIO	VIRGO
31	4:23 AM GEMINI	SAGITTARIUS	SCORPIO	VIRGO	LEO	PISCES	VIRGO	SCORPIO	VIRGO
NOV.									
1		SAGITTARIUS	SCORPIO	VIRGO	LEO	PISCES	VIRGO	SCORPIO	VIRGO
2	12:41 PM CANCER	SAGITTARIUS	SCORPIO	VIRGO	LEO	PISCES	VIRGO	SCORPIO	VIRGO
3		SAGITTARIUS	SCORPIO	VIRGO	LEO	PISCES	VIRGO	SCORPIO	VIRGO
4	6:39 PM LEO	SAGITTARIUS	SCORPIO	VIRGO	LEO	PISCES	VIRGO	SCORPIO	VIRGO
5		SAGITTARIUS	SCORPIO	VIRGO	LEO	PISCES	VIRGO	SCORPIO	VIRGO
6	10:26 PM VIRGO	SAGITTARIUS	SCORPIO	VIRGO	LEO	PISCES	VIRGO	SCORPIO	VIRGO
7		SAGITTARIUS	SCORPIO	VIRGO	LEO	PISCES	VIRGO	SCORPIO	VIRGO
8		SAGITTARIUS	SCORPIO	VIRGO	LEO	PISCES	VIRGO	SCORPIO	VIRGO
9	0:12 AM LIBRA	SAGITTARIUS	SCORPIO	VIRGO	LEO	PISCES	VIRGO	SCORPIO	VIRGO
10		SAGITTARIUS	SCORPIO	VIRGO	LEO	PISCES	VIRGO	SCORPIO	VIRGO
11	1:22 AM SCORPIO	SAGITTARIUS	SCORPIO	VIRGO	LEO	PISCES	VIRGO	SCORPIO	VIRGO
12		SAGITTARIUS	SCORPIO	VIRGO	LEO	PISCES	VIRGO	SCORPIO	VIRGO
13	2:52 AM SAGITTARIUS	SAGITTARIUS	SCORPIO	VIRGO	LEO	PISCES	VIRGO	SCORPIO	VIRGO
14		SCORPIO	SCORPIO	VIRGO	LEO	PISCES	VIRGO	SCORPIO	VIRGO
15	6:49 AM CAPRICORN	SCORPIO	SCORPIO	VIRGO	LEO	PISCES	VIRGO	SCORPIO	VIRGO
16		SCORPIO	SCORPIO	VIRGO	LEO	PISCES	VIRGO	SCORPIO	VIRGO
17	1:59 PM AQUARIUS	SCORPIO	SCORPIO	VIRGO	LEO	PISCES	VIRGO	SCORPIO	VIRGO
18		SCORPIO	SCORPIO	VIRGO	LEO	PISCES	VIRGO	SCORPIO	VIRGO
19		SCORPIO	SCORPIO	VIRGO	LEO	PISCES	VIRGO	SCORPIO	VIRGO
20	1:13 AM PISCES	SCORPIO	SCORPIO	VIRGO	LEO	PISCES	VIRGO	SCORPIO	VIRGO
21		SCORPIO	SAGITTARIUS	VIRGO	LEO	PISCES	VIRGO	SCORPIO	VIRGO
22	2:00 PM ARIES	SCORPIO	SAGITTARIUS	VIRGO	LEO	PISCES	VIRGO	SCORPIO	VIRGO

1967

OCT.	MOON FROM IN	MERCURY	VENUS	MARS	JUPITER	SATURN	URANUS	NEPTUNE	PLUTO
25		SCORPIO	VIRGO	CAPRICORN	VIRGO	ARIES	VIRGO	SCORPIO	VIRGO
26	2:41 AM LEO	SCORPIO	VIRGO	CAPRICORN	VIRGO	ARIES	VIRGO	SCORPIO	VIRGO
27		SCORPIO	VIRGO	CAPRICORN	VIRGO	ARIES	VIRGO	SCORPIO	VIRGO
28	8:33 AM VIRGO	SCORPIO	VIRGO	CAPRICORN	VIRGO	ARIES	VIRGO	SCORPIO	VIRGO
29		SCORPIO	VIRGO	CAPRICORN	VIRGO	ARIES	VIRGO	SCORPIO	VIRGO
30	10:44 AM LIBRA	SCORPIO	VIRGO	CAPRICORN	VIRGO	ARIES	VIRGO	SCORPIO	VIRGO
31		SCORPIO	VIRGO	CAPRICORN	VIRGO	ARIES	VIRGO	SCORPIO	VIRGO
NOV.									
1	10:40 AM SCORPIO	SCORPIO	VIRGO	CAPRICORN	VIRGO	ARIES	VIRGO	SCORPIO	VIRGO
2		SCORPIO	VIRGO	CAPRICORN	VIRGO	ARIES	VIRGO	SCORPIO	VIRGO
3	10:14 AM SAGITTARIUS	SCORPIO	VIRGO	CAPRICORN	VIRGO	ARIES	VIRGO	SCORPIO	VIRGO
4		SCORPIO	VIRGO	CAPRICORN	VIRGO	ARIES	VIRGO	SCORPIO	VIRGO
5	11:04 AM CAPRICORN	SCORPIO	VIRGO	CAPRICORN	VIRGO	ARIES	VIRGO	SCORPIO	VIRGO
6		SCORPIO	VIRGO	CAPRICORN	VIRGO	ARIES	VIRGO	SCORPIO	VIRGO
7	3:15 PM AQUARIUS	SCORPIO	VIRGO	CAPRICORN	VIRGO	ARIES	VIRGO	SCORPIO	VIRGO
8		SCORPIO	VIRGO	CAPRICORN	VIRGO	ARIES	VIRGO	SCORPIO	VIRGO
9	10:56 PM PISCES	SCORPIO	VIRGO	CAPRICORN	VIRGO	ARIES	VIRGO	SCORPIO	VIRGO
10		SCORPIO	LIBRA	CAPRICORN	VIRGO	ARIES	VIRGO	SCORPIO	VIRGO
11		SCORPIO	LIBRA	CAPRICORN	VIRGO	ARIES	VIRGO	SCORPIO	VIRGO
12	10:25 AM ARIES	SCORPIO	LIBRA	CAPRICORN	VIRGO	ARIES	VIRGO	SCORPIO	VIRGO
13		SCORPIO	LIBRA	CAPRICORN	VIRGO	ARIES	VIRGO	SCORPIO	VIRGO
14	11:04 PM TAURUS	SCORPIO	LIBRA	CAPRICORN	VIRGO	ARIES	VIRGO	SCORPIO	VIRGO
15		SCORPIO	LIBRA	CAPRICORN	VIRGO	ARIES	VIRGO	SCORPIO	VIRGO
16		SCORPIO	LIBRA	CAPRICORN	VIRGO	ARIES	VIRGO	SCORPIO	VIRGO
17	11:37 AM GEMINI	SCORPIO	LIBRA	CAPRICORN	VIRGO	ARIES	VIRGO	SCORPIO	VIRGO
18		SCORPIO	LIBRA	CAPRICORN	VIRGO	ARIES	VIRGO	SCORPIO	VIRGO
19	11:00 PM CANCER	SCORPIO	LIBRA	CAPRICORN	VIRGO	ARIES	VIRGO	SCORPIO	VIRGO
20		SCORPIO	LIBRA	CAPRICORN	VIRGO	ARIES	VIRGO	SCORPIO	VIRGO
21		SCORPIO	LIBRA	CAPRICORN	VIRGO	ARIES	VIRGO	SCORPIO	VIRGO
22	8:52 AM LEO	SCORPIO	LIBRA	CAPRICORN	VIRGO	ARIES	VIRGO	SCORPIO	VIRGO

SCORPIO

OCT.	MOON FROM IN	MERCURY	VENUS	MARS	JUPITER	SATURN	URANUS	NEPTUNE	PLUTO
24		LIBRA	SAGITTARIUS	VIRGO	VIRGO	ARIES	LIBRA	SCORPIO	VIRGO
25	8:25 PM CAPRICORN	LIBRA	SAGITTARIUS	VIRGO	VIRGO	ARIES	LIBRA	SCORPIO	VIRGO
26		LIBRA	SAGITTARIUS	VIRGO	VIRGO	ARIES	LIBRA	SCORPIO	VIRGO
27	10:46 PM AQUARIUS	LIBRA	SAGITTARIUS	VIRGO	VIRGO	ARIES	LIBRA	SCORPIO	VIRGO
28		LIBRA	SAGITTARIUS	VIRGO	VIRGO	ARIES	LIBRA	SCORPIO	VIRGO
29		LIBRA	SAGITTARIUS	VIRGO	VIRGO	ARIES	LIBRA	SCORPIO	VIRGO
30	3:56 AM PISCES	LIBRA	SAGITTARIUS	VIRGO	VIRGO	ARIES	LIBRA	SCORPIO	VIRGO
31		LIBRA	SAGITTARIUS	VIRGO	VIRGO	ARIES	LIBRA	SCORPIO	VIRGO
NOV.									
1	11:58 AM ARIES	LIBRA	SAGITTARIUS	VIRGO	VIRGO	ARIES	LIBRA	SCORPIO	VIRGO
2		LIBRA	SAGITTARIUS	VIRGO	VIRGO	ARIES	LIBRA	SCORPIO	VIRGO
3	10:05 PM TAURUS	LIBRA	SAGITTARIUS	VIRGO	VIRGO	ARIES	LIBRA	SCORPIO	VIRGO
4		LIBRA	SAGITTARIUS	VIRGO	VIRGO	ARIES	LIBRA	SCORPIO	VIRGO
5		LIBRA	SAGITTARIUS	VIRGO	VIRGO	ARIES	LIBRA	SCORPIO	VIRGO
6	9:36 AM GEMINI	LIBRA	SAGITTARIUS	VIRGO	VIRGO	ARIES	LIBRA	SCORPIO	VIRGO
7		LIBRA	SAGITTARIUS	VIRGO	VIRGO	ARIES	LIBRA	SCORPIO	VIRGO
8	10:07 PM CANCER	LIBRA	SAGITTARIUS	VIRGO	VIRGO	ARIES	LIBRA	SCORPIO	VIRGO
9		SCORPIO	SAGITTARIUS	VIRGO	VIRGO	ARIES	LIBRA	SCORPIO	VIRGO
10		SCORPIO	SAGITTARIUS	LIBRA	VIRGO	ARIES	LIBRA	SCORPIO	VIRGO
11	10:49 PM LEO	SCORPIO	SAGITTARIUS	LIBRA	VIRGO	ARIES	LIBRA	SCORPIO	VIRGO
12		SCORPIO	SAGITTARIUS	LIBRA	VIRGO	ARIES	LIBRA	SCORPIO	VIRGO
13	9:04 PM VIRGO	SCORPIO	SAGITTARIUS	LIBRA	VIRGO	ARIES	LIBRA	SCORPIO	VIRGO
14		SCORPIO	SAGITTARIUS	LIBRA	VIRGO	ARIES	LIBRA	SCORPIO	VIRGO
15		SCORPIO	CAPRICORN	LIBRA	VIRGO	ARIES	LIBRA	SCORPIO	VIRGO
16	3:22 AM LIBRA	SCORPIO	CAPRICORN	LIBRA	LIBRA	ARIES	LIBRA	SCORPIO	VIRGO
17		SCORPIO	CAPRICORN	LIBRA	LIBRA	ARIES	LIBRA	SCORPIO	VIRGO
18	6:01 AM SCORPIO	SCORPIO	CAPRICORN	LIBRA	LIBRA	ARIES	LIBRA	SCORPIO	VIRGO
19		SCORPIO	CAPRICORN	LIBRA	LIBRA	ARIES	LIBRA	SCORPIO	VIRGO
20	6:12 AM SAGITTARIUS	SCORPIO	CAPRICORN	LIBRA	LIBRA	ARIES	LIBRA	SCORPIO	VIRGO
21		SCORPIO	CAPRICORN	LIBRA	LIBRA	ARIES	LIBRA	SCORPIO	VIRGO
22	5:43 AM CAPRICORN	SCORPIO	CAPRICORN	LIBRA	LIBRA	ARIES	LIBRA	SCORPIO	VIRGO

1969

OCT.	MOON FROM IN	MERCURY	VENUS	MARS	JUPITER	SATURN	URANUS	NEPTUNE	PLUTO
24		LIBRA	LIBRA	CAPRICORN	LIBRA	TAURUS	LIBRA	SCORPIO	VIRGO
25	0:28 AM TAURUS	LIBRA	LIBRA	CAPRICORN	LIBRA	TAURUS	LIBRA	SCORPIO	VIRGO
26		LIBRA	LIBRA	CAPRICORN	LIBRA	TAURUS	LIBRA	SCORPIO	VIRGO
27	8:23 AM GEMINI	LIBRA	LIBRA	CAPRICORN	LIBRA	TAURUS	LIBRA	SCORPIO	VIRGO
28		LIBRA	LIBRA	CAPRICORN	LIBRA	TAURUS	LIBRA	SCORPIO	VIRGO
29	7:43 PM CANCER	LIBRA	LIBRA	CAPRICORN	LIBRA	TAURUS	LIBRA	SCORPIO	VIRGO
30		LIBRA	LIBRA	CAPRICORN	LIBRA	TAURUS	LIBRA	SCORPIO	VIRGO
31		LIBRA	LIBRA	CAPRICORN	LIBRA	TAURUS	LIBRA	SCORPIO	VIRGO
NOV.									
1	6:38 AM LEO	LIBRA	LIBRA	CAPRICORN	LIBRA	TAURUS	LIBRA	SCORPIO	VIRGO
2		SCORPIO	LIBRA	CAPRICORN	LIBRA	TAURUS	LIBRA	SCORPIO	PLUTO
3	7:13 PM VIRGO	SCORPIO	LIBRA	CAPRICORN	LIBRA	TAURUS	LIBRA	SCORPIO	VIRGO
4		SCORPIO	LIBRA	CAPRICORN	LIBRA	TAURUS	LIBRA	SCORPIO	VIRGO
5		SCORPIO	LIBRA	AQUARIUS	LIBRA	TAURUS	LIBRA	SCORPIO	VIRGO
6	5:08 AM LIBRA	SCORPIO	LIBRA	AQUARIUS	LIBRA	TAURUS	LIBRA	SCORPIO	VIRGO
7		SCORPIO	LIBRA	AQUARIUS	LIBRA	TAURUS	LIBRA	SCORPIO	VIRGO
8	11:18 AM SCORPIO	SCORPIO	LIBRA	AQUARIUS	LIBRA	TAURUS	LIBRA	SCORPIO	VIRGO
9		SCORPIO	LIBRA	AQUARIUS	LIBRA	TAURUS	LIBRA	SCORPIO	VIRGO
10	2:33 PM SAGITTARIUS	SCORPIO	LIBRA	AQUARIUS	LIBRA	TAURUS	LIBRA	SCORPIO	VIRGO
11		SCORPIO	SCORPIO	AQUARIUS	LIBRA	TAURUS	LIBRA	SCORPIO	VIRGO
12	4:26 PM CAPRICORN	SCORPIO	SCORPIO	AQUARIUS	LIBRA	TAURUS	LIBRA	SCORPIO	VIRGO
13		SCORPIO	SCORPIO	AQUARIUS	LIBRA	TAURUS	LIBRA	SCORPIO	VIRGO
14	6:12 PM AQUARIUS	SCORPIO	SCORPIO	AQUARIUS	LIBRA	TAURUS	LIBRA	SCORPIO	VIRGO
15		SCORPIO	SCORPIO	AQUARIUS	LIBRA	TAURUS	LIBRA	SCORPIO	VIRGO
16	8:58 PM PISCES	SCORPIO	SCORPIO	AQUARIUS	LIBRA	TAURUS	LIBRA	SCORPIO	VIRGO
17		SCORPIO	SCORPIO	AQUARIUS	LIBRA	TAURUS	LIBRA	SCORPIO	VIRGO
18		SCORPIO	SCORPIO	AQUARIUS	LIBRA	TAURUS	LIBRA	SCORPIO	VIRGO
19	1:22 AM ARIES	SCORPIO	SCORPIO	AQUARIUS	LIBRA	TAURUS	LIBRA	SCORPIO	VIRGO
20		SCORPIO	SCORPIO	AQUARIUS	LIBRA	TAURUS	LIBRA	SCORPIO	VIRGO
21	7:34 AM TAURUS	SAGITTARIUS	SCORPIO	AQUARIUS	LIBRA	TAURUS	LIBRA	SCORPIO	VIRGO
22		SAGITTARIUS	SCORPIO	AQUARIUS	LIBRA	TAURUS	LIBRA	SCORPIO	VIRGO

1970

Date	MOON FROM IN	MERCURY	VENUS	MARS	JUPITER	SATURN	URANUS	NEPTUNE	PLUTO
OCT.									
24	2:27 PM VIRGO	LIBRA	SCORPIO	LIBRA	SCORPIO	TAURUS	LIBRA	SCORPIO	VIRGO
25		LIBRA	SCORPIO	LIBRA	SCORPIO	TAURUS	LIBRA	SCORPIO	VIRGO
26		SCORPIO	SCORPIO	LIBRA	SCORPIO	TAURUS	LIBRA	SCORPIO	VIRGO
27	2:48 AM LIBRA	SCORPIO	SCORPIO	LIBRA	SCORPIO	TAURUS	LIBRA	SCORPIO	VIRGO
28		SCORPIO	SCORPIO	LIBRA	SCORPIO	TAURUS	LIBRA	SCORPIO	VIRGO
29	1:10 PM SCORPIO	SCORPIO	SCORPIO	LIBRA	SCORPIO	TAURUS	LIBRA	SCORPIO	VIRGO
30		SCORPIO	SCORPIO	LIBRA	SCORPIO	TAURUS	LIBRA	SCORPIO	VIRGO
31	9:27 PM SAGITTARIUS	SCORPIO	SCORPIO	LIBRA	SCORPIO	TAURUS	LIBRA	SCORPIO	VIRGO
NOV.									
1		SCORPIO	SCORPIO	LIBRA	SCORPIO	TAURUS	LIBRA	SCORPIO	VIRGO
2		SCORPIO	SCORPIO	LIBRA	SCORPIO	TAURUS	LIBRA	SCORPIO	VIRGO
3	3:56 AM CAPRICORN	SCORPIO	SCORPIO	LIBRA	SCORPIO	TAURUS	LIBRA	SCORPIO	VIRGO
4		SCORPIO	SCORPIO	LIBRA	SCORPIO	TAURUS	LIBRA	SCORPIO	VIRGO
5	8:23 AM AQUARIUS	SCORPIO	SCORPIO	LIBRA	SCORPIO	TAURUS	LIBRA	SCORPIO	VIRGO
6		SCORPIO	SCORPIO	LIBRA	SCORPIO	TAURUS	LIBRA	SCORPIO	VIRGO
7	11:42 AM PISCES	SCORPIO	SCORPIO	LIBRA	SCORPIO	TAURUS	LIBRA	SAGITTARIUS	VIRGO
8		SCORPIO	SCORPIO	LIBRA	SCORPIO	TAURUS	LIBRA	SAGITTARIUS	VIRGO
9	1:42 PM ARIES	SCORPIO	SCORPIO	LIBRA	SCORPIO	TAURUS	LIBRA	SAGITTARIUS	VIRGO
10		SCORPIO	SCORPIO	LIBRA	SCORPIO	TAURUS	LIBRA	SAGITTARIUS	VIRGO
11	3:53 PM TAURUS	SCORPIO	SCORPIO	LIBRA	SCORPIO	TAURUS	LIBRA	SAGITTARIUS	VIRGO
12		SCORPIO	SCORPIO	LIBRA	SCORPIO	TAURUS	LIBRA	SAGITTARIUS	VIRGO
13	7:08 PM GEMINI	SCORPIO	SCORPIO	LIBRA	SCORPIO	TAURUS	LIBRA	SAGITTARIUS	VIRGO
14		SAGITTARIUS	SCORPIO	LIBRA	SCORPIO	TAURUS	LIBRA	SAGITTARIUS	VIRGO
15		SAGITTARIUS	SCORPIO	LIBRA	SCORPIO	TAURUS	LIBRA	SAGITTARIUS	VIRGO
16	0:50 AM CANCER	SAGITTARIUS	SCORPIO	LIBRA	SCORPIO	TAURUS	LIBRA	SAGITTARIUS	VIRGO
17		SAGITTARIUS	SCORPIO	LIBRA	SCORPIO	TAURUS	LIBRA	SAGITTARIUS	VIRGO
18	9:47 AM LEO	SAGITTARIUS	SCORPIO	LIBRA	SCORPIO	TAURUS	LIBRA	SAGITTARIUS	VIRGO
19		SAGITTARIUS	SCORPIO	LIBRA	SCORPIO	TAURUS	LIBRA	SAGITTARIUS	VIRGO
20	10:07 PM VIRGO	SAGITTARIUS	SCORPIO	LIBRA	SCORPIO	TAURUS	LIBRA	SAGITTARIUS	VIRGO
21		SAGITTARIUS	SCORPIO	LIBRA	SCORPIO	TAURUS	LIBRA	SAGITTARIUS	VIRGO
22		SAGITTARIUS	SCORPIO	LIBRA	SCORPIO	TAURUS	LIBRA	SAGITTARIUS	VIRGO

1971

Date	MOON FROM IN	MERCURY	VENUS	MARS	JUPITER	SATURN	URANUS	NEPTUNE	PLUTO
OCT.									
25		SCORPIO	SCORPIO	AQUARIUS	SAGITTARIUS	GEMINI	LIBRA	SAGITTARIUS	LIBRA
26	7:05 PM AQUARIUS	SCORPIO	SCORPIO	AQUARIUS	SAGITTARIUS	GEMINI	LIBRA	SAGITTARIUS	LIBRA
27		SCORPIO	SCORPIO	AQUARIUS	SAGITTARIUS	GEMINI	LIBRA	SAGITTARIUS	LIBRA
28	11:41 PM PISCES	SCORPIO	SCORPIO	AQUARIUS	SAGITTARIUS	GEMINI	LIBRA	SAGITTARIUS	LIBRA
29		SCORPIO	SCORPIO	AQUARIUS	SAGITTARIUS	GEMINI	LIBRA	SAGITTARIUS	LIBRA
30		SCORPIO	SCORPIO	AQUARIUS	SAGITTARIUS	GEMINI	LIBRA	SAGITTARIUS	LIBRA
31	1:18 AM ARIES	SCORPIO	SCORPIO	AQUARIUS	SAGITTARIUS	GEMINI	LIBRA	SAGITTARIUS	LIBRA
NOV.									
1		SCORPIO	SCORPIO	AQUARIUS	SAGITTARIUS	GEMINI	LIBRA	SAGITTARIUS	LIBRA
2	1:02 AM TAURUS	SCORPIO	SCORPIO	AQUARIUS	SAGITTARIUS	GEMINI	LIBRA	SAGITTARIUS	LIBRA
3		SCORPIO	SCORPIO	AQUARIUS	SAGITTARIUS	GEMINI	LIBRA	SAGITTARIUS	LIBRA
4	1:10 AM GEMINI	SCORPIO	SCORPIO	AQUARIUS	SAGITTARIUS	GEMINI	LIBRA	SAGITTARIUS	LIBRA
5		SCORPIO	SCORPIO	AQUARIUS	SAGITTARIUS	GEMINI	LIBRA	SAGITTARIUS	LIBRA
6	3:07 AM CANCER	SCORPIO	SAGITTARIUS	AQUARIUS	SAGITTARIUS	GEMINI	LIBRA	SAGITTARIUS	LIBRA
7		SAGITTARIUS	SAGITTARIUS	PISCES	SAGITTARIUS	GEMINI	LIBRA	SAGITTARIUS	LIBRA
8	8:29 AM LEO	SAGITTARIUS	SAGITTARIUS	PISCES	SAGITTARIUS	GEMINI	LIBRA	SAGITTARIUS	LIBRA
9		SAGITTARIUS	SAGITTARIUS	PISCES	SAGITTARIUS	GEMINI	LIBRA	SAGITTARIUS	LIBRA
10	5:54 PM VIRGO	SAGITTARIUS	SAGITTARIUS	PISCES	SAGITTARIUS	GEMINI	LIBRA	SAGITTARIUS	LIBRA
11		SAGITTARIUS	SAGITTARIUS	PISCES	SAGITTARIUS	GEMINI	LIBRA	SAGITTARIUS	LIBRA
12		SAGITTARIUS	SAGITTARIUS	PISCES	SAGITTARIUS	GEMINI	LIBRA	SAGITTARIUS	LIBRA
13	6:24 AM LIBRA	SAGITTARIUS	SAGITTARIUS	PISCES	SAGITTARIUS	GEMINI	LIBRA	SAGITTARIUS	LIBRA
14		SAGITTARIUS	SAGITTARIUS	PISCES	SAGITTARIUS	GEMINI	LIBRA	SAGITTARIUS	LIBRA
15	6:54 PM SCORPIO	SAGITTARIUS	SAGITTARIUS	PISCES	SAGITTARIUS	GEMINI	LIBRA	SAGITTARIUS	LIBRA
16		SAGITTARIUS	SAGITTARIUS	PISCES	SAGITTARIUS	GEMINI	LIBRA	SAGITTARIUS	LIBRA
17		SAGITTARIUS	SAGITTARIUS	PISCES	SAGITTARIUS	GEMINI	LIBRA	SAGITTARIUS	LIBRA
18	6:48 AM SAGITTARIUS	SAGITTARIUS	SAGITTARIUS	PISCES	SAGITTARIUS	GEMINI	LIBRA	SAGITTARIUS	LIBRA
19		SAGITTARIUS	SAGITTARIUS	PISCES	SAGITTARIUS	GEMINI	LIBRA	SAGITTARIUS	LIBRA
20	4:55 PM CAPRICORN	SAGITTARIUS	SAGITTARIUS	PISCES	SAGITTARIUS	GEMINI	LIBRA	SAGITTARIUS	LIBRA
21		SAGITTARIUS	SAGITTARIUS	PISCES	SAGITTARIUS	GEMINI	LIBRA	SAGITTARIUS	LIBRA
22		SAGITTARIUS	SAGITTARIUS	PISCES	SAGITTARIUS	GEMINI	LIBRA	SAGITTARIUS	LIBRA

1972

OCT.	MOON FROM IN	MERCURY	VENUS	MARS	JUPITER	SATURN	URANUS	NEPTUNE	PLUTO
24	9:44 AM GEMINI	SCORPIO	VIRGO	LIBRA	CAPRICORN	GEMINI	LIBRA	SAGITTARIUS	LIBRA
25		SCORPIO	VIRGO	LIBRA	CAPRICORN	GEMINI	LIBRA	SAGITTARIUS	LIBRA
26	10:21 AM CANCER	SCORPIO	VIRGO	LIBRA	CAPRICORN	GEMINI	LIBRA	SAGITTARIUS	LIBRA
27		SCORPIO	VIRGO	LIBRA	CAPRICORN	GEMINI	LIBRA	SAGITTARIUS	LIBRA
28	1:43 PM LEO	SCORPIO	VIRGO	LIBRA	CAPRICORN	GEMINI	LIBRA	SAGITTARIUS	LIBRA
29		SCORPIO	VIRGO	LIBRA	CAPRICORN	GEMINI	LIBRA	SAGITTARIUS	LIBRA
30	7:46 PM VIRGO	SCORPIO	VIRGO	LIBRA	CAPRICORN	GEMINI	LIBRA	SAGITTARIUS	LIBRA
31		SAGITTARIUS	LIBRA	LIBRA	CAPRICORN	GEMINI	LIBRA	SAGITTARIUS	LIBRA
NOV.									
1		SAGITTARIUS	LIBRA	LIBRA	CAPRICORN	GEMINI	LIBRA	SAGITTARIUS	LIBRA
2	5:28 AM LIBRA	SAGITTARIUS	LIBRA	LIBRA	CAPRICORN	GEMINI	LIBRA	SAGITTARIUS	LIBRA
3		SAGITTARIUS	LIBRA	LIBRA	CAPRICORN	GEMINI	LIBRA	SAGITTARIUS	LIBRA
4	5:00 PM SCORPIO	SAGITTARIUS	LIBRA	LIBRA	CAPRICORN	GEMINI	LIBRA	SAGITTARIUS	LIBRA
5		SAGITTARIUS	LIBRA	LIBRA	CAPRICORN	GEMINI	LIBRA	SAGITTARIUS	LIBRA
6		SAGITTARIUS	LIBRA	LIBRA	CAPRICORN	GEMINI	LIBRA	SAGITTARIUS	LIBRA
7	5:24 AM SAGITTARIUS	SAGITTARIUS	LIBRA	LIBRA	CAPRICORN	GEMINI	LIBRA	SAGITTARIUS	LIBRA
8		SAGITTARIUS	LIBRA	LIBRA	CAPRICORN	GEMINI	LIBRA	SAGITTARIUS	LIBRA
9	6:05 PM CAPRICORN	SAGITTARIUS	LIBRA	LIBRA	CAPRICORN	GEMINI	LIBRA	SAGITTARIUS	LIBRA
10		SAGITTARIUS	LIBRA	LIBRA	CAPRICORN	GEMINI	LIBRA	SAGITTARIUS	LIBRA
11		SAGITTARIUS	LIBRA	LIBRA	CAPRICORN	GEMINI	LIBRA	SAGITTARIUS	LIBRA
12	5:50 AM AQUARIUS	SAGITTARIUS	LIBRA	LIBRA	CAPRICORN	GEMINI	LIBRA	SAGITTARIUS	LIBRA
13		SAGITTARIUS	LIBRA	LIBRA	CAPRICORN	GEMINI	LIBRA	SAGITTARIUS	LIBRA
14	2:38 PM PISCES	SAGITTARIUS	LIBRA	LIBRA	CAPRICORN	GEMINI	LIBRA	SAGITTARIUS	LIBRA
15		SAGITTARIUS	LIBRA	LIBRA	CAPRICORN	GEMINI	LIBRA	SAGITTARIUS	LIBRA
16	7:30 PM ARIES	SAGITTARIUS	LIBRA	SCORPIO	CAPRICORN	GEMINI	LIBRA	SAGITTARIUS	LIBRA
17		SAGITTARIUS	LIBRA	SCORPIO	CAPRICORN	GEMINI	LIBRA	SAGITTARIUS	LIBRA
18	8:57 PM TAURUS	SAGITTARIUS	LIBRA	SCORPIO	CAPRICORN	GEMINI	LIBRA	SAGITTARIUS	LIBRA
19		SAGITTARIUS	LIBRA	SCORPIO	CAPRICORN	GEMINI	LIBRA	SAGITTARIUS	LIBRA
20	8:39 PM GEMINI	SAGITTARIUS	LIBRA	SCORPIO	CAPRICORN	GEMINI	LIBRA	SAGITTARIUS	LIBRA
21		SAGITTARIUS	LIBRA	SCORPIO	CAPRICORN	GEMINI	LIBRA	SAGITTARIUS	LIBRA
22	8:19 PM CANCER	SAGITTARIUS	LIBRA	SCORPIO	CAPRICORN	GEMINI	LIBRA	SAGITTARIUS	LIBRA

1973

OCT.	MOON FROM IN	MERCURY	VENUS	MARS	JUPITER	SATURN	URANUS	NEPTUNE	PLUTO
24		SCORPIO	SAGITTARIUS	TAURUS	AQUARIUS	CANCER	LIBRA	SAGITTARIUS	LIBRA
25	5:29 PM SCORPIO	SCORPIO	SAGITTARIUS	TAURUS	AQUARIUS	CANCER	LIBRA	SAGITTARIUS	LIBRA
26		SCORPIO	SAGITTARIUS	TAURUS	AQUARIUS	CANCER	LIBRA	SAGITTARIUS	LIBRA
27		SCORPIO	SAGITTARIUS	TAURUS	AQUARIUS	CANCER	LIBRA	SAGITTARIUS	LIBRA
28	3:06 AM SAGITTARIUS	SCORPIO	SAGITTARIUS	TAURUS	AQUARIUS	CANCER	LIBRA	SAGITTARIUS	LIBRA
29		SCORPIO	SAGITTARIUS	TAURUS	AQUARIUS	CANCER	LIBRA	SAGITTARIUS	LIBRA
30	2:52 PM CAPRICORN	SCORPIO	SAGITTARIUS	ARIES	AQUARIUS	CANCER	LIBRA	SAGITTARIUS	LIBRA
31		SCORPIO	SAGITTARIUS	ARIES	AQUARIUS	CANCER	LIBRA	SAGITTARIUS	LIBRA
NOV.									
1		SCORPIO	SAGITTARIUS	ARIES	AQUARIUS	CANCER	LIBRA	SAGITTARIUS	LIBRA
2	3:33 AM AQUARIUS	SCORPIO	SAGITTARIUS	ARIES	AQUARIUS	CANCER	LIBRA	SAGITTARIUS	LIBRA
3		SCORPIO	SAGITTARIUS	ARIES	AQUARIUS	CANCER	LIBRA	SAGITTARIUS	LIBRA
4	3:17 PM PISCES	SCORPIO	SAGITTARIUS	ARIES	AQUARIUS	CANCER	LIBRA	SAGITTARIUS	LIBRA
5		SCORPIO	SAGITTARIUS	ARIES	AQUARIUS	CANCER	LIBRA	SAGITTARIUS	LIBRA
6	11:38 PM ARIES	SCORPIO	CAPRICORN	ARIES	AQUARIUS	CANCER	LIBRA	SAGITTARIUS	LIBRA
7		SCORPIO	CAPRICORN	ARIES	AQUARIUS	CANCER	LIBRA	SAGITTARIUS	LIBRA
8		SCORPIO	CAPRICORN	ARIES	AQUARIUS	CANCER	LIBRA	SAGITTARIUS	LIBRA
9	3:17 AM TAURUS	SCORPIO	CAPRICORN	ARIES	AQUARIUS	CANCER	LIBRA	SAGITTARIUS	LIBRA
10		SCORPIO	CAPRICORN	ARIES	AQUARIUS	CANCER	LIBRA	SAGITTARIUS	LIBRA
11	5:31 AM GEMINI	SCORPIO	CAPRICORN	ARIES	AQUARIUS	CANCER	LIBRA	SAGITTARIUS	LIBRA
12		SCORPIO	CAPRICORN	ARIES	AQUARIUS	CANCER	LIBRA	SAGITTARIUS	LIBRA
13	6:22 AM CANCER	SCORPIO	CAPRICORN	ARIES	AQUARIUS	CANCER	LIBRA	SAGITTARIUS	LIBRA
14		SCORPIO	CAPRICORN	ARIES	AQUARIUS	CANCER	LIBRA	SAGITTARIUS	LIBRA
15	7:31 AM LEO	SCORPIO	CAPRICORN	ARIES	AQUARIUS	CANCER	LIBRA	SAGITTARIUS	LIBRA
16		SCORPIO	CAPRICORN	ARIES	AQUARIUS	CANCER	LIBRA	SAGITTARIUS	LIBRA
17	10:43 AM VIRGO	SCORPIO	CAPRICORN	ARIES	AQUARIUS	CANCER	LIBRA	SAGITTARIUS	LIBRA
18		SCORPIO	CAPRICORN	ARIES	AQUARIUS	CANCER	LIBRA	SAGITTARIUS	LIBRA
19	4:13 PM LIBRA	SCORPIO	CAPRICORN	ARIES	AQUARIUS	CANCER	LIBRA	SAGITTARIUS	LIBRA
20		SCORPIO	CAPRICORN	ARIES	AQUARIUS	CANCER	LIBRA	SAGITTARIUS	LIBRA
21		SCORPIO	CAPRICORN	ARIES	AQUARIUS	CANCER	LIBRA	SAGITTARIUS	LIBRA
22	0:22 AM SCORPIO	SCORPIO	CAPRICORN	ARIES	AQUARIUS	CANCER	LIBRA	SAGITTARIUS	LIBRA

1974   SCORPIO

	MOON FROM IN	MERCURY	VENUS	MARS	JUPITER	SATURN	URANUS	NEPTUNE	PLUTO
OCT.									
24		SCORPIO	LIBRA	LIBRA	PISCES	CANCER	LIBRA	SAGITTARIUS	LIBRA
25	11:02 AM PISCES	SCORPIO	LIBRA	LIBRA	PISCES	CANCER	LIBRA	SAGITTARIUS	LIBRA
26		SCORPIO	LIBRA	LIBRA	PISCES	CANCER	LIBRA	SAGITTARIUS	LIBRA
27	10:33 PM ARIES	LIBRA	SCORPIO	LIBRA	PISCES	CANCER	LIBRA	SAGITTARIUS	LIBRA
28		LIBRA	SCORPIO	LIBRA	PISCES	CANCER	LIBRA	SAGITTARIUS	LIBRA
29		LIBRA	SCORPIO	SCORPIO	PISCES	CANCER	LIBRA	SAGITTARIUS	LIBRA
30	7:22 AM TAURUS	LIBRA	SCORPIO	SCORPIO	PISCES	CANCER	LIBRA	SAGITTARIUS	LIBRA
31		LIBRA	SCORPIO	SCORPIO	PISCES	CANCER	LIBRA	SAGITTARIUS	LIBRA
NOV.									
1	1:32 PM GEMINI	LIBRA	SCORPIO	SCORPIO	PISCES	CANCER	LIBRA	SAGITTARIUS	LIBRA
2		LIBRA	SCORPIO	SCORPIO	PISCES	CANCER	LIBRA	SAGITTARIUS	LIBRA
3	6:06 PM CANCER	LIBRA	SCORPIO	SCORPIO	PISCES	CANCER	LIBRA	SAGITTARIUS	LIBRA
4		LIBRA	SCORPIO	SCORPIO	PISCES	CANCER	LIBRA	SAGITTARIUS	LIBRA
5	9:22 PM LEO	LIBRA	SCORPIO	SCORPIO	PISCES	CANCER	LIBRA	SAGITTARIUS	LIBRA
6		LIBRA	SCORPIO	SCORPIO	PISCES	CANCER	LIBRA	SAGITTARIUS	LIBRA
7		LIBRA	SCORPIO	SCORPIO	PISCES	CANCER	LIBRA	SAGITTARIUS	LIBRA
8	0:07 AM VIRGO	LIBRA	SCORPIO	SCORPIO	PISCES	CANCER	LIBRA	SAGITTARIUS	LIBRA
9		LIBRA	SCORPIO	SCORPIO	PISCES	CANCER	LIBRA	SAGITTARIUS	LIBRA
10	3:07 AM LIBRA	LIBRA	SCORPIO	SCORPIO	PISCES	CANCER	LIBRA	SAGITTARIUS	LIBRA
11		LIBRA	SCORPIO	SCORPIO	PISCES	CANCER	LIBRA	SAGITTARIUS	LIBRA
12	6:49 AM SCORPIO	SCORPIO	SCORPIO	SCORPIO	PISCES	CANCER	LIBRA	SAGITTARIUS	LIBRA
13		SCORPIO	SCORPIO	SCORPIO	PISCES	CANCER	LIBRA	SAGITTARIUS	LIBRA
14	11:57 AM SAGITTARIUS	SCORPIO	SCORPIO	SCORPIO	PISCES	CANCER	LIBRA	SAGITTARIUS	LIBRA
15		SCORPIO	SCORPIO	SCORPIO	PISCES	CANCER	LIBRA	SAGITTARIUS	LIBRA
16	7:41 PM CAPRICORN	SCORPIO	SCORPIO	SCORPIO	PISCES	CANCER	LIBRA	SAGITTARIUS	LIBRA
17		SCORPIO	SCORPIO	SCORPIO	PISCES	CANCER	LIBRA	SAGITTARIUS	LIBRA
18		SCORPIO	SCORPIO	SCORPIO	PISCES	CANCER	LIBRA	SAGITTARIUS	LIBRA
19	6:13 AM AQUARIUS	SCORPIO	SCORPIO	SCORPIO	PISCES	CANCER	LIBRA	SAGITTARIUS	LIBRA
20		SCORPIO	SAGITTARIUS	SCORPIO	PISCES	CANCER	LIBRA	SAGITTARIUS	LIBRA
21	7:06 PM PISCES	SCORPIO	SAGITTARIUS	SCORPIO	PISCES	CANCER	LIBRA	SAGITTARIUS	LIBRA
22		SCORPIO	SAGITTARIUS	SCORPIO	PISCES	CANCER	SCORPIO	SAGITTARIUS	LIBRA

1975

	MOON FROM IN	MERCURY	VENUS	MARS	JUPITER	SATURN	URANUS	NEPTUNE	PLUTO
OCT.									
25	3:49 AM CANCER	LIBRA	VIRGO	CANCER	ARIES	LEO	SCORPIO	SAGITTARIUS	LIBRA
26		LIBRA	VIRGO	CANCER	ARIES	LEO	SCORPIO	SAGITTARIUS	LIBRA
27	10:20 AM LEO	LIBRA	VIRGO	CANCER	ARIES	LEO	SCORPIO	SAGITTARIUS	LIBRA
28		LIBRA	VIRGO	CANCER	ARIES	LEO	SCORPIO	SAGITTARIUS	LIBRA
29	2:01 PM VIRGO	LIBRA	VIRGO	CANCER	ARIES	LEO	SCORPIO	SAGITTARIUS	LIBRA
30		LIBRA	VIRGO	CANCER	ARIES	LEO	SCORPIO	SAGITTARIUS	LIBRA
31	3:17 PM LIBRA	LIBRA	VIRGO	CANCER	ARIES	LEO	SCORPIO	SAGITTARIUS	LIBRA
NOV.									
1		LIBRA	VIRGO	CANCER	ARIES	LEO	SCORPIO	SAGITTARIUS	LIBRA
2	3:53 PM SCORPIO	LIBRA	VIRGO	CANCER	ARIES	LEO	SCORPIO	SAGITTARIUS	LIBRA
3		LIBRA	VIRGO	CANCER	ARIES	LEO	SCORPIO	SAGITTARIUS	LIBRA
4	4:46 PM SAGITTARIUS	LIBRA	VIRGO	CANCER	ARIES	LEO	SCORPIO	SAGITTARIUS	LIBRA
5		LIBRA	VIRGO	CANCER	ARIES	LEO	SCORPIO	SAGITTARIUS	LIBRA
6	7:14 PM CAPRICORN	LIBRA	VIRGO	CANCER	ARIES	LEO	SCORPIO	SAGITTARIUS	LIBRA
7		SCORPIO	VIRGO	CANCER	ARIES	LEO	SCORPIO	SAGITTARIUS	LIBRA
8		SCORPIO	VIRGO	CANCER	ARIES	LEO	SCORPIO	SAGITTARIUS	LIBRA
9	2:49 AM AQUARIUS	SCORPIO	VIRGO	CANCER	ARIES	LEO	SCORPIO	SAGITTARIUS	LIBRA
10		SCORPIO	LIBRA	CANCER	ARIES	LEO	SCORPIO	SAGITTARIUS	LIBRA
11	2:04 PM PISCES	SCORPIO	LIBRA	CANCER	ARIES	LEO	SCORPIO	SAGITTARIUS	LIBRA
12		SCORPIO	LIBRA	CANCER	ARIES	LEO	SCORPIO	SAGITTARIUS	LIBRA
13		SCORPIO	LIBRA	CANCER	ARIES	LEO	SCORPIO	SAGITTARIUS	LIBRA
14	2:46 AM ARIES	SCORPIO	LIBRA	CANCER	ARIES	LEO	SCORPIO	SAGITTARIUS	LIBRA
15		SCORPIO	LIBRA	CANCER	ARIES	LEO	SCORPIO	SAGITTARIUS	LIBRA
16	3:05 PM TAURUS	SCORPIO	LIBRA	CANCER	ARIES	LEO	SCORPIO	SAGITTARIUS	LIBRA
17		SCORPIO	LIBRA	CANCER	ARIES	LEO	SCORPIO	SAGITTARIUS	LIBRA
18		SCORPIO	LIBRA	CANCER	ARIES	LEO	SCORPIO	SAGITTARIUS	LIBRA
19	1:14 AM GEMINI	SCORPIO	LIBRA	CANCER	ARIES	LEO	SCORPIO	SAGITTARIUS	LIBRA
20		SCORPIO	LIBRA	CANCER	ARIES	LEO	SCORPIO	SAGITTARIUS	LIBRA
21	9:35 AM CANCER	SCORPIO	LIBRA	CANCER	ARIES	LEO	SCORPIO	SAGITTARIUS	LIBRA
22		SCORPIO	LIBRA	CANCER	ARIES	LEO	SCORPIO	SAGITTARIUS	LIBRA

1976

	MOON FROM IN	MERCURY	VENUS	MARS	JUPITER	SATURN	URANUS	NEPTUNE	PLUTO
OCT.									
24		LIBRA	SAGITTARIUS	SCORPIO	TAURUS	LEO	SCORPIO	SAGITTARIUS	LIBRA
25	0:16 AM SAGITTARIUS	LIBRA	SAGITTARIUS	SCORPIO	TAURUS	LEO	SCORPIO	SAGITTARIUS	LIBRA
26		LIBRA	SAGITTARIUS	SCORPIO	TAURUS	LEO	SCORPIO	SAGITTARIUS	LIBRA
27	1:01 AM CAPRICORN	LIBRA	SAGITTARIUS	SCORPIO	TAURUS	LEO	SCORPIO	SAGITTARIUS	LIBRA
28		LIBRA	SAGITTARIUS	SCORPIO	TAURUS	LEO	SCORPIO	SAGITTARIUS	LIBRA
29	5:13 AM AQUARIUS	LIBRA	SAGITTARIUS	SCORPIO	TAURUS	LEO	SCORPIO	SAGITTARIUS	LIBRA
30		SCORPIO	SAGITTARIUS	SCORPIO	TAURUS	LEO	SCORPIO	SAGITTARIUS	LIBRA
31	12:58 PM PISCES	SCORPIO	SAGITTARIUS	SCORPIO	TAURUS	LEO	SCORPIO	SAGITTARIUS	LIBRA
NOV.									
1		SCORPIO	SAGITTARIUS	SCORPIO	TAURUS	LEO	SCORPIO	SAGITTARIUS	LIBRA
2		SCORPIO	SAGITTARIUS	SCORPIO	TAURUS	LEO	SCORPIO	SAGITTARIUS	LIBRA
3	0:12 AM ARIES	SCORPIO	SAGITTARIUS	SCORPIO	TAURUS	LEO	SCORPIO	SAGITTARIUS	LIBRA
4		SCORPIO	SAGITTARIUS	SCORPIO	TAURUS	LEO	SCORPIO	SAGITTARIUS	LIBRA
5	12:40 PM TAURUS	SCORPIO	SAGITTARIUS	SCORPIO	TAURUS	LEO	SCORPIO	SAGITTARIUS	LIBRA
6		SCORPIO	SAGITTARIUS	SCORPIO	TAURUS	LEO	SCORPIO	SAGITTARIUS	LIBRA
7		SCORPIO	SAGITTARIUS	SCORPIO	TAURUS	LEO	SCORPIO	SAGITTARIUS	LIBRA
8	1:09 AM GEMINI	SCORPIO	SAGITTARIUS	SCORPIO	TAURUS	LEO	SCORPIO	SAGITTARIUS	LIBRA
9		SCORPIO	SAGITTARIUS	SCORPIO	TAURUS	LEO	SCORPIO	SAGITTARIUS	LIBRA
10	1:10 PM CANCER	SCORPIO	SAGITTARIUS	SCORPIO	TAURUS	LEO	SCORPIO	SAGITTARIUS	LIBRA
11		SCORPIO	SAGITTARIUS	SCORPIO	TAURUS	LEO	SCORPIO	SAGITTARIUS	LIBRA
12	11:39 PM LEO	SCORPIO	SAGITTARIUS	SCORPIO	TAURUS	LEO	SCORPIO	SAGITTARIUS	LIBRA
13		SCORPIO	SAGITTARIUS	SCORPIO	TAURUS	LEO	SCORPIO	SAGITTARIUS	LIBRA
14		SCORPIO	SAGITTARIUS	SCORPIO	TAURUS	LEO	SCORPIO	SAGITTARIUS	LIBRA
15	6:49 AM VIRGO	SCORPIO	CAPRICORN	SCORPIO	TAURUS	LEO	SCORPIO	SAGITTARIUS	LIBRA
16		SCORPIO	CAPRICORN	SCORPIO	TAURUS	LEO	SCORPIO	SAGITTARIUS	LIBRA
17	10:54 AM LIBRA	SAGITTARIUS	CAPRICORN	SCORPIO	TAURUS	LEO	SCORPIO	SAGITTARIUS	LIBRA
18		SAGITTARIUS	CAPRICORN	SCORPIO	TAURUS	LEO	SCORPIO	SAGITTARIUS	LIBRA
19	11:29 AM SCORPIO	SAGITTARIUS	CAPRICORN	SCORPIO	TAURUS	LEO	SCORPIO	SAGITTARIUS	LIBRA
20		SAGITTARIUS	CAPRICORN	SCORPIO	TAURUS	LEO	SCORPIO	SAGITTARIUS	LIBRA
21	11:11 AM SAGITTARIUS	SAGITTARIUS	CAPRICORN	SAGITTARIUS	TAURUS	LEO	SCORPIO	SAGITTARIUS	LIBRA
22		SAGITTARIUS	CAPRICORN	SAGITTARIUS	TAURUS	LEO	SCORPIO	SAGITTARIUS	LIBRA

1977

	MOON FROM IN	MERCURY	VENUS	MARS	JUPITER	SATURN	URANUS	NEPTUNE	PLUTO
OCT.									
24	2:41 AM ARIES	SCORPIO	LIBRA	CANCER	CANCER	LEO	SCORPIO	SAGITTARIUS	LIBRA
25		SCORPIO	LIBRA	CANCER	CANCER	LEO	SCORPIO	SAGITTARIUS	LIBRA
26	11:44 AM TAURUS	SCORPIO	LIBRA	CANCER	CANCER	LEO	SCORPIO	SAGITTARIUS	LIBRA
27		SCORPIO	LIBRA	LEO	CANCER	LEO	SCORPIO	SAGITTARIUS	LIBRA
28	10:48 PM GEMINI	SCORPIO	LIBRA	LEO	CANCER	LEO	SCORPIO	SAGITTARIUS	LIBRA
29		SCORPIO	LIBRA	LEO	CANCER	LEO	SCORPIO	SAGITTARIUS	LIBRA
30		SCORPIO	LIBRA	LEO	CANCER	LEO	SCORPIO	SAGITTARIUS	LIBRA
31	11:19 AM CANCER	SCORPIO	LIBRA	LEO	CANCER	LEO	SCORPIO	SAGITTARIUS	LIBRA
NOV.									
1		SCORPIO	LIBRA	LEO	CANCER	LEO	SCORPIO	SAGITTARIUS	LIBRA
2		SCORPIO	LIBRA	LEO	CANCER	LEO	SCORPIO	SAGITTARIUS	LIBRA
3	0:12 AM LEO	SCORPIO	LIBRA	LEO	CANCER	LEO	SCORPIO	SAGITTARIUS	LIBRA
4		SCORPIO	LIBRA	LEO	CANCER	LEO	SCORPIO	SAGITTARIUS	LIBRA
5	10:30 AM VIRGO	SCORPIO	LIBRA	LEO	CANCER	LEO	SCORPIO	SAGITTARIUS	LIBRA
6		SCORPIO	LIBRA	LEO	CANCER	LEO	SCORPIO	SAGITTARIUS	LIBRA
7	5:06 PM LIBRA	SCORPIO	LIBRA	LEO	CANCER	LEO	SCORPIO	SAGITTARIUS	LIBRA
8		SCORPIO	LIBRA	LEO	CANCER	LEO	SCORPIO	SAGITTARIUS	LIBRA
9	7:38 PM SCORPIO	SCORPIO	LIBRA	LEO	CANCER	LEO	SCORPIO	SAGITTARIUS	LIBRA
10		SAGITTARIUS	LIBRA	LEO	CANCER	LEO	SCORPIO	SAGITTARIUS	LIBRA
11	8:16 PM SAGITTARIUS	SAGITTARIUS	SCORPIO	LEO	CANCER	LEO	SCORPIO	SAGITTARIUS	LIBRA
12		SAGITTARIUS	SCORPIO	LEO	CANCER	LEO	SCORPIO	SAGITTARIUS	LIBRA
13	8:02 PM CAPRICORN	SAGITTARIUS	SCORPIO	LEO	CANCER	LEO	SCORPIO	SAGITTARIUS	LIBRA
14		SAGITTARIUS	SCORPIO	LEO	CANCER	LEO	SCORPIO	SAGITTARIUS	LIBRA
15	9:30 PM AQUARIUS	SAGITTARIUS	SCORPIO	LEO	CANCER	LEO	SCORPIO	SAGITTARIUS	LIBRA
16		SAGITTARIUS	SCORPIO	LEO	CANCER	LEO	SCORPIO	SAGITTARIUS	LIBRA
17		SAGITTARIUS	SCORPIO	LEO	CANCER	LEO	SCORPIO	SAGITTARIUS	LIBRA
18	1:10 AM PISCES	SAGITTARIUS	SCORPIO	LEO	CANCER	VIRGO	SCORPIO	SAGITTARIUS	LIBRA
19		SAGITTARIUS	SCORPIO	LEO	CANCER	VIRGO	SCORPIO	SAGITTARIUS	LIBRA
20	8:32 AM ARIES	SAGITTARIUS	SCORPIO	LEO	CANCER	VIRGO	SCORPIO	SAGITTARIUS	LIBRA
21		SAGITTARIUS	SCORPIO	LEO	CANCER	VIRGO	SCORPIO	SAGITTARIUS	LIBRA
22	6:08 PM TAURUS	SAGITTARIUS	SCORPIO	LEO	CANCER	VIRGO	SCORPIO	SAGITTARIUS	LIBRA

1978

SCORPIO

MOON FROM	IN	MERCURY	VENUS	MARS	JUPITER	SATURN	URANUS	NEPTUNE	PLUTO
OCT.									
24		SCORPIO	SCORPIO	SCORPIO	LEO	VIRGO	SCORPIO	SAGITTARIUS	LIBRA
25		SCORPIO	SCORPIO	SCORPIO	LEO	VIRGO	SCORPIO	SAGITTARIUS	LIBRA
26	7:59 AM VIRGO	SCORPIO	SCORPIO	SCORPIO	LEO	VIRGO	SCORPIO	SAGITTARIUS	LIBRA
27		SCORPIO	SCORPIO	SCORPIO	LEO	VIRGO	SCORPIO	SAGITTARIUS	LIBRA
28	6:04 PM LIBRA	SCORPIO	SCORPIO	SCORPIO	LEO	VIRGO	SCORPIO	SAGITTARIUS	LIBRA
29		SCORPIO	SCORPIO	SCORPIO	LEO	VIRGO	SCORPIO	SAGITTARIUS	LIBRA
30		SCORPIO	SCORPIO	SCORPIO	LEO	VIRGO	SCORPIO	SAGITTARIUS	LIBRA
31	0:40 AM SCORPIO	SCORPIO	SCORPIO	SCORPIO	LEO	VIRGO	SCORPIO	SAGITTARIUS	LIBRA
NOV.									
1		SCORPIO	SCORPIO	SCORPIO	LEO	VIRGO	SCORPIO	SAGITTARIUS	LIBRA
2	4:59 AM SAGITTARIUS	SCORPIO	SCORPIO	SCORPIO	LEO	VIRGO	SCORPIO	SAGITTARIUS	LIBRA
3		SCORPIO	SCORPIO	SAGITTARIUS	LEO	VIRGO	SCORPIO	SAGITTARIUS	LIBRA
4	7:51 AM CAPRICORN	SAGITTARIUS	SCORPIO	SAGITTARIUS	LEO	VIRGO	SCORPIO	SAGITTARIUS	LIBRA
5		SAGITTARIUS	SCORPIO	SAGITTARIUS	LEO	VIRGO	SCORPIO	SAGITTARIUS	LIBRA
6	10:15 AM AQUARIUS	SAGITTARIUS	SCORPIO	SAGITTARIUS	LEO	VIRGO	SCORPIO	SAGITTARIUS	LIBRA
7		SAGITTARIUS	SCORPIO	SAGITTARIUS	LEO	VIRGO	SCORPIO	SAGITTARIUS	LIBRA
8	1:13 PM PISCES	SAGITTARIUS	SCORPIO	SAGITTARIUS	LEO	VIRGO	SCORPIO	SAGITTARIUS	LIBRA
9		SAGITTARIUS	SCORPIO	SAGITTARIUS	LEO	VIRGO	SCORPIO	SAGITTARIUS	LIBRA
10	5:03 PM ARIES	SAGITTARIUS	SCORPIO	SAGITTARIUS	LEO	VIRGO	SCORPIO	SAGITTARIUS	LIBRA
11		SAGITTARIUS	SCORPIO	SAGITTARIUS	LEO	VIRGO	SCORPIO	SAGITTARIUS	LIBRA
12	10:30 PM TAURUS	SAGITTARIUS	SCORPIO	SAGITTARIUS	LEO	VIRGO	SCORPIO	SAGITTARIUS	LIBRA
13		SAGITTARIUS	SCORPIO	SAGITTARIUS	LEO	VIRGO	SCORPIO	SAGITTARIUS	LIBRA
14		SAGITTARIUS	SCORPIO	SAGITTARIUS	LEO	VIRGO	SCORPIO	SAGITTARIUS	LIBRA
15	5:43 AM GEMINI	SAGITTARIUS	SCORPIO	SAGITTARIUS	LEO	VIRGO	SCORPIO	SAGITTARIUS	LIBRA
16		SAGITTARIUS	SCORPIO	SAGITTARIUS	LEO	VIRGO	SCORPIO	SAGITTARIUS	LIBRA
17	3:12 PM CANCER	SAGITTARIUS	SCORPIO	SAGITTARIUS	LEO	VIRGO	SCORPIO	SAGITTARIUS	LIBRA
18		SAGITTARIUS	SCORPIO	SAGITTARIUS	LEO	VIRGO	SCORPIO	SAGITTARIUS	LIBRA
19		SAGITTARIUS	SCORPIO	SAGITTARIUS	LEO	VIRGO	SCORPIO	SAGITTARIUS	LIBRA
20	3:20 AM LEO	SAGITTARIUS	SCORPIO	SAGITTARIUS	LEO	VIRGO	SCORPIO	SAGITTARIUS	LIBRA
21		SAGITTARIUS	SCORPIO	SAGITTARIUS	LEO	VIRGO	SCORPIO	SAGITTARIUS	LIBRA
22	3:57 PM VIRGO	SAGITTARIUS	SCORPIO	SAGITTARIUS	LEO	VIRGO	SCORPIO	SAGITTARIUS	LIBRA

1979

MOON FROM	IN	MERCURY	VENUS	MARS	JUPITER	SATURN	URANUS	NEPTUNE	PLUTO
OCT.									
25	7:00 PM CAPRICORN	SCORPIO	SCORPIO	LEO	VIRGO	VIRGO	SCORPIO	SAGITTARIUS	LIBRA
26		SCORPIO	SCORPIO	LEO	VIRGO	VIRGO	SCORPIO	SAGITTARIUS	LIBRA
27		SCORPIO	SCORPIO	LEO	VIRGO	VIRGO	SCORPIO	SAGITTARIUS	LIBRA
28	0:18 AM AQUARIUS	SCORPIO	SCORPIO	LEO	VIRGO	VIRGO	SCORPIO	SAGITTARIUS	LIBRA
29		SCORPIO	SCORPIO	LEO	VIRGO	VIRGO	SCORPIO	SAGITTARIUS	LIBRA
30	3:27 AM PISCES	SCORPIO	SCORPIO	LEO	VIRGO	VIRGO	SCORPIO	SAGITTARIUS	LIBRA
31		SAGITTARIUS	SCORPIO	LEO	VIRGO	VIRGO	SCORPIO	SAGITTARIUS	LIBRA
NOV.									
1	4:53 AM ARIES	SAGITTARIUS	SCORPIO	LEO	VIRGO	VIRGO	SCORPIO	SAGITTARIUS	LIBRA
2		SAGITTARIUS	SCORPIO	LEO	VIRGO	VIRGO	SCORPIO	SAGITTARIUS	LIBRA
3	6:21 AM TAURUS	SAGITTARIUS	SCORPIO	LEO	VIRGO	VIRGO	SCORPIO	SAGITTARIUS	LIBRA
4		SAGITTARIUS	SCORPIO	LEO	VIRGO	VIRGO	SCORPIO	SAGITTARIUS	LIBRA
5	8:35 AM GEMINI	SAGITTARIUS	SAGITTARIUS	LEO	VIRGO	VIRGO	SCORPIO	SAGITTARIUS	LIBRA
6		SAGITTARIUS	SAGITTARIUS	LEO	VIRGO	VIRGO	SCORPIO	SAGITTARIUS	LIBRA
7	1:48 PM CANCER	SAGITTARIUS	SAGITTARIUS	LEO	VIRGO	VIRGO	SCORPIO	SAGITTARIUS	LIBRA
8		SAGITTARIUS	SAGITTARIUS	LEO	VIRGO	VIRGO	SCORPIO	SAGITTARIUS	LIBRA
9	10:36 PM LEO	SAGITTARIUS	SAGITTARIUS	LEO	VIRGO	VIRGO	SCORPIO	SAGITTARIUS	LIBRA
10		SAGITTARIUS	SAGITTARIUS	LEO	VIRGO	VIRGO	SCORPIO	SAGITTARIUS	LIBRA
11		SAGITTARIUS	SAGITTARIUS	LEO	VIRGO	VIRGO	SCORPIO	SAGITTARIUS	LIBRA
12	10:39 AM VIRGO	SAGITTARIUS	SAGITTARIUS	LEO	VIRGO	VIRGO	SCORPIO	SAGITTARIUS	LIBRA
13		SAGITTARIUS	SAGITTARIUS	LEO	VIRGO	VIRGO	SCORPIO	SAGITTARIUS	LIBRA
14	11:20 PM LIBRA	SAGITTARIUS	SAGITTARIUS	LEO	VIRGO	VIRGO	SCORPIO	SAGITTARIUS	LIBRA
15		SAGITTARIUS	SAGITTARIUS	LEO	VIRGO	VIRGO	SCORPIO	SAGITTARIUS	LIBRA
16		SAGITTARIUS	SAGITTARIUS	LEO	VIRGO	VIRGO	SCORPIO	SAGITTARIUS	LIBRA
17	10:37 AM SCORPIO	SAGITTARIUS	SAGITTARIUS	LEO	VIRGO	VIRGO	SCORPIO	SAGITTARIUS	LIBRA
18		SAGITTARIUS	SAGITTARIUS	LEO	VIRGO	VIRGO	SCORPIO	SAGITTARIUS	LIBRA
19	6:53 PM SAGITTARIUS	SCORPIO	SAGITTARIUS	LEO	VIRGO	VIRGO	SCORPIO	SAGITTARIUS	LIBRA
20		SCORPIO	SAGITTARIUS	VIRGO	VIRGO	VIRGO	SCORPIO	SAGITTARIUS	LIBRA
21		SCORPIO	SAGITTARIUS	VIRGO	VIRGO	VIRGO	SCORPIO	SAGITTARIUS	LIBRA
22	1:10 AM CAPRICORN	SCORPIO	SAGITTARIUS	VIRGO	VIRGO	VIRGO	SCORPIO	SAGITTARIUS	LIBRA

Date	MOON FROM IN	MERCURY	VENUS	MARS	JUPITER	SATURN	URANUS	NEPTUNE	PLUTO
OCT.									
24		SCORPIO	VIRGO	SAGITTARIUS	VIRGO	LIBRA	SCORPIO	SAGITTARIUS	LIBRA
25	2:59 PM GEMINI	SCORPIO	VIRGO	SAGITTARIUS	VIRGO	LIBRA	SCORPIO	SAGITTARIUS	LIBRA
26		SCORPIO	VIRGO	SAGITTARIUS	VIRGO	LIBRA	SCORPIO	SAGITTARIUS	LIBRA
27	4:46 PM CANCER	SCORPIO	VIRGO	SAGITTARIUS	VIRGO	LIBRA	SCORPIO	SAGITTARIUS	LIBRA
28		SCORPIO	VIRGO	SAGITTARIUS	LIBRA	LIBRA	SCORPIO	SAGITTARIUS	LIBRA
29	10:09 PM LEO	SCORPIO	VIRGO	SAGITTARIUS	LIBRA	LIBRA	SCORPIO	SAGITTARIUS	LIBRA
30		SCORPIO	VIRGO	SAGITTARIUS	LIBRA	LIBRA	SCORPIO	SAGITTARIUS	LIBRA
31		SCORPIO	LIBRA	SAGITTARIUS	LIBRA	LIBRA	SCORPIO	SAGITTARIUS	LIBRA
NOV.									
1	7:36 AM VIRGO	SCORPIO	LIBRA	SAGITTARIUS	LIBRA	LIBRA	SCORPIO	SAGITTARIUS	LIBRA
2		SCORPIO	LIBRA	SAGITTARIUS	LIBRA	LIBRA	SCORPIO	SAGITTARIUS	LIBRA
3	7:43 PM LIBRA	SCORPIO	LIBRA	SAGITTARIUS	LIBRA	LIBRA	SCORPIO	SAGITTARIUS	LIBRA
4		SCORPIO	LIBRA	SAGITTARIUS	LIBRA	LIBRA	SCORPIO	SAGITTARIUS	LIBRA
5		SCORPIO	LIBRA	SAGITTARIUS	LIBRA	LIBRA	SCORPIO	SAGITTARIUS	LIBRA
6	8:14 AM SCORPIO	SCORPIO	LIBRA	SAGITTARIUS	LIBRA	LIBRA	SCORPIO	SAGITTARIUS	LIBRA
7		SCORPIO	LIBRA	SAGITTARIUS	LIBRA	LIBRA	SCORPIO	SAGITTARIUS	LIBRA
8	8:35 PM SAGITTARIUS	SCORPIO	LIBRA	SAGITTARIUS	LIBRA	LIBRA	SCORPIO	SAGITTARIUS	LIBRA
9		SCORPIO	LIBRA	SAGITTARIUS	LIBRA	LIBRA	SCORPIO	SAGITTARIUS	LIBRA
10		SCORPIO	LIBRA	SAGITTARIUS	LIBRA	LIBRA	SCORPIO	SAGITTARIUS	LIBRA
11	7:35 AM CAPRICORN	SCORPIO	LIBRA	SAGITTARIUS	LIBRA	LIBRA	SCORPIO	SAGITTARIUS	LIBRA
12		SCORPIO	LIBRA	SAGITTARIUS	LIBRA	LIBRA	SCORPIO	SAGITTARIUS	LIBRA
13	4:04 PM AQUARIUS	SCORPIO	LIBRA	SAGITTARIUS	LIBRA	LIBRA	SCORPIO	SAGITTARIUS	LIBRA
14		SCORPIO	LIBRA	SAGITTARIUS	LIBRA	LIBRA	SCORPIO	SAGITTARIUS	LIBRA
15	10:22 PM PISCES	SCORPIO	LIBRA	SAGITTARIUS	LIBRA	LIBRA	SCORPIO	SAGITTARIUS	LIBRA
16		SCORPIO	LIBRA	SAGITTARIUS	LIBRA	LIBRA	SCORPIO	SAGITTARIUS	LIBRA
17		SCORPIO	LIBRA	SAGITTARIUS	LIBRA	LIBRA	SCORPIO	SAGITTARIUS	LIBRA
18	1:01 AM ARIES	SCORPIO	LIBRA	SAGITTARIUS	LIBRA	LIBRA	SCORPIO	SAGITTARIUS	LIBRA
19		SCORPIO	LIBRA	SAGITTARIUS	LIBRA	LIBRA	SCORPIO	SAGITTARIUS	LIBRA
20	1:59 AM TAURUS	SCORPIO	LIBRA	SAGITTARIUS	LIBRA	LIBRA	SCORPIO	SAGITTARIUS	LIBRA
21		SCORPIO	LIBRA	SAGITTARIUS	LIBRA	LIBRA	SCORPIO	SAGITTARIUS	LIBRA
22	1:44 AM GEMINI	SCORPIO	LIBRA	SAGITTARIUS	LIBRA	LIBRA	SCORPIO	SAGITTARIUS	LIBRA

1981

Date	MOON FROM IN	MERCURY	VENUS	MARS	JUPITER	SATURN	URANUS	NEPTUNE	PLUTO
OCT.									
24	7:57 PM LIBRA	LIBRA	SAGITTARIUS	VIRGO	LIBRA	LIBRA	SCORPIO	SAGITTARIUS	LIBRA
25		LIBRA	SAGITTARIUS	VIRGO	LIBRA	LIBRA	SCORPIO	SAGITTARIUS	LIBRA
26		LIBRA	SAGITTARIUS	VIRGO	LIBRA	LIBRA	SCORPIO	SAGITTARIUS	LIBRA
27	6:37 AM SCORPIO	LIBRA	SAGITTARIUS	VIRGO	LIBRA	LIBRA	SCORPIO	SAGITTARIUS	LIBRA
28		LIBRA	SAGITTARIUS	VIRGO	LIBRA	LIBRA	SCORPIO	SAGITTARIUS	LIBRA
29	6:54 PM SAGITTARIUS	LIBRA	SAGITTARIUS	VIRGO	LIBRA	LIBRA	SCORPIO	SAGITTARIUS	LIBRA
30		LIBRA	SAGITTARIUS	VIRGO	LIBRA	LIBRA	SCORPIO	SAGITTARIUS	LIBRA
31		LIBRA	SAGITTARIUS	VIRGO	LIBRA	LIBRA	SCORPIO	SAGITTARIUS	LIBRA
NOV.									
1	7:48 AM CAPRICORN	LIBRA	SAGITTARIUS	VIRGO	LIBRA	LIBRA	SCORPIO	SAGITTARIUS	LIBRA
2		LIBRA	SAGITTARIUS	VIRGO	LIBRA	LIBRA	SCORPIO	SAGITTARIUS	LIBRA
3	7:47 PM AQUARIUS	LIBRA	SAGITTARIUS	VIRGO	LIBRA	LIBRA	SCORPIO	SAGITTARIUS	LIBRA
4		LIBRA	SAGITTARIUS	VIRGO	LIBRA	LIBRA	SCORPIO	SAGITTARIUS	LIBRA
5		LIBRA	SAGITTARIUS	VIRGO	LIBRA	LIBRA	SCORPIO	SAGITTARIUS	LIBRA
6	4:38 AM PISCES	LIBRA	CAPRICORN	VIRGO	LIBRA	LIBRA	SCORPIO	SAGITTARIUS	LIBRA
7		LIBRA	CAPRICORN	VIRGO	LIBRA	LIBRA	SCORPIO	SAGITTARIUS	LIBRA
8	9:31 AM ARIES	LIBRA	CAPRICORN	VIRGO	LIBRA	LIBRA	SCORPIO	SAGITTARIUS	LIBRA
9		LIBRA	CAPRICORN	VIRGO	LIBRA	LIBRA	SCORPIO	SAGITTARIUS	LIBRA
10	11:08 AM TAURUS	SCORPIO	CAPRICORN	VIRGO	LIBRA	LIBRA	SCORPIO	SAGITTARIUS	LIBRA
11		SCORPIO	CAPRICORN	VIRGO	LIBRA	LIBRA	SCORPIO	SAGITTARIUS	LIBRA
12	10:48 AM GEMINI	SCORPIO	CAPRICORN	VIRGO	LIBRA	LIBRA	SCORPIO	SAGITTARIUS	LIBRA
13		SCORPIO	CAPRICORN	VIRGO	LIBRA	LIBRA	SCORPIO	SAGITTARIUS	LIBRA
14	10:34 AM CANCER	SCORPIO	CAPRICORN	VIRGO	LIBRA	LIBRA	SCORPIO	SAGITTARIUS	LIBRA
15		SCORPIO	CAPRICORN	VIRGO	LIBRA	LIBRA	SCORPIO	SAGITTARIUS	LIBRA
16	12:01 PM LEO	SCORPIO	CAPRICORN	VIRGO	LIBRA	LIBRA	SCORPIO	SAGITTARIUS	LIBRA
17		SCORPIO	CAPRICORN	VIRGO	LIBRA	LIBRA	SAGITTARIUS	SAGITTARIUS	LIBRA
18	5:01 PM VIRGO	SCORPIO	CAPRICORN	VIRGO	LIBRA	LIBRA	SAGITTARIUS	SAGITTARIUS	LIBRA
19		SCORPIO	CAPRICORN	VIRGO	LIBRA	LIBRA	SAGITTARIUS	SAGITTARIUS	LIBRA
20		SCORPIO	CAPRICORN	VIRGO	LIBRA	LIBRA	SAGITTARIUS	SAGITTARIUS	LIBRA
21	1:29 AM LIBRA	SCORPIO	CAPRICORN	VIRGO	LIBRA	LIBRA	SAGITTARIUS	SAGITTARIUS	LIBRA
22		SCORPIO	CAPRICORN	VIRGO	LIBRA	LIBRA	SAGITTARIUS	SAGITTARIUS	LIBRA

SCORPIO

	MOON FROM IN	MERCURY	VENUS	MARS	JUPITER	SATURN	URANUS	NEPTUNE	PLUTO
OCT.									
24	3:52 PM AQUARIUS	LIBRA	LIBRA	SAGITTARIUS	SCORPIO	LIBRA	SAGITTARIUS	SAGITTARIUS	LIBRA
25		LIBRA	LIBRA	SAGITTARIUS	SCORPIO	LIBRA	SAGITTARIUS	SAGITTARIUS	LIBRA
26		LIBRA	LIBRA	SAGITTARIUS	SCORPIO	LIBRA	SAGITTARIUS	SAGITTARIUS	LIBRA
27	3:29 AM PISCES	LIBRA	SCORPIO	SAGITTARIUS	SCORPIO	LIBRA	SAGITTARIUS	SAGITTARIUS	LIBRA
28		LIBRA	SCORPIO	SAGITTARIUS	SCORPIO	LIBRA	SAGITTARIUS	SAGITTARIUS	LIBRA
29	12:39 PM ARIES	LIBRA	SCORPIO	SAGITTARIUS	SCORPIO	LIBRA	SAGITTARIUS	SAGITTARIUS	LIBRA
30		LIBRA	SCORPIO	SAGITTARIUS	SCORPIO	LIBRA	SAGITTARIUS	SAGITTARIUS	LIBRA
31	5:17 PM TAURUS	LIBRA	SCORPIO	SAGITTARIUS	SCORPIO	LIBRA	SAGITTARIUS	SAGITTARIUS	LIBRA
NOV.									
1		LIBRA	SCORPIO	CAPRICORN	SCORPIO	LIBRA	SAGITTARIUS	SAGITTARIUS	LIBRA
2	8:00 PM GEMINI	LIBRA	SCORPIO	CAPRICORN	SCORPIO	LIBRA	SAGITTARIUS	SAGITTARIUS	LIBRA
3		LIBRA	SCORPIO	CAPRICORN	SCORPIO	LIBRA	SAGITTARIUS	SAGITTARIUS	LIBRA
4	9:28 PM CANCER	SCORPIO	SCORPIO	CAPRICORN	SCORPIO	LIBRA	SAGITTARIUS	SAGITTARIUS	LIBRA
5		SCORPIO	SCORPIO	CAPRICORN	SCORPIO	LIBRA	SAGITTARIUS	SAGITTARIUS	LIBRA
6	11:17 PM LEO	SCORPIO	SCORPIO	CAPRICORN	SCORPIO	LIBRA	SAGITTARIUS	SAGITTARIUS	LIBRA
7		SCORPIO	SCORPIO	CAPRICORN	SCORPIO	LIBRA	SAGITTARIUS	SAGITTARIUS	LIBRA
8		SCORPIO	SCORPIO	CAPRICORN	SCORPIO	LIBRA	SAGITTARIUS	SAGITTARIUS	LIBRA
9	2:42 AM VIRGO	SCORPIO	SCORPIO	CAPRICORN	SCORPIO	LIBRA	SAGITTARIUS	SAGITTARIUS	LIBRA
10		SCORPIO	SCORPIO	CAPRICORN	SCORPIO	LIBRA	SAGITTARIUS	SAGITTARIUS	LIBRA
11	8:05 AM LIBRA	SCORPIO	SCORPIO	CAPRICORN	SCORPIO	LIBRA	SAGITTARIUS	SAGITTARIUS	LIBRA
12		SCORPIO	SCORPIO	CAPRICORN	SCORPIO	LIBRA	SAGITTARIUS	SAGITTARIUS	LIBRA
13	2:56 PM SCORPIO	SCORPIO	SCORPIO	CAPRICORN	SCORPIO	LIBRA	SAGITTARIUS	SAGITTARIUS	LIBRA
14		SCORPIO	SCORPIO	CAPRICORN	SCORPIO	LIBRA	SAGITTARIUS	SAGITTARIUS	LIBRA
15		SCORPIO	SCORPIO	CAPRICORN	SCORPIO	LIBRA	SAGITTARIUS	SAGITTARIUS	LIBRA
16	0:10 AM SAGITTARIUS	SCORPIO	SCORPIO	CAPRICORN	SCORPIO	LIBRA	SAGITTARIUS	SAGITTARIUS	LIBRA
17		SCORPIO	SCORPIO	CAPRICORN	SCORPIO	LIBRA	SAGITTARIUS	SAGITTARIUS	LIBRA
18	11:13 AM CAPRICORN	SCORPIO	SCORPIO	CAPRICORN	SCORPIO	LIBRA	SAGITTARIUS	SAGITTARIUS	LIBRA
19		SCORPIO	SAGITTARIUS	CAPRICORN	SCORPIO	LIBRA	SAGITTARIUS	SAGITTARIUS	LIBRA
20		SCORPIO	SAGITTARIUS	CAPRICORN	SCORPIO	LIBRA	SAGITTARIUS	SAGITTARIUS	LIBRA
21	0:42 AM AQUARIUS	SCORPIO	SAGITTARIUS	CAPRICORN	SCORPIO	LIBRA	SAGITTARIUS	SAGITTARIUS	LIBRA
22		SAGITTARIUS	SAGITTARIUS	CAPRICORN	SCORPIO	LIBRA	SAGITTARIUS	SAGITTARIUS	LIBRA

1983

	MOON FROM IN	MERCURY	VENUS	MARS	JUPITER	SATURN	URANUS	NEPTUNE	PLUTO
OCT.									
24	4:17 AM GEMINI	LIBRA	VIRGO	VIRGO	SAGITTARIUS	SCORPIO	SAGITTARIUS	SAGITTARIUS	LIBRA
25		LIBRA	VIRGO	VIRGO	SAGITTARIUS	SCORPIO	SAGITTARIUS	SAGITTARIUS	LIBRA
26	9:48 AM CANCER	LIBRA	VIRGO	VIRGO	SAGITTARIUS	SCORPIO	SAGITTARIUS	SAGITTARIUS	LIBRA
27		SCORPIO	VIRGO	VIRGO	SAGITTARIUS	SCORPIO	SAGITTARIUS	SAGITTARIUS	LIBRA
28	1:28 PM LEO	SCORPIO	VIRGO	VIRGO	SAGITTARIUS	SCORPIO	SAGITTARIUS	SAGITTARIUS	LIBRA
29		SCORPIO	VIRGO	VIRGO	SAGITTARIUS	SCORPIO	SAGITTARIUS	SAGITTARIUS	LIBRA
30	4:11 PM VIRGO	SCORPIO	VIRGO	VIRGO	SAGITTARIUS	SCORPIO	SAGITTARIUS	SAGITTARIUS	LIBRA
31		SCORPIO	VIRGO	VIRGO	SAGITTARIUS	SCORPIO	SAGITTARIUS	SAGITTARIUS	LIBRA
NOV.									
1	6:45 PM LIBRA	SCORPIO	VIRGO	VIRGO	SAGITTARIUS	SCORPIO	SAGITTARIUS	SAGITTARIUS	LIBRA
2		SCORPIO	VIRGO	VIRGO	SAGITTARIUS	SCORPIO	SAGITTARIUS	SAGITTARIUS	LIBRA
3	9:29 PM SCORPIO	SCORPIO	VIRGO	VIRGO	SAGITTARIUS	SCORPIO	SAGITTARIUS	SAGITTARIUS	LIBRA
4		SCORPIO	VIRGO	VIRGO	SAGITTARIUS	SCORPIO	SAGITTARIUS	SAGITTARIUS	LIBRA
5		SCORPIO	VIRGO	VIRGO	SAGITTARIUS	SCORPIO	SAGITTARIUS	SAGITTARIUS	LIBRA
6	1:41 AM SAGITTARIUS	SCORPIO	VIRGO	VIRGO	SAGITTARIUS	SCORPIO	SAGITTARIUS	SAGITTARIUS	SCORPIO
7		SCORPIO	VIRGO	VIRGO	SAGITTARIUS	SCORPIO	SAGITTARIUS	SAGITTARIUS	SCORPIO
8	8:22 AM CAPRICORN	SCORPIO	VIRGO	VIRGO	SAGITTARIUS	SCORPIO	SAGITTARIUS	SAGITTARIUS	SCORPIO
9		SCORPIO	VIRGO	VIRGO	SAGITTARIUS	SCORPIO	SAGITTARIUS	SAGITTARIUS	SCORPIO
10	7:00 PM AQUARIUS	SCORPIO	LIBRA	VIRGO	SAGITTARIUS	SCORPIO	SAGITTARIUS	SAGITTARIUS	SCORPIO
11		SCORPIO	LIBRA	VIRGO	SAGITTARIUS	SCORPIO	SAGITTARIUS	SAGITTARIUS	SCORPIO
12		SCORPIO	LIBRA	VIRGO	SAGITTARIUS	SCORPIO	SAGITTARIUS	SAGITTARIUS	SCORPIO
13	7:37 AM PISCES	SCORPIO	LIBRA	VIRGO	SAGITTARIUS	SCORPIO	SAGITTARIUS	SAGITTARIUS	SCORPIO
14		SCORPIO	LIBRA	VIRGO	SAGITTARIUS	SCORPIO	SAGITTARIUS	SAGITTARIUS	SCORPIO
15	7:53 PM ARIES	SAGITTARIUS	LIBRA	VIRGO	SAGITTARIUS	SCORPIO	SAGITTARIUS	SAGITTARIUS	SCORPIO
16		SAGITTARIUS	LIBRA	VIRGO	SAGITTARIUS	SCORPIO	SAGITTARIUS	SAGITTARIUS	SCORPIO
17		SAGITTARIUS	LIBRA	VIRGO	SAGITTARIUS	SCORPIO	SAGITTARIUS	SAGITTARIUS	SCORPIO
18	5:30 AM TAURUS	SAGITTARIUS	LIBRA	VIRGO	SAGITTARIUS	SCORPIO	SAGITTARIUS	SAGITTARIUS	SCORPIO
19		SAGITTARIUS	LIBRA	LIBRA	SAGITTARIUS	SCORPIO	SAGITTARIUS	SAGITTARIUS	SCORPIO
20	12:06 PM GEMINI	SAGITTARIUS	LIBRA	LIBRA	SAGITTARIUS	SCORPIO	SAGITTARIUS	SAGITTARIUS	SCORPIO
21		SAGITTARIUS	LIBRA	LIBRA	SAGITTARIUS	SCORPIO	SAGITTARIUS	SAGITTARIUS	SCORPIO
22	4:07 PM CANCER	SAGITTARIUS	LIBRA	LIBRA	SAGITTARIUS	SCORPIO	SAGITTARIUS	SAGITTARIUS	SCORPIO

SCORPIO

OCT.	MOON FROM IN	MERCURY	VENUS	MARS	JUPITER	SATURN	URANUS	NEPTUNE	PLUTO
24	5:43 AM SCORPIO	SCORPIO	SAGITTARIUS	CAPRICORN	CAPRICORN	SCORPIO	SAGITTARIUS	SAGITTARIUS	SCORPIO
25		SCORPIO	SAGITTARIUS	CAPRICORN	CAPRICORN	SCORPIO	SAGITTARIUS	SAGITTARIUS	SCORPIO
26	6:12 AM SAGITTARIUS	SCORPIO	SAGITTARIUS	CAPRICORN	CAPRICORN	SCORPIO	SAGITTARIUS	SAGITTARIUS	SCORPIO
27		SCORPIO	SAGITTARIUS	CAPRICORN	CAPRICORN	SCORPIO	SAGITTARIUS	SAGITTARIUS	SCORPIO
28	9:19 AM CAPRICORN	SCORPIO	SAGITTARIUS	CAPRICORN	CAPRICORN	SCORPIO	SAGITTARIUS	SAGITTARIUS	SCORPIO
29		SCORPIO	SAGITTARIUS	CAPRICORN	CAPRICORN	SCORPIO	SAGITTARIUS	SAGITTARIUS	SCORPIO
30	4:17 PM AQUARIUS	SCORPIO	SAGITTARIUS	CAPRICORN	CAPRICORN	SCORPIO	SAGITTARIUS	SAGITTARIUS	SCORPIO
31		SCORPIO	SAGITTARIUS	CAPRICORN	CAPRICORN	SCORPIO	SAGITTARIUS	SAGITTARIUS	SCORPIO
NOV.									
1		SCORPIO	SAGITTARIUS	CAPRICORN	CAPRICORN	SCORPIO	SAGITTARIUS	SAGITTARIUS	SCORPIO
2	3:00 AM PISCES	SCORPIO	SAGITTARIUS	CAPRICORN	CAPRICORN	SCORPIO	SAGITTARIUS	SAGITTARIUS	SCORPIO
3		SCORPIO	SAGITTARIUS	CAPRICORN	CAPRICORN	SCORPIO	SAGITTARIUS	SAGITTARIUS	SCORPIO
4	3:52 PM ARIES	SCORPIO	SAGITTARIUS	CAPRICORN	CAPRICORN	SCORPIO	SAGITTARIUS	SAGITTARIUS	SCORPIO
5		SCORPIO	SAGITTARIUS	CAPRICORN	CAPRICORN	SCORPIO	SAGITTARIUS	SAGITTARIUS	SCORPIO
6		SCORPIO	SAGITTARIUS	CAPRICORN	CAPRICORN	SCORPIO	SAGITTARIUS	SAGITTARIUS	SCORPIO
7	4:23 AM TAURUS	SAGITTARIUS	SAGITTARIUS	CAPRICORN	CAPRICORN	SCORPIO	SAGITTARIUS	SAGITTARIUS	SCORPIO
8		SAGITTARIUS	SAGITTARIUS	CAPRICORN	CAPRICORN	SCORPIO	SAGITTARIUS	SAGITTARIUS	SCORPIO
9	3:17 PM GEMINI	SAGITTARIUS	SAGITTARIUS	CAPRICORN	CAPRICORN	SCORPIO	SAGITTARIUS	SAGITTARIUS	SCORPIO
10		SAGITTARIUS	SAGITTARIUS	CAPRICORN	CAPRICORN	SCORPIO	SAGITTARIUS	SAGITTARIUS	SCORPIO
11		SAGITTARIUS	SAGITTARIUS	CAPRICORN	CAPRICORN	SCORPIO	SAGITTARIUS	SAGITTARIUS	SCORPIO
12	0:33 AM CANCER	SAGITTARIUS	SAGITTARIUS	CAPRICORN	CAPRICORN	SCORPIO	SAGITTARIUS	SAGITTARIUS	SCORPIO
13		SAGITTARIUS	SAGITTARIUS	CAPRICORN	CAPRICORN	SCORPIO	SAGITTARIUS	SAGITTARIUS	SCORPIO
14	7:22 AM LEO	SAGITTARIUS	CAPRICORN	CAPRICORN	CAPRICORN	SCORPIO	SAGITTARIUS	SAGITTARIUS	SCORPIO
15		SAGITTARIUS	CAPRICORN	CAPRICORN	CAPRICORN	SCORPIO	SAGITTARIUS	SAGITTARIUS	SCORPIO
16	12:18 PM VIRGO	SAGITTARIUS	CAPRICORN	AQUARIUS	CAPRICORN	SCORPIO	SAGITTARIUS	SAGITTARIUS	SCORPIO
17		SAGITTARIUS	CAPRICORN	AQUARIUS	CAPRICORN	SCORPIO	SAGITTARIUS	SAGITTARIUS	SCORPIO
18	2:46 PM LIBRA	SAGITTARIUS	CAPRICORN	AQUARIUS	CAPRICORN	SCORPIO	SAGITTARIUS	SAGITTARIUS	SCORPIO
19		SAGITTARIUS	CAPRICORN	AQUARIUS	CAPRICORN	SCORPIO	SAGITTARIUS	SAGITTARIUS	SCORPIO
20	3:53 PM SCORPIO	SAGITTARIUS	CAPRICORN	AQUARIUS	CAPRICORN	SCORPIO	SAGITTARIUS	SAGITTARIUS	SCORPIO
21		SAGITTARIUS	CAPRICORN	AQUARIUS	CAPRICORN	SCORPIO	SAGITTARIUS	SAGITTARIUS	SCORPIO
22	4:57 PM SAGITTARIUS	SAGITTARIUS	CAPRICORN	AQUARIUS	CAPRICORN	SCORPIO	SAGITTARIUS	CAPRICORN	SCORPIO

1985

OCT.	MOON FROM IN	MERCURY	VENUS	MARS	JUPITER	SATURN	URANUS	NEPTUNE	PLUTO
24		SCORPIO	LIBRA	VIRGO	AQUARIUS	SCORPIO	SAGITTARIUS	CAPRICORN	SCORPIO
25	2:09 PM ARIES	SCORPIO	LIBRA	VIRGO	AQUARIUS	SCORPIO	SAGITTARIUS	CAPRICORN	SCORPIO
26		SCORPIO	LIBRA	VIRGO	AQUARIUS	SCORPIO	SAGITTARIUS	CAPRICORN	SCORPIO
27		SCORPIO	LIBRA	VIRGO	AQUARIUS	SCORPIO	SAGITTARIUS	CAPRICORN	SCORPIO
28	2:11 AM TAURUS	SCORPIO	LIBRA	LIBRA	AQUARIUS	SCORPIO	SAGITTARIUS	CAPRICORN	SCORPIO
29		SCORPIO	LIBRA	LIBRA	AQUARIUS	SCORPIO	SAGITTARIUS	CAPRICORN	SCORPIO
30	2:36 PM GEMINI	SCORPIO	LIBRA	LIBRA	AQUARIUS	SCORPIO	SAGITTARIUS	CAPRICORN	SCORPIO
31		SCORPIO	LIBRA	LIBRA	AQUARIUS	SCORPIO	SAGITTARIUS	CAPRICORN	SCORPIO
NOV.									
1		SAGITTARIUS	LIBRA	LIBRA	AQUARIUS	SCORPIO	SAGITTARIUS	CAPRICORN	SCORPIO
2	3:12 AM CANCER	SAGITTARIUS	LIBRA	LIBRA	AQUARIUS	SCORPIO	SAGITTARIUS	CAPRICORN	SCORPIO
3		SAGITTARIUS	LIBRA	LIBRA	AQUARIUS	SCORPIO	SAGITTARIUS	CAPRICORN	SCORPIO
4	3:12 AM LEO	SAGITTARIUS	LIBRA	LIBRA	AQUARIUS	SCORPIO	SAGITTARIUS	CAPRICORN	SCORPIO
5		SAGITTARIUS	LIBRA	LIBRA	AQUARIUS	SCORPIO	SAGITTARIUS	CAPRICORN	SCORPIO
6	9:34 PM VIRGO	SAGITTARIUS	LIBRA	LIBRA	AQUARIUS	SCORPIO	SAGITTARIUS	CAPRICORN	SCORPIO
7		SAGITTARIUS	LIBRA	LIBRA	AQUARIUS	SCORPIO	SAGITTARIUS	CAPRICORN	SCORPIO
8		SAGITTARIUS	LIBRA	LIBRA	AQUARIUS	SCORPIO	SAGITTARIUS	CAPRICORN	SCORPIO
9	1:14 AM LIBRA	SAGITTARIUS	LIBRA	LIBRA	AQUARIUS	SCORPIO	SAGITTARIUS	CAPRICORN	SCORPIO
10		SAGITTARIUS	SCORPIO	LIBRA	AQUARIUS	SCORPIO	SAGITTARIUS	CAPRICORN	SCORPIO
11	1:53 AM SCORPIO	SAGITTARIUS	SCORPIO	LIBRA	AQUARIUS	SCORPIO	SAGITTARIUS	CAPRICORN	SCORPIO
12		SAGITTARIUS	SCORPIO	LIBRA	AQUARIUS	SCORPIO	SAGITTARIUS	CAPRICORN	SCORPIO
13	1:12 AM SAGITTARIUS	SAGITTARIUS	SCORPIO	LIBRA	AQUARIUS	SCORPIO	SAGITTARIUS	CAPRICORN	SCORPIO
14		SAGITTARIUS	SCORPIO	LIBRA	AQUARIUS	SCORPIO	SAGITTARIUS	CAPRICORN	SCORPIO
15	1:10 AM CAPRICORN	SAGITTARIUS	SCORPIO	LIBRA	AQUARIUS	SCORPIO	SAGITTARIUS	CAPRICORN	SCORPIO
16		SAGITTARIUS	SCORPIO	LIBRA	AQUARIUS	SCORPIO	SAGITTARIUS	CAPRICORN	SCORPIO
17	3:54 AM AQUARIUS	SAGITTARIUS	SCORPIO	LIBRA	AQUARIUS	SCORPIO	SAGITTARIUS	CAPRICORN	SCORPIO
18		SAGITTARIUS	SCORPIO	LIBRA	AQUARIUS	SAGITTARIUS	SAGITTARIUS	CAPRICORN	SCORPIO
19	10:04 AM PISCES	SAGITTARIUS	SCORPIO	LIBRA	AQUARIUS	SAGITTARIUS	SAGITTARIUS	CAPRICORN	SCORPIO
20		SAGITTARIUS	SCORPIO	LIBRA	AQUARIUS	SAGITTARIUS	SAGITTARIUS	CAPRICORN	SCORPIO
21	8:00 PM ARIES	SAGITTARIUS	SCORPIO	LIBRA	AQUARIUS	SAGITTARIUS	SAGITTARIUS	CAPRICORN	SCORPIO
22		SAGITTARIUS	SCORPIO	LIBRA	AQUARIUS	SAGITTARIUS	SAGITTARIUS	CAPRICORN	SCORPIO

SCORPIO

1986

MOON FROM	IN	MERCURY	VENUS	MARS	JUPITER	SATURN	URANUS	NEPTUNE	PLUTO
OCT.									
24		SCORPIO	SCORPIO	AQUARIUS	PISCES	SAGITTARIUS	SAGITTARIUS	CAPRICORN	SCORPIO
25	1:04 PM LEO	SCORPIO	SCORPIO	AQUARIUS	PISCES	SAGITTARIUS	SAGITTARIUS	CAPRICORN	SCORPIO
26		SCORPIO	SCORPIO	AQUARIUS	PISCES	SAGITTARIUS	SAGITTARIUS	CAPRICORN	SCORPIO
27	11:42 PM VIRGO	SCORPIO	SCORPIO	AQUARIUS	PISCES	SAGITTARIUS	SAGITTARIUS	CAPRICORN	SCORPIO
28		SCORPIO	SCORPIO	AQUARIUS	PISCES	SAGITTARIUS	SAGITTARIUS	CAPRICORN	SCORPIO
29		SCORPIO	SCORPIO	AQUARIUS	PISCES	SAGITTARIUS	SAGITTARIUS	CAPRICORN	SCORPIO
30	6:29 AM LIBRA	SCORPIO	SCORPIO	AQUARIUS	PISCES	SAGITTARIUS	SAGITTARIUS	CAPRICORN	SCORPIO
31		SCORPIO	SCORPIO	AQUARIUS	PISCES	SAGITTARIUS	SAGITTARIUS	CAPRICORN	SCORPIO
NOV.									
1	9:21 AM SCORPIO	SCORPIO	SCORPIO	AQUARIUS	PISCES	SAGITTARIUS	SAGITTARIUS	CAPRICORN	SCORPIO
2		SCORPIO	SCORPIO	AQUARIUS	PISCES	SAGITTARIUS	SAGITTARIUS	CAPRICORN	SCORPIO
3	10:25 AM SAGITTARIUS	SCORPIO	SCORPIO	AQUARIUS	PISCES	SAGITTARIUS	SAGITTARIUS	CAPRICORN	SCORPIO
4		SCORPIO	SCORPIO	AQUARIUS	PISCES	SAGITTARIUS	SAGITTARIUS	CAPRICORN	SCORPIO
5	11:05 AM CAPRICORN	SCORPIO	SCORPIO	AQUARIUS	PISCES	SAGITTARIUS	SAGITTARIUS	CAPRICORN	SCORPIO
6		SCORPIO	SCORPIO	AQUARIUS	PISCES	SAGITTARIUS	SAGITTARIUS	CAPRICORN	SCORPIO
7	12:47 PM AQUARIUS	SCORPIO	SCORPIO	AQUARIUS	PISCES	SAGITTARIUS	SAGITTARIUS	CAPRICORN	SCORPIO
8		SCORPIO	SCORPIO	AQUARIUS	PISCES	SAGITTARIUS	SAGITTARIUS	CAPRICORN	SCORPIO
9	4:44 PM PISCES	SCORPIO	SCORPIO	AQUARIUS	PISCES	SAGITTARIUS	SAGITTARIUS	CAPRICORN	SCORPIO
10		SCORPIO	SCORPIO	AQUARIUS	PISCES	SAGITTARIUS	SAGITTARIUS	CAPRICORN	SCORPIO
11	11:35 PM ARIES	SCORPIO	SCORPIO	AQUARIUS	PISCES	SAGITTARIUS	SAGITTARIUS	CAPRICORN	SCORPIO
12		SCORPIO	SCORPIO	AQUARIUS	PISCES	SAGITTARIUS	SAGITTARIUS	CAPRICORN	SCORPIO
13		SCORPIO	SCORPIO	AQUARIUS	PISCES	SAGITTARIUS	SAGITTARIUS	CAPRICORN	SCORPIO
14	8:12 AM TAURUS	SCORPIO	SCORPIO	AQUARIUS	PISCES	SAGITTARIUS	SAGITTARIUS	CAPRICORN	SCORPIO
15		SCORPIO	SCORPIO	AQUARIUS	PISCES	SAGITTARIUS	SAGITTARIUS	CAPRICORN	SCORPIO
16	7:30 PM GEMINI	SCORPIO	SCORPIO	AQUARIUS	PISCES	SAGITTARIUS	SAGITTARIUS	CAPRICORN	SCORPIO
17		SCORPIO	SCORPIO	AQUARIUS	PISCES	SAGITTARIUS	SAGITTARIUS	CAPRICORN	SCORPIO
18		SCORPIO	SCORPIO	AQUARIUS	PISCES	SAGITTARIUS	SAGITTARIUS	CAPRICORN	SCORPIO
19	7:25 AM CANCER	SCORPIO	SCORPIO	AQUARIUS	PISCES	SAGITTARIUS	SAGITTARIUS	CAPRICORN	SCORPIO
20		SCORPIO	SCORPIO	AQUARIUS	PISCES	SAGITTARIUS	SAGITTARIUS	CAPRICORN	SCORPIO
21	8:13 PM LEO	SCORPIO	SCORPIO	AQUARIUS	PISCES	SAGITTARIUS	SAGITTARIUS	CAPRICORN	SCORPIO
22		SCORPIO	SCORPIO	AQUARIUS	PISCES	SAGITTARIUS	SAGITTARIUS	CAPRICORN	SCORPIO

1987

MOON FROM	IN	MERCURY	VENUS	MARS	JUPITER	SATURN	URANUS	NEPTUNE	PLUTO
OCT.									
24	7:47 PM SAGITTARIUS	SCORPIO	SCORPIO	LIBRA	ARIES	SAGITTARIUS	SAGITTARIUS	CAPRICORN	SCORPIO
25		SCORPIO	SCORPIO	LIBRA	ARIES	SAGITTARIUS	SAGITTARIUS	CAPRICORN	SCORPIO
26	11:34 PM CAPRICORN	SCORPIO	SCORPIO	LIBRA	ARIES	SAGITTARIUS	SAGITTARIUS	CAPRICORN	SCORPIO
27		SCORPIO	SCORPIO	LIBRA	ARIES	SAGITTARIUS	SAGITTARIUS	CAPRICORN	SCORPIO
28		SCORPIO	SCORPIO	LIBRA	ARIES	SAGITTARIUS	SAGITTARIUS	CAPRICORN	SCORPIO
29	2:35 AM AQUARIUS	SCORPIO	SCORPIO	LIBRA	ARIES	SAGITTARIUS	SAGITTARIUS	CAPRICORN	SCORPIO
30		SCORPIO	SCORPIO	LIBRA	ARIES	SAGITTARIUS	SAGITTARIUS	CAPRICORN	SCORPIO
31	5:19 AM PISCES	SCORPIO	SCORPIO	LIBRA	ARIES	SAGITTARIUS	SAGITTARIUS	CAPRICORN	SCORPIO
NOV.									
1		SCORPIO	SCORPIO	LIBRA	ARIES	SAGITTARIUS	SAGITTARIUS	CAPRICORN	SCORPIO
2	8:45 AM ARIES	LIBRA	SCORPIO	LIBRA	ARIES	SAGITTARIUS	SAGITTARIUS	CAPRICORN	SCORPIO
3		LIBRA	SCORPIO	LIBRA	ARIES	SAGITTARIUS	SAGITTARIUS	CAPRICORN	SCORPIO
4	1:02 PM TAURUS	LIBRA	SAGITTARIUS	LIBRA	ARIES	SAGITTARIUS	SAGITTARIUS	CAPRICORN	SCORPIO
5		LIBRA	SAGITTARIUS	LIBRA	ARIES	SAGITTARIUS	SAGITTARIUS	CAPRICORN	SCORPIO
6	7:10 PM GEMINI	LIBRA	SAGITTARIUS	LIBRA	ARIES	SAGITTARIUS	SAGITTARIUS	CAPRICORN	SCORPIO
7		LIBRA	SAGITTARIUS	LIBRA	ARIES	SAGITTARIUS	SAGITTARIUS	CAPRICORN	SCORPIO
8		LIBRA	SAGITTARIUS	LIBRA	ARIES	SAGITTARIUS	SAGITTARIUS	CAPRICORN	SCORPIO
9	4:17 AM CANCER	LIBRA	SAGITTARIUS	LIBRA	ARIES	SAGITTARIUS	SAGITTARIUS	CAPRICORN	SCORPIO
10		LIBRA	SAGITTARIUS	LIBRA	ARIES	SAGITTARIUS	SAGITTARIUS	CAPRICORN	SCORPIO
11	3:52 PM LEO	LIBRA	SAGITTARIUS	LIBRA	ARIES	SAGITTARIUS	SAGITTARIUS	CAPRICORN	SCORPIO
12		SCORPIO	SAGITTARIUS	LIBRA	ARIES	SAGITTARIUS	SAGITTARIUS	CAPRICORN	SCORPIO
13		SCORPIO	SAGITTARIUS	LIBRA	ARIES	SAGITTARIUS	SAGITTARIUS	CAPRICORN	SCORPIO
14	4:48 AM VIRGO	SCORPIO	SAGITTARIUS	LIBRA	ARIES	SAGITTARIUS	SAGITTARIUS	CAPRICORN	SCORPIO
15		SCORPIO	SAGITTARIUS	LIBRA	ARIES	SAGITTARIUS	SAGITTARIUS	CAPRICORN	SCORPIO
16	4:09 PM LIBRA	SCORPIO	SAGITTARIUS	LIBRA	ARIES	SAGITTARIUS	SAGITTARIUS	CAPRICORN	SCORPIO
17		SCORPIO	SAGITTARIUS	LIBRA	ARIES	SAGITTARIUS	SAGITTARIUS	CAPRICORN	SCORPIO
18	11:44 PM SCORPIO	SCORPIO	SAGITTARIUS	LIBRA	ARIES	SAGITTARIUS	SAGITTARIUS	CAPRICORN	SCORPIO
19		SCORPIO	SAGITTARIUS	LIBRA	ARIES	SAGITTARIUS	SAGITTARIUS	CAPRICORN	SCORPIO
20		SCORPIO	SAGITTARIUS	LIBRA	ARIES	SAGITTARIUS	SAGITTARIUS	CAPRICORN	SCORPIO
21	4:14 AM SAGITTARIUS	SCORPIO	SAGITTARIUS	LIBRA	ARIES	SAGITTARIUS	SAGITTARIUS	CAPRICORN	SCORPIO
22		SCORPIO	SAGITTARIUS	LIBRA	ARIES	SAGITTARIUS	SAGITTARIUS	CAPRICORN	SCORPIO

1988

Date	MOON FROM / IN	MERCURY	VENUS	MARS	JUPITER	SATURN	URANUS	NEPTUNE	PLUTO
OCT.									
24	8:22 PM TAURUS	LIBRA	VIRGO	PISCES	GEMINI	SAGITTARIUS	SAGITTARIUS	CAPRICORN	SCORPIO
25		LIBRA	VIRGO	PISCES	GEMINI	SAGITTARIUS	SAGITTARIUS	CAPRICORN	SCORPIO
26	10:07 PM GEMINI	LIBRA	VIRGO	PISCES	GEMINI	SAGITTARIUS	SAGITTARIUS	CAPRICORN	SCORPIO
27		LIBRA	VIRGO	PISCES	GEMINI	SAGITTARIUS	SAGITTARIUS	CAPRICORN	SCORPIO
28		LIBRA	VIRGO	PISCES	GEMINI	SAGITTARIUS	SAGITTARIUS	CAPRICORN	SCORPIO
29	2:42 AM CANCER	LIBRA	VIRGO	PISCES	GEMINI	SAGITTARIUS	SAGITTARIUS	CAPRICORN	SCORPIO
30		LIBRA	LIBRA	PISCES	GEMINI	SAGITTARIUS	SAGITTARIUS	CAPRICORN	SCORPIO
31	11:25 AM LEO	LIBRA	LIBRA	PISCES	GEMINI	SAGITTARIUS	SAGITTARIUS	CAPRICORN	SCORPIO
NOV.									
1		LIBRA	LIBRA	PISCES	GEMINI	SAGITTARIUS	SAGITTARIUS	CAPRICORN	SCORPIO
2	11:25 PM VIRGO	LIBRA	LIBRA	ARIES	GEMINI	SAGITTARIUS	SAGITTARIUS	CAPRICORN	SCORPIO
3		LIBRA	LIBRA	ARIES	GEMINI	SAGITTARIUS	SAGITTARIUS	CAPRICORN	SCORPIO
4		LIBRA	LIBRA	ARIES	GEMINI	SAGITTARIUS	SAGITTARIUS	CAPRICORN	SCORPIO
5	12:15 PM LIBRA	LIBRA	LIBRA	ARIES	GEMINI	SAGITTARIUS	SAGITTARIUS	CAPRICORN	SCORPIO
6		LIBRA	LIBRA	ARIES	GEMINI	SAGITTARIUS	SAGITTARIUS	CAPRICORN	SCORPIO
7	11:39 PM SCORPIO	SCORPIO	LIBRA	ARIES	GEMINI	SAGITTARIUS	SAGITTARIUS	CAPRICORN	SCORPIO
8		SCORPIO	LIBRA	ARIES	GEMINI	SAGITTARIUS	SAGITTARIUS	CAPRICORN	SCORPIO
9		SCORPIO	LIBRA	ARIES	GEMINI	SAGITTARIUS	SAGITTARIUS	CAPRICORN	SCORPIO
10	8:53 AM SAGITTARIUS	SCORPIO	LIBRA	ARIES	GEMINI	SAGITTARIUS	SAGITTARIUS	CAPRICORN	SCORPIO
11		SCORPIO	LIBRA	ARIES	GEMINI	SAGITTARIUS	SAGITTARIUS	CAPRICORN	SCORPIO
12	4:23 PM CAPRICORN	SCORPIO	LIBRA	ARIES	GEMINI	SAGITTARIUS	SAGITTARIUS	CAPRICORN	SCORPIO
13		SCORPIO	LIBRA	ARIES	GEMINI	CAPRICORN	SAGITTARIUS	CAPRICORN	SCORPIO
14	9:46 PM AQUARIUS	SCORPIO	LIBRA	ARIES	GEMINI	CAPRICORN	SAGITTARIUS	CAPRICORN	SCORPIO
15		SCORPIO	LIBRA	ARIES	GEMINI	CAPRICORN	SAGITTARIUS	CAPRICORN	SCORPIO
16		SCORPIO	LIBRA	ARIES	GEMINI	CAPRICORN	SAGITTARIUS	CAPRICORN	SCORPIO
17	1:37 AM PISCES	SCORPIO	LIBRA	ARIES	GEMINI	CAPRICORN	SAGITTARIUS	CAPRICORN	SCORPIO
18		SCORPIO	LIBRA	ARIES	GEMINI	CAPRICORN	SAGITTARIUS	CAPRICORN	SCORPIO
19	3:50 AM ARIES	SCORPIO	LIBRA	ARIES	GEMINI	CAPRICORN	SAGITTARIUS	CAPRICORN	SCORPIO
20		SCORPIO	LIBRA	ARIES	GEMINI	CAPRICORN	SAGITTARIUS	CAPRICORN	SCORPIO
21	5:41 AM TAURUS	SCORPIO	LIBRA	ARIES	GEMINI	CAPRICORN	SAGITTARIUS	CAPRICORN	SCORPIO
22		SCORPIO	LIBRA	ARIES	GEMINI	CAPRICORN	SAGITTARIUS	CAPRICORN	SCORPIO

1989

Date	MOON FROM / IN	MERCURY	VENUS	MARS	JUPITER	SATURN	URANUS	NEPTUNE	PLUTO
OCT.									
24		LIBRA	SAGITTARIUS	LIBRA	CANCER	CAPRICORN	CAPRICORN	CAPRICORN	SCORPIO
25		LIBRA	SAGITTARIUS	LIBRA	CANCER	CAPRICORN	CAPRICORN	CAPRICORN	SCORPIO
26	9:01 AM LIBRA	LIBRA	SAGITTARIUS	LIBRA	CANCER	CAPRICORN	CAPRICORN	CAPRICORN	SCORPIO
27		LIBRA	SAGITTARIUS	LIBRA	CANCER	CAPRICORN	CAPRICORN	CAPRICORN	SCORPIO
28	9:50 PM SCORPIO	LIBRA	SAGITTARIUS	LIBRA	CANCER	CAPRICORN	CAPRICORN	CAPRICORN	SCORPIO
29		LIBRA	SAGITTARIUS	LIBRA	CANCER	CAPRICORN	CAPRICORN	CAPRICORN	SCORPIO
30		LIBRA	SAGITTARIUS	LIBRA	CANCER	CAPRICORN	CAPRICORN	CAPRICORN	SCORPIO
31	10:11 AM SAGITTARIUS	SCORPIO	SAGITTARIUS	LIBRA	CANCER	CAPRICORN	CAPRICORN	CAPRICORN	SCORPIO
NOV.									
1		SCORPIO	SAGITTARIUS	LIBRA	CANCER	CAPRICORN	CAPRICORN	CAPRICORN	SCORPIO
2	9:53 PM CAPRICORN	SCORPIO	SAGITTARIUS	LIBRA	CANCER	CAPRICORN	CAPRICORN	CAPRICORN	SCORPIO
3		SCORPIO	SAGITTARIUS	LIBRA	CANCER	CAPRICORN	CAPRICORN	CAPRICORN	SCORPIO
4		SCORPIO	SAGITTARIUS	LIBRA	CANCER	CAPRICORN	CAPRICORN	CAPRICORN	SCORPIO
5	7:11 AM AQUARIUS	SCORPIO	SAGITTARIUS	SCORPIO	CANCER	CAPRICORN	CAPRICORN	CAPRICORN	SCORPIO
6		SCORPIO	CAPRICORN	SCORPIO	CANCER	CAPRICORN	CAPRICORN	CAPRICORN	SCORPIO
7	1:02 PM PISCES	SCORPIO	CAPRICORN	SCORPIO	CANCER	CAPRICORN	CAPRICORN	CAPRICORN	SCORPIO
8		SCORPIO	CAPRICORN	SCORPIO	CANCER	CAPRICORN	CAPRICORN	CAPRICORN	SCORPIO
9	3:50 PM ARIES	SCORPIO	CAPRICORN	SCORPIO	CANCER	CAPRICORN	CAPRICORN	CAPRICORN	SCORPIO
10		SCORPIO	CAPRICORN	SCORPIO	CANCER	CAPRICORN	CAPRICORN	CAPRICORN	SCORPIO
11	3:56 PM TAURUS	SCORPIO	CAPRICORN	SCORPIO	CANCER	CAPRICORN	CAPRICORN	CAPRICORN	SCORPIO
12		SCORPIO	CAPRICORN	SCORPIO	CANCER	CAPRICORN	CAPRICORN	CAPRICORN	SCORPIO
13	3:43 PM GEMINI	SCORPIO	CAPRICORN	SCORPIO	CANCER	CAPRICORN	CAPRICORN	CAPRICORN	SCORPIO
14		SCORPIO	CAPRICORN	SCORPIO	CANCER	CAPRICORN	CAPRICORN	CAPRICORN	SCORPIO
15	4:33 PM CANCER	SCORPIO	CAPRICORN	SCORPIO	CANCER	CAPRICORN	CAPRICORN	CAPRICORN	SCORPIO
16		SCORPIO	CAPRICORN	SCORPIO	CANCER	CAPRICORN	CAPRICORN	CAPRICORN	SCORPIO
17	8:20 PM LEO	SCORPIO	CAPRICORN	SCORPIO	CANCER	CAPRICORN	CAPRICORN	CAPRICORN	SCORPIO
18		SCORPIO	CAPRICORN	SCORPIO	CANCER	CAPRICORN	CAPRICORN	CAPRICORN	SCORPIO
19		SAGITTARIUS	CAPRICORN	SCORPIO	CANCER	CAPRICORN	CAPRICORN	CAPRICORN	SCORPIO
20	3:56 AM VIRGO	SAGITTARIUS	CAPRICORN	SCORPIO	CANCER	CAPRICORN	CAPRICORN	CAPRICORN	SCORPIO
21		SAGITTARIUS	CAPRICORN	SCORPIO	CANCER	CAPRICORN	CAPRICORN	CAPRICORN	SCORPIO
22	3:24 PM LIBRA	SAGITTARIUS	CAPRICORN	SCORPIO	CANCER	CAPRICORN	CAPRICORN	CAPRICORN	SCORPIO

1990 SCORPIO

	MOON		MERCURY	VENUS	MARS	JUPITER	SATURN	URANUS	NEPTUNE	PLUTO
	FROM	IN								
OCTOBER										
24			SCORPIO	LIBRA	GEMINI	LEO	CAPRICORN	CAPRICORN	CAPRICORN	SCORPIO
25			SCORPIO	LIBRA	GEMINI	LEO	CAPRICORN	CAPRICORN	CAPRICORN	SCORPIO
26	8:56 AM	AQUARIUS	SCORPIO	SCORPIO	GEMINI	LEO	CAPRICORN	CAPRICORN	CAPRICORN	SCORPIO
27			SCORPIO	SCORPIO	GEMINI	LEO	CAPRICORN	CAPRICORN	CAPRICORN	SCORPIO
28	5:59 PM	PISCES	SCORPIO	SCORPIO	GEMINI	LEO	CAPRICORN	CAPRICORN	CAPRICORN	SCORPIO
29			SCORPIO	SCORPIO	GEMINI	LEO	CAPRICORN	CAPRICORN	CAPRICORN	SCORPIO
30	10:50 PM	ARIES	SCORPIO	SCORPIO	GEMINI	LEO	CAPRICORN	CAPRICORN	CAPRICORN	SCORPIO
31			SCORPIO	SCORPIO	GEMINI	LEO	CAPRICORN	CAPRICORN	CAPRICORN	SCORPIO
NOVEMBER										
1			SCORPIO	SCORPIO	GEMINI	LEO	CAPRICORN	CAPRICORN	CAPRICORN	SCORPIO
2	0:38 AM	TAURUS	SCORPIO	SCORPIO	GEMINI	LEO	CAPRICORN	CAPRICORN	CAPRICORN	SCORPIO
3			SCORPIO	SCORPIO	GEMINI	LEO	CAPRICORN	CAPRICORN	CAPRICORN	SCORPIO
4	0:44 AM	GEMINI	SCORPIO	SCORPIO	GEMINI	LEO	CAPRICORN	CAPRICORN	CAPRICORN	SCORPIO
5			SCORPIO	SCORPIO	GEMINI	LEO	CAPRICORN	CAPRICORN	CAPRICORN	SCORPIO
6	0:41 AM	CANCER	SCORPIO	SCORPIO	GEMINI	LEO	CAPRICORN	CAPRICORN	CAPRICORN	SCORPIO
7			SCORPIO	SCORPIO	GEMINI	LEO	CAPRICORN	CAPRICORN	CAPRICORN	SCORPIO
8	2:55 AM	LEO	SCORPIO	SCORPIO	GEMINI	LEO	CAPRICORN	CAPRICORN	CAPRICORN	SCORPIO
9			SCORPIO	SCORPIO	GEMINI	LEO	CAPRICORN	CAPRICORN	CAPRICORN	SCORPIO
10	7:34 AM	VIRGO	SCORPIO	SCORPIO	GEMINI	LEO	CAPRICORN	CAPRICORN	CAPRICORN	SCORPIO
11			SAGITTARIUS	SCORPIO	GEMINI	LEO	CAPRICORN	CAPRICORN	CAPRICORN	SCORPIO
12	4:09 PM	LIBRA	SAGITTARIUS	SCORPIO	GEMINI	LEO	CAPRICORN	CAPRICORN	CAPRICORN	SCORPIO
13			SAGITTARIUS	SCORPIO	GEMINI	LEO	CAPRICORN	CAPRICORN	CAPRICORN	SCORPIO
14			SAGITTARIUS	SCORPIO	GEMINI	LEO	CAPRICORN	CAPRICORN	CAPRICORN	SCORPIO
15	3:00 AM	SCORPIO	SAGITTARIUS	SCORPIO	GEMINI	LEO	CAPRICORN	CAPRICORN	CAPRICORN	SCORPIO
16			SAGITTARIUS	SCORPIO	GEMINI	LEO	CAPRICORN	CAPRICORN	CAPRICORN	SCORPIO
17	2:41 PM	SAGITTARIUS	SAGITTARIUS	SCORPIO	GEMINI	LEO	CAPRICORN	CAPRICORN	CAPRICORN	SCORPIO
18			SAGITTARIUS	SCORPIO	GEMINI	LEO	CAPRICORN	CAPRICORN	CAPRICORN	SCORPIO
19			SAGITTARIUS	SAGITTARIUS	GEMINI	LEO	CAPRICORN	CAPRICORN	CAPRICORN	SCORPIO
20	3:20 AM	CAPRICORN	SAGITTARIUS	SAGITTARIUS	GEMINI	LEO	CAPRICORN	CAPRICORN	CAPRICORN	SCORPIO
21			SAGITTARIUS	SAGITTARIUS	GEMINI	LEO	CAPRICORN	CAPRICORN	CAPRICORN	SCORPIO
22	3:52 PM	AQUARIUS	SAGITTARIUS	SAGITTARIUS	GEMINI	LEO	CAPRICORN	CAPRICORN	CAPRICORN	SCORPIO

1991

	MOON		MERCURY	VENUS	MARS	JUPITER	SATURN	URANUS	NEPTUNE	PLUTO
	FROM	IN								
OCTOBER										
24			SCORPIO	VIRGO	SCORPIO	VIRGO	AQUARIUS	CAPRICORN	CAPRICORN	SCORPIO
25	10:10 AM	GEMINI	SCORPIO	VIRGO	SCORPIO	VIRGO	AQUARIUS	CAPRICORN	CAPRICORN	SCORPIO
26			SCORPIO	VIRGO	SCORPIO	VIRGO	AQUARIUS	CAPRICORN	CAPRICORN	SCORPIO
27	12:38 PM	CANCER	SCORPIO	VIRGO	SCORPIO	VIRGO	AQUARIUS	CAPRICORN	CAPRICORN	SCORPIO
28			SCORPIO	VIRGO	SCORPIO	VIRGO	AQUARIUS	CAPRICORN	CAPRICORN	SCORPIO
29	3:21 PM	LEO	SCORPIO	VIRGO	SCORPIO	VIRGO	AQUARIUS	CAPRICORN	CAPRICORN	SCORPIO
30			SCORPIO	VIRGO	SCORPIO	VIRGO	AQUARIUS	CAPRICORN	CAPRICORN	SCORPIO
31	6:48 PM	VIRGO	SCORPIO	VIRGO	SCORPIO	VIRGO	AQUARIUS	CAPRICORN	CAPRICORN	SCORPIO
NOVEMBER										
1			SCORPIO	VIRGO	SCORPIO	VIRGO	AQUARIUS	CAPRICORN	CAPRICORN	SCORPIO
2	11:13 PM	LIBRA	SCORPIO	VIRGO	SCORPIO	VIRGO	AQUARIUS	CAPRICORN	CAPRICORN	SCORPIO
3			SCORPIO	VIRGO	SCORPIO	VIRGO	AQUARIUS	CAPRICORN	CAPRICORN	SCORPIO
4			SAGITTARIUS	VIRGO	SCORPIO	VIRGO	AQUARIUS	CAPRICORN	CAPRICORN	SCORPIO
5	5:10 AM	SCORPIO	SAGITTARIUS	VIRGO	SCORPIO	VIRGO	AQUARIUS	CAPRICORN	CAPRICORN	SCORPIO
6			SAGITTARIUS	VIRGO	SCORPIO	VIRGO	AQUARIUS	CAPRICORN	CAPRICORN	SCORPIO
7	1:22 PM	SAGITTARIUS	SAGITTARIUS	VIRGO	SCORPIO	VIRGO	AQUARIUS	CAPRICORN	CAPRICORN	SCORPIO
8			SAGITTARIUS	VIRGO	SCORPIO	VIRGO	AQUARIUS	CAPRICORN	CAPRICORN	SCORPIO
9			SAGITTARIUS	LIBRA	SCORPIO	VIRGO	AQUARIUS	CAPRICORN	CAPRICORN	SCORPIO
10	0:17 AM	CAPRICORN	SAGITTARIUS	LIBRA	SCORPIO	VIRGO	AQUARIUS	CAPRICORN	CAPRICORN	SCORPIO
11			SAGITTARIUS	LIBRA	SCORPIO	VIRGO	AQUARIUS	CAPRICORN	CAPRICORN	SCORPIO
12	1:07 PM	AQUARIUS	SAGITTARIUS	LIBRA	SCORPIO	VIRGO	AQUARIUS	CAPRICORN	CAPRICORN	SCORPIO
13			SAGITTARIUS	LIBRA	SCORPIO	VIRGO	AQUARIUS	CAPRICORN	CAPRICORN	SCORPIO
14			SAGITTARIUS	LIBRA	SCORPIO	VIRGO	AQUARIUS	CAPRICORN	CAPRICORN	SCORPIO
15	1:34 AM	PISCES	SAGITTARIUS	LIBRA	SCORPIO	VIRGO	AQUARIUS	CAPRICORN	CAPRICORN	SCORPIO
16			SAGITTARIUS	LIBRA	SCORPIO	VIRGO	AQUARIUS	CAPRICORN	CAPRICORN	SCORPIO
17	11:09 AM	ARIES	SAGITTARIUS	LIBRA	SCORPIO	VIRGO	AQUARIUS	CAPRICORN	CAPRICORN	SCORPIO
18			SAGITTARIUS	LIBRA	SCORPIO	VIRGO	AQUARIUS	CAPRICORN	CAPRICORN	SCORPIO
19	4:50 PM	TAURUS	SAGITTARIUS	LIBRA	SCORPIO	VIRGO	AQUARIUS	CAPRICORN	CAPRICORN	SCORPIO
20			SAGITTARIUS	LIBRA	SCORPIO	VIRGO	AQUARIUS	CAPRICORN	CAPRICORN	SCORPIO
21			SAGITTARIUS	LIBRA	SCORPIO	VIRGO	AQUARIUS	CAPRICORN	CAPRICORN	SCORPIO
22	7:23 PM	GEMINI	SAGITTARIUS	LIBRA	SCORPIO	VIRGO	AQUARIUS	CAPRICORN	CAPRICORN	SCORPIO

SCORPIO

1992

	MOON FROM / IN	MERCURY	VENUS	MARS	JUPITER	SATURN	URANUS	NEPTUNE	PLUTO
OCTOBER									
23	9:40 AM LIBRA	SCORPIO	SAGITTARIUS	CANCER	LIBRA	AQUARIUS	CAPRICORN	CAPRICORN	SCORPIO
24		SCORPIO	SAGITTARIUS	CANCER	LIBRA	AQUARIUS	CAPRICORN	CAPRICORN	SCORPIO
25	11:05 AM SCORPIO	SCORPIO	SAGITTARIUS	CANCER	LIBRA	AQUARIUS	CAPRICORN	CAPRICORN	SCORPIO
26		SCORPIO	SAGITTARIUS	CANCER	LIBRA	AQUARIUS	CAPRICORN	CAPRICORN	SCORPIO
27	2:30 PM SAGITTARIUS	SCORPIO	SAGITTARIUS	CANCER	LIBRA	AQUARIUS	CAPRICORN	CAPRICORN	SCORPIO
28		SCORPIO	SAGITTARIUS	CANCER	LIBRA	AQUARIUS	CAPRICORN	CAPRICORN	SCORPIO
29	9:19 PM CAPRICORN	SAGITTARIUS	SAGITTARIUS	CANCER	LIBRA	AQUARIUS	CAPRICORN	CAPRICORN	SCORPIO
30		SAGITTARIUS	SAGITTARIUS	CANCER	LIBRA	AQUARIUS	CAPRICORN	CAPRICORN	SCORPIO
31		SAGITTARIUS	SAGITTARIUS	CANCER	LIBRA	AQUARIUS	CAPRICORN	CAPRICORN	SCORPIO
NOVEMBER									
1	7:44 AM AQUARIUS	SAGITTARIUS	SAGITTARIUS	CANCER	LIBRA	AQUARIUS	CAPRICORN	CAPRICORN	SCORPIO
2		SAGITTARIUS	SAGITTARIUS	CANCER	LIBRA	AQUARIUS	CAPRICORN	CAPRICORN	SCORPIO
3	8:13 AM PISCES	SAGITTARIUS	SAGITTARIUS	CANCER	LIBRA	AQUARIUS	CAPRICORN	CAPRICORN	SCORPIO
4		SAGITTARIUS	SAGITTARIUS	CANCER	LIBRA	AQUARIUS	CAPRICORN	CAPRICORN	SCORPIO
5		SAGITTARIUS	SAGITTARIUS	CANCER	LIBRA	AQUARIUS	CAPRICORN	CAPRICORN	SCORPIO
6	8:20 AM ARIES	SAGITTARIUS	SAGITTARIUS	CANCER	LIBRA	AQUARIUS	CAPRICORN	CAPRICORN	SCORPIO
7		SAGITTARIUS	SAGITTARIUS	CANCER	LIBRA	AQUARIUS	CAPRICORN	CAPRICORN	SCORPIO
8	6:20 PM TAURUS	SAGITTARIUS	SAGITTARIUS	CANCER	LIBRA	AQUARIUS	CAPRICORN	CAPRICORN	SCORPIO
9		SAGITTARIUS	SAGITTARIUS	CANCER	LIBRA	AQUARIUS	CAPRICORN	CAPRICORN	SCORPIO
10		SAGITTARIUS	SAGITTARIUS	CANCER	LIBRA	AQUARIUS	CAPRICORN	CAPRICORN	SCORPIO
11	1:50 AM GEMINI	SAGITTARIUS	SAGITTARIUS	CANCER	LIBRA	AQUARIUS	CAPRICORN	CAPRICORN	SCORPIO
12		SAGITTARIUS	SAGITTARIUS	CANCER	LIBRA	AQUARIUS	CAPRICORN	CAPRICORN	SCORPIO
13	7:20 AM CANCER	SAGITTARIUS	CAPRICORN	CANCER	LIBRA	AQUARIUS	CAPRICORN	CAPRICORN	SCORPIO
14		SAGITTARIUS	CAPRICORN	CANCER	LIBRA	AQUARIUS	CAPRICORN	CAPRICORN	SCORPIO
15	11:24 AM LEO	SAGITTARIUS	CAPRICORN	CANCER	LIBRA	AQUARIUS	CAPRICORN	CAPRICORN	SCORPIO
16		SAGITTARIUS	CAPRICORN	CANCER	LIBRA	AQUARIUS	CAPRICORN	CAPRICORN	SCORPIO
17	2:29 PM VIRGO	SAGITTARIUS	CAPRICORN	CANCER	LIBRA	AQUARIUS	CAPRICORN	CAPRICORN	SCORPIO
18		SAGITTARIUS	CAPRICORN	CANCER	LIBRA	AQUARIUS	CAPRICORN	CAPRICORN	SCORPIO
19	5:04 PM LIBRA	SAGITTARIUS	CAPRICORN	CANCER	LIBRA	AQUARIUS	CAPRICORN	CAPRICORN	SCORPIO
20		SAGITTARIUS	CAPRICORN	CANCER	LIBRA	AQUARIUS	CAPRICORN	CAPRICORN	SCORPIO
21	3:53 PM SCORPIO	SAGITTARIUS	CAPRICORN	CANCER	LIBRA	AQUARIUS	CAPRICORN	CAPRICORN	SCORPIO

1993

	MOON FROM / IN	MERCURY	VENUS	MARS	JUPITER	SATURN	URANUS	NEPTUNE	PLUTO
OCTOBER									
23		SCORPIO	LIBRA	SCORPIO	LIBRA	AQUARIUS	CAPRICORN	CAPRICORN	SCORPIO
24	4:18 PM PISCES	SCORPIO	LIBRA	SCORPIO	LIBRA	AQUARIUS	CAPRICORN	CAPRICORN	SCORPIO
25		SCORPIO	LIBRA	SCORPIO	LIBRA	AQUARIUS	CAPRICORN	CAPRICORN	SCORPIO
26		SCORPIO	LIBRA	SCORPIO	LIBRA	AQUARIUS	CAPRICORN	CAPRICORN	SCORPIO
27	4:40 AM ARIES	SCORPIO	LIBRA	SCORPIO	LIBRA	AQUARIUS	CAPRICORN	CAPRICORN	SCORPIO
28		SCORPIO	LIBRA	SCORPIO	LIBRA	AQUARIUS	CAPRICORN	CAPRICORN	SCORPIO
29	5:21 PM TAURUS	SCORPIO	LIBRA	SCORPIO	LIBRA	AQUARIUS	CAPRICORN	CAPRICORN	SCORPIO
30		SCORPIO	LIBRA	SCORPIO	LIBRA	AQUARIUS	CAPRICORN	CAPRICORN	SCORPIO
31		SCORPIO	LIBRA	SCORPIO	LIBRA	AQUARIUS	CAPRICORN	CAPRICORN	SCORPIO
NOVEMBER									
1	5:14 AM GEMINI	SCORPIO	LIBRA	SCORPIO	LIBRA	AQUARIUS	CAPRICORN	CAPRICORN	SCORPIO
2		SCORPIO	LIBRA	SCORPIO	LIBRA	AQUARIUS	CAPRICORN	CAPRICORN	SCORPIO
3	3:26 PM CANCER	SCORPIO	LIBRA	SCORPIO	LIBRA	AQUARIUS	CAPRICORN	CAPRICORN	SCORPIO
4		SCORPIO	LIBRA	SCORPIO	LIBRA	AQUARIUS	CAPRICORN	CAPRICORN	SCORPIO
5	11:07 PM LEO	SCORPIO	LIBRA	SCORPIO	LIBRA	AQUARIUS	CAPRICORN	CAPRICORN	SCORPIO
6		SCORPIO	LIBRA	SCORPIO	LIBRA	AQUARIUS	CAPRICORN	CAPRICORN	SCORPIO
7		SCORPIO	LIBRA	SCORPIO	LIBRA	AQUARIUS	CAPRICORN	CAPRICORN	SCORPIO
8	3:48 AM VIRGO	SCORPIO	LIBRA	SCORPIO	LIBRA	AQUARIUS	CAPRICORN	CAPRICORN	SCORPIO
9		SCORPIO	SCORPIO	SAGITTARIUS	LIBRA	AQUARIUS	CAPRICORN	CAPRICORN	SCORPIO
10	5:43 AM LIBRA	SCORPIO	SCORPIO	SAGITTARIUS	SCORPIO	AQUARIUS	CAPRICORN	CAPRICORN	SCORPIO
11		SCORPIO	SCORPIO	SAGITTARIUS	SCORPIO	AQUARIUS	CAPRICORN	CAPRICORN	SCORPIO
12	6:01 AM SCORPIO	SCORPIO	SCORPIO	SAGITTARIUS	SCORPIO	AQUARIUS	CAPRICORN	CAPRICORN	SCORPIO
13		SCORPIO	SCORPIO	SAGITTARIUS	SCORPIO	AQUARIUS	CAPRICORN	CAPRICORN	SCORPIO
14	6:21 AM SAGITTARIUS	SCORPIO	SCORPIO	SAGITTARIUS	SCORPIO	AQUARIUS	CAPRICORN	CAPRICORN	SCORPIO
15		SCORPIO	SCORPIO	SAGITTARIUS	SCORPIO	AQUARIUS	CAPRICORN	CAPRICORN	SCORPIO
16	8:35 AM CAPRICORN	SCORPIO	SCORPIO	SAGITTARIUS	SCORPIO	AQUARIUS	CAPRICORN	CAPRICORN	SCORPIO
17		SCORPIO	SCORPIO	SAGITTARIUS	SCORPIO	AQUARIUS	CAPRICORN	CAPRICORN	SCORPIO
18	2:09 PM AQUARIUS	SCORPIO	SCORPIO	SAGITTARIUS	SCORPIO	AQUARIUS	CAPRICORN	CAPRICORN	SCORPIO
19		SCORPIO	SCORPIO	SAGITTARIUS	SCORPIO	AQUARIUS	CAPRICORN	CAPRICORN	SCORPIO
20	11:28 PM PISCES	SCORPIO	SCORPIO	SAGITTARIUS	SCORPIO	AQUARIUS	CAPRICORN	CAPRICORN	SCORPIO
21		SCORPIO	SCORPIO	SAGITTARIUS	SCORPIO	AQUARIUS	CAPRICORN	CAPRICORN	SCORPIO

1994

SCORPIO

OCTOBER	MOON FROM	IN	MERCURY	VENUS	MARS	JUPITER	SATURN	URANUS	NEPTUNE	PLUTO
24	5:16 PM	CANCER	LIBRA	SCORPIO	LEO	SCORPIO	PISCES	CAPRICORN	CAPRICORN	SCORPIO
25			LIBRA	SCORPIO	LEO	SCORPIO	PISCES	CAPRICORN	CAPRICORN	SCORPIO
26			LIBRA	SCORPIO	LEO	SCORPIO	PISCES	CAPRICORN	CAPRICORN	SCORPIO
27	4:05 AM	LEO	LIBRA	SCORPIO	LEO	SCORPIO	PISCES	CAPRICORN	CAPRICORN	SCORPIO
28			LIBRA	SCORPIO	LEO	SCORPIO	PISCES	CAPRICORN	CAPRICORN	SCORPIO
29	11:22 AM	VIRGO	LIBRA	SCORPIO	LEO	SCORPIO	PISCES	CAPRICORN	CAPRICORN	SCORPIO
30			LIBRA	SCORPIO	LEO	SCORPIO	PISCES	CAPRICORN	CAPRICORN	SCORPIO
31	2:47 PM	LIBRA	LIBRA	SCORPIO	LEO	SCORPIO	PISCES	CAPRICORN	CAPRICORN	SCORPIO
NOVEMBER										
1			LIBRA	SCORPIO	LEO	SCORPIO	PISCES	CAPRICORN	CAPRICORN	SCORPIO
2	3:20 PM	SCORPIO	LIBRA	SCORPIO	LEO	SCORPIO	PISCES	CAPRICORN	CAPRICORN	SCORPIO
3			LIBRA	SCORPIO	LEO	SCORPIO	PISCES	CAPRICORN	CAPRICORN	SCORPIO
4	2:47 PM	SAGITTARIUS	LIBRA	SCORPIO	LEO	SCORPIO	PISCES	CAPRICORN	CAPRICORN	SCORPIO
5			LIBRA	SCORPIO	LEO	SCORPIO	PISCES	CAPRICORN	CAPRICORN	SCORPIO
6	3:03 PM	CAPRICORN	LIBRA	SCORPIO	LEO	SCORPIO	PISCES	CAPRICORN	CAPRICORN	SCORPIO
7			LIBRA	SCORPIO	LEO	SCORPIO	PISCES	CAPRICORN	CAPRICORN	SCORPIO
8	5:49 PM	AQUARIUS	LIBRA	SCORPIO	LEO	SCORPIO	PISCES	CAPRICORN	CAPRICORN	SCORPIO
9			LIBRA	SCORPIO	LEO	SCORPIO	PISCES	CAPRICORN	CAPRICORN	SCORPIO
10			LIBRA	SCORPIO	LEO	SCORPIO	PISCES	CAPRICORN	CAPRICORN	SCORPIO
11	0:05 AM	PISCES	SCORPIO	SCORPIO	LEO	SCORPIO	PISCES	CAPRICORN	CAPRICORN	SCORPIO
12			SCORPIO	SCORPIO	LEO	SCORPIO	PISCES	CAPRICORN	CAPRICORN	SCORPIO
13	9:45 AM	ARIES	SCORPIO	SCORPIO	LEO	SCORPIO	PISCES	CAPRICORN	CAPRICORN	SCORPIO
14			SCORPIO	SCORPIO	LEO	SCORPIO	PISCES	CAPRICORN	CAPRICORN	SCORPIO
15	9:45 PM	TAURUS	SCORPIO	SCORPIO	LEO	SCORPIO	PISCES	CAPRICORN	CAPRICORN	SCORPIO
16			SCORPIO	SCORPIO	LEO	SCORPIO	PISCES	CAPRICORN	CAPRICORN	SCORPIO
17			SCORPIO	SCORPIO	LEO	SCORPIO	PISCES	CAPRICORN	CAPRICORN	SCORPIO
18	10:42 AM	GEMINI	SCORPIO	SCORPIO	LEO	SCORPIO	PISCES	CAPRICORN	CAPRICORN	SCORPIO
19			SCORPIO	SCORPIO	LEO	SCORPIO	PISCES	CAPRICORN	CAPRICORN	SCORPIO
20	11:22 PM	CANCER	SCORPIO	SCORPIO	LEO	SCORPIO	PISCES	CAPRICORN	CAPRICORN	SCORPIO
21			SCORPIO	SCORPIO	LEO	SCORPIO	PISCES	CAPRICORN	CAPRICORN	SCORPIO
22			SCORPIO	SCORPIO	LEO	SCORPIO	PISCES	CAPRICORN	CAPRICORN	SCORPIO

1995

OCTOBER	MOON FROM	IN	MERCURY	VENUS	MARS	JUPITER	SATURN	URANUS	NEPTUNE	PLUTO
24			LIBRA	SCORPIO	SAGITTARIUS	SAGITTARIUS	PISCES	CAPRICORN	CAPRICORN	SCORPIO
25			LIBRA	SCORPIO	SAGITTARIUS	SAGITTARIUS	PISCES	CAPRICORN	CAPRICORN	SCORPIO
26	0:57 AM	SAGITTARIUS	LIBRA	SCORPIO	SAGITTARIUS	SAGITTARIUS	PISCES	CAPRICORN	CAPRICORN	SCORPIO
27			LIBRA	SCORPIO	SAGITTARIUS	SAGITTARIUS	PISCES	CAPRICORN	CAPRICORN	SCORPIO
28	2:16 AM	CAPRICORN	LIBRA	SCORPIO	SAGITTARIUS	SAGITTARIUS	PISCES	CAPRICORN	CAPRICORN	SCORPIO
29			LIBRA	SCORPIO	SAGITTARIUS	SAGITTARIUS	PISCES	CAPRICORN	CAPRICORN	SCORPIO
30	4:24 AM	AQUARIUS	LIBRA	SCORPIO	SAGITTARIUS	SAGITTARIUS	PISCES	CAPRICORN	CAPRICORN	SCORPIO
31			LIBRA	SCORPIO	SAGITTARIUS	SAGITTARIUS	PISCES	CAPRICORN	CAPRICORN	SCORPIO
NOVEMBER										
1	8:18 AM	PISCES	LIBRA	SCORPIO	SAGITTARIUS	SAGITTARIUS	PISCES	CAPRICORN	CAPRICORN	SCORPIO
2			LIBRA	SCORPIO	SAGITTARIUS	SAGITTARIUS	PISCES	CAPRICORN	CAPRICORN	SCORPIO
3	2:22 PM	ARIES	LIBRA	SAGITTARIUS	SAGITTARIUS	SAGITTARIUS	PISCES	CAPRICORN	CAPRICORN	SCORPIO
4			SCORPIO	SAGITTARIUS	SAGITTARIUS	SAGITTARIUS	PISCES	CAPRICORN	CAPRICORN	SCORPIO
5	10:36 PM	TAURUS	SCORPIO	SAGITTARIUS	SAGITTARIUS	SAGITTARIUS	PISCES	CAPRICORN	CAPRICORN	SCORPIO
6			SCORPIO	SAGITTARIUS	SAGITTARIUS	SAGITTARIUS	PISCES	CAPRICORN	CAPRICORN	SCORPIO
7			SCORPIO	SAGITTARIUS	SAGITTARIUS	SAGITTARIUS	PISCES	CAPRICORN	CAPRICORN	SCORPIO
8	8:36 AM	GEMINI	SCORPIO	SAGITTARIUS	SAGITTARIUS	SAGITTARIUS	PISCES	CAPRICORN	CAPRICORN	SCORPIO
9			SCORPIO	SAGITTARIUS	SAGITTARIUS	SAGITTARIUS	PISCES	CAPRICORN	CAPRICORN	SCORPIO
10	8:58 PM	CANCER	SCORPIO	SAGITTARIUS	SAGITTARIUS	SAGITTARIUS	PISCES	CAPRICORN	CAPRICORN	SCORPIO
11			SCORPIO	SAGITTARIUS	SAGITTARIUS	SAGITTARIUS	PISCES	CAPRICORN	CAPRICORN	SAGITTARIUS
12			SCORPIO	SAGITTARIUS	SAGITTARIUS	SAGITTARIUS	PISCES	CAPRICORN	CAPRICORN	SAGITTARIUS
13	9:38 AM	LEO	SCORPIO	SAGITTARIUS	SAGITTARIUS	SAGITTARIUS	PISCES	CAPRICORN	CAPRICORN	SAGITTARIUS
14			SCORPIO	SAGITTARIUS	SAGITTARIUS	SAGITTARIUS	PISCES	CAPRICORN	CAPRICORN	SAGITTARIUS
15	9:03 AM	VIRGO	SCORPIO	SAGITTARIUS	SAGITTARIUS	SAGITTARIUS	PISCES	CAPRICORN	CAPRICORN	SAGITTARIUS
16			SCORPIO	SAGITTARIUS	SAGITTARIUS	SAGITTARIUS	PISCES	CAPRICORN	CAPRICORN	SAGITTARIUS
17			SCORPIO	SAGITTARIUS	SAGITTARIUS	SAGITTARIUS	PISCES	CAPRICORN	CAPRICORN	SAGITTARIUS
18	5:19 AM	LIBRA	SCORPIO	SAGITTARIUS	SAGITTARIUS	SAGITTARIUS	PISCES	CAPRICORN	CAPRICORN	SAGITTARIUS
19			SCORPIO	SAGITTARIUS	SAGITTARIUS	SAGITTARIUS	PISCES	CAPRICORN	CAPRICORN	SAGITTARIUS
20	9:41 AM	SCORPIO	SCORPIO	SAGITTARIUS	SAGITTARIUS	SAGITTARIUS	PISCES	CAPRICORN	CAPRICORN	SAGITTARIUS
21			SCORPIO	SAGITTARIUS	SAGITTARIUS	SAGITTARIUS	PISCES	CAPRICORN	CAPRICORN	SAGITTARIUS
22	10:57 AM	SAGITTARIUS	SCORPIO	SAGITTARIUS	SAGITTARIUS	SAGITTARIUS	PISCES	CAPRICORN	CAPRICORN	SAGITTARIUS

SCORPIO

OCTOBER	MOON FROM IN	MERCURY	VENUS	MARS	JUPITER	SATURN	URANUS	NEPTUNE	PLUTO
23	11:51 PM ARIES	LIBRA	VIRGO	LEO	CAPRICORN	ARIES	AQUARIUS	CAPRICORN	SAGITTARIUS
24		LIBRA	VIRGO	LEO	CAPRICORN	ARIES	AQUARIUS	CAPRICORN	SAGITTARIUS
25		LIBRA	VIRGO	LEO	CAPRICORN	ARIES	AQUARIUS	CAPRICORN	SAGITTARIUS
26	3:12 AM TAURUS	LIBRA	VIRGO	LEO	CAPRICORN	ARIES	AQUARIUS	CAPRICORN	SAGITTARIUS
27		SCORPIO	VIRGO	LEO	CAPRICORN	ARIES	AQUARIUS	CAPRICORN	SAGITTARIUS
28	8:36 AM GEMINI	SCORPIO	VIRGO	LEO	CAPRICORN	ARIES	AQUARIUS	CAPRICORN	SAGITTARIUS
29		SCORPIO	LIBRA	LEO	CAPRICORN	ARIES	AQUARIUS	CAPRICORN	SAGITTARIUS
30	4:57 PM CANCER	SCORPIO	LIBRA	VIRGO	CAPRICORN	ARIES	AQUARIUS	CAPRICORN	SAGITTARIUS
31		SCORPIO	LIBRA	VIRGO	CAPRICORN	ARIES	AQUARIUS	CAPRICORN	SAGITTARIUS
NOVEMBER									
1		SCORPIO	LIBRA	VIRGO	CAPRICORN	ARIES	AQUARIUS	CAPRICORN	SAGITTARIUS
2	4:17 AM LEO	SCORPIO	LIBRA	VIRGO	CAPRICORN	ARIES	AQUARIUS	CAPRICORN	SAGITTARIUS
3		SCORPIO	LIBRA	VIRGO	CAPRICORN	ARIES	AQUARIUS	CAPRICORN	SAGITTARIUS
4	4:58 PM VIRGO	SCORPIO	LIBRA	VIRGO	CAPRICORN	ARIES	AQUARIUS	CAPRICORN	SAGITTARIUS
5		SCORPIO	LIBRA	VIRGO	CAPRICORN	ARIES	AQUARIUS	CAPRICORN	SAGITTARIUS
6		SCORPIO	LIBRA	VIRGO	CAPRICORN	ARIES	AQUARIUS	CAPRICORN	SAGITTARIUS
7	4:30 AM LIBRA	SCORPIO	LIBRA	VIRGO	CAPRICORN	ARIES	AQUARIUS	CAPRICORN	SAGITTARIUS
8		SCORPIO	LIBRA	VIRGO	CAPRICORN	ARIES	AQUARIUS	CAPRICORN	SAGITTARIUS
9	1:03 PM SCORPIO	SCORPIO	LIBRA	VIRGO	CAPRICORN	ARIES	AQUARIUS	CAPRICORN	SAGITTARIUS
10		SCORPIO	LIBRA	VIRGO	CAPRICORN	ARIES	AQUARIUS	CAPRICORN	SAGITTARIUS
11	6:27 PM SAGITTARIUS	SCORPIO	LIBRA	VIRGO	CAPRICORN	ARIES	AQUARIUS	CAPRICORN	SAGITTARIUS
12		SCORPIO	LIBRA	VIRGO	CAPRICORN	ARIES	AQUARIUS	CAPRICORN	SAGITTARIUS
13	11:45 PM CAPRICORN	SCORPIO	LIBRA	VIRGO	CAPRICORN	ARIES	AQUARIUS	CAPRICORN	SAGITTARIUS
14		SCORPIO	LIBRA	VIRGO	CAPRICORN	ARIES	AQUARIUS	CAPRICORN	SAGITTARIUS
15		SAGITTARIUS	LIBRA	VIRGO	CAPRICORN	ARIES	AQUARIUS	CAPRICORN	SAGITTARIUS
16	0:15 AM AQUARIUS	SAGITTARIUS	LIBRA	VIRGO	CAPRICORN	ARIES	AQUARIUS	CAPRICORN	SAGITTARIUS
17		SAGITTARIUS	LIBRA	VIRGO	CAPRICORN	ARIES	AQUARIUS	CAPRICORN	SAGITTARIUS
18	3:01 AM PISCES	SAGITTARIUS	LIBRA	VIRGO	CAPRICORN	ARIES	AQUARIUS	CAPRICORN	SAGITTARIUS
19		SAGITTARIUS	LIBRA	VIRGO	CAPRICORN	ARIES	AQUARIUS	CAPRICORN	SAGITTARIUS
20	6:35 AM ARIES	SAGITTARIUS	LIBRA	VIRGO	CAPRICORN	ARIES	AQUARIUS	CAPRICORN	SAGITTARIUS
21		SAGITTARIUS	LIBRA	VIRGO	CAPRICORN	ARIES	AQUARIUS	CAPRICORN	SAGITTARIUS

1997

OCTOBER	MOON FROM IN	MERCURY	VENUS	MARS	JUPITER	SATURN	URANUS	NEPTUNE	PLUTO
23	0:11 AM LEO	SCORPIO	SAGITTARIUS	SAGITTARIUS	AQUARIUS	ARIES	AQUARIUS	CAPRICORN	SAGITTARIUS
24		SCORPIO	SAGITTARIUS	SAGITTARIUS	AQUARIUS	ARIES	AQUARIUS	CAPRICORN	SAGITTARIUS
25	12:00 PM VIRGO	SCORPIO	SAGITTARIUS	SAGITTARIUS	AQUARIUS	ARIES	AQUARIUS	CAPRICORN	SAGITTARIUS
26		SCORPIO	SAGITTARIUS	SAGITTARIUS	AQUARIUS	ARIES	AQUARIUS	CAPRICORN	SAGITTARIUS
27		SCORPIO	SAGITTARIUS	SAGITTARIUS	AQUARIUS	ARIES	AQUARIUS	CAPRICORN	SAGITTARIUS
28	1:06 AM LIBRA	SCORPIO	SAGITTARIUS	SAGITTARIUS	AQUARIUS	ARIES	AQUARIUS	CAPRICORN	SAGITTARIUS
29		SCORPIO	SAGITTARIUS	SAGITTARIUS	AQUARIUS	ARIES	AQUARIUS	CAPRICORN	SAGITTARIUS
30	1:16 PM SCORPIO	SCORPIO	SAGITTARIUS	SAGITTARIUS	AQUARIUS	ARIES	AQUARIUS	CAPRICORN	SAGITTARIUS
31		SCORPIO	SAGITTARIUS	SAGITTARIUS	AQUARIUS	ARIES	AQUARIUS	CAPRICORN	SAGITTARIUS
NOVEMBER									
1	11:28 PM SAGITTARIUS	SCORPIO	SAGITTARIUS	SAGITTARIUS	AQUARIUS	ARIES	AQUARIUS	CAPRICORN	SAGITTARIUS
2		SCORPIO	SAGITTARIUS	SAGITTARIUS	AQUARIUS	ARIES	AQUARIUS	CAPRICORN	SAGITTARIUS
3		SCORPIO	SAGITTARIUS	SAGITTARIUS	AQUARIUS	ARIES	AQUARIUS	CAPRICORN	SAGITTARIUS
4	7:32 AM CAPRICORN	SCORPIO	SAGITTARIUS	SAGITTARIUS	AQUARIUS	ARIES	AQUARIUS	CAPRICORN	SAGITTARIUS
5		SCORPIO	CAPRICORN	SAGITTARIUS	AQUARIUS	ARIES	AQUARIUS	CAPRICORN	SAGITTARIUS
6	1:34 PM AQUARIUS	SCORPIO	CAPRICORN	SAGITTARIUS	AQUARIUS	ARIES	AQUARIUS	CAPRICORN	SAGITTARIUS
7		SCORPIO	CAPRICORN	SAGITTARIUS	AQUARIUS	ARIES	AQUARIUS	CAPRICORN	SAGITTARIUS
8	5:36 PM PISCES	SAGITTARIUS	CAPRICORN	SAGITTARIUS	AQUARIUS	ARIES	AQUARIUS	CAPRICORN	SAGITTARIUS
9		SAGITTARIUS	CAPRICORN	CAPRICORN	AQUARIUS	ARIES	AQUARIUS	CAPRICORN	SAGITTARIUS
10	7:45 PM ARIES	SAGITTARIUS	CAPRICORN	CAPRICORN	AQUARIUS	ARIES	AQUARIUS	CAPRICORN	SAGITTARIUS
11		SAGITTARIUS	CAPRICORN	CAPRICORN	AQUARIUS	ARIES	AQUARIUS	CAPRICORN	SAGITTARIUS
12	8:46 PM TAURUS	SAGITTARIUS	CAPRICORN	CAPRICORN	AQUARIUS	ARIES	AQUARIUS	CAPRICORN	SAGITTARIUS
13		SAGITTARIUS	CAPRICORN	CAPRICORN	AQUARIUS	ARIES	AQUARIUS	CAPRICORN	SAGITTARIUS
14	10:06 PM GEMINI	SAGITTARIUS	CAPRICORN	CAPRICORN	AQUARIUS	ARIES	AQUARIUS	CAPRICORN	SAGITTARIUS
15		SAGITTARIUS	CAPRICORN	CAPRICORN	AQUARIUS	ARIES	AQUARIUS	CAPRICORN	SAGITTARIUS
16		SAGITTARIUS	CAPRICORN	CAPRICORN	AQUARIUS	ARIES	AQUARIUS	CAPRICORN	SAGITTARIUS
17	1:33 AM CANCER	SAGITTARIUS	CAPRICORN	CAPRICORN	AQUARIUS	ARIES	AQUARIUS	CAPRICORN	SAGITTARIUS
18		SAGITTARIUS	CAPRICORN	CAPRICORN	AQUARIUS	ARIES	AQUARIUS	CAPRICORN	SAGITTARIUS
19	8:39 AM LEO	SAGITTARIUS	CAPRICORN	CAPRICORN	AQUARIUS	ARIES	AQUARIUS	CAPRICORN	SAGITTARIUS
20		SAGITTARIUS	CAPRICORN	CAPRICORN	AQUARIUS	ARIES	AQUARIUS	CAPRICORN	SAGITTARIUS
21	7:34 PM VIRGO	SAGITTARIUS	CAPRICORN	CAPRICORN	AQUARIUS	ARIES	AQUARIUS	CAPRICORN	SAGITTARIUS

1998

SCORPIO

DAY	MOON FROM — IN	MERCURY	VENUS	MARS	JUPITER	SATURN	URANUS	NEPTUNE	PLUTO
OCTOBER									
24		SCORPIO	LIBRA	VIRGO	PISCES	TAURUS	AQUARIUS	CAPRICORN	SAGITTARIUS
25	12:06 PM CAPRICORN	SCORPIO	SCORPIO	VIRGO	PISCES	TAURUS	AQUARIUS	CAPRICORN	SAGITTARIUS
26		SCORPIO	SCORPIO	VIRGO	PISCES	ARIES	AQUARIUS	CAPRICORN	SAGITTARIUS
27	9:45 PM AQUARIUS	SCORPIO	SCORPIO	VIRGO	PISCES	ARIES	AQUARIUS	CAPRICORN	SAGITTARIUS
28		SCORPIO	SCORPIO	VIRGO	PISCES	ARIES	AQUARIUS	CAPRICORN	SAGITTARIUS
29		SCORPIO	SCORPIO	VIRGO	PISCES	ARIES	AQUARIUS	CAPRICORN	SAGITTARIUS
30	3:59 AM PISCES	SCORPIO	SCORPIO	VIRGO	PISCES	ARIES	AQUARIUS	CAPRICORN	SAGITTARIUS
31		SCORPIO	SCORPIO	VIRGO	PISCES	ARIES	AQUARIUS	CAPRICORN	SAGITTARIUS
NOVEMBER									
1	6:28 AM ARIES	SCORPIO	SCORPIO	VIRGO	PISCES	ARIES	AQUARIUS	CAPRICORN	SAGITTARIUS
2		SAGITTARIUS	SCORPIO	VIRGO	PISCES	ARIES	AQUARIUS	CAPRICORN	SAGITTARIUS
3	6:13 AM TAURUS	SAGITTARIUS	SCORPIO	VIRGO	PISCES	ARIES	AQUARIUS	CAPRICORN	SAGITTARIUS
4		SAGITTARIUS	SCORPIO	VIRGO	PISCES	ARIES	AQUARIUS	CAPRICORN	SAGITTARIUS
5	5:12 AM GEMINI	SAGITTARIUS	SCORPIO	VIRGO	PISCES	ARIES	AQUARIUS	CAPRICORN	SAGITTARIUS
6		SAGITTARIUS	SCORPIO	VIRGO	PISCES	ARIES	AQUARIUS	CAPRICORN	SAGITTARIUS
7	5:40 AM CANCER	SAGITTARIUS	SCORPIO	VIRGO	PISCES	ARIES	AQUARIUS	CAPRICORN	SAGITTARIUS
8		SAGITTARIUS	SCORPIO	VIRGO	PISCES	ARIES	AQUARIUS	CAPRICORN	SAGITTARIUS
9	9:34 AM LEO	SAGITTARIUS	SCORPIO	VIRGO	PISCES	ARIES	AQUARIUS	CAPRICORN	SAGITTARIUS
10		SAGITTARIUS	SCORPIO	VIRGO	PISCES	ARIES	AQUARIUS	CAPRICORN	SAGITTARIUS
11	5:38 PM VIRGO	SAGITTARIUS	SCORPIO	VIRGO	PISCES	ARIES	AQUARIUS	CAPRICORN	SAGITTARIUS
12		SAGITTARIUS	SCORPIO	VIRGO	PISCES	ARIES	AQUARIUS	CAPRICORN	SAGITTARIUS
13		SAGITTARIUS	SCORPIO	VIRGO	PISCES	ARIES	AQUARIUS	CAPRICORN	SAGITTARIUS
14	4:59 AM LIBRA	SAGITTARIUS	SCORPIO	VIRGO	PISCES	ARIES	AQUARIUS	CAPRICORN	SAGITTARIUS
15		SAGITTARIUS	SCORPIO	VIRGO	PISCES	ARIES	AQUARIUS	CAPRICORN	SAGITTARIUS
16	5:42 PM SCORPIO	SAGITTARIUS	SCORPIO	VIRGO	PISCES	ARIES	AQUARIUS	CAPRICORN	SAGITTARIUS
17		SAGITTARIUS	SCORPIO	VIRGO	PISCES	ARIES	AQUARIUS	CAPRICORN	SAGITTARIUS
18		SAGITTARIUS	SAGITTARIUS	VIRGO	PISCES	ARIES	AQUARIUS	CAPRICORN	SAGITTARIUS
19	6:14 AM SAGITTARIUS	SAGITTARIUS	SAGITTARIUS	VIRGO	PISCES	ARIES	AQUARIUS	CAPRICORN	SAGITTARIUS
20		SAGITTARIUS	SAGITTARIUS	VIRGO	PISCES	ARIES	AQUARIUS	CAPRICORN	SAGITTARIUS
21	5:46 PM CAPRICORN	SAGITTARIUS	SAGITTARIUS	VIRGO	PISCES	ARIES	AQUARIUS	CAPRICORN	SAGITTARIUS
22		SAGITTARIUS	SAGITTARIUS	VIRGO	PISCES	ARIES	AQUARIUS	CAPRICORN	SAGITTARIUS

1999

DAY	MOON FROM — IN	MERCURY	VENUS	MARS	JUPITER	SATURN	URANUS	NEPTUNE	PLUTO
OCTOBER									
24	2:26 PM TAURUS	SCORPIO	VIRGO	CAPRICORN	ARIES	TAURUS	AQUARIUS	AQUARIUS	SAGITTARIUS
25		SCORPIO	VIRGO	CAPRICORN	ARIES	TAURUS	AQUARIUS	AQUARIUS	SAGITTARIUS
26	2:34 PM GEMINI	SCORPIO	VIRGO	CAPRICORN	ARIES	TAURUS	AQUARIUS	AQUARIUS	SAGITTARIUS
27		SCORPIO	VIRGO	CAPRICORN	ARIES	TAURUS	AQUARIUS	AQUARIUS	SAGITTARIUS
28	3:10 PM CANCER	SCORPIO	VIRGO	CAPRICORN	ARIES	TAURUS	AQUARIUS	AQUARIUS	SAGITTARIUS
29		SCORPIO	VIRGO	CAPRICORN	ARIES	TAURUS	AQUARIUS	AQUARIUS	SAGITTARIUS
30	5:48 PM LEO	SCORPIO	VIRGO	CAPRICORN	ARIES	TAURUS	AQUARIUS	AQUARIUS	SAGITTARIUS
31		SAGITTARIUS	VIRGO	CAPRICORN	ARIES	TAURUS	AQUARIUS	AQUARIUS	SAGITTARIUS
NOVEMBER									
1	11:08 PM VIRGO	SAGITTARIUS	VIRGO	CAPRICORN	ARIES	TAURUS	AQUARIUS	AQUARIUS	SAGITTARIUS
2		SAGITTARIUS	VIRGO	CAPRICORN	ARIES	TAURUS	AQUARIUS	AQUARIUS	SAGITTARIUS
3		SAGITTARIUS	VIRGO	CAPRICORN	ARIES	TAURUS	AQUARIUS	AQUARIUS	SAGITTARIUS
4	6:58 AM LIBRA	SAGITTARIUS	VIRGO	CAPRICORN	ARIES	TAURUS	AQUARIUS	AQUARIUS	SAGITTARIUS
5		SAGITTARIUS	VIRGO	CAPRICORN	ARIES	TAURUS	AQUARIUS	AQUARIUS	SAGITTARIUS
6	4:47 PM SCORPIO	SAGITTARIUS	VIRGO	CAPRICORN	ARIES	TAURUS	AQUARIUS	AQUARIUS	SAGITTARIUS
7		SAGITTARIUS	VIRGO	CAPRICORN	ARIES	TAURUS	AQUARIUS	AQUARIUS	SAGITTARIUS
8		SAGITTARIUS	VIRGO	CAPRICORN	ARIES	TAURUS	AQUARIUS	AQUARIUS	SAGITTARIUS
9	4:16 AM SAGITTARIUS	SAGITTARIUS	LIBRA	CAPRICORN	ARIES	TAURUS	AQUARIUS	AQUARIUS	SAGITTARIUS
10		SCORPIO	LIBRA	CAPRICORN	ARIES	TAURUS	AQUARIUS	AQUARIUS	SAGITTARIUS
11	5:01 PM CAPRICORN	SCORPIO	LIBRA	CAPRICORN	ARIES	TAURUS	AQUARIUS	AQUARIUS	SAGITTARIUS
12		SCORPIO	LIBRA	CAPRICORN	ARIES	TAURUS	AQUARIUS	AQUARIUS	SAGITTARIUS
13		SCORPIO	LIBRA	CAPRICORN	ARIES	TAURUS	AQUARIUS	AQUARIUS	SAGITTARIUS
14	5:47 AM AQUARIUS	SCORPIO	LIBRA	CAPRICORN	ARIES	TAURUS	AQUARIUS	AQUARIUS	SAGITTARIUS
15		SCORPIO	LIBRA	CAPRICORN	ARIES	TAURUS	AQUARIUS	AQUARIUS	SAGITTARIUS
16	4:22 PM PISCES	SCORPIO	LIBRA	CAPRICORN	ARIES	TAURUS	AQUARIUS	AQUARIUS	SAGITTARIUS
17		SCORPIO	LIBRA	CAPRICORN	ARIES	TAURUS	AQUARIUS	AQUARIUS	SAGITTARIUS
18	10:58 PM ARIES	SCORPIO	LIBRA	CAPRICORN	ARIES	TAURUS	AQUARIUS	AQUARIUS	SAGITTARIUS
19		SCORPIO	LIBRA	CAPRICORN	ARIES	TAURUS	AQUARIUS	AQUARIUS	SAGITTARIUS
20		SCORPIO	LIBRA	CAPRICORN	ARIES	TAURUS	AQUARIUS	AQUARIUS	SAGITTARIUS
21	1:27 AM TAURUS	SCORPIO	LIBRA	CAPRICORN	ARIES	TAURUS	AQUARIUS	AQUARIUS	SAGITTARIUS
22		SCORPIO	LIBRA	CAPRICORN	ARIES	TAURUS	AQUARIUS	AQUARIUS	SAGITTARIUS

SCORPIO

	MOON FROM	IN	MERCURY	VENUS	MARS	JUPITER	SATURN	URANUS	NEPTUNE	PLUTO
OCTOBER										
22	10:53 AM	VIRGO	SCORPIO	SAGITTARIUS	VIRGO	GEMINI	TAURUS	AQUARIUS	AQUARIUS	SAGITTARIUS
23			SCORPIO	SAGITTARIUS	VIRGO	GEMINI	TAURUS	AQUARIUS	AQUARIUS	SAGITTARIUS
24	2:31 PM	LIBRA	SCORPIO	SAGITTARIUS	VIRGO	GEMINI	TAURUS	AQUARIUS	AQUARIUS	SAGITTARIUS
25			SCORPIO	SAGITTARIUS	VIRGO	GEMINI	TAURUS	AQUARIUS	AQUARIUS	SAGITTARIUS
26	7:24 PM	SCORPIO	SCORPIO	SAGITTARIUS	VIRGO	GEMINI	TAURUS	AQUARIUS	AQUARIUS	SAGITTARIUS
27			SCORPIO	SAGITTARIUS	VIRGO	GEMINI	TAURUS	AQUARIUS	AQUARIUS	SAGITTARIUS
28			SCORPIO	SAGITTARIUS	VIRGO	GEMINI	TAURUS	AQUARIUS	AQUARIUS	SAGITTARIUS
29	2:41 AM	SAGITTARIUS	SCORPIO	SAGITTARIUS	VIRGO	GEMINI	TAURUS	AQUARIUS	AQUARIUS	SAGITTARIUS
30			SCORPIO	SAGITTARIUS	VIRGO	GEMINI	TAURUS	AQUARIUS	AQUARIUS	SAGITTARIUS
31	1:03 PM	CAPRICORN	SCORPIO	SAGITTARIUS	VIRGO	GEMINI	TAURUS	AQUARIUS	AQUARIUS	SAGITTARIUS
NOVEMBER										
1			SCORPIO	SAGITTARIUS	VIRGO	GEMINI	TAURUS	AQUARIUS	AQUARIUS	SAGITTARIUS
2			SCORPIO	SAGITTARIUS	VIRGO	GEMINI	TAURUS	AQUARIUS	AQUARIUS	SAGITTARIUS
3	1:42 AM	AQUARIUS	SCORPIO	SAGITTARIUS	VIRGO	GEMINI	TAURUS	AQUARIUS	AQUARIUS	SAGITTARIUS
4			SCORPIO	SAGITTARIUS	LIBRA	GEMINI	TAURUS	AQUARIUS	AQUARIUS	SAGITTARIUS
5	2:14 PM	PISCES	SCORPIO	SAGITTARIUS	LIBRA	GEMINI	TAURUS	AQUARIUS	AQUARIUS	SAGITTARIUS
6			SCORPIO	SAGITTARIUS	LIBRA	GEMINI	TAURUS	AQUARIUS	AQUARIUS	SAGITTARIUS
7			LIBRA	SAGITTARIUS	LIBRA	GEMINI	TAURUS	AQUARIUS	AQUARIUS	SAGITTARIUS
8	0:03 AM	ARIES	LIBRA	SAGITTARIUS	LIBRA	GEMINI	TAURUS	AQUARIUS	AQUARIUS	SAGITTARIUS
9			SCORPIO	SAGITTARIUS	LIBRA	GEMINI	TAURUS	AQUARIUS	AQUARIUS	SAGITTARIUS
10	6:13 AM	TAURUS	SCORPIO	SAGITTARIUS	LIBRA	GEMINI	TAURUS	AQUARIUS	AQUARIUS	SAGITTARIUS
11			SCORPIO	SAGITTARIUS	LIBRA	GEMINI	TAURUS	AQUARIUS	AQUARIUS	SAGITTARIUS
12	9:28 AM	GEMINI	SCORPIO	SAGITTARIUS	LIBRA	GEMINI	TAURUS	AQUARIUS	AQUARIUS	SAGITTARIUS
13			SCORPIO	CAPRICORN	LIBRA	GEMINI	TAURUS	AQUARIUS	AQUARIUS	SAGITTARIUS
14	11:22 AM	CANCER	SCORPIO	CAPRICORN	LIBRA	GEMINI	TAURUS	AQUARIUS	AQUARIUS	SAGITTARIUS
15			SCORPIO	CAPRICORN	LIBRA	GEMINI	TAURUS	AQUARIUS	AQUARIUS	SAGITTARIUS
16	1:20 PM	LEO	SCORPIO	CAPRICORN	LIBRA	GEMINI	TAURUS	AQUARIUS	AQUARIUS	SAGITTARIUS
17			SCORPIO	CAPRICORN	LIBRA	GEMINI	TAURUS	AQUARIUS	AQUARIUS	SAGITTARIUS
18	4:16 PM	VIRGO	SCORPIO	CAPRICORN	LIBRA	GEMINI	TAURUS	AQUARIUS	AQUARIUS	SAGITTARIUS
19			SCORPIO	CAPRICORN	LIBRA	GEMINI	TAURUS	AQUARIUS	AQUARIUS	SAGITTARIUS
20	8:36 PM	LIBRA	SCORPIO	CAPRICORN	LIBRA	GEMINI	TAURUS	AQUARIUS	AQUARIUS	SAGITTARIUS
21			SCORPIO	CAPRICORN	LIBRA	GEMINI	TAURUS	AQUARIUS	AQUARIUS	SAGITTARIUS

2001

	MOON FROM	IN	MERCURY	VENUS	MARS	JUPITER	SATURN	URANUS	NEPTUNE	PLUTO
OCTOBER										
23	8:27 PM	AQUARIUS	LIBRA	LIBRA	CAPRICORN	CANCER	GEMINI	AQUARIUS	AQUARIUS	SAGITTARIUS
24			LIBRA	LIBRA	CAPRICORN	CANCER	GEMINI	AQUARIUS	AQUARIUS	SAGITTARIUS
25			LIBRA	LIBRA	CAPRICORN	CANCER	GEMINI	AQUARIUS	AQUARIUS	SAGITTARIUS
26	8:57 AM	PISCES	LIBRA	LIBRA	CAPRICORN	CANCER	GEMINI	AQUARIUS	AQUARIUS	SAGITTARIUS
27			LIBRA	LIBRA	CAPRICORN	CANCER	GEMINI	AQUARIUS	AQUARIUS	SAGITTARIUS
28	9:16 PM	ARIES	LIBRA	LIBRA	AQUARIUS	CANCER	GEMINI	AQUARIUS	AQUARIUS	SAGITTARIUS
29			LIBRA	LIBRA	AQUARIUS	CANCER	GEMINI	AQUARIUS	AQUARIUS	SAGITTARIUS
30			LIBRA	LIBRA	AQUARIUS	CANCER	GEMINI	AQUARIUS	AQUARIUS	SAGITTARIUS
31	7:49 AM	TAURUS	LIBRA	LIBRA	AQUARIUS	CANCER	GEMINI	AQUARIUS	AQUARIUS	SAGITTARIUS
NOVEMBER										
1			LIBRA	LIBRA	AQUARIUS	CANCER	GEMINI	AQUARIUS	AQUARIUS	SAGITTARIUS
2	4:14 PM	GEMINI	LIBRA	LIBRA	AQUARIUS	CANCER	GEMINI	AQUARIUS	AQUARIUS	SAGITTARIUS
3			LIBRA	LIBRA	AQUARIUS	CANCER	GEMINI	AQUARIUS	AQUARIUS	SAGITTARIUS
4	10:45 PM	CANCER	LIBRA	LIBRA	AQUARIUS	CANCER	GEMINI	AQUARIUS	AQUARIUS	SAGITTARIUS
5			LIBRA	LIBRA	AQUARIUS	CANCER	GEMINI	AQUARIUS	AQUARIUS	SAGITTARIUS
6			LIBRA	LIBRA	AQUARIUS	CANCER	GEMINI	AQUARIUS	AQUARIUS	SAGITTARIUS
7	3:35 AM	LEO	LIBRA	LIBRA	AQUARIUS	CANCER	GEMINI	AQUARIUS	AQUARIUS	SAGITTARIUS
8			SCORPIO	LIBRA	AQUARIUS	CANCER	GEMINI	AQUARIUS	AQUARIUS	SAGITTARIUS
9	6:50 AM	VIRGO	SCORPIO	SCORPIO	AQUARIUS	CANCER	GEMINI	AQUARIUS	AQUARIUS	SAGITTARIUS
10			SCORPIO	SCORPIO	AQUARIUS	CANCER	GEMINI	AQUARIUS	AQUARIUS	SAGITTARIUS
11	8:54 AM	LIBRA	SCORPIO	SCORPIO	AQUARIUS	CANCER	GEMINI	AQUARIUS	AQUARIUS	SAGITTARIUS
12			SCORPIO	SCORPIO	AQUARIUS	CANCER	GEMINI	AQUARIUS	AQUARIUS	SAGITTARIUS
13	10:46 AM	SCORPIO	SCORPIO	SCORPIO	AQUARIUS	CANCER	GEMINI	AQUARIUS	AQUARIUS	SAGITTARIUS
14			SCORPIO	SCORPIO	AQUARIUS	CANCER	GEMINI	AQUARIUS	AQUARIUS	SAGITTARIUS
15	1:52 PM	SAGITTARIUS	SCORPIO	SCORPIO	AQUARIUS	CANCER	GEMINI	AQUARIUS	AQUARIUS	SAGITTARIUS
16			SCORPIO	SCORPIO	AQUARIUS	CANCER	GEMINI	AQUARIUS	AQUARIUS	SAGITTARIUS
17	7:41 PM	CAPRICORN	SCORPIO	SCORPIO	AQUARIUS	CANCER	GEMINI	AQUARIUS	AQUARIUS	SAGITTARIUS
18			SCORPIO	SCORPIO	AQUARIUS	CANCER	GEMINI	AQUARIUS	AQUARIUS	SAGITTARIUS
19			SCORPIO	SCORPIO	AQUARIUS	CANCER	GEMINI	AQUARIUS	AQUARIUS	SAGITTARIUS
20	4:56 AM	AQUARIUS	SCORPIO	SCORPIO	AQUARIUS	CANCER	GEMINI	AQUARIUS	AQUARIUS	SAGITTARIUS
21			SCORPIO	SCORPIO	AQUARIUS	CANCER	GEMINI	AQUARIUS	AQUARIUS	SAGITTARIUS

SCORPIO

2002

MOON FROM	IN	MERCURY	VENUS	MARS	JUPITER	SATURN	URANUS	NEPTUNE	PLUTO
OCTOBER									
23 7:18 PM	GEMINI	LIBRA	SCORPIO	LIBRA	LEO	GEMINI	AQUARIUS	AQUARIUS	SAGITTARIUS
24		LIBRA	SCORPIO	LIBRA	LEO	GEMINI	AQUARIUS	AQUARIUS	SAGITTARIUS
25		LIBRA	SCORPIO	LIBRA	LEO	GEMINI	AQUARIUS	AQUARIUS	SAGITTARIUS
26 6:11 AM	CANCER	LIBRA	SCORPIO	LIBRA	LEO	GEMINI	AQUARIUS	AQUARIUS	SAGITTARIUS
27		LIBRA	SCORPIO	LIBRA	LEO	GEMINI	AQUARIUS	AQUARIUS	SAGITTARIUS
28 5:21 PM	LEO	LIBRA	SCORPIO	LIBRA	LEO	GEMINI	AQUARIUS	AQUARIUS	SAGITTARIUS
29		LIBRA	SCORPIO	LIBRA	LEO	GEMINI	AQUARIUS	AQUARIUS	SAGITTARIUS
30 7:00 PM	VIRGO	LIBRA	SCORPIO	LIBRA	LEO	GEMINI	AQUARIUS	AQUARIUS	SAGITTARIUS
31		SCORPIO	SCORPIO	LIBRA	LEO	GEMINI	AQUARIUS	AQUARIUS	SAGITTARIUS
NOVEMBER									
1 8:29 PM	LIBRA	SCORPIO	SCORPIO	LIBRA	LEO	GEMINI	AQUARIUS	AQUARIUS	SAGITTARIUS
2		SCORPIO	SCORPIO	LIBRA	LEO	GEMINI	AQUARIUS	AQUARIUS	SAGITTARIUS
3 8:11 PM	SCORPIO	SCORPIO	SCORPIO	LIBRA	LEO	GEMINI	AQUARIUS	AQUARIUS	SAGITTARIUS
4		SCORPIO	SCORPIO	LIBRA	LEO	GEMINI	AQUARIUS	AQUARIUS	SAGITTARIUS
5 8:02 PM	SAGITTARIUS	SCORPIO	SCORPIO	LIBRA	LEO	GEMINI	AQUARIUS	AQUARIUS	SAGITTARIUS
6		SCORPIO	SCORPIO	LIBRA	LEO	GEMINI	AQUARIUS	AQUARIUS	SAGITTARIUS
7 10:00 PM	CAPRICORN	SCORPIO	SCORPIO	LIBRA	LEO	GEMINI	AQUARIUS	AQUARIUS	SAGITTARIUS
8		SCORPIO	SCORPIO	LIBRA	LEO	GEMINI	AQUARIUS	AQUARIUS	SAGITTARIUS
9		SCORPIO	SCORPIO	LIBRA	LEO	GEMINI	AQUARIUS	AQUARIUS	SAGITTARIUS
10 1:26 AM	AQUARIUS	SCORPIO	SCORPIO	LIBRA	LEO	GEMINI	AQUARIUS	AQUARIUS	SAGITTARIUS
11		SCORPIO	SCORPIO	LIBRA	LEO	GEMINI	AQUARIUS	AQUARIUS	SAGITTARIUS
12 12:43 PM	PISCES	SCORPIO	SCORPIO	LIBRA	LEO	GEMINI	AQUARIUS	AQUARIUS	SAGITTARIUS
13		SCORPIO	SCORPIO	LIBRA	LEO	GEMINI	AQUARIUS	AQUARIUS	SAGITTARIUS
14		SCORPIO	SCORPIO	LIBRA	LEO	GEMINI	AQUARIUS	AQUARIUS	SAGITTARIUS
15 0:39 AM	ARIES	SCORPIO	SCORPIO	LIBRA	LEO	GEMINI	AQUARIUS	AQUARIUS	SAGITTARIUS
16		SCORPIO	SCORPIO	LIBRA	LEO	GEMINI	AQUARIUS	AQUARIUS	SAGITTARIUS
17 1:25 PM	TAURUS	SCORPIO	SCORPIO	LIBRA	LEO	GEMINI	AQUARIUS	AQUARIUS	SAGITTARIUS
18		SCORPIO	SCORPIO	LIBRA	LEO	GEMINI	AQUARIUS	AQUARIUS	SAGITTARIUS
19		SAGITTARIUS	SCORPIO	LIBRA	LEO	GEMINI	AQUARIUS	AQUARIUS	SAGITTARIUS
20 1:26 AM	GEMINI	SAGITTARIUS	SCORPIO	LIBRA	LEO	GEMINI	AQUARIUS	AQUARIUS	SAGITTARIUS
21		SAGITTARIUS	SCORPIO	LIBRA	LEO	GEMINI	AQUARIUS	AQUARIUS	SAGITTARIUS
22 11:49 AM	CANCER	SAGITTARIUS	SCORPIO	LIBRA	LEO	GEMINI	AQUARIUS	AQUARIUS	SAGITTARIUS

2003

MOON FROM	IN	MERCURY	VENUS	MARS	JUPITER	SATURN	URANUS	NEPTUNE	PLUTO
OCTOBER									
23 4:28 AM	LIBRA	LIBRA	SCORPIO	PISCES	VIRGO	CANCER	AQUARIUS	AQUARIUS	SAGITTARIUS
24		SCORPIO	SCORPIO	PISCES	VIRGO	CANCER	AQUARIUS	AQUARIUS	SAGITTARIUS
25 5:10 AM	SCORPIO	SCORPIO	SCORPIO	PISCES	VIRGO	CANCER	AQUARIUS	AQUARIUS	SAGITTARIUS
26		SCORPIO	SCORPIO	PISCES	VIRGO	CANCER	AQUARIUS	AQUARIUS	SAGITTARIUS
27 4:56 AM	SAGITTARIUS	SCORPIO	SCORPIO	PISCES	VIRGO	CANCER	AQUARIUS	AQUARIUS	SAGITTARIUS
28		SCORPIO	SCORPIO	PISCES	VIRGO	CANCER	AQUARIUS	AQUARIUS	SAGITTARIUS
29 5:38 AM	CAPRICORN	SCORPIO	SCORPIO	PISCES	VIRGO	CANCER	AQUARIUS	AQUARIUS	SAGITTARIUS
30		SCORPIO	SCORPIO	PISCES	VIRGO	CANCER	AQUARIUS	AQUARIUS	SAGITTARIUS
31 8:42 AM	AQUARIUS	SCORPIO	SCORPIO	PISCES	VIRGO	CANCER	AQUARIUS	AQUARIUS	SAGITTARIUS
NOVEMBER									
1		SCORPIO	SCORPIO	PISCES	VIRGO	CANCER	AQUARIUS	AQUARIUS	SAGITTARIUS
2 2:53 PM	PISCES	SCORPIO	SCORPIO	PISCES	VIRGO	CANCER	AQUARIUS	AQUARIUS	SAGITTARIUS
3		SCORPIO	SAGITTARIUS	PISCES	VIRGO	CANCER	AQUARIUS	AQUARIUS	SAGITTARIUS
4		SCORPIO	SAGITTARIUS	PISCES	VIRGO	CANCER	AQUARIUS	AQUARIUS	SAGITTARIUS
5 0:04 AM	ARIES	SCORPIO	SAGITTARIUS	PISCES	VIRGO	CANCER	AQUARIUS	AQUARIUS	SAGITTARIUS
6		SCORPIO	SAGITTARIUS	PISCES	VIRGO	CANCER	AQUARIUS	AQUARIUS	SAGITTARIUS
7 11:30 AM	TAURUS	SCORPIO	SAGITTARIUS	PISCES	VIRGO	CANCER	AQUARIUS	AQUARIUS	SAGITTARIUS
8		SCORPIO	SAGITTARIUS	PISCES	VIRGO	CANCER	AQUARIUS	AQUARIUS	SAGITTARIUS
9		SCORPIO	SAGITTARIUS	PISCES	VIRGO	CANCER	AQUARIUS	AQUARIUS	SAGITTARIUS
10 0:15 AM	GEMINI	SCORPIO	SAGITTARIUS	PISCES	VIRGO	CANCER	AQUARIUS	AQUARIUS	SAGITTARIUS
11		SCORPIO	SAGITTARIUS	PISCES	VIRGO	CANCER	AQUARIUS	AQUARIUS	SAGITTARIUS
12 1:11 PM	CANCER	SAGITTARIUS	SAGITTARIUS	PISCES	VIRGO	CANCER	AQUARIUS	AQUARIUS	SAGITTARIUS
13		SAGITTARIUS	SAGITTARIUS	PISCES	VIRGO	CANCER	AQUARIUS	AQUARIUS	SAGITTARIUS
14		SAGITTARIUS	SAGITTARIUS	PISCES	VIRGO	CANCER	AQUARIUS	AQUARIUS	SAGITTARIUS
15 0:49 AM	LEO	SAGITTARIUS	SAGITTARIUS	PISCES	VIRGO	CANCER	AQUARIUS	AQUARIUS	SAGITTARIUS
16		SAGITTARIUS	SAGITTARIUS	PISCES	VIRGO	CANCER	AQUARIUS	AQUARIUS	SAGITTARIUS
17 9:37 AM	VIRGO	SAGITTARIUS	SAGITTARIUS	PISCES	VIRGO	CANCER	AQUARIUS	AQUARIUS	SAGITTARIUS
18		SAGITTARIUS	SAGITTARIUS	PISCES	VIRGO	CANCER	AQUARIUS	AQUARIUS	SAGITTARIUS
19 2:43 PM	LIBRA	SAGITTARIUS	SAGITTARIUS	PISCES	VIRGO	CANCER	AQUARIUS	AQUARIUS	SAGITTARIUS
20		SAGITTARIUS	SAGITTARIUS	PISCES	VIRGO	CANCER	AQUARIUS	AQUARIUS	SAGITTARIUS
21 4:25 PM	SCORPIO	SAGITTARIUS	SAGITTARIUS	PISCES	VIRGO	CANCER	AQUARIUS	AQUARIUS	SAGITTARIUS
22		SAGITTARIUS	SAGITTARIUS	PISCES	VIRGO	CANCER	AQUARIUS	AQUARIUS	SAGITTARIUS

2004

	MOON										
	FROM	**IN**	**MERCURY**	**VENUS**	**MARS**	**JUPITER**	**SATURN**	**URANUS**	**NEPTUNE**	**PLUTO**
OCTOBER										
22			SCORPIO	VIRGO	LIBRA	LIBRA	CANCER	PISCES	AQUARIUS	SAGITTARIUS
23	0:14 AM	PISCES	SCORPIO	VIRGO	LIBRA	LIBRA	CANCER	PISCES	AQUARIUS	SAGITTARIUS
24			SCORPIO	VIRGO	LIBRA	LIBRA	CANCER	PISCES	AQUARIUS	SAGITTARIUS
25	5:25 AM	ARIES	SCORPIO	VIRGO	LIBRA	LIBRA	CANCER	PISCES	AQUARIUS	SAGITTARIUS
26			SCORPIO	VIRGO	LIBRA	LIBRA	CANCER	PISCES	AQUARIUS	SAGITTARIUS
27	12:38 PM	TAURUS	SCORPIO	VIRGO	LIBRA	LIBRA	CANCER	PISCES	AQUARIUS	SAGITTARIUS
28			SCORPIO	VIRGO	LIBRA	LIBRA	CANCER	PISCES	AQUARIUS	SAGITTARIUS
29	10:12 PM	GEMINI	SCORPIO	LIBRA	LIBRA	LIBRA	CANCER	PISCES	AQUARIUS	SAGITTARIUS
30			SCORPIO	LIBRA	LIBRA	LIBRA	CANCER	PISCES	AQUARIUS	SAGITTARIUS
31			SCORPIO	LIBRA	LIBRA	LIBRA	CANCER	PISCES	AQUARIUS	SAGITTARIUS
NOVEMBER										
1	9:54 AM	CANCER	SCORPIO	LIBRA	LIBRA	LIBRA	CANCER	PISCES	AQUARIUS	SAGITTARIUS
2			SCORPIO	LIBRA	LIBRA	LIBRA	CANCER	PISCES	AQUARIUS	SAGITTARIUS
3	10:33 PM	LEO	SCORPIO	LIBRA	LIBRA	LIBRA	CANCER	PISCES	AQUARIUS	SAGITTARIUS
4			SAGITTARIUS	LIBRA	LIBRA	LIBRA	CANCER	PISCES	AQUARIUS	SAGITTARIUS
5			SAGITTARIUS	LIBRA	LIBRA	LIBRA	CANCER	PISCES	AQUARIUS	SAGITTARIUS
6	10:01 AM	VIRGO	SAGITTARIUS	LIBRA	LIBRA	LIBRA	CANCER	PISCES	AQUARIUS	SAGITTARIUS
7			SAGITTARIUS	LIBRA	LIBRA	LIBRA	CANCER	PISCES	AQUARIUS	SAGITTARIUS
8	6:24 PM	LIBRA	SAGITTARIUS	LIBRA	LIBRA	LIBRA	CANCER	PISCES	AQUARIUS	SAGITTARIUS
9			SAGITTARIUS	LIBRA	LIBRA	LIBRA	CANCER	PISCES	AQUARIUS	SAGITTARIUS
10	11:06 PM	SCORPIO	SAGITTARIUS	LIBRA	LIBRA	LIBRA	CANCER	PISCES	AQUARIUS	SAGITTARIUS
11			SAGITTARIUS	LIBRA	SCORPIO	LIBRA	CANCER	PISCES	AQUARIUS	SAGITTARIUS
12			SAGITTARIUS	LIBRA	SCORPIO	LIBRA	CANCER	PISCES	AQUARIUS	SAGITTARIUS
13	0:57 AM	SAGITTARIUS	SAGITTARIUS	LIBRA	SCORPIO	LIBRA	CANCER	PISCES	AQUARIUS	SAGITTARIUS
14			SAGITTARIUS	LIBRA	SCORPIO	LIBRA	CANCER	PISCES	AQUARIUS	SAGITTARIUS
15	1:34 AM	CAPRICORN	SAGITTARIUS	LIBRA	SCORPIO	LIBRA	CANCER	PISCES	AQUARIUS	SAGITTARIUS
16			SAGITTARIUS	LIBRA	SCORPIO	LIBRA	CANCER	PISCES	AQUARIUS	SAGITTARIUS
17	2:40 AM	AQUARIUS	SAGITTARIUS	LIBRA	SCORPIO	LIBRA	CANCER	PISCES	AQUARIUS	SAGITTARIUS
18			SAGITTARIUS	LIBRA	SCORPIO	LIBRA	CANCER	PISCES	AQUARIUS	SAGITTARIUS
19	5:39 AM	PISCES	SAGITTARIUS	LIBRA	SCORPIO	LIBRA	CANCER	PISCES	AQUARIUS	SAGITTARIUS
20			SAGITTARIUS	LIBRA	SCORPIO	LIBRA	CANCER	PISCES	AQUARIUS	SAGITTARIUS
21	11:12 AM	ARIES	SAGITTARIUS	LIBRA	SCORPIO	LIBRA	CANCER	PISCES	AQUARIUS	SAGITTARIUS

2005

	MOON										
	FROM	**IN**	**MERCURY**	**VENUS**	**MARS**	**JUPITER**	**SATURN**	**URANUS**	**NEPTUNE**	**PLUTO**
OCTOBER										
23			SCORPIO	SAGITTARIUS	TAURUS	LIBRA	LEO	PISCES	AQUARIUS	SAGITTARIUS
24	4:50 PM	LEO	SCORPIO	SAGITTARIUS	TAURUS	LIBRA	LEO	PISCES	AQUARIUS	SAGITTARIUS
25			SCORPIO	SAGITTARIUS	TAURUS	LIBRA	LEO	PISCES	AQUARIUS	SAGITTARIUS
26			SCORPIO	SAGITTARIUS	TAURUS	SCORPIO	LEO	PISCES	AQUARIUS	SAGITTARIUS
27	5:29 AM	VIRGO	SCORPIO	SAGITTARIUS	TAURUS	SCORPIO	LEO	PISCES	AQUARIUS	SAGITTARIUS
28			SCORPIO	SAGITTARIUS	TAURUS	SCORPIO	LEO	PISCES	AQUARIUS	SAGITTARIUS
29	5:16 PM	LIBRA	SCORPIO	SAGITTARIUS	TAURUS	SCORPIO	LEO	PISCES	AQUARIUS	SAGITTARIUS
30			SAGITTARIUS	SAGITTARIUS	TAURUS	SCORPIO	LEO	PISCES	AQUARIUS	SAGITTARIUS
31			SAGITTARIUS	SAGITTARIUS	TAURUS	SCORPIO	LEO	PISCES	AQUARIUS	SAGITTARIUS
NOVEMBER										
1	2:30 AM	SCORPIO	SAGITTARIUS	SAGITTARIUS	TAURUS	SCORPIO	LEO	PISCES	AQUARIUS	SAGITTARIUS
2			SAGITTARIUS	SAGITTARIUS	TAURUS	SCORPIO	LEO	PISCES	AQUARIUS	SAGITTARIUS
3	8:56 AM	SAGITTARIUS	SAGITTARIUS	SAGITTARIUS	TAURUS	SCORPIO	LEO	PISCES	AQUARIUS	SAGITTARIUS
4			SAGITTARIUS	SAGITTARIUS	TAURUS	SCORPIO	LEO	PISCES	AQUARIUS	SAGITTARIUS
5	1:18 PM	CAPRICORN	SAGITTARIUS	CAPRICORN	TAURUS	SCORPIO	LEO	PISCES	AQUARIUS	SAGITTARIUS
6			SAGITTARIUS	CAPRICORN	TAURUS	SCORPIO	LEO	PISCES	AQUARIUS	SAGITTARIUS
7	4:32 PM	AQUARIUS	SAGITTARIUS	CAPRICORN	TAURUS	SCORPIO	LEO	PISCES	AQUARIUS	SAGITTARIUS
8			SAGITTARIUS	CAPRICORN	TAURUS	SCORPIO	LEO	PISCES	AQUARIUS	SAGITTARIUS
9	7:24 PM	PISCES	SAGITTARIUS	CAPRICORN	TAURUS	SCORPIO	LEO	PISCES	AQUARIUS	SAGITTARIUS
10			SAGITTARIUS	CAPRICORN	TAURUS	SCORPIO	LEO	PISCES	AQUARIUS	SAGITTARIUS
11	10:23 PM	ARIES	SAGITTARIUS	CAPRICORN	TAURUS	SCORPIO	LEO	PISCES	AQUARIUS	SAGITTARIUS
12			SAGITTARIUS	CAPRICORN	TAURUS	SCORPIO	LEO	PISCES	AQUARIUS	SAGITTARIUS
13			SAGITTARIUS	CAPRICORN	TAURUS	SCORPIO	LEO	PISCES	AQUARIUS	SAGITTARIUS
14	2:03 AM	TAURUS	SAGITTARIUS	CAPRICORN	TAURUS	SCORPIO	LEO	PISCES	AQUARIUS	SAGITTARIUS
15			SAGITTARIUS	CAPRICORN	TAURUS	SCORPIO	LEO	PISCES	AQUARIUS	SAGITTARIUS
16	7:11 AM	GEMINI	SAGITTARIUS	CAPRICORN	TAURUS	SCORPIO	LEO	PISCES	AQUARIUS	SAGITTARIUS
17			SAGITTARIUS	CAPRICORN	TAURUS	SCORPIO	LEO	PISCES	AQUARIUS	SAGITTARIUS
18	2:43 PM	CANCER	SAGITTARIUS	CAPRICORN	TAURUS	SCORPIO	LEO	PISCES	AQUARIUS	SAGITTARIUS
19			SAGITTARIUS	CAPRICORN	TAURUS	SCORPIO	LEO	PISCES	AQUARIUS	SAGITTARIUS
20			SAGITTARIUS	CAPRICORN	TAURUS	SCORPIO	LEO	PISCES	AQUARIUS	SAGITTARIUS
21	1:11 AM	LEO	SAGITTARIUS	CAPRICORN	TAURUS	SCORPIO	LEO	PISCES	AQUARIUS	SAGITTARIUS
22			SAGITTARIUS	CAPRICORN	TAURUS	SCORPIO	LEO	PISCES	AQUARIUS	SAGITTARIUS

SCORPIO

2006

	MOON FROM	IN	MERCURY	VENUS	MARS	JUPITER	SATURN	URANUS	NEPTUNE	PLUTO
OCTOBER										
23			SCORPIO	LIBRA	SCORPIO	SCORPIO	LEO	PISCES	AQUARIUS	SAGITTARIUS
24	1:54 PM	SAGITTARIUS	SCORPIO	SCORPIO	SCORPIO	SCORPIO	LEO	PISCES	AQUARIUS	SAGITTARIUS
25			SCORPIO	SCORPIO	SCORPIO	SCORPIO	LEO	PISCES	AQUARIUS	SAGITTARIUS
26	10:48 PM	CAPRICORN	SCORPIO	SCORPIO	SCORPIO	SCORPIO	LEO	PISCES	AQUARIUS	SAGITTARIUS
27			SCORPIO	SCORPIO	SCORPIO	SCORPIO	LEO	PISCES	AQUARIUS	SAGITTARIUS
28			SCORPIO	SCORPIO	SCORPIO	SCORPIO	LEO	PISCES	AQUARIUS	SAGITTARIUS
29	5:18 AM	AQUARIUS	SCORPIO	SCORPIO	SCORPIO	SCORPIO	LEO	PISCES	AQUARIUS	SAGITTARIUS
30			SCORPIO	SCORPIO	SCORPIO	SCORPIO	LEO	PISCES	AQUARIUS	SAGITTARIUS
31	9:12 AM	PISCES	SCORPIO	SCORPIO	SCORPIO	SCORPIO	LEO	PISCES	AQUARIUS	SAGITTARIUS
NOVEMBER										
1			SCORPIO	SCORPIO	SCORPIO	SCORPIO	LEO	PISCES	AQUARIUS	SAGITTARIUS
2	10:47 AM	ARIES	SCORPIO	SCORPIO	SCORPIO	SCORPIO	LEO	PISCES	AQUARIUS	SAGITTARIUS
3			SCORPIO	SCORPIO	SCORPIO	SCORPIO	LEO	PISCES	AQUARIUS	SAGITTARIUS
4	11:06 AM	TAURUS	SCORPIO	SCORPIO	SCORPIO	SCORPIO	LEO	PISCES	AQUARIUS	SAGITTARIUS
5			SCORPIO	SCORPIO	SCORPIO	SCORPIO	LEO	PISCES	AQUARIUS	SAGITTARIUS
6	11:47 AM	GEMINI	SCORPIO	SCORPIO	SCORPIO	SCORPIO	LEO	PISCES	AQUARIUS	SAGITTARIUS
7			SCORPIO	SCORPIO	SCORPIO	SCORPIO	LEO	PISCES	AQUARIUS	SAGITTARIUS
8	2:47 PM	CANCER	SCORPIO	SCORPIO	SCORPIO	SCORPIO	LEO	PISCES	AQUARIUS	SAGITTARIUS
9			SCORPIO	SCORPIO	SCORPIO	SCORPIO	LEO	PISCES	AQUARIUS	SAGITTARIUS
10	9:35 PM	LEO	SCORPIO	SCORPIO	SCORPIO	SCORPIO	LEO	PISCES	AQUARIUS	SAGITTARIUS
11			SCORPIO	SCORPIO	SCORPIO	SCORPIO	LEO	PISCES	AQUARIUS	SAGITTARIUS
12			SCORPIO	SCORPIO	SCORPIO	SCORPIO	LEO	PISCES	AQUARIUS	SAGITTARIUS
13	8:20 AM	VIRGO	SCORPIO	SCORPIO	SCORPIO	SCORPIO	LEO	PISCES	AQUARIUS	SAGITTARIUS
14			SCORPIO	SCORPIO	SCORPIO	SCORPIO	LEO	PISCES	AQUARIUS	SAGITTARIUS
15	9:15 PM	LIBRA	SCORPIO	SCORPIO	SCORPIO	SCORPIO	LEO	PISCES	AQUARIUS	SAGITTARIUS
16			SCORPIO	SCORPIO	SCORPIO	SCORPIO	LEO	PISCES	AQUARIUS	SAGITTARIUS
17			SCORPIO	SAGITTARIUS	SCORPIO	SCORPIO	LEO	PISCES	AQUARIUS	SAGITTARIUS
18	9:48 AM	SCORPIO	SCORPIO	SAGITTARIUS	SCORPIO	SCORPIO	LEO	PISCES	AQUARIUS	SAGITTARIUS
19			SCORPIO	SAGITTARIUS	SCORPIO	SCORPIO	LEO	PISCES	AQUARIUS	SAGITTARIUS
20	8:16 PM	SAGITTARIUS	SCORPIO	SAGITTARIUS	SCORPIO	SCORPIO	LEO	PISCES	AQUARIUS	SAGITTARIUS
21			SCORPIO	SAGITTARIUS	SCORPIO	SCORPIO	LEO	PISCES	AQUARIUS	SAGITTARIUS
22			SCORPIO	SAGITTARIUS	SCORPIO	SCORPIO	LEO	PISCES	AQUARIUS	SAGITTARIUS

2007

	MOON FROM	IN	MERCURY	VENUS	MARS	JUPITER	SATURN	URANUS	NEPTUNE	PLUTO
OCTOBER										
23	8:25 PM	ARIES	SCORPIO	VIRGO	CANCER	SAGITTARIUS	VIRGO	PISCES	AQUARIUS	SAGITTARIUS
24			LIBRA	VIRGO	CANCER	SAGITTARIUS	VIRGO	PISCES	AQUARIUS	SAGITTARIUS
25	8:06 PM	TAURUS	LIBRA	VIRGO	CANCER	SAGITTARIUS	VIRGO	PISCES	AQUARIUS	SAGITTARIUS
26			LIBRA	VIRGO	CANCER	SAGITTARIUS	VIRGO	PISCES	AQUARIUS	SAGITTARIUS
27	7:12 PM	GEMINI	LIBRA	VIRGO	CANCER	SAGITTARIUS	VIRGO	PISCES	AQUARIUS	SAGITTARIUS
28			LIBRA	VIRGO	CANCER	SAGITTARIUS	VIRGO	PISCES	AQUARIUS	SAGITTARIUS
29	7:51 PM	CANCER	LIBRA	VIRGO	CANCER	SAGITTARIUS	VIRGO	PISCES	AQUARIUS	SAGITTARIUS
30			LIBRA	VIRGO	CANCER	SAGITTARIUS	VIRGO	PISCES	AQUARIUS	SAGITTARIUS
31	11:49 PM	LEO	LIBRA	VIRGO	CANCER	SAGITTARIUS	VIRGO	PISCES	AQUARIUS	SAGITTARIUS
NOVEMBER										
1			LIBRA	VIRGO	CANCER	SAGITTARIUS	VIRGO	PISCES	AQUARIUS	SAGITTARIUS
2			LIBRA	VIRGO	CANCER	SAGITTARIUS	VIRGO	PISCES	AQUARIUS	SAGITTARIUS
3	7:46 AM	VIRGO	LIBRA	VIRGO	CANCER	SAGITTARIUS	VIRGO	PISCES	AQUARIUS	SAGITTARIUS
4			LIBRA	VIRGO	CANCER	SAGITTARIUS	VIRGO	PISCES	AQUARIUS	SAGITTARIUS
5	6:48 PM	LIBRA	LIBRA	VIRGO	CANCER	SAGITTARIUS	VIRGO	PISCES	AQUARIUS	SAGITTARIUS
6			LIBRA	VIRGO	CANCER	SAGITTARIUS	VIRGO	PISCES	AQUARIUS	SAGITTARIUS
7			LIBRA	VIRGO	CANCER	SAGITTARIUS	VIRGO	PISCES	AQUARIUS	SAGITTARIUS
8	7:19 AM	SCORPIO	LIBRA	VIRGO	CANCER	SAGITTARIUS	VIRGO	PISCES	AQUARIUS	SAGITTARIUS
9			LIBRA	LIBRA	CANCER	SAGITTARIUS	VIRGO	PISCES	AQUARIUS	SAGITTARIUS
10	8:00 PM	SAGITTARIUS	LIBRA	LIBRA	CANCER	SAGITTARIUS	VIRGO	PISCES	AQUARIUS	SAGITTARIUS
11			LIBRA	LIBRA	CANCER	SAGITTARIUS	VIRGO	PISCES	AQUARIUS	SAGITTARIUS
12			LIBRA	LIBRA	CANCER	SAGITTARIUS	VIRGO	PISCES	AQUARIUS	SAGITTARIUS
13	8:02 AM	CAPRICORN	LIBRA	LIBRA	CANCER	SAGITTARIUS	VIRGO	PISCES	AQUARIUS	SAGITTARIUS
14			LIBRA	LIBRA	CANCER	SAGITTARIUS	VIRGO	PISCES	AQUARIUS	SAGITTARIUS
15	6:31 PM	AQUARIUS	LIBRA	LIBRA	CANCER	SAGITTARIUS	VIRGO	PISCES	AQUARIUS	SAGITTARIUS
16			LIBRA	LIBRA	CANCER	SAGITTARIUS	VIRGO	PISCES	AQUARIUS	SAGITTARIUS
17			LIBRA	LIBRA	CANCER	SAGITTARIUS	VIRGO	PISCES	AQUARIUS	SAGITTARIUS
18	2:16 AM	PISCES	LIBRA	LIBRA	CANCER	SAGITTARIUS	VIRGO	PISCES	AQUARIUS	SAGITTARIUS
19			LIBRA	LIBRA	CANCER	SAGITTARIUS	VIRGO	PISCES	AQUARIUS	SAGITTARIUS
20	6:25 AM	ARIES	LIBRA	LIBRA	CANCER	SAGITTARIUS	VIRGO	PISCES	AQUARIUS	SAGITTARIUS
21			LIBRA	LIBRA	CANCER	SAGITTARIUS	VIRGO	PISCES	AQUARIUS	SAGITTARIUS
22	7:20 AM	TAURUS	LIBRA	LIBRA	CANCER	SAGITTARIUS	VIRGO	PISCES	AQUARIUS	SAGITTARIUS

2008

SCORPIO

	MOON FROM	IN	MERCURY	VENUS	MARS	JUPITER	SATURN	URANUS	NEPTUNE	PLUTO
OCTOBER										
22			LIBRA	SAGITTARIUS	SCORPIO	CAPRICORN	VIRGO	PISCES	AQUARIUS	SAGITTARIUS
23	2:41 PM	VIRGO	LIBRA	SAGITTARIUS	SCORPIO	CAPRICORN	VIRGO	PISCES	AQUARIUS	SAGITTARIUS
24			LIBRA	SAGITTARIUS	SCORPIO	CAPRICORN	VIRGO	PISCES	AQUARIUS	SAGITTARIUS
25	9:49 PM	LIBRA	LIBRA	SAGITTARIUS	SCORPIO	CAPRICORN	VIRGO	PISCES	AQUARIUS	SAGITTARIUS
26			LIBRA	SAGITTARIUS	SCORPIO	CAPRICORN	VIRGO	PISCES	AQUARIUS	SAGITTARIUS
27			LIBRA	SAGITTARIUS	SCORPIO	CAPRICORN	VIRGO	PISCES	AQUARIUS	SAGITTARIUS
28	6:48 AM	SCORPIO	LIBRA	SAGITTARIUS	SCORPIO	CAPRICORN	VIRGO	PISCES	AQUARIUS	SAGITTARIUS
29			LIBRA	SAGITTARIUS	SCORPIO	CAPRICORN	VIRGO	PISCES	AQUARIUS	SAGITTARIUS
30	5:42 PM	SAGITTARIUS	LIBRA	SAGITTARIUS	SCORPIO	CAPRICORN	VIRGO	PISCES	AQUARIUS	SAGITTARIUS
31			LIBRA	SAGITTARIUS	SCORPIO	CAPRICORN	VIRGO	PISCES	AQUARIUS	SAGITTARIUS
NOVEMBER										
1			LIBRA	SAGITTARIUS	SCORPIO	CAPRICORN	VIRGO	PISCES	AQUARIUS	SAGITTARIUS
2	6:14 AM	CAPRICORN	LIBRA	SAGITTARIUS	SCORPIO	CAPRICORN	VIRGO	PISCES	AQUARIUS	SAGITTARIUS
3			LIBRA	SAGITTARIUS	SCORPIO	CAPRICORN	VIRGO	PISCES	AQUARIUS	SAGITTARIUS
4	7:03 PM	AQUARIUS	SCORPIO	SAGITTARIUS	SCORPIO	CAPRICORN	VIRGO	PISCES	AQUARIUS	SAGITTARIUS
5			SCORPIO	SAGITTARIUS	SCORPIO	CAPRICORN	VIRGO	PISCES	AQUARIUS	SAGITTARIUS
6			SCORPIO	SAGITTARIUS	SCORPIO	CAPRICORN	VIRGO	PISCES	AQUARIUS	SAGITTARIUS
7	5:44 AM	PISCES	SCORPIO	SAGITTARIUS	SCORPIO	CAPRICORN	VIRGO	PISCES	AQUARIUS	SAGITTARIUS
8			SCORPIO	SAGITTARIUS	SCORPIO	CAPRICORN	VIRGO	PISCES	AQUARIUS	SAGITTARIUS
9	12:27 PM	ARIES	SCORPIO	SAGITTARIUS	SCORPIO	CAPRICORN	VIRGO	PISCES	AQUARIUS	SAGITTARIUS
10			SCORPIO	SAGITTARIUS	SCORPIO	CAPRICORN	VIRGO	PISCES	AQUARIUS	SAGITTARIUS
11	3:06 PM	TAURUS	SCORPIO	SAGITTARIUS	SCORPIO	CAPRICORN	VIRGO	PISCES	AQUARIUS	SAGITTARIUS
12			SCORPIO	CAPRICORN	SCORPIO	CAPRICORN	VIRGO	PISCES	AQUARIUS	SAGITTARIUS
13	3:12 PM	GEMINI	SCORPIO	CAPRICORN	SCORPIO	CAPRICORN	VIRGO	PISCES	AQUARIUS	SAGITTARIUS
14			SCORPIO	CAPRICORN	SCORPIO	CAPRICORN	VIRGO	PISCES	AQUARIUS	SAGITTARIUS
15	2:53 PM	CANCER	SCORPIO	CAPRICORN	SCORPIO	CAPRICORN	VIRGO	PISCES	AQUARIUS	SAGITTARIUS
16			SCORPIO	CAPRICORN	SAGITTARIUS	CAPRICORN	VIRGO	PISCES	AQUARIUS	SAGITTARIUS
17	4:09 PM	LEO	SCORPIO	CAPRICORN	SAGITTARIUS	CAPRICORN	VIRGO	PISCES	AQUARIUS	SAGITTARIUS
18			SCORPIO	CAPRICORN	SAGITTARIUS	CAPRICORN	VIRGO	PISCES	AQUARIUS	SAGITTARIUS
19	8:14 PM	VIRGO	SCORPIO	CAPRICORN	SAGITTARIUS	CAPRICORN	VIRGO	PISCES	AQUARIUS	SAGITTARIUS
20			SCORPIO	CAPRICORN	SAGITTARIUS	CAPRICORN	VIRGO	PISCES	AQUARIUS	SAGITTARIUS
21			SCORPIO	CAPRICORN	SAGITTARIUS	CAPRICORN	VIRGO	PISCES	AQUARIUS	SAGITTARIUS

2009

	MOON FROM	IN	MERCURY	VENUS	MARS	JUPITER	SATURN	URANUS	NEPTUNE	PLUTO
OCTOBER										
23	1:40 AM	CAPRICORN	LIBRA	LIBRA	LEO	AQUARIUS	VIRGO	PISCES	AQUARIUS	CAPRICORN
24			LIBRA	LIBRA	LEO	AQUARIUS	VIRGO	PISCES	AQUARIUS	CAPRICORN
25	2:09 PM	AQUARIUS	LIBRA	LIBRA	LEO	AQUARIUS	VIRGO	PISCES	AQUARIUS	CAPRICORN
26			LIBRA	LIBRA	LEO	AQUARIUS	VIRGO	PISCES	AQUARIUS	CAPRICORN
27			LIBRA	LIBRA	LEO	AQUARIUS	VIRGO	PISCES	AQUARIUS	CAPRICORN
28	2:46 AM	PISCES	SCORPIO	LIBRA	LEO	AQUARIUS	VIRGO	PISCES	AQUARIUS	CAPRICORN
29			SCORPIO	LIBRA	LEO	AQUARIUS	VIRGO	PISCES	AQUARIUS	CAPRICORN
30	12:58 PM	ARIES	SCORPIO	LIBRA	LEO	AQUARIUS	LIBRA	PISCES	AQUARIUS	CAPRICORN
31			SCORPIO	LIBRA	LEO	AQUARIUS	LIBRA	PISCES	AQUARIUS	CAPRICORN
NOVEMBER										
1	7:46 PM	TAURUS	SCORPIO	LIBRA	LEO	AQUARIUS	LIBRA	PISCES	AQUARIUS	CAPRICORN
2			SCORPIO	LIBRA	LEO	AQUARIUS	LIBRA	PISCES	AQUARIUS	CAPRICORN
3	11:54 PM	GEMINI	SCORPIO	LIBRA	LEO	AQUARIUS	LIBRA	PISCES	AQUARIUS	CAPRICORN
4			SCORPIO	LIBRA	LEO	AQUARIUS	LIBRA	PISCES	AQUARIUS	CAPRICORN
5			SCORPIO	LIBRA	LEO	AQUARIUS	LIBRA	PISCES	AQUARIUS	CAPRICORN
6	2:44 AM	CANCER	SCORPIO	LIBRA	LEO	AQUARIUS	LIBRA	PISCES	AQUARIUS	CAPRICORN
7			SCORPIO	LIBRA	LEO	AQUARIUS	LIBRA	PISCES	AQUARIUS	CAPRICORN
8	5:24 AM	LEO	SCORPIO	SCORPIO	LEO	AQUARIUS	LIBRA	PISCES	AQUARIUS	CAPRICORN
9			SCORPIO	SCORPIO	LEO	AQUARIUS	LIBRA	PISCES	AQUARIUS	CAPRICORN
10	8:31 AM	VIRGO	SCORPIO	SCORPIO	LEO	AQUARIUS	LIBRA	PISCES	AQUARIUS	CAPRICORN
11			SCORPIO	SCORPIO	LEO	AQUARIUS	LIBRA	PISCES	AQUARIUS	CAPRICORN
12	12:23 PM	LIBRA	SCORPIO	SCORPIO	LEO	AQUARIUS	LIBRA	PISCES	AQUARIUS	CAPRICORN
13			SCORPIO	SCORPIO	LEO	AQUARIUS	LIBRA	PISCES	AQUARIUS	CAPRICORN
14	5:25 PM	SCORPIO	SCORPIO	SCORPIO	LEO	AQUARIUS	LIBRA	PISCES	AQUARIUS	CAPRICORN
15			SCORPIO	SCORPIO	LEO	AQUARIUS	LIBRA	PISCES	AQUARIUS	CAPRICORN
16			SAGITTARIUS	SCORPIO	LEO	AQUARIUS	LIBRA	PISCES	AQUARIUS	CAPRICORN
17	0:23 AM	SAGITTARIUS	SAGITTARIUS	SCORPIO	LEO	AQUARIUS	LIBRA	PISCES	AQUARIUS	CAPRICORN
18			SAGITTARIUS	SCORPIO	LEO	AQUARIUS	LIBRA	PISCES	AQUARIUS	CAPRICORN
19	10:02 AM	CAPRICORN	SAGITTARIUS	SCORPIO	LEO	AQUARIUS	LIBRA	PISCES	AQUARIUS	CAPRICORN
20			SAGITTARIUS	SCORPIO	LEO	AQUARIUS	LIBRA	PISCES	AQUARIUS	CAPRICORN
21	10:12 PM	AQUARIUS	SAGITTARIUS	SCORPIO	LEO	AQUARIUS	LIBRA	PISCES	AQUARIUS	CAPRICORN
22			SAGITTARIUS	SCORPIO	LEO	AQUARIUS	LIBRA	PISCES	AQUARIUS	CAPRICORN

2010

	MOON FROM	IN	MERCURY	VENUS	MARS	JUPITER	SATURN	URANUS	NEPTUNE	PLUTO
OCTOBER										
23			SCORPIO	SCORPIO	SCORPIO	PISCES	LIBRA	ARIES	AQUARIUS	CAPRICORN
24			SCORPIO	SCORPIO	SCORPIO	PISCES	LIBRA	ARIES	AQUARIUS	CAPRICORN
25	6:49 AM	GEMINI	SCORPIO	SCORPIO	SCORPIO	PISCES	LIBRA	ARIES	AQUARIUS	CAPRICORN
26			SCORPIO	SCORPIO	SCORPIO	PISCES	LIBRA	ARIES	AQUARIUS	CAPRICORN
27	2:15 PM	CANCER	SCORPIO	SCORPIO	SCORPIO	PISCES	LIBRA	ARIES	AQUARIUS	CAPRICORN
28			SCORPIO	SCORPIO	SAGITTARIUS	PISCES	LIBRA	ARIES	AQUARIUS	CAPRICORN
29	7:40 PM	LEO	SCORPIO	SCORPIO	SAGITTARIUS	PISCES	LIBRA	ARIES	AQUARIUS	CAPRICORN
30			SCORPIO	SCORPIO	SAGITTARIUS	PISCES	LIBRA	ARIES	AQUARIUS	CAPRICORN
31	10:52 PM	VIRGO	SCORPIO	SCORPIO	SAGITTARIUS	PISCES	LIBRA	ARIES	AQUARIUS	CAPRICORN
NOVEMBER										
1			SCORPIO	SCORPIO	SAGITTARIUS	PISCES	LIBRA	ARIES	AQUARIUS	CAPRICORN
2			SCORPIO	SCORPIO	SAGITTARIUS	PISCES	LIBRA	ARIES	AQUARIUS	CAPRICORN
3	0:20 AM	LIBRA	SCORPIO	SCORPIO	SAGITTARIUS	PISCES	LIBRA	ARIES	AQUARIUS	CAPRICORN
4			SCORPIO	SCORPIO	SAGITTARIUS	PISCES	LIBRA	ARIES	AQUARIUS	CAPRICORN
5	1:17 AM	SCORPIO	SCORPIO	SCORPIO	SAGITTARIUS	PISCES	LIBRA	ARIES	AQUARIUS	CAPRICORN
6			SCORPIO	SCORPIO	SAGITTARIUS	PISCES	LIBRA	ARIES	AQUARIUS	CAPRICORN
7	3:29 AM	SAGITTARIUS	SCORPIO	SCORPIO	SAGITTARIUS	PISCES	LIBRA	ARIES	AQUARIUS	CAPRICORN
8			SCORPIO	LIBRA	SAGITTARIUS	PISCES	LIBRA	ARIES	AQUARIUS	CAPRICORN
9	8:38 AM	CAPRICORN	SAGITTARIUS	LIBRA	SAGITTARIUS	PISCES	LIBRA	ARIES	AQUARIUS	CAPRICORN
10			SAGITTARIUS	LIBRA	SAGITTARIUS	PISCES	LIBRA	ARIES	AQUARIUS	CAPRICORN
11	5:33 PM	AQUARIUS	SAGITTARIUS	LIBRA	SAGITTARIUS	PISCES	LIBRA	ARIES	AQUARIUS	CAPRICORN
12			SAGITTARIUS	LIBRA	SAGITTARIUS	PISCES	LIBRA	ARIES	AQUARIUS	CAPRICORN
13			SAGITTARIUS	LIBRA	SAGITTARIUS	PISCES	LIBRA	ARIES	AQUARIUS	CAPRICORN
14	5:25 AM	PISCES	SAGITTARIUS	LIBRA	SAGITTARIUS	PISCES	LIBRA	ARIES	AQUARIUS	CAPRICORN
15			SAGITTARIUS	LIBRA	SAGITTARIUS	PISCES	LIBRA	ARIES	AQUARIUS	CAPRICORN
16	6:00 PM	ARIES	SAGITTARIUS	LIBRA	SAGITTARIUS	PISCES	LIBRA	ARIES	AQUARIUS	CAPRICORN
17			SAGITTARIUS	LIBRA	SAGITTARIUS	PISCES	LIBRA	ARIES	AQUARIUS	CAPRICORN
18			SAGITTARIUS	LIBRA	SAGITTARIUS	PISCES	LIBRA	ARIES	AQUARIUS	CAPRICORN
19	5:05 AM	TAURUS	SAGITTARIUS	LIBRA	SAGITTARIUS	PISCES	LIBRA	ARIES	AQUARIUS	CAPRICORN
20			SAGITTARIUS	LIBRA	SAGITTARIUS	PISCES	LIBRA	ARIES	AQUARIUS	CAPRICORN
21	1:47 PM	GEMINI	SAGITTARIUS	LIBRA	SAGITTARIUS	PISCES	LIBRA	ARIES	AQUARIUS	CAPRICORN
22			SAGITTARIUS	LIBRA	SAGITTARIUS	PISCES	LIBRA	ARIES	AQUARIUS	CAPRICORN

2011

	MOON FROM	IN	MERCURY	VENUS	MARS	JUPITER	SATURN	URANUS	NEPTUNE	PLUTO
OCTOBER										
23			SCORPIO	SCORPIO	LEO	TAURUS	LIBRA	ARIES	AQUARIUS	CAPRICORN
24	10:50 AM	LIBRA	SCORPIO	SCORPIO	LEO	TAURUS	LIBRA	ARIES	AQUARIUS	CAPRICORN
25			SCORPIO	SCORPIO	LEO	TAURUS	LIBRA	ARIES	AQUARIUS	CAPRICORN
26	10:09 AM	SCORPIO	SCORPIO	SCORPIO	LEO	TAURUS	LIBRA	ARIES	AQUARIUS	CAPRICORN
27			SCORPIO	SCORPIO	LEO	TAURUS	LIBRA	ARIES	AQUARIUS	CAPRICORN
28	9:46 AM	SAGITTARIUS	SCORPIO	SCORPIO	LEO	TAURUS	LIBRA	ARIES	AQUARIUS	CAPRICORN
29			SCORPIO	SCORPIO	LEO	TAURUS	LIBRA	ARIES	AQUARIUS	CAPRICORN
30	11:40 AM	CAPRICORN	SCORPIO	SCORPIO	LEO	TAURUS	LIBRA	ARIES	AQUARIUS	CAPRICORN
31			SCORPIO	SCORPIO	LEO	TAURUS	LIBRA	ARIES	AQUARIUS	CAPRICORN
NOVEMBER										
1	5:09 PM	AQUARIUS	SCORPIO	SCORPIO	LEO	TAURUS	LIBRA	ARIES	AQUARIUS	CAPRICORN
2			SAGITTARIUS	SAGITTARIUS	LEO	TAURUS	LIBRA	ARIES	AQUARIUS	CAPRICORN
3			SAGITTARIUS	SAGITTARIUS	LEO	TAURUS	LIBRA	ARIES	AQUARIUS	CAPRICORN
4	2:19 AM	PISCES	SAGITTARIUS	SAGITTARIUS	LEO	TAURUS	LIBRA	ARIES	AQUARIUS	CAPRICORN
5			SAGITTARIUS	SAGITTARIUS	LEO	TAURUS	LIBRA	ARIES	AQUARIUS	CAPRICORN
6	2:03 PM	ARIES	SAGITTARIUS	SAGITTARIUS	LEO	TAURUS	LIBRA	ARIES	AQUARIUS	CAPRICORN
7			SAGITTARIUS	SAGITTARIUS	LEO	TAURUS	LIBRA	ARIES	AQUARIUS	CAPRICORN
8			SAGITTARIUS	SAGITTARIUS	LEO	TAURUS	LIBRA	ARIES	AQUARIUS	CAPRICORN
9	2:46 AM	TAURUS	SAGITTARIUS	SAGITTARIUS	LEO	TAURUS	LIBRA	ARIES	AQUARIUS	CAPRICORN
10			SAGITTARIUS	SAGITTARIUS	LEO	TAURUS	LIBRA	ARIES	AQUARIUS	CAPRICORN
11	3:11 PM	GEMINI	SAGITTARIUS	SAGITTARIUS	VIRGO	TAURUS	LIBRA	ARIES	AQUARIUS	CAPRICORN
12			SAGITTARIUS	SAGITTARIUS	VIRGO	TAURUS	LIBRA	ARIES	AQUARIUS	CAPRICORN
13			SAGITTARIUS	SAGITTARIUS	VIRGO	TAURUS	LIBRA	ARIES	AQUARIUS	CAPRICORN
14	2:20 AM	CANCER	SAGITTARIUS	SAGITTARIUS	VIRGO	TAURUS	LIBRA	ARIES	AQUARIUS	CAPRICORN
15			SAGITTARIUS	SAGITTARIUS	VIRGO	TAURUS	LIBRA	ARIES	AQUARIUS	CAPRICORN
16	11:18 AM	LEO	SAGITTARIUS	SAGITTARIUS	VIRGO	TAURUS	LIBRA	ARIES	AQUARIUS	CAPRICORN
17			SAGITTARIUS	SAGITTARIUS	VIRGO	TAURUS	LIBRA	ARIES	AQUARIUS	CAPRICORN
18	5:20 PM	VIRGO	SAGITTARIUS	SAGITTARIUS	VIRGO	TAURUS	LIBRA	ARIES	AQUARIUS	CAPRICORN
19			SAGITTARIUS	SAGITTARIUS	VIRGO	TAURUS	LIBRA	ARIES	AQUARIUS	CAPRICORN
20	8:17 PM	LIBRA	SAGITTARIUS	SAGITTARIUS	VIRGO	TAURUS	LIBRA	ARIES	AQUARIUS	CAPRICORN
21			SAGITTARIUS	SAGITTARIUS	VIRGO	TAURUS	LIBRA	ARIES	AQUARIUS	CAPRICORN
22	8:59 PM	SCORPIO	SAGITTARIUS	SAGITTARIUS	VIRGO	TAURUS	LIBRA	ARIES	AQUARIUS	CAPRICORN

2012

SCORPIO

	MOON FROM	IN	MERCURY	VENUS	MARS	JUPITER	SATURN	URANUS	NEPTUNE	PLUTO
OCTOBER										
23			SCORPIO	VIRGO	SAGITTARIUS	GEMINI	SCORPIO	ARIES	PISCES	CAPRICORN
24	6:01 AM	PISCES	SCORPIO	VIRGO	SAGITTARIUS	GEMINI	SCORPIO	ARIES	PISCES	CAPRICORN
25			SCORPIO	VIRGO	SAGITTARIUS	GEMINI	SCORPIO	ARIES	PISCES	CAPRICORN
26	2:32 PM	ARIES	SCORPIO	VIRGO	SAGITTARIUS	GEMINI	SCORPIO	ARIES	PISCES	CAPRICORN
27			SCORPIO	VIRGO	SAGITTARIUS	GEMINI	SCORPIO	ARIES	PISCES	CAPRICORN
28			SCORPIO	LIBRA	SAGITTARIUS	GEMINI	SCORPIO	ARIES	PISCES	CAPRICORN
29	1:16 AM	TAURUS	SAGITTARIUS	LIBRA	SAGITTARIUS	GEMINI	SCORPIO	ARIES	PISCES	CAPRICORN
30			SAGITTARIUS	LIBRA	SAGITTARIUS	GEMINI	SCORPIO	ARIES	PISCES	CAPRICORN
31	1:41 PM	GEMINI	SAGITTARIUS	LIBRA	SAGITTARIUS	GEMINI	SCORPIO	ARIES	PISCES	CAPRICORN
NOVEMBER										
1			SAGITTARIUS	LIBRA	SAGITTARIUS	GEMINI	SCORPIO	ARIES	PISCES	CAPRICORN
2			SAGITTARIUS	LIBRA	SAGITTARIUS	GEMINI	SCORPIO	ARIES	PISCES	CAPRICORN
3	2:44 AM	CANCER	SAGITTARIUS	LIBRA	SAGITTARIUS	GEMINI	SCORPIO	ARIES	PISCES	CAPRICORN
4			SAGITTARIUS	LIBRA	SAGITTARIUS	GEMINI	SCORPIO	ARIES	PISCES	CAPRICORN
5	2:40 PM	LEO	SAGITTARIUS	LIBRA	SAGITTARIUS	GEMINI	SCORPIO	ARIES	PISCES	CAPRICORN
6			SAGITTARIUS	LIBRA	SAGITTARIUS	GEMINI	SCORPIO	ARIES	PISCES	CAPRICORN
7	11:36 PM	VIRGO	SAGITTARIUS	LIBRA	SAGITTARIUS	GEMINI	SCORPIO	ARIES	PISCES	CAPRICORN
8			SAGITTARIUS	LIBRA	SAGITTARIUS	GEMINI	SCORPIO	ARIES	PISCES	CAPRICORN
9			SAGITTARIUS	LIBRA	SAGITTARIUS	GEMINI	SCORPIO	ARIES	PISCES	CAPRICORN
10	4:36 AM	LIBRA	SAGITTARIUS	LIBRA	SAGITTARIUS	GEMINI	SCORPIO	ARIES	PISCES	CAPRICORN
11			SAGITTARIUS	LIBRA	SAGITTARIUS	GEMINI	SCORPIO	ARIES	PISCES	CAPRICORN
12	6:11 AM	SCORPIO	SAGITTARIUS	LIBRA	SAGITTARIUS	GEMINI	SCORPIO	ARIES	PISCES	CAPRICORN
13			SAGITTARIUS	LIBRA	SAGITTARIUS	GEMINI	SCORPIO	ARIES	PISCES	CAPRICORN
14	5:53 AM	SAGITTARIUS	SCORPIO	LIBRA	SAGITTARIUS	GEMINI	SCORPIO	ARIES	PISCES	CAPRICORN
15			SCORPIO	LIBRA	SAGITTARIUS	GEMINI	SCORPIO	ARIES	PISCES	CAPRICORN
16	5:36 AM	CAPRICORN	SCORPIO	LIBRA	SAGITTARIUS	GEMINI	SCORPIO	ARIES	PISCES	CAPRICORN
17			SCORPIO	LIBRA	CAPRICORN	GEMINI	SCORPIO	ARIES	PISCES	CAPRICORN
18	7:11 AM	AQUARIUS	SCORPIO	LIBRA	CAPRICORN	GEMINI	SCORPIO	ARIES	PISCES	CAPRICORN
19			SCORPIO	LIBRA	CAPRICORN	GEMINI	SCORPIO	ARIES	PISCES	CAPRICORN
20	11:56 AM	PISCES	SCORPIO	LIBRA	CAPRICORN	GEMINI	SCORPIO	ARIES	PISCES	CAPRICORN
21			SCORPIO	LIBRA	CAPRICORN	GEMINI	SCORPIO	ARIES	PISCES	CAPRICORN

2013

	MOON FROM	IN	MERCURY	VENUS	MARS	JUPITER	SATURN	URANUS	NEPTUNE	PLUTO
OCTOBER										
23	10:37 PM	CANCER	SCORPIO	SAGITTARIUS	VIRGO	CANCER	SCORPIO	ARIES	PISCES	CAPRICORN
24			SCORPIO	SAGITTARIUS	VIRGO	CANCER	SCORPIO	ARIES	PISCES	CAPRICORN
25			SCORPIO	SAGITTARIUS	VIRGO	CANCER	SCORPIO	ARIES	PISCES	CAPRICORN
26	11:13 AM	LEO	SCORPIO	SAGITTARIUS	VIRGO	CANCER	SCORPIO	ARIES	PISCES	CAPRICORN
27			SCORPIO	SAGITTARIUS	VIRGO	CANCER	SCORPIO	ARIES	PISCES	CAPRICORN
28	10:46 PM	VIRGO	SCORPIO	SAGITTARIUS	VIRGO	CANCER	SCORPIO	ARIES	PISCES	CAPRICORN
29			SCORPIO	SAGITTARIUS	VIRGO	CANCER	SCORPIO	ARIES	PISCES	CAPRICORN
30			SCORPIO	SAGITTARIUS	VIRGO	CANCER	SCORPIO	ARIES	PISCES	CAPRICORN
31	7:23 AM	LIBRA	SCORPIO	SAGITTARIUS	VIRGO	CANCER	SCORPIO	ARIES	PISCES	CAPRICORN
NOVEMBER										
1			SCORPIO	SAGITTARIUS	VIRGO	CANCER	SCORPIO	ARIES	PISCES	CAPRICORN
2	12:36 PM	SCORPIO	SCORPIO	SAGITTARIUS	VIRGO	CANCER	SCORPIO	ARIES	PISCES	CAPRICORN
3			SCORPIO	SAGITTARIUS	VIRGO	CANCER	SCORPIO	ARIES	PISCES	CAPRICORN
4	3:15 PM	SAGITTARIUS	SCORPIO	SAGITTARIUS	VIRGO	CANCER	SCORPIO	ARIES	PISCES	CAPRICORN
5			SCORPIO	CAPRICORN	VIRGO	CANCER	SCORPIO	ARIES	PISCES	CAPRICORN
6	4:45 PM	CAPRICORN	SCORPIO	CAPRICORN	VIRGO	CANCER	SCORPIO	ARIES	PISCES	CAPRICORN
7			SCORPIO	CAPRICORN	VIRGO	CANCER	SCORPIO	ARIES	PISCES	CAPRICORN
8	6:31 PM	AQUARIUS	SCORPIO	CAPRICORN	VIRGO	CANCER	SCORPIO	ARIES	PISCES	CAPRICORN
9			SCORPIO	CAPRICORN	VIRGO	CANCER	SCORPIO	ARIES	PISCES	CAPRICORN
10	9:37 PM	PISCES	SCORPIO	CAPRICORN	VIRGO	CANCER	SCORPIO	ARIES	PISCES	CAPRICORN
11			SCORPIO	CAPRICORN	VIRGO	CANCER	SCORPIO	ARIES	PISCES	CAPRICORN
12			SCORPIO	CAPRICORN	VIRGO	CANCER	SCORPIO	ARIES	PISCES	CAPRICORN
13	2:40 AM	ARIES	SCORPIO	CAPRICORN	VIRGO	CANCER	SCORPIO	ARIES	PISCES	CAPRICORN
14			SCORPIO	CAPRICORN	VIRGO	CANCER	SCORPIO	ARIES	PISCES	CAPRICORN
15	9:50 AM	TAURUS	SCORPIO	CAPRICORN	VIRGO	CANCER	SCORPIO	ARIES	PISCES	CAPRICORN
16			SCORPIO	CAPRICORN	VIRGO	CANCER	SCORPIO	ARIES	PISCES	CAPRICORN
17	7:08 PM	GEMINI	SCORPIO	CAPRICORN	VIRGO	CANCER	SCORPIO	ARIES	PISCES	CAPRICORN
18			SCORPIO	CAPRICORN	VIRGO	CANCER	SCORPIO	ARIES	PISCES	CAPRICORN
19			SCORPIO	CAPRICORN	VIRGO	CANCER	SCORPIO	ARIES	PISCES	CAPRICORN
20	6:24 AM	CANCER	SCORPIO	CAPRICORN	VIRGO	CANCER	SCORPIO	ARIES	PISCES	CAPRICORN
21			SCORPIO	CAPRICORN	VIRGO	CANCER	SCORPIO	ARIES	PISCES	CAPRICORN
22	6:58 PM	LEO	SCORPIO	CAPRICORN	VIRGO	CANCER	SCORPIO	ARIES	PISCES	CAPRICORN

	MOON FROM	IN	MERCURY	VENUS	MARS	JUPITER	SATURN	URANUS	NEPTUNE	PLUTO
OCTOBER										
23	4:11 PM	SCORPIO	LIBRA	LIBRA	SAGITTARIUS	LEO	SCORPIO	ARIES	PISCES	CAPRICORN
24			LIBRA	SCORPIO	SAGITTARIUS	LEO	SCORPIO	ARIES	PISCES	CAPRICORN
25	11:41 PM	SAGITTARIUS	LIBRA	SCORPIO	SAGITTARIUS	LEO	SCORPIO	ARIES	PISCES	CAPRICORN
26			LIBRA	SCORPIO	CAPRICORN	LEO	SCORPIO	ARIES	PISCES	CAPRICORN
27			LIBRA	SCORPIO	CAPRICORN	LEO	SCORPIO	ARIES	PISCES	CAPRICORN
28	5:04 AM	CAPRICORN	LIBRA	SCORPIO	CAPRICORN	LEO	SCORPIO	ARIES	PISCES	CAPRICORN
29			LIBRA	SCORPIO	CAPRICORN	LEO	SCORPIO	ARIES	PISCES	CAPRICORN
30	8:53 AM	AQUARIUS	LIBRA	SCORPIO	CAPRICORN	LEO	SCORPIO	ARIES	PISCES	CAPRICORN
31			LIBRA	SCORPIO	CAPRICORN	LEO	SCORPIO	ARIES	PISCES	CAPRICORN
NOVEMBER										
1	11:38 AM	PISCES	LIBRA	SCORPIO	CAPRICORN	LEO	SCORPIO	ARIES	PISCES	CAPRICORN
2			LIBRA	SCORPIO	CAPRICORN	LEO	SCORPIO	ARIES	PISCES	CAPRICORN
3	1:54 PM	ARIES	LIBRA	SCORPIO	CAPRICORN	LEO	SCORPIO	ARIES	PISCES	CAPRICORN
4			LIBRA	SCORPIO	CAPRICORN	LEO	SCORPIO	ARIES	PISCES	CAPRICORN
5	4:34 PM	TAURUS	LIBRA	SCORPIO	CAPRICORN	LEO	SCORPIO	ARIES	PISCES	CAPRICORN
6			LIBRA	SCORPIO	CAPRICORN	LEO	SCORPIO	ARIES	PISCES	CAPRICORN
7	8:46 PM	GEMINI	LIBRA	SCORPIO	CAPRICORN	LEO	SCORPIO	ARIES	PISCES	CAPRICORN
8			LIBRA	SCORPIO	CAPRICORN	LEO	SCORPIO	ARIES	PISCES	CAPRICORN
9			SCORPIO	SCORPIO	CAPRICORN	LEO	SCORPIO	ARIES	PISCES	CAPRICORN
10	3:39 AM	CANCER	SCORPIO	SCORPIO	CAPRICORN	LEO	SCORPIO	ARIES	PISCES	CAPRICORN
11			SCORPIO	SCORPIO	CAPRICORN	LEO	SCORPIO	ARIES	PISCES	CAPRICORN
12	1:45 PM	LEO	SCORPIO	SCORPIO	CAPRICORN	LEO	SCORPIO	ARIES	PISCES	CAPRICORN
13			SCORPIO	SCORPIO	CAPRICORN	LEO	SCORPIO	ARIES	PISCES	CAPRICORN
14			SCORPIO	SCORPIO	CAPRICORN	LEO	SCORPIO	ARIES	PISCES	CAPRICORN
15	2:09 AM	VIRGO	SCORPIO	SCORPIO	CAPRICORN	LEO	SCORPIO	ARIES	PISCES	CAPRICORN
16			SCORPIO	SCORPIO	CAPRICORN	LEO	SCORPIO	ARIES	PISCES	CAPRICORN
17	2:31 PM	LIBRA	SCORPIO	SAGITTARIUS	CAPRICORN	LEO	SCORPIO	ARIES	PISCES	CAPRICORN
18			SCORPIO	SAGITTARIUS	CAPRICORN	LEO	SCORPIO	ARIES	PISCES	CAPRICORN
19			SCORPIO	SAGITTARIUS	CAPRICORN	LEO	SCORPIO	ARIES	PISCES	CAPRICORN
20	0:32 AM	SCORPIO	SCORPIO	SAGITTARIUS	CAPRICORN	LEO	SCORPIO	ARIES	PISCES	CAPRICORN
21			SCORPIO	SAGITTARIUS	CAPRICORN	LEO	SCORPIO	ARIES	PISCES	CAPRICORN
22	7:20 AM	SAGITTARIUS	SCORPIO	SAGITTARIUS	CAPRICORN	LEO	SCORPIO	ARIES	PISCES	CAPRICORN

2015

	MOON FROM	IN	MERCURY	VENUS	MARS	JUPITER	SATURN	URANUS	NEPTUNE	PLUTO
OCTOBER										
23	0:19 AM	PISCES	LIBRA	VIRGO	VIRGO	VIRGO	SAGITTARIUS	ARIES	PISCES	CAPRICORN
24			LIBRA	VIRGO	VIRGO	VIRGO	SAGITTARIUS	ARIES	PISCES	CAPRICORN
25	1:23 AM	ARIES	LIBRA	VIRGO	VIRGO	VIRGO	SAGITTARIUS	ARIES	PISCES	CAPRICORN
26			LIBRA	VIRGO	VIRGO	VIRGO	SAGITTARIUS	ARIES	PISCES	CAPRICORN
27	1:08 AM	TAURUS	LIBRA	VIRGO	VIRGO	VIRGO	SAGITTARIUS	ARIES	PISCES	CAPRICORN
28			LIBRA	VIRGO	VIRGO	VIRGO	SAGITTARIUS	ARIES	PISCES	CAPRICORN
29	1:25 AM	GEMINI	LIBRA	VIRGO	VIRGO	VIRGO	SAGITTARIUS	ARIES	PISCES	CAPRICORN
30			LIBRA	VIRGO	VIRGO	VIRGO	SAGITTARIUS	ARIES	PISCES	CAPRICORN
31	4:10 AM	CANCER	LIBRA	VIRGO	VIRGO	VIRGO	SAGITTARIUS	ARIES	PISCES	CAPRICORN
NOVEMBER										
1			LIBRA	VIRGO	VIRGO	VIRGO	SAGITTARIUS	ARIES	PISCES	CAPRICORN
2	10:49 AM	LEO	SCORPIO	VIRGO	VIRGO	VIRGO	SAGITTARIUS	ARIES	PISCES	CAPRICORN
3			SCORPIO	VIRGO	VIRGO	VIRGO	SAGITTARIUS	ARIES	PISCES	CAPRICORN
4	9:24 PM	VIRGO	SCORPIO	VIRGO	VIRGO	VIRGO	SAGITTARIUS	ARIES	PISCES	CAPRICORN
5			SCORPIO	VIRGO	VIRGO	VIRGO	SAGITTARIUS	ARIES	PISCES	CAPRICORN
6			SCORPIO	VIRGO	VIRGO	VIRGO	SAGITTARIUS	ARIES	PISCES	CAPRICORN
7	10:15 AM	LIBRA	SCORPIO	VIRGO	VIRGO	VIRGO	SAGITTARIUS	ARIES	PISCES	CAPRICORN
8			SCORPIO	LIBRA	VIRGO	VIRGO	SAGITTARIUS	ARIES	PISCES	CAPRICORN
9	11:04 PM	SCORPIO	SCORPIO	LIBRA	VIRGO	VIRGO	SAGITTARIUS	ARIES	PISCES	CAPRICORN
10			SCORPIO	LIBRA	VIRGO	VIRGO	SAGITTARIUS	ARIES	PISCES	CAPRICORN
11			SCORPIO	LIBRA	VIRGO	VIRGO	SAGITTARIUS	ARIES	PISCES	CAPRICORN
12	10:15 AM	SAGITTARIUS	SCORPIO	LIBRA	VIRGO	VIRGO	SAGITTARIUS	ARIES	PISCES	CAPRICORN
13			SCORPIO	LIBRA	LIBRA	VIRGO	SAGITTARIUS	ARIES	PISCES	CAPRICORN
14	7:22 PM	CAPRICORN	SCORPIO	LIBRA	LIBRA	VIRGO	SAGITTARIUS	ARIES	PISCES	CAPRICORN
15			SCORPIO	LIBRA	LIBRA	VIRGO	SAGITTARIUS	ARIES	PISCES	CAPRICORN
16			SCORPIO	LIBRA	LIBRA	VIRGO	SAGITTARIUS	ARIES	PISCES	CAPRICORN
17	2:25 AM	AQUARIUS	SCORPIO	LIBRA	LIBRA	VIRGO	SAGITTARIUS	ARIES	PISCES	CAPRICORN
18			SCORPIO	LIBRA	LIBRA	VIRGO	SAGITTARIUS	ARIES	PISCES	CAPRICORN
19	7:23 PM	PISCES	SCORPIO	LIBRA	LIBRA	VIRGO	SAGITTARIUS	ARIES	PISCES	CAPRICORN
20			SCORPIO	LIBRA	LIBRA	VIRGO	SAGITTARIUS	ARIES	PISCES	CAPRICORN
21	10:13 AM	ARIES	SAGITTARIUS	LIBRA	LIBRA	VIRGO	SAGITTARIUS	ARIES	PISCES	CAPRICORN
22			SAGITTARIUS	LIBRA	LIBRA	VIRGO	SAGITTARIUS	ARIES	PISCES	CAPRICORN

LOOK TO THE STARS...
with these exciting horoscope guides for 2001-2003!

Published each year, TOTAL HOROSCOPES provide complete yearly, daily, and weekly forecasts featuring: quick sun sign identification for the cusp-born; your rising sign; moon tables; fishing and planting guides; lucky numbers; hints for mates; and much more!

__ARIES	0-515-12815-5/ $5.99
__TAURUS	0-515-12816-3/ $5.99
__GEMINI	0-515-12817-1/ $5.99
__CANCER	0-515-12818-X/ $5.99
__LEO	0-515-12819-8/ $5.99
__VIRGO	0-515-12820-1/ $5.99
__LIBRA	0-515-12821-X/ $5.99
__SCORPIO	0-515-12822-8/ $5.99
__SAGITTARIUS	0-515-12823-6/ $5.99
__CAPRICORN	0-515-12824-4/ $5.99
__AQUARIUS	0-515-12825-2/ $5.99
__PISCES	0-515-12826-0/ $5.99

Published each year, SUPER HOROSCOPES feature the most comprehensive, candid, and insightful astrological information in trade format, including: compatibility guides; pertinent suggestions about happiness, romance, business, and health; yearly and daily forecasts for each sign with advice and comments; and much more!

__ARIES	0-425-17451-4/ $7.99
__TAURUS	0-425-17452-2/ $7.99
__GEMINI	0-425-17453-0/ $7.99
__CANCER	0-425-17454-9/ $7.99
__LEO	0-425-17455-7/ $7.99
__VIRGO	0-425-17456-5/ $7.99
__LIBRA	0-425-17457-3/ $7.99
__SCORPIO	0-425-17458-1/ $7.99
__SAGITTARIUS	0-425-17459-X/ $7.99
__CAPRICORN	0-425-17460-3/ $7.99
__AQUARIUS	0-425-17461-1/ $7.99
__PISCES	0-425-17462-X/ $7.99

TO ORDER CALL: 1-800-788-6262, ext. 1. Refer to Ad # 918

Penguin Putnam Inc.
375 Hudson Street
New York, NY 10014

*Prices subject to change